More praise for

ATROCITIES

by Matthew White

"Full of fascinating information about parts of the world little-known to most Westerners."
—*Washington Post*

"With its stylishly lurid graphics and goofy asides, [*Atrocities*] . . . arrives trailing some impressive scholarly affirmation." —Jennifer Schuessler, *New York Times*

"White explains the hows and whys rather brilliantly." —*Telegraph* (UK)

"Sometimes, a little humor is indispensable. Matthew White uses it elegantly in the title of his fascinating new, big and easy-to-read reference book. [*Atrocities: The 100 Deadliest Episodes in Human History*] is a bright door stopper and mind opener."
—Bill Blakemore, ABC News

"Despite being a kind of encyclopedia of evil, it actually manages to be a fascinating read thanks to White's keen grasp of history and his wry take on the villains of the past. It helps that White is careful to respect the victims who died at the hands of others and correct the record when necessary about the identities of those who were responsible for so much misery." —Randy Dotinga, *Christian Science Monitor*

"Undeniably compelling. The author . . . has put together a serious—and seriously interesting—collection of events that have resulted in massive loss of human life." —*Booklist*

ATROCITIES

THE 100 DEADLIEST EPISODES IN HUMAN HISTORY

Matthew White

W. W. NORTON & COMPANY

NEW YORK   LONDON

For information about permission to reproduce selections from this book, write to Permissions, W. W. Norton & Company, Inc., 500 Fifth Avenue, New York, NY 10110

For information about special discounts for bulk purchases, please contact W. W. Norton Special Sales at specialsales@wwnorton.com or 800-233-4830

Manufacturing by RR Donnelley, Harrisonburg, VA
Book design by Daniel Lagin
Production manager: Anna Oler

Library of Congress Cataloging-in-Publication Data

White, Matthew.
[Great big book of horrible things]
Atrocities : the 100 deadliest episodes in human history / Matthew White.
    pages cm
"Originally published under the title The great big book of horrible things : the definitive chronicle of history's 100 worst atrocities"—Title page verso.
Includes bibliographical references and index.
ISBN 978-0-393-34523-0 (pbk.)
1. Atrocities—History. 2. Massacres—History. 3. War crimes—History.
4. World history. I. Title.
D24.W45 2013
909—dc23   2013003071

W. W. Norton & Company, Inc.
500 Fifth Avenue, New York, N.Y. 10110
www.wwnorton.com

W. W. Norton & Company Ltd.
Castle House, 75/76 Wells Street, London W1T 3QT

1 2 3 4 5 6 7 8 9 0

To my mother, who gave me my sense of humor,
and my father, who gave me my sense of justice

CONTENTS

LIST OF MAPS

FOREWORD

TRADITIONAL HISTORY IS ABOUT KINGS AND ARMIES RATHER THAN PEOPLE. Empires rose, empires fell, entire populations were enslaved or annihilated, and no one seemed to think there was anything wrong with it. Because of this lack of curiosity among traditional scholars about the human cost of historical extravaganzas, a curious person had nowhere to go to answer such basic questions as whether the twentieth century was really the most violent in history or whether religion, nationalism, anarchy, Communism, or monarchy killed the most people.

During the past decade, though, historians and laypeople alike have gone to the sprawling website of a guy on the Internet, Matthew White—self-described atrocitologist, necrometrician, and quantifier of hemoclysms. White is a representative of that noble and underappreciated profession, the librarian, and he has compiled the most comprehensive, disinterested, and statistically nuanced estimates available of the death tolls of history's major catastrophes. In *Atrocities*, White now combines his numerical savvy with the skills of a good storyteller to present a new history of civilization, a history whose protagonists are not great emperors but their unsung victims—millions and millions and millions of them.

White writes with a light touch and a dark wit that belies a serious moral purpose. His scorn is directed at the stupidity and callousness of history's great leaders, at the statistical innumeracy and historical ignorance of various ideologues and propagandists, and at the indifference of traditional history to the magnitude of human suffering behind momentous events.

—Steven Pinker

INTRODUCTION

NO ONE LIKES STATISTICS AS MUCH AS I DO. I MEAN THAT LITERALLY. I CAN never find anyone who wants to listen to me recite statistics.

Well, there is one exception. For several years, I've maintained the Historical Atlas of the Twentieth Century, a history website on which, among other things, I've analyzed statistics of changing literacy, urban populations, casualties of war, industrial workforce, population density, and infant mortality. Of those, the numbers that people want to argue about are casualties.

Boy do they want to argue.

From the moment I first posted a tentative list of the twenty-five largest cities in 1900, the twenty bloodiest wars, and the one hundred most important artworks of the twentieth century, I was swamped by e-mails wondering how, why, and where I got my casualty statistics. And why isn't this other atrocity listed? And which country killed the most? Which ideology? And just who the hell do I think I am, accusing the Turks of doing such things?

After many years of this, my website has become a major clearinghouse for body counts, so believe me when I say that I have heard every debate on the subject. Let's get something out of the way right now. Everything you are about to read is disputed. There is no point in loading the narrative with every "supposedly" or "allegedly" or "according to some sources" that it deserves. Nor will I make you slog through every alternative version of events that has ever been suggested.

There is no atrocity in history that every person in the world agrees on. Someone somewhere will deny it ever happened, and someone somewhere will insist it did. For example, I am convinced that the Holocaust happened, but that Herod's Massacre of the Innocents did not. It would be easy to find people who disagree with me on both.

Atrocitology is at the center of most major historical disputes. People don't argue about nice history. They argue about who killed whose grandfather. They try to draw lessons from the past and speculate about who is the most Hitleresque politician coming over the horizon. On a particularly contentious topic, two historians from the opposite poles of politics can cover the same ground yet appear to be discussing two entirely different planets. Sometimes you can't find any overlap in the narratives, and it becomes nearly impossible to fuse them into a seamless middle ground. All I can say is that I have tried to follow the consensus of scholars, but when I support a minority view, I will tell you so.

Most people writing a book about history's worst atrocities would describe the "One Hundred Worst Things I Can Recall at the Moment." They would include the Holocaust, slavery, 9/11, Wounded Knee, Jeffrey Dahmer, Hiroshima, Jack the Ripper, the Iraq War, the Kennedy assassination, Pickett's Charge, and so on. Unfortunately, just brainstorming a list like that will usually reflect an author's biases rather than a proper historical balance. That particular list makes it look like almost everything bad in history was done either to or by Americans rather recently, which implies that Americans are intrinsically, cosmically more important than anyone else.

Other lists might make it seem like everything bad can be associated with one root cause (resources, racism, religion, for example), one culture (Communists, the West, Muslims), or one method (war, exploitation, taxation). Most people acquire their knowledge of atrocities haphazardly—a TV documentary, a few movies, a political website, a tourist brochure, and that angry man at the end of the bar—and then proceed to make judgments about the world based on those few examples. I'm hoping to offer a broader and more balanced range of examples to use when arguing about history.

To be fair to all sides, I have carefully selected one hundred events with the largest man-made death tolls, regardless of who was involved or why they did it. To emphasize the statistical basis of this list, I devote more space to describing the deadliest events, while quickly summarizing the lesser events. A death toll of several million gets several pages, while a death toll of a few hundred thousand gets a few paragraphs. *The* deadliest event gets the longest chapter.

One of the standard ways to skew the data is to decide up front that certain kinds of killing are worse than others, so only those are counted. Gassing ethnic minorities is worse than bombing cities, which is just as bad as shooting prisoners of war, which is worse than machine-gunning enemy troops, which is better than plundering colonial natives, so massacres and famines are counted but not air raids and battles. Or maybe it's the other way around. In any case, my philosophy is that I wouldn't want to die in any of these ways, so I count all killings, regardless of how they happened or to whom.

You might wonder how I can possibly know the number who died in an atrocity. After all, wars are messy and confusing, and people can easily disappear without a trace. The participants happily lie about numbers in order to look brave, noble, or tragic. Reporters and historians can be biased or gullible.

The best answer would vary on a case-by-case basis, but the short answer is money. Even if a general is reluctant to tell the newspapers how many men he lost in a bungled offensive, he still has to tell the accountants to drop 4,000 men from the payroll. Even if a dictator tries to hide how many civilians died in a massive resettlement, his finance minister will still note the disappearance of 100,000 taxpayers. A customs official at the harbor will be collecting duties on each cargo of new slaves, and someone has to pay to have the bodies carted away after every massacre. Head counts (and by extension, body counts) are not just an academic exercise; they have been an important part of government financing for centuries.

Obviously these death tolls have a significant margin of error, but a list of history's one hundred biggest body counts is not entirely guesswork. For one thing, big events leave big footprints. Even though no one will ever know exactly how many Inca or Romans died in the fall of their civilizations, histories describe big battles and massacres, and archaeological excavations suggest a massive decline of the population. These events killed a lot of people even if "a lot" can't be defined precisely.

At the top of the scale, a million here and a million there barely moves an event's rank a couple of notches along the list. Some people would disagree with my estimate that Stalin killed 20 million people, but even if you claim (as some do) that he killed 50 million, that would move him from Number 6 to Number 2. On the other hand, defending Stalin by claiming (as others do) that he killed a mere 3 million will drop him down to only Number 29, so for my purposes, there's not much point in arguing about the exact number. Stalin will be on my list, regardless.

At the same time, some events won't reach the lower threshold no matter how much we dispute the precise numbers. An exact body count is hard to come by for Castro's regime in Cuba, but no one has ever suggested that he killed the hundreds of thousands necessary to be considered for a slot on my list. Many infamous brutes such as François "Papa Doc" Duvalier, Vlad the Impaler, Caligula, and Augusto Pinochet easily fall short, as do many well-known conflicts, such as the Arab-Israeli wars and the Anglo-Boer War.

Some people would bring more cleverness to this task than I do. They might track the world's worst multicide back to some distant root cause and declare *that* to be the most horrible thing people ever did. They might blame influential people for all of the evil done by those who followed them. They would blame Jesus for the Crusades, Darwin for the Holocaust, Marx for the Gulag, and Marco Polo for the destruction of the Aztecs.

Unfortunately this approach ignores the nature of historical causality. Yes, you can take an event (let's say, the September 11, 2001, terrorist attacks) and track back through the chain of cause and effect to show how this is the natural result of, say, the 1953 coup against the prime minister of Iran, but you can just as easily track that same event back to the First World War, the Wright brothers, D. B. Cooper, Muhammad ibn Abd al-Wahhab, Henry Ford, the Russian conquest of Turkistan, Levittown, the founding of Yale University, Elisha Otis, the Holocaust, and the opening of the Erie Canal. So many threads of causality feed into any individual event that you can usually find a way to connect any two things you want.

Aside from morbid fascination, is there any reason to know the one hundred highest body counts of history? Four reasons come to mind:

First, things that happen to a lot of people are usually more important than things that happen to only a few people. If I'm in bed with the flu, no one cares, but if half of the city is stricken with the flu, it's a medical emergency. If I lose my job, that's my bad luck; if thousands of people lose their jobs, the economy crashes. A few murders a week is business as usual in a big city police department; twenty murders a day is a civil war.

Second, killing a person is the most you can do to him. It affects him more than teaching him, robbing him, healing him, hiring him, marrying him, or imprisoning him—for the simple reason that death is the most complete and permanent change you can inflict. A killer can easily undo the work of a teacher or a doctor, but neither a doctor nor a teacher can undo the work of a killer.*

Therefore, just by default, my one hundred multicides had a maximum impact on an enormous number of people. Without too much debate, I can easily label these to be among history's most significant events.

You may be tempted to dismiss the impact of these events as solely negative, but that's an artificial distinction. Destruction and creation are intimately intertwined. The fall of the Roman Empire cleared the way for medieval Europe. The Second World War created the Cold War and democratic regimes in Germany, Italy, and Japan. The Napoleonic Wars inspired works by Tolstoy, Tchaikovsky, and Goya. I'm not saying that the *1812 Overture* was worth the half-million lives lost in the Russian Campaign, morally speaking. I'm just saying that as a plain historical fact, there would be no jazz, gospel, or rock and roll without slavery, and everyone born in the postwar Baby Boom of 1946–64 owes their existence to World War II.

A third reason to consider is that we sometimes forget the human impact of historic events. Yes, these things happened a long time ago, and all of those people would be dead now anyway, but there comes a point where we have to realize that a clash of cultures did more than blend cuisines, vocabularies, and architectural styles. It also caused a lot of very personal suffering.

The fourth and certainly most practical reason to gather body counts is for risk assessment and problem solving. If we study history to avoid repeating the mistakes of the past, it helps to know what those mistakes were, and that includes *all* of the mistakes, not just the ones that support certain pet ideas. It's easy to solve the problem of human violence if we focus only on the seven atrocities that prove our point, but a list of the hundred worst presents more of a challenge. A person's grand unified theory of human violence should explain most of the multicides on this list or else he might need to reconsider. In fact, the

---

* "The evil that men do lives after them; The good is oft interred with their bones." (William Shakespeare, *Julius Caesar*, Act 3, Scene II)

next time somebody declares that he knows the cause of or solution to human violence, you can probably open this book at random and immediately find an event that is not explained by his theory.

Despite my skepticism about any common thread running through all one hundred atrocities, I still found some interesting tendencies. Let me share with you the three biggest lessons I learned while working on this list:

1. Chaos is deadlier than tyranny. More of these multicides result from the breakdown of authority rather than the exercise of authority. In comparison to a handful of dictators such as Idi Amin and Saddam Hussein who exercised their absolute power to kill hundreds of thousands, I found more and deadlier upheavals like the Time of Troubles, the Chinese Civil War, and the Mexican Revolution where no one exercised enough control to stop the death of millions.

2. The world is very disorganized. Power structures tend to be informal and temporary, and many of the big names in this book (for example, Stalin, Cromwell, Tamerlane, Caesar) exercised supreme authority without holding a regular job in the government. Most wars don't start neatly with declarations and mobilizations and end with surrenders and treaties. They tend to build up from escalating incidents of violence, fizzle out when everyone is too exhausted to continue, and are followed by unpredictable aftershocks. Soldiers and nations happily change sides in the middle of wars, sometimes in the middle of battles. Most nations are not as neatly delineated as you might expect. In fact, some nations at war (I call them *quantum states*) don't quite exist and don't quite not exist; instead they hover in limbo until somebody wins the war and decides their fate, which is then retroactively applied to earlier versions of the nation.

3. War kills more civilians than soldiers. In fact, the army is usually the safest place to be during a war. Soldiers are protected by thousands of armed men, and they get the first choice of food and medical care. Meanwhile, even if civilians are not systematically massacred, they are usually robbed, evicted, or left to starve; however, their stories are usually left untold. Most military histories skim lightly over the massive suffering of the ordinary, unarmed civilians caught in the middle, even though theirs is the most common experience of war.*

---

* For example, standard reference works such as *The World Almanac* and Wikipedia meticulously list the number of American soldiers, sailors, and marines killed in each of America's wars, while ignoring civilian deaths among merchant seamen, passengers, refugees, runaway slaves, and, of course, Indians and settlers along the frontier.

The Ascent of Manslaughter

Where do we start? People have been killing each other ever since they came down from the trees, and I wouldn't be surprised to find bodies stashed up in the branches as well. Some of the earliest human bones show fractures that must have come from weapons. Early inscriptions boast of thousands of enemies slaughtered. The oldest holy books record battles in which the followers of one angry god smite the followers of some other angry god; however, the small tribes and villages caught in these ancient wars didn't have enough potential victims to be killed on a scale that could compare with today. It took many centuries of human history before people were gathered in large enough populations to be killed by the hundreds of thousands, so the earliest of history's one hundred worst atrocities didn't occur until the Persians built an empire that spanned the known world.

ATROCITIES

SECOND PERSIAN WAR

Death toll: 300,000[1]
Rank: 96
Type: clash of cultures
Broad dividing line: Persians vs. Greeks
Time frame: 480–479 BCE
Location: Greece
Major state participants: Persian Empire, Athens, Sparta
Who usually gets the most blame: Xerxes

Prequel: The First Persian War

When the land-based Persian Empire, which had conquered everyone it could reach, from Pakistan to Egypt, came up against the seafaring Greeks, the Persians scooped up several Greek colonies on the Ionian coast of Asia Minor (modern Turkey). Many years of quiet subservience passed, but then the Greek ruler of the Ionian city of Miletus got ambitious. He threw off Persian rule and asked for help from free Greek cities overseas—first Sparta (which refused), then Athens (which agreed). A joint Greek army of Ionians and Athenians marched inland and attacked the Persian provincial capital at Sardis, which they briefly occupied and accidentally burned down. Within a couple of years, however, the revolt was put down, and the Athenians hurried home to lie low and hope that the Persians hadn't noticed them.

Shah Darius of Persia, however, had not gotten where he was by letting insults pass unpunished, and he assigned a servant to remind him every day to remember the Athenians. Darius decided he needed to conquer the independent Greek states on the European mainland that were stirring up trouble among his Greek subjects; however, the first assault directly across the sea failed. The Athenians beat his army badly and drove it away at the Battle of Marathon.

Second Persian War

Ten years later, a new shah, Xerxes, gathered levies (peasant draftees) from all over the empire into the largest army ever seen,* too large to move by boat. Taking the overland route up through the Balkans and down into Greece, he forced his way past all barriers, man-made and natural. He crossed the Dardanelles strait on a floating bridge made of boats; then his engineers dug a canal across the dangerous Acte Peninsula, home of Mount Athos.

With the Persians bearing down on them, a scratch army of 4,900 Greeks under Spartan leadership tried to slow them at the mountain pass of Thermopylae, while the Greek fleet stopped an amphibious end run at the nearby strait of Artemisia. The Greek phalanx, the traditional Greek battle formation in which heavily armored spearmen lined up into a human wall of shields and spearheads, easily held against repeated Persian assaults. After a few days of tough fighting, however, the Persians found another way around Thermopylae, so they outflanked and slaughtered the last defenders blocking their way. The Persian army moved into the Greek heartland, taking Athens after the inhabitants had fled to nearby islands.

When all seemed lost, the Athenian fleet met the Persian warships in the narrow channel between the island of Salamis and the mainland. In the confusing swirl of galleys darting, ramming, and splintering, the Persians lost over two hundred ships and 40,000 sailors. With the Greeks now in control of the sea, the huge and hungry Persian army was cut off from supplies.

Xerxes returned to Persia with part of his army, leaving behind a smaller force to live off the land and finish the conquest. This army hunkered down for the winter in northern Greece and then moved south again in the spring, reoccupying Athens. After frantic diplomacy by the displaced Athenians, the Greek city-states finally agreed to combine their armies. The two forces met at Plataea, where the Greek phalanx overwhelmed the Persians. The survivors made their long, painful retreat back to Persia, losing thousands along the way. Meanwhile, the Athenian fleet shot across the Aegean Sea and finished off the remaining Persian ships with an amphibious attack on their naval camp at Mycale in Ionia.[2]

Legacy

Almost every list of decisive battles or turning points in history begins with something from the Persian Wars, so you might already know that Greek victory rescued Western

---

* No one knows how many. Herodotus reported that the force numbered 2,640,000 soldiers and sailors, including 1,700,000 infantry, but no one believes it.

Civilization and the concept of individual freedom from the faceless Oriental hordes who are the villains of Victorian histories and recent movies.

On the other hand, let's not get carried away. Being conquered by the Persians would not have been the end of the world. By the standards of the day, the Persians were rather benign conquerors. For example, they were one of the only people in history to be nice to the Jews. They allowed the Jews to return to Palestine and rebuild their temple, instead of massacring or deporting them as the Assyrians, Babylonians, Romans, Spaniards, Cossacks, Russians, and Germans did at various other junctures of history. Even with a Persian victory at Salamis, free Greeks would have remained in Sicily, Italy, and Marseilles. Greek civilization would later prove vibrant enough to survive—and eventually usurp—a half millennium of Roman rule. There's no reason why the Greeks couldn't get through a few generations of Persian rule intact.

ALEXANDER THE GREAT

Death toll: 500,000 died, including 250,000 civilians massacred[1]
Rank: 70
Type: world conqueror
Broad dividing line: Macedonians vs. Persians
Time frame: ruled 336–325 BCE
Location: Middle East
Who usually gets the most blame: Alexander III of Macedon

THE BATTLE BETWEEN EAST AND WEST WENT IN TWO PHASES. THE PERSIAN Wars decided that the West would survive, but Alexander the Great ensured that the West would dominate.

Alexander's father, King Philip II of Macedon in northeastern Greece, redesigned the phalanx by strengthening the solid infantry block with longer spears and covering its flanks with archers and cavalry. He conquered Greece with his new army but was assassinated before he could turn against the Persian Empire. His twenty-year-old son, Alexander III, then took over and put down a couple of immediate revolts with what would come to be characteristic ruthlessness—one revolt to the north by the tribes of Thrace; then one to the south by the strongest Greek city, Thebes. Having covered his back, Alexander crossed into Asia Minor (Turkey) and destroyed the Persian provincial garrison when it tried to block his path at the Granicus River. He then began an epic march across the Middle East.

Alexander was recklessly direct, as shown in the story of the Gordian knot, a mystical tangle of rope kept in a temple in Asia Minor. A prophecy foretold that whoever could undo the knot would rule Asia, but Alexander refused to be distracted by the impossibility of the task. He simply drew his sword and cut through the knot. His characteristic battle strategy was similar. He aimed for what appeared to be the strongest part of the enemy line and attacked straight into it. The tactic was risky, and he accumulated an impressive collection of battle wounds from a variety of weapons, but Macedonian kings were expected to lead by personal example.[2]

After maneuvering through the pass between Asia Minor and Syria, Alexander discovered that Shah Darius III of Persia had slipped his full army behind him, cutting the Macedonians off at Issus. With hardly a thought, Alexander spotted a weakness in the Persian line and charged into it with his cavalry. The Persians broke ranks and were slaughtered as they ran, abandoning their baggage train to the Macedonians, including the Persian empress and her daughter.

Alexander moved south to capture the ports that allowed the Persian fleet to threaten his lines of communication. The Phoenician port of Tyre had been built safely on an offshore island, beyond the reach of countless earlier armies. The Macedonians, however, settled in and spent the next several months building a causeway out to the island. Once Alexander connected the mainland to the island, Tyre fell to assault. Alexander massacred the men and sold the women and children into slavery.

When Alexander visited Egypt, he was hailed as a god, and he no doubt agreed. In 331 BCE, at the mouth of the Nile River he laid the groundwork for Alexandria, a new city of culture and learning that would soon be the home of the greatest library in the ancient world, the greatest lighthouse, the original Museum (Temple of the Muses), and just about every scholar for the next several centuries.

At Gaugamela in northern Mesopotamia (Iraq), the Persians threw their largest army yet again against Alexander's smaller army on flat open ground where their numbers should have had the advantage. The Persians had gathered elephants, scythed chariots, and several hundred thousand exotic levies from all across the Middle East. Alexander defeated them anyway. He then seized the royal Persian city of Persepolis, which he burned in a drunken accident, and hounded the fugitive Darius to his death deep in the wilderness.[3]

Alexander disappeared off the edge of the map, fighting tribes in their mountain strongholds in central Asia. With those taken, he moved south into India and beat the native kings and their war elephants. Finally, his exhausted soldiers realized he would not turn around until he reached the edge of the world. The army mutinied and forced him to return home.

Alexander took his soldiers home the hard way, across the scorching desert on the coast of Iran. Some say it was a brilliant move to stay resupplied by the navy while taking the most direct route possible. Others say he was punishing his men for making him go home. In any case, two-thirds of his army died by the time they returned to civilization.[4]

AGE OF WARRING STATES

Death toll: 1.5 million[1]
Rank: 40
Type: failed state
Broad dividing line: Qin vs. Chu
Time frame: 475–221 BCE
Location: China
Who usually gets the most blame: a string of increasingly vicious kings, culminating with Zheng of Qin

Prologue: Spring and Autumn Period (ca. 770–475 BCE)

To understand where China went, you should appreciate where it began. During the Zhou dynasty (ca. 1050 BCE–256 BCE) a nominal emperor ruled the whole of China, but he was more like a hereditary pope—a vestige of an ancient, almost forgotten era, a spiritual presence rather than a true monarch. Real power rested with feudatory states that incorporated pieces of the old empire. Below that level was the standard feudal arrangement of lesser lords and peasants.

The Chinese during the Spring and Autumn Period were a very well-mannered people, but their solution to every moral dilemma seemed to be ritual suicide. Let's role-play a couple of actual scenarios found in the history books:[2]

You are a noble of a minor rank who has been ordered by your lord, the prince of Jin, to assassinate his state minister for a serious transgression. When you discover that your target has been wrongly accused, you will

    A. Do your job and kill him anyway, as soldiers have been doing for centuries.
    B. Not kill him, and then hide because your lord will be quite angry.
    C. Not kill him, and then commit suicide for betraying your lord's trust.

You are a noble of the state of Chu, and you firmly believe that your prince is embarking on a dangerous policy that will turn out badly for him. You will

    A. Keep your mouth shut and not risk angering him.
    B. Convince him to change his mind, and then bask in his gratitude.

C. Convince him to change his mind, and then cut off your own feet for having disagreed with him.

If you answered (c) to these questions, you would have enjoyed the Spring and Autumn Period. Answer (c) was the chosen solution among the actual individuals in the history books.

During the Spring and Autumn Period, states fought for prestige rather than conquest. Usually, a defeated Chinese king was allowed to keep his title and lands as long as he acknowledged the magnificence of the man who beat him.

One episode probably says it all: After a decisive victory, a chariot of the Jin army was chasing a chariot of the defeated Chu army when the fugitive chariot got stuck in a ditch. The pursuing chariot pulled up alongside so the Jin charioteer could helpfully advise his enemy on how to free the chariot. When the chariot was up and running again, the chase resumed. The fleeing chariot easily reached the safety of the Chu army.[3]

The Age of Warring States (ca. 475–221 BCE)

Chinese war-making turned cold-blooded after 473 BCE. For years, the two states of Wu and Yueh had been fighting each other whenever they had a spare moment. The king of Wu had won the previous round and followed the tradition of being a gracious winner, leaving the state of Yueh intact as long as its people acknowledged Wu's magnificence. Then in 473 BCE, while Wu was off fighting elsewhere, the king of Yueh snuck in and took Wu's capital. Fair enough—Yueh won that round. Wu admitted defeat and agreed that Yueh was now top dog; however, instead of leaving it at that, Yueh stripped his broken enemy of his lands and stashed him in a humiliating new kingdom consisting of a river island with three hundred inhabitants. The king of Wu refused to accept this shame and committed suicide.

The Spring and Summer Period had ended with the kingdom of Jin foremost among the others, but now a civil war ripped it apart. Three independent kingdoms (Han, Zhao, and Wei) emerged from the chaos in 403 BCE.

In time, "war became a business of wholesale slaughter, unmitigated by acts or gestures of chivalry which was considered as a folly hopelessly out-of-date by the people of the time. In the battlefield killing pure and simple was encouraged. A soldier was rewarded according to the number of human heads or, when these became too cumbersome, the number of human ears that he could produce after the battle. Ten thousand was considered a modest casualty list for a single campaign; twenty or thirty thousand was quite common. The wanton murder of prisoners of war, unthinkable in the former age, became a practice by no means unusual, it being considered the best, the surest, and the cheapest way of weakening a rival state."[4]

The warring states were helped along by the invention of crossbows. About the same time, battle tactics shifted from chariots to cavalry. Increasingly the Chinese made weapons and armor from iron rather than bronze. All of these innovations made war cheaper, meaning everyone could get involved, not just the nobility.

Rise of Qin

By the 360s BCE, only eight feudal states were still on the board, chief among them Wei in the central north. Wei had reduced the kingdoms of Han, Lu, and Sung to vassals, which provoked a counter-alliance of two more kingdoms, Zhao and Qi, to keep Wei under control. This briefly created an equilibrium in which no one state was strong enough to expand, so peace broke out.

Most states were compressed in the center of China along the Yellow River, small in size but densely populated; however, a couple of outer states held vast frontier territories with large armies hardened by battles with barbarians in the wilderness. In the west, backing up against the open steppe, was Qin (pronounced "chin"). This land was good for raising horses, and the kingdom was inhabited by tough, no-nonsense people who were considered crude by the rest of China. One ancient critic described their music as nothing more than beating clay jars with thigh bones and chanting, "Woo! Woo! Woo!"

Duke Hsiao ruled Qin from 361 to 338 BCE, guided by his minister Lord Shang. Together they organized a totalitarian state to maximize the state's agricultural output and war-making abilities. They abolished the nobility and replaced it with a professional army in which soldiers were promoted for bravery rather than connections. They crushed dissent. They restricted travel. These reforms gave Duke Hsiao the most powerful army in China, which he used in a surprise attack that broke Wei's hegemony in 351 BCE.

Lord Shang's reforms stirred up a lot of anger inside Qin, so when Duke Hsiao died, Shang's enemies hunted him down. He tried to flee anonymously, but his own laws made unauthorized travel impossible. He didn't get very far before an innkeeper turned him over to the authorities for failure to produce the right documents. Shang was hauled off and torn apart with chariots. His reforms, however, stayed in place.[5]

In 316 the Qin kingdom annexed the barbarian lands of Shu and Pa, which added thousands of tribal warriors to the army.[6] By now, most of the initiative in international relations lay with Qin, and the other kingdoms could only respond. The only other state powerful enough to have its own foreign policy was Chu, a large kingdom that was expanding into forests of the southern frontier.

To keep Qin from expanding eastward into the Chinese heartland, the states that lined up north to south on Qin's eastern border joined Chu in a "vertical" alliance—*hezong* in Chinese. Qin leapfrogged this barrier to advance down the Yellow River and link up with the states on the other side in a "horizontal" alliance, called *lianheng*.

The wars came quickly after this, from all directions, and it would take dozens of pages to sort them out in any meaningful way. The general flavor can be sampled from one incident in 260 BCE, in which ruthless cunning defeated honor. At Changping in northwestern China, a Zhao army in a good defensive position faced the army of Qin, which could only settle down and wait. As the wait dragged on with no resolution in sight, Qin agents started a whispering campaign about how those Zhao cowards were avoiding battle. Eventually, the Zhao king was stung by the rumors of cowardice, so he replaced his cautious general with one he thought more honorable. This new general set out to attack, but as soon as he left his fortifications, the Qin army lurched forward and easily surrounded the Zhao force. The Zhao general laid down his weapons and surrendered, but Qin soldiers killed every last member of the Zhao force anyway.

Endgame

In 256 BCE, Qin soldiers marched into Loyang and deposed the last Zhou emperor.[7] No replacement was appointed, and after this China didn't even pretend to be one country.

In 247 BCE, at the age of thirteen, Prince Zheng came to the throne of Qin when his father the king died. Most members of the court expected him to be easily manipulated, so they conspired all around him. His mother, Queen Dowager Zhao Ji, renowned as a great beauty and graceful dancer, was given control of the government until Zheng came of age. She shared this regency with Prime Minister Lu Buwei, who was rumored to be Zheng's real father.

To free himself from his entanglement with the queen dowager, the prime minister "found a man named Lao Ai who had an unusually large penis, and made him a servant in his household. Then, when an occasion arose, he had suggestive music performed and, instructing Lao Ai to stick his penis though the center of a wheel made of paulownia wood, had him walk about with it, making certain that a report of this reached the ears of the queen dowager so as to excite her interest."[8]

The queen dowager quickly fell in love with Lao, which opened the happy couple to great risks, so they came up with a scheme to keep it secret. Lao arranged to be accused of a crime for which the punishment was castration, but he and the queen bribed the gelder to leave Lao's mighty genitalia intact and pluck out his beard instead. Now that everyone thought he was a eunuch, Lao could openly and legally become part of the queen's household.[9]

Eventually, they had two children together, whom they kept carefully hidden from her son, the king. Knowing the danger they were in, they planned a coup against Zheng and secured personal command of nearby troops using forged documents. Unfortunately, Zheng was way ahead of them. When Lao's troops arrived at the royal chamber, King Zheng had his own troops ready in an ambush. Lao barely escaped the trap and fled. With a price of one million copper coins on his head, Lao was quickly captured and sentenced to die. The queen dowager was forced to watch while her lover was torn apart with chariots. Their two secret sons were tied in sacks and beaten to death.

There was more to come. Most of the stories of King Zheng's youth involved him narrowly surviving or cleverly discovering assassination plots. One assassin, the courtier Jing Ke, was revealed when a dagger fell out of the map he was unrolling. A blind lute player, Gao Jianli, tried clobbering Zheng with a lead-weighted lute when he got close enough, but he missed. A lesser man than King Zheng would have turned reclusive and twitchy by this point, but a lesser man would never have earned a place in history by uniting the Warring States.

By the age of thirty, Zheng had become the undisputed master of his kingdom. His mother was helpless in exile. Prime Minister Lu Buwei had been forced to commit suicide. All other ministers were cowed. In one final, busy decade, the kingdom of Qin swept the board clean. Han fell in 230 BCE, Wei in 225 BCE. Qin then conquered Chu (223 BCE), Yan and Zhao (both 222 BCE), and Qi (221 BCE), completing the unification of China. Zheng took a new title, First Emperor; his story continues in a later chapter (see "Qin Shi Huang Di").

FIRST PUNIC WAR

Death toll: 400,000[1]
Rank: 81
Type: hegemonial war
Broad dividing line: Rome vs. Carthage
Time frame: 264–241 BCE
Location: western Mediterranean
Who usually gets the most blame: Carthage (a classic example of the winners writing the history books)
Another damn: Roman conquest

A BOATLOAD OF UNEMPLOYED MERCENARIES CALLED THE MAMERTINES seized Messina in Sicily, murdering the town's leaders and taking their women for themselves. That was bad enough, but then the Mamertines began raiding some of their neighbors for loot and extorting from the rest. Sicily was mostly under the local control of tribes and city-states, but Carthage and Syracuse had staked out large spheres of influence, and Roman-ruled Italy was within shouting distance across the straight from Messina. All three major powers in the region wanted to drive the Mamertines out and restore the peaceful status quo, but politics complicated the situation. When Syracuse moved to attack the freebooters, Carthage naturally took the other side. Then the Mamertines worried that the price for Carthaginian help was too high, so they asked Rome to help them get rid of the Carthaginians. This quickly escalated into a general war for control of Sicily.[2]

The Roman army—veterans toughened by the conquest of Italy—won almost every land battle in Sicily, but the Carthaginian navy was far superior in numbers, seamanship, and boatbuilding to anything the Romans could launch. As a result, they could land fresh mercenary armies anywhere on the island and intercept Roman reinforcements being shipped over from the mainland. It created a stalemate.*

---

* What made the Roman army so successful? First, the Romans were meticulous organizers who standardized every aspect of war-making—camping, supply, marching, pay, rewards, discipline—so that no mistakes or delays would keep them from getting at the enemy.

Second, they broke the solid phalanx that most armies used at that time into smaller blocks of

The Romans soon came up with new naval tactics that played to their strengths. They turned sea battles into land battles by inventing the corvus (crow), a pivoted and hinged gangplank located at the front of the boat. Rather than rely on the difficult tactic of ramming enemy ships, the Romans used grappling hooks to drag their ship alongside a target ship. Then the corvus dropped, its spike crashing down and hooking through the deck of the enemy ship. Then heavily armed Roman soldiers rushed across the plank to slaughter the crew.

In 255 BCE, after securing Sicily and clearing the Carthaginians off the sea, the Romans landed an army in North Africa, but they were stopped by the powerful walls around the city of Carthage. Then a freshly hired army of Greek mercenaries and war elephants landed and beat the Romans. The Romans evacuated the survivors from Africa, but a sudden storm hit, sinking 248 ships of the Roman fleet off Cape Pachynus, sending 100,000 rowers, marines, and soldiers to the bottom.[3] It was the worst maritime disaster in human history.*

The war then returned to Sicily. Now the Romans had the advantage on both land and sea, but two more unexpected storms destroyed two more Roman fleets in quick succession, giving the Carthaginians an opportunity to hold the Romans to a stalemate. Finally, in 241 BCE, by the Aegates Islands off western Sicily, the Romans destroyed the Carthaginian fleet, which was bringing supplies to the army. With their last army trapped and starving, Carthage agreed to peace on Roman terms, which included reparations, ransom, and Sicily.

---

several hundred men (maniples at first; cohorts after a major reorganization in 107 BCE) that could maneuver and adjust to circumstances on the battlefield more flexibly. These blocks were then assembled into legions of around 5,000 men apiece.

Roman soldiers usually began a battle by advancing calmly, tossing a volley of heavy javelins (*pila*; singular: *pilum*) into the massed enemy and then closing in with swords. The pila were so heavy that even if an enemy soldier blocked it with his shield, it would still imbed and drag the shield down with its extra weight.

* If not *the* worst, then tied for first place with the loss of Kublai Khan's fleet by storm off the coast of Japan in 1281, which reportedly also killed 100,000.

QIN SHI HUANG DI

Death toll: a million[1]
Rank: 46
Type: despot
Broad dividing line: First Emperor vs. tradition
Time frame: 221–210 BCE
Location: China
Who usually gets the most blame: Qin Shi Huang Di (born Zheng)

The First Emperor

Once Zheng became lord of all China, he invented a brand new title by which he is known to history: First (Shi) August (Huang) Emperor (Di) of China (Qin).

At his side, Prime Minister Li Si set new standards for all of the conniving, ruthless chief counselors in history. Li Si had very definite ideas on how to remodel China into a peaceful and orderly empire for all eternity. He had the ear of the First Emperor and plenty of suggestions. For the most part, these reforms spread Qin's well-established totalitarian system into the newly conquered lands.

To keep power out of the hands of ambitious nobles, Shi Huang Di broke up the old aristocracy and abolished feudalism. After collecting weapons from the defeated nobles, he divided his domain into thirty-six commanderies run by officials he appointed. For each commandery, the First Emperor had three autonomous officials running part of the government: a governor running the civil branch, an independent military commander, and an inspector to spy on the other two. For lower jobs, he created a professional civil service that was filled by applicants who had passed impartial tests of their education.

To spread unity across the previously warring states, the First Emperor reduced all regional variations to one official version of everything. He standardized Chinese writing to the system in use today. He reissued money and decreed one system of weights and measurement. He required all wagons to have the same axle length so they would fit on the new roads he built all over China, roads that made it easier for him to rush his armies to any hot spot.

Whenever Shi Huang Di tried to make changes, academics fussed and insisted that there was no precedent—the law forbade it. Well, the obvious solution was to remove all those pesky precedents and start from scratch. He ordered every book in China brought to him, and he had all of them, except for a few technical manuals, burned. When scholars howled at this, he buried 460 of them alive so he wouldn't have to listen to their howling anymore. Many years later, after Shi Huang Di was safely gone, scholars gathered and tried to write down whatever they could remember of the lost literature.[2]

Sealing Himself In

The First Emperor needed to protect the northern frontier against raids by the nomadic horsemen known as the Xiongnu (who were once believed to have been forerunners of the Huns, but now are not). He connected several local walls that blocked strategic passes into one big wall dividing the known world into Us and Them. To build this wall, he sent a general to the frontier with 300,000 soldiers and a million conscripted laborers, most of whom were said to have died in the construction. A steady flow of workmen traveled north to replace the dead. Legend says that every stone in the wall cost a human life.

The purpose of the Great Wall wasn't to keep the Xiongnu from crossing. It was easy enough for them to prop a ladder up against any long unmanned stretch. But they couldn't get horses up the ladder and over the wall, so they would have to invade China on foot, without the military advantage that made them so formidable.

Although Shi Huang Di was the first to build *a* Great Wall of China, he didn't build *the* Great Wall of China. The wall has been expanded, dismantled, neglected, and rebuilt so many times in the past two thousand years that the current wall stretching across north China is newer—a mere five hundred years old or so—and often follows a very different path than the original.[3]

Search for the Secret of Eternal Life

When he gave himself the title of First Emperor, Shi Huang Di intended that all subsequent emperors would continue the naming scheme. His son would become Er Shi Huang Di (Second Emperor), followed by the Third, Fourth, and so on. However, deep down, Shi Huang Di really wanted to become the Only Emperor. He spent a great deal of effort seeking immortality.

The court alchemist told the emperor that mercury was the key to eternal life, and provided him with potions that would grant him eternal life. Shi Huang Di also sent the Taoist sorcerer Xu Fu to search eastward for the secret of immortality. The Eight Immortals, Taoist saints who had learned the secrets of the universe, were said to live on Penglai Mountain beyond the eastern seas. Xu Fu was given a fleet of sixty ships, five thousand crewmen, accompanied by three thousand virgin boys and girls because it was believed that their purity would aid the quest. Several years after he had disappeared over the horizon, Xu Fu returned and reported that a large and frightening sea monster blocked the way, so Shi Huang Di sent a boatload of archers to kill the monster. Then Xu Fu tried again, but he was never heard from again.

Modern historians trying to make sense of this tale suggest that Xu Fu simply discovered Japan and settled down. Archaeology shows that Chinese culture began to appear in Japan around this time.[4]

Failure in the Search for Eternal Life

When Shi Huang Di died in 210 BCE on a tour of the provinces—possibly poisoned by the mercury in his magic elixirs—Li Si kept the news secret for two months until he could return to the capital and tie up some loose ends. Among them, he had to strip command from a dangerously conservative general and to force Shi Huang Di's eldest son to commit suicide. To keep the empire from dissolving into chaos, Li Si kept up a pretense of a live ruler by arriving at the emperor's carriage every day and ducking behind the curtain to consult with him. A wagonload of fish joined the entourage to disguise the smell of the emperor's corpse.[5]

The First Emperor had begun building his tomb many years earlier, employing seven hundred thousand workmen on the project and working many of them to death. The tomb complex measured three miles across, reputedly protected with booby-trapped crossbows. To protect the secret locations, the men who installed these were locked in the tomb as well. In 1974, excavation uncovered an underground army of eight thousand terra cotta statues of soldiers guarding the tomb, and that may be only a small part of treasures buried there. The tomb is reputed to contain a replica of the world floating in a sea of mercury, and a 2006 soil analysis suggests that a substantial amount of mercury is still buried in the unexcavated section.[6]

Once Li Si removed all of the conservatives from any possible influence over the succession, he announced the death of the emperor and allowed the throne to pass to a prince who agreed with all of the radical changes of the previous decade. Er Shi Huang Di (the Second Emperor), however, ruled only a few years before China fell into civil war.

How Bad Was He?

As with most ancient individuals, there are only a handful of original sources, all filtered through centuries of copying and recopying, censoring, fictionalizing, moralizing, and sensationalizing, so there's a very good chance that everything we know about Shi Huang Di is wrong, or at least more complicated than we are led to believe. If you go around burying scholars alive, you won't fare well in the writings of subsequent scholars.[7]

We can't be certain how many people he killed, but for the sake of ranking, I'm following the common accusation of a million.

SECOND PUNIC WAR

Death toll: 770,000[1]
Rank: 58
Type: hegemonial war
Broad dividing line: Rome vs. Carthage
Time frame: 218–202 BCE
Location: western Mediterranean
Who usually gets the most blame: Hannibal
Another damn: Roman conquest

B Y NOW ALMOST ALL OF THE COASTAL REGIONS OF THE WESTERN MEDITER-ranean had fallen under the domination of either Carthage or Rome. These competing empires were divided by the Ebro River in Spain until the city of Saguntum in the Carthaginian sphere switched sides and asked for Roman protection. Hannibal, the Carthaginian general on the spot, would allow none of that, so he stormed and sacked Saguntum. Then, before the Romans could do much more than complain and issue their formal declaration of war, Hannibal marched a Carthaginian army from Spain, up the coast, and over the Alps into Italy.

Over the next few years, a series of Roman armies tried to stop Hannibal, but each was defeated in turn. More than just defeated—annihilated. At Trebia in northern Italy, Hannibal faked a retreat, which lured the Romans out of a strong defensive position to be ambushed in a shallow river. At Lake Trasimene, three Roman legions were enticed along the lakeside road and ambushed in a morning fog. By now, the Romans were wise to Hannibal's tricks and refused to meet him in battle for another year.[2]

Finally, the Romans fielded their largest army ever, eight Roman legions plus allies and cavalry—80,000 men in all—and fought Hannibal on open ground, in broad daylight, at Cannae in southern Italy. Hannibal stood to meet them with an army around half their size. He stationed two heavy blocks of infantry on small elevations in the field and connected them with a flexible line of light infantry in the center. When the Romans attacked into his line, Hannibal's flanks held while the center was pushed backward. This created a funnel that drew the Roman army into the center. The Roman front line shoved against the Carthaginians while the Roman back lines shoved against their front lines, and soon the Romans bunched up too tightly to wield their weapons effectively. Meanwhile, Hannibal's cavalry chased away the Roman horsemen and sealed the open back of the funnel, trapping the entire Roman army in a crowded killing field. The Romans were systematically butchered for the rest of the day until none were left standing.[3]

In two years, the Romans had lost 150,000 men at Hannibal's hands. Roman allies began to defect after this. Syracuse tossed in with Carthage and defended itself against Roman retaliation using an awesome (and probably mythical) collection of war engines devised by the mathematician Archimedes—improved catapults, a mechanical claw that grabbed ships and dashed them against the rocks, and a mirror that focused the sun's rays into a deadly heat beam. Eventually, however, Roman discipline and martial skill defeated Greek ingenuity. Syracuse was taken, and Archimedes was killed during the sacking of the city.

Unable to defeat the Carthaginians in Italy, the Romans sent an army under Scipio to take Spain away from them. After a protracted war that cut Carthage off from this vital source of wealth and manpower, Hasdrubal, the Carthaginian commander in Spain, broke contact and followed his brother Hannibal's path into Italy. Along the way, two Roman armies converged on his army and cornered it on rocky, uneven ground at the Metaurus River in Italy, where he found it difficult to deploy his battle lines. The Roman armies wiped out Hasdrubal before he could add his army to Hannibal's, and a Roman rider flung his severed head into his brother's camp.

Eventually, Scipio's Romans landed in North Africa, which forced Hannibal to abandon Italy and hurry back to defend his homeland. Scipio convinced the Numidian neighbors of Carthage—suppliers of prime cavalry—to switch to the Roman side, and then he destroyed the last Carthaginian army at Zama when Hannibal's war elephants panicked and stampeded back into Carthaginian lines. The ensuing peace treaty put the entire western Mediterranean under Roman control.

North Sea

Baltic Sea

BRITAIN

Elbe

Germans

Suebi

Atlantic Ocean

Eburones

Belgae

Rhine

Alesia
(battle 52 BCE)

Danube

The white areas designate
the extent of direct Roman
control as of 133 BCE

Avaricum
(battle 52 BCE)

Aedui

Sequani

Helvetians

GAUL

ALPS

Po

Aquileia

Rhône

ITALY

Narbonne

Massalia
(Marseille)

Metaurus R.
(battle 207 BCE)

Adriatic Sea

Ebro

Tiber

Rome

Marsi

SPAIN

Appian Way

Samnites

Saguntum

Capua

Cannae
(battle 216 BCE)

Tarentum

Mediterranean Sea

Tyrrhenian Sea

Cartagena

Messina

SICILY

Gadir
(Cadiz)

Carthage

Syracuse

NUMIDIA

Zama
(battle 202 BCE)

AFRICA

THE ROMAN REPUBLIC & DOMINIONS

ca. 133 BCE

0   200   400   600   800   1000   kilometers

0   100   200   300   400   500   600   miles

Scythians

DACIA

Danube

THRACE

MACEDONIA

Pergamum

ASIA

Delphi

Athens

Ephesus

Aegean Sea

Rhodes

Crete

Mediterranean Sea

Cyrene

CYRENAICA

Crimea

Black Sea

Sinope

BYTHNIA

PONTUS

Asia Minor

CAPPADOCIA

TAURUS MTS.

CILICIA

Cyprus

Antioch

Jerusalem

Alexandria

EGYPT

Nile

CAUCASUS MTS.

Caspian Sea

ARMENIA

Tigranocerta
(battle 69 BCE)

ZAGROS MTS.

MESOPOTAMIA

Tigris

Euphrates

Syrian Desert

GLADIATORIAL GAMES

Death toll: 3.5 million[1]
Rank: 28
Type: ritual killing
Broad dividing line: net and trident vs. sword and shield
Time frame: from at least 264 BCE to ca. 435 CE
Location: Roman Empire
Who usually gets the most blame: Romans

GLADIATORIAL COMBAT IS SUCH AN INCOMPREHENSIBLY ALIEN ACTIVITY that we usually turn to sports analogies in order to describe it—but just this once, let's try not to. It's true that some gladiators became as famous as today's football players, but most died shamefully and anonymously. The point of the games was to celebrate the death of outcasts. A skilled fight was merely an entertaining bonus.

Gladiatorial combat began in the distant mists of time somewhere in Italy as rites to honor the dead. The Romans claimed to have picked up the practice from the neighboring Etruscan people, but there's no other evidence for an Etruscan origin, so historians nowadays lean toward blaming another extinct Italian people, the Samnites, who did leave behind evidence of gladiatorial combat.[2]

Sacrificing prisoners of war and spilling their blood on the graves of great warriors was practiced worldwide. It transferred their power to the heroes and got a bit of revenge at the same time. Occasionally, however, prisoners were made to fight each other. Not only was this more entertaining than simply cutting their throats over the grave, but also it shifted the burden of killing from the priests to fellow prisoners. It allowed an ostentatious show of mercy for one lucky winner chosen by the gods to survive. Ancient murals in Mexico of prisoners fighting show that this practice developed independently outside the Mediterranean; however, only the Romans took it to such excess. In fact, the general absence of gladiatorial combat outside the Roman world suggests that it probably is *not* the inevitable manifestation of some sort of universal human bloodlust.

The Romans made the games an integral part of civic life, a spectacle that hardened the citizenry against the sight of blood and pain while eliminating excess prisoners of war and criminals. As a warrior people with enemies in all directions, the Romans had to become accustomed to violent death from an early age. The games taught by example how to face death with courage and dignity; they reinforced the importance of being Roman by showing hated slaves, criminals, and foreigners getting torn apart.[3]

Roman games were usually organized to honor the memory of a great and noble Roman. A high-ranking sponsor paid for the games and offered spectators free entry. The audience was sorted and seated by class: the imperial box, senators together in the front rows, enfranchised Roman citizens with their peers, and women in the back rows, way up at the top.

The first recorded fight was three matches among six slaves to honor Brutus Pera after a battle in 264 BCE. Over time, the size of the contests escalated. Titus Flamininus presented seventy-four matches a century later, and Julius Caesar planned 320 pairs in 65 BCE. As with anything that becomes too popular, the original purpose became diluted. As the republic declined, the games became more entertainment than ritual as ambitious politicians competed in offering flashier spectacles for the public. They hoped that an especially grand show would be remembered by the voters come election time. Julius Caesar was an expert politician and a master of pleasing the crowds. He sometimes armed fighters with outlandish weapons or gilded armor. He arranged mock battles with real bloodshed, including a reenactment of the fall of Troy. He was one of the first sponsors to reenact sea battles in artificial lakes, and the very first to display a giraffe in Rome.[4]

The arena was usually the largest building in any Roman city, and the importance of the games in Roman life was highlighted in 80 CE with the construction of the largest arena ever—the Flavian Amphitheater, or Colosseum—in Rome. The most visible and distinctive symbol of Roman magnificence, the Colosseum could seat up to sixty thousand spectators. A team of sailors hoisted a massive canopy to shade the crowd. Underground tunnels, chambers, and mechanisms positioned and lifted animals, equipment, and scenery into view. When the games were over, the Colosseum efficiently sent the audience away through seventy-six exits.

Until the Nazis built their death camps, the Colosseum may have been the smallest site of the most killings in history, with more killings per acre than any battlefield or prison. In 2007, a worldwide poll declared the Colosseum to be one of the New Seven Wonders of the World.

A Day on the Sand

The morning of a festival day usually began with interesting animals from all over the known world—crocodiles, elephants, leopards, hippos, moose, ostriches, reindeer, or rhinos—being brought into the arena to be displayed and slaughtered by dozens or hundreds. Vicious bears, bulls, lions, or wolves might be made to fight each other for the spectacle, or hunters might dispatch them for the crowd with bows and spears. Specialized performers, such as bullfighters, might fight animals face-to-face according to traditional rituals.

The slaughter of animals in the arena served the extra purpose of allowing the sponsor to provide the people with a splendid feast of roasted bull, deer, or elephant. The meat was fed to the multitudes in open-air banquets after the show.[5]

Five thousand wild animals and four thousand domestic animals were killed to celebrate the opening of the Colosseum. Trajan killed eleven thousand animals to celebrate his Dacian triumph in 107 CE.[6] The demand for more spectacles drove the most impressive species in the empire to extinction. The last European lions were killed around 100 CE. The North African elephant disappeared during the second century CE. Hyrcanian tigers, aurochs, Western wisents, and Barbary lions barely survived the Roman era in a few remote wastelands, but they never recovered and eventually went extinct in later centuries.[7]

Around midday, criminals were publicly executed, as a warning to others, often by fire or by beasts turned loose on them. Sometimes criminals were just thrown together in large batches with simple weapons and told to kill each other. At other times, Roman imagination created lively punishments that fit the crime. Some prisoners were executed by acting out some of the grislier myths: Hercules burning, Icarus falling from the sky, Hippolytus dragged by horses, Actaeon turned into a deer and ripped apart by dogs. These were considered valuable lessons on the mysterious ways of the gods.

The real show didn't begin until the afternoon, when the skilled gladiators were brought out. Gladiators began as criminals, slaves, and prisoners of war, but they were trained in special schools, *ludi*, so that they would put on the best show possible. Some combat was just a matter of making one hundred Gauls fight one hundred Arabs in a mock battle, which would instruct citizen soldiers on what to expect on the frontier; however, much of the time the gladiators fought in single combat so that the audience could savor their fighting skills without distractions.

The games began with the *editor* checking to make sure the weapons were real. Gladiatorial armor was designed to decrease the risk of slight wounds in favor of a clean killing by protecting the arms and face while leaving the chest and neck exposed. Visored helmets hid the faces of the gladiators and kept deaths in the arena anonymous and impersonal. Fighters were outfitted like barbarians or mythical warriors in traditional styles of arms and armor such as the Samnite and the Thracian, named after enemy tribes. A *secutor* fought with a sword and heavy rectangular shield, his sword arm encased in an armored sleeve (*manica*). The trident man (*retiarius*) used a net to grapple with a *murmillo*, a gladiator who wore scaly armor and a fish-shaped helmet in a fanciful reenactment of Neptune fighting a sea monster.

When a gladiator disabled his opponent, the audience would vote on the loser's fate from the stands by giving thumb gestures.* If the crowd was convinced that the defeated

---

* No one knows for sure what the thumb signals were. They are commonly labeled "thumbs up" and "thumbs down," but for all we know, they might have been "thumb extended" and "thumb retracted"

fighter had done his best, it would often spare his life. In fact, the tombstones of successful gladiators frequently listed fight statistics that included wins, ties, and losses, so a single loss wasn't always a career-ending calamity. It has been estimated that only 20 percent of combats resulted in death during Augustus's era, but under some of the later emperors, 50 percent of combats resulted in death.[8]

A rare but special event was the *munera sine missione*, "offerings without reprieve," a series of playoffs from which only one fighter would emerge alive. Early in the first century CE, Augustus banned the practice, considering it cruel to not allow a brave fighter the chance for a reprieve, but later emperors revived it for its dramatic appeal.

Endgame

Gladiators were trained in how to die with grace. A defeated fighter was expected to offer his neck for the final stab without a lot of embarrassing weeping, fleeing, or begging for mercy.[9]

After every fight to death, attendants disguised as underworld gods came out and made sure the dead man wasn't faking. Mercury with a winged hat and sandals poked the loser with a hot iron to see if he flinched. Charun, an Etruscan demon with pointy ears and a vulture's nose, whacked the forehead of the fallen with a mallet.* Then slaves hauled the body away and sprinkled fresh sand over the pools of blood.[10]

Out of sight, in the arena's morgue, attendants working under the strict eye of a supervising official stripped the valuable armor from the body and slit the dead fighter's throat to ensure no deception. Because gladiators were slaves and criminals, their bodies were usually dumped into rubbish pits, but one of the perks of becoming a successful gladiator was the prospect of a decent burial paid for by grateful fans or sponsors, or by fighters pooling money in burial clubs.[11]

With luck, skill, or charisma, a successful gladiator might retire from his career alive and free. Retired gladiators often became trainers or highly paid contract fighters. Others hired out as thugs, bodyguards, and enforcers.

Because Romans considered compassion a weakness, their philosophers rarely opposed the games on those grounds. Some of Cicero's writings complain of gimmicky games he considered vulgar and sadistic, but he still approved of well-played games that illustrated traditional Roman values of strength and honor.[12] Naturally, the most unpleasant emperors (for example, Caligula and Commodus) enjoyed watching men

---

instead. The direct evidence is vague. (Desmond Morris, *Gestures: Their Origins and Distribution* [New York: Scarborough, 1980], pp. 186–193)

* This ritual survived for centuries, oddly, in the Vatican, where a dead pope was traditionally tapped on the forehead with a silver hammer to make sure he's really dead.

hack each other apart and sometimes joined in the fun, but even emperors with better reputations showed proper Roman bloodlust. Emperor Claudius often ordered the loser's helmet to be removed when the final blow was delivered so he could watch the agony on the dying man's face. Marcus Aurelius, on the other hand, disliked the fights and tried to organize games with blunted weapons and as few killings as possible.

Early Christians opposed gladiatorial fighting as a rival religious ritual that had martyred a couple of thousand Christians during the first three centuries of the Christian Era.[13] The games lost some popularity after the empire turned Christian and compassion became a virtue. Constantine tried to abolish gladiatorial combat by edict in 325 CE, but the abolition was sporadically enforced. After the Germanic invaders dismantled the Western Roman Empire, however, there was no longer a need for Romans to toughen up by watching men die. The new barbarian kings generally put a stop to gladiatorial combat whenever they took over. The last recorded fight at the Colosseum occurred around 435 CE, although public animal fights continued there for nearly a century more.

ROMAN SLAVE WARS

Death toll: 1 million[1]
Rank: 46
Type: slave revolts
Broad dividing line: slaves vs. masters
Time frame: 134–71 BCE
Location: Sicily and Italy
Traditional translation of the name: Servile Wars (*bellum servile*)
Who usually gets the most blame: Roman slave drivers
Another damn: rebellion against Rome
Economic factors: slaves, grain

First Servile War (134–131 BCE)

In their continuous wars of conquest, the Romans acquired hundreds of thousands of prisoners and confiscated vast estates from enemies all over the world, all of which they auctioned off to Roman speculators. This was especially true in Sicily, where the Punic Wars had broken the old Carthaginian and Greek aristocracy, replacing it with huge plantations worked by slaves for the profit of Roman landlords. By the second century BCE, Sicily had become the granary of the republic.

In 134 BCE, the slaves of a wealthy Roman planter outside the Sicilian town of Henna killed their master. The murder put not only the killers under the threat of crucifixion, but also, by Roman law, every slave in the household. Faced with this gruesome penalty for merely being in the wrong place at the wrong time, all of the slaves fled into the mountains. There they attached themselves to another runaway, a former Syrian slave originally named Eunus but now rechristened with the loftier royal name Antiochus. He had taken over a mountain shrine to the earth goddess Demeter. By hiding a nut filled with sulfur and fire in his mouth, Eunus breathed flames when he spoke, which amazed his followers and convinced them he spoke for the goddess.

Here grew a community of runaway slaves that supported itself by robbing travelers and plantations. It swelled to 2,000 followers as more slaves flocked to the temple of Demeter. Their general, a Greek slave named Achaeus, traveled around the island recruiting soldiers for the cause, attracting a number of free farmers who disliked the plantation owners as much as any slave. This rebel army then beat the Roman praetor (governor) of Sicily and his hastily assembled militia. That boosted Eunus's following tenfold and more.

Elsewhere, another infestation of runaways formed around Cleon, a slave who had been born in Cilicia (now southern Turkey). He soon agreed to recognize Eunus as the king of Sicily. By now 70,000 slaves were under arms.

Because the Romans were tied up with wars elsewhere, they couldn't give the rebellious slaves their undivided attention. Still, they managed to dispatch a new consular army every year to fight the rebels. Roman law decreed that all rebellious slaves taken alive had to be crucified, but local authorities considered that a waste of valuable property. Instead, they returned captured slaves to their master for discipline, which usually meant whipping rather than death. Eventually Publius Rupilius, the latest consul* in charge of crushing the rebellion, took it upon himself to crucify any slaves he captured alive, eventually nailing up 20,000.

Finally both Roman consuls took their combined armies into the heart of rebel territory and besieged Henna for two years. When the rebels were finally starved out and crushed, Eunus was taken back to Rome. However, he was not publicly strangled in the manner of an honorable foreign enemy. Instead, he died forgotten in prison some time later. Similarly, Publius Rupilius was not given all the pomp and glory of a full Roman triumph because beating mere slaves didn't count as a *true* victory.[2]

Second Servile War (104–100 BCE)

While the big plantations prospered, small, free farmers all across Sicily were being forced into slavery by the crushing debt they owed to lenders and large land owners. Because so many of these new slaves had been subjugated via shady deals, the Roman governor of

---

* The highest elected official in the Roman Republic, a consul served as chief executive and supreme commander. There were always two consuls, and both were replaced every year so that they couldn't accumulate too much power. Other Roman magistrates (tribune, quaestor, aedile, praetor, for example, in roughly the ascending order of power) were also elected for one year and assigned lesser duties.

Everyone who served a term as a magistrate automatically earned a lifetime seat in the Senate, where the ultimate authority of the government lay. This meant that every member of the Senate had had at least one year of practical experience overseeing the unglamorous daily activities that kept the city and the empire operating smoothly, such as building and maintaining roads and sewers, collecting taxes, judging lawsuits, and commanding frontier garrisons.

This system kept power divided between many hands. It churned out large numbers of experienced administrators who could readily be assigned any task—military, civil, or judicial—with plenty of replacements on hand if they failed. Unfortunately, it also meant that there was no single head of state to keep ambitious politicians from killing each other to get ahead (literally—Roman politics was brutal). Over time, power in Rome tended to coalesce around factions and personalities rather than constitutional offices.

Sicily, Publius Licinius Nerva, established a court to hear claims. He proved too efficient for his own good. After he had freed about eight hundred wrongly enslaved people, the local planters bullied him into dropping the issue. The governor backed down and told any plaintiffs who still had cases pending that they would have to remain slaves. They rose in rebellion instead.

The rebel slave Salvius took control of the uprising under the new name Tryphon. By sheer numerical superiority, the slaves quickly took over most of the large country estates. Most towns shut their gates in time and remained Roman; however, the rebels kept food from reaching the towns, and famine followed.

The governor had only unskilled militia at his disposal, and these were beaten outside the town of Morgantia. The town itself was saved from capture only when the Romans offered freedom to any town slaves who helped defend the walls.

Needing more men, the governor came to an agreement with one of the bandit gangs that ranged freely in the mountains—a pardon for the bandits in exchange for crushing the slaves—but this too failed to break the rebellion.

By now Sicily had two slave rebellions, and the two leaders, Salvius of the interior and Athenion in the west, agreed to rule jointly. Soon after, 14,000 Roman veterans arrived from the mainland. Although outnumbered, they beat the combined slave armies by superior discipline, but the Roman general did not press his advantage and the slaves escaped into the mountains. The general was replaced for his failure, but the next year, his replacement was himself replaced for doing no better. Finally a third general, the consul Manius Aquillius, wiped out the slave armies in two years of hard combat. Manius Aquillius also personally killed the enemy commander, Athenion, face-to-face in the middle of the battle—a rare feat in history.[3]

Third Servile War (73–71 BCE)

You've heard of this one.

Spartacus was born in Thrace (now Bulgaria) and served in the Roman army until he deserted and turned to banditry. After being caught, he was sold to the gladiatorial school in Capua. There he was put through the customarily brutal training until he and about seventy of his fellow gladiators escaped into the countryside.

His band quickly grew to a thousand escaped slaves and knocked back the first Roman legion sent to punish them. Then they camped in the natural fortress formed by the dormant volcanic crater of Vesuvius. When a new Roman legion cornered Spartacus in this hideout, his army slid down a sheer cliff face on ropes made from vines. Then Spartacus snuck around and attacked his besiegers. The Romans had unwisely camped in a narrow defile, and without either the time or space to properly deploy, they were badly bloodied by Spartacus and his army.

Convinced now of the gravity of the uprising, the Roman Senate sent four legions to crush the rebels. Spartacus headed north, hoping to escape from Italy over the Alps, where his followers would split up to make their separate ways home; however, his army preferred to stay and loot Italy, so Spartacus turned south again and raped and murdered his way back down the peninsula. He beat every Roman contingent that went against him. With each victory, Spartacus gathered more weapons to arm his followers, who now numbered in the tens of thousands.

Spartacus eventually arrived at the very tip of Italy, where he planned to cross over to Sicily and detach that island from the Roman Empire. He had negotiated with pirates to ferry his army in exchange for allowing them to use the Sicilian ports, but at the last minute the pirates backed out of the deal, stranding the gladiators on the mainland. Meanwhile, the Roman war effort came under the command of Marcus Licinius Crassus, the richest man in Rome, who financed a new army. Crassus built a massive wall across the toe of Italy, which his 32,000 troops occupied, to hold the 100,000 rebels in the south and starve them through the winter.

Spartacus crucified a random Roman prisoner in front of his army to remind his men of the horrible fate that awaited them if they lost, and then they tried to break through the wall. This failed. He tried again, but only one-third of the rebels escaped with Spartacus. The rest were left behind to be leisurely wiped out by the Romans whenever they got around to it.

His forces now seriously weakened, Spartacus was harried up and down southern Italy while his army was whittled away. A second Roman general, Pompey, arrived to steal the glory from his political enemy Crassus. Going into his last battle with little hope of success, Spartacus slit the throat of his horse, declaring that if he lost, he wouldn't need a horse, and if he won, he'd have his pick of the finest horse in Rome.

The gladiator army stood for one last battle and was swept off the field by Crassus, but Pompey took all of the credit by getting in the way of the rebels' retreat and slaughtering them as they fled. Six thousand prisoners were nailed to crosses up and down the Appian Way, the highway connecting Rome with southeast Italy, to die slowly, their bodies rotting down to scattered bones as a warning to other disgruntled slaves. Spartacus probably wasn't among them. He was never heard from again, but his body was likely among the tens of thousands piled up on the battlefield.[4]

What's Next?

After dealing with all of the Slave Wars together, we will jump back a bit to catch up on what's been happening elsewhere in the Roman Empire.

For the next few chapters, our path will diverge from mainstream history. We have entered an era of Roman history when the wars themselves are less important than who's fighting them. During the last few generations of the Roman Republic, ambitious Roman generals will kill hundreds of thousands of foreigners simply to raise their own public profile. Most modern historians of Rome follow the political ups and downs of these generals at Rome rather than their military ups and downs on the frontier. We, on the other hand, will be looking more at the hundreds of thousands of foreigners who were killed to make Rome great.

WAR OF THE ALLIES

Death toll: 300,000[1]
Rank: 96
Type: ethnic civil war
Broad dividing line: Romans vs. Italians
Time frame: 91–88 BCE
Location: Italy
Traditional translation of the name: Social War (*bellum sociale*)
Who usually gets the most blame: Romans
Another damn: rebellion against Rome

THE PEOPLES OF CENTRAL ITALY HAD FOUGHT AS ALLIES OF THE ROMANS IN their wars of conquest, supplying as much as half of the manpower in their armies, but all of the power and the glory of the conquests went to the City of Rome. Allied officers serving in Roman armies were subject to draconian Roman punishments without the right of appeal that Roman citizens had. Roman magistrates passing through allied towns exercised dictatorial authority, and only citizens of Rome had any say in Roman policy or protection from Roman power. So the Italian allies petitioned to be recognized as citizens. They found an ally in Marcus Livius Drusus, a Roman tribune who argued their case in city politics, but every time the vote came up, the Senate shot it down. When Drusus was assassinated as part of the cutthroat politics of the city, the Italian allies abandoned the cooperative approach and went to plan B. Eight tribes, notably the Samnites and Marsi, set up a rival republic ("Italia") with its capital in the town of Corfinium, east of Rome.

Rome immediately mobilized its army to put a stop to this. With enemies in all directions, the two Roman consuls in 90 BCE split the 150,000-man army and headed off separately. Publius Rutilius Lupus went north, Lucius Julius Caesar south. In the north, Rutilius bungled several battles and was eventually killed, but his adviser, the veteran general and alpha Roman of the era, Gaius Marius, took over and led this army to victory over the Marsi. In the south, the Roman army took a beating but managed to hold the Italians to a draw.*

---

* Among the Roman forces in the southern theater, Lucius Cornelius Sulla emerged as a leader to rival Marius. They would eventually fight their own civil war over who ran Rome, and each would end up as dictator for a while.

For the first time since Hannibal's day, Rome had enemies within reach of the city gates. Realizing that winning the war would be harder than they had anticipated, Rome granted concessions to any allies who remained or resumed being loyal. The next year, both consuls took their armies north together and scored a conspicuous victory over the rebellious Italians.

Eventually, the war was extinguished when Rome granted the rebellious allies the right to vote for the Roman government. The catch was that the votes had to be cast in person in the city of Rome itself. At first glance, this was not quite the compromise that Rome claimed because most allied citizens couldn't be bothered to trek all the way to Rome on election day. Early on, most of their votes were never cast; however, candidates eventually learned it was worth the cost to have their supporters carted in from distant communities for the election season, and in time it became quite a rowdy holiday.[2]

THIRD MITHRIDATIC WAR

Death toll: 400,000 at least[1]
Rank: 81
Type: hegemonial war
Broad dividing line: Rome vs. Pontus
Time frame: 73–63 BCE
Location: Asia Minor (modern Turkey)
Who usually gets the most blame: Mithridates
Another damn: Roman conquest

AFTER THE CARTHAGINIANS, THE KINGDOM OF PONTUS, WHICH ENCIRcled much of the Black Sea and had its capital at Sinope on the north coast of Asia Minor, put up the most stubborn resistance to Roman expansion.

Prelude: The First Mithridatic War (89–85 BCE)

While the Romans were busy with the revolt of the allies in Italy, King Mithridates of Pontus took advantage of the distraction to encroach on the Roman sphere of influence in the east. After he overran Rome's allied kingdoms of Bithynia (to the west) and Cappadocia (to the south), their refugee kings convinced the Romans to come to their rescue. As soon as the Romans declared war, however, the Pontic army occupied the Roman province of Asia (the western edge of present-day Turkey). Mithridates ordered all Italians living in these lands—80,000 merchants, sailors, travelers, family members, even Italian-born slaves—killed and their property seized.

Mithridates crossed over to Greece for another easy conquest until Rome solved its problem with the Italian allies and retaliated. Lucius Cornelius Sulla—now a Roman consul—arrived and beat the Pontics in several battles, killing over 150,000 of them;[2] however, the terms of peace he imposed on Mithridates were light because Sulla wanted to get home quickly and shore up his power base in Rome.

To pay for new armies, the warring sides looted the holiest shrines in Greece. Mithridates plundered the island of Delos, birthplace of Apollo and Artemis, while Rome plundered the Oracle at Delphi and Olympia, site of the Olympic Games. Each army hauled away cartloads of precious art to be auctioned for hard cash.[3]

Second Mithridatic War (83–82 BCE)

The Second Mithridatic War was a border skirmish and hardly worth mentioning except that you would probably be confused if the story jumped from the first to the third war without an explanation. Mithridates started rebuilding his army in order to put down some local rebellions, but the local Roman commander thought this new manpower was going to be directed against Rome. After the first clashes, however, they settled the problem diplomatically.

Third—and Deadliest—Mithridatic War (73–63 BCE)

By now, most kings in the Mediterranean had come to terms with the fact that Rome was in charge. They cleared every major policy decision with their Roman ambassador first. Monarchs without sons sometimes went further and simply left their kingdoms to Rome in their wills, but when the king of Bithynia bequeathed his kingdom to Rome, Mithridates declared the will a Roman forgery and occupied Bithynia again. He expected that the Romans would be too busy chasing Spartacus to stop him.

The Roman Senate dispatched Lucius Licinius Lucullus to fix the Pontic problem, but when he arrived, he found the local Roman forces to be an undisciplined rabble in no condition for a hard campaign. He took some time whipping them into shape, but this left another Roman commander in the area, Marcus Aurelius Cotta, on his own to be defeated at Chalcedon and besieged at Cyzicus by Mithridates. With an army that was still barely trained, Lucullus marched out and scared the Pontics into abandoning the siege.

In the subsequent campaign, Lucullus systematically destroyed the Pontic army and overran Asia Minor. Mithridates fled east to his son-in-law, King Tigranes of Armenia, who refused Roman extradition requests. In 69 BCE, Lucullus fought his way into Armenia by way of upper Mesopotamia with a campaign that killed about 100,000 Armenians. The fortune looted from the Armenian capital Tigranocerta made Lucullus the richest man in Rome, and his extravagant lifestyle became legendary after he returned home and began spending it.

Mithridates now fled to his lands on the north shore of the Black Sea, where his son, Machares, ruled, but Machares did not want to antagonize Rome and refused to take up arms. Never a sentimentalist, Mithridates killed Machares and took personal control of his territory. He rebuilt his army by recruiting Scythian horsemen from the Ukrainian steppe.

In Asia Minor, Lucullus made enemies among his fellow countrymen as he consolidated control of Rome's conquests. To relieve the crushing poverty of these war-torn lands, he unilaterally abolished some of the heaviest debts that the colonials owed Roman moneylenders and tax farmers, independent contractors who squeezed the local populations on behalf of the Roman government. This angered many powerful financiers. His soldiers also disliked Lucullus for being stingy with his loot, so they refused to go any further during his latest campaign. This opened the door for a Pontic counteroffensive to reclaim a lot of the lost territory. Lucullus's enemies in Rome took this opportunity to have him recalled and replaced by Pompey (66 BCE), who then grabbed all of the glory by administering the last blow to the dying Kingdom of Pontus.

As the world closed in around him, Mithridates poisoned his daughters and wives to keep them from being captured and humiliated. He then tried to kill himself by poison, but this failed because he had spent a lifetime developing an immunity to the poisons commonly used by assassins. Finally, one of his generals finished the job with a sword.

GALLIC WAR

Death toll: 700,000[1]
Rank: 61
Type: war of conquest
Broad dividing line: Romans vs. Gauls, Germans
Time frame: 58–51 BCE
Location: Gaul (France)
Who usually gets the most blame: Caesar
Another damn: Roman conquest

Helvetii

The surest way to please the voters of Rome was to bring back plenty of loot from foreign conquests and distribute it liberally throughout the city. By the time of the late Roman Republic, however, the empire was too big for the two ruling consuls to go rampaging all over the world, racking up wealth and glory in foreign wars during the single year allotted them. Instead, they got their chance as proconsuls, former consuls who were appointed by the Senate as governors of troublesome (but potentially lucrative) frontier provinces. A popular consul would be rewarded with a lush province to squeeze, while an unpopular one might be given a vast stretch of rocky desert full of scruffy, unprofitable nomads. After serving out his extremely popular term as consul, Gaius Julius Caesar was given four legions and the job of governing several peaceful northern Roman provinces, notably southern Gaul (now southern France).

Caesar was itching for an excuse—any excuse—to start conquering and looting, so he was delighted when the Celtic Helvetians asked permission to migrate across the Roman protectorate in Gaul in 58 BCE. Caesar refused the request, the Helvetians went ahead anyway, and Caesar jumped in front of them with six legions.* He built a long wall across their path near Lake Geneva and waited. The Helvetians waited too.

When the Helvetians tried to maneuver around Caesar, he caught them crossing a river and smashed their rear guard. Then he pursued them closely, allowing them no rest and killing any stragglers, until he accidentally outreached his supply lines. As he pulled back, the Helvetians turned around and pursued him, until the Romans made a stand on a

---

* The Roman Senate officially assigned Caesar only four legions. After that, Caesar raised new legions himself, financed with the loot from Gaul.

hill near the major Gallic town of Bibracte in central France. They repulsed the Helvetian attacks, counterattacked, and destroyed them.

According to documents that Caesar found in the abandoned Helvetian camp, 368,000 Helvetians (one-fourth of them warriors) had set out, but now only 110,000 were left. He resettled the survivors back in their old home (now Switzerland) to prevent the Germans from expanding into the empty land.[2]

It was already too late for that.

Ariovistus

To the north, two Gallic tribes of the Rhine Valley, the Aedui and the Sequani, were having a war, so the Sequani hired the Suebi, a German tribe under Ariovistus, to come help. After the Aedui were beaten, however, Ariovistus wouldn't leave. He seized a third of the Sequani territory, where he settled 120,000 of his own people. Then Ariovistus increased his claim to two-thirds of the Sequani territory.

Caesar, however, was not going to let the Germans assemble a powerful new territory so close to the Roman frontier, so in response to pleas from the Aedui, he demanded the Suebi withdraw. When Ariovistus sneered at the request, Caesar took 30,000 men north in September. The two sides parleyed and maneuvered for a while, until the Roman camp at Vosges found itself surrounded by 70,000 screaming Germans. The Romans calmly formed their lines and attacked. They routed the Suebi and chased them fifteen miles in close pursuit. Having lost 25,000 men, the Suebi escaped back across the Rhine, and Ariovistus was soon rumored to be dead, probably killed in disgrace by his own people.

Probing Outward

For the next year, Caesar stayed in the north battling the Belgae, a major coalition of Gallic tribes that was arming itself to block Roman expansion. In June 56 BCE, Caesar built a wooden bridge over the Rhine in ten days, the first ever to span the river. This awe-inspiring feat of engineering intimidated most of the local tribes into giving him hostages as a token of surrender. Caesar had to spend only eighteen days across the river burning the towns of the one tribe that resisted him. He destroyed the bridge upon retreat rather than leave it as an unguarded back door into the empire.

Caesar crossed over to Britain in 55 BCE to see whether it was worth conquering. He took only two legions, either because he planned no more than a reconnoiter or because he arrogantly assumed that two would be enough to subjugate the island. In any case, the British proved more formidable than he had expected. He ran dangerously low on supplies but raided out from his beachhead and destroyed some villages to show he wasn't going to be bullied into a retreat. Then he retreated to the mainland.

By now, Caesar had picked up two new legions for a total of eight. In the winter of 54–53 BCE, King Ambiorix of the Germanic Eburones tricked the local Roman forces into accepting safe passage across his territory, but then he ambushed them. Most of a Roman legion was wiped out, losing its eagle—the visible symbol of the legion and a powerful talisman. The survivors fled back to their camp and committed suicide rather than become prisoners of the Germans.

Caesar arrived and retaliated by destroying every village and farm in the territory of the Eburones. Although most of the people fled and hid from direct Roman vengeance, they now starved in the winter. Caesar also gave the neighboring tribes permission to do whatever they wanted to to the Eburones. Although we don't know exactly what these tribes did, it was certainly awful. History never mentions the Eburones again.

By 53 BCE, Caesar had ten legions. From the north, he turned around and swept through Gaul again, making sure all of the tribes knew who was in charge. He crushed a string of stubborn Gallic tribes one by one, selling women and children to the slavers who followed his army everywhere it went. Plutarch reports that a million Gauls were taken captive during Caesar's campaigns. The flood of cheap slaves into Italy eventually impoverished the Roman working class, which in turn undermined the democratic foundations of the republic.

The campaign complete, Caesar was able to declare the whole region to be Roman territory. Although every Gallic army that had stood up to the Romans had been beaten, the Gauls decided to take one last shot at driving away the invaders. A large coalition of previously pacified tribes rose in revolt under Vercingetorix, chieftain of the Arverni tribe. To starve the Romans, the Gauls destroyed any supplies they couldn't remove or defend, and the subsequent siege of the Gallic capital at Avaricum was almost as punishing for the Romans outside as for the Gauls inside. Through twenty-seven days of heavy rain, the Romans tried to assemble wheeled siege towers to take the town, while Gallic raiders tried to disrupt their building. Finally, the siege engines were ready, and a Roman assault overran the walls. The conquerors killed everyone inside. Caesar reported no survivors: "Neither old men nor women nor children. Of the whole population—about forty thousand—a bare eight hundred who rushed out of the town at the first alarm got safely through to Vercingetorix."

Vercingetorix had remained at large during the siege of Avaricum, winning several small battles before Caesar cornered him in the stronghold at Alesia. Once again the Romans camped in a ring around the enemy fortress and began building siege engines. After the Romans fought off an attempt by Gauls outside the perimeter to break the siege, Vercingetorix gave up. He threw himself on Caesar's mercy, and although Caesar had a reputation for forgiving his enemies, this time Caesar held firm. Vercingetorix was stashed in jail for a few years until the festive day of Caesar's triumphal procession, when he was dragged out, paraded through the streets of Rome, and ritually strangled at the end.

Legacy

The stubborn and incorruptible Marcus Porcius Cato, one of the last senators in Rome to believe in the republic, vigorously opposed Caesar's war. He felt that Caesar had launched it under false pretenses and that he should be turned over to the Germans for punishment. Other powerful men in Rome also opposed Caesar, but mostly because his ambition to become dictator conflicted with their own ambition to do the same.

Not only had the war covered Caesar with wealth and glory, but also it had left him with a veteran army of unrivaled size, fully bribed in his favor with the loot from Gaul. Even though no one in Rome could stop him from becoming dictator of the republic, it still took a few years of civil war before all of the doubters were convinced. However, just as Caesar settled in to enjoy the fruits of his victory, he was assassinated. His lieutenants fought each other for a few more years, but eventually the last man standing, Caesar's nephew Octavianus, inherited the Caesarian mantle under the title Augustus, and Rome became a proper empire.

ANCIENT INNUMERACY

JUST HOW RELIABLE ARE OLD ATROCITY STATISTICS? "NOT VERY" IS THE TRA-ditional answer. Some modern historians dismiss ancient atrocity statistics as a matter of course, simply because the supporting evidence (if there ever was any) is now lost. They explain that these statistics come from innumerate and largely illiterate societies lacking the modern ability to count large numbers of people and keep accurate records. Conquerors liked to brag about their exploits, and the vast hordes of the enemy army grew with each retelling. Body counts for individual battles are suspiciously lopsided, with huge piles of enemy dead produced at a cost of a few scratches to the winning side. Civilization before the Enlightenment was rather flexible when it came to historic accuracy, and ancient historians never let the truth get in the way of a good story.

As historian Catherine Rubincam puts it, "Ancient historians were not like modern historians, especially in their handling of numbers."[1]

Unfortunately the contrast is not always so clear-cut. In later sections of this book, we will see that modern numbers often aren't much better. For example, it's quite common to run across estimates of 100,000 Iraqi soldiers killed in the 1991 Gulf War, even though the Americans found only 577 dead bodies and captured only 800 wounded among their 37,000 prisoners.[2] For the most recent Iraq War, estimates of the number killed in the five years or so following the 2003 invasion run anywhere from 85,000[3] to 1.2 million.[4] Compared to that range of guesses, the question of whether 25,000 or 50,000 Romans were killed at Cannae doesn't look so bad.

I tend to give ancient records the benefit of the doubt. Our ancestors knew how to count sheep, cattle, and money, so why would they suddenly forget when it came to counting people? Ancient people were literate enough to have left behind extensive graffiti as one of their most common relics. We usually accept the word of ancient historians when they list a chronology of events or itemize a kingdom's budget, so why are we more skeptical when they count bodies?

Let's put this on a scale of 1 to 10. Most modern scholars assume that ancient body counts have a reliability score of 2 (the ancients just plugged in any old number that sounded impressive), compared with modern estimates, which are presumed to have a reliability score of 9 (meticulously counted and cross-referenced against official records). This would easily justify ignoring the numbers in ancient histories.

On the other hand, I suspect that the reliability of ancient numbers might score closer to 4 (subpar, but estimated by people who at least knew how to keep accounting records and count into the thousands without smoke pouring from their ears). More to the point, I might assign a reliability score of 7 for most modern estimates (a score based on scattered records, and a lot of fudging to fill in the gaps). This makes it a lot harder to draw a line of plausibility between them. If we believe the questionable death tolls from Hiroshima, Stalin's Russia, or the Korean War, then we shouldn't get too skeptical about Alexander the Great.

My rule of thumb is that if at least one modern historian treats an ancient body count as credible, then I won't dismiss it out of hand. We don't have to accept every number the ancients throw at us, but doubting an ancient death toll just because it sounds fishy isn't enough.

For comparison, consider the Holocaust. Right now, everybody knows the Holocaust happened. If we have any doubts, we can pick up the phone and call someone who was there. At some point, however, there won't be any eyewitnesses left to ask. We will have to rely on archives as proof. But in 2037, a budget cut will shut down one of the major American archives, which will go into a warehouse and crumble. Then a big war in the Middle East will destroy the Holocaust archives in Israel, and twenty years later a new anti-Semitic dictator in Russia will purge his country's archives. And let's not forget the Great Computer Crash of 2022, which will wipe out all of the documents that had been meticulously digitized.

Eventually, the proof will have eroded so much that we can only take some historian's word for it that all those people were killed, which is exactly the same problem we face with ancient atrocities. Future skeptics will openly question how Hitler could have possibly killed 6 million Jews with such primitive weapons: Why, that's more people than lived in any city on the planet at the time, all packed into these half-dozen little camps? Impossible! Six million Jews could have fought back and beaten the Nazis with their bare hands. . . .

There is a tendency to dismiss a lot of uncomfortable history as hearsay, but when you get down to it, all history is hearsay. We owe it to the victims to not doubt too readily.

XIN DYNASTY

Death toll: 10 million
Rank: 14
Type: dynastic dispute
Broad dividing line: Han dynasty (legitimate) vs. Wang Mang (usurper) vs. the Red Eyebrows (rebels)
Time frame: 9–24 CE
Location: China
Who usually gets the most blame: Wang Mang
Another damn: Chinese dynasty collapsing

Happy Families Are All Alike

Contrary to what you would expect, traditional monarchies tend to be matriarchal. Let's say you're the emperor. Since inheritance passes through the male line, blood relatives of your father are all slotted neatly into the succession, which makes them all rivals. There is no reason for them to look out for your best interests. In palace intrigues, don't count on help from your younger brother, because he's next in line for the throne. Your father's brother is third in line. If anything happens to you, they all move up a step.

On the other hand, women who have married into the imperial family have a more precarious position. The empress's only connection to the court might be her relationship to you. If you die and your uncle inherits the throne, then your mother and wife are going to get shoved aside. The best they and their families could hope for is exile; the worst could be a bloody purge. For that reason, the families of your wife or mother are natural allies who will watch your back. The history of empires is replete with powerful dowager empresses, the wives of dead emperors, trying to hold onto power. One way to reduce the influence of your in-laws is to stay in the family and marry sisters (the Egyptian way) or cousins (the European way), but the Chinese had strict laws against incest that required the emperor to marry outside his lineage.

(You won't like this next part. It has a confusing profusion of ancient dates and Chinese names,* but you don't need to stash them into your long-term memory. Just get a feel for the general texture of the events.)

---

* A possibly too detailed explanation of Chinese emperors' names:
    First things first. In the Far East, the family name comes first. Wang Mang's father was Wang Wan. Mao Zedong's brother was Mao Zetan.

Shortly after the death of the First Emperor (see "Qin Shi Huang Di"), China fell into civil war from which a new dynasty, the Han, emerged as the sole power. For almost two centuries, a reunified China moved along smoothly under the Han dynasty. When Emperor Yuan (which translates as the "Primary Emperor") died in 33 BCE, his son, Emperor Cheng (the "Successful Emperor"), came to the throne and ruled quietly for the next twenty-six years. Cheng relied on his mother's family, the Wangs, to staff his court. For example, command of the army went to the empress's brother Wang Feng in 33 BCE and passed to Wang Yin (22 BCE), Wang Shang (15 BCE), Wang Gen (12 BCE), and finally to the empress's nephew Wang Mang in 8 BCE. There was nothing unusual in this, but when Emperor Cheng died without a living son in 7 BCE, the influence of the Wangs abruptly ended.

The throne then passed to Cheng's twenty-year-old nephew, his half-brother's sickly son, the new Emperor Ai (the "Lamentable Emperor"). Cheng had been the son of Yuan's Empress Wang, but Ai was Yuan's grandson by way of another woman, his consort, Princess Fu, who now began to elevate her family to high posts in the empire. Emperor Ai, however, was homosexual and died childless in 1 BCE. Ai's twenty-two-year-old commander of the army and probable lover, Dong Xian, was too slow in the subsequent scramble for power, so he was removed and driven to suicide by the resurgent Dowager Empress Wang. The Wangs set about purging all the Dongs that Dong Xian had hired, along with all of the Fus that Dowager Princess Fu had put into government.[1]

The throne then passed to a nine-year-old cousin, Emperor Ping (the "Peaceful Emperor"), and Dowager Empress Wang appointed her brother's son, Wang Mang, as regent. If you glance back a couple of paragraphs, you will see Wang Mang listed as army commander for the last year of Emperor Cheng's reign. The Wangs reclaimed all of the positions they had lost six years earlier. The regent Wang Mang married his daughter to the child emperor in order to solidify his hold on power.

Wang Mang's son, Wang Yu, worried that this power grab would eventually backfire and that Emperor Ping would purge the Wangs once he got old enough to plot and scheme on his own. To cover himself against that eventuality, Wang Yu conspired with the

---

Emperors usually began life with a personal name, such as Liu Xiu, meaning Xiu of the Liu family. Later, as reigning emperors, they were known simply as the emperor or something like that. After they died, historians gave them a formal name by which they are known to posterity, such as Emperor Guangwu. The formal name often means something descriptive in Chinese, in this case "Complete-Martial." In every history book I've seen, these formal names pass into English without translation—Yuan, Cheng, Ai, Ping—but it might be easier for you to keep the characters straight if you think of them translated—Primary, Successful, Lamentable, Peaceful.

If it helps, just think of European history played out by characters named the Sun King and the Virgin Queen instead of Louis and Elizabeth.

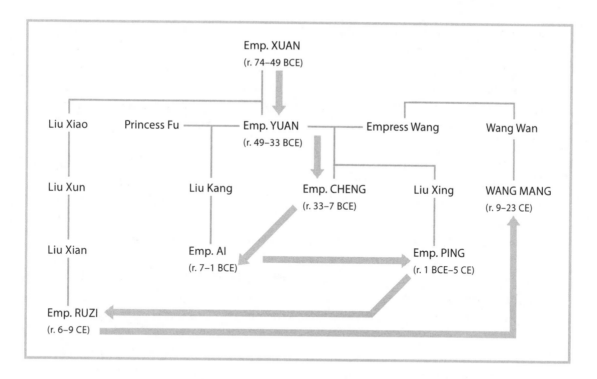

emperor's maternal clan, the Wei family, to remove his father from both the regency and the land of the living. When Wang Mang discovered this, he ordered his son to commit suicide and then wiped out all of the Weis except for the emperor's mom. The emperor, now thirteen years old, resented Wang Mang for killing all of his uncles and cousins, but he died before he could act on the resentment. Everyone suspected that Wang Mang had poisoned him. This was 6 CE.[2]

Okay. Start paying attention again.

The Brand New Dynasty

The story so far: The Han dynasty had unified and stabilized China for two hundred years. Then it hit a bump in the imperial succession. Wang Mang, former army commander and nephew of the dowager empress, was regent of China, but the young emperor he was supposed to be taking care of had just died mysteriously. Naturally, this thirteen-year-old emperor left no children behind. In fact, there were no surviving male offspring of any of the four previous emperors, all the way back to Emperor Yuan (with whom we started this story), so Wang Mang backed up a generation and looked into the offspring of an earlier emperor. He handpicked the youngest one he could find to be the new emperor, a one-year-old prince, Ruzi (which translates as "Infant"). Wang Mang, of course, stayed on as regent until the new prince reached adulthood, which didn't seem likely in the hands of these people.

In 9 CE, Wang Mang tired of waiting for the baby emperor to get old enough to be worth killing, so he packed off Ruzi to an early retirement. (That's not a euphemism. Ruzi survived another sixteen years on a comfortable estate.) Wang Mang declared himself to be the first emperor of a new dynasty, called, appropriately, the Xin dynasty (the "New" dynasty).

As brutal as this history sounds, these few years of Han dynasty backstabbing killed what—a hundred people at most? This by itself doesn't earn a place on my list. The problem is that it distracted the imperial household from tending to the necessary business of running the empire, and it undermined the legitimacy of the court. China had burned through three child emperors in sixteen years and was now in the hands of a usurper.

Wang Mang was a strict Confucian fundamentalist, so much so that he executed three sons, a nephew, and a grandson for breaking various laws,[3] and he spent an inordinate amount of his reign trying to restore lost rituals and procedures of the ancients. He claimed to have conveniently discovered a lost manuscript of Confucius that supported all of his reforms.

Being a traditionalist, he returned to older forms of cash used when Confucius was around. Spades, knives,* and shells supplemented coinage for the first time in hundreds of years. He ended up issuing so many different kinds of money that no one could acquire the familiarity they needed to spot counterfeits, so the people didn't trust any of the money in circulation. The economy sputtered to a halt.

As a usurper himself, Wang Mang knew firsthand that emperors should not trust their ministers, so he kept a tight rein on his subordinates. Because he refused to delegate many important but tedious tasks, the work never got done. For example, Wang tried to restructure the pay scale of the civil service, but he got so wrapped up in the details that the civil servants went without pay for years on end. Naturally, they turned to other sources of income, most of them illegal.

Like so many idealists across history, Wang wanted to restore the lost good old days when (so he imagined) big families of free citizens on small farms formed the backbone of society. To this end, Wang tried to break up the big estates of the nobility. He set a maximum for the amount of land any family could own, and then redistributed the surplus land to their neighbors. This earned him no friends.

---

* Not spades and knives *literally*. The ancient Chinese minted coins that were shaped like shovel heads and knife blades before settling on modern disk-shaped coinage.

Mandate of Heaven

Traditional Chinese political philosophy puts great stock in the Mandate of Heaven. Under this theory, Heaven will favor a just emperor with peace and prosperity, but if the ruler is *not* favored with peace and prosperity, then clearly Heaven finds him odious. It is perfectly acceptable—indeed, a sacred duty—to overthrow an ill-favored emperor. Heaven quickly showed its displeasure at Wang Mang.

The Yellow River (or Huang Ho) is definitely the deadliest geographic feature known to man. As the center of trade and irrigation, the river keeps China alive, but far too often the silt-choked river clogs with sediments and overflows its banks, carving a new path to the sea across the adjacent plain and whichever hapless towns and villages might stand in the way. Several floods of the Yellow River have the distinction of being the only natural disasters in history to have killed over a million people. Including the subsequent famine and disease, 7 million died in the flood of 1332–33; 900,000 to 2 million, in 1887; and 1 to 4 million, in 1931.[4]

With the Chinese government distracted by palace intrigues, civil engineers fell behind in repairing the irrigation systems that were vital to life in China, among them the levees that kept the Yellow River in its banks. In 4 CE, the Yellow River jumped out of its riverbed, spreading flood and famine. In 11 CE, it jumped again.[5]

Wang Mang's Xin dynasty might have survived if it hadn't been for these disruptions. When divine anger began to show itself, a prophecy that the Han dynasty would be restored to power started circulating. Secret societies soon sprang up.

Red Eyebrow Rebellion

In 17 CE, a new gang of rebels started a life of banditry in the coastal provinces of the lower Yellow River that had been hit hardest by the floods. Called the Red Eyebrows after the streaks of red war paint they smeared on their foreheads, the rebels knocked down all of the armies the Xin dynasty sent against them. Finally, Wang Mang sent a giant force to crush them, which scored a few successes and inflicted a lot of retribution on rebel sympathizers, until the Red Eyebrows destroyed the Xin army at Chengchang in 23 CE. The Red Eyebrows scrounged up Liu Penzi, a fourteen-year-old member of the Liu clan (the former ruling family of the Han dynasty), whom they declared emperor.[6]

Meanwhile, several smaller bands of rebels in central China between the Yellow and Yangtze Rivers fell under the spell of another branch of the Liu family and consolidated into a larger threat, called the Lulin, or Greenwood, Army after the rugged mountain (Lu-lin, translated as "green wood") that had served as their first refuge. The Greenwood chief was Liu Yan, a sixth-generation descendant of a former Han emperor, but ironically he proved far too competent and charismatic to keep his supporters. The other Greenwood leaders preferred a weak nonentity whom they could manipulate, so they conspired and connived and elevated Liu Yan's third cousin, Liu Xuan, to the rank of declared emperor instead.[7]

Wang Mang sent another massive army, said to be almost 500,000, although it probably wasn't, to crush the Greenwood forces, said to number less than 10,000, although that probably wasn't true either. In June 23 CE, as the Xin army besieged a Greenwood garrison in the town of Kunyang, Liu Xiu, younger brother of the former leader Liu Yan, gathered fresh rebels in the countryside and moved to relieve the siege. The Xin commander underestimated the strength of the approaching rebels and took an arrogantly trivial force to brush them aside. When the Greenwood rebels beat this small unit, the Xin soldiers fled back toward the main army, spreading panic and pessimism. Then the Greenwood forces inside Kunyang attacked out the town gates, while the rebel forces outside the town followed up their victory. A sudden thunderstorm and flash flood added to the confusion, and the Xin army fled and was massacred in retreat.[8]

Having lost two major armies in a single year, Wang Mang was doomed. In the race to reach the capital at Chang'an (Xian nowadays), the Greenwood Army arrived before the Red Eyebrows, so their candidate, Liu Xuan, became the leader of the restored Han dynasty. Chang'an fell after determined block-by-block defense. As the palace burned, Wang Mang was beheaded and cut into pieces so that everyone could have a keepsake.[9]

The New Han

Before Liu Xuan had a chance to settle in and enjoy being emperor, conspiracies began to surround him. The former Infant Emperor Ruzi was wooed out of retirement by a couple of minor noblemen, but their attempt to seize power failed. They were all executed.

To play it safe, Xuan quickly found an excuse to have his former rival, Liu Yan, executed as well.

Then several generals plotted to kidnap Xuan. They too were discovered and most of them were executed, but one of the survivors managed to chase Xuan out of Chang'an. Xuan regrouped with loyal generals and retook the city. Xuan was hardly back on his throne when the Red Eyebrows arrived and took Chang'an for themselves, installing their own emperor, Liu Penzi. The Red Eyebrows captured Emperor Liu Xuan but merely demoted him to lesser nobility and sent him away to herd horses so as not to stir up resentment. Soon, however, the people began to speak wistfully about the days when Xuan was in charge, so he was dragged into a dungeon and strangled.[10]

Liu Yan's brother, Liu Xiu, was off fighting on the frontier. A legendarily prudent man, Liu Xiu had been lying low since Liu Yan's execution on trumped-up charges a couple of years earlier, but with Xuan out of the picture, he declared himself emperor (25 CE) and marched his army against the Red Eyebrows. It was a tough campaign, but Liu Xiu prevailed and took Chang'an in 27 CE. He pursued the retreating Red Eyebrows and finally trapped them with overwhelming numbers. Sick of all of the killing, Liu Xiu held back the attack and offered generous terms of surrender: a general amnesty, a nice estate for ex-Emperor Penzi, and no mass executions. They accepted.

Liu Xiu's restored Han dynasty would survive for another two centuries. He became known to posterity as the "Complete and Martial Emperor"—in Chinese, Emperor Guangwu.

Population Plummet

Despite a few temporary interruptions, China has existed as a political entity longer than any other nation on earth, and the civil servants of the Chinese Empire have been keeping detailed records for centuries. Many have been lost to fire, flood, war, and mice, but some fragments, copies, and summaries survive. Among them are sporadic census records going back several dynasties. Surprisingly, summaries of the Chinese census of 2 CE are largely intact, giving us the oldest reliable population figures of any society in history. Admittedly, there are a few discrepancies in the data, but most scholars accept that the population of China in 2 CE was around 57,671,400.

After that, census records show that China was in serious trouble. The recorded population plunged to 21 million in 57 CE, bounced up to 34 million in 75 CE, then worked its way up to 43 million by 88 CE. I know that's a lot of numbers to spring on the unsuspecting reader in one sentence, but the upshot is that China appears to have lost close to 37 million people in a half century of war, flood, and famine, and the count was still almost 13 million short as the century came to a close. As bad as that looks, it's likely that many of the 37 million missing people were still alive but hiding from tax collectors. The reduced census count of 57 CE probably indicates the government's inability to find every person in China after a period of widespread unrest rather than a pure death toll.

Even so, most scholars believe that there is an actual population loss of many millions hidden somewhere in there. Depending on whom you read, the real population decline in China during the first century could be anywhere from 8 to 43 million. Scrounging around, I was able to find several different estimates. I have chosen the low-middle estimate of 10 million as a reasonable compromise.[11]

ROMAN-JEWISH WARS

Death toll: 350,000
Rank: 94
Type: religious uprising, colonial rebellion
Broad dividing line: Jews vs. Romans
Time frame: 66–74 and 132–135 CE
Location: Palestine
Who usually gets the most blame: Romans
Another damn: rebellion against Rome

First Jewish Revolt (66–74 CE)

Following Alexander the Great's conquests, Greeks had settled over the Middle East, where they usually formed an alien upper class resented by the natives. In Caesarea, the chief city of Roman Palestine, Greeks and Jews were always exchanging insults, but sometimes the heckling escalated to full-scale riots. After one round of riots, the Roman governor demanded that the Jewish community pay for all of the damages. The Jews, however, claimed that the Greeks were to blame for sacrificing some birds on the steps of a synagogue in the first place, so they refused. No problem; the Roman governor simply took the money out of the temple treasury in Jerusalem.

Jews all over the country rose up in anger at the blasphemy. Radical nationalists—the Zealots—easily chased the small Roman garrison into Syria. In the first flush of victory, it looked like God had restored the Jewish nation to its former glory until Emperor Nero sent a full army under Vespasian to put down the uprising. His Roman legions systematically eradicated the rebels in Galilee with sieges, massacres, and political maneuvering, and eventually they closed in on Jerusalem.

The war was interrupted in 68 when Roman generals fed up with Nero's antics overthrew him, and one after another, every Roman general in the empire marched his legions on Rome to claim the throne for himself. Vespasian proved to be the last and most permanent of the four emperors proclaimed during this year and a half of chaos.

Emperor Vespasian turned the Jewish rebellion over to his son Titus, who surrounded Jerusalem. Siege engines were difficult to build in Palestine because trees were scarce and scraggly, but sheer Roman stubbornness kept Jerusalem sealed off for two years and brought its defenders toward the edge of starvation. Every day the Romans captured desperate foraging parties of Zealots outside the walls and nailed them up in plain view of the defenders. When Jerusalem finally fell in 70 CE, the Romans massacred the population and reduced the temple in Jerusalem to rubble. The five-foot-tall seven-branched gold candlestick that had graced the temple was hauled off to Rome and triumphantly paraded for the people.

Most of the city walls were demolished, but Titus ordered a short, impressive stretch of the temple-complex wall preserved as a lesson to future rebels that even the thickest walls can't withstand the Roman army. This wall fragment (now known as the Western or Wailing Wall) is the holiest spot in Judaism, which proves that the *real* lesson for future rebellions is either (a) faith can indeed withstand the Roman army or (b) if you start to demolish a holy site, finish the damn job.*

The last 960 Zealots retreated to the mountain fortress of Masada. The defenders watched helplessly as the Romans began to methodically build a massive ramp up the mountain in order to roll their siege engines into range. Knowing they were doomed, the trapped Zealots drew lots. The losers killed the winners and then drew lots again. The losers killed the winners, and so on, until only one defender was left alive to commit the unpardonable sin of suicide.

Bar Kokhba Revolt (132–135 CE)

The destruction caused by the first revolt was centered mostly on Jerusalem, and much of Palestine remained unravaged. Peace and prosperity gradually returned.[1] Then the Romans tried to assimilate the province into the larger Mediterranean cultural melting pot. Around 132, Emperor Hadrian banned genital mutilation throughout the empire, which sounds like an excellent idea until we remember that Judaism requires circumcision. Hadrian quickly revised his order to make an exception for Jews. Unfortunately, Hadrian also chose this moment to start rebuilding Jerusalem as a modern Roman city with a temple of Jupiter where the temple of Yahweh had stood.

The Jews would not accept any of this, and they rose up under Simon ben Kosiba, who gained the messianic nickname Bar Kokhba, "Son of the Star."[2] The rebels were strongest in the countryside, where they built fortified strongholds interlaced with hidden access tunnels. The Romans sent three legions to put down the rebellion. It was a hard campaign, and one of the legions disappears from the history books after this, probably wiped out by the rebels. The war is said to have destroyed fifty strongholds and 985 villages. It was so destructive that we still don't have the whole story or too many relics, just a few caves discovered in the cliffs near the Dead Sea. These caves housed the last of the rebels, and archaeologists named them after their most distinctive contents: the Cave of Scrolls, the

---

* The other side of this wall is the third holiest site in Islam, so people will probably be fighting over it for the rest of human existence.

Cave of Arrows, the Cave of Letters (including some written by Bar Kokhba), and the Cave of Horrors (forty skeletons, entire families dead of starvation), among others.

When the fighting was over, most of the Jews in Palestine were killed, exiled, or enslaved, and this time the Romans made certain there would not be a next time. The Romans depopulated much of the territory and restocked it with more cooperative ethnicities. The Jews were exiled from Palestine, and the Diaspora, the scattering of Jews across the globe, began.

Death Toll

Ancient historians claim that as many as 2 million Jews were killed in these and other revolts. The contemporary Jewish historian Josephus reported that 1,197,000 people were killed during the siege of Jerusalem in the first revolt, although Tacitus estimated a death toll of half that: 600,000.[3] Cassius Dio[4] reports that a total of 580,000 Jews were killed in battle during the second revolt. Ancient historians report the death toll for other rebellions by Jewish minorities in Cyrene and Cyprus (not included here) as 220,000 and 240,000.[5] These unbelievable claims are usually held up as the perfect example of why not to trust the numbers in ancient histories.

Realistically, maybe one-fifth to one-half of the inhabitants of Palestine died in each of the revolts, but that's still not a complete answer because no one knows how many people lived there to begin with. Estimates of the pre-revolt population of Palestine run anywhere from 0.5 million to 6 million. Religious historians tend to favor the high numbers, which are based on written sources like the works of Josephus; archaeologists favor the low numbers, which are based on land use and population densities.[6] In any case, a reasonable estimate would be something like 350,000 deaths all told, which would be around one-third if the original population was 1 million, or one-half if it was 700,000, or one-fourth if it was 1.4 million. No matter what anyone says, it's unlikely that the ancient population of the area came anywhere close to 2 million, which was the number of inhabitants at the time of independence in 1948.

THE THREE KINGDOMS OF CHINA

Death toll: 34 million missing
Rank: 25
Type: failed state
Broad dividing line and major state participants: Wu vs. Wei vs. Shu
Time frame: 189–280 CE
Location: China
Other state participants: Han (before), Jin (after)
Who usually gets the most blame: eunuchs, Cao Cao
Another damn: Chinese dynasty collapsing

> The empire, long divided, must unite; long united, must divide. Thus it
> has ever been . . .

—opening lines of *Romance of the Three Kingdoms*

The Story in One Hundred Words or Less

As the Han dynasty grew more corrupt, peasant revolts unleashed chaos. Warlords carved up the empire among themselves. From this turmoil, three kingdoms gradually emerged:

1. The Kingdom of Wei, led by the devious Cao Cao (pronounced "tsow-tsow")
2. The Kingdom of Wu, led by the ambitious Sun Quan (pronounced "soon-chew-ann")
3. The Kingdom of Shu, led by the virtuous Liu Bei (pronounced "lyoo-bay")

Over the next century, the Three Kingdoms fought each other in shifting alliances. Heroes rose and fell. Finally, China was reunified.

R3K

The era of the Three Kingdoms has a special place in Chinese culture as a kind of Trojan War, Wild West, and Camelot all rolled into one. It was a conveniently mysterious time into which any saga could be dropped without a lot of backstory. It was a violent, chaotic era when men made their own destiny, when a person's moral strength was tested in the crucible of war, when adventure was just down the road or over the next hill. Eventually, in the fourteenth century during the Ming dynasty, Luo Guanzhong bundled all of the accumulated stories together into *Romance of the Three Kingdoms*, one of the three* most important novels in Chinese literature.

In Chinese culture, a name from the era of the Three Kingdoms will likely spark memories of a character from the novel rather than the real historical individual. Cao Cao is a scheming villain. The Zhang brothers who founded the Yellow Turbans are sorcerers and con men. Sun Quan's sister Sun Shangxiang is the archetype of all tomboy princesses who are surprisingly skilled in the martial arts. Guan Yu, companion and blood brother of Liu Bei, was posthumously promoted to Chinese god of war, so you just *know* he displayed some awe-inspiring martial prowess in *Romance*.[1]

As with most historical novels, the characters from *Romance* interact much more directly than they probably did in real life, all having rich personal friendships, loves, and vendettas to drive the story forward. They can be divided into heroes and villains more neatly than real people usually can be. The story is consistently popular; the 2007 film *Red Cliff* directed by John Woo and based on events from the Three Kingdoms is the highest-grossing film in Chinese history.[2]

Now let's back up and see how this age of chaos unfolded.

The Beginning: Yellow Turban Rebellion (184–188 CE)

The first version of the Han dynasty had fallen to Wang Mang (see "Xin Dynasty") because imperial in-laws held too much power, so when Liu Xiu (Emperor Guangwu) restored the Han dynasty, he tried something different. This time the emperor surrounded himself with eunuchs, who were (literally) cut off from all family connections and presumably would be loyal only to the emperor. Unfortunately, in practice, the eunuchs proved even more selfish than the imperial in-laws because they had to enjoy their power *right now*, rather than bank it away for their children. During the reign of Emperor Ling (156–189 CE), a clique of palace eunuchs, the Ten Regular Attendants, controlled the government and looted the empire for their own personal gain.

At the time, China was in the grips of a deadly epidemic, until a team of wandering Taoist healers, Zhang Jiao and his brothers, developed a cure. Considering the state of medicine in this era, if their cure actually worked, then the disease may have been imaginary or something that ordinarily went away on its own. Maybe their cure was a placebo or just a rumor. There's even a slim chance it was some esoteric folk wisdom that is now lost. In any case, as the brothers traveled throughout the empire tending the sick,

---

* The Chinese like precise numerical lists. We will see this tendency several times in this book.

they accumulated a large, grateful following. They listened to complaints of suffering and injustice, and they offered hope. In time they became leaders of a large secret society of discontented commoners. Passwords and rituals bound them together, and every member recruited more members from trusted friends and neighbors.

Finally the Zhang brothers rose up against the tyrannical power of the palace eunuchs. For identification in battle, the rebels wore yellow headscarves (traditionally but misleadingly translated into English as "Yellow Turbans"). They scored tremendous success in the beginning, defeating at least three major armies thrown against them.

Other revolts erupted in the wake of the Yellow Turban success. The Five Pecks of Rice Rebellion (so called because that was the initiation fee for membership to the secret society) established a theocratic kingdom in Sichuan in 184. Although this kingdom was destroyed rather quickly, the movement eventually turned into the Way of the Celestial Masters, a Taoist cult that has fluctuated in and out of respectability across Chinese history.

Within a year, however, the main Yellow Turban uprising had been beaten down and a half-million Chinese were dead, including the Zhang brothers.[3] Independent bands lingered, and every time it looked like the last of them was crushed, another insurgency would erupt somewhere else. This finally ended when the last 300,000 armed rebels (along with civilian dependents, reportedly a million people in total) surrendered to the Han general Cao Cao, who kept this force under arms as a special unit under his own command.

The End of the World

In 189 Emperor Ling died without a direct heir, but Ling's widow, the empress regent, and her brother He Jin, the army commander, elevated one of Ling's relatives as Emperor Shao. The Ten Regular Attendants opposed the new emperor, so Shao summoned He Jin and the army to the capital at Luoyang on the Yellow River plain to scare them into obedience. As the army camped outside Luoyang, the Ten Regulars forged an imperial order instructing General He Jin to meet with his sister in the palace. Once he was away from his army, the eunuchs had him ambushed and killed. They displayed his head from the city walls to frighten the army, but this only made the soldiers angry. The army stormed the city and massacred all of the eunuchs, depantsing every man they found who wanted to be spared so they could look for genitalia.[4]

With leaderless soldiers and pantless bureaucrats running amok in the capital city, chaos spread throughout China. General Dong Zhuo pulled his army off the northern frontier and moved to Luoyang, defeating everyone who stood in his way. He replaced Emperor Shao with Shao's younger brother, ruling as Emperor Xian. More armies converged on the capital to drive away Dong Zhuo, who burned Luoyang to the ground and retreated to the secondary capital at Chang'an. Within a year, Dong Zhou was assassinated by an ambitious subordinate, who kept Emperor Xian as a hostage and a pawn in the civil war that was sweeping across China.

By now, all of the large armies that had been raised to put down the Yellow Turbans had turned on each other. At first, two types of contenders fought for control of China. Landowning nobility raised peasant armies to quell local rebellions and ward off other ambitious aristocrats. Soon, however, these amateur armies were bumping up against the professional armies led by career officers who had recently been stationed on the frontier. Most of these conflicts ended in favor of the professionals, and soon the civil war was entirely in the hands of rootless armies instead of the nobility.

> There are five possible operations for any army. If you can fight, fight; if you cannot fight, defend; if you cannot defend, flee; if you cannot flee, surrender; if you cannot surrender, die. These five courses are open to you, and a hostage would be useless. Now return and tell your master.
>
> —Sima Yi to Gongsun Yuan's emissary,
> *Romance of the Three Kingdoms*

Red Cliffs

After a few years, Emperor Xian escaped his captors and took refuge with Cao Cao, which conferred legitimacy on his war band. By 207, Cao Cao had beaten a string of rivals and united the Yellow River plain under his puppet emperor. In an earlier time, this would have been enough to count as a reunification of China, but the Chinese people had been expanding southward over the past few centuries, and these new frontier territories remained outside his control. These southern states combined their armies to repel any expansion southward by Cao Cao.

When Cao Cao invaded in 208, he met the allied armies of the south at Red Cliffs, a rugged gorge of the Yangtze River. For a couple of days, the two forces watched each other across the river. Finally Cao Cao piled his army into boats and tried an amphibious assault against the opposite bank, but halfway there, the wind shifted, blowing his boats back to his side of the river. The enemy now launched fire ships on the new wind; these collided with Cao Cao's boats and spread fire and chaos throughout the invasion force. With his fleet destroyed, Cao Cao abandoned the Yangtze and returned north.

China's split now solidified into the Three Kingdoms:

1. Cao Cao's Wei Kingdom on the Yellow River plain inherited most of the Han imperial apparatus.

2. Sun Quan's Wu Kingdom occupied most of southern China along the lower Yangtze River valley and toward Indochina.

3. Liu Bei's Shu Kingdom was tucked into the broad Sichuan basin around the upper Yangtze River.

Each of these kingdoms claimed to be loyal to the emperor and the legitimate continuation of the Han dynasty, unlike the other two territories run by rebellious usurpers. Liu Bei of Shu was the only warlord with actual roots in the imperial family, although it was a distant connection at best.

Reshuffle

When Cao Cao died in 220, he was still technically a subject of the Han emperor; however, his son Cao Pi (pronounced sort of like "soppy") deposed Emperor Xian in favor of himself. This made the Wei Kingdom's break with the old days official. It also provoked Liu Bei into declaring Shu a sovereign kingdom. Not to be left out, Sun Quan declared Wu an independent kingdom. In due time, these kingdoms were passed to their offspring.

The dominant personality of this phase of history was General Zhuge Liang of Shu, one of the architects of the victory at Red Cliffs. Folklore credits his sorcery in calling up the wind which spread the fire that destroyed Cao Cao's fleet. The Chinese remember Zhuge as a master tactician and the legendary inventor of many clever gadgets, such as a repeating crossbow, the box kite, the sky lantern, the dumpling, and a couple of things called the wooden ox and the gliding horse, which were traditionally pictured as gravity-driven walking machines but nowadays are assumed to have been two kinds of wheelbarrows.[5] He is anachronistically credited with being the first general to use gunpowder, which he supposedly learned from a wandering Taoist sage—even though gunpowder didn't appear until almost a millennium in the future. Basically, Zhuge gets the credit for every novelty that appeared in China during Late Antiquity.

Over the next decade, General Zhuge attacked northward against the Kingdom of Wei, year after year. He attacked five times and was beaten back five times. Why does his complete failure to accomplish anything concern us? Because fighting off Zhuge Liang brought General Sima Yi of Wei to prominence as the savior of the kingdom.

Now that the Kingdom of Wei owed its survival to a war hero in the Sima family, the Sima star was rising while the Cao star was setting. As the throne passed along from one Cao offspring to another, the emperors became less and less impressive, with shorter reigns, and the kingdom depended more and more on the grizzled General Sima Yi to keep things going. Finally, in 251, during the reign of the fifth Cao, Sima Yi declared himself emperor of the new Jin dynasty and executed all of the Caos he could find on charges of treason. Sima Yi died within a year, but his legacy survived under his grandson. Over the next fifteen years Sima's Jin dynasty conquered southern China, bringing an end to the Three Kingdoms Era.

> The empire, long united, must divide; long divided, must unite. Thus it has ever been . . .
>
> —penultimate lines of *Romance of the Three Kingdoms*

Warning: Math Ahead

During the century of peace and prosperity under the later Han dynasty, the Chinese population grew magnificently, but when that peace dissolved, the population crashed. The Han census of 140 CE counted 9.7 million households and almost 50 million individuals living in the empire. When the Jin dynasty counted the inhabitants in the reunified empire in 280 CE, after a century of civil war, their census found only 2.5 million households and 16 million individuals.[6]

The 34 million missing people were probably not all dead, but how do we turn this lone solid statistic into a credible death toll? Usually, if I have a lot of different estimates for a death toll, I prefer to average them out using the median, but in this case, there is only the one number—take it or leave it. On the other hand, I've discovered a rough shortcut that sometimes produces a sensible middle ground out of wildly differing estimates: the geometric mean of the upper and lower limits of plausibility often approximates the average of many more mundane estimates.[7]

In this case, the absolute maximum plausible death toll is obvious: maybe all those 34 million missing people actually died in the collapse of Han civilization. Now, what's the absolute minimum who could have died? For a population drop to be this noticeable, a half million at the very least must have died. That would come to 1 percent of China's population, and only about 6,500 a year. The geometric mean of these two numbers is around 4.1 million, which is the death toll I've used to rank this event.

FALL OF THE WESTERN ROMAN EMPIRE

Death toll: 7 million[1]

Rank: 19

Type: failed state

Broad dividing line: Rome vs. the barbarians

Time frame: 395–455 CE

Location: western Europe

Major state participants: Eastern Roman Empire, Western Roman Empire

Major non-state participants: Alans, Angles, Burgundians, Franks, Heruli, Huns, Ostrogoths, Saxons, Vandals, Visigoths

Who usually gets the most blame: decadent Romans, barbarous Germans, Attila the Hun

T HE DECLINE AND FALL OF THE ROMAN EMPIRE IS THE ARCHETYPE OF EVERY collapse in human history. It is the giant metaphorical mirror we hold up to whichever era we live in. If we can find some parallel, no matter how superficial, between Rome and today, then we can predict and pontificate about whatever dangerous road we are traveling. If we point out only the similarities between, say, the Iraq War and the Spanish-American War, then a few history buffs might nod in recognition and turn the page, but if we find similarities between the Iraq War and the fall of Rome, then we can easily spread panic and alarm throughout the population, thereby earning our hefty pundit salaries.

A Really, Really Short History of the Roman Empire before the Fall

The Roman Republic became the Roman Empire with the accession of Augustus in 14 BCE. For the next few centuries the imperial apparatus muddled along, surviving every threat. The emperors ran the gamut from the criminally insane to the honest and sensible in an almost predictable pattern. A few decades of decent emperors would be interrupted when the succession fell to a dangerous psychotic. After a brief reign of terror, he would be assassinated, and a short, sharp civil war would sort out all of the claimants. Then a new string of reasonably competent emperors would restore calm. Sure, it's messier than the television attack ads and colorful sex scandals that determine who gets to run the typical modern democracy, but it worked well enough for generations.

After several centuries of this, the Roman Empire was very different from the Rome of popular imagination, where Julius Caesar raced a chariot against Pontius Pilate, and Caligula was smothered at Pompeii, while Spartacus seduced Cleopatra.* The newer empire was Christian, and it no longer had much to do with the city of Rome. Emperors came from the Romanized populations of the provinces rather than the city itself. In fact, the empire's ethnicity was becoming blended and homogenized. Latin had replaced the indigenous languages across much of western Europe, and every free man in the empire was legally a citizen, subject to a uniform set of laws. These new Romans even wore trousers on occasion rather than togas. They were turning medieval.

For administrative convenience, the empire was usually split into two autonomous halves—the Western Roman Empire headquartered in Milan, and the Eastern Roman Empire headquartered in Constantinople. The system in place near the end made sense on paper but never worked. The emperor of each half (titled Caesar) selected and groomed his preferred successor (titled Augustus), and the succession was supposed to pass peacefully from one to the other without interruption. In practice, however, the death of an emperor often created a power vacuum, a civil war, and a usurper, with the throne eventually passing to the most audacious. Often the Caesar of the other half had practical approval of the choice since he was the one with armies at his command when the throne became available. This kept the two halves linked rather than drifting apart. It was common for close kinsmen to rule both halves at the same time, such as the brothers Valens and Valentinian, who became East and West Caesar in 364.

Goths Arrive

When a dangerous new breed of barbarian, the Huns, appeared on the northeastern horizon of the civilized world in the late 300s, all of the Germanic tribes in their path fled or surrendered. The Visigoths escaped across the Danube River, the northern border of the Roman Empire, and begged Eastern Emperor Valens to save them. He allowed them to settle along the south bank as federates, a kind of subordinate vassal living in an autonomous enclave. The Visigoths placed the emphasis on autonomous, while the local Roman officials preferred to stress the subordinate part of the equation. Pretty soon, disagreements turned into open revolt.

In 378, Valens marched the Roman army against the Visigoths, who were approaching the Roman city of Adrianople and planning a pillage. Valens arrived with 40,000 troops, camped for the night, and then advanced against the Gothic infantry, who had drawn up

---

* I never claimed popular imagination was very accurate.

in a circle of wagons. Valens attacked in proper legionary order, but the laager held until Gothic cavalry arrived and enveloped his army. The encircled Romans were squeezed, crushed, and annihilated, resulting in the worst Roman defeat in recent memory. They never even found the emperor's body. It was somewhere in the pile, just one anonymous corpse amid the tens of thousands.

Peace Returns to Constantinople

Although it's customary to treat the Battle of Adrianople as the beginning of the end for Rome, nothing else happened for a generation. The Western emperor (Valentinian's son Gratian) gave the Eastern Empire and his sister to one of the few high generals of good Roman family, Theodosius, who ruled competently for twenty years.

Theodosius was a bit of a thug. He once massacred seven thousand inhabitants of Thessalonica because a mob there lynched one of his generals for imprisoning a popular charioteer, but it's worth noting that the empire was not swirling irrevocably down the drain at this point. The Romans were still capable of producing a strong emperor who would be remembered for what he did rather than for what was done to him.

Theodosius contained the Visigoths and settled them back into their little enclave. The Battle of Adrianople had shown the tactical superiority of the Gothic method of combat (armored cavalry fighting with lances) over the traditional Roman legion, so Theodosius began a massive recruiting of barbarians into the Roman army.

His reign is more notable for religious rather than political events. A firm Christian, Theodosius outlawed paganism and transferred the title of supreme pontiff (high priest) from the emperor to the bishop of Rome. He put a stop to pagan rituals like the Olympic Games and allowed Christian mobs to destroy ancient shrines such as the Serapeum, which was part of the library complex in Alexandria. The sacred flame of the Vestal Virgins in Rome was extinguished after a thousand years of careful tending. Pagans warned that this would anger the gods and bring nothing but trouble. Apparently they were right.

Despite ominous portents, Roman civilization was still thriving intellectually at this point. Saint Augustine, the theologian who stands second only to Saint Paul in creating the Christianity we know today, came to prominence during this era. Augustine had spent his youth enjoying the pleasures of the flesh; then he grew up, got religion in 386 CE, and ruined it for everyone else. He worked over the problem of free will, developed original sin, damned unbaptized babies, outlawed sex, and turned Christianity from a popular movement into a postgraduate philosophy course. Whenever your eyes glaze over while studying religion, or whenever you find yourself wondering where Jesus said *that*, that's Saint Augustine at work.

Christianity was well established throughout the Roman sphere by this time. All of the Germanic tribes lined up along the border had converted long ago, but unfortunately the empire had declared their version, Arianism, a heresy for disagreeing over the Trinity. Arians believed that the Son didn't exist until the Father created him, unlike the Catholics of the Roman Empire, who believed that Father and Son coexisted eternally. It doesn't really matter except that people will fight about anything.

Politics in Milan

Meanwhile, the Western Roman Empire was torn by internal disputes. Twice recently, ambitious generals had assassinated the Western emperor and Theodosius had to intervene to remove the usurper. The first time, when Gratian was killed in 383, Theodosius restored the line of the legitimate family (Valentinian II), but the second time, in 394, he kept the Western Empire for himself. For one year—and for the last time—a single emperor ruled a unified empire from Britain to Arabia.

When Theodosius died in 395, the empire was divided between his two sons. His eleven-year-old son, Honorius, got the Western Empire, while the slightly older Arcadius got the Eastern. Honorius would rule for the next three decades, until 423, during which the important collapsing began, so let's blame it all on him, even if he was only eleven years old.

The man who really ran the Western Empire was the general and regent, Stilicho. He is usually described as a Vandal general in Roman service, but he was born and raised a Roman. Although his father was a Vandal chieftain commanding auxiliaries in the Roman army, Stilicho's mother was pure Roman. In any case, Stilicho's background was not unusual. Most high army commanders by this time were only a generation or so removed from barbarian mercenary ancestors.

All Hell Breaks Loose

In the Eastern Empire, before Theodosius was cold, the Visigoths under Alaric decided to move. Like most savages, the Goths were rather vague on the concept of institutions, but they believed strongly in personal bonds. With Theodosius dead, they considered themselves freed from their agreement to settle down peacefully. They pulled up stakes and began marauding up and down the Balkans against light, ineffective Roman resistance. By 402 the Visigoths had broken through to Italy. With an enemy army on the civilized side of the Alps for the first time in six hundred years, Honorius (now eighteen) removed the court from Milan, which was dangerously exposed on a wide plain, to Ravenna, on the coast behind impassable swamps. Stilicho beat the Visigoths, who pulled back to reconsider their options.

With so much of the Roman army in Italy chasing Visigoths, the northern frontier was lightly defended, so in 406, a big barbarian horde—mostly the Germanic Vandals and

Suebi, along with the Iranian Alans—crossed the frozen Rhine River at Mainz without opposition. They rampaged across Gaul, burning, killing, and raping, until they crossed the Pyrenees into Spain. The poet Orientius, bishop of Auch, described it a few years later:

> Some lay as food for dogs; for many a burning roof
> Both took their soul, and cremated their corpse.
> Through the villages and villas, through the countryside and market-place,
> Through all the regions, on all the roads, in this place and that, there was Death, Misery,
>   Destruction, Burning, and Mourning.
> The whole of Gaul smoked on a single funeral pyre.[2]

Stopping the invasion was not the highest priority at court. Honorius was more worried that Stilicho was becoming too powerful, so he had him assassinated in 408.

Seeing the chaos unfold on the continent, Constantine, the commander of the Roman army in Britain, declared himself emperor of the Western Empire. He crossed into Gaul to assert his claim, leaving the Britons to fend for themselves under an independence they didn't want.

With loyal troops so scarce, Honorius was in no position to fight Constantine. Instead, he was forced to accept him as co-emperor, but before Emperor Constantine III could settle in and enjoy himself, one of his own generals rebelled and raised a third emperor. After this, it gets even more complicated. Other garrisons took sides and pretty soon all

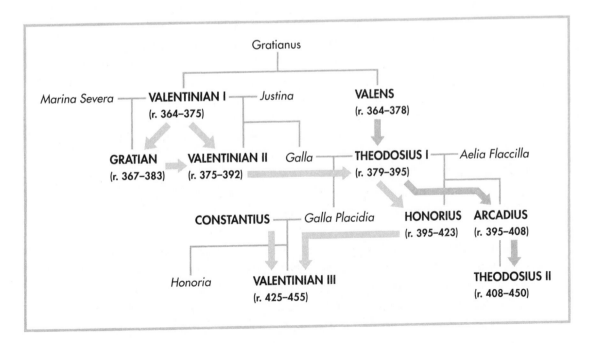

of the Romans in northwest Europe were fighting each other. Eventually, however, all of the Roman usurpers and their families were safely dead. Severed heads were hoisted triumphantly on poles all across the land—Constantine's among them.

Safe for the moment, Honorius now had to promote Constantius, a loyal general who had saved his skin in the recent conflict, to co-emperor. Meanwhile, two other tribes had slipped into the unguarded Roman provinces behind the Vandals. The Franks, who had earlier settled as federates in the Rhine delta, now spread deeper into the land that would eventually be named after them (France). The Burgundians did likewise, ending up in Burgundy. Local Roman officials were forced to pay tribute to these tribes until someone could come and chase them away. It would take longer than anyone suspected.

Although the continent still remained under (nominal) Roman control, Emperor Honorius sent a letter to the Britons declaring them officially on their own. There was nothing he could do for them. Over the next few decades, tribe after tribe of barbarians— Picts, Scots, Angles, Saxons, and Jutes—from several directions—Ireland, Scotland, and Denmark—took advantage of the opportunity and plunged Britain into a violent, unchronicled age. With no real defender riding to their rescue, the helpless Britons had to dream one, and the legend of King Arthur was born.

The Sack of Rome

Meanwhile Alaric returned with his Visigoths and extorted a massive ransom from the city of Rome in 409. When he presented his demands at the gates of the city, the Romans were shocked. What had he left for them to keep? "Your lives," he answered.

This kept Alaric financed for about a year, but then he returned, seized the city, and looted for several days in 410. Although Rome wasn't the capital anymore and the looting was more robbery than wanton destruction, the fall of Rome shocked the civilized world. Clearly whatever was happening was more than just another dynastic dispute.

The Roman Empire is like the dinosaurs. Both are more famous for being gone than for having survived all those centuries; however, the city of Rome had remained unpillaged by foreigners for eight hundred years (390 BCE–410 CE). This is extraordinary, even by modern standards. For a sense of perspective, consider some other capital cities that foreign troops have occupied at one time or another in the past four hundred years—only half the number of years Rome remained unconquered:

Addis Ababa (1936), Athens (1826, 1941), Baghdad (1623, 1638, 1917, 2003), Beijing (1644, 1860, 1900, 1937, 1945), Berlin (1760, 1806, 1945), Brussels (1914, 1940), Buenos Aires (1806), Cairo (1799, 1882), Copenhagen (1807, 1940), Delhi (1761, 1783, 1803, 1857), Havana (1762, 1898), Kabul (1738, 1839, 1879, 1979, 2001), London (1688), Madrid (1706, 1710, 1808), Manila (1762, 1898, 1942), Mexico City (1845, 1863), Moscow (1605, 1610, 1812), Nanjing (1937), Paris (1814, 1871, 1940), Philadelphia (1777), Pretoria (1900), Rome (1798, 1808, 1849, 1943, 1944), Seoul (1910, 1945, 1950, 1951), Tehran (1941), Tokyo (1945), Vienna (1805, 1809, 1938, 1945), Washington (1814)

Unraveling

By now, trouble was so thick that individual problems had to wait in line for the chance to come crashing down on the empire. Compared to the other choices hanging over Rome, the Visigoths didn't look so bad after all. Sure, they looted Rome and killed Emperor Valens, but at least they weren't the Huns or the Vandals. From this point on, the Visigoths played the role of Rome's friendly barbarians.

Among the booty carried off from Rome was Emperor Honorius's twenty-year-old sister, Galla Placidia, and to solidify the growing alliance between the empire and the Visigoths, they were allowed to keep her. She married Athaulf, the new king who had succeeded Alaric, and the tribe was resettled in southern Gaul and given generous rights to tax local Roman citizens.

Eventually Athaulf was murdered by a servant in a coup, and the widow Placidia was bound and paraded through town in humiliation.[3] When a new Visigothic king put down the uprising, Placidia made her way back to Ravenna, where Honorius married her to his co-emperor Constantius, who didn't live very long either.

After Honorius died in 423, a usurper, Johannes, took over until the Eastern emperor's army arrived to place Valentinian, the six-year-old nephew of Honorius and son of Constantius, on the throne in 425. Valentinian III would be the last Roman emperor to spend any length of time on the Western throne, although he never quite became the actual master of the empire. His mother, Galla Placidia, ruled as regent, and she was eminently qualified. After all, she was the daughter, wife, mother, sister, granddaughter, aunt, and niece of emperors, so at least she knew her way around the palace. As the years progressed, however, the general Flavius Aetius came to exercise more and more power.

By now, the barbarians had divided Spain among themselves and broken the local Roman army, so the empire called in a favor from the Visigoths, who rode to Spain and wiped out the Asding tribe of Vandals, leaving only the Siling tribe to carry on the proud Vandal name.

Meanwhile, the Roman commander in North Africa, Boniface, was up to something. Galla Placidia wasn't sure what he was planning, but he seemed to be consolidating more power than a provincial could be allowed, so she summoned him back to Italy to explain. When Boniface stayed put, she sent a Roman army to insist, so Boniface offered half of

North Africa to the Siling Vandals in exchange for their help. Still under pressure from the Visigoths, the Vandals gladly abandoned Spain and crossed the Strait of Gibraltar in 429. Suddenly faced with two enemies in Africa, Placidia reconciled with Boniface, who promptly turned against the Vandals.

The Vandals, however, easily routed every Roman army sent against them and began the systematic conquest of North Africa, city by city. One Vandal siege trapped Saint Augustine in the city of Hippo, where he died in 430 still besieged. In 439, the Vandals finally took the provincial capital, Carthage. This gave them control of the grain supply that fed Rome at this point in history. By now, they had built a fleet with which to raid up and down the Mediterranean coast, attacking peaceful seaside communities that hadn't seen a pirate fleet in five hundred years.[4]

Attila

By this time, the Huns had arrived at the river frontiers of the Roman Empire and began to strike into the Balkans. An ecclesiastical chronicler described it: "There were so many murders and blood-lettings that the dead could not be numbered. Ay, for they took captive the churches and monasteries and slew the monks and maidens in great quantities."[5] The Eastern emperor, Theodosius II, surrendered the south bank of the Danube to Hun control and paid a huge ransom for the Huns to not come any closer, but the Western emperor had too many other priorities and not enough cash to protect his half. The Huns camped across the Danube and raided into Roman Pannonia (western Hungary) for a quick pillage now and then to keep in practice.

Back in Italy, the empire's attention was diverted by one of the most destructive episodes of sibling rivalry in history. Valentinian's sister Honoria became romantically involved with the manager of her estates, which was politically dangerous, so they conspired to overthrow her brother before he found out. Unfortunately they were too late; he already knew. Valentinian beheaded her lover and would have done the same to his sister except that Placidia intervened. The imperial family then tried to force Honoria into marriage with an aged and safe senator, but she adamantly refused. Finally everyone agreed that Honoria would be packed off to Constantinople for safe keeping.

Having lost the first round, Honoria secretly wrote to Attila, king of the Huns, to propose a marriage alliance, entrusting her eunuch to take the letter to Attila, along with her ring to guarantee authenticity. When this new plot was discovered, the Eastern emperor Theodosius II quickly dumped the problem back on Ravenna, shipping Honoria home with the advice that his cousin Valentinian should agree to the marriage for political expediency. Placidia agreed, but Valentinian was furious. It took all of Placidia's influence just to talk him out of killing his sister for the trouble she had caused; however, both Placidia and Theodosius II died about this time, which left the final decision to Valentinian, who would have nothing to do with any such union. Honoria was married to a minor Roman and exiled; she disappears from history after this.[6]

Unfortunately Attila was not so easy to remove. He had been promised an imperial bride, and dammit, someone had better pay up. He rode against the empire to claim Honoria, along with an expected dowry of half the empire. Attacking over the Rhine, Attila swept across the north of Gaul, leaving behind a reputation for destructiveness that would last over a thousand years. A chronicler described the opening gambit: "The Huns, issuing from Pannonia, reached the town of Metz on the vigil of the feast of Easter, devastating the whole country. They gave the city to the flames and slew the people with the edge of the sword, and did to death the priests of the Lord before the holy altars."[7]

The Huns advanced as far as Orleans, which withstood their siege, so they rode off to find an easier target. Soon the combined army of Romans and Visigoths under the command of Aetius caught up with the Huns and beat them at the Battle of the Catalaunian Plains in 451. This was the last victory ever achieved by the Western Roman army, and we know almost nothing about it. Not only have archaeologists never found the site, but also they don't even know where to start looking. In the histories that have come down to us, the sizes of the armies and the mountains of dead have been exaggerated beyond recognition.[8]

After a retreat and regroup, Attila crossed the Alps into Italy, destroying the city of Aquileia and driving the survivors into hiding in the marshes of a nearby lagoon, where they would build a new city, Venice. As the Huns headed deeper into Italy, another looting of Rome looked likely, but Attila changed his mind after meeting with local notables, such as Pope Leo. No one knows why Attila turned back and went home, but candidates include everything from the miraculous appearance of Saints Peter and Paul, to an outbreak of plague, to the realization that he had overstretched his resources, to a simple payoff.

Back in Barbarianland in 453, Attila died drunk in bed on his wedding night after a great effusion of blood from his nose. Within a year, all of the Germanic vassals had thrown off the yoke of the Huns, who quickly retreated to the Ukrainian steppe.[9]

By this time, General Aetius had become too powerful and a threat to Valentinian. One day in 454, when Aetius was delivering a financial report to the emperor, Valentinian leapt off the throne, sword in hand, and cut his general down then and there. Aetius was avenged six months later when soldiers loyal to him assassinated Valentinian.

Soon afterward, King Gaiseric of the Vandals landed an army at Ostia and attacked up the Tiber River, capturing Rome. The Vandals gave it a much more thorough shakedown than the Visigoths had, attaching their name to the whole concept of aimless destruction. When they sailed back to Carthage after a fourteen-day pillage, they carried off centuries' worth of collected treasures, such as the gold candlestick looted from Jerusalem, and thousands of prisoners, including Valentinian's widow and daughters.

The lesser prisoners went straight into the slave markets, while the imperial family remained hostages.[10]

Closing Time

For all practical purposes, that was the end of the Western Roman Empire. The name would linger for another generation, but the nation ceased being a viable entity in 455 with the extinction of the Theodosian dynasty and the Vandal sack of Rome. There was no kernel of safe, productive territory from which to recruit and finance a new army. Over the next few decades, the German conquerors assembled small kingdoms out of the pieces of the empire. There would be many more battles, assassinations, betrayals, sieges, and massacres before the process was complete, but you don't have to know them. All that matters is that Rome was gone, and armies were looting places that hadn't been looted for hundreds of years.

With the death of Attila, a couple of German tribes that had been vassals of the Huns—the Ostrogoths and the Heruli—now had the chance to act as independent players in the ruins of the empire. Having been subordinate for so long, they almost missed the chance to get a piece of the carcass, but with all of the other tribes pushed westward by the Romans and Huns into Gaul and Spain, the Heruli and Ostrogoths had free rein to move in and take Italy itself.

The Roman Empire had been so important for so long that no one could imagine a world without it. For the next twenty-one years, the conquerors kept up the pretense of a Roman Empire, when, in fact, quarreling generals ran the show behind a string of puppet front men known as the Phantom Emperors. Eventually the rising German strongman in Italy, a Herul named Odovacer, consolidated his hold over the peninsula. In 476, Odovacer retired the current emperor, a thirteen-year-old nonentity named Romulus Augustus,* to his country estates, leaving the office of Caesar empty.

And that was that.

Why Did Rome Fall?

The best way to understand the fall of Rome is to skip the first half of any book on the subject. Yes, background and long-term trends are important, but some historians go so far back looking for the cause that they make it sound like Rome was tumbling toward its inevitable fall right from the start. When I first started researching this chapter, I read the

---

* No account of the fall of Rome is complete without noting the irony of the last emperor being named after the founder of Rome plus the first emperor.

literature and dutifully took notes about Valerian, Marcus Aurelius, and Diocletian before I realized that these people predate the fall by as much as two centuries. That's like finding the cause of the collapse of the Soviet Union in something that Catherine the Great did.

Let's start by setting some commonsense rules:

A proper explanation should apply to the fifth century rather than the first, so paganism, gladiators, and Nero's fiddling are clearly out of the question. Because the empire had long ago stopped being run from its eponymous city, any cause that is too closely tied to Rome—such as lead poisoning in the city's water supply or malaria in the swamps of southern Italy—would also be doubtful. Likewise, saying that the empire was too big is not very convincing because it was no bigger in the fifth century than it was in the first.

A hundred years ago, racial theories of Rome's collapse were popular—mongrelization weakened the race, and so on—but that's just projecting the worries of one era back onto another. Nowadays you might hear explanations based on climate change, tropical diseases, or killer asteroids because those are the things we worry about.

Anything having to do with reduced fertility or general degradation of the ruling class is doubtful because the Roman Empire was not a strict monarchy that was passed from father to son to grandson. It was more of a military dictatorship in which power was passed from a dead emperor to an experienced relative or respected colleague. Nor was Rome especially snobby. When the empire ran low on Italian patricians to run the show, provincial commoners filled in.

As with the whole dinosaurs-became-birds crowd, some claim that Rome never "fell"; it merely became something else. The eastern half survived another thousand years as the Byzantine Empire, and rulers calling themselves Caesars existed into the twentieth century, albeit as kaisers and czars. And let's not forget that the most powerful spiritual leader in the world still supervises his hundreds of millions of followers from Rome.

No, Really. Why Did Rome Fall?

You may find it disappointing to learn that most historians avoid grand, cosmic explanations for the fall of Rome and instead offer narrowly specific—almost petty—causes, either one at a time or in various combinations:

The most popular explanation blames a failure of leadership. Rome never developed a smooth system for passing the imperium from one emperor to the next, which stirred up a small civil war almost every time an emperor died. Emperors lacked any legitimacy other than having commanded the biggest army, and ambitious generals had little personal loyalty to their sovereign. Thus, when the crisis hit, Rome got an unfortunate series of usurpers, children, and lightweights on the throne who were more afraid of their own armies than of the barbarians.[11]

Second, cavalry became the major means of fighting wars, but Rome had been built and maintained by infantry.* Because the Romans responded to these new cavalry tactics by hiring alien mercenaries rather than training native Romans to fight this way, the army became less and less committed to the survival of the empire. The Roman army had always had a certain selfish opportunism that led to countless coups and mutinies, but as long as the army was mostly Roman, the soldiers hesitated leaving the door open for an unopposed barbarian invasion. Hunnish and Gothic mercenaries had no such qualms.[12]

Third, moving the primary capital to Constantinople tightened Roman control of the East, but it also marginalized the West. Armies that were conveniently placed to protect the new capital weren't very helpful in protecting the West. During the peak of Roman strength, the armies guarding the long river frontiers in central Europe were supported by taxes from the sophisticated urban economy of the eastern Mediterranean. When the empire was split into eastern and western halves, the East inherited the cash cow and a shorter frontier, while the West inherited the expense of guarding a long border with proceeds from a more primitive economy.[13] Eventually, the West simply couldn't afford to defend itself.

Fourth, the conversion to Christianity (after 313) created internal divisions and alienated pagan traditionalists. When the position of high priest became separate from the position of emperor, it diluted popular support for the government. The emperor lost half of his legitimacy. The people were less inclined to render unto Caesar once he stopped being a living god. This also helps to explain why China—where the emperor kept his divinity—was eventually reconstituted as a unified nation.[14]

The Big Picture

> If a man were called to fix the period in the history of the world, during
> which the condition of the human race was most happy and prosperous,

---

* Why did this shift take place? There is no easy answer. It would be nice if a new invention suddenly made cavalry superior to infantry, like maybe stirrups, which gave horsemen a sturdier platform for fighting, allowing them to shoot arrows with greater stability and to brace themselves to attack with a lance. Ancient cavalry lacked stirrups, but medieval horsemen had them—indeed, knights couldn't joust without stirrups. This means the stirrup arrived at some point in the early Dark Ages. If we could somehow prove that the Huns brought the stirrup to Europe, this would easily explain their military superiority and the fall of Rome in one simple lesson (stirrups!), which means we could knock off class early. This line of thought has tempted some historians into trying to identify stirrups in every stray scrap of metal found in Hunnish graves; unfortunately, adequate evidence of the stirrup doesn't show up in Europe until a few centuries too late for the Huns. (Otto Maenchen-Helfen, *World of the Huns: Studies in Their History and Culture* [Berkeley: University of California Press, 1973], pp. 206–207; Hildinger, *Warriors of the Steppe*, p. 19)

he would, without hesitation, name that which elapsed from the death of Domitian to the accession of Commodus [96–180 CE]. The vast extent of the Roman Empire was governed by absolute power, under the guidance of virtue and wisdom. The armies were restrained by the firm but gentle hand of four successive emperors, whose characters and authority commanded involuntary respect. The forms of the civil administration were carefully preserved by Nerva, Trajan, Hadrian, and the Antonines, who delighted in the image of liberty, and were pleased with considering themselves as the accountable ministers of the laws. Such princes deserved the honor of restoring the republic, had the Romans of their days been capable of enjoying a rational freedom.

— **Edward Gibbon,** *Decline and Fall of the Roman Empire*

Edward Gibbon's *Decline and Fall of the Roman Empire* is widely considered the greatest history book ever written in English. This annoys modern historians because (1) they know a lot more about history today than Gibbon did, and (2) they're jealous. Some have criticized Gibbon for praising Rome so highly, since the Romans had war, illiteracy, hunger, disease, slavery, and repressed women. Well, so did the era in which Gibbon wrote (1776–88), so shut up; he's right. Many fields of human activity didn't return to Roman-era levels until the nineteenth century.

The empire created real peace across a huge area for hundreds of years. My one hundred bloodiest events include seven conflicts fought in the Mediterranean region in the four centuries before Augustus, but only one during the four centuries after him.

Historians used to consider the fall of Rome a sharp fault line that split the ancient and medieval worlds, but since the 1970s, academia has been experimenting with a new viewpoint. Nowadays, the whole span from 200 to 800 CE is considered a single transitional period called Late Antiquity. As part of this, there is also a tendency to downplay the violence associated with the barbarian invasions—as well as frowning on calling them barbarians. In fact, some scholars argue that the whole fall of the Western Roman Empire is overrated as a milestone, and that the changes sweeping Europe were mostly the peaceful immigration of wandering tribes, who imposed a new ruling class but were culturally assimilated in a couple of generations.[15]

This view is especially popular among the English, Americans, and Germans since they are the descendants of the aforementioned barbarians, who would now seem less barbaric. In the larger sense, it's just another one of those shifts in historiography in which former savages (Vandals, Mongols, Zulus, Vikings) are rehabilitated while former paragons of civilization (Romans, British) are denigrated. Every now and then scholars grow bored with overrated golden ages, and they gain a renewed interest in former dark ages. It happens all the time. It's never permanent, and we shouldn't take it too seriously.

Under this new paradigm, there is also a tendency not to differentiate between each storm front that pounded away at Mediterranean civilization. Whether Huns, Goths, Avars, Vikings, Magyars, or Arabs, it's all part of the same megatrend. While this helps to keep the whole matter in context, it obscures the fact that the fall of Rome in the fifth century was the hurricane.

The fall of Rome is arguably the most important geopolitical event in Western history. Without the shattering of the empire, the Romanized populations of western Europe would not have evolved separate identities. Instead of French, Spanish, Italian, and Portuguese, there would be only Romans in these lands (speaking something very similar to Italian). This neo-Roman homeland would also have included Britain, North Africa, and the south bank of the Danube, whose Romanized populations were later absorbed, assimilated, and replaced by Anglo-Saxon, Arab, and Slavic invaders. Imagine a single ethnic group filling all of the lands from Liverpool to Libya with a two-thousand-year history of unity. It would have rivaled China as the most ancient, most populous country on earth.

How Many People Died?

The numbers are pure speculation, but almost every archaeological site across Europe shows a steep decline in the number of artifacts discovered in fifth-century layers. Copper coins, broken tiles, rusty tools, nails, broken glass, cobblestones, graffiti, cracked bricks, tombstones, and pottery shards are found in countless ruins, foundations, mounds, middens, and dumps from the Roman era all across western Europe. Then in layers dating to after the arrival of the Saxons, Franks, and Goths, archaeologists find fewer new deposits. In some cases, the sites dry up altogether, and regions that formerly had a lot of little towns, villas, and villages appear reduced to a handful of fortified strongholds.

When archaeologists find less stuff, it generally means one of four things:

1. Fewer people.
2. The same number of people but less stuff per person.
3. The same quantity of both people and stuff, but the stuff is less durable.
4. Everything was the same, but we're looking in the wrong places.

Of these four possibilities, the simplest is the first, and that is usually considered the default position unless special evidence points to one of the other three possibilities. On the other hand, these four explanations are not mutually exclusive. The reduced number of people might be greatly impoverished, leaving behind even fewer artifacts per person. As these sites leave less debris, it becomes harder to find them for study.[16]

Most demographers believe that the population of the Roman provinces in Europe reached a peak of 30 or 40 million in 200 CE, and then fell by one-third, or even one-half, during the entire period of decline, bottoming out at 20 million or so in 600 CE. The loss at the core of this period, during the fifth century, is sometimes estimated as one-fourth or one-fifth of the population. Most of this decline would not be the direct result of violence, but rather the result of famine and disease spread by the disruption of society.[17]

JUSTINIAN

Death toll: zillions
Rank: 59
Type: despot
Broad dividing line: Romans vs. barbarians (rematch)
Time frame: ruled 527–65
Location: Mediterranean
Major state participants: Eastern Roman (Byzantine) Empire, Gothic kingdom, Vandal kingdom
Who usually gets the most blame: Justinian and Theodora

Life at Court

Procopius, the official historian in the court of Emperor Justinian in Constantinople, kept two sets of books. By day he wrote public histories that showered praise on the emperor, but at night he would pull out his secret history and describe what *really* happened. Much of what we think we know about this era depends on whether you consider Procopius a liar.[1]

Justinian was born in 483 to a peasant family somewhere in the Balkans, and he always spoke the Eastern Empire's Greek with a barbarous accent. Justinian would have passed unknown to history if his Uncle Justin hadn't joined the palace guard in Constantinople and worked his way up through the ranks to become commander. From there, Uncle Justin easily made himself emperor in 518 when the old emperor died childless.

Having no children himself, Justin adopted his nephew Justinian as his chief assistant and heir. As Justin tottered into senility, Justinian became the true ruler of the empire long before he officially inherited the throne at the age of forty-four.

Justinian's wife, Empress Theodora, has been reviled across history for her sexuality. According to Procopius, she worked her way up from being a child prostitute to performing live sex acts on stage, eventually becoming a high-class courtesan, where she caught the eye and other anatomical parts of the heir apparent. Procopius spares us no detail of her sexual escapades. When Edward Gibbon wrote his chapter dealing with Theodora, he was too embarrassed to actually describe her activities in common English. Instead, he cloaks her tales from innocent eyes with quotations in raw Greek and commentary in Latin.[2]

According to less interesting (and probably more accurate) historians, however, she was an ordinary actress with a talent for comedy and uninhibited sexy roles. The daughter of the circus bear keeper, Theodora was in her mid-twenties, with at least one child out of wedlock, when she became involved with the middle-aged Justinian. When he ascended the throne, she moved up with him. Justinian considered her a valuable partner, and all imperial edicts were issued in both their names.[3]

Life among the high and mighty in Constantinople involved the usual collection of plots, schemes, and assassinations. Theodora set a standard of easy sexuality among the ruling class, and she was the only person at court to show a backbone when the Nika riots swept the capital and left tens of thousands dead. Thanks to Procopius, we have a vivid record of it all, and it would make a great television series; however, most sober, sensible history books concentrate on the less sordid aspects of Justinian's reign:

- He thoroughly codified Roman law, which has formed the basis of European law ever since.
- He built the Hagia Sophia church in Constantinople, one of the architectural marvels of the world.
- He put the finishing touches on orthodox Christianity and erased the last traces of Mediterranean paganism.
- Bubonic plague arrived in Europe for the first time and in just a few years wiped out as much as one-fourth of the people in the Mediterranean area.

But since this book deals with massive man-made death and destruction, let's skip all that and follow his armies west. Justinian maintained an aggressive foreign policy designed to turn back the clock to the glory days of the Roman Empire, and that's where he racked up his highest body counts.

Western Wars (535–554)

Justinian has a reputation among historians for picking extremely talented assistants, seemingly from out of the blue. Early in his reign, he began to favor a junior officer on the Persian front, Belisarius, with promotions over more experienced officers. Belisarius never let him down. Now Belisarius launched an armada against the Vandal kingdom in North Africa, with 15,000 ground forces, 32,000 sailors, his wife Antonina as his right-hand administrator, and the historian Procopius as his spymaster.

The Romans landed on the desert coast, far from the center of Vandal power, but Belisarius quickly rolled over all resistance and took Carthage. He crossed the first enemy kingdom off his list and returned home to bask in the appreciation of his sovereign.[4] In Belisarius's triumphal parade he carried the solid gold menorah that Titus had taken to Rome and the Vandals had relayed to Carthage. Afraid of the curse that seemed to follow the temple treasury everywhere it went, Justinian returned it to Jerusalem, and that's the last anyone has heard of it.

The Gothic War

Within a year, Belisarius was back in the West to put down a mutiny of the troops he had left in charge of Africa. Then he turned toward the Gothic kingdom of Italy and systematically worked his way northward. Palermo was taken with a sea assault. Naples fell soon afterward when the Romans snuck past the Gothic defenses and into the city through an abandoned aqueduct.[5]

The pope threw open the gates of Rome to Belisarius, but in December 536 the Goths arrived and besieged the Roman force inside Rome. Neither side had enough troops to cover the twelve miles of walls that surrounded the city, so the siege was rather Homeric, with skirmishes and sorties on the open land outside guarded gates, while spies and agents could easily sneak in and out to gather intelligence and arrange betrayals.

The Roman position inside the city deteriorated as supplies dwindled, but so did the condition of the besieging Goths. The siege could have gone either way, until Antonina and Procopius recruited fresh troops in Naples and hurried north to reinforce Belisarius. In February, Gothic King Witigis called a time-out to negotiate a compromise, but Belisarius stalled and used the three-month armistice to move troops within striking distance of the Gothic capital at Ravenna.

Justinian now worried that his general was getting too powerful, so he sent another army from Constantinople under the eunuch Narses to coordinate with Belisarius. Although Narses had no military experience, he proved surprisingly adept. He fought his way up the Lombard plain and took Milan, which he then left in the hands of a subordinate.

Unfortunately, having two headstrong generals in joint command of the same army confused their subordinates. When a Gothic counterattack besieged Milan and brought it to the brink of starvation, the nearby Roman relief force wouldn't budge until orders arrived from both Belisarius and Narses.

By then it was too late. Gothic King Witigis had offered safe passage to the Roman general inside Milan if he surrendered, but this offer did not extend to the city's civilians, whom Witigis planned to punish for betraying him. The Roman general tried to reject the offer, but his soldiers were hungry and forced him to accept. As the Roman garrison abandoned Milan, the Goths moved in and destroyed the city, slaughtering all of the men—300,000, according to contemporary histories—and dragging off the women.

Another Gothic War

By now Italy was so devastated that it needed time to recover before anyone would consider it worth fighting over again. Everyone with weapons came to an agreement about who got control of what, and they all returned to their corners to catch their breath.

In 541, Totila, Gothic king of Italy, resumed the war and scored a three-year winning streak, so Justinian sent Belisarius back to Italy for a second round. As the armies attacked back and forth, the city of Rome switched hands several times, until finally in 548, Belisarius got caught on the wrong side of palace intrigues in Constantinople and was pushed into retirement.

The eunuch Narses arrived to take over the war in 552. He killed Totila in battle and retook Rome. The next king of the Goths was also defeated and killed the next year. Taking advantage of the chaos, the Franks and Alamanni invaded Italy from the north in August 553. Narses defeated them as well and settled the remnant of the invading horde in Italy. Finally, with the Romans in control of the situation, the war came to an end.

Death Toll

Procopius claimed that Justinian killed a myriad myriads of myriads in total across his entire reign, which, when translated literally from Greek, means $10,000^3$, or 1 trillion people.[6] Since a myriad cubed is over a hundred times the population of the planet today, Procopius is probably mistaken. In the *Decline and Fall of the Roman Empire*, Edward Gibbon suggests that one of those myriads accidentally snuck in and should be ignored, reducing the total dead from war, pestilence, and famine under Justinian to a mere 100 million.

Generations of historians have accepted Gibbon's compromise as true, and I found nineteenth-century authors who put Justinian into the standardized list of monsters in history.[7] However, the original population of the Eastern Roman Empire wasn't big enough to lose 100 million. Modern historians believe it began with around 26 million people (not counting Italy and Tunisia), and much of the authenticated population decline under Justinian came from bubonic plague.[8]

Procopius also claims that raiding by Slavs and Avars into the Balkans removed 200,000 inhabitants from the Eastern Roman Empire every year, through either death or slavery, which would come to a total toll of 6.4 million people throughout Justinian's thirty-two-year reign. Gibbon, for one, doubts that number since the area under attack probably couldn't even support that many people.[9]

According to Procopius, 5 million died in the African war and 15 million in the Italian war. Every historian—even the ones who are cautious about throwing numbers around—agrees that Italy was devastated by the reconquest. For the sake of ranking, I'm blaming Justinian's western wars for three-quarters of a million deaths. This comes to 15 percent of the 5 million people who probably lived in Italy and Tunisia.[10] It's just a guess.

GOGURYEO-SUI WARS

Death toll: 600,000[1]
Rank: 67
Type: wars of conquest
Broad dividing line: Sui China vs. Goguryeo
Time frame: 598 and 612
Location: Korea
Who usually gets the most blame: China

AFTER A FEW CENTURIES OF DIVISION, CHINA WAS REUNITED UNDER THE
Sui dynasty, but the northern Korean kingdom of Goguryeo decided to raid across
the border one last time before the new rulers got organized. The Chinese emperor
responsible for the reunification, Wendi,* was furious and retaliated in 598 with a massive invasion designed to conquer Korea all the way down to the tip. He sent an army of
300,000 across the Liao River, Goguryeo's Manchurian border, and down the Korean
peninsula toward the capital at Pyongyang. The invasion went very badly. The Chinese
apparently forgot that July and August are the rainy season in Manchuria. The roads were
muddy and the fleet that accompanied the army was battered by storms. Whenever the
Chinese ships docked, Goguryean troops attacked them, until finally the Goguryeo navy
sailed out and smashed the Chinese armada. Meanwhile, Korean guerrillas harassed the
Chinese army all the way in, and then all the way out, and the Chinese lost most of their
men along the way.[2]

It took awhile for China to recover from the disaster, but Wendi's son, Yangdi,† his
successor and probable assassin, tried again in 612. He recruited a million soldiers and
many times that number of support personnel. He repaired and expanded the Grand Canal
that connected the Yellow and Yangtze Rivers in order to bring men and supplies from
south to north. He established massive stockpiles and gathered coastal transportation to
shadow the army as it moved over land. As long as his army stayed within an easy wagon
ride of the coast, the Chinese navy could keep the forces supplied.

---

* Wendi translates as the "Civil" (*wen*) "Emperor" (*di*), but you'll find it easiest to remember his name
  if you pronounce it like the girl in *Peter Pan* or the fast-food hamburger chain.
† His formal posthumous name means the "Slothful" (*yang*) "Emperor" (*di*). Obviously, at some point,
  he annoyed the wrong Chinese historian.

The Chinese crossed the Liao River again with 305,000 troops, but when progress slowed, the fleet zipped ahead and landed a large force of marines to take Pyongyang castle. After scattering the defenders, the Chinese marines broke ranks to loot, which left them exposed to a Goguryeo ambush in which the marines were slaughtered and chased off. Only a couple of thousand made it safely back to the fleet.[3]

The Chinese army, meanwhile, pushed onward. For a time, the Goguryeo and Sui commanders played mind games, trying to lure one another into negotiations in order to spring a trap or gather intelligence. Finally, the Goguryean commander Eulji closed this phase by sending a rude poem to his Sui counterpart, and the campaign resumed. After pushing south, the Chinese began crossing the Salsu River. The Goguryeans, however, had secretly dammed the river above the crossing, and when the Sui army was halfway across the deceptively shallow water, the Goguryeans released the flood. Thousands of Chinese drowned, and the rest fled. Of the 305,000 Chinese soldiers who had invaded Korea, only 2,700 returned.[4]

The repeated defeats in Korea fatally weakened the Sui dynasty. It didn't last much longer and would shortly be replaced by the Tang dynasty.

MIDEAST SLAVE TRADE

Death toll: 18.5 million (18 million from Africa and 0.5 million from Europe)
Rank: 8
Type: commercial exploitation
Broad dividing line: Arabs enslaving Africans, mostly
Time frame: seventh to nineteenth centuries
Location: Middle East
Who usually gets the most blame: Arab slave traders, African middlemen, Barbary pirates
Summarized in two words: Eunuchs . . . ick
Economic factors: slaves, gold, salt

Background: Slavery in General

Throughout most of recorded history, almost every person was legally subordinate to someone else. Children were at the mercy of their father; husbands ruled over their wives; commoners cringed under the nobility. Most state-level societies have had formal hierarchies connecting all individuals. The Romans maintained complex patron-client relationships with interrelated obligations among all free persons—citizens, foreigners, and freedmen. European feudalism had many layers of lord and vassal, while serfs were bonded to the land.

Slaves were the most extreme type of subordinate. While most members of a lord-peasant or patron-client relationship had reciprocal rights and duties, the master-slave relationship was simpler and entirely one-sided. A master could do anything he wanted to his slave, and a slave could do nothing without the permission of his master. It was totally legal for a master to beat a slave to death well into the eighteenth century, even among peoples we would normally consider civilized, such as Virginians.[1] On the scale of personhood, running from serf to freeholder to lord, a slave was at the bottom, one step below mule.* On the plus side, slavery was not widely considered a permanent condition.

Most societies didn't go out of their way to get slaves; they merely acquired them accidentally, and they were often at a loss as to what to do with them. Usually, a person was enslaved only after a string of abnormally bad luck. Being captured in a war, convicted

---

* The main distinction being that it was usually illegal to rape your mule.

of a crime, abandoned as a child, and taken to pay a debt were the customary paths into bondage, and for the first three, the alternative to slavery was usually death.

Everyday housework created the steadiest demand for slaves, but as the supply of slaves fluctuated with the fortunes of wars, there might sometimes be a glut. In those cases, three of the customary dumping grounds for surplus, expendable people were mines, prostitution, and human sacrifice, depending on the culture.

In some societies, the economy got along fine with a minimum number of slaves. In medieval Europe, for example, there was no shortage of labor; land was the resource in short supply, so moving enslaved farm workers into a region didn't boost output. On the other hand, in some slave-saturated societies, such as nineteenth-century Sudan, every household that rose above the barest poverty owned at least one slave girl to wash, sew, cook, and clean.

Demand for slaves occasionally surged, sending slave traders out to the fringes of civilization, wherever large populations existed without strong armies to protect the people from being kidnapped. The most famous surge filled the labor shortage that followed the discovery of America, but I will discuss that later (see "Atlantic Slave Trade"). For much of history, the biggest markets for slaves—mostly girls needed for housework—were the wealthy kingdoms of the Middle East, and the deepest reservoir of available people was Africa. Over the centuries, millions of slaves were shipped out from seaports along the East African coast and on desert caravans crossing the Sahara.

East Africa

The slave trade along Africa's east coast goes back as far as we have records. In the days of the Pharaohs, shipments of new slaves flowed steadily up the Red Sea to Egypt, most likely from Eritrea and Somalia. By the tenth century, Arab sailors had established a chain of trading posts down the African coast as far south as Kilwa (now in Tanzania). Many of these posts were offshore islands that had as little contact with the mainland as possible. By 1300, the southern reach of Arab traders had extended to Sofala (now in Mozambique).

After the Portuguese found their way around the southern cape of Africa in 1493, they quickly used their superior firepower to bundle all of these slave stations into their rapidly expanding empire. However, in 1653, a fleet from the southern Arabian sultanate of Oman, armed with weaponry equal to anything the Europeans had, captured the northern slave ports. With one foot in Arabia and the other in Africa, Oman became a bipolar nation based on the slave trade, anchored at the island of Zanzibar in Tanzania.

In 1780, the Omanis captured the rival slave market of Kilwa and diverted Kilwa's trade to their own routes. By 1834, sixty-five hundred slaves per year were being exported from Zanzibar. By the 1840s, the number had doubled.[2] In 1859, nineteen thousand slaves were recorded arriving at Zanzibar from the interior. After 1840, the ruler of Oman moved his court from the Arabian Peninsula to the richer and more cosmopolitan city of Zanzibar, which became independent of its Arab trading partner in 1845. By 1871 the sultan derived a fourth of his income from the slave trade.[3]

It wasn't until the European exploration of Africa in the nineteenth century that detailed descriptions of slaving in the heart of Africa emerged. Every day, somewhere deep in Africa, slavers would select a vulnerable village and creep into striking distance. With a sudden attack, the raiders shot down any men capable of resistance and seized the women and children to be herded off to begin their new life of servitude.

On the exploratory safaris that opened up the Dark Continent, Europeans usually followed the slave trails into Africa, which were often the only trade routes that connected the coasts and the interior. Christian missionaries heading deeper into unexplored Africa encountered long columns of slaves, mostly women, scarred by whips, chained by the neck, being driven toward the coasts. Explorers retracing paths they had followed on an earlier trip often found districts that had lost half of their villages to slavers since the last visit. A British superintendent of missionaries estimated that "four or five lives were lost for every slave delivered safe at Zanzibar."[4]

By the 1860s, the African slaver Tippu Tip was plundering an area deep in the interior, beyond the African lakes in the eastern Congo. His reach became a virtual kingdom, predatory and unstoppable, pillaging up and down the Congo River until Belgians carving out their own empire bought him off. In Kenya, near Lake Rudolf, slavers operated in the 1890s until the British established a protectorate over the region. One European reported that "an Arab who has lately returned from Lake Nyasa informed me that he has traveled for seventeen days through a country covered with ruined towns and villages . . . and where now no living soul is to be seen."[5]

In the late nineteenth century, worldwide demand for ivory surged, as did the price, which temporarily made slaves more valuable as porters to carry the elephant tusks to the coast, rather than as a distinct commodity. Porters were taken from inland villages and sold overseas when their job was done.[6]

To feed the slave caravans crossing the Tsavo River region in Kenya, traders hunted the big game into local extinction. With their usual food sources gone and caravan trails littered with the bodies of exhausted slaves, the local lions quickly discovered that humans were good eating. Then after the slaves stopped coming, the lions of Tsavo satisfied their newfound taste for humans by eating dozens of railroad workers, which temporarily halted the expansion of British control in the colony. In 1898 the most brazen man-eaters were killed; the wild game returned eventually, and the remaining lions went back to avoiding people.[7]

Arriving at the coasts, the slaves were delivered to traders for shipment overseas. A British visitor described the slaves at a market on the Indian Ocean in the late 1860s: ". . . all young boys and girls, some of them mere babies . . . Skeletons, with a diseased skin drawn tight over them, eyeballs left hideously prominent by the falling away of the surrounding flesh, chests shrunk and bent, joints unnaturally swelled and horribly knotty by contrast with the wretched limbs between them, voices dry and hard, and 'distantly near' like those of a nightmare . . ."[8]

Small Arab trading vessels ferried the slaves from East Africa to the Middle East. A British captain on anti-slave patrol* stopped a local boat carrying slaves on the Indian Ocean. Male slaves were chained above decks, in the open. Below decks were the women. "On the bottom of the [boat] was a pile of stones as ballast, and on these stones, without even a mat, were twenty-three women huddled together, one or two with infants in their arms. These women were literally doubled up, there being no room to sit erect."[9]

North Africa

When the Arabs introduced camels into North Africa in the Middle Ages, it became a lot easier to cross the Sahara and see what lay on the other side. Those who made the trip usually came back with slaves. Throughout the Middle Ages, the nomadic Bedouin in the Sahara raided the settled communities along the southern edge of the desert, in the band of savannah known as the Sahel, gathering slaves to be hauled to markets on the Mediterranean. By 1300, however, the Sahel had developed a line of powerful kingdoms, such as Ghana and Mali, along the edge of the desert that could stand up to the Bedouin. Unfortunately, rather than forming a barrier to slave raids into deeper parts of Africa, these kingdoms became the new middlemen, raiding farther south for fresh slaves to send north.

When raiding didn't work, the Bedouin traded salt they found in the desert for slaves and gold from the Sahel. From the scattered records we have, it seems to have been a thriving business. In 1353, the Muslim travel writer Ibn Battuta returned to the Mediterranean coast on a caravan hauling 600 female slaves.

By the 1700s, at least 1,500 slaves per year were being taken north, the number peaking at as many as 3,000 per year in the late 1800s. As British warships closed off the Atlantic slave trade in the nineteenth century, the slaves that would have been sent to America were sent north instead, across the desert. Because Libya remained free of European control longer than any other stretch of North African coast, Benghazi and Tripoli became the major outlets of the Saharan slave trade in the nineteenth century.

By the late 1850s, slaves accounted for two-thirds of the value carried on all of the caravans across the Sahara.[10] The trade was so lucrative that most rulers would use any excuse to arrest a subject and sell her into slavery.

It was a brutal crossing. One European traveler crossed the Sahara in the 1800s on a large caravan that lost three or four slaves to exhaustion, disease, thirst, and heat stroke

---

* I will discuss the details of the abolition movement in the chapter on the Atlantic slave trade.

for every survivor who arrived at market. Entire caravans with hundreds of slaves often disappeared in the desert.

Even if we put aside morality for the moment and look at this from a simple profit motive, it seems wasteful to allow so many slaves to die. You would think the slave dealers would want to protect their investment, but as one contemporary explained, the slave trade was like the ice trade. A certain amount of melting away was acceptable because the final product fetched a high-enough price to cover the losses. It wasn't even much of an investment to begin with. At their source, slaves were cheap. In the central Sahel, a single horse was worth twenty slaves.[11]

Abolition in the Middle East was imposed by outside forces, not by an upwelling of local goodwill. Europeans began to have moral qualms about slavery in the late eighteenth century, so when they took control of Africa in the next century, they put a stop to the international traffic in slaves. Local slavery persisted, however, even to the present day, and perhaps a couple of hundred thousand slaves are still being held in Mauritania and Sudan, although their governments deny it.

Eunuchs

Eunuchs were especially useful for guarding the harem—the large assemblage of wives and concubines that every Asian potentate collected. Eunuchs had all of the physical strength of men but none of the sex drive, so they could be trusted not to help themselves to the women and not to produce families to put on the throne in place of the emperor. The disadvantage is that the population of eunuchs was not self-sustaining. They had to be continuously resupplied from elsewhere.

Islam forbids the mutilation of slaves, but rather than let a mere technicality interfere with the demand for eunuchs, Muslims assigned that task to the infidels. The slaves were castrated either by pagans in Africa shortly after being caught or by the Jews and Christians living in the Muslim world.

Eunuch-using societies preferred to castrate boys before puberty. This left them childlike in sex drive, voice, and appearance, unlike castrated adults, who still looked and acted more like men. Slave boys were taken aside, supposedly to be circumcised—as was customary for all males in the Muslim world—but this was a trick to get the knife close enough to strike without the boy struggling. When the barber surgeon got the knife near, he would grab and sever the boy's entire genitalia instead of just the foreskin.[12]

Eunuchs received a different procedure according to their race. White eunuchs had only their testicles snipped off, but black eunuchs had the whole apparatus—testes, scrotum, and penis—cut away and cauterized with boiling hot butter, leaving just a hole for urination.

Because the final sale of eunuchs came at the end of a long process of raids, caravans, and markets, with their numbers winnowed by disease, brutal discipline, and drowning all along the way, a British consul in the nineteenth century estimated that 100,000 Sudanese had died to produce the 500 eunuchs in Cairo—a loss of 200 lives for each eunuch.[13]

As we've seen in the chapters on, for example, the Xin dynasty, the fall of Rome, the Three Kingdoms, and Justinian, royal women were often the center of a web of family intrigue, and ambitious eunuchs would often turn their access to the harem to their own advantage. Eunuchs were not under all of the legal restrictions that kept women repressed, so they could move easily between the world of men and the world of women, serving as useful facilitators and front men. All across the Old World, eunuchs made a lot of history.

Corsairs

Because of the religious divide between the Christian northern and Muslim southern shores of the Mediterranean Sea, the opposite coasts were considered fair game for slave raids. As a rule, both Christians and Muslims did not enslave members of their own religions. Well, actually, they did this quite often, but it was considered wrong . . . not illegal as such, but certainly impolite. Snatching citizens of a fellow Christian or Muslim country could cause all sorts of diplomatic problems. On the other hand, kidnapping infidels was almost a sacred duty.

Generally, the Barbary pirates or corsairs from North Africa were the worst offenders in the Mediterranean trade. A pirate fleet would pounce on any rich and vulnerable ships to seize cargo, crew, and passengers for sale at one of the Barbary ports in North Africa such as Algiers, Tunis, or Tripoli. Most of the people pulled off the ship would be sold ashore, but prosperous or important prisoners were set aside to be ransomed back to their families or governments. Eventually, most seafaring nations in Europe established consulates in the Barbary cities to expedite the ransoming.

Crewmen captured on ships might be bribed or tortured into assisting the corsair fleet in attacking their seaside hometowns. They would be used as a familiar face to talk their way past the town's defenses. Even without trickery, a small fishing village was no match for a pirate fleet. Corsairs would swoop in from the sea, round up entire villages, and haul the inhabitants away into slavery. Sometimes pirates stayed ashore for a few days to see if any rich relatives were willing to ransom their prisoners. Because of primitive communications, the corsairs could usually count on several days of safe looting before local authorities could mobilize enough strength to chase them off.

The largest hauls in slaves came from raids against the coastal communities of Italy, Spain, and Greece, although attacks in the Atlantic Ocean were not unknown. Around 1625, a corsair raid against Reykjavik, Iceland, enslaved 400 men, women, and children; in 1631, another raid enslaved 237 from Baltimore, Ireland.[14] Those who were too young, old, or weak might be thrown overboard on the way back to Africa, but the majority of captives were taken to the market. Women were usually sold into harems, while men often became galley slaves.

At this point in history, rowing galleys created the biggest demand for cheap, expendable labor in the Mediterranean. In the ancient world, free men had rowed galleys for wages, but by the Middle Ages it had become slave work. Galley slaves were usually worked to death without a second thought. Chained to their benches, the slaves pulled the oars continuously, constantly, in the sun, in the rain, and then through much of the night. Not even able to lie down for sleep, the slaves could only catch an occasional nap while slumped over their oars. In battles and storms, galley slaves went down with the ship. At the Battle of Lepanto between Ottoman Turkey and Spain in 1571, more than 10,000 Christian galley slaves drowned, shackled in the bellies of the Turkish warships.

Western naval technology eventually surpassed that of the corsairs. By the early 1800s, European and American warships were systematically retaliating against any Barbary ports that continued to harbor pirates. The North African cities were forced to crack down on the corsairs, and the Mediterranean became safe for commerce.

Mamelukes

Slaves served as the backbone of many Muslim armies. The Ottoman Turks (ca. 1450–1900) required Christian peasant communities in the Balkans to surrender a quota of young boys to be raised as Muslims and trained as soldiers. The Egyptians of the same period usually bought Circassian boys from the Caucasus Mountains. These boys were kept isolated from the outside world during their childhood as they learned war craft and Islam. They were counted as slaves, the personal property of the sultan. Although legally freed upon reaching adulthood, they could never leave the sultan's service. They would live their entire lives as soldiers in a barracks. Their own children were sent away and forbidden from following in their fathers' line of work. When these soldiers got too old for combat, they would be moved into support duties and eventually into a comfortable retirement, with slaves assigned to keep them happy.

Called Mamelukes after the Arabic word for slave, these slave soldiers had no family, tribal affiliations, or property to interfere with their loyalty to the sultan. On the other hand, they tended to have more loyalty to their comrades than to the crown, and Muslim dynasties were under constant threat of a coup by Mamelukes if they pushed them too hard.[15]

I don't count Mamelukes in the statistics of this megadeath because I consider them, morally, to be more a type of draftee than a type of slave. The restrictions imposed on the average Mameluke were more in line with military duty than with slavery.

Numbers

Slavery in the Muslim world has not been studied as deeply as slavery in Christendom, so there are fewer trustworthy numbers. In *Islam's Black Slaves*, Ronald Segal reported estimates of either 11.5 million or 14 million African slaves shipped to the Muslim world. Other estimates run from 10 to 25 million live slaves imported.

How many Africans died in the slave trade? Although many anecdotes point to dozens of dead slaves for every live one delivered, these may be isolated incidents. Overall, there is no solid proof that the eastern trade was either more or less deadly than the western trade, so I'm going to apply the western ratio from that chapter and declare that three slaves died for every two transported. That would come to 18 million deaths to produce 12 million live slaves.

Robert C. Davis estimated that between 1.0 and 1.25 million European Christians were enslaved by Muslims on the Barbary Coast between 1530 and 1780.[16] Few ever saw their homes again, and we probably should count at least half of them as dead. Because of cruelty and hard labor, the death rate among these slaves was nearly six times the death rate among a free population,[17] and attrition eroded their numbers.

AN LUSHAN REBELLION

Death toll: 36 million missing
Rank: 13
Type: military uprising
Broad dividing line: the frontier military vs. the central government
Time frame: 755–63
Location: China
Who usually gets the most blame: An Lushan mostly, but also the dotty and infatuated Emperor Xuanzong

CHINA UNDER THE TANG DYNASTY REACHED FARTHER WEST THAN AT ANY time before or since. This Chinese expansion coincided with the eruption of Arab empire builders all across the Middle East, leading to history's only battle between Chinese and Arab armies, at the Talas River in central Asia in 751.

Somewhere in the rugged borderland between these expanding cultures, probably near Bukhara in Turkistan, An Lushan was born around 703. His mother was descended from an important Turkic clan. His father, probably a soldier of Sogdian descent (medieval kin to the Pashtuns who dominate Afghanistan today), died when Lushan was young. His mother remarried into the family of a prominent nomadic warlord.

When rival tribesmen assassinated the khan of that particular batch of Turks in 716, the An clan found itself on the wrong side of tribal intrigues and fled eastward, into the outlying provinces of the Chinese Empire, where it came under the protection of a friendly Turkish warlord. For a while, young Lushan lived at the edge of the law, until he was caught stealing sheep. Sentenced to death, the twenty-year-old thief tried to bargain with Governor Zhang Shougui even as the executioner raised the club to bash his skull in. "Does the great lord wish to destroy the barbarians?" he asked. "Why kill a brave warrior?" Seeing his point, the governor put An to use as a scout.

On the Way Up

In 733, when the Tang emperor transferred Governor Zhang to the northeast to replace a commander who had been defeated and killed by the Khitan (the local barbarians),*

---

* Ironically, because the Khitan briefly ruled part of China when the West first took an interest in the Far East, the English language originally named China after these non-Chinese people: *Cathay.*

An Lushan followed. He proved adept at the fast cavalry raids that characterized frontier warfare. Although short-tempered and impetuous when dealing with subordinates, An was always good-natured and quite likeable when dealing with superiors. He rose through the ranks, becoming Zhang's lieutenant and eventually his adopted son. Even so, An was going from stout, to stocky, to morbidly obese, and Zhang frequently chewed him out in public over it. Then, in 736, while Zhang was visiting the capital, An had to deal with an attack by the Khitan and Hsi (the other local barbarians) on his own and was badly defeated. When Zhang returned from the capital fuming, he sentenced An to death, but realizing this might not go over well, he expelled An from the army instead. Within a year, however, An was reinstated.[1]

In 742, the emperor gave An his own frontier province to defend. He kept a steady stream of tribute flowing from his frontier command back to the capital—camels, dogs, falcons, horses, and, best of all, bags of heads taken from Khitan chieftains. Some accused him of collecting these heads from enemy leaders he had lured into negotiations under a truce before springing a trap on them. But results mattered, and the emperor gave him two additional provinces to protect, making a solid fiefdom of three territories in the northeast, near the Great Wall. More would be added later.[2]

An Lushan became a frequent and welcome visitor at the palace in Chang'an, where he played the fat buffoon for the amusement of the courtiers. He became a special favorite of the emperor's favorite young concubine, Yang Guifei. She even pretended to adopt him as a son in a mock ceremony where the monstrously obese An was presented to his new mom in a diaper. Rumors swirled that Lushan and Guifei were lovers, but she has been remembered across time as one of the four great beauties of Chinese history, while he couldn't even walk without draping his arms over servants who held up his enormous bulk, so . . . ick.[3]

Based on the fabled love between the emperor and his lady, and the continued high regard the emperor felt for An, historians consider an affair unlikely. Yang Guifei had originally been married to one of the emperor's sons (but not one of the sons who shows up later in this story), until the infatuated seventy-year-old emperor dissolved the marriage and stashed Yang in a nunnery for a couple of years to restore her lost virginity. The romance of Emperor Xuanzong and Yang Guifei became the stuff of legends.

Things Go Wrong

In 751, An Lushan led his army and Hsi allies against the Khitan, but after a long, dusty journey, the Hsi chieftain demanded a rest, so An had him killed. The Hsi contingent deserted, and on the way out, they warned the Khitan that the Chinese were coming. When the exhausted Chinese pressed on, they stumbled into a Khitan ambush and were slaughtered. An Lushan barely escaped with his battered army. Upon returning to camp, he executed several surviving officers, while others fled to the hills to wait for his anger to cool.[4]

When the emperor's chief minister died in 752, he was succeeded by a cousin of Yang

Guifei, Yang Guozhong, who immediately began to blame all of the problems of the empire on his predecessor. An Lushan, tarnished by his friendship with the previous minister, quickly got on the bad side of Minister Yang, who whispered rumors into the emperor's ear. Emperor Xuanzong sent a trusted eunuch out to spy on An, but a healthy bribe made sure the emperor got a glowing report on the loyalty of his general. Even so, the emperor felt that An's loyalty should be examined at close hand, and he summoned him back to court. An Lushan suspected that if he left his army and returned to the capital, he would be stripped of his authority at the very least, and possibly imprisoned, exiled, or killed. An thanked the emperor for the invitation, but said he wasn't felling well. Then the emperor gave a bride to An's son, along with an order for An Lushan to return and attend the wedding. An refused and, realizing that he was running out of excuses, rebelled. He issued a flimsy cover story that the emperor had secretly begged him to get rid of the prime minister, and in December 755 he set out for the capital with an army of 100,000, traveling by night, eating at daybreak.[5]

Suffering an irritating skin disease and nearly blind, An Lushan had lost whatever good humor he may have once had. He was prone to unreasonable rages during which he would have subordinates dismembered.[6] After he pulled his army away from the border, his old territories rose in counter-revolt behind him, but that didn't matter. All he cared about was reaching the capital. To keep his soldiers loyal, he allowed a quick rape, looting, and slaughter in each captured city, but always pressed on. In January, An's army crossed the icy Yellow River and captured the secondary capital at Luoyang, where he proclaimed himself emperor.[7]

The main imperial army of 80,000 was gathering at Tongguan Pass, but An's arrival drove its forward units back in disorder. Then the rebel advance stalled before the pass. The armies waited, but this delay gave palace eunuchs in Chang'an enough time to plot against the imperial generals. Maybe they had a good reason to plot, maybe they didn't. Who knows? I mean, they're palace eunuchs; plotting is what they do best. Regardless of the reason, they convinced Emperor Xuanzong to have his generals executed.

Finally, in July, after a huge battle of horsemen and archers, the imperial army was defeated and the pass lay open. Emperor Xuanzong fled the capital on a highway choked by desperate and demoralized imperial soldiers who were looking for a scapegoat. The prime minister, Yang Guozhong, was dragged from his wagon and stomped to death. Then the soldiers stopped the emperor's caravan and demanded the death of the concubine, Yang Guifei, whom they suspected of being An Lushan's accomplice and lover. Xuanzong reluctantly allowed it, and imperial soldiers hauled her away. She was strangled and dumped in a ditch, while the emperor continued on his way.[8]

The Next Generation

The flight of the emperor was as good as an abdication in the eyes of his ambitious third son, Suzong, who then declared himself emperor. Ex-emperor Xuanzong spent the rest of his life in closely guarded retirement.

After the rebels took the capital of Chang'an, An Lushan began to consolidate his power, but he had made far too many enemies within his own entourage to survive much longer. One of his advisers, having been flogged in punishment for some offense, conspired with An Lushan's son, An Qingxu. They approached An Lushan's favorite eunuch, whom Lushan had personally castrated many years earlier in a fit of anger. This eunuch stabbed An Lushan in his sleep with his own sword, but it took a lot of messy effort to cut through all of the layers of fat. An Lushan screamed and struggled, but eventually succumbed. He was buried under his tent, and the army was told he died of illness.[9]

Within a few months, an imperial counterattack recaptured the capital on behalf of the new emperor, Suzong.[10] As the rebels fell back, An Qingxu was deposed by his lieutenant Shi Siming. An Qingxu was quickly put on trial for the murder of his father and strangled. Shi continued the rebellion for several years, followed by his son, and so on, until the last of his family was caught and killed.

In the end, the Tang dynasty survived only by bringing in outsiders like the Tibetans and Uighurs to fight their battles for them, for a price. China had to cede its western territories—the desert colonies in the Tarim Basin—to its new allies. The days when Chinese garrisons maintained direct control over the road to the west would not return for hundreds of years.

Poets' War

The An Lushan Rebellion stands high in the cultural history of China because two of their greatest poets lived and wrote during this time. This gives us an interesting glimpse into the Chinese attitude toward war. It is much more pacifistic than, for example, *Beowulf*, which was written about the same time in England.

Li Po was an enthusiastic drinker and drifter, an alchemist and Taoist mystic, who lived a lucky life full of ups and downs. In his mid-fifties when the war began, he was considered the greatest poet of his era. He attached himself to Prince Lin, sixteenth son of the emperor, but in 756, the prince was accused of plotting to establish an independent kingdom and was executed. Li Po was tossed into prison, but an old soldier he had helped thirty years before had now risen to high command in the loyalist army. This commander released Li and employed him as his secretary. Soon, however, the charges were restored, and Li Po was exiled to the southern barbarian province of Yelang. He dawdled and visited with friends along the way, so even after three years, he had still not arrived at his destination. Then a general amnesty arrived, so Li turned around and went back home to east China. While staying at a relative's house, he died. Legend has it that while drinking wine in a boat on the river, he tried to grab the moon's reflection on the surface and tumbled in, which is probably the poet's equivalent of dying bravely in battle.[11]

> *In the battlefield men grapple each other and die;*
> *The horses of the vanquished utter lamentable cries to heaven,*
> *While ravens and kites peck at human entrails,*
> *Carry them up in their flight, and hang them on the branches of dead trees.*
> *So, men are scattered and smeared over the desert grass,*
> *And the generals have accomplished nothing.*
> *Oh, nefarious war! I see why arms*
> *Were so seldom used by the benign sovereigns.*

> **—Li Po, "Nefarious War"**[12]

Younger than Li Po by eleven years, Tu Fu had a cloud of bad luck following him around. After failing the exams necessary for a career in the civil service, he wandered and eventually befriended Li, acquiring a reputation as a promising poet. Returning to the court, he married and tried for five years to get a job with the government. Just as he landed a minor position, An Lushan attacked, and Tu Fu fled the capital only to be captured by bandits. After escaping them, he wandered ragged and hungry, eventually connecting again with the exiled court. He secured a minor job as a censor, but his hardships caused the deaths of some of his children by hunger and illness. After losing this job, he resumed wandering aimlessly. He too is said to have died drinking on a boat, by overindulgence after a ten-day fast.[13]

> *The war-chariots rattle,*
> *The war-horses whinny;*
> *To each man a bow and a quiver at his belt.*
> *Father, mother, son, wife, stare at them going,*
> *Till dust shall have buried the bridge at Hsien-yang.*
> *We trot with them and cry and catch at their long sleeves,*
> *But the sound of our crying goes up to the clouds;*
> *For every time a bystander asks the men a question,*
> *The men can only answer us that they have to go.*

> **—Tu Fu, "A Song of War-Chariots"**[14]

Bai Juyi belonged to the next generation of poets, born a few years after the war had ended, but his epic *Song of Everlasting Sorrow* told of the tragic love between Emperor Xuanzong and Yang Guifei. After her death, the emperor is said to have moped around, and then hired a medium to summon her spirit. They reminisce over old times, and Xuanzong is really, really sorry about tossing her to angry soldiers. Finally they agree that they are destined to reunite on the other side.

Bai Juyi says it better than I do, however. He did not consider this his best work, but it became very popular among romantic young girls.[15]

The king has sought the darkness of his hands,
Veiling the eyes that looked for help in vain,
And as he turns to gaze upon the slain,
His tears, her blood, are mingled on the sands

—Bai Juyi, "The Song of Everlasting Sorrow"[16]

Numbers

The census taken in China in the year 754 recorded a population of 52,880,488. After ten years of civil war, the census of 764 found only 16,900,000 people in China.

What happened to 36 million people? Is a loss of two-thirds in one decade even possible? Perhaps. Peasants often lived at the very edge of starvation, so the slightest disruption could cause a massive die-off, particularly if they depended on large irrigation systems. As we saw with the Xin dynasty and the Three Kingdoms, this was not the only population collapse in Chinese history, and many authorities quote these numbers with a minimum of doubt. On the other hand, these numbers could also represent a decline in the central government's ability to find every taxpayer rather than an actual population collapse.[17]

More convincing, though less dramatically precise, is the count of households. In the seven counts before An Lushan's Rebellion, the census repeatedly found between 8 and 9 million households, and then, in the seven counts following the rebellion, the census consistently found no more than 4 million. Even a century after the revolt, in 845, the Chinese civil service could find only 4,955,151 taxpaying households, a long drop from the 9,069,154 households recorded in 755.[18] This indicates that the actual population collapse may have been closer to one-half, or 26 million. For the sake of ranking, however, I'm being conservative and cutting this in half, counting only 13 million dead in the An Lushan Rebellion. Even so, it still ranks among the twenty deadliest multicides in human history.

MAYAN COLLAPSE

Death toll: over 2 million missing
Rank: 46
Type: failed state
Broad dividing line: some awful unknown force, like the weather or Cthulu, against the Mayans
Time frame: 790–909
Location: Yucatan Peninsula, Mexico, and Guatemala
Who usually gets the most blame: Most people suspect that the Mayans somehow brought it on themselves
The unanswerable question everyone asks: Where did everyone go?

T HE MAYANS BUILT A FASCINATING AND COMPLEX CIVILIZATION FROM scratch, prospered for several centuries, and then abandoned it, without even saying good-bye. From being builders and mathematicians on a grand scale, they went back to being quiet subsistence gardeners, leaving behind huge jungle-encrusted ruins to mystify later generations. For over a century and a half, we've been trying to figure out why.

The three most popular explanations among archaeologists are:

1. Drought. In this scenario, the Mayan disappearance was driven by climate, and there wasn't much the Mayans could have done to prevent it.
2. Systematic ecological collapse. This scenario focuses on the poor choices the Mayans made in the management of resources. For example, they may have cut down too many forests, which parched and eroded the soil.
3. Politics and war. In this case, the Mayans more or less killed each other off.

Other explanations are occasionally floated but easily shot down. Perhaps a new disease killed off all of the Mayans—but, as we will see in later chapters, the Western Hemisphere was unfamiliar with pandemic diseases before the Europeans brought them. Or maybe the Mayans were wiped out by foreign invaders—but there has been no evidence of an abrupt, widespread appearance of foreign artifacts in any of the sites. How about a volcano or earthquake? No, the collapse wasn't quick enough; it took almost a century to unfold. This is a classic locked-room mystery.

This is also a classic Rorschach test. With such sketchy evidence, the temptation is to pick whatever scenario supports one's underlying worldview. Do you want to demonstrate that humans are forever at the mercy of nature? Then the Mayans succumbed to drought. Want to teach us to manage our resources better? Then the Mayans carelessly destroyed their environment. Want a backstory for your novel about dreadful supernatural forces? Then the Mayans meddled in occult matters and unleashed demonic forces from the darkening void. I bet you can guess which one I'm going with.

Most scholars don't pick one explanation to the exclusion of the others. Several destructive forces were obviously wearing away at Mayan civilization, but in keeping with the theme of this book, we will focus on war.

War to End All Wars

Arthur Demarest of Vanderbilt University is the major proponent of war as the agent of the Mayan collapse. According to his scenario, the rivalry between cities spun out of control in the middle of the eighth century. Excavations show that the Mayan kings built greater palaces, demanded more pomp and ritual, and displayed flashier adornment to amaze and awe their competitors. Unfortunately, their escalating ambition may have removed the limits that had kept earlier wars from becoming too destructive. War shifted from ritualistic contests of honor and prestige to wholesale butchery and robbery. It chewed up resources and distracted the Mayans from more productive activities, such as trade and farming.

Through much of the Classic Period, Mayan communities were laid out in a lazy sprawl, and the peasants farmed the best land available. Then Mayan cities in the Late Classic Period showed signs of trouble. The settlements pulled back and concentrated into easily defended hills surrounded by palisades. These were not always near the most productive farmland, so harvests suffered. War intensified, as indicated by archaeological evidence of a more violent society.

In the ruined city of Cancuen, Guatemala, Demarest found thirty-one skeletons of men, children, and women (two of them pregnant) dismembered and dumped into a cistern around 800 CE. Jewelry of jade, jaguar teeth, and Pacific shells indicates that these people were nobility, killed for some reason other than robbery. In a shallow grave nearby were skeletons of the last king and queen of the city. Demarest also found unfinished defensive walls, scattered spearheads, and another dozen skeletons here and there with markings of spear and ax wounds. This was the end of Cancuen. Nothing later than this massacre has been found in the ruins.[1]

The most interesting feature in the ruins of Chunchucmil is a stone wall encircling the center of the site and visible in aerial photos. Dating to sometime in the Late Classic

Period, the wall was constructed over every road, plaza, and building in its path, using stones plundered from nearby structures. It appears to have been built urgently to keep something out, without regard to aesthetics or architectural preservation. Unfinished and C-shaped, the wall was apparently the last feature built at the site, but the builders never closed the circle. Something interrupted the construction, and that was the end of Chunchucmil.

Although evidence varies from site to site, archaeologists often come up empty when looking for an alternative, purely natural explanation of the Mayan collapse. In the Petexbatun region of the Southern Lowlands, Lori Wright (Texas A&M) examined Mayan bones from the end of the Classic Period, but found that the people were well nourished. Nick Dunning (University of Cincinnati) studied soil core samples but found no evidence of climate change. These findings tend to point away from drought and famine as the primary cause of the disappearance; however, excavations have uncovered evidence of growing poverty in the land: less imported pottery and a lower quality of artifacts.[2]

We can track the collapse of the Mayan civilization with eerie precision. At abandoned cities all across the Mayan homeland, monumental inscriptions fizzle out as the ninth century progresses. They don't stop in mid-sentence with an "arrgh" and a splash of blood, but at each site, there comes a point where nothing new is added to the generally mundane inscriptions from before the final crisis hit. The last dates recorded at Pomona and Aguateca correspond to our 790 CE. Over the next decade, Palenque, Bonampak, and Yaxha fell silent. In the first quarter of the 800s, seven more notable cities stopped inscribing their history; five more stopped in the second quarter. Another eight fell silent by 889. The last date chiseled at Chichen Itza was in 898. Uxmal kept going until 907, but after Tonina stopped recording in 909, the Classic Mayans had nothing more to say.

Death Toll

Even though we aren't sure whether chronic warfare was the primary cause of the collapse, we're pretty sure it was the result. Whether a specific scenario begins with a bad harvest, a volcanic cloud, or failed rains, it always seems to end up with the Mayans fighting over dwindling resources.

How many died as a direct consequence of war? For the entire civilization to disappear, the body count must have been substantial. Throughout this book, cultures have been able to bounce back even after losing as much as one-fourth of their people, so it was probably more than that.

Of course, no one knows what the population of the Mayans was at the classic peak of their civilization, but estimates run anywhere from 3 to 14 million.[3] On top of that, no one is sure how many were left after the worst had happened. B. L. Turner II estimated that an original population of almost 3 million in 800 dropped to less than 1 million by 1000. Richard E. W. Adams estimated that the population peaked at 12 to 14 million and crashed to 1.8 million afterward.[4]

For the sake of ranking, I'm being conservative and assuming that one-third of the minimum population was killed in their final conflicts. This comes to an even million.

THE CRUSADES

Death toll: 3 million[1]
Rank: 30
Type: holy war
Broad dividing line: West Christians ("Franks") vs. Muslims ("Saracens") vs. East Christians ("Greeks")
Time frame: 1095–1291
Location: Levant
Who usually gets the most blame: definitely *not* Richard the Lionheart and Saladin

Truce of God

When Arab conquerors overran the Middle East in the seventh century, they ended up controlling the birthplace of the Christian faith. These new overlords usually let their Christian subjects live in peace and allowed Christian pilgrims easy access to their holy sites, but every now and then a new Muslim king or dynasty burning with an extra dose of fanaticism would launch a persecution. It got especially bad under Caliph (Arabic for "successor") al-Hakim of Egypt, who harassed Christians and destroyed churches throughout his domain, including Christendom's holiest shrine, the Church of the Holy Sepulchre in Jerusalem, in 1009. Even though subsequent caliphs returned to a policy of tolerance, new seeds of mistrust had been sown.[2]

Then in 1071, a new team of empire-building Muslims, the Seljuk Turks, wiped out the Byzantine army at the Battle of Manzikert, which opened up the remaining Byzantine provinces in Asia to conquest. The Byzantine emperor asked the West to save him, but it took many years of indifference before the West finally realized that letting all of Asia fall to the Turks would be a mistake. Meanwhile, the Turks moved south to take Palestine from the Egyptians. As the tide of battle rolled back and forth, Jerusalem changed hands a few times, with at least one massacre of the mostly Muslim ruling class of the city. Christian pilgrims from Europe found themselves caught in a dangerous war zone and returned home with tales of abuse at Muslim hands.

Through most of its early history, Christianity had frowned on war. Saint Augustine had established strict and nearly impossible criteria for declaring and fighting a just war. The church calendar forbade fighting on so many holy days that even officially approved combat was off limits for almost half the year. By the second millennium, the Roman

Catholic Church had imposed so many limitations on war-making that it was difficult for the western European aristocracy to get a really good war going.

Not that they didn't try. Some of the larger states, such as the German Empire, which had imposed rules of civilized behavior on the nobility, were weakening, leading to more and more local disputes being settled by force of arms. Too many unemployed sons of the nobility were wandering around Europe, brawling and fighting, killing each other and innocent bystanders.

Pope Urban II hoped to channel their energy into more acceptable activities, like killing infidels. With a stirring speech at the 1095 Council of Clermont, he encouraged the warrior class of Europe to take up the cross and plant it once again in the Holy Land. It seemed like a good task to keep all those spare knights busy, and it would guarantee the safety of pilgrims. Pope Urban assured them that anyone who took up a crusade would earn valuable spiritual bonus points to boost their score on Judgment Day. The volunteers pledged to see it through to the end, or may God strike them dead.[3]

First Crusade

Meanwhile, a wandering holy man, Peter the Hermit, was preaching directly to the people about the need to free the Holy Land from the Saracens. This People's Crusade fired the imagination of Europe and attracted a massive following of men and women, soldiers and civilians, all sworn to free the Holy Land.

But first they decided to get rid of the infidels among them, so they rampaged through the Jewish communities in the Rhineland. A thousand Jews were killed or driven to suicide in Mainz. In Worms, crusaders broke into the bishop's palace and slaughtered 800 Jews who had been given refuge there. More Jews were massacred in Speir, Cologne, and Prague before the crusaders set out for the Holy Land.

As these mobs of armed pilgrims crossed Europe, they tended to commandeer supplies from the communities along their path, secure in the knowledge that God held their quest in the highest favor. The local people, however, had a different opinion and fights broke out. One large crusader band that was killing Jews and plundering supplies across Germany was wiped out by the king of Hungary as it crossed the border. Finally, the first wave of crusaders arrived outside Constantinople, and the Byzantine emperor quickly ferried them across the straits to Asia before they could cause any trouble.

The Turks, meanwhile, had been hearing frightening rumors that a vast horde from the west was bearing down on them. The rumor became reality when the Byzantines dumped the People's Crusade in Asia and pointed them toward the Saracens. The crusaders flowed forward, and soon surrounded Nicaea, a Greek city the Turks had recently taken. The Turkish sultan gathered his forces and set out to break the siege. They approached cautiously and skirmished tentatively. Finally, the full armies clashed, but it was not much of a battle. The inexperienced and incompetent mob of Franks was easily wiped out, leaving thousands dead on the field and tens of thousands more on route to the slave markets.[4]

When the next wave of crusaders arrived, the Turks shrugged. They were still congratulating each other on how easy it had been to dispatch the first batch; however, the second wave comprised the more level-headed and prudent crusaders. The first wave had been overeager and unprepared. The second wave was neither. These were the ones who had stayed behind and put some effort into planning and preparation. They sharpened their swords, transferred their estates to competent caretakers, and loaded up on provisions. They put less faith in God and a stout heart, and more in horseflesh and steel.

After crossing into Asia, three columns of Franks converged on the Turks, who mistakenly put all of their effort into fighting the first column they came across, at Dorylaeum in July 1097. When the second column suddenly arrived on their flank, the Turks were surprised, tired, and running out of arrows. Then the third column showed up behind them, and the Turks were slaughtered and scattered in confusion. The sultan fled, abandoning his servants, treasury, and baggage train.[5]

With the Turks broken, the Franks marched across Asia Minor, reclaiming the lost territory of the Byzantines and pushing toward Syria. There weren't enough crusaders to totally surround the great city of Antioch, so they camped outside for several months trying to figure out what to do next. Eventually, scouts reported that a Saracen relief force was coming to break the siege, but then, at the last minute, the crusader spy network inside the city paid off. That night, assisted by a Christian Armenian resident of Antioch, a strike force scaled the walls, killed the sentries, and flung open the gates for the waiting army.[6]

When the Turkish relief force arrived and found the crusaders inside the city, they surrounded the city for a siege of their own. But just as the crusaders lost all hope, they discovered, hidden under the floor of an ancient church, the actual* spearhead that had been thrust into Christ's side at Calvary. Heartened by this powerful talisman, they sallied beyond the gates to fight the Turks.

The long march had killed most of the Franks' horses, so now they fought on foot, which accidentally turned out to their advantage. Unlike their Saracen counterparts, European knights trained to fight both on horse and on foot, but the Turks had never come up against heavily armored foot soldiers before. Without big warhorses to hit, Turkish arrows had little effect, and when the crusaders closed in with the Saracen light infantry, they butchered the Muslims.[7]

The First Crusade had never developed a strict command structure. It usually operated as a collection of allied armies voluntarily cooperating (or not) according to consensus, but Prince Bohemond of Taranto had been the practical commander of the crusaders

---

* Probably not.

so far.[8] Now Bohemond settled down to rule Antioch, while Count Raymond of Toulouse and Godfrey of Bouillon led the Crusade south toward Jerusalem.

In December 1098, crusaders took the town of Ma'arra after a month-long siege and slaughtered some 20,000 Saracen captives. By now, with two years of hard marching behind them, the crusaders were exhausted and starving. They had lost most of their horses, and the countryside had been stripped of food. The hungriest crusaders followed the massacre at Ma'arra by roasting and feeding on the bodies of dead Muslims.*[9]

Finally, Jerusalem was besieged and captured in July 1099. The crusaders looted the city and killed 70,000 people in the streets—Muslims mostly, but also anyone who looked Muslim. Jews who had taken refuge in a synagogue were burned inside. The chroniclers wrote of crusaders wading through blood as deep as their horses' bridles—an exaggeration obviously, but we can certainly imagine them splashing through sticky puddles of blood leaking from bodies in the streets.

Style of War

In history books, the Crusades are usually numbered as a sequence of distinct events, but they only looked like that from Europe. What we usually call the First or Seventh Crusade is really the first or seventh large wave of new recruits rounded up and marched out from Europe. This doesn't mean that peace reigned in Palestine between officially designated Crusades. In Asia, war came and went on its own schedule based on local circumstances.

In both armies, the knights were a specialized minority who fought from horseback. Wrapped head to toe in light chain mail, they fought with a lance, sword, axe, or mace, bobbing and ducking behind a large shield that bore the brunt of the enemy's blows. Each knight was at the head of a team of noncombatant support personnel—squires, pages, grooms—and supplemented by light infantry and archers.

The Seljuk Turks were recent arrivals from the steppe who fought mostly as mounted archers. The older nations of the Mideast, such as the Fatimids of Egypt, fought much the same way as the Europeans. Neither style of fighting had a clear advantage. European knights were more heavily armored but slower than the Turks. European crossbows had

---

* This episode of cannibalism seems to be both the one thing that almost all Muslims know about the Crusades and the one thing that almost no Christians know about the Crusades. Once you understand that discrepancy, you will begin to see how difficult it is to write unbiased history. People retell the stories they like and forget the rest. By the way, this story isn't mere propaganda. At least three contemporary sources describe it, most plausibly in a report to the pope by a commander in the field. Most crusader cannibalism seems to have been the work of an armed mob of mad guerrilla pilgrims known as the *tafurs*, who often did this sort of thing just to be tough.

a longer range but a slower rate of fire than the short bows of the Turks. On open ground, the Turks had the advantage, but at close quarters and in siegecraft the Franks did.

Some of the more dedicated crusaders formed into orders of fighting monks to escort and protect pilgrims in the Holy Land. Headquartered in Jerusalem at the Temple Mount and the Amalfitan Hospital, these Templars and Hospitallers kept monastic vows of poverty and chastity, and then worked off all that pent-up energy by smiting the heathens. Because the Templars controlled movement to the Holy Land, they invented the letter of credit, whereby pilgrims would leave cash at an office of the order in Europe and carry a receipt to be redeemed at any other office of the order worldwide. As the only Europeans who understood the dark art of moving money around, the Templars acquired a sinister reputation.

The Crusades into the Holy Land coincided with a couple of other efforts to expand Christendom: the Christian reconquest of Muslim Spain and the Teutonic conquest of the pagan Baltic Sea. All three efforts exchanged personnel and learned from one another. The Second Crusaders even stopped in Spain on the way to Palestine and helped the local Christians by capturing Lisbon from the Moors.

Second Crusade

Almost a half century passed, and the crusaders were settled comfortably into four crusader states: Edessa, Tripoli, Jerusalem, and Antioch. The Holy Land was firmly in control of the children of the First Crusaders, but then the new Saracen ruler, Zengi, consolidated an empire in Syria and reduced the crusader states to three by capturing Edessa, the inmost outpost of Christendom. Europe organized a second crusade to take it back (1147), and this time kings jumped on the bandwagon—Philip Augustus of France, Conrad III of Germany. However, the royal dilettantes of the Second Crusade were not as dangerous as the hungry, landless adventurers of the First Crusade, so they didn't make a dent in the surrounding Saracens.

Third Crusade

After Zengi's death, the empire was passed around to several young Zengids until Saladin, a Kurdish general acting as regent, decided to rule in his own name instead. At first, Saladin maintained peaceful relations with the Christians on the Levantine coast, but then a crusader lord, Reginald of Chatillon, ambushed a Muslim caravan and seized Saladin's sister. Saladin avenged the offense with a new jihad that climaxed in a massive Saracen victory at the Battle of Hattin. This opened the way for Saladin to capture Jerusalem along with many Templar prisoners, whom he put to death.

Losing Jerusalem convinced Europe to get serious about crusading again. In 1190, Richard the Lionheart, the brand new king of England, set out from Marseilles with King Philip II of France. The Holy Roman Empire in central Europe was supposed to supply the backbone of the expedition, but shortly after crossing into Asia Minor, Emperor Frederick Barbarossa slipped in a river he was fording and was pinned underwater by the weight of his armor, drowning.

History likes the Third Crusade. This was the classy crusade, where wise and virtuous kings hacked each other apart with honor and style. There was none of that wading through rivers of blood after capturing every city. In the Third Crusade, all of the rivers of blood came from people who jolly well knew what they were getting into. After an especially good fight, a victor might simply salute his stunned and helpless opponent instead of sliding a dagger into the eye slot of his helmet to finish him off.

OK. It probably wasn't nearly as sporting as later stories imagine, but both sides in the Third Crusade received good press. Saladin is one of the most beloved warlords in Muslim history, and many otherwise somber historians describe him in unusually affectionate language; "when he smiled, he could light up a room" is an actual quote from a recent history.[10] Dante imagined Saladin in the minimum-security wing of Hell, where decent heathens are merely quarantined rather than boiled in lava. Richard the Lionheart, meanwhile, has gone down as one of the most beloved kings in English history (with one of history's greatest nicknames) based entirely on his crusading. He barely even visited his own kingdom, which he impoverished to support his holy war. Philip II stuck around only long enough to earn his points with the pope, and then he hurried home to France.

In reality, Saladin's sense of honor was flexible. After Hattin, two leading crusaders were brought before him in chains. He fed the first one, explaining that the rules of hospitality now forbade him from killing a prisoner who had been given food and drink by his captor. The other prisoner—Reginald of Chatillon, whom Saladin was planning to kill for breaking the truce—lunged for a cup of wine and downed it before anyone could stop him. Reginald thought, Aha! I'm safe! But Saladin killed him anyway because no one likes a smart-ass.[11]

Richard, too, was not completely chivalrous. After taking Acre from the Muslims, Richard gave Saladin a week to come to terms. When the deadline passed, Richard dragged his 2,700 Saracen prisoners of war outside the city gates and beheaded them, along with 300 of their family members. Freed from this encumbrance, the full crusader army rode off to battle.

The two titans fought only one pitched battle. After a frustrating campaign of maneuver, the armies finally met at Arsuf. Richard held his anxious knights back under a shower of Arab arrows until the right moment presented itself. Then, the Lionheart released a cavalry charge that broke the enemy ranks and slaughtered them. The victory, however, went nowhere because Richard had to hurry home to save his wobbly throne from his brother and save his fiefs in France from his onetime comrade, Philip II. Jerusalem would remain in Muslim hands.

Fourth Crusade

By now, Christendom had realized that Palestine could not stand alone; its larger neighbors, Egypt and Syria, conquered it too easily. No empire in recorded history has ever been anchored on Palestine, so the next wave of crusaders (mobilized by Pope Innocent III) decided to take Egypt by sea and build on that.

When this new batch of crusaders arrived in Venice, it turned out that they didn't have enough money to pay for their trip to the Orient. Being businessmen above all else, the Venetians said, No problem, the crusaders could earn the money by taking the Adriatic port of Zara away from Hungary. The city was duly assaulted and turned over to the Venetians.

The pope immediately excommunicated the entire crusader force for this assault on fellow Christians, and several leaders backed out of the enterprise, but the bulk of the crusaders pushed on. Faced with crusader stubbornness, the pope backed down and took the crusaders back into the church.

Because every wave of crusaders had, like locusts, left a trail of desolation as it made its way through the Byzantine Empire, the Byzantines were reluctant to let the crusaders pass again. The crusaders themselves had mixed feelings about the Byzantines. Sure, these Greeks were Christians, but they were also schismatics who practiced their own alien version of the religion in defiance of the pope. Rather than negotiate rights of passage this time, the crusaders found an exiled Byzantine prince who claimed the throne, and in 1204 they seized Constantinople on his behalf. When he turned stingy about paying them for their support, however, the Franks installed one of their own as king. Thus, the last city left unlooted from the Ancient Era was thoroughly ransacked, and many precious books, pieces of art, and archives from the Greco-Roman zenith disappeared—burned, trampled, melted, smashed, or stolen.

As payment for ferrying the crusaders into battle against Byzantium, Venice took four big bronze horses to decorate Saint Mark's Square, plus a scattering of easily defensible islands to control the trade of the eastern Mediterranean.

While western Europeans occupied the strategic core of the Byzantine Empire, three backwater provinces remained under Greek rule. Over the next few decades these parts painfully reassembled themselves into the Byzantine Empire, finally retaking Constantinople from the Franks in 1261.

Somewhere in the midst of all of this activity, the whole business of attacking the Saracens completely slipped everyone's mind.[12]

Children's Crusade

In 1212 a new outbreak of crusading fever swept Europe as a couple of wandering child evangelists stirred up the youth of France and Germany with impassioned pleas and sermons. Enthusiastic mobs of young people followed them in devotion from town to town. As with most medieval history, we have only a few sentences written at the time and many pages of embellished tales written a generation later as our source of information, so no one is sure exactly what happened, but apparently thousands of children—teenagers, more likely—ran away from home and took to the road, determined to free the Holy Land after their elders had failed. Many never made it out of Europe, and most were never seen again.

The most common story is that a column of 20,000 eager French children descended on the port of Marseilles, where they were told transportation awaited them. They embarked on ships and sailed off to do God's bidding—except that it was a trick: the shipmasters sold them all in Mediterranean slave markets instead. Another wave of 30,000 German youngsters made the hazardous crossing over Alpine passes; many were lost along the way. Some drifted over to Genoa, where they gave up and settled down. Others pressed on. When the survivors gathered in Rome to be blessed by the pope, he thanked them for their piety, but seeing their pitiful condition, sent them home.[13]

Fifth Crusade and Beyond

By now, the crusader movement was fizzling out, and the European presence on the Levantine shore was down to three coastal enclaves—Acre, Tripoli, and Antioch. A new outburst of crusaders under King Louis of France (later Saint Louis) tried to conquer Egypt. They took the port of Damietta and won some battles as they moved deeper into Egypt, but in the end, they simply lacked the stamina to keep moving forward. While withdrawing from Cairo, the king and his army were captured and held for ransom.

The next Crusade, the Sixth, was a disappointment for everyone involved. With Mongols bearing down on the Muslim world from the Far East, the Saracens had to keep their armies freed up and ready to meet the next raid from the east. They needed to keep the crusader states in their rear quiet, and the price for this was returning control of Jerusalem to the Franks.

So the crusaders got Jerusalem back, but they got it through diplomacy and didn't get to kill anyone. Even so, it was a temporary measure and Jerusalem was shortly back in Muslim hands. Meanwhile, the crusader state of Antioch fell to the Mongols.

In 1289, Tripoli fell to the Egyptians, leaving only Acre in crusader hands. Then in 1291, a band of Christian pilgrims from Acre brawled with Syrian merchants, and the sultan of Egypt demanded compensation for the Muslims killed. When the price proved beyond the means of the Christian community, the sultan attacked and removed this last crusader state from the map.

Legacy

Some historians say that the Crusades drove a wedge between Christianity and Islam that still exists to this day, but let's be realistic. Neither of these religions gets along with *anybody*. It would be difficult to find any time in history when their followers weren't killing each other—and even if you could, that would only be because they were resting up and getting ready for another round.

However, by putting huge numbers of western European aristocrats in close contact with the sophisticated Orient, the Crusades were able to jump-start Western Civilization—in a happy history book that would be the main legacy of the Crusades. For our purposes, however, the main legacy was a harshening of the Christian religion. For the next five hundred years—until the Enlightenment tamed it—western Christianity had an unfortunate tendency to direct violence against unbelievers.

We will see other religious wars in this book, but those will be wars about people—people trying to impose their beliefs, people wanting to be left alone, people being punished, people being rescued. The Crusades were about a place: the Holy Land.[14]

While fighting over land is quite common, the land in dispute usually provides some practical resource—minerals, crops, harbors, farms, strategic location, exploitable labor, or sheer size. Palestine has none of these. The sole resource of the Holy Land is heritage. There's no gold, no oil, very little fertile land, and few natives, nothing but sacred sites, so in essence, the Crusades killed 3 million people in a fight to control the tourist trade.

RELIGIOUS KILLING

THE STRANGEST THING ABOUT RELIGIOUS CONFLICTS IS THAT SOME PEOPLE deny they ever happen. They will say the Crusades were about economics and the Inquisition was a consolidation of power. They will deny that anyone fights over religion, despite the fact that the participants freely admit to fighting over religion.

Obviously, no war is 100 percent religious (or 100 percent anything) in motivation, but we can't duck the fact that some conflicts involve more religion than others. So how can we decide when religion is the real cause of a conflict and not just a convenient cover story?

Well, for starters, if the only difference between the two sides is religion, then it is a safe bet that the conflict is religious. Serbs, Croats, and Bosniacs are basically the same people except for religion. Ditto the Dutch and the Flemings. In the French Wars of Religion, the partition of India, the Troubles in Northern Ireland, and the war in Lebanon, people who looked alike, spoke the same languages, and lived in the same communities were at each other's throats only because they followed different religions.

Another consideration: How easily can you describe a conflict without mentioning religion? The American Civil War certainly had religious elements to it—John Brown's fanaticism, Lincoln's inaugural address, "The Battle Hymn of the Republic"—but you could easily write a detailed history of the war without mentioning any of these. Contrast that with, for example, the Crusades. Could you even get one paragraph into it without mentioning the pope, the Holy Land, or Jerusalem? You can argue that the Crusades were about something other than religion, but try writing two pages without bringing it up.

Finally, if the parties declare religious motives, we should at least consider the possibility that they are telling the truth. Religion is so central to a person's worldview that most big decisions have some sort of religious consideration. Even if the warmonger-in-chief is using religion only as a convenient and cynical excuse to stir up the masses, the main reason he does that is because *it works*. You never see warmongers rallying armies to destroy an enemy that spells or shaves differently, because those are stupid reasons to fight a war. A different religion by contrast is usually accepted as a perfectly fine reason to kill someone. If it weren't, why would people rally behind it?

Still, not every conflict between different religions is a religious conflict, especially when there are multiple differences between the conflicting groups. In the European conquest of the Americas, the desire to convert the natives fell far behind the desire to rob them. The Pacific war between the Japanese and the Americans is easily explained as a geopolitical power struggle. When the Turks pushed into Europe, religion played a role in motivating both attackers and defenders, but it was secondary to the simple empire-building that was occurring along *all* the borders of the empire.

For this list, let's count only conflicts and oppressions in which religion is widely considered the *primary* reason for the conflict, along with human sacrifices and ritual killings.

The Thirty Deadliest Religious Killings

Taiping Rebellion (1850–64)
Twenty million died in a messianic uprising of Chinese Christians.

Thirty Years War (1618–48)
Seven and a half million died as Catholics and Protestants fought for control of Germany.

Holocaust (ca.1938–45; see "Second World War")
Nazi Germany killed 5.5 million Jews all across Europe. Even though the Nazis claimed to be killing Jews for racial reasons, the only substantive difference between the victims of the Holocaust and those left untouched was their ancestral religion. It was the climax of several centuries of European anti-Semitism.*

Mahdi Revolt (1881–98)
Five and a half million Sudanese died during this fundamentalist Muslim uprising.

Gladiatorial Games (264 BCE–435 CE)
Perhaps 3.5 million gladiators were killed to honor the Roman ancestors.

---

* Confusing the issue is the ambiguity of Hitler's religion. In public, Hitler was a Catholic. He spoke kindly of Christ and was never excommunicated. Many of his followers proudly considered themselves to be Christians fighting against godless Communism. Whatever Hitler's long-term plans for Christianity may have been, he treated it more gently and with more respect than he did Communism, Judaism, or homosexuality.

Hitler's personal religion is hard to nail down. Hard-core Nazis preferred to label themselves *gottgläubiger*, "god-believers," as a formal break from Christianity, and the broad category that best fits Hitler is Deism, the belief in an impersonal higher power, based on reason and nature, without revelation or miracles. This puts him in the same general belief system as Benjamin Franklin, Mark Twain, Voltaire, and Thomas Jefferson, although clearly at the other end of the moral spectrum.

French Wars of Religion (1562–98)

Three million people died in the wars between the Catholics and Protestants of France.

Crusades (1095–1291)

For two hundred years, European Christians tried to wrest control of the Holy Land from the Muslims. Perhaps 3 million people died in these wars.

Fang La Rebellion (1120–22)

Two million died in a peasant revolt in China that started with friction between a Taoist emperor and a Manichaean minority.

Aztec Human Sacrifice (1440–1524)

The Aztecs sacrificed some 1.2 million people.

Albigensian Crusade (1208–49)

Around 1 million people in the south of France were killed in this war to exterminate the Cathar heresy.

Panthay Rebellion (1855–73)

A rebellion of Muslims in southeast China killed a million.

Hui Rebellion (1862–78)

Another rebellion of Muslims in northwest China killed 640,000.

Partition of India (1947)

Mob violence killed 500,000 Hindus and Muslims.

Cromwell's Invasion of Ireland (1649–52)

Cromwell killed 300,000 to 500,000 Irish in his invasion.

Roman-Jewish Wars (66–74 and 130–136 CE)

A series of messianic revolts against Roman authority led to maybe 350,000 deaths.

The Bible

There are two sides to the debate about the atrocities described in the Bible: (1) God is merciful and everything described in the Bible is absolutely, inerrantly true, but the number of people slaughtered by the Israelites was wildly exaggerated, and those people deserved it anyway. (2) The Bible was written by mere mortals who made plenty of mistakes so you can't believe everything you read there, but look at all of the people killed by so-called holy men in so-called holy wars in the so-called Holy Land.

Consider, for example, the city of Ai. The Bible states quite clearly that Joshua killed all 12,000 people in the city at the orders of God. If you are a fundamentalist, you have a lot of explaining to do, but if you are a heathen, you can simply point out that Ai means "ruin," and archaeologists have determined that the town was destroyed long before the Israelites arrived in Palestine, so the Bible is wrong. This means neither side in the debate can comfortably use the Bible to support their interpretation of history.

Be that as it may, if we total the nasty bits of scripture, we'll find 1,167,000 mass killings by humans specifically enumerated in the Bible. Perhaps a quarter of these (ca. 300,000) are historically plausible and religiously motivated.[1]

Japan (1587–1660)

During the Shimabara Rebellion of 1637–38, the Christian rebel force of 20,000 fighting men and 17,000 women and children was wiped out, leaving only 105 survivors. Overall, the Catholic Church counts 3,125 named and 200,000 to 300,000 unnamed martyrs in Japan from this period.[2]

Bosnia (1992–95)

When the predominantly Muslim republic of Bosnia-Herzegovina broke away from Yugoslavia, local Christian Serbs and the government in Belgrade tried to stop them. Two hundred thousand people died in the ensuing civil war.[3]

Sati (outlawed in 1829)

The sacrifice of a widow on the funeral pyre of her husband was common practice in India, particularly in Bengal, where authorities recorded 8,000 satis between 1815 and 1828. Perhaps 60,000 or so widows were burned alive all across India during the preceding century, and a couple of hundred thousand since the Middle Ages.[4]

English Civil War (1642–46)

In the struggle between the Puritans of Parliament and the High-Church supporters of the King, 190,000 Englishmen died, including, at the end, the king himself.[5]

Lebanon (1975–90)

The country of Lebanon was originally carved out of French Syria to give local Christians a country where they could be a (slim) majority. By 1975, the national majority had shifted to the Muslims, so a civil war erupted over power sharing. One hundred fifty thousand people were killed.[6]

Algeria (1992–2002)

Up to 150,000 died in a civil war that began when the military junta refused to hand over the government to Muslim fundamentalist parties that had won the recent elections.[7]

Vietnam (1820–85)

A total of some 130,000 Catholic missionaries and converts were killed under persecution by several generations of Vietnamese rulers.[8]

Russia (1919)

As many as 115,000 Jews were killed in pogroms by anti-Bolshevik soldiers in Ukraine during the Russian Civil War.[9]

Byzantine Empire (ca. 845–55)

The Byzantine empress Theodora (not Justinian's wife, this Theodora was the widow of

Emperor Theophilus, the regent for Michael III, and a saint) hunted down and killed 100,000 Paulicians, followers of a Gnostic heresy.[10]

Dutch Revolt (1566–1609)

The Protestants of the northern Netherlands rebelled against their Spanish rulers. The Spanish duke of Alva boasted of executing 18,600 rebels after he was sent to put down the uprising. In all, 100,000 people died in the revolt, including 8,000 in the sack of Antwerp. The Protestant lands became the independent Dutch Republic, while the Catholic south stayed loyal to Spain and eventually became Belgium.[11]

Ukraine (1648–54)

During a rebellion against Poland, Cossacks under Bogdan Chmielnicki massacred as many as 100,000 Jews and wiped out three hundred Jewish communities.[12]

Eastern Roman Empire (514–18)

When Emperor Anastasius appointed Monophysite bishops (who believed that the divine and human aspects of Christ were separate) rather than Chalcedonian bishops (who believed that the divine and human aspects of Christ were unified), General Vitalian (a Chalcedonian) rose in rebellion against him. Sixty-five thousand people died in what Edward Gibbon called the first religious war.[13]

Witch Hunts (1400–1800)

Sixty thousand accused witches were burned or otherwise executed all across Europe.[14]

Thuggee (until the nineteenth century)

This mystical cult of thieves and stranglers may have sacrificed around 50,000 travelers to the goddess Kali.*

In God We Trust

If we categorize the entries in this list according to which religions came into conflict, we get this simplified breakdown:

Christian vs. Christian: 9

Muslim vs. Christian: 3

Christian vs. Jewish: 3

---

* Recent scholarship tends to treat the Thugs mostly as bandit gangs with a lot of superstitions rather than as cultists; however, the traditional view considers human sacrifice to be the Thugs' primary motivation, so I have included them on this list. (Mike Dash, *Thug: The True Story of India's Murderous Cult* [London: Granta Books, 2005])

Eastern vs. Christian: 3

Jewish vs. pagan: 2

Muslim vs. Chinese: 2

Muslim vs. Muslim: 2

Human sacrifice in India: 2

Human sacrifice in Mexico: 1

Ritual killing in Rome: 1

Muslim vs. Hindu: 1

Manichaean vs. Taoist: 1

We can probably go even farther and group them into four larger categories: indigenous human sacrifice (4), monotheistic religions fighting each other (17), heathens fighting monotheistic religions (8), and heathens stirring up trouble all by themselves (1). In early history, the majority of religious killings involved sacrificing people to bribe and placate the dangerous forces of the universe. Then, Judaism and its offshoots, Christianity and Islam, devised a worldview where a single all-powerful god required a strict, uncompromising belief rather than tangible offerings. After that, religious killings tended to arise from the friction of incompatible beliefs.

Notice that followers of Eastern religions haven't often killed each other over who has the better god. Nor have pagans, shamanists, and animists. These relatively flexible religions usually keep calm until they bump up against rigid monotheists.

Although most of us favor religious tolerance, that is a losing strategy in the end. Monotheism's intolerance of rival beliefs is one of the main reasons why it has succeeded in replacing the more relaxed indigenous religions of Europe, Africa, America, and the Middle East.

FANG LA REBELLION

Death toll: 2 million[1]
Rank: 37
Type: peasant revolt
Broad dividing line: Song dynasty vs. rebels
Time frame: 1120–22
Location: China
Who usually gets the most blame: Chu Mien
Another damn: Chinese peasant revolt

L IKE NERO AND HITLER, EMPEROR HUIZONG OF CHINA WAS AN ARTIST, except that Huizong was a rather good one. His art still hangs in museums around the world. He savored the finer things in life—poetry, birdsong, scented palaces with lacquered furniture, gardens of fine stones, rare flowers, and fountains. To please him, his ministers scoured the country seizing the most splendid objects for the emperor's enjoyment. They plundered tombs and broke into wealthy villas to search for hidden treasure. One very greedy procurement officer, Chu Mien, was especially bad at squeezing the populace, and his agents seized a grove of lacquer trees that belonged to Fang La.

Fang La lived in the town of Muzhou in the coastal province of Zhejiang. Noted for his generosity, Fang La was the community leader of the local Vegetarian Demon Worshippers, which is what the Chinese called the Manichaeans.

Founded by the prophet Mani in Persia in the third century CE, Manichaeism is an extinct religion that believed in an eternal conflict between the forces of good and evil. Christianity probably lifted the whole notion of heaven and hell from them, this being neither Jewish nor Greco-Roman, but very Manichaean. Because Manichaeans believed that good and evil were equally strong and evenly balanced, their enemies accused them of playing both sides of the street and worshipping the devil. The Persian authorities threw Mani in jail for the rest of his life after he came up with this religion. Despite persecution, Mani's teachings spread along the caravan routes throughout Asia and into China.

The indigenous religions of China tend to fall into two traditions. Confucianism (based on the teachings of Confucius) is a code of social behavior, while Taoism (based on the teachings of Lao-Tzu) is a mystical cosmology that tries to explain the universe. Both originated in China's semi-mythical past of the fifth century BCE. Neither religion expects their followers to follow one faith to the exclusion of all others, and it has been said that traditional (pre-Communist) Chinese were Confucianist in public and Taoist in private.[2] Buddhism, the other common religion of China, originated in India (also in the fifth century BCE), but easily adapted and attached itself to the native Chinese culture without much fuss.

Emperor Huizong was not only a patron of the arts but also a devout Taoist and one of the few Chinese emperors to go out of his way to outlaw Buddhism, which he considered an unhealthy foreign influence. The emperor had also been trying to eradicate Manichaeism for the same reason. Chinese officials discouraged several practices associated with this Persian religion, such as vegetarianism and the wearing of white. When Fang La was shaken down by Chu Mien, he found a deep well of Manichaean resentment to tap and a religious network that could be used to organize and plan a revolt.

The rebels succeeded at first with hit-and-run tactics against the local militia, but then veteran troops from the frontier arrived under the eunuch general Tong Guan. These professional soldiers easily beat Fang La's army in several open battles, so the rebels retreated to caves where they resisted all assaults. To deflate popular support for the rebels, Tong Guan renounced the government's authority to seize property on a whim. Finally, in May 1121, a local woman led the imperial troops into the caves, and they captured Fang and his family. The rebellion continued for a couple of years after this, but the imperial forces eventually mopped up the remaining resistance.

Unfortunately, pulling troops off the frontier had fatally weakened the empire, and Jurchen barbarians from Manchuria broke through the Great Wall to overrun north China. The Song dynasty retreated and regrouped in the south, only half as big as it was when the dynasty began.[3]

GENGHIS KHAN

Death toll: 40 million[1]
Rank: 2
Type: world conqueror
Broad dividing line: Mongols vs. civilization
Time frame: lived ca. 1162–1227, but didn't strike out against the world until 1206
Location: Asian interior (the largest contiguous empire ever created)
Who usually gets the most blame: Genghis Khan
Another damn: Mongol invasion
The unanswerable question everyone asks: He couldn't have been this destructive, could he?

HIDDEN AWAY IN THE BACK OF BEYOND, MONGOLIA IS A HARSH, DUSTY wilderness that's synonymous with remote. It's where you find dinosaur bones and shaggy nomads and none of the major fast-food franchises. Modern Mongolia is a tiny football-shaped country that has been kicked around by larger countries for hundreds of years, but the Mongolians comfort themselves with the knowledge that once upon a time they produced the absolutely baddest badass in human history: Genghis Khan.

Of course, the Mongolians can't actually brag about his wholesale butchery—in fact, they vigorously deny it—so they emphasize his courage, his audacity, his splendor, his cunning, his occasional acts of charity, along with the admittedly useful feat of temporarily bridging East and West into a single political entity. They point out all of the helpful inventions (such as pasta and gunpowder, maybe) that passed back and forth across this vast, unprecedented empire. They proudly use him to decorate their banknotes, vodka bottles, beer bottles, shops, hotels, street signs, and chocolate bars.[2]

Some Westerners buy into this. When a recent genetic study indicated that Genghis Khan might have 16 million living descendants, many reports described him as a "prolific lover," not a serial rapist.*[3] Throughout the best-selling *Genghis Khan and the Making of the Modern World*, Jack Weatherford often writes like a defense counsel picking away at the prosecution's case: "Although the army of Genghis Khan killed at an unprecedented

---

* Keep in mind that even with 16 million descendants, Genghis Khan hasn't replaced the number of people he killed.

rate . . . they deviated from standard practice of the times in an important and surprising way. The Mongols did not torture, mutilate, or maim."[4] After an arrow from the walls of the besieged city of Nishapur killed his son-in-law, Genghis Khan allowed his widowed daughter to decide the fate of the city: "She *reportedly* decreed death for all. . . . According to widely circulated *but unverified stories*, she ordered soldiers to pile the heads . . . in three separate pyramids—one each for the men, the women, and the children. Then she *supposedly* ordered that the dogs, the cats . . . be put to death so that no living creature would survive the murder [*sic*] of her husband" (emphasis added).[5]

Personally, I find it unsettling to see the victims of Genghis Khan shrugged off as easily as Holocaust-deniers ignore the Jews, and then to realize that hundreds of years from now, some historians will be rehabilitating Hitler's reputation.

But it's not really a black or white issue. No world leader can get as far as Genghis Khan without a certain amount of charisma, adaptability, and competence. If we spend several generations stereotyping a ruler as a dim-witted, bloodthirsty savage, then sooner or later iconoclastic researchers will realize that there's more to the story than our simplistic stereotypes.

Angry Orphan

Who was this man named Genghis Khan? Well, for starters, that's not his name; it's a title meaning "Universal Leader." It isn't even a very good transliteration into English because we tend to pronounce both of the g's the same. Across the centuries, the "Universal" part has been rendered in English as Zingis (1700s), Jenghiz (1800s), Genghis (1900s), and Chinggis (2000s), and even though my spell-checker prefers Genghis, we should start getting used to Chinggis.

But let's begin with Temujin, since that was his actual name. He was born insignificantly, somewhere in Mongolia, sometime around 1162, to one among several rival tribes on the steppe. When Temujin was nine, a rival tribe, the Tatars, murdered his father, and the family had to flee into exile. Temujin had to fight for supremacy within his family; he killed his older half-brother, ostensibly for stealing the game he took in a hunt. Temujin got married at the age of sixteen, but a rival tribe kidnapped his wife. Although he got her back quickly, she turned out to be pregnant, so the paternity of that son, his eldest, was always in doubt. Eventually, Temujin linked up with a chieftain who was most notorious for occasionally boiling the flesh off live prisoners in a cauldron.

Personally charismatic, Temujin gathered followers from among other dispossessed individuals, which meant that these followers owed everything they had to him, not to an accident of birth.[6] Temujin valued loyalty so highly that even when disloyalty among his enemies worked to his advantage, the culprit was punished. At one city, the soldiers of the garrison snuck down and opened the gates for his army to flood in. Chinggis Khan had them executed for their treachery.

Temujin heard of the legendary beauty of a Tatar princess, so he had his followers hunt her down. His soldiers swooped in and chased away her fiancé. They carried the princess back to Temujin, who took her as one of his many wives. Some time later, at a court gathering, he saw his bride go white with terror. Glancing around, Temujin saw only one unfamiliar face in the crowd, so he had this man seized and interrogated. It was the former fiancé, who just wanted to look at her one more time. Temujin had him beheaded.

When Chinggis Khan finally beat the Tatars, he is said to have lined up all of the men and boys alongside a wagon and ordered his followers to kill every Tatar male who stood taller than the lynch pin of the wagon wheel; however, this attempt to exterminate the tribe that killed his father was either pure myth or less than successful. Tatars eventually formed such a major part of his armies that the terms *Tatar* and *Mongol* became almost interchangeable among Europeans.[7]

Most of Temujin's career was spent consolidating the tribes of the Mongolian grasslands into a single fighting nation. Temujin incorporated conquered tribes into his army by scattering them across his organization. The Mongols came to be more of an army than an actual ethnicity, a fusion of diverse clans that abandoned their petty feuds and grudges and subordinated themselves to Temujin. After many hard years of killing, a gathering of the freshly unified tribes of Mongolia in 1206 proclaimed Temujin to be Chinggis Khan, ruler of the world. The title was only a little bit premature.

Steppenwolves

War colleges and polemophiles* have a special warm spot for the Mongols. These horsemen combined the big-sky freedom of cowboys with the shock and awe of a blitzkrieg. Like a modern army, Mongol horse archers relied on mobility and projectiles to annihilate their enemies, so they inspire more professional admiration and daydreams than do plodding lines of peasant pikemen.

Among the nomadic herdsmen of the Eurasian steppe, boys old enough to walk were old enough to ride, so they became expert horsemen at an early age. Because the management of a herd was so much like battle itself, all men were trained in the arts of war by default. The herdsmen would circle their herds of sheep, cattle, and goats on fast ponies, leading a herd in a chosen direction, splitting it into smaller sections, and selecting a few

---

* Don't look it up. It's not a real word. From the Greek, *polemos*, "war," and *philos*, "beloved," it means a nonprofessional who frequently reads, watches, and discusses war books, films, and articles—or more succinctly: a guy.

head of livestock to pick off for the day's meal. The techniques for slaughtering cattle and sheep worked just as well for slaughtering people. The archers rode up close enough to send a volley into the massed enemy, and then veered off before the enemy could retaliate. They would keep this up all day, thinning the enemy ranks and creating gaps that could be slowly widened, wedging the mob apart into smaller, bite-sized groups.[8]

Adding to the tactical skills of the nomads was their amazing long-distance mobility. Peasant armies were tied to the land—both defending it and working it—and they could spare only a handful of their adult males for long-distance campaigning. The nomads, however, lived in carts and tents and lived off cattle, goats, and sheep. They could simply uproot their entire nation and drag it along wherever they went. In the quiet times between battles, they could still tend their herds and their families, thriving wherever there was enough pasture to support them.

This ability to hurry from place to place made Mongol armies seem much larger than they really were, which is why the word *ordu*, originally a Mongol military unit, has come into English as *horde*, a huge mob.

Many historians openly admire Chinggis Khan's mastery of psychological warfare. By wiping out every population that resisted him, Chinggis Khan hoped to terrify future enemies into immediate submission, thereby saving countless lives—well, except for the thousands he originally massacred to make his point, obviously.[9] And excluding the towns that bravely tried to stand up to him; obviously they got massacred as well. And sometimes a town surrendered without a fight, but then Chinggis Khan decided that leaving behind a garrison was too much trouble, so he just killed everyone instead. And of course, many, many refugees—terrified of these propaganda stories—died of hunger, disease, and exhaustion while fleeing the Mongol onslaught. So when you add it all up, his propaganda probably didn't save nearly as many lives as some historians say it did.

Mongol weapons were the finest of their kind anywhere in the world, and the composite bow was the deadliest weapon known to man for many centuries. It originated in distant antiquity, but the Mongols became the masters of it.

Bend a stick over your knee until it breaks. That is the kind of pressure a bow is put through every time you shoot an arrow. The best solution is to build the bow with materials that enhance the performance and counteract the specific problems facing critical points along the curve. Inside the bend needs a material that compresses and recoils sharply without breaking. Horn is ideal for that. The curved outside of the bend needs an elastic material that stretches without losing its snap. That would be sinew, the tough connective tissue joining muscle and bone. Then bind all of the parts tightly with glue (from boiled hooves) that can take the repeated strain, and you've got a composite bow, made entirely from materials the Mongols could get from their herds.[10]

Why didn't the whole world field armies trained and equipped along the Mongol model? Since archery and horsemanship take years of training to master, it took years to replace each lost soldier on the Mongol side. Also, campaigning exhausted and killed horses faster than most societies could replace them.* In addition, the food surplus of farming societies was useful for producing huge, expendable infantry regiments armed with easy weapons like pikes, axes, and crossbows. To these solid lines of infantry, a sedentary, civilized nation could add a mobile strike force of armored knights on heavy warhorses, who might not have been as fast or as numerous as a nomadic horde but could usually chase them out of the neighborhood before they did too much damage.

China

China at this time was split in half. The southern part was still under the Song dynasty, a purely Chinese manifestation renowned for its art, poetry, and justice. It didn't get conquered until the onslaught of Chinggis Khan's grandson, Kublai Khan, so it doesn't concern us here.† Northern China was under the relatively benign rule of alien conquerors from the north, Jurchen warlords ruling from Beijing as the Jin dynasty.

In 1211, about 100,000 Mongols with 300,000 horses crossed the Gobi desert and overwhelmed the Jin cavalry at the pass known as Badger's Mouth on the northern edge of Chinese territory. One Mongol column swept down quickly enough to take the secondary Jin capital at Mukden (now Shenyang), but the primary capital at Beijing held against their first attack and subsequent siege. While waiting for the city to surrender, the Mongols devastated the countryside. Although Chinggis Khan had no siege machines, he discovered another way to take some of the other walled cities scattered across northern China. He rounded up every civilian he could find and herded them ahead of his assault teams as human shields while the Mongols advanced safely behind them. Either the defenders wasted all of their arrows killing noncombatants, or they refused to shoot and surrendered instead—a win-win for Chinggis Khan.

After a year, the Jin paid him off, and Chinggis Khan abandoned his siege of Beijing. Feeling dangerously exposed to the frontier, the Jin emperor moved the court south from Beijing to Kaifeng, behind the Yellow River. Some Chinese army units, however, took this

---

* For example, even though South Africa is a relatively hospitable habitat for horses, two-thirds of the half-million horses that the British army used to fight the Boers in 1899–1902 died in that war, most of them from overwork, disease, and malnutrition. (Keegan, *History of Warfare* [1993], pp. 187–188) During the American Civil War, approximately three horses died for every two men who did, even though this was an infantry war in which few horses were exposed directly to battle. (Margaret Elsinor Derry, *Horses in Society: A Story of Animal Breeding and Marketing, 1800–1920* [Toronto: University of Toronto Press, 2006], p. 121)

† And Kublai Khan wanted to capture this profitable region intact, so he was less destructive than his grandfather.

as a sign of weakness and betrayal and then defected to the Mongols, bringing many alien but useful military skills into the Mongol camp, such as siegecraft for taking fortifications. Now that the Mongols had the ability to take Beijing, they resumed the attack. The city was taken, looted, and burned in May 1215, but Chinggis Khan was so indifferent to the value of cities that he didn't even attend the capture, leaving it to a turncoat Chinese general instead.

Reportedly, 60,000 women flung themselves from the walls of Beijing to avoid rape. That number is probably an exaggeration, but the full extent of the devastation was obvious. A year later, a scout from Khwarezm, the next land on Chinggis Khan's to-do list, investigated the site to confirm the horrible fate of this great city. "He reported that the bones of the slaughtered formed mountains, that the soil was greasy with human fat, that some of his entourage died from the diseases spread by rotting bodies."[11]

The Mongol attempts to conquer the remnant of the Jin empire beyond the Yellow River failed as Mongol resources were stretched thin and Jin resources were easily concentrated, but this bothered Chinggis Khan not at all. For the next several years, he regarded northern China more as a no-man's-land to be ruthlessly plundered rather than as a conquered province to be administered and taxed. He hadn't quite learned to appreciate the value of urban economies.[12]

Death of Khwarezm

Long ago the barren desert region now covered by all of the 'stans of Central Asia hosted a string of oasis cities along the caravan routes between Persia and China. Supported by irrigated orchards and gardens, this was the thriving cultural center of Islam known as Khwarezm. The city of Bukhara is said to have had a population of 300,000 and a library of 45,000 volumes, among them 200 written by a native son, Ibn Sina, the greatest scientist of medieval Islam.[13] Merv, the hometown of poet Omar Khayyam, had ten libraries containing a total of 150,000 handwritten volumes.[14] Today, if you look on a map, you won't see Khwarezm anymore. Here's why.

For a few years after the fall of northern China, Chinggis Khan and Sultan Muhammad of Khwarezm played diplomatic games, exchanging gifts, envoys, embassies, and pleasant letters in order to shame one another with their own unsurpassed magnificence. Certain gifts or forms of address would imply superiority, which meant the other had to reply with more splendor or admit defeat. Finally, in 1219, the sultan tired of this one-upmanship. When a splendid caravan of Mongol envoys and merchants arrived at the Khwarezmi city of Utrar, the local governor, with the connivance of the sultan, accused them of being spies and had them all killed. When Chinggis Khan sent ambassadors to the court of the sultan of Khwarezm in the city of Bukhara to demand compensation and punishment, the sultan killed one ambassador and plucked out the beards of the other two, which was even more insulting in central Asian culture.[15] Chinggis Khan then rode west with an army numbering between 100,000 and 150,000. The forward scouting units were traveling at sixty miles per day.

In the first clash of armies, the Khwarezmians were routed, leaving a reported 160,000 dead on the field. Utrar, site of the first insult, was besieged for five months. Finally, one of the besieged commanders tried to flee through a side gate. The Mongols caught him and executed him for treachery, but this opened the gate for the Mongol army to rush in. The governor barricaded himself in the inner fortress, which held for a further month. When he was captured, Chinggis Khan had molten silver poured into his eyes and ears.[16] The city was looted and burned. The eradication of the city was so complete that archaeologists did not discover its exact location until very recently.

The city of Balkh surrendered without a fight, but Chinggis Khan slaughtered the inhabitants anyway so his troops wouldn't have to watch their backs when they moved on to the next town.[17]

Then Bukhara fell. The Muslim historian Ibn al-Athir described it as "a day of horror. There was nothing to be heard but the sobbing of men, women, and children torn apart forever, the Mongol troops sharing out the population. The barbarians did violence to the modesty of the women under the eyes of all their unfortunate menfolk, who in their powerlessness could only weep."[18]

Gurganj withstood a five-month siege, beginning in 1220. Finally, prisoners taken in previous conquests were forced to fill the moats with dirt and debris and undermine the walls. After the walls crashed down, the city was overrun quarter by quarter, street by street, in slow, desperate combat. The defenders threw buckets of flaming petroleum onto the buildings in the path of the invaders. Three thousand Mongols tried to cross the river, but Muslim soldiers on the bridge held against them, and the Mongols were killed to a man. When the city finally fell in April 1221, the river was diverted through broken dikes to erase every trace of the city.[19] The women and children were sold into slavery, and 100,000 captives with useful skills were sent back to China. Everyone else was herded out onto the plain and killed. According to the historian Juvaini, 50,000 soldiers killed twenty-four people apiece, for a total of 1.2 million dead.

At city after city, rather than face defenders on the walls directly, Chinggis Khan herded captive men, women, and children from the surrounding countryside and suburbs ahead of his armies, where they took direct hits from the defenders' arrows.

One woman hoped to save herself by crying out while being attacked that she had swallowed a pearl to hide it from looters. It didn't work. She was quickly gutted and her entrails were searched. All of the other corpses from that day forward were opened up and inspected.[20] At another town, the Mongol general heard that the living hid among the dead so he ordered all of the native corpses beheaded and the heads stacked up just to be sure.

Nishapur fell to another column of Mongols in April. Its people were killed, and the town was demolished and plowed over. According to the medieval historian Sayfi, 1,747,000 people were killed at Nishapur. This is probably far more people than lived in the city, but it suggests the scale of the massacre. If a million is the medieval way of saying "the highest number you can possibly imagine," then the number who died at Nishapur was clearly much more than you can possibly imagine.

When the Mongols sent a messenger to demand the surrender of Herat, the leaders of the city had him killed, which is usually considered an unwise move when dealing with Mongols. Fortunately, the city's governor was killed early in the subsequent siege, and the townsfolk immediately surrendered and blamed the misunderstanding on him. The people were spared, but the Mongols executed the Turkish garrison of 12,000. Unfortunately, the people of Herat pushed their luck too far. After Chinggis Khan moved on to new conquests, the Heratis rose up against the Mongol garrison, so Chinggis Khan returned and wiped them out.

The first Mongol scouting party to reach Merv was driven off, and the prisoners taken in the skirmish were paraded through the streets and publicly executed. Then the main Mongol force arrived and camped outside the city walls. The city was swollen with refugees from the countryside, with many times its normal population of 70,000. After six days, the town surrendered, and the Mongol commander ordered the citizens to assemble outside the walls. The wealthiest were tortured into revealing the whereabouts of all their hidden treasure. Four hundred artisans and some children were kept for future use. The rest of the population was wiped out. Afterward, a cleric explored the ruins and counted the bodies, calculating the total number of dead at 1.3 million. The Mongols destroyed the dam that supplied the irrigation for the area. No city was ever rebuilt on that site.[21]

Further Expansions

Chinggis Khan returned to China to clean up the annoying enclaves that had survived his earlier conquest. He spent a brief period trying to resolve his ongoing war against the reduced Jin empire, but that came to nothing, so he turned instead against the Tanguts—Tibetans who had moved down from the Himalayas and founded caravan cities in the oases between China and Khwarezm. City after city fell to his hordes, and no mercy was recorded for the captives. Tanguts tried to flee to the mountains and hide in caves, but few succeeded. Bonefields littered the desert for many years afterward.

As the king of the Tanguts tried to negotiate the safe surrender of his besieged capital, Ningxia, in 1227, the aged Chinggis Khan felt his own death approach. His last orders saw to it that the Tanguts would not outlast him. Ningxia was taken and the population exterminated.

Meanwhile, two of Chinggis Khan's most trusted generals, Subotai and Jebe, had chased the refugee Sultan Muhammad of Khwarezm deep into Persia, but he died before they caught him. So the expedition wouldn't be a total waste, the Mongols took the Persian city of Qazwin while they were in the neighborhood. "The inhabitants fought back in the streets, knife in hand, killing many Mongols, but their desperate resistance could not fend off a general massacre in which there perished more than forty thousand people."[22] Then the Mongols pushed northward into Azerbaijan and Georgia, destroying countless towns, and crossed the Caucasus into the steppe of Russia and Ukraine. The advance columns were closing in on Poland when word came that Chinggis Khan had died, so the attack was halted as the leaders returned to decide the succession.

Chinggis Khan was buried in a secret tomb, somewhere deep in the Mongol homeland. Any witnesses who happened across his funeral procession were seized and killed to prevent them from reporting the location. After the body was buried with his accumulated wealth, the slaves who carried him were ambushed and slaughtered to hide the location forever. His grave has never been found, but it haunts archaeology as one of the world's greatest career-boosting possibilities.

Was It Even Possible?

For now let's forget the incredible body counts reported for individual atrocities and focus instead on overall estimates from modern demographers. By all accounts, the population of Asia crashed during Chinggis Khan's wars of conquest. China had the most to lose, so China lost the most—anywhere from 30 to 60 million. The Jin dynasty ruling northern China recorded 7.6 million households in the early thirteenth century. In 1234 the first census under the Mongols recorded 1.7 million households in the same area. In his biography of Chinggis Khan, John Man interprets these two data points as a population decline from 60 million to 10 million. In *The Atlas of World Population History*, Colin McEvedy estimates that the population of China declined by 35 million as the Mongols subjugated the country during the thirteenth century. In *The Mongols*, historian David Morgan estimates the Chinese population (in both the north and the south) as 100 million before the conquest and 70 million after.[23]

John Man makes a rough guess that 1,250,000 people were killed in Khwarezm in two years—one-fourth of the 5 million original inhabitants. McEvedy states that the population of Iran declined by 1.5 million; the population of Afghanistan dropped by some 750,000, while European Russia lost 500,000.[24]

One of the most common arguments about Chinggis Khan is that he just couldn't have been this destructive, could he? He had such primitive weapons, and there were far fewer people to kill in those days, so how could he kill more people than Stalin and World War I combined? There has been a recent trend to rehabilitate his reputation by dismissing all of the horror stories as propaganda. It's interesting to watch the debate go back and forth over time as each expert weighs in:

J. D. Durand, 1960: "A considerable decrease of population in the north might have been caused by the struggle between the Chinese and the Mongol invader.... Still the sheer magnitude of the decrease in the north, not balanced by any corresponding increase in the south, creates a suspicion that the census in the north was very defective."[25]

Rene Grousset, 1972: "Courtesies having been observed in respect to strict historical objectivity, let us make no bones about our horror at the appalling butchery."[26]

David Morgan, 1986: "Professor Bernard Lewis, something of a revisionist on this matter of the Mongol horrors, has suggested that in the twentieth century we are better able to judge man's destructive capacity than were our Victorian forebears, to whom the Mongol conquests seemed terrible beyond normal human experience.... [H]e feels... we should resist the temptation to believe that the Mongols, whose apparatus of destruction was so primitive compared with what was available to Hitler, could have devastated the Islamic world so totally."[27]

David Morgan, 1986 (speaking for himself): "It is true that what we hear most about is the slaughter and demolition of the great cities of [eastern Persia]. But more serious . . . was the effect of the Mongol invasions on agriculture. . . . [S]ome of [the irrigation systems] were destroyed during the invasions, and without effective irrigation much of the land would soon revert to desert. But a more long-term consideration is that [these systems], even if not actually destroyed, quickly cease to operate if they are not constantly maintained. Hence if peasants were killed in large numbers, or fled from their land and stayed away, land would suffer irreparable damage simply through neglect."[28]

Jack Weatherford, 2004: "The Mongols operated a virtual propaganda machine that consistently inflated the number of people killed in battle and spread fear wherever its words carried."[29] "Although accepted as fact and repeated through the generations, the numbers have no basis in reality. It would be physically difficult to slaughter that many cows or pigs, which wait passively for their turn. Overall, those who were supposedly slaughtered outnumbered the Mongols by ratios of up to fifty to one. The people could have merely run away, and the Mongols would not have been able to stop them."[30]

John Man, 2004: "*One million three hundred thousand?* . . . Many historians doubt this because it sounds simply incredible. But we know from the last century's horrors that mass slaughter comes easily . . . 800,000 were killed in the Rwanda genocide of 1994 . . . over just three months. . . . For a Mongol, an unresisting prisoner would have been easier to dispatch than a sheep. A sheep is killed with care, in order not to spoil the meat. . . . There was no need to take such trouble with the inhabitants of Merv, who were of less value than a sheep. It takes only seconds to slit a throat, and move onto the next."[31]

The important point to notice is that the exact same evidence can easily be interpreted in opposite directions. A recorded drop in the population between censuses is either an accurate reflection of a massive decline or an indication that the census was flawed. Either the Holocaust shows how difficult it is to kill huge numbers of people or it proves how easy it is. A full confession to killing thousands is either the truth or mere boastfulness.

There's a word for this shifting interpretation of underlying facts: *paradigm*. This is the theoretical framework within which theories, laws, and generalizations are formulated.[32] If your ruling paradigm declares that human populations do not crash abruptly, then the only way to interpret the census is to assume an error in the data. If your paradigm declares that only the industrial efficiency of the gas chambers made the Holocaust possible, then obviously spear-waving barbarians can't kill millions, regardless of what the chronicles say. In 1994, when a million people were massacred in Rwanda in three months, mostly with machetes, the paradigm shifted to accept the idea that gas chambers are not necessary for genocide.

Admittedly, history is biased by the available sources, and many of the stories that have come down to us are likely exaggerations. Unfortunately, when you dismiss too much history as mere propaganda, you find yourself caught in a paranoid cycle where you will not trust what anyone says, and you will believe only what you want to believe. Maybe the relentless bad press that surrounds Chinggis Khan means only that history was written by his victims. On the other hand, that's to be expected when everyone who interacted with him ended up as a victim.

Did Everybody Do It?

Whenever you start denigrating a notable person from the past, you will be told that those were different times. Everybody did it. You can't judge the past by modern standards, his defenders will say. Everybody else was just as bad.

Is this true? Were all the people of the Middle Ages as barbarous as Chinggis Khan? Well, unfortunately for the defenders of Chinggis Khan, the rebuttal is almost too easy. The career of the Universal Leader spanned almost the same years as a man who was nearly as famous, nearly as influential, and completely the opposite. Let's consider the biography of a contemporary who *didn't* kill as many people as Chinggis Khan:

In 1206—the same year that the Mongol tribes proclaimed their warlord Temujin to be Chinggis Khan—a twenty-three-year-old ascetic arrived in Rome. Like Temujin, Giovanni di Bernardone is more commonly known by another name, in this case, Francesco, the Frenchman, even though he was from the Italian town of Assisi.* Unlike Temujin, Francesco's early attempts at soldiering were simply a matter of duty to his hometown, and they proved less than legendary. He was captured by forces from Perugia at the age of twenty and spent a year as a prisoner of war before a truce secured his release. He tried again in the next war, but he was sent home from this campaign with a serious fever. Charming,

---

* His father admired the French, and nicknamed his son after them.

witty, and pleasure-loving in his youth, Francesco turned to religion and philosophy after his experience of war and near brush with death.

After dedicating the next few years to prayer and study, Francis of Assisi concluded that all nature manifested the benevolence of God. He considered all living creatures to be the brothers of mankind. Giving away all his worldly goods and tending to the sick and poor, he made it a point to live his life as Jesus had. Francis of Assisi founded a monastic order, the Franciscans, dedicated to poverty and good works, although his contribution was mostly that of a charismatic example rather than a methodical organizer. Unlike the severe scourges-and-scorpions holy men that every religion churns up, Francis was always good-humored and pleasant.

Francis is the first person recorded to have spontaneously sprouted the stigmata, the five wounds of Christ. Inventing this new way of being mystically weird is probably a point against him, but Saint Francis of Assisi exemplifies the best of Christianity. He died in 1226, a year before Chinggis Khan did. No gravediggers were slaughtered to hide the tomb of Saint Francis. It's now a major pilgrimage site and one of the world's great tourist traps.

ALBIGENSIAN CRUSADE

Death toll: 1 million[1]
Rank: 46
Type: religious war
Broad dividing line: Catholics vs. Cathars
Time frame: 1208–29
Location: southern France
Who usually gets the most blame: Pope Innocent III, Simon de Montfort

A Perfect Storm

Catharism was a persistent heresy that survived several centuries of attempted eradication all across Christendom. Cathars believed that Jesus was not of this corrupt world but was a purely divine entity, a phantom. He had come to replace the vicious, vengeful God of the Old Testament who had created our flawed universe. The word *Cathar* came from the Greek word for purity, and Cathars believed that all people should strive to separate themselves from the corruption of the material world to reach a condition called Perfect. They also believed that humans needed no intermediaries to receive Jesus's salvation, which obviously did not go over well with the Roman Catholic Church. After many centuries of persecution, the Cathars were finally exterminated in their last stronghold in the south of France in the thirteenth century.

Crusade

Sovereignty was complicated in the Languedoc region of southern France. Although the French king had ultimate dominion over the region, outsiders like the kings of England and Spain had some valuable fiefdoms scattered around the area as well. Feudal lords had even more autonomy here than most of their peers elsewhere.

The lack of central authority attracted heretics. Cathars—called Albigensians here—weren't the majority in Languedoc, but they were a tolerated minority. Enough local lords, such as the powerful Count Raymond VI of Toulouse, considered them useful, peaceful citizens and gave them protection. This annoyed the Catholic Church, which accused the Cathars of the usual atrocities—sodomy, devil worship, baby stealing, and desecration of holy objects. In May 1207 Raymond was excommunicated by the church for being uncooperative in its efforts to eradicate the Cathars.

In January 1208, Rome sent an envoy into the region to try to convince Raymond to stamp out the heretics. After unsuccessful and angry negotiations, unknown assassins killed the papal representative while he was returning home. The church blamed Raymond.

Pope Innocent III now preached a full crusade against the heretics. This was especially popular in northern France because anyone who took up the cross against the Cathars would earn the same spiritual bonus points with God as fighting in the Holy Land—without having to take a long, queasy sea voyage or eat disgusting foreign foods. Ten thousand of them gathered in Lyon.

Beziers

The crusaders attacked the city of Beziers first. It was well fortified and well supplied, and everyone expected it to withstand a siege, but on the first day, as the crusaders were setting up the camp, several shiftless camp followers—cooks, drivers, and so on—went down to a shaded creek beneath the city walls to rest and cool off.

Defenders on the wall started exchanging insults with the northern riffraff, and tempers frayed. The townsmen decided to go outside and teach the stray northerners a lesson. Unfortunately, during this sortie, they left the town gate wide open, filled with cheering civilians. Others in the crusader camp spotted the fight. They grabbed their clubs and rushed over to join the melee, finally chasing the townsmen back inside and following hard on their heels. As northerners got inside the gate, soldiers from the town rushed down from the city walls to drive them out. Distracted by the brawl, no one noticed that some of the more quick-witted crusaders had snuck in and propped ladders up against the suddenly unguarded walls.

And that was the end of Beziers.

As the crusaders eradicated this hotbed of heresy, the leader of the Catholic forces, Simon de Montfort, was asked how they could tell the heretics from the orthodox. His solution was simple: "Kill them all; God will know his own."* Thousands of civilians took sanctuary in the town church, but the crusaders followed them inside and slaughtered them anyway. Although most of the townspeople were Catholic, all of the inhabitants of Beziers—20,000 people—were massacred regardless of religion.[2]

Root and Branch

Town after town fell to the crusaders. After the water supply to Carcassonne was cut, the inhabitants surrendered and were exiled with just the clothes they wore. The mountain

---

* Like most quotes from history, we don't have this on tape or written in Simon's own hand, so half the historians you ask will swear he never said any such thing.

fortress of Minerve near Beziers lost its water supply when crusader catapults destroyed the fortified tunnel to the town's well. After Minerve surrendered, the Cathars were forcibly converted to Catholicism, except for 140 who refused and were burned.

After the capture of Bram, every member of the Cathar garrison had his eyes gouged out and his nose and upper lip sliced off. Only one soldier was left with a single eye intact in order to guide the faceless men back to spread fear in Cathar territory.[3]

Raymond of Toulouse had been keeping a low profile, riding along in support of the crusade, but after a year of watching his domain become ravaged, he switched sides. After Toulouse withstood a siege by Simon de Montfort, Raymond counterattacked, retaking much of the lost territory and bringing Montfort under siege. The next year, the Catholics had the upper hand and ended up outside Toulouse again. Because Raymond was the vassal and brother-in-law of King Peter II of Aragon in northern Spain, this king now joined the fight against the crusaders.

Languedoc became a maelstrom of battle, and Toulouse changed hands several times before it was all done, but the war dragged on, year after year, without a final knockout blow. Because the pope required only forty days of crusading to earn God's favor, the holy mobs that came south every summer for the campaign season would pack up and go home six weeks later, leaving Simon de Montfort alone in Languedoc to face the Cathar counterattack.[4]

The war lasted longer than its major participants. King Peter II of Spain was killed in battle at Muret in 1213. In 1218, Simon de Montfort was killed outside Toulouse by a stone from a catapult manned by women of the town. Raymond fled to England for a time, then went to Rome to plead his case; he returned to fight and finally died in 1222.

During the 1220s the war continued under a new generation of leaders, sons of Simon and Raymond, but one by one the last Cathar strongholds fell and stayed down. In 1226, King Louis VIII of France pledged himself to the crusade, and now the full French army overwhelmed the heretics in one tough year of campaigning. The king then negotiated acceptable terms with the principal nobles of the south, and the Treaty of Paris ended hostilities in 1229.[5]

In 1229, Rome established the Inquisition in Toulouse to make sure none of the supposed converts were secretly practicing their old heretical ways. Sporadic rebellions and uprisings continued in the hinterlands for several decades. Apostates were hunted down. Relapsed or stubborn Cathars were burned—the last of them in 1321.[6]

HULAGU'S INVASION

Death toll: 800,000[1]
Rank: 55
Type: conquest
Broad dividing line: Mongols vs. Arabs
Time frame: 1255–60
Location: Middle East
Who usually gets the most blame: Hulagu
Another damn: Mongol invasion

I T ANNOYED THE GREAT KHAN MONGKE, GRANDSON OF CHINGGIS KHAN, that the Muslim minority scattered around his empire considered the caliph in Baghdad—secular ruler of Iraq and spiritual leader of all Sunni Muslims—to be more important than the great khan himself. This could not be tolerated. The caliph had to go.

Rumors of invasion preparations soon came to the ears of the Order of the Assassins, a mysterious Muslim cult in the mountain fortress of Alamut in Persia, who trained specialized killers to strike down enemies all over the world. Although the Assassins were no friends of the caliph, when it became obvious that the Mongols were getting ready to invade westward, the Assassins dispatched 400 of their best to cut down Mongke. The plan failed, and in 1253, Mongke ordered his brother Hulagu to retaliate.

In 1256, after a few years of preparation and hard riding, the Mongols arrived, but a new grand master was in charge of the Assassins, and he quickly surrendered to avoid the worst. He accompanied the Mongols on a circuit of the Assassins' castles, ordering them to surrender, which brought an end to the Order. The grand master was initially treated well for his cooperation, but eventually his Mongol attendants found an excuse to kick and beat him to death.

The next year, Hulagu sent messengers to Baghdad insisting that the caliph tear down the city walls, fill the moat, and come groveling to Hulagu to offer his subservience. The caliph was in the middle of a power struggle among some of his officials and couldn't find the time to respond, so Hulagu advanced.

The Mongols arrived at Baghdad in January 1258, and within a week it was obvious that further resistance was pointless. The caliph and his generals surrendered, and Hulagu ordered the city destroyed. Although Hulagu himself followed the traditional tribal shamanism of the Mongols, his mother, favorite wife, and chief general were all Nestorian

Christians from central Asia, so the Christian population of the city was going to be spared the worst. They were told to take refuge in their church, which was then declared off-limits during the subsequent sack.

The rest of the city's population was killed. Books from the great library were dumped in the Tigris River, which ran black with ink and red with blood. Because the Mongols believed it was bad luck to spill royal blood onto the earth, they rolled the caliph in a carpet and trampled him to death with horses. This extinguished the line of caliphs that stretched all the way back to Muhammad.

Persian historians later claimed that 800,000 died in the sacking of Baghdad, but in diplomatic correspondence with King Louis IX of France, Hulagu himself reported that he had killed 200,000.

The Mongols then swept through Syria, accepting the surrender of the Arab cities of Damascus and Aleppo and the crusader state of Antioch. The Mongol tide was about to wash over Egypt when word arrived that the Great Khan Mongke had died. Hulagu returned to Mongolia to settle the succession, leaving behind a subordinate to continue the conquest. Egyptian Mamelukes soundly beat these Mongols and killed their general at the Battle of Goliath Spring (Ayn Jalut) in Palestine, the farthest the Mongols would ever reach in this part of the world.[2]

HUNDRED YEARS WAR

Death toll: 3.5 million
Rank: 28
Type: dynastic dispute
Broad dividing line: France vs. England
Time frame: 1337–1453
Location: France
Who usually gets the most blame: Nowadays the Hundred Years War is usually treated as an act of nature (that is, just one of those things), inevitable and not really anyone's *fault*.
Trick question: How long did it last?

> But if the cause be not good, the king himself hath a heavy reckoning to make, when all those legs and arms and heads, chopped off in battle, shall join together at the latter day and cry all "We died at such a place;" some swearing, some crying for a surgeon, some upon their wives left poor behind them, some upon the debts they owe, some upon their children rawly left. I am afeard there are few die well that die in a battle; for how can they charitably dispose of any thing, when blood is their argument? Now, if these men do not die well, it will be a black matter for the king that led them to it; whom to disobey were against all proportion of subjection.
>
> —William Shakespeare, *Henry V*

Edwardian War (1337–60)

Ever since the Norman Conquest of England in 1066, England had been ruled by—and let's not mince words here—Frenchmen. Historians call them English, but most of the English nobility spoke French as their primary language. The laws of England were written in French. The English nobility had major fiefs and summer homes in France, and the king of England often owned as much of France as did the French king. They were French in everything but geography.

When the king of France died childless in 1328, his first cousin, King Edward III of England, put in a claim to be his replacement. Instead, the French nobility picked a weakling they could dominate, rather than a powerful king, such as Edward would be. Of course this infuriated Edward.

Because local wars and intrigues kept him busy, Edward didn't launch his war to assert his claim for ten years. By that time, he had an exciting new weapon in his arsenal. He had first encountered the longbow while fighting peasants in the wild borderlands alongside Wales. Made from the yew tree and tall as a man, the longbow required enormous strength to pull, but with it, a trained archer could put an arrow through an inch of solid oak at two hundred yards and plate armor at one hundred yards. Impressed at how easily the longbow killed his best knights and disrupted his attacks, Edward made these archers an integral part of his own army.

Since medieval warfare was rarely secret, the French, aware of the impending war, had assembled a fleet and were getting ready to attack first, but the English fleet cornered the French ships at Sluys, the port of Bruges, in 1340. Archers crammed aboard the English fleet swept the crews off the French ships and left the English in control of the channel. "The fish drank so much French blood, it was said afterward, that if God had given them the power of speech they would have spoken in French."[1]

After the English landed in France in 1346, the two armies maneuvered around each other in the north of France for several months, trying to corner the other in the most advantageous battlefield. King Edward realized that the best tactical use of his strengths was to set up dismounted knights, foot soldiers, and archers in a defensive hedgehog bristling with spears, swords, and battle-axes, and then to get the French to attack. Finally, at Crecy, the English took a strong position atop a hill and waited for the French to come. As the battle was joined, the French knights were so eager to get at the English that they rode over their own retreating crossbowmen to get to the front lines. In the first round, their big heavy warhorses were ideal targets for the English arrows. Then the dismounted and heavily armored French knights slogged, slipped, and struggled up the muddy slopes, all the while being cut down by English archers. When it was all over the French losses were staggering, leaving their nobility badly depleted.

To solidify their control over northern France, the English brought the English Channel port of Calais under a long and frustrating siege. Finally, the leading citizens of the starving town offered to surrender. The English were planning the customary massacre of the defenders as the penalty for causing them so much trouble, but the town's leaders willingly offered themselves up to be killed if only the people would be spared. Their courage moved the heart of the English queen, who obviously did not know the first thing about the proper way of waging war. She pestered her husband to show mercy. Edward relented—probably with a weary sigh—so the leaders and people of Calais were expelled instead of killed. Then the city was thoroughly Anglicized.

With the north secure, the war moved south. In 1356, King Edward's son, Edward the Black Prince, marauded inward from English-controlled Aquitaine on the western coast of France, leading his army 260 miles across the center of France, burning towns and castles in order to provoke the French king into coming to stop him. When the English arrived at the Loire River, however, they discovered that the French had destroyed the bridges, stranding the English 160 miles from the safety of the English Channel. They turned around to go home, but the French army caught up at Poitiers in September. The 7,000 Englishmen were outnumbered by as many as five to one.

Because horses were large, vulnerable targets for the English archers, the French chose to advance on foot. Their first wave arrived exhausted and was cut to pieces. While trying to retreat, they blundered into the second wave, which was thrown into chaos as well. Finally King John I of France regrouped and led the third and largest wave toward the English position, just as the English charged out to press their advantage. The English overwhelmed the French nobility and drove them into headlong retreat toward the safety of the town of Poitiers, but when the fleeing French arrived, they found the gates shut. The English cavalry caught up and easily massacred the tired survivors of the battle. France was running out of knights and options.[2]

Among the captives from the Battle of Poitiers were King John of France and his son, who were taken to England, where the Black Prince gave them a royal tour and they were cheered by the populace. (Just because they were at war, that was no reason to be uncivil to a guest.) Negotiations for his release never quite worked out, and the French king died still captive in London in 1364.

After a truce was negotiated in 1360, the English army was supposed to pack up and go home, but huge numbers of suddenly unemployed mercenaries didn't have nice homes to return to. They had enjoyed living off the conquered French and refused to give it up. Instead, they stayed behind and roamed the countryside in predatory armies, looting, raping, and extorting.

Caroline War (1369–89)

As King Edward of England grew old and feeble, he began to neglect the English position on the continent. After a nine-year truce, the new French king, Charles V, decided to resume the war and see if history had shifted in France's favor.

The pendulum of chance was definitely swinging back toward the French. England's Black Prince came down with a wasting disease and died in 1376. When his father the king followed one year later, the English throne went to Richard, the ten-year-old son of the Black Prince, rather than to a battle-tested warrior. The French pressed their growing advantage, and except for a few coastal enclaves, they cleared the English off the continent.

By the 1380s, the French had fixed their English problem and were raiding ports along the English coast.

Interlude of Insanity and Peace (1389–1415)

After the death of Charles V in 1380, the French throne went to his twelve-year-old son, Charles the Mad. He didn't start with that nickname, but in 1392 a mysterious illness made his hair and nails fall out. While still feverish and slightly delirious, Charles VI went riding with his entourage. A sudden noise startled him into drawing his sword and hacking through everyone he saw. He slew four attendants before he could be stopped.

His bouts of odd behavior came and went, but they became progressively longer and worse as he got older. He alternated between a listless stupor and frantic gaiety. Once he accidentally set fire to himself and several friends while playing a shaggy wild man at a masked ball, and his life was saved by a quick-thinking duchess who smothered him under her skirts. On his bad days, he urinated in his clothes, smashed furniture, and allowed his children to go ragged with neglect. For a while he believed he was made out of glass and would break if jostled.[3]

Charles was too crazy to lead France at war, so peace broke out. Instead, the French royal family spent the next few decades killing each other in court intrigues as various relatives of the king fought over who was really in charge. Although Isabella, the German-born French queen, had been passionately in love with Charles at first, and continued trying to make an heir with him despite his dangerous behavior, she eventually started an affair with the king's brother, the duke of Orleans. It continued until agents of the king's uncle, Philip the Proud, duke of Burgundy, cut the king's brother down in the streets of Paris.

Hank Cinq

After almost a full generation of peace, the new king of England, Henry V, decided to press the issue yet again. Hoping to take advantage of the chaos at the French court, Henry invaded France in 1415. After taking the port of Harfleur in a bloody assault (Shakespeare: "Once more into the breach . . ."), he hunted the French army on a long march through mud, rain, and clammy autumn weather. Disease and malnutrition slowed and weakened his army, and then the French army stood in his way, ready to fight, at Agincourt.

Although outnumbered two to one (at least), the English took up a strong defensive position on a narrow field, with both flanks anchored in the woods. There they waited and tormented the French with clouds of arrows from English longbows. Angered beyond reason, the main line of dismounted French knights attacked while still under a deadly hail of arrows. When the two opposing lines of heavy infantry finally closed, the French were already tired, frustrated, and fewer. They were slaughtered.

Meanwhile, behind the English line, a mob of French peasants raided Henry's camp to loot and steal. With chaos unfolding behind him, Henry worried that the French prisoners of war under loose guard in his camp might rearm and attack his rear, so he ordered them killed. The English nobility refused to commit such a dastardly deed, so Henry told his archers—who were peasants and less squeamish about violating the rules of chivalry—to kill the prisoners. About the same time, the French army fled the field from Henry's front and gave the English their victory.[4]

With yet another slaughter of the French nobility complete, Henry was able to dictate the terms of peace. King Charles VI (the Mad) of France agreed that Henry should get the throne next, and to seal the deal, Henry married Charles's daughter, Catherine.

Here ends Shakespeare's patriotic drama of Henry V's glorious crusade—on a high note with England triumphant. Unfortunately, King Henry died before King Charles did, which left his baby son as the new king, Henry VI, of England. The treaty's status was uncertain.

Burgundy Breaks with France

John the Fearless, the latest duke of Burgundy, had stayed out of the Agincourt campaign because his house was still feuding with the rest of the French royal family over who should get France after Charles the Mad died. In 1418, Burgundian forces seized Paris from King Charles's garrison to show he was serious.

The next year, the king's teenage son, the dauphin (crown prince), met John the Fearless on the bridge at Montereau to negotiate a settlement, but the prince sprung a trap and killed him instead. Annoyed by the betrayal, the next duke of Burgundy switched to the English side of the war, bringing Paris with him. The dauphin fled to the countryside, so when Charles the Mad died in 1422, the dauphin was not able to upgrade his title to king. The English held Paris for their claimant to the French throne, the baby King Henry.

Joan of Arc

About this time (1429), a teenage peasant girl heard the disembodied voices of saints commanding her to arm herself, saddle up, and save France. This being the Middle Ages, Joan of Arc was not sedated and wheeled into a hospital room by worried relatives. Instead, she obeyed the voices and sought out the fugitive French court. After convincing the dauphin that she really did have saints whispering in her ear, Joan led an army against the English forces besieging Orleans, a vital crossing of the Loire River that (you will recall) had stopped Attila the Hun's rampage a thousand years earlier (see "Fall of the Western Roman Empire").

Actually, the French situation at Orleans was not all that bad, nor did the English have an overwhelming advantage. The siege probably could have been broken if anyone had bothered to try; however, the French had all but given up. Morale was shot, and they had passively accepted that the city would fall. Joan's arrival revived the French spirits. The French attacked and drove away the English.

After the war moved into open country, Joan hounded the English army, waiting for a weakness to appear. Finally, at Patay, she caught the English before they had completely staked out their defensive line. The French attack slaughtered the English and captured most of their leaders. This opened the path to the city of Rheims, where new kings were traditionally crowned, so the dauphin became King Charles VII of France.*

In 1430, the Burgundians captured Joan and sold her to the English, who then rounded up compliant churchmen from Paris to put her on trial. Joan was found guilty of wearing men's clothes and burned alive as a witch.

Joan's major contribution to the war had been to figure out that the French knights could beat the English hedgehog formation if they would stop being such idiots. The French code of chivalry demanded that they not back down from a fight, no matter how unfavorable their situation. The common theme running through the French defeats at Crecy, Poitiers, and Agincourt was a French charge against a strong English defensive position. It never occurred to the French to wait until they caught the English at a disadvantage. Joan had the moral authority to convince the knights to modify their rigid rules and to put more thought into their attacks. With divinely inspired encouragement, the French began to apply actual tactics to their war effort.[5]

Endgame

In 1435, Burgundy dropped its alliance with England. The war continued for almost twenty more years, but as the English territory on the continent eroded, the battleground

---

* In Joan's entourage rode Gilles de Rais, marshal of France, earning glory as one of his nation's greatest warriors, but he eventually earned greater fame as one of the deadliest serial killers in human history. After retiring from military service to his estates in 1435, he began kidnapping, sodomizing, and disemboweling young boys. When he was caught in 1440, he confessed in vivid and convincing detail to 150 murders. He was quickly tried, convicted, and strangled, although the heresy and ritual blasphemy he committed during his murders shocked his contemporaries more than the murders themselves. All in all, a savage footnote to a savage era. (Wilson, *Mammoth Book of the History of Murder*, pp. 51–59)

shrunk as well. These smaller English holdings resulted in lower tax payments, which supported smaller armies that avoided taking any risks. When taxes were raised in England, the peasants rose up in anger. When taxes were lowered, the foreign mercenaries in the English army went home.

Battles became fewer until the last battle was fought at Castillon in 1451, which also made history as the first battle in western Europe where guns made a difference. French cannon and muskets outfired the English longbows, opening a new era of warfare. Meanwhile, England got distracted by its own dynastic dispute (War of the Roses, 1455–85; death toll, 100,000), which kept the English too busy to invade France anymore.

Legacy

The Hundred Years War split France and England into two distinct countries, something that wasn't always apparent before. On a map, the big change was that there were no longer huge bits of England in France.

The main cultural legacy was that the English people started to abandon the Frenchness that had been hanging around since the Norman Conquest. As the wars dragged on, the English kings learned to stir up the bloodlust of their people by appealing to their patriotism and exhalting English culture over French. In 1362, Parliament was opened in English for the first time. Court proceedings were conducted in English after this as well. In 1404, out of a growing sense of nationalism, England decreed that negotiations with the French would be in neutral Latin instead of the enemy's French.

On the French side, the main result was political. The war had bled the French nobility white, and few were left alive to contest the power of the king. The final phase of the war had concentrated power in the Crown and made France about as close to a centralized monarchy as you would find anywhere in Europe at the time. France became the most powerful nation in Europe, and would remain so for the next four hundred years.

Death Toll

In 1937, the sociologist Pitirim Sorokin added and multiplied several variables to estimate that the English and French armies lost a combined total of 185,250 men on the battlefields of the Hundred Years War.[6] Others have estimated that 40 percent of the French nobility died in each of the battles of Agincourt and Crecy.[7] That's only a small part of the suffering.

Wars of that era were not all chivalry and jousting tournaments. Rather than getting tied down besieging impregnable castles, medieval armies would often launch a *chevauchée*, a relentless and devastating raid through enemy territory that left a path of bodies and desolation in its wake. Enough such raids would break morale, spread chaos, and deny resources to the enemy. An effective *chevauchée* might even provoke the defenders of the castle into coming out and fighting like men.

France began the war with a population of around 20 million and ended up with only half of that a hundred years later.[8] This was also the era of the Black Death, so there's no easy way to determine how many of the 10 million or so missing people died from the war and not the plague; most authorities who mention this population collapse also acknowledge that chronic warfare was a contributing factor. As Robert S. Lopez put it, in *The Cambridge Economic History of Europe from the Decline of the Roman Empire*, "In France war was perhaps an even worse calamity than the Black Death."[9] Translating this into mathematics implies that war may have caused more than half of the population decline:

war loss > ½ (minimum population loss: 7 million) = at least 3.5 million

FALL OF THE YUAN DYNASTY

Death toll: 30 million missing
Rank: 17
Type: native uprising
Broad dividing line: Chinese vs. Mongols
Time frame: ca. 1340–70
Location: China
Who usually gets the most blame: Mongols
Another damn: Chinese dynasty collapsing

A S THE GENERATIONS PASSED, THE MONGOLS GOT BETTER AT RULING China—but let's face it, they couldn't have gotten any worse. Eventually peace and prosperity returned, and a century after Chinggis Khan's initial conquest, the Chinese population had rebounded somewhat. The khans conquered southern China, settled into Beijing as the Yuan dynasty, and behaved like proper emperors rather than uncouth barbarians. Soon they learned to appreciate the luxuries of the civilized world and the taxes that paid for these.

Even so, the Mongols remained aliens in China and treated the native Chinese as a race of conquered servants. All of the top jobs went to Mongols, who had less familiarity with what was necessary to run a civilization. The Mongols especially fell behind in maintaining the irrigation systems along the Yellow River. The river broke through the dykes in 1288, then again in 1332–33, killing 7 million. Another flood of the Yellow River in 1344 ruined the Grand Canal, which ran almost a thousand miles north to south and connected trade across China's various west-to-east river networks. This meant that grain could no longer be shipped safely by barge from the rice fields of the south to the capital. Instead, grain shipments went over the open sea, where they were vulnerable to pirate attacks. When the coastal province of Zhejiang rebelled under Fang Kuo-chen in 1348, his pirate fleet began to interrupt these shipments in the waters alongside his territory.[1]

Red Turban Rebellion

In 1351, to fix these problems, the Mongol emperor Toghon Temur of China drafted 150,000 peasants and set them to work taming the Yellow River. He also stationed 20,000 soldiers to keep the peasants in line. Forced into slave labor, these disgruntled workers fell under the influence of the militant White Lotus sect of Buddhists and their military arm, the Red Turbans.[2] The White Lotus focused its worship on Maitreya, the Future Buddha, who would descend from heaven and create paradise after the King of Light had prepared the way. Soon after the leader of the Red Turbans, Han Shantong, launched a rebellion against the Mongols, the authorities caught and killed him, but not before he convinced his followers that his son, Han Liner, would make an excellent King of Light.[3]

However, the man who would turn out to be the next ruler of China was hiding elsewhere. Among the countless orphans left after the flood of 1344 was a sixteen-year-old peasant boy, Zhu Yuanzhang. The son of a tax evader and the grandson of a sorcerer, Zhu took refuge in a Buddhist monastery after gradually losing his family one by one to flood, famine, poverty, and plague.

Mongol field commanders putting down the Red Turban uprising had an unfortunate tendency to burn random Buddhist temples and report back to Beijing that they had just destroyed another rebel stronghold. After Zhu's temple was destroyed, the twenty-three-year-old was left homeless, so he joined a nearby Red Turban force commanded by Kuo Tzu-hsing. Within a year, Zhu Yuanzhang was entrusted with an independent command. After Kuo Tzu-hsing died in 1354, his successors launched a couple of extremely unsuccessful attacks against the east-central city of Nanjing during which the rest of the Red Turban leaders in that part of the country were killed. Zhu was the last surviving commander and became the new leader of the war band.[4] When Nanjing finally fell in April 1356, Zhu made it his capital and proclaimed himself emperor of the new Ming ("Bright") dynasty, ruling over middle China.

Zhu wasn't the only claimant to the Chinese throne. In 1355, Han Liner, King of Light among the Red Turbans in the north, was strong enough to declare himself a legitimate successor to the long-gone Song dynasty. Meanwhile the leadership of the Red Turbans in the south went through a string of assassinations that eliminated several claimants and left Chen Youliang in charge. He proclaimed himself emperor of the restored Han dynasty and reached a deal with Zhu Yuanzhang to divide China so they could focus on consolidating control over their territories.

As the Red Turban commanders took over more and more of China, Mongol control shrank to Beijing and little else. The Mongols, however, were not totally out of the picture yet. In 1359, they raided south and broke Han Liner's power base. Finally, in 1368, Zhu Yuanzhang chased the last Mongols out of Beijing and back across the Great Wall, which allowed the native Chinese to turn to the important business of deciding which of them would be the new emperor of a united China. This required another civil war.

Ming-Han War

Because of the last Mongol attack, Han Liner of the pseudo-Song dynasty was no longer a viable candidate, but to finalize this state of affairs, Zhu arranged a fatal boating accident for him in 1367. This meant that the fate of China came down to either Zhu Yuanzhang (Ming dynasty) or Chen Youliang (Han dynasty), and the battle lines moved to the Yangtze River, where amphibious assaults were conducted up and down the river. For a while, Chen gained the upper hand by using the tall, fortified sterncastles of his massive three-story warships to attack over the walls of riverside cities. Then in 1363, Zhu Yuanzhang arrived with 200,000 men aboard an unknown number of small ships to break Chen's siege of Nanchang. Chen withdrew his fleet of 300,000 men aboard 150 gigantic tower ships to the deeper, wider waters of Lake Poyang, where an important tributary flowed into the Yangtze River, and where he hoped to have more room (at the time, around 2,000 square miles, or the size of Delaware)[5] to maneuver.

The subsequent fight on the lake, which stretched from late August to early October 1363, is usually considered the largest naval battle (in terms of personnel) in history. Throughout September, the heavy Han ships huddled in the center of the lake, chained together for added solidity, harassed on all sides by the smaller, more numerous Ming vessels, which looked for an opportunity to board or set fire to the enemy. At first the Han vessels inflicted more damage than their attackers, but under the late summer sun, water levels fell and the shallows turned to swamps, shifting the advantage from Chen's giant ships to Zhu's lighter vessels. Eventually, Zhu's fleet moved upriver and got a favorable wind and current. They sent fireships packed with gunpowder downwind and downriver into Chen's fleet, blowing up dozens of ships and killing 60,000 men. The fleets continued to skirmish until finally, a month later, Chen Youliang tried again to break out of the lake. This time, he was killed by an arrow in the skull during the ensuing battle.

Zhu Yuanzhang soon mopped up all remaining opposition and established his undisputed control of China as the Hongwu ("Vastly Martial") emperor.[6]

Necrometry

According to *The Cambridge History of China*, the post-Mongol recovery of China's population peaked in 1340 at 19.9 million households and 90 million people, but was reduced by late Yuan warfare to 13 million households and 60 million people by the end of the dynasty in 1368.[7] In other words, 30 million people disappeared in the mayhem. Even though that source specifically blames the population crash on warfare, I still feel obliged to split the body count among floods, famine, bubonic plague, and war. Let's assign one-fourth (7.5 million) of the total to each of these causes.

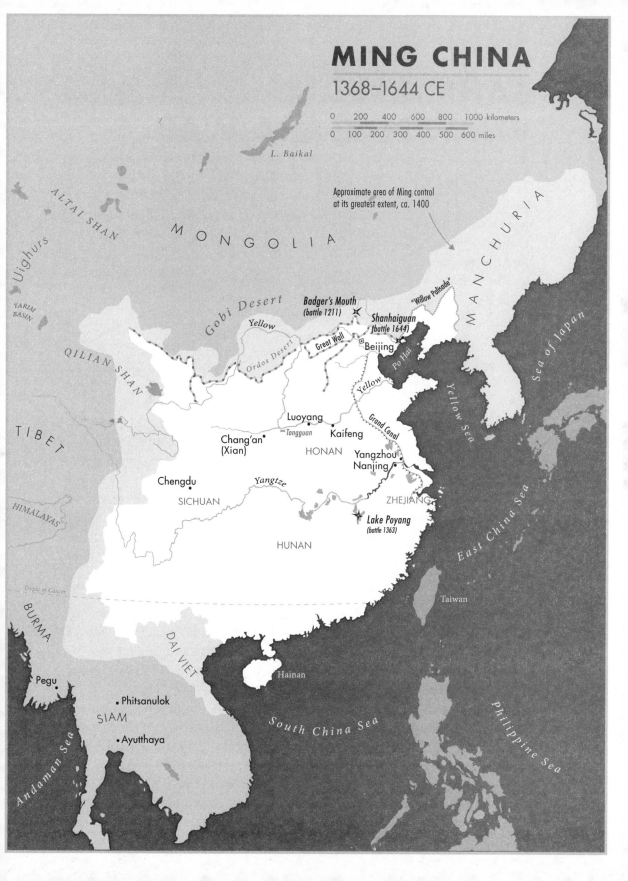

MING CHINA
1368–1644 CE

0 200 400 600 800 1000 kilometers
0 100 200 300 400 500 600 miles

L. Baikal

ALTAI SHAN

Uighurs

TARIM
BASIN

MONGOLIA

Gobi Desert

QILIAN SHAN

Yellow

Ordos Desert

Great Wall

Badger's Mouth
(battle 1211)

Shanhaiguan
(battle 1644)

"Willow Palisade"

Approximate area of Ming control
at its greatest extent, ca. 1400

MANCHURIA

Sea of Japan

Beijing

Po Hai

Yellow

Yellow Sea

TIBET

HIMALAYAS

Chang'an
(Xian)

Tongguan

Luoyang

Kaifeng

HONAN

Grand Canal

Yangzhou
Nanjing

Chengdu

Yangtze

SICHUAN

ZHEJIANG

Lake Poyang
(battle 1363)

East China Sea

HUNAN

Tropic of Cancer

Taiwan

BURMA

Pegu

Phitsanulok

SIAM

Ayutthaya

DAI VIET

Hainan

South China Sea

Andaman Sea

Philippine Sea

BAHMANI-VIJAYANAGARA WAR

Death toll: 500,000
Rank: 70
Type: clash of cultures
Broad dividing line: Muslims vs. Hindus
Time frame: 1366
Location: southern India
Major state participants: Bahmani sultanate, Vijayanagara empire
Who usually gets the most blame: the other side
The unanswerable question everyone asks: Huh?

MUSLIMS FROM CENTRAL ASIA BEGAN THE SERIOUS CONQUEST OF INDIA around 1000, and the passing centuries saw plenty of misery spread by the advancing armies—50,000 massacred here, 100,000 massacred there—but never enough in one place at one time to make my top one hundred list.

By the fourteenth century, the Muslims controlled most of the subcontinent. On the leading edge of Muslim expansion was the Bahmani sultanate in west-central India. Facing it, the last stronghold of Hindu sovereignty was an empire centered on the city of Vijayanagar, in the south. The primary battleground for these two was the Raichur Doab, a wedge of land between the confluence of the Krishna and Tungabhadra Rivers in central India.

While pushing back against the Muslims, Bukka Raya I of Vijayanagar captured the fortified town of Mudkal in the Raichur Doab and killed its entire garrison. Only one man escaped to report the slaughter to his sovereign, Muhammad Shah, Bahmani sultan in the town of Kulbarga, who was so grief-stricken by the news that he ordered the sole survivor killed as punishment for abandoning his comrades.

Muhammad marched south across the Krishna River and swore he would not rest until he had killed at least 100,000 Hindus in revenge. At the first clash, the Hindu forces were routed, and they fled in a headlong panic to the safety of the nearby fortress of Adoni, abandoning their camp and camp followers to be massacred by the Bahmani.[1]

Without bothering to take Adoni, Muhammad Shah crossed the Tungabhadra River into the enemy heartland, which had never before been invaded by Muslims, and he brought cannons, another first for south India. The next battle was a tough, all-day fight until around four o'clock, when the Vijayanagaran army broke and ran. Indian soldiers were usually accompanied and attended by their families in camp, but these were now abandoned in the confusion. Once again, Muhammad Shah ordered a general massacre of all the Hindu camp followers, sparing not even the pregnant or newborn.

For the next three months, he chased Bukka Raya all over his domains, defeating every Vijayanagaran attempt to stand against him, and killing every local resident who fell into his hands, regardless of age or sex. Then he brought the city of Vijayanagar under seige.

After a frustrating month, it became clear that Vijayanagar could hold out as long as necessary, so Muhammad withdrew, harassed the whole way out by the Hindu army in close pursuit. The two armies crossed north of the Tungabhadra River, back into the Raichur Doab. Finally, Muhammad Shah stopped for the night and waited for the Hindu force to arrive and camp nearby—as the two armies had been doing since the retreat started. Around midnight, however, Bahmani forces snuck back and sprang a trap on their pursuers, killing 10,000 in the dark and scattering the rest. Muhammad proceeded to lay waste to the surrounding territory with genocidal fury, killing every inhabitant he could find.

Sick of the devastation, Hindu religious leaders and Vijayanagaran military officers begged Bukka Raya to negotiate an end to the war. He sent ambassadors to explain to Muhammad Shah that, until now, it had been the custom in south India to not kill prisoners and civilians. Muhammad Shah's own officers also pointed out to him that he had sworn to kill a hundred thousand Hindus—not *all* of them. When Bukka Raya agreed to apologize and pay reparations, Muhammad Shah returned home across the Krishna River.[2]

Death Toll

The Muslim historian Firishtah estimated the number of dead on the Hindu side as over 500,000.[3] We probably shouldn't take this literally, but it's a plausible order of magnitude. Of all the individual wars during the Muslim conquest of India, this is one of only two for which the reported death toll passes the threshold for being on my list (see "Aurangzeb" for the other).

TIMUR

Death toll: 17 million[1]
Rank: 9
Type: world conqueror
Broad dividing line: Timur vs. everyone he could get to
Time frame: ruled 1370–1405
Location: central Asia, the eye of the hurricane being Samarkand
Who usually gets the most blame: Timur; also called Tamburlaine (old version) or Tamerlane (newer version) from his insulting nickname, Timur Lenk ("the Lame")
Another damn: Mongol invasion

The Man You Love to Hate

Throughout medieval Europe, traveling actors lived at the edge of society. They had to conform to rules of behavior and please their powerful sponsors among the nobility, so they would never dare to challenge the authorities. According to the strict guidelines of medieval drama, the bad guy always died in the end—often horribly, usually repentant. Theater was supposed to reinforce society's norms.

Then came the Renaissance, and in the commercial center of London, successful playwrights learned that they could afford to challenge the rules. Christopher Marlowe wrote a play, *Tamburlaine the Great*, about an emperor of the Orient, a glorious monster, destroyer of cities, and despoiler of women. Tamburlaine strutted larger than life across the stage, and reveled in his wealth, his schemes, and his magnificent power. When the play ends, the villain is unrepentant and triumphant over all of his enemies, surrounded by worshipful followers. No one had ever seen anything like it. Audiences adored it, and it became the first theatrical hit in recorded history.

Somewhere in the audience, a young actor, beginning playwright, and friend of Marlowe's named William Shakespeare realized that he too could probably make a living writing big, bloody dramas. That, however, is another story.[2] The question that concerns us is, who was this magnificent villain known to Marlowe as Tamburlaine?

First and foremost, he was the type of barbarian warlord that people told stories about. To his admirers, he was sort of a warrior trickster. As a young bandit in the central Asian wilderness, he had his soldiers build unnecessary campfires in a circle around the enemy to convince them they were outnumbered. He had his horsemen drag branches to kick up a larger dust cloud. When invading India, he strapped bundles of kindling onto camels.

As the enemy elephants charged, his men chased flaming camels right into the elephants' faces, who then panicked and stampeded back over the shocked Indian army.

Legendary villainy also swirled around him. When the Christian garrison of Sivas in Armenia asked about terms of surrender, Timur swore no blood would be shed. After they surrendered, he remained true to his word and buried them alive instead.

An Arab contemporary was reminded mostly of animal predators when describing Timur's followers: "leopards of Turkistan, tigers of Balkhshan, hawks of Dasht and Khata, Mongol vultures, Jata eagles, vipers of Khajend," and people in many other dangerous nations labeled as hounds, lions, hyenas, and crocodiles. It was a cosmopolitan army that grew more formidable with each conquest.[3]

Timur's biography abounds with such colorful anecdotes that skeptics question everything said about him, but many of his chroniclers knew him personally as diplomats, allies, or favored scholars. Most of the stories come to us, if not firsthand, then as close to it as scholarship in the manuscript era allows. For example, if you are curious about how we know things like medieval casualty statistics, here's a story: Once, as Timur's army set off to pursue a fleeing enemy, each soldier placed a stone in a pile. When they returned from battle, each man took a stone off the pile. By counting the remaining stones, Timur knew exactly and immediately how many men he had lost.[4]

The most confusing aspect of Timur's biography is that he simply attacked every which way, with no specific long-term plan other than conquest. Part of this was economic. Loot sustained armies in those days, so obviously he had to find a steady supply of rich enemies to rob. Part was geographic. Being in central Asia meant that he had enemies in all directions and no borders anchored securely against a coastline.

Land of Confusion

After Chinggis Khan died in 1227, his unified empire survived only briefly before sons, grandsons, and generals broke it down into more manageable quarters—the Yuan dynasty, the Il-Khans, the Chagatai Khanate, and the Golden Horde. For another generation or two, these four khanates cooperated as a kind of loose crime syndicate. Each quarter-empire had a frontier abutting rich foreigners who could be invaded and plundered, so theoretically they had no reason to quarrel with each other. Within a few decades, this friendly arrangement broke down as well, and the Chinggisids (the heirs of Chinggis) were at each others' throats. Timur was born into this chaos sometime around 1336. We will meet each of these khanates in turn as Timur sets out to conquer them and re-create the empire of Chinggis Khan.

Timur's clan of Mongols had gone native and adopted the Turkic language and Muslim religion during the previous generation. They lived in what had once been part of the unhappy land of Khwarezm, which had been so thoroughly devastated by the Mongols but had later become the inheritance of Chinggis Khan's second son, Chagatai. By Timur's day, rival khans were fighting each other for control.

Timur started his career as a minor bandit. As a young man, he took arrow wounds in his right hand and knee while either fighting glorious battles (his story) or stealing sheep (his enemies' story), leaving him with a limp and a stiff arm the rest of his life.[5] Despite these infirmities, he gathered enough followers to form an impressive army of freebooters. Eventually, his reputation as an up-and-coming warlord brought him to the attention of the alpha khan, Tughlak, who made him governor of Transoxiana.

In the years following Tughlak's death in 1366, Timur outfought his rivals and took the throne of Samarkand. It's all very complicated, but there were assassinations involved, as well as pitched battles and marriages. To puff up his pedigree, he claimed to be descended from Chinggis Khan and Muhammad's son-in-law, Ali, but no one really believes any of that nowadays, unless it was a coincidence. (Both Chinggis Khan and Ali produced a lot of unrecorded descendants. You might be one.)

Timur scrounged up a documented relative of Chinggis Khan to sit on the throne of Samarkand, while Timur himself took the more modest title of Amir (Lord) and pulled levers from behind the curtain. No one was fooled by this arrangement, and most histories neglect to mention that Timur was not, technically, the ruler of his empire.

Sometimes it can be difficult to tell Chinggis Khan and Timur apart. They seem to blend together into a generic Mongol warlord template, but there are substantial differences. Timur was a devoted Muslim, and he struck more deeply into the Middle East, against places you are more likely to have heard of: Delhi and Damascus instead of Nishapur and Bukhara.

Also unlike Chinggis Khan, Timur liked cities—well, his own cities at least. He turned his capital of Samarkand into one of the most beautiful cities of the world. Impressed by an onion dome he had seen after capturing Damascus, he had it replicated in Samarkand. From there the style spread into Russia (the Kremlin) and India (the Taj Mahal).[6]

For other cities, however, his preferred form of architecture was the tower of skulls. After consolidating his hold in Samarkand, Timur set out to decorate the world with these.

Campaigns: Southwest (1381–84)

In the generations since Chinggis Khan destroyed it in 1221, the city of Herat was reborn, becoming a wealthy and cultured stop on the Silk Road. During his earlier days as a wandering mercenary, Timur worked for the ruling dynasty of Herat, and now he tried to negotiate a marriage alliance. The current ruler agreed in principle but stalled on the details. Then Timur's spies discovered that Herat was strengthening its defenses, a clearly provocative act. Timur stormed across three hundred miles of rough desert and mountains to surround the city. Knowing the fate that awaited an unsuccessful defense, Herat gave up without a fight and was granted mercy.[7]

With his army mobilized and having traveled so far west, Timur continued his offensive. The Persian quarter of Chinggis Khan's empire had become the realm of the Il-Khans, but they fizzled out about the same time as the Chagatai dynasty. Exploiting this power vacuum, Timur invaded Persia with what would come to be characteristic cruelty.

At the town of Isfizar, Timur sealed 2,000 prisoners into a tower to die of starvation. The nearby town of Zaranj carried bad memories for Timur since this was where he had received his debilitating wounds, so even though the residents surrendered without a fight, Zaranj was put to the sword and torch.[8]

Southwest (1386–88)

Timur went home to rest awhile before he invaded Persia again. After taking the city of Isfahan in central Iran, he installed a garrison and was ready to grant mercy, but the people rose up and killed the garrison. Timur stormed the city again and wiped out the inhabitants, stacking up their severed heads as a warning to others who might resist him. The nearby city of Shiraz took the hint and surrendered immediately. A Muslim historian exploring Isfahan shortly afterward counted twenty-eight towers of 1,500 heads each before he stopped circling the ruins. The likely total was close to 70,000.[9]

Although we think of the past as a more brutal era than today, it's worth noting that many of Timur's soldiers were appalled at the order to massacre civilians and fellow Muslims; however, Timur demanded a certain number of heads from each unit—or else. Officers were appointed to keep the count. The more squeamish soldiers bought their quota from comrades with fewer qualms. At first, the price of a head was twenty dinars, but as the massacre progressed and the supply rose to meet demand, the price plunged to half a dinar.[10]

Northwest (1390–91)

A Mongol dynasty calling itself the Golden Horde had inherited the European quarter of Chinggis Khan's empire, west of the Ural Mountains, spanning the steppes of Russia and Ukraine. There had been a dynastic dispute in the 1370s, and for a while Timur let Toktamish, the outcast contender for leadership, sleep on his sofa until he could find a job (metaphorically speaking). Timur helped him regain the throne of the Golden Horde, but then the two Chinggisids had a falling out. Shortly after Timur withdrew from his first raid into Persia, Toktamish snuck in behind him and took Tabriz, a city Timur had been saving for later.

Clearly Eurasia was not big enough for the two of them. Timur struck due north into the unknown wilderness of Siberia, and then turned left, sneaking up on his enemy through the vast forests of Russia. In June 1391 Timur's army—100,000 men and women*—came crashing down on the Golden Horde at the Battle of Kunduzcha. After a fierce fight, Toktamish fled, with Timur's hordes in close pursuit. According to the Persian chronicler Sharaf ad-Din Ali Yazdi, "For the space of forty leagues whither they were pursued nothing could be seen but rivers of blood and the plains covered with dead bodies."[11]

Although Toktamish escaped, his major cities—Sarai and Astrakhan—were taken and looted.

Southwest (1393)

Persia again.

Northwest (1395)

Toktamish again.

Southeast (1398–99)

In the summer of 1398 Timur set out to punish his fellow Muslim, the sultan of Delhi, for tolerating all cultures and letting Hindus walk around free, which Timur considered an affront to Islam. By December, he had crossed all of the mountains, deserts, and rivers that separated India from the rest of the world, and led his army down onto the plain of Punjab. As he pushed on through India, he accumulated thousands of Hindu prisoners to be brought home as slaves.

Timur's army overwhelmed the forces of the sultan under the walls of Delhi, defeating their war elephants with the flaming camel tactic described earlier. During the battle, Timur heard his prisoners cheering the Indian attacks, so he had them killed—100,000 of them, according to the chronicles. He originally planned to spare Delhi, but as his soldiers looted and raped their way across the fallen city, fights and scuffles broke out with the inhabitants. This coalesced into a full riot against the invaders, which Timur put down with typical ruthlessness. Around 50,000 citizens were massacred, and their heads were stacked up outside the four corners of the city. He then hauled off all the treasure that had accumulated in this great capital over the years, along with tens of thousands of new slaves.

---

* Timur was unique in allowing women to fight in his army, but probably not too many. (Marozzi, *Tamerlane*, p. 102)

West (1400–4)

In October 1400, Timur struck west. Having reduced Persia from great empire to mere shortcut, he swept through and attacked beyond it. He took all of the major cities in his path, and buried alive the garrison of Sivas. He destroyed Aleppo and piled up 20,000 heads. Then he pillaged, burned, and depopulated Damascus in March 1401.

Showing uncharacteristic mercy, he resettled some defeated Turkmen soldiers in Syria. Homesick, they tried to sneak back to their native land, supporting themselves by robbery. Timur caught them near the city Damghan and piled their bloody heads out in the countryside. A Spanish diplomat to Timur's court described passing them: "Outside Damghanat the distance of a bowshot we noticed two towers, built as tall as the height to which one might cast up a stone which were entirely constructed from men's skulls set in clay. Besides these there were other two similar towers, but these appeared already fallen to the ground in decay." These towers were said to emit supernatural flames in the night for years after that.[12]

A small force sent to secure Baghdad had made no headway, so Timur returned with his full army and beseiged it for six weeks. On an unbearably hot day, when the defenders retreated to the shade, Timur struck. After the city was secured, Timur ordered every one of his warriors to bring him a severed head—some sources say two. Only clergy and scholars were spared the massacre. When it turned out that there were fewer inhabitants of Baghdad than Timur's quota, heads were taken from the Mongols' own camp followers, prostitutes, and personal slaves, because no one dared defy a command from Timur. The Mongols leveled every secular building and surrounded the ruins with 120 towers, assembled from 90,000 heads altogether, while Timur made a pilgrimage to a nearby shrine to pray.[13]

The westward invasion brought Timur into conflict with the Ottoman Turks, who were busy erasing the last vestiges of the Byzantine Empire. The Turkish sultan, Bayezid the Thunderbolt, had crushed a string of enemies in both Europe and Asia, and all he needed to cap off his career and be proclaimed the greatest warrior in the history of Islam was to take Constantinople, seat of empire, valve of the Black Sea, and gateway to Europe that had held against Muslim invaders for centuries.

Then, in 1402, Timur's hordes came thundering out of the east and Bayezid had to abandon his siege of Constantinople to stop him. Bayezid marched out with a huge battle-hardened army and caught up with Timur at Ankara. It was a tough battle, and several units of Bayezid's disgruntled conscripts switched over to Timur's side, throwing the Ottoman position into chaos. Bayezid was defeated and captured along with his entourage. Timur had unwittingly saved Europe from the Turks for half a century.

Many stories are told of the humiliation that the ex-sultan suffered at the hands of Timur. They say Bayezid was kept on public display in a cage, that his wife was forced to serve meals to the court naked, that Timur used him as a footstool.* These stories are probably not true because they didn't appear until late in history. The earliest available historians claimed that Bayezid was well treated.

Upon reaching the far coast of Anatolia (the peninsula of Turkey), Timur laid siege to the Knights of Rhodes in the Christian city of Smyrna, which held for a few weeks and then fell to the customary massacre and pillage. When a Christian fleet later arrived to assist the knights by breaking the siege, Timur taunted them and proved that they were too late by catapulting the severed heads of the former defenders onto their ships.

Amir Timur

Timur had great respect for scholars and attracted many to his court. He commissioned magnificent Korans from the finest calligraphers. He was also a chess master, and the most complicated version of the game is still named after him. In Tamerlane chess, the board has nearly twice as many spaces as regular chess and more pieces, such as elephants that jump two squares diagonally and giraffes that move one diagonal and three straight.

Like most tyrants, Timur imposed strict and swift justice in his domains, and he was not prone to weighing subtleties. When Timur returned from his war against the west and heard that the governor of Samarkand had been oppressive and greedy in his absence, Timur had the governor hanged. All of this man's ill-gotten gains were taken into the treasury. There's no great surprise in any of this, but Timur then hanged an influential friend of the governor's who had tried to buy the governor's freedom. Then Timur hanged yet another official who had interceded on behalf of the governor. After that, everyone got the message.[14]

His simplistic approach to problem solving shows up again and again: "Timur now gave orders that a street should be built to pass right through Samarqand, which should have shops opened on either side of it in which every kind of merchandise should be sold, and this new street was to go from one side of the city through to the other side, traversing the heart of the township. . . . No heed was paid to the complaint of persons to whom the property here might belong, and those whose houses thus were demolished suddenly had to quit with no warning, carrying away with them their goods and chattels as best they might."[15]

Endgame

Now seventy-one, Timur had crushed the two most powerful empires in Asia: Delhi and the Ottomans. He had conquered in every direction but one: eastward into China. The

---

* However, this is not why we call a padded footstool an ottoman.

native Ming dynasty led by Zhu Yuanzhang had recently tossed the Mongols out of China, and Timur decided that this could not be allowed to stand. With a new army, he set out to restore the empire of Chinggis Khan, but old age caught up with him and he died in 1405 before he got his army across the border.

The significance of Timur's conquests—however huge, bloody, and colorful—is minor and full of ironies. He was a devout Muslim who almost exclusively destroyed Muslim enemies, and it was the losers in his wars who established true legacies while Samarkand became a desert backwater under forgotten khans.[16] The Ottomans regrouped and dominated the Middle East for a half millennium. The Golden Horde and its Tatar successors blocked Russian expansion into the steppe for several centuries. Timur's most lasting impact is that one branch of his descendants forged its own destiny as the Mughals of India (see "Aurangzeb" for details).

One final story is told about Timur. It involves his own severed head. In 1941, hoping to make the definitive portrait of Timur, the Soviet scientist Mikhail Gerasimov opened his tomb and took away his skull for facial reconstruction. Locals had warned him that a curse awaited any lord who disturbed the tomb of Lord Timur. Gerasimov scoffed and proceeded with his tomb robbery. Within a couple of days, the curse came true, and Germany invaded the Soviet Union.

The new Central Asian nation of Uzbekistan is rehabilitating Timur as a national hero. A magnificent equestrian statue of him now dominates the main square of the capital city, Tashkent, replacing the bust of Karl Marx that had been there in the late Soviet era, which had replaced the earlier statue of Stalin, which replaced the original tsarist statue of Konstantin Kaufman, Russian conqueror of Central Asia. Apparently, this plaza has never honored a likeable person.[17]

CHINESE CONQUEST OF VIETNAM

Death toll: probably not 7 million[1]
Rank: 61
Type: war of conquest
Broad dividing line: China vs. Vietnam
Time frame: 1406–28
Location: Vietnam (also called Dai Viet or Annam at the time)
Who usually gets the most blame: China

WHEN HO QUY LY, THE CHIEF MINISTER OF DAI VIET (MEDIEVAL VIETNAM), usurped the throne in 1400, he smoothed it over diplomatically with his neighbors—especially China—by swearing that no heir remained from the previous Tran dynasty. Then an outcast Tran prince ruined everything by showing up in China to ask the Ming for their help in restoring his family to the throne. The Chinese mobilized 800,000 troops in their southern provinces during the summer of 1406 and invaded Vietnam.

In previous invasions southward, Chinese troops experienced difficulty defeating the war elephants of Southeast Asian armies, but now they had horses disguised as lions and primitive guns shooting fire arrows to drive them back. The Chinese invaders overran most of the country, and in the middle of 1407, they captured and executed the current king of Vietnam, Ho Quy Ly's son. They put their man on the throne, restoring the Tran dynasty.[2]

But then the Chinese wouldn't go home. They began to establish new administrative districts with tax offices, salt offices to enforce the monopoly, Confucian schools, and Buddhist registries. When the king of Vietnam insisted that it really was time for the Chinese to leave, war erupted. It was a confusing rebellion, with a new leader of the Tran dynasty popping up every time the Chinese killed the old one. In 1413, the last of these, Tran De Qui Khoang, was beaten in battle and captured, later committing suicide.

The Chinese took direct control of Vietnam and set out to eradicate the native culture. "Chinese dress and customs were imposed on the people; women were compelled to wear short pants and vests; people had to wear long hair; public instructions were taught in

Chinese while Vietnamese books were suppressed."[3] The people were brutally overworked to extract the country's resources.

An aristocratic landowner, Le Loi, rose in rebellion, but his forces were quickly scattered by the Ming in 1418. He regrouped and rebuilt his army deep in the inaccessible mountains. They hid in remote areas of the country, moving out occasionally to ambush Chinese forces for supplies. If that didn't work, they ate their horses or scrounged wild rice and grass.

Over the next ten years, Le Loi wore down the Chinese by attacking isolated garrisons and supply convoys and then retreating into the mountains when larger forces arrived. By paying off corruptible officials, Le Loi gained additional supplies and breathing space. Finally, the Chinese gave up and abandoned the country to Le Loi, who established the Le dynasty in 1428.

AZTEC HUMAN SACRIFICE

Death toll: 1.2 million
Rank: 45
Type: human sacrifice
Broad dividing line: priests vs. prisoners
Time frame: ca. 1440–1521
Location: Mexico
Who usually gets the most blame: Aztecs
The unanswerable question everyone asks: Didn't they notice that the sun came up every morning even if they didn't sacrifice to it?

IN 1521, BEATEN BY AN UPRISING OF AZTECS, RETREATING FROM TENOCHTITlan (today's Mexico City) in a panic, the Spaniards under Cortés watched helplessly from a distance as natives killed their captured comrades:

> There was sounded the dismal drum of [Huitzilopochtli] and many other shells and horns and things like trumpets and the sound of them all was terrifying, and we all looked toward the lofty pyramid . . . and saw that our comrades . . . were being carried by force up the steps . . .
>
> We saw them place plumes on the heads of many of them and with things like fans in their hands they forced them to dance before [Huitzilopochtli] and after they had danced they immediately placed them on their backs on some rather narrow stones . . . and with some knives they sawed open their chests and drew out their palpitating hearts and offered them to their idols.
>
> They kicked the bodies down the steps, and the Indian butchers who were waiting below cut off the arms and feet and flayed the skin off the faces and prepared it afterward like glove leather with the beards on . . . and the flesh they ate in *chilmole*.[1]

Human sacrifice is a worldwide phenomenon, but nowhere else has it ever been recorded on the vast scale that was found among the Aztecs of central Mexico. In Aztec myth, the sun, Huitzilopochtli, was born when one of the gods leapt into a fire; afterward the other gods gave their blood to heal and feed this burning god. Aztec sacrifice reenacted the original sacrifice of the gods, and without new blood, the sun would die. In fact, most of the gods in the Aztec pantheon lived on human blood. Only Queztalcoatl, the Feathered Serpent, opposed human sacrifice, but the other gods had forced him into exile.

The Aztecs were a warrior people above all else. They had emerged as a small tribe surrounded by hostile neighbors, but they fought their way outward and forged an empire stretching from sea to sea in central Mexico. To thank the gods for their good fortune, and to bribe them into continuing their favors, the Aztecs offered the blood of prisoners taken in battle.

In fact, the capture of sacrificial victims was so important that Aztec battle soon bent to that purpose. In these Flower Wars, Aztecs followed strict rules when attacking their neighbors, beginning by pleasantly negotiating with their enemies a time and place for the battle. Combat followed ancient rituals—a bonfire, music, dancing, and finally a massed charge. Fighting was face to face, hand to hand, with mostly nonlethal weapons because Aztecs preferred not to damage the merchandise. Enemies were pulled out of the line, bound, and dragged back to Tenochtitlan. Aztec warriors worked their way up the social hierarchy by capturing prisoners alive to be sacrificed.[2]

The largest number of sacrifices took place in Tenochtitlan, a city built on islands in a lake, at the Great Temple dedicated to Huitzilopochtli, the god of the sun and war. Doped prisoners by the dozens or hundreds were marched up to the top of the pyramid. At the top, in view of the gods and the city, a team of priests each grabbed a limb or head and pulled the victim down. The sacrificial priest sawed out the prisoner's beating heart with an obsidian knife and then burned it on the altar.[3]

The priest then pushed the body down the stairs, where it was dismantled, jointed, cooked, and carved. The owner of the sacrificed prisoner got the choicest cuts of meat to be served at a family banquet, while a stew made from the leftovers fed the masses. Pumas, wolves, and jaguars in the zoo gnawed the bones.

Another ritual known as the Flaying of Men was held in honor of the god Xipe Totec. It began with an ordinary day of cutting out hearts atop a pyramid, after which the bodies were butchered for a family feast. The next day, an honored prisoner was tethered to a stone and given blunt weapons with which he would fight four Eagle and Jaguar Knights, who had sharp weapons so the outcome of the battle was never in doubt. After the prisoner was killed, the priests cut him open, and the celebrants ate him. His sponsor took a bowl of blood to all of the temples to paint the mouths of the idols. He would then wear the skin of the dead man for twenty days as it rotted away. Finally, the skin was ritually discarded in a cave at the temple and the celebrant was cleansed.

Children were sacrificed to Tlaloc, the rain god. Babies born with certain physical characteristics on astrologically significant days were especially prized, but any child would do. Their throats were slit after the priest made them cry and collected their tears. Unlike other sacrifices, which were considered festive occasions, the Aztecs accompanied the killing of children with loud wailing, and the priests considered it a grim, dirty business. Aztecs avoided the places of child sacrifice whenever they could.[4]

Women were sacrificed to the mother goddess, Xilonen. The central woman in the ritual became the goddess and was beheaded as she danced. She was then skinned. Her heart was extracted and burned. A favored warrior wore her skin throughout the next year, and he became the goddess.[5]

Victims dedicated to the Fire God, Xuihtecuhutli, were sedated and cast into a fire. Priests then hooked them—scorched but still alive—and hauled them out so their beating hearts could be excised.

If we're looking for a single person to blame for the scale of Aztec sacrifice, a candidate would be Tlacaelel, chief adviser to three successive rulers. A Spanish chronicler reported that he "invented devilish, cruel and frightful sacrifices."[6]

Tlacaelel supervised the rededication of the Grand Temple for King Ahuitzotl in 1487 during which sacrificial victims lined up in four queues stretching out along the causeways that bound together the islands of Tenochtitlan. It took four teams four days to kill all of the prisoners as the blood pooled and clotted at the base of the pyramid. Later historians tried to turn these clues into an actual number, first arriving at some 80,000 victims, but nowadays calculated as 14,000 to 20,000.[7]

Why So Many?

Aztec human sacrifice is so completely unfathomable that most scholars don't even try to explain it. The Aztecs sacrificed people for religious reasons and that's that. Among the few who try to find a secular cause for it, most prefer something similar to the reason for Roman gladiatorial games—a warrior people toughening themselves up while dehumanizing and demoralizing their enemies.

Every now and then, someone will try to connect Aztec sacrifice to the lack of domesticated food animals in pre-Colombian America,* which would have sent the natives scrounging for an alternative source of protein. Small populations could hunt and fish wild animals, but in a region as densely populated as central Mexico, the only large animals in abundance were other people. To get to this protein, the Mexicans needed their gods' permission to kill and eat their neighbors, so the Aztecs shared the hearts and blood with their gods and got to keep the meat for themselves.[8]

This is the most sensible explanation for Aztec sacrifice and also the least popular. In fact, you would be hard-pressed to find any authority anywhere who believes this theory.[9] But the so-called cannibal kingdom hypothesis has a good deal in its favor. For starters,

---

* Most of the big, tasty animals in the Americas went extinct as soon as the first people arrived. There's probably a connection.

why was history's only urban culture without large food animals also the only urban culture that regularly ate human flesh? Why did history never produce rampant cannibalism in any urban culture that has goats, sheep, cattle, or pigs? Is this a mere coincidence?

Most scholars say yes and offer up numerous counter-arguments. They accuse the Spaniards of lying in order to justify conquering the savage heathens. They accuse Westerners of being unable to understand mysterious native folkways and explain that it was considered an honor to be given to the gods. They treat the statement that the Aztecs had no food animals as an insult to a perfectly nutritious cuisine that included bugs, lizards, and snails. Both anthropologists and vegetarians point out that meat is unnecessary for healthy living. Then everyone reminds us that the Spanish Inquisition killed people too, so who are *we* to condemn the Aztecs?[10]

Why do so few writers look beyond "religious reasons" for a cause? I suspect that *trying* to explain Aztec sacrifice means that we *need* to explain it, which would imply that it is somehow abnormal, which might upset widely held views about native cultures. This might then lead us to accept outdated Eurocentric notions about heathen savages and the superiority of Western Christendom. It's a slippery slope many scholars want to avoid.

However, the scale of Aztec human sacrifice was so far beyond most religious killings that it probably requires a special explanation. The Spanish Inquisition (32,000 killed)[11] and the witch hunts (60,000 killed)[12] simply can't compare to the Aztec sacrifice. Those European atrocities killed only enough enemies to make their point. The Aztecs went into overdrive. Even gladiatorial combat among the Romans killed at around half the annual rate as the Aztecs—and that was spread across a much larger area, among a population at least four times larger. Although human sacrifice was common in tribes and villages worldwide, most societies kept the numbers small and outgrew it as soon as they were forced to live close together in cities. The Chinese of the Shang dynasty, for example, sacrificed a mere 13,000 humans in 250 years (1300–1050 BCE).[13]

Homicide tends to disrupt the cooperative and orderly behavior that society needs to function. Although I hesitate to generalize about *all* of the atrocities in this book, I've noticed that most mass killings either occur after societies break down or are directed against specific enemies on behalf of someone in power. Unnecessarily killing hundreds of thousands of random neighbors on the whim of invisible beings will rip a society apart, unless someone important is getting something very tangible out of it. I think it was meat.

Death Toll

The extent of human sacrifice under the Aztecs is the subject of rancorous debate, and many scholars contend that the whole thing has been exaggerated—no more than a handful they say, and only on big holidays.[14] But the evidence remains. The Aztecs proudly displayed the heads of their victims on public skull racks with neatly arranged and easily counted rows. The skull rack in Tenochtitlan held 136,000 skulls according to Spanish eyewitness Andres de Tapia. The skull rack in Xocotlan had over 100,000 skulls according to Spanish eyewitness Bernal Díaz. That's almost a quarter of a million right there.[15]

The body count has been estimated as anything from 15,000 (Sherburne Cook) to 250,000 (Woodrow Borah) per year.[16] The nineteenth-century historian William Prescott insisted that the Aztecs sacrificed at least 20,000, possibly 50,000, people per year over the course of two centuries.[17] At the other end are revisionists who insist that the Aztecs hardly ever sacrificed anyone, no matter what those lying Spaniards said. Bartolome de las Casas and Voltaire claimed that only about 150 Mexicans were sacrificed each year, and that the Spaniards exaggerated in order to justify their conquest.[18] In any case, an estimate of 15,000 or 20,000 a year (total of about 1.2 to 1.6 million) seems to be the most widely repeated one.[19]

ATLANTIC SLAVE TRADE

Death toll: 16 million[1]

Rank: 10

Type: commercial exploitation, racism

Broad dividing line: Europeans enslaving Africans

Time frame: 1452–1807

Location: from Africa to the Americas

Major supplying nations: Ashanti, Benin, Dahomey, Kongo, Lunda, Oyo

Major seafaring nations: France, Great Britain, Netherlands, Portugal, Spain, United States

Major receiving colonies: Brazil, Carolina, Cuba, Georgia, Jamaica, Maryland, Saint-Domingue, Virginia

Who usually gets the most blame: European slave traders, African middlemen, and American planters

Economic factors: slaves, sugar, gold

B Y THE EARLY 1400S, THE EUROPEANS HAD DEVELOPED REVOLUTIONARY new oceangoing ships that could travel anywhere at all, regardless of the wind, currents, distance, or direction. Mariners started looking around to see what they could find. The Spanish and Portuguese stumbled across several archipelagos in the eastern Atlantic: the Azores, Canaries, and Madeira. The Portuguese also began to poke southward along the coast of Africa, looking for the source of the gold that had steadily trickled out of Africa since the beginning of recorded history. Eventually, they connected with western African kingdoms on the Gulf of Guinea, and picked up some gold from native traders. Almost as an afterthought, they took some slaves too.

Although slaves had always been a major African export (see "Mideast Slave Trade"), there was not much of a market for them in Europe. The land already had enough serfs, and it was much easier to hire domestic servants from the local peasantry than to import them from another continent. Eventually, the Portuguese discovered there was money to be made putting masses of slaves to work on sugar plantations in recently discovered tropical Atlantic islands such as Madeira and Cape Verde. This established the model for future expansion.[2]

The discovery of America pushed slavery into the center of the European economy. With Native Americans dying off from devastating new diseases against which they had no inborn immunity (see "Conquest of the Americas"), the New World was facing a serious labor shortage. A whole hemisphere of land was worthless because there was no one to work it. After a few experimental plantations in the Caribbean proved that growing sugar with African slaves would turn a profit, the Spanish crown opened the New World to Portuguese slave traders in 1513.

Collection

The Europeans didn't capture the slaves themselves. Deadly tropical diseases and grouchy native kings discouraged Europeans from probing too deeply into the African mainland. For most of the slaving era, the only permanent European presence in western Africa was a dozen or so coastal forts. These were established to prevent rival Europeans from encroaching on the trade, not to conquer the natives. The first of these was the Portuguese fort of Elmina (now in Ghana), established in 1482 and named after the mines that were thought to supply the gold.* For over a century, slaving remained a purely Portuguese activity, but in the 1630s, Dutch warships challenged and thoroughly defeated the Portuguese all across the globe. This broke the Portuguese monopoly, and the rest of Europe swarmed in and set up slaving stations up and down the African coast.

Native kingdoms like Ashanti, Oyo, and Kongo became profitable middlemen in the slave trade, and their kings grew rich and magnificent off the tribute, taxes, and kickbacks that kept the trade flowing. In return for slaves, Africa got the usual trade goods (copper and brass trinkets, textiles, pots, kettles, knives, and cowrie shells)† plus some more interesting ones (guns, rum). Most important in the long run, Africa got maize, which became a staple crop all across the continent, even deep inland.

At first, the local Africans traded whatever slaves they had on hand. Most of them were criminals, adulterers, or debtors, but as demand grew, African coastal kingdoms would start new wars specifically to capture prisoners to sell as slaves. Eventually, native slave traders were raiding inland to kidnap fresh slaves. After capturing a village, the traders usually killed or abandoned the elderly and infants because there was no market for them. The remaining villagers would be dragged away for sale.[3]

---

* The gold was actually panned from river deposits.

† Shells were used as currency in Africa. Some people today might take the attitude of how silly it was to sell humans in exchange for worthless trinkets like shells, but when you get down to it, shells are no more intrinsically worthless than, say, gold. After all, aside from being pretty and shiny, what good is gold? In fact, shells have a lot in common with gold. Both are easy to identify, hard to fake, rare enough to be valuable, but common enough to be used as a medium of exchange.

Newly harvested slaves would be herded back to the coast in coffles (chained caravans) along trails hundreds of miles long, on journeys that often lasted months. Slaves were shackled together at the neck, wrists, or ankles, maybe attached to the man in front of him with a yoke on his neck or to the man beside him with chains on his wrist. They were prodded, beaten, and kicked to keep them moving, and the weak would be killed if they fell so they couldn't recover later and escape. The major slave trails were littered with bones.[4]

Because American slaves were usually set to work in the fields, big strong men were the most highly valued. About 90 percent of the slaves shipped to America were adults or teenagers, and men outnumbered women by two to one. Women often fetched a high enough price in Africa to keep them from being sold overseas.[5]

About half of the slaves died while being marched to the coast or while waiting for a buyer.[6] The survivors of the march would be collected in coastal slave prisons, or barracoons, until a ship came along. Some barracoons were solid fortresses where slaves were stashed in dungeons. Others were open corrals or cattle pens, with slaves manacled out in the sun. All barracoons were overcrowded, filthy, and buzzing with flies.

European slave ships prowled the coast, looking for the best deals. They would buy a few slaves here and a few there; it often took several months for a ship to assemble a full cargo of slaves crammed below decks. In many places, European ships anchored off the coast while native traders brought slaves out on canoes. Elsewhere, European buyers would come ashore to inspect and haggle. They poked and prodded slaves as they would any other animals. Because proven fertility would make them more valuable, women were inspected for stretch marks and other signs of childbearing. Ages might be estimated by the quality of the teeth, but sellers sometimes shaved heads to hide gray hair. When the sale was final, slaves were branded with hot irons to mark ownership. Then they were herded on board the ships naked because clothes would just add one more thing to get filthy on the trip to the New World.

Slaves that no one wanted were often killed on the spot. Keeping them alive increased maintenance costs, and letting them go would encourage future slaves to make themselves flagrantly unmarketable. As one contemporary account described it:

> The traders frequently beat those negroes which are objected to by the captains, and use them with great severity. It matters not whether they are refused on account of age, illness, deformity or for any other reason. At New Calabar, in particular, the traders have frequently been known to put them to death. Instances have happened at that place, that the traders, when negroes have been objected to, have dropped their canoes under the stern of the vessel, and instantly beheaded them, in sight of the captain.[7]

Middle Passage

Olaudah Equiano, "a slave who lived to tell the tale,"[8] later described his first impression of a European slave ship in the late 1700s:

> When I looked round the ship too and saw a large furnace of copper boiling, and a multitude of black people of every description chained together, every one of their countenances expressing dejection and sorrow, I no longer doubted of my fate and quite overpowered with horror and anguish, I fell motionless on the deck and fainted. . . . I asked if we were not to be eaten by those white men with horrible looks, red faces and long hair?[9]

Typically two to four hundred slaves were carried on each ship. They were chained below decks in pairs, ankle to ankle, wrist to wrist, lying side by side with about half the space assigned to convicts or soldiers being transported during the same era.[10] Buckets were set up in the corner as toilets, but a slave had to get there while still chained to his neighbor. Many didn't make it to the bucket on time, and slave ships always stank of human waste.

Men and women were chained in different parts of the ship for both disciplinary and moral reasons. In a classic example of values dissonance, ship captains were fine with slavery but appalled at the possibility of sexual activity on board. Captains also suspected that male slaves became less docile and more protective when they had women among them.[11]

The voyage typically lasted two to three months. Slaves were not especially mistreated on the ships. They were kept reasonably healthy with plenty of water and starchy food: beans, biscuits, plantains, rice, and yams. If a slave tried a hunger strike, his mouth was wedged open for forced feeding. Once land was safely out of sight and beyond temptation, slaves might be brought above deck in small, manageable groups to stretch and dance. They were usually released from their chains as the voyage progressed.[12]

Overall, 40 percent of all slaves (4.65 million) were shipped by the Portuguese, and 35 percent (4 million) were sent to the Portuguese colony of Brazil. The trade peaked in the 1700s, when nearly 6 million slaves were transported by all nations. During the 1780s an average of 80,000 new slaves were arriving in America every year. By this time, the British dominated the trade. In the eighteenth century, the British shipped around 2.5 million.[13]

The slave and sugar economy was so lucrative that every seafaring European country tried to get a piece of it, even those we don't normally think of as heartless slave drivers, such as the Danes. The Danish West Indian and Guinea Company had two slave stations in Africa where they gathered workers for Denmark's colony in the Virgin Islands. In all, 28,000 slaves were transported on Danish ships.

In total, some 10 to 12 million slaves were transported across the Atlantic.[14] Probably

10 to 15 percent of them died in transit, often from dysentery, scurvy, and smallpox.[15] The dead were thrown overboard without ceremony, and sharks followed the ships hoping for an easy meal.[16]

It's been noted that the death rate of crews on slave ships was often the same as the death rate among slaves, a point that is sometimes used as proof that slaves were not treated all that badly. Unfortunately, this is more an indication of how badly the crews were treated. The slave trade numbed men to brutality. The crewmen on slave ships were widely considered the worst scum of the docks. They were paid the least and were more likely to settle quarrels with knives or be hanged by their captain.[17]

Because Europeans were especially susceptible to the fevers lurking along the coasts of Africa, the slave ships were considered the most dangerous assignment a sailor could get. They even sang about it: "Beware and take care of the Bight of Benin / Few come out, though many go in."[18]

Disbursement

Witnesses said that you could always smell a slave ship sailing into a harbor. After weeks on the oceans, they stank of the stale urine, sweat, vomit, and feces from three hundred confined humans, and the warm Caribbean breezes spread the stench over the whole town. Slavers usually arrived with great ceremony—cannon blasts or special bells—to gather buyers and alert the authorities. They hoped to unload and disburse their dangerous cargo before the new slaves got their bearings.

After a doctor inspected the slaves for contagious diseases, they were offloaded to warehouses and slave jails to be prepared for sale. New slaves were fattened up, washed, and oiled to be more attractive than the wretched skeletons that originally staggered off the ship. They would be displayed, inspected, and auctioned. When the sale was final, the slaves were often branded by their new owners with hot irons.

During the first year on the plantation, Africans were broken, trained, and acclimated. New slaves were usually assigned relatively easy jobs until they were toughened up ("seasoned") and sent into the sugar fields for the really hard work. Even so, probably a third of all new slaves died during seasoning.[19] Although Africans as a race had previously been exposed to all of the Old World diseases, developing some genetic immunity, Africans as individuals were often vulnerable. Jumbling hundreds of people from all over Africa into one crowded plantation exposed many new slaves to smallpox, measles, malaria, or yellow fever for the very first time.

It wasn't pure biology driving the death rate. Sugar cultivation was especially brutal to the body, from handling the knife-like leaves of the sugar cane in the fields to the boiling cauldrons in the refinery. Slaves were overworked, underfed, and overcrowded. Shackled if they tried to flee and beaten for any infraction, most slaves quickly acquired heavy scars around their ankles and crisscrossing their backs. Many of the folkways that had allowed Africans to avoid disease back home—proper care or isolation for the sick, proper disposal of the dead, food preparation, waste removal, clean housing, shade, rest—were a luxury in the American plantations. Only the hardiest Africans survived the shock of the first few years.[20]

In the deadly islands of the Caribbean, the slaves died faster than they could reproduce, which meant the population was not self-sustaining. The workforce had to be continuously propped up by new imports. Even though 864,000 slaves had been imported into the French colony of Saint-Domingue (Haiti) between 1680 and 1791, the black population in 1789 numbered only 435,000. Despite the arrival of 750,000 slaves in Jamaica from 1655 to 1807, only 310,000 were alive to be freed when Britain abolished slavery in 1834. Compare that to the English-speaking lands on the North American mainland, where the 427,500 slaves imported from Africa had mostly survived and bred up to 1.4 million by 1810.[21]

Because of this constant replenishment from Africa, the islands acquired more African culture than did the American mainland. Language and religion in the Caribbean tend to be a synthesis of European and African elements in the form of creoles and voodoo, whereas black North Americans speak with a slight accent and are mostly Protestants.

The biggest consumer of slave labor was sugar production, which employed 55 percent of the new slaves arriving from Africa, but there were fortunes to be made in other tropical products such as coffee (which grabbed 18 percent of the new slaves), cotton (5 percent), and cocoa (3 percent). Of course, new slaves were assigned throughout the economy, from working in mines (9 percent) to serving as household staff (9 percent).[22] Later generations of slaves born in America were often trained in urban trades such as carpentry, brick-making, or blacksmithing.

Once they were acclimated in America, the death rate eased off, but slaves still had a life expectancy many years less than the free people of the same community.

Judgment

In both Africa and America in the early days of the trade, slavery was not necessarily considered a permanent condition. Most of the first slaves imported in Virginia were indentured servants who were released after their terms of servitude (ten years was typical) had expired. That soon changed.

Three shifts in the winds of history made the Western slave trade stand out for its cruelty. The first was the rise of global capitalism in the fifteenth century. This broke the cultural and emotional connections between masters and slaves who had lived among each other in the same communities for generations. It turned slaves into mere commodities to be bought and sold in anonymous bulk across wide distances.

Second was racism. "We" have always been better than "them," but through most of human history, "we" were a tiny tribe—Saxons, Athenians, Venetians, Judeans, whatever—in a big sea of "them." The Greeks, for example, lumped all non-Greeks—black/white, literate/illiterate, clothed/naked—into the catch-all category of *barbaroi*. With so many of "them" out there, there was a limit to the amount of damage "we" could do. Only later did "we" expand to include *everyone* who looks like us, bundled together in opposition to everyone who looks different.

The slave trade largely invented racism, this division of humanity into groups organized solely by physical appearance. A feedback cycle developed where so many Africans lived as slaves in the New World that slavery seemed like the obvious, natural condition for Africans. Once Europeans began to associate dark skin with slavery, every dark-skinned person was assumed to be a slave, and if he wasn't, well, then he should be.[23] If owners liberated too many African slaves after a period of servitude, it would create a class of free blacks in which runaways could hide. The slave owners had to vigorously oppose the growth of an independent, unregulated free black community. Then they had to justify these actions by appealing to racist ideology.[24]

Third, the rise of liberal notions of inborn personal dignity removed many intermediate forms of inequality such as serfdom, concubinage, and apprenticeship. These diverse classes and castes had once filled the gap between the slave and the freeborn with a series of small steps rather than an impassible chasm. Slavery in nineteenth-century America was no worse than slavery in seventeenth-century America, but as the rights of common citizens expanded, the contrast with slaves became more glaring.

Abolition

In 1781, the British slave ship *Zong* was lost somewhere near Jamaica, stranded in a calm and losing slaves to fevers and bad planning. The captain's investment was draining away. Unfortunately, insurance wouldn't cover slaves who died of natural causes on board the vessel itself, but it would pay for cargo lost at sea or jettisoned to lighten the load or conserve dwindling resources, something shippers routinely did with livestock. The captain started tossing dozens of sick slaves overboard. Over several days, 132 slaves drowned in this way. When the captain got back to land, he filed an insurance claim for the lost slaves. When the insurance company refused to pay, the captain sued.[25]

The lawsuit almost passed without notice, as had so many earlier cases, but a small legal notice in the newspaper brought it to the attention of abolitionists, who made a fuss. This didn't affect the case, but it helped mobilize the forces of abolition.

The very fact that there were abolitionists at all was a victory for both the Enlightenment and the Protestant Reformation. Across the previous millennia, the harshest criticism that any major religion had leveled against slavery was an occasional suggestion to treat slaves better. Aside from that, scripture was more likely to cite slavery approvingly, as a model for the relationship between man and God. The Old Testament cursed the descendants of Canaan to slavery. Saints Peter and Paul instructed slaves to obey their masters. In 1452, Pope Nicholas V issued the *Dum Diversas*, which granted Catholic countries "full and free permission to invade, search out, capture, and subjugate the Saracens and pagans and any other unbelievers and enemies of Christ wherever they may be . . . and to reduce their persons into perpetual slavery." In fact, until well into the 1800s, most missionary societies considered slavery to be beneficial because it brought pagan Africans into the warm bosom of Christendom.[26]

The splintering of Christianity, however, had created a far left wing dedicated to the equality of all people. Several of these splinter groups, first the Mennonites (1688), then the Quakers (1696), then the more numerous Methodists (1774), began to come out against the very existence of slavery. In 1775, Quakers in Philadelphia organized the first abolitionist society in America. English Quakers established their country's first antislavery society in 1783.

This radical fringe would have been easily ignored had it not been for the wider acceptance of liberal ideals during the Enlightenment of the eighteenth century. Although Enlightenment philosophers usually dismissed Christianity as mere superstition, they agreed with the Quakers that all men are born free and equal. As liberalism infiltrated society, it became harder to stay silent about slavery. By the late 1700s, the leading minds of Western Civilization (Bentham, Hume, Locke, Montesquieu, Rousseau, Voltaire, for example) had recognized the injustice of slavery.

Of all aspects of slavery, it was easiest to agitate public sympathy against the slave trade, which destroyed lives, broke apart families, and subjected innocent victims to such obvious suffering and indignity. This was the first element of Western slavery to crumble to moral assault.

After years of parliamentary debate, the British finally outlawed the international slave trade in 1807, and most other civilized countries followed their lead over the next decade. Some, like Spain and Portugal, had to be bullied into it by other countries and would only pass toothless laws that they didn't even enforce; however, even more important than placing new laws on the books, the British committed their fleet to patrolling the coast of Africa and arresting all slave traders as pirates, regardless of nationality.

For several decades, the Atlantic Ocean saw a steady game of cops and robbers, and like most activities outside the law, slaving became even more brutal. To avoid being captured with slaves aboard, some slave ships shackled their cargo to a single long chain. If a patrol boat came into view, the first slave was pushed overboard, and the chain carried all of the slaves into the ocean, one after another. The incriminating evidence would be deep underwater by the time the Royal Navy boarded the ship.[27]

Between 1820 and 1870, the British navy seized almost 1,600 ships and freed 150,000 slaves.[28] Most of them were offloaded at Freetown in Sierra Leone because it would be impossible to return them to their scattered, inland homelands. The much smaller American navy soon joined the slave patrol and over time offloaded 6,000 liberated slaves at Monrovia in Liberia.[29]

Abolition, Phase Two

Technically, that's the end of this chapter. On my list of one hundred multicides, I count only deaths caused by the slave trade during capture, transport, and seasoning, and not the deaths of slaves after they were settled, so this megadeath ends with the abolition of the transoceanic trade; however, let's bring the story to its full conclusion.

The day-to-day practice of slavery, which kept workers in bondage to a single owner, proved harder to eradicate than the international slave trade. Remember, this was the era of serfdom, workhouses, and sweatshops, so the average man in power cared little about the ordinary worker, regardless of his race or condition of servitude. As long as slavery was maintained with minimal standards of decency, and, more important, kept quiet and out of sight, most people were willing to let it stand.

Although the driving force of abolitionism was moral, it wouldn't have made much headway without economic changes. At the beginning of the modern era, so many business ventures involved slaves at some point in the process that no one could abolish slavery without losing a lot of money. An investor who was morally opposed to profiting from slavery would be shut out of making money from shipping, textiles, tobacco, sugar, banking, insurance, and mining. Then in the mid-1700s, the emerging industrial economies began to produce plenty of money without using slaves. Suddenly, the abolition of slavery wouldn't bankrupt as many important people, so it became a lot easier to take a moral stand.

Why did the Industrial Revolution push out slavery? It's not that slaves couldn't do the work. Slaves could be found working as factory hands, miners, and skilled tradesmen in cities and towns throughout the Western Hemisphere—and doing a perfectly fine job of it. Factories often treated their workers like slaves anyway, so using actual slaves was not a problem.

The real problem was that slaves were a long-term investment that tied up capital and became riskier as the economy became more dynamic. With markets always fluctuating, it was easier to just hire and fire free labor as needed, rather than raise slaves from babies for jobs that might be gone when they were old enough to work. Only agricultural production was steady enough, year by year, to make it feasible to acquire a workforce years before it would be put to use.[30]

Also, plantations were more self-sufficient than cities, making it a lot cheaper to keep slaves. Food, water, housing, and firewood were easily available on farms, so in bad times it was possible to hunker down and wait for the economy to improve. Keeping slaves in an urban economy meant renting shelter, importing food, and buying fuel. That's money flowing out even when there's no money coming in. It was easier to pay workers a wage and let them worry about their own upkeep.*

By 1800, Western Civilization had divided regionally, all-or-nothing, on the issue of slavery. Unless a region absolutely depended on slaves to maintain the economy, harassed local leaders usually knuckled under to the moral badgering of the abolitionists and just freed the damn slaves—anything to get the Quakers off their backs.

Within the first generation of the abolitionist movement, slavery disappeared from the world's most urbanized economies. In Great Britain, a landmark case in 1772 concerning the slave James Somerset decided that slavery could not be enforced under English law. The northern American states and territories abolished slavery between 1777 (Vermont) and 1804 (New Jersey). The revolutionary government of France abolished slavery at home almost as soon as it took power (1791) and in the colonies after much debate (1794).

In warmer regions where cash crops grown by slaves were the mainstay of the local economy, slavery survived these opening battles. Fearing both bankruptcy and the unleashing of thousands of unsupervised savages into their helpless communities, the slave owners stood stubbornly against any reform. Politics polarized. Tempers flared. Negotiated emancipation became nearly impossible in the regions where slavery was most deeply rooted, and it was only violent upheavals that finally shook it loose.

In 1791, the slaves in the French colony of Saint-Domingue rebelled while the motherland was distracted by the French Revolution. It took hundreds of thousands of lives and many years, but in the end, they established Haiti as the second independent country in the Western Hemisphere (see "Haitian Slave Revolt").

In 1802, Napoleon reestablished slavery in the remaining French colonies. Only after the violent overthrow of the restored monarchy and the founding of the Second Republic in 1848 did France permanently abolish slavery in all of its colonies.

The British parliament abolished slavery in all of the British colonies in 1833. This was probably the only major emancipation that was accomplished without fighting.

In the United States, the North-South divide over slavery intensified and touched every aspect of public life. In 1845, for example, the pro-slavery factions of the Baptists split off and formed the Southern Baptist Convention, currently the second largest religious body in the United States.†

Every new territorial acquisition by the United States had to be allocated to either the

---

* This sounds like wage labor was even more cruel than slavery. Well, yes, it was, except that free laborers were allowed to get married, keep their children, fight back, go to court, go to school, go to church, avoid church, save money, spend money, drink beer, drink whiskey, drink too much, read, move, and own their own pants. But, yes, aside from all that . . .

† For the record, the Southern Baptists are no longer in favor of slavery. They renounced it in 1995.

slave or the free section of the country. The future balance of power depended on North and South packing potential new states with like-minded settlers. The dispute eventually produced a political party, the Republicans, whose unifying principle was its opposition to the expansion of slavery. When this party was voted into office in 1860, the slave owners rebelled, and over a half-million people died in the ensuing civil war.

In Cuba, slavery wasn't shaken loose until its first unsuccessful war of independence, the Ten Years War. By the time the insurrection was put down in 1878, too many slaves had escaped to hunt them all down again, so the Spanish government decided not to argue with any slaves who had guns. (In technical terms, the peace treaty granted freedom to any slave who had fought for either side in the war—in other words, those who had guns.) The rest were set free eight years later.

In 1888, more than a century after the beginning of the abolitionist movement, Brazil became the last Western nation to abolish slavery during a political upheaval that included the overthrow of the monarchy, although the lineup probably wasn't what you would expect. Instead of elitists (monarchists and slave owners) versus liberals (republicans and abolitionists), the upheaval saw nationalists (republicans and slave owners preferring local control) allied against internationalists (monarchists and abolitionists trying to fit into global civilization).

In *Atrocities*, slavery stands unique as one of the few atrocities that has been utterly and completely . . . well, *eradicated* is too optimistic a word . . . let's say *marginalized*. Although forms of slavery still exist here and there in dark pockets, nations as a whole do not practice it anymore. A nation can openly torture prisoners, shoot dissidents, invade neighbors, beat women to death, or work children in sweatshops without apology, and it will still get its seat in the United Nations, no questions asked; however, not one of them will dare to legalize slavery. Pure and unadulterated slavery is the strongest taboo in international law.

It's a start at least.

CONQUEST OF THE AMERICAS

Death toll: 15 million
Rank: 11
Type: colonial conquest
Broad dividing line: Europeans vs. Native Americans
Time frame: beginning in 1492
Location: Western Hemisphere
Primary participants: Aztecs, Carib, Incas, Spaniards, Taino
Secondary participants: Americans, Blackfoot, Cherokee, Cheyenne, Creeks, English, Iroquois, Pequot, Powhatan, Shoshone, Sioux
Who usually gets the most blame: Columbus, conquistadors, Custer*
Economic factors: gold, silver

Nobody Expects the Spanish Inquisition

You would be hard-pressed to find a nation less suited to peaceful first contact with an alien culture than Renaissance Spain. For over seven hundred years, this peninsula had been torn between Christian and Muslim cultures, European and African armies, into a kaleidoscope of angry kingdoms, duchies, and emirates. Spain didn't even exist as a nation until two lesser kingdoms were fused by the marriage of their monarchs in 1469.

In Spain, the crusader mentality was alive and unlikely to take prisoners. Grenada, the last Muslim stronghold in the peninsula, didn't fall to Christian conquerors until 1492, the same year that Spain expelled its Jews. By that time, the Spanish Inquisition had been set up to make sure there were no hidden infidels mocking decent people from behind a mask of piety. Heretics were broken and burned by the thousands.

The Mediterranean Sea was a battleground between the Christian and Muslim fleets,

---

* The key word is *usually*. This is not a list of who *deserves* the most blame. Custer is the most notorious Indian killer in American history, but he was hardly the worst. He has come to exemplify the American side of the Indian Wars, but his unpardonable sin wasn't shooting up the odd Indian village here and there; it was getting beaten. Andrew Jackson killed more, but he won all of his battles, so he's on the twenty-dollar bill.

so European mariners began to explore the Atlantic, hoping to bypass the hated Saracens and connect with the riches of the Orient. The Portuguese took the obvious route, down the coast of Africa, while the Spaniards took a gamble on the direct route, straight across the open ocean to the other side of the globe. Christopher Columbus imagined, planned, and led the 1492 expedition, which probably would have disappeared in the wide, endless ocean if he had been right about the next stop being Asia. As luck would have it, islands off the coast of an entirely unsuspected pair of continents gave him a safe landfall before his supplies ran out. He thought it was Asia, but within a decade or so, subsequent explorers proved it to be a completely New World.

Waiting for Columbus

In one of the great contrasts of history, the people who greeted Columbus, the Taino (or Arawak) of the Bahamas, were among the gentlest people ever recorded. As Columbus described them, "They neither carry nor know anything of arms, for I showed them swords, and they took them by the blade and cut themselves through ignorance."[1] "They are a loving people, without covetousness, and fit for anything . . . there is no better land nor people. They love their neighbours as themselves, and their speech is the sweetest and gentlest in the world, and always with a smile."[2]

Well naturally the first thing Columbus did was to size them up for plunder. "They would make fine servants,"[3] he noted. "With fifty men they can all be subjugated and made to do what is required of them."[4]

He then poked southward, deeper into the West Indies, inquiring after any spare gold they might have lying around. He explored the larger islands—Cuba, Hispaniola—and found little worth stealing except for more natives. Always on the lookout for opportunity, he noted, "From here, in the name of the Blessed Trinity, we can send all the slaves that can be sold."[5] To prove his point, Columbus kidnapped a few natives to take back to Spain as specimens. Then he left a small settlement on Hispaniola and sailed back to Spain with the wonderful news.

The Snake in Paradise

Let's take a moment to appreciate the wonderful bounty that was laid out before the Spaniards, free for the taking, starting with the most important item for a sailor finishing a couple of months on the open ocean. The women, Columbus reported, were "naked as the day they were born," with "no more embarrassment than animals."[6] Once we've contemplated that, let's notice that the natives had almost no metals—certainly no brass, tin, steel, iron, or bronze—no metals at all *except* gold and silver, which were soft and shiny and easy to work. That means the Native Americans had spent several centuries digging and panning all of the precious metals they could find, accumulating treasures conveniently within reach, but had failed to invent a way to defend them.

It would be misleading to characterize the Spaniards as lions among sheep, but they were definitely lions among coyotes—both being predators, but in a far different league. Native Americans could be as cruel and vicious as any of the world's peoples. The Aztecs were sacrificing 15,000 fellow humans atop their pyramids every year (see "Aztec Human Sacrifice"). Even before Columbus arrived, the gentle Taino were being gradually but inexorably driven off their islands by the Carib, who gave their name not only to the sea but also to their characteristic diet: *cannibalism*. The Incas sacrificed children on mountains. The Iroquois delighted in cutting and burning captives.

Be that as it may, most natives didn't quite have what it took to be unstoppable killing machines. Aztec warfare was ritualistic, with the purpose of collecting live prisoners to be sacrificed. The Indians of the North American plains became known for counting coup, the ritual of bravery in which they attacked only to tag the enemy, not to kill him. The Spaniards took war a lot more seriously.

The Spanish conquistadors went into battle with steel swords, which could easily kill by severing an arm or a head, unlike the native clubs and stone hatchets that required repeated battering to incapacitate an enemy. Spanish armor, especially helmets, made it even more difficult for the Indians to score a hit. The Spaniards used horses and hunting dogs, terrifying monsters that could easily chase down, trample, or tear apart fleeing warriors. European crossbows were easier to aim and shoot than native bows and arrows. Cannons shook the earth and shredded enemy mobs. The arquebus, or primitive musket, of the conquistadors was too slow and inaccurate to have much of a military effect unless there were a lot of them, but don't underestimate the psychological impact of a crack of thunder, followed by the man beside you dropping mysteriously dead.[7]

The West Indies

We know so little about Christopher Columbus. We don't know when or where he was born, where he first landed in America, what he looked like, or where he is buried. Obviously that hasn't stopped us from filling in the gaps with guesses, imagination, and speculation, even if it contradicts the little we do know. No matter what historians tell us, we continue to believe in the Christopher Columbus we want, not the one who existed. This is equally true whether we want Columbus to be a hero or a villain.

Every few years, a book comes out that promises to demythify Columbus and expose him for the son of a bitch he was, and the oddest thing is that this has been happening for hundreds of years, right from the start. The most important primary source of what little we know of the life of Columbus are the writings of Bartolome de las Casas, Dominican priest and zealous defender of the Indians. The only reason we have, for example, the log of Columbus's first voyage is because las Casas had a copy in his personal papers. Las Casas originally admired Columbus and was among the wild crowds that cheered his return to Spain, but after las Casas moved to America, he made it his driving goal in life to publicize and denounce the cruelties his fellow countrymen inflicted on the Indians. Columbus and his peers are often defended with the argument that you can't judge the past by modern standards, but it's important to remember that "modern standards" existed in Columbus's day in the person of las Casas and others like him.

Columbus returned to Hispaniola in early 1494, outfitted by the Spanish crown with a fleet of seventeen ships to stake out an empire. He discovered that the small settlement he had planted on his first voyage had been wiped out after a dispute with the natives, but that didn't matter. This new expedition had 1,500 fresh Europeans, along with tools, seeds, and livestock, ready to subjugate the New World. With Columbus came his two brothers to share his good fortune.

Columbus gave the natives strict quotas of gold to bring to him, and for several months he required the Taino to abandon their fields and pan gold in the hills, which sparked a famine that killed 50,000. He also rounded up 1,500 natives and penned them for sale as slaves. After stuffing as many as he could into ships heading back to Spain, he used the remainder locally.[8]

Columbus had spent so much of his life as a sea captain that he preferred ruling by edict and immediate punishment. Eventually his summary executions of occasional Spaniards annoyed the colonists. Disagreements over whether to treat the natives as slaves (Columbus's view) or loyal subjects (the Crown's view) divided the colony as well. When an auditor arrived from Spain, among the first sights to greet him were corpses swinging from ropes. The Columbus brothers were clapped in chains and shipped home to answer charges. The crown still had enough faith in Columbus to forgive him and continue to use him as an explorer, but he was never again given command on land.

The Caribbean

Soon the Spaniards began to parcel out the New World according to a system called *encomiendo* (trusteeship). In theory, the Indians remained in possession of the land under the supervision of a benevolent European trustee. You can guess how well that worked in practice.[9]

In 1502 Brother Nicholas de Ovando of a Spanish military-religious order arrived in Hispanola with 2,500 settlers. He invited all of the native chiefs to a splendid banquet in their honor, and then killed them. He easily enslaved the remaining leaderless natives. The next year, Ponce de Leon put down a rebellion on the tip of Hispanola with a massacre of 7,000 Taino.[10] As Spaniards spread throughout Hispanola, the recorded population of the island quickly plunged from 60,000 (1509) to 11,000 (1518).

With the natives dying from overwork, unfamiliar diseases, and strict discipline, the Spaniards began raiding neighboring islands for new labor. When those islands ran out of people, they harvested slaves from the next island over, and then the next, until all of the Indians of the West Indies were either enslaved or, increasingly, dead.

The brutality didn't go unnoticed or unopposed. As early as 1511, a Dominican priest in the Spanish colonies, Antonio de Montesinos, was arguing desperately that the Indians should be treated with common decency.[11]

Central America

For several years navigators had been bumping up against a large landmass southwest of the Indies, one with rivers so big they had to be draining a full continent. An early attempt to settle this region was abandoned as soon as the Spaniards saw the jungle and its menacing natives. Onboard was Vasco de Balboa, who decided to settle in Hispaniola instead, where he did poorly as a plantation owner.

In 1508, when another, larger Spanish force set out to conquer the western mainland, Balboa stowed away among the expedition's supplies in order to escape his creditors. Although the expedition leader's first instinct was to dump the trespasser at the next island, Balboa convinced him that his earlier experience on the mainland would be useful.

The expedition landed in Panama, founded a town, killed some natives, and began to prowl around, snatching gold wherever the explorers found it. When the leader of the expedition began to tax the settlers' gold, Balboa led a mutiny that put him in charge. Soon a new governor arrived from Hispaniola to take control of the colony, but Balboa seized him and pushed him off to sea in a leaky boat that was never seen again.

While exploring deep inland, bartering or stealing gold baubles and jewelry from the natives, Balboa heard stories of another ocean, beyond the mainland, so he set out to see if this could be a new passage to Asia. He hacked his way onward, battling tribe after tribe and stripping them of their gold and pearls. When he found that the men of one tribe dressed as women, he had his attack dogs rip them apart. Finally, in 1513, he arrived at the Pacific Ocean, the first European to see it from that side.

It was the zenith of his career. A new royal governor, Pedrarias, soon replaced and beheaded Balboa. This man proved to be even more ruthless than Balboa, wiping out almost all of the local natives in his search for gold.[12]

Mexico

Several expeditions to Mexico, both planned and accidental, had already come to grief in the face of native hostility, but Governor Velásquez of Cuba was willing to try again. In 1519, he asked Hernán Cortés, one of Cuba's wealthiest settlers, to investigate stories of this mysterious land to the west. Cortés was supposed to make contact, arrange trade, and report back, but as preparations progressed Velásquez noticed that Cortés was a bit too enthusiastic about the assignment, outfitting a much larger and more heavily armed expedition than Velásquez had in mind.

Finally, the governor realized that the first man to reach Mexico would have virgin land to plunder, and he had just handed the opportunity to an untrustworthy rival. At the last minute, he tried to withdraw his permission for the expedition, but Cortés's brother-in-law had Velásquez's messenger waylaid and killed, which allowed Cortés the chance to escape. Now, technically in mutiny against the lawful authority, Cortés had no place to go but forward.

Shortly after first landing in Mexico in Yucatan, the Spaniards found a stranded compatriot from an earlier, failed expedition who knew his way around the country, as well as the local Mayan language. He led Cortés northward toward the Aztec Empire. As they sailed along the coast, one native village welcomed Cortés and gave him several women to do with as he pleased, one of whom, Malinche, proved especially useful. She spoke both Mayan and Nahuatl, the Aztec language, and eventually learned Spanish. More important, after being sold into slavery by her stepfather and passed through several hands, she was not especially loyal to her people. All accounts describe her as beautiful and intelligent, standing beside Cortés at all councils, whispering advice into his ear. She eventually bore Cortés a son, and then disappeared into history.

Finally disembarking at Veracruz, the Spaniards set out on foot. During the march inland, Cortés and his 500 soldiers defeated the collected armies of the Tlaxcala, deadly enemies of the Aztecs. Awed by the Spaniards' might, the Tlaxcala quickly switched to the winning side and welcomed Cortés as their ally. In October 1519, Cortés pushed onward, now reinforced by 3,000 Tlaxcala. He attacked the Aztec holy city of Cholula, killing 3,000 citizens and burning the city.

Finally, Cortés marched along a wide causeway into the Aztec capital of Tenochtitlan, a magnificent city of pyramids, fish ponds, and gardens along interlaced canals, built on islands at the center of a lake. Gold trinkets, bangles, and ornaments were to be seen everywhere. Although no one actually knows how many people lived there, every historian agrees that Tenochtitlan was larger than any European city at that time except Constantinople.[13]

At their first meeting, the Aztec emperor Montezuma invited Cortés to stay as an honored guest in the palace, but over the next few weeks, Cortés began to restrict and control the emperor, making Montezuma an imprisoned puppet. Then news arrived that another Spanish force had landed at the coast with orders from Velásquez to bring Cortés under control. Cortés rushed back and beat the newcomers in battle, but his stories of the great city of gold convinced the survivors to join him.

Meanwhile, the Spanish garrison that Cortés had left in Tenochtitlan had interrupted a religious festival, either to murder and rob wealthy Aztecs (the native story) or to prevent a human sacrifice (the Spanish story). When Cortés returned, he found the Aztecs in rebellion and his countrymen besieged and starving in the palace. Cortés hauled Montezuma out onto a balcony to appeal for calm, but the emperor was pelted with stones and killed. Then Cortés was chased out of town in a running battle. Most of the Spaniards were captured and sacrificed during the retreat. Their screams as they were cut open by priests could be heard in the night by their fleeing comrades.[14]

As the remaining Spaniards recuperated among the Tlaxcala, an invisible ally destroyed the Aztecs for them. Smallpox is an Old World disease that leaves its survivors scarred but immune from further infections. Over the generations, Europeans inherited resistance to the disease from these survivors, and by the sixteenth century, smallpox was a disease of children in Europe. Adults rarely died from it unless they belonged to a population that had never been exposed to it before. Now, this disease and others like it—measles, flu, tuberculosis, for example—were wiping out the susceptible populations of the Western Hemisphere. The epidemic that hit the Aztecs killed their new king and uncounted thousands more.

The Spaniards built a fleet of portable boats and returned to Tenochtitlan with 80,000 Tlaxcalan allies. Cortés's invasion force then attacked across the ponds and canals of Tenochtitlan against a determined house-by-house defense. Cortés fought his way back in, rooting out the resistance, dismantling the city as he went. Some 200,000 Aztecs died in the fight to save their city. By the time it was over, the canals were choked with bodies, and Cortés had extinguished a major world civilization, but he was wealthy beyond imagination.

Peru

The Inca Empire, which stretched along the mountainous spine of South America, was the most advanced native political entity in the Americas. As many miles in length as the United States is in width, Incan Peru was a land of llamas and alpacas, stone fortresses and terraced farms gently layered into the mountainsides. For their first few decades in the New World, the Spaniards didn't even know it was there, until Francisco Pizarro, an illiterate former associate of Balboa's, sailed south from Panama to explore the Pacific coast of South America. Encountering a native trading vessel, he yanked a few Indians off to serve as guides and translators. Soon he sailed into the native port of Tumbes and was hospitably received. He learned of the vast Inca Empire that stretched up and down the coast, but more important, Pizarro noticed how wealthy and vulnerable these people were.

After a pleasant visit, the Europeans took leave of their native hosts and the race was on. The town's governor sent runners to the Inca king with news of the strangers, while Pizarro returned to Spain with his report.

The king of Spain gave Pizarro permission to conquer the Incas, and in 1531, Pizarro retraced his earlier path. This time, however, Pizarro discovered that Tumbes had been looted and devastated. As the Spaniards marched inland without opposition, they noticed that the villages along their route were missing their men.

Smallpox had arrived ahead of the Spaniards. About the time of Pizarro's first visit, the disease was spreading throughout the interior, killing the Inca king and his heir apparent. His two remaining sons had spent much of the intervening years fighting for control of the empire and conscripting every able-bodied man they could lay their hands on. The winner, Atahualpa, had been expecting the Spaniards to arrive at some point, but he considered them less dangerous than his own family members.

Francisco Pizarro and two hundred Spaniards took over the deserted town of Cajamarca. They arranged a meeting with Atahualpa, who arrived in the main square with 80,000 troops in full splendor, marching with drums, plumes, spears, and stone hatchets.

The Incas, however, discovered the plaza mysteriously empty. A Dominican friar approached to negotiate, offering Atahualpa a choice: convert to Christianity or be attacked. This was the standard legal offer that preceded all wars against the heathens. Christians were forbidden from fighting fellow Christians without a good reason, or at least a plausible excuse, but heathens were fair game at any time, so the rule was simple: confirm their heathenism and then attack.

When Atahualpa failed to take this threat from two hundred scruffy strangers seriously, hidden Spaniards raked the plaza with gunfire and attacked the crowded Incas with horses and sabers, killing 8,000 Incas with barely a scratch to themselves. Pizarro personally seized Atahualpa and dragged him off his litter into captivity. Forced to buy back his liberty, Atahualpa agreed to fill a room with gold and silver ransom. Precious art collected by the empire for centuries was turned over to the Spaniards, who melted and hammered it down for easy shipment.

Even after the ransom was paid, the Spaniards kept Atahualpa imprisoned. Atahualpa realized that he was expendable as long as other potential rulers were free and alive, so he issued orders to wipe out the imperial family up and down the empire. His brother and rival, Huascar, was among those killed. Not only was this no help, but also it gave Pizarro an excuse to get rid of Atahualpa. The Inca king was sentenced to be burned at the stake, but he was told that if he converted to Christianity, he would be given a lighter sentence. Atahualpa agreed, so the Spaniards strangled him instead.[15]

Cities of Gold and Mountains of Silver

It took many hard years of fighting for the Spaniards to secure control over all of Peru. A rebel prince of the Incas took refuge in the mountain fortress of Machu Picchu and the Spaniards had to reduce his territory step-by-step. Meanwhile, a steady stream of fresh conquistadors arrived to grab a piece of the action. Even before Peru was pacified, the conquistadors began fighting among themselves, but in time, Spanish control of Peru was secure.

Then in 1549, Spaniards discovered a mountain of silver ore at Potosi (now in southern Bolivia). Over the generations that followed, native laborers were systematically drafted from neighboring districts to dig into the mountain until they dropped. Mining accidents killed dozens at a time, while mercury vapors eroded the nervous systems of other miners. Workers died by the tens of thousands, but the silver of Potosi funded Spanish ambitions for the next century.[16]

One of the Spanish adventurers who drifted through Potosi, a minor nobleman and soldier of fortune named Lope de Aguirre, was arrested in 1551 and found guilty of abusing the Indians. Considering that the ordinary brutality of Potosi was killing workers by the truckload, you can imagine how badly a person would have to behave in order to be prosecuted. When Judge Francisco de Esquivel sentenced Aguirre to a flogging despite his rank, Aguirre swore vengeance. For three years Aguirre hunted Esquivel, allowing him no safe haven, chasing him to Lima, to Quito, and finally to Cuzco. Esquivel had even taken to wearing a chain mail vest at all times in case Aguirre found him. It didn't help. In Cuzco, Aguirre caught up with Esquivel, snuck into the heavily guarded mansion of the viceroy of Peru, and killed the judge with a head wound.

Aguirre's military skill was soon needed to put down a rebellion of mutinous Spaniards, so the Crown pardoned him for the murder of the governor. In 1559 he joined a Spanish military expedition from Peru over the Andes into the forbidding and pestilent Amazon jungle—and he brought his teenage daughter Elvira along as well. Rumors had been circulating of El Dorado, a kingdom of gold somewhere in the unexplored wilderness. Although Aguirre started low in the chain of command, a series of internal squabbles, stabbings, executions, and mysterious accidents left him in charge of the expedition. The remaining Spaniards hacked and blasted their way through the Amazonian tribes downriver for thousands of miles without finding the golden land they had been promised.

After cutting through the last underbrush and Indians, Aguirre reemerged into Spanish territory on the other side of South America, and almost immediately stole Margarita Island on the Caribbean coast from the Spanish garrison. While trying to establish an independent empire on Margarita, he saw plots and schemes everywhere, and he ended up killing almost everyone in his entourage. When he tried to expand his operation into Panama, the authorities moved in and rooted him out. As the Spanish forces closed in, Aguirre's last act was to kill his daughter so no one else could have her. The authorities cut Aguirre's body into four parts and distributed them for display all over Spanish America.

North America

By the time the English, French, and Dutch began to stake out colonies in North America, the worst was over for the main centers of native civilization. In the grand scheme of things, the centuries of continuous wars between the North American Indians and the Anglo-Americans were secondary to the devastation wrought on the densely populated Meso-American, Andean, and Caribbean heartlands. Be that as it may, the United States is the world's current hegemon, and the eradication of the Native Americans is generally considered America's greatest national sin, so people argue about Wounded Knee more than they argue about Atahualpa.

A quick rundown of the sixteen deadliest events of the Anglo-American frontier should give the flavor of who did what to whom:

March 22, 1622: The Powhatans killed 347 English settlers—men, women, and children—a third of the Virginia colony's population, with coordinated attacks up and down the James River.

1623: After negotiating a peace treaty with the rebellious Chiskiack tribe on the Potomac River, the English brought out wine to toast the end of hostilities. It was poisoned, and 200 Chiskiack leaders keeled over dead. The English slaughtered the survivors.[17]

May 26, 1637: Connecticut militia surrounded a Pequot town on the Mystic River, setting fire to the houses and burning the trapped villagers. Around 600 Pequots, mostly women and children, died in the flames or were shot down as they tried to escape.[18]

1675–76, King Philip's War: In the usual pattern of frontier warfare, one killing led to three killings, which led to a full raid, until everyone was killing someone. Entire villages were wiped out, and captives were skinned, scalped, burned, and dismembered by both sides. Three thousand Indians and 600 settlers were killed, and the head of Metacom, the Wampanoag leader known to the settlers as King Philip, was displayed on a pole in Plymouth for many years afterward.[19]

August 8, 1757: After being surrounded by overwhelming force, the British-American garrison of Fort William Henry in New York agreed to surrender its fort and weapons to the French in exchange for safe passage home. The native Abenaki allies of the French didn't like those terms, so they attacked the unarmed British column in the open, killing a couple of hundred of the easier targets—women, children, the sick, the wounded, and so on.

July 1778: A raid by Loyalists and Iroquois into the Wyoming Valley of Pennsylvania killed 360 settlers.[20]

November 4, 1791: Miami and Wabash Indians under Little Turtle attacked a column led by Arthur St. Clair in the Northwest Territory, killing 623 U.S. soldiers and two dozen civilian camp followers.[21]

August 30, 1813: Creek Indians of the Red Stick faction captured Fort Mims in Alabama and massacred up to 500 frightened white settlers and noncombatant Creeks of the rival White Stick faction who had taken refuge there.[22]

March 27, 1814: General Andrew Jackson's soldiers killed more than 500 Creek warriors in the Battle of Horseshoe Bend in Alabama.[23]

1837–38, Trail of Tears: President Andrew Jackson expelled all of the Indians still living east of the Mississippi River and herded them into new lands in the West. Because the Cherokee had recently lived in peace with the Americans and were still numerous and prosperous, they had much more to lose and were especially hard hit in this ethnic cleansing. Some 18,000 Cherokee were cast out of their homeland in and around Georgia, and at least 4,000, possibly 8,000, died of cold, hunger, exhaustion, or disease before they got to Oklahoma.[24]

August 18, 1862: Santee Sioux attacked small family farms up and down the Minnesota frontier, killing and mutilating 400 settlers in the opening raids. Altogether, some 800 settlers died as fighting continued over the next month. As punishment, 38 Indians were hanged in the largest mass execution in American history.[25]

January 29, 1863: California militia killed about 250 Shoshoni villagers, including 90 women and children, on Bear River in Idaho.

November 29, 1864: Colorado militia attacked a peaceful village on Sand Creek suddenly at dawn and massacred 163 Cheyenne.[26]

January 23, 1870: The U.S. Army attacked a village of Piegan Blackfeet in Montana, killing 173, including 90 women and 50 children.[27]

June 25, 1876, Battle of the Little Bighorn: While attacking a large Indian encampment, Custer's Seventh Cavalry was driven off, cornered, and wiped out by Sioux and Cheyenne. The toll was 267 U.S. soldiers killed.

December 29, 1890, Wounded Knee: A refugee band of Miniconjou Sioux, mostly women and children, had surrendered to the U.S. Army. While the prisoners were being disarmed, shots were fired. Confusion erupted, and everyone with a gun started using it, including army machine-gunners overlooking the refugees. When the smoke cleared, 128 (officially) or 300 (unofficially) Sioux and 25 U.S. soldiers were dead. It was the last major event of the Indian Wars.[28]

For those of you keeping score at home, that comes to:

Massacre or ethnic cleansing by whites against Indians: 7

Massacre or ethnic cleansing by Indians against whites: 4

War or battle in which the Indians badly beat the whites: 3

War or battle in which the whites badly beat the Indians: 2

This indicates that blatant atrocities outnumbered honest warfare by about two to one—and I'm using a *very* loose definition of honest warfare that includes taking no prisoners. Although the North American Indian Wars are too complicated to be explained in a short narrative summary, the most decisive turning point was 1815. Before then, the Indians were players in larger geopolitical conflicts between the French, British, Spanish, and Americans. This gave individual tribes powerful allies, protectors, and sponsors. After 1815, however, all of the white nations had settled their differences, and the Indians were on their own against the advancing Americans.

Amazonia

The Amazonian rain forest became the world's last haven for unassimilated Indians, but these tribes were largely destroyed in the twentieth century. Out of an original 230 surviving Indian tribes in Brazil in 1900, eighty-seven went extinct by 1957. During the same period, the Indian population of Brazil crashed from 1 million to 200,000.[29] The story for each tribe was usually the same. Some vital resource—gold, oil, rubber, hydroelectric potential—would be discovered deep in the jungle, and civilization would come crashing down on the local inhabitants in order to exploit it. The forest would be tamed and cleared, along with any animal or Indian life that got in the way.

Many of the Indians disappeared without any record, but some genocides happened recently enough to be well documented. The Ache Indians of Paraguay fell to repeated massacre, rape, and robbery when a new road was cut into their territory in 1968. The Yanomami on the border between Brazil and Venezuela were overrun by gold miners in the 1980s and devastated by new diseases, rape, gunfights, and the chemical runoff from mining, which poisoned the streams.

Distemper Tyrannis

European cruelties were responsible for only a fraction of the Indians who died during the conquest of the Americas. Disease took the rest. For centuries the large, intertwined populations of Eurasia and Africa had been exchanging diseases with each other across trade routes, giving the Old World races improved levels of resistance as generation after generation was naturally selected for those who could survive smallpox, measles, and influenza. The Native Americans, however, were biologically naive and totally susceptible. Entire villages died of these new diseases shortly after first contact.

Should we condemn the Europeans for these deaths by disease? It's a tricky moral point, and naturally you find partisans of all extremes.

On one side, you'll find the argument that most Indians died of disease, and disease isn't genocide, period. The defense rests.

> Stephen Katz: "When mass death occurred among the Indians of America . . . it was almost without exception caused by microbes, not militia . . . that is, this depopulation happened unwittingly rather than by design, even transpiring in direct opposition to the expressed and self interested will of the white empire-builder or settler."[30]

In fact, earlier generations saw the land as being swept clean by the hand of God to make way for the newcomers. Tragic, yes, but it was germs not men that killed the Indians. By this viewpoint, European resistance to disease was a manifestation of an innate superiority.

> Governor Winthrop of colonial Massachusetts: "God hath therefore cleared our title to this place."[31]

On the other hand, some writers want to blame the Europeans entirely for the disease that arrived with them. They accuse the Europeans of being unclean—physically, spiritually, and morally—and the diseases they brought with them would almost seem to be a symptom of thoroughly sick culture:

> David Stannard: "Roadside ditches, filled with stagnant water, served as public latrines in the [Spanish] cities of the fifteenth century. . . . Along with the stench and repulsive appearance of the openly displayed dead, human and animal alike, a modern visitor to a European city in this era would be repelled by the appearance and vile aromas given by the living as well. Most people never bathed, not once in an entire lifetime. Almost everyone had his or her brush with smallpox and other deforming diseases that left survivors partially blinded, pock-marked, or crippled."[32]

Most writers grudgingly accept that we can't really *blame* the Europeans for being immune to the diseases that killed the natives, but it's hardly playing fair, is it?

James Loewen: " 'One can only speculate what the outcome of the rivalry might have been if the impact of European diseases on the American population had not been so devastating. . . .' After all, Native Americans had driven off Samuel de Champlain when he had tried to settle in Massachusetts in 1606. The following year, Abenakis had helped expel the first Plymouth Company settlement from Maine."[33]

Jared Diamond: "Infectious diseases played a decisive role in European conquests . . . by decimating many peoples on other continents. For example, a smallpox epidemic devastated the Aztecs after the failure of the first Spanish attack in 1520 and killed Cuitl[a]huac, the Aztec emperor who briefly succeeded Montezuma. . . . The most populous and highly organized native societies of North America, the Mississippian chiefdoms, disappeared in that way between 1492 and the late 1600s, even before Europeans themselves made their first settlement on the Mississippi River."[34]

In many ways, it doesn't matter what killed the Indians because we usually add death by disease and famine into the total cost of wars and repressions anyway. Anne Frank died of typhus, not poison gas, but she's still counted as a victim of the Holocaust. The same standard should apply to the Amerindian population collapse, as long as the deaths occurred *after* their society had already been disrupted by direct European hostility. If a tribe was enslaved or driven off its lands, the associated increase in the number of deaths by disease would definitely count toward the atrocity; however, if someone merely sneezed on a tribe at first contact, it should not count.

Consider the Powhatans of Virginia. In the book *American Holocaust*, David Stannard claims that their population was 100,000 before contact, but European "depredations and disease" reduced this population to a mere 14,000 by the time the English settled Jamestown in 1607.[35] Now, let's be fair. Should we blame the English for 86,000 deaths that occurred before they even arrived? Stannard mentions pre-Jamestown depredations, but as far as I can tell, the handful of European ventures into the Virginia region before 1607 were too small to do much depredating. Until Jamestown, the Europeans usually got the worst of it. For, example, a small Spanish mission was wiped out by natives in 1571, and England's Roanoke Colony mysteriously disappeared around 1589.

If the Europeans had arrived with the most benign intentions and behaved like perfect guests, or if Carib mariners had been the ones to discover Europe instead of the opposite, then the Indians would still have been exposed to unfamiliar diseases and the population would still have been scythed by massive epidemics. In that case, society would regard it in the same category as the Black Death: bad luck.*

---

* Did the Europeans deliberately spread smallpox among the Indians? Most rumors of this appeared long after the alleged events. The only actual documentation of such a thing is an exchange of letters

That said, the mere fact that disease was the primary agent of death doesn't absolve the Europeans. Whatever reduced the residual 14,000 Powhatans of 1607 to just about zero definitely counts because by that time, English hostility and land grabs were taking their toll. In most of the atrocities listed in this book, starvation and disease did most of the dirty work but I still count them as atrocities. If I were to limit the tally to the number of deaths by direct violence, the Holocaust killed fewer than 3 million Jews, and the toll from the American Civil War wouldn't be high enough to make the list.[36]

How Many Died?

In 1542, las Casas estimated that the Spaniards had killed more than 12 million Native Americans and probably as many as 15 million in the first fifty years of contact. Despite five hundred years of additional research, that's still as good as any estimate that has followed.

A few other researchers have attempted to supply better numbers. In *American Holocaust*, Stannard estimates the total cost of the near extermination of the American Indians as 100 million dead. In *Statistics of Democide*, Rudolph J. Rummel suggests a range of 9,723,000 to 24,838,000 democides inflicted on the Native Americans before 1900, including 2 to 15 million during the Colonial Era.[37]

Usually, I prefer the median of all available estimates as my death toll. I figure that if I lined up all of our experts, and then started marking out the extremes—using the highest to cancel out the lowest, the second highest against the second lowest, eventually closing in on the center—I would have a number that is more defensible than one that stands alone at the upper or lower edge. The problem here is that there are only three reasonably authoritative estimates, all wildly different. Using the same trick I sometimes used for medieval Chinese estimates, I could decide to go with the geometric mean (14 million) of Rummel's absolute minimum (2 million) and Stannard's absolute maximum (100 million).

Can't we do any better?

The crux of the problem is that no one has the foggiest notion of how many Native Americans were around before the Europeans came along and began to both count them and kill them. As *The New York Public Library American History Desk Reference* puts it, "Estimates of the Native American population of the Americas, all completely unscientific, range from 15 to 60 million."[38] And even this cynical assessment is wrong. The estimates range from 8 to 145 million.[39] Most writers pick the estimate that best supports whatever

---

among British authorities in 1763 exploring the possibility of giving the enemy tribes blankets from smallpox patients. Whether they actually went through with this scheme is not recorded. A smallpox epidemic certainly hit the target Indians soon after, but the very fact that there were convenient smallpox patients in the hospital shows that the disease was already on hand, spreading through traditional human contact.

thesis they're pushing. The number of Indians is directly proportional to how destructive they want the Europeans to be.

For what it's worth, an estimate of around 40 million original inhabitants seems to be a popular choice among the authorities who aren't screaming from a soapbox.[40]

So how did I arrive at the 15 million in the heading of this chapter? I've assumed that the New World began with 40 million people, but after the Europeans arrived, the Amerindian population crashed and bottomed out at around 5 million.

The next step is to determine how many of these 35 million deaths should count as indictable killings resulting from violence and oppression, both direct (war, murder, execution) and indirect (famine, aggravated disease). Obviously, some were and some weren't. We can't apportion the death toll with any kind of certainty, but no matter how much I fiddle with the numbers, I can't get the indictable genocides much lower than 10 million or much higher than 20 million. I split the difference.[41]

GENOCIDE

WAS THE DESTRUCTION OF THE AMERICAN INDIANS GENOCIDE? WELL, the Indians were in the way, and the Europeans got rid of them. It became genocide in effect if not intent.

At almost every step of the way, powerful factions deliberately killed unassimilated Indians, and this troubled their consciences no more than clearing the forests or hunting down dangerous predators. Across most of the hemisphere, Europeans and Africans completely replaced the Amerindians, and even where the native gene stock has survived, their descendants adopted Western languages and religions.

The G Word

Since genocide is the worst accusation you can throw at a nation, every oppression gets called genocide at some point or another. Merely calling it a purge or massacre doesn't seem to be enough. Then, because genocide is such an insult, every accusation is vigorously denied, usually by insisting that the killing was a legitimate act of war, the death toll was lower, the enemy deserved it, or the deaths weren't deliberate. A long history of international law prohibiting the murder of civilians hasn't actually prevented the murder of civilians, but it has made us quite good at coming up with excuses.

After a half century of arguing about the meaning of *genocide*, the word has lost its sharp edges, but let's define it narrowly here to mean the attempted eradication of an ethnic group by violence. Let's further define ethnicity as a group identity you have no control over. You are born into it; you share it with your family, and it does not change no matter what may happen later in your life. Because *genocide* comes from the same root as *genetics*, common sense would indicate that genocide is the killing of a people based on their ancestry, not their religion, wealth, education, or political beliefs.

By this definition, the Nagasaki bombing, killings by the Khmer Rouge regime, and the Katyn massacre were *not* genocides—the Nagasaki bombing because surrender was an option, the Cambodia killings because they were political and within a single ethnicity, and the Katyn massacre (see "Joseph Stalin") because the scale was not large enough to count as "attempted eradication."

One defining characteristic of genocide is the single-minded devotion with which the oppressors eradicate the target group. The oppressors are not satisfied with killing just anyone who rises up and resists—they make it a point to hunt down and wipe out every man, woman, child, baby, and dog. If you belong to the target demographic, you will be killed no matter how much you beg for mercy; girls, however, are often spared, raped, and enslaved because they aren't important enough to be killed.

Taking revenge against an entire family for the crimes of one member doesn't count as genocide either, even though it often looks like it.

Notice that about half of the genocides listed below were successful. The target group was thoroughly eliminated and replaced by the perpetrators, at least in the regions under attack. Most of today's largest ethnicities have gotten where they are by wiping out their rivals. Other genocides were unsuccessful. The victims bounced back, and the only lasting result was the bitter memory of tens of thousands of senseless deaths.

Thirty-One Notable Genocides:

Native American Indians: 15,000,000 may have died at the hands of European conquerors.

Along with the collapse of the native population up and down the Western Hemisphere, hundreds of individual tribes simply disappeared:

> The Arrohattoc of Virginia were gone by 1669.
> The Apalachee of Florida died out in the 1700s.
> The Yazoo of Mississippi died out after 1729.
> The Powhatan language of Virginia went extinct in the 1790s.
> The Timucua of Florida disappeared shortly after 1821.
> Shanawdithit, the last known Beothuk of Newfoundland, died in 1829.
> During the 1870s, the Argentines wiped out the Araucanian Indians to open the Pampas to white settlement.[1]
> Ishi, the last Yahi of California, died in 1916.[2]
> The Clackamas of Oregon were gone by the 1920s.
> The Natchez language of Louisiana died out in the 1930s.
> The Catawban language family of the Carolinas went extinct in the 1960s.

The pattern of destruction for each tribe was much the same. The first white visitors were welcomed with cautious hospitality. Soon, contact with the Europeans infected the natives with catastrophic illnesses. Then whalers, soldiers, settlers, or miners raided the tribe for slave labor or supplies. The Indians stole horses, cattle, or tools. Thieves and trespassers were killed. The other side retaliated. Peace returned for a while. War followed that. Eventually, the local whites decided that the only solution was to remove the natives completely. Cooperative Indians were rounded up and sent away, while uncooperative ones were hunted down and killed. The few pitiful survivors were taken under the protection of a charity, where they were housed in a shed out back and taught to sing hymns. The last members of the tribe were considered a sad, drunken curiosity and were allowed to die without perpetuating their culture or bloodline.

Holocaust: 5,500,000 Jews were killed[3] (see "Second World War" for details).

Because the word *genocide* was coined in 1944 specifically to describe what Hitler was doing inside conquered Europe, this is the one event that counts as genocide no matter how you define it. In fact, most people use the word to mean any activity that reminds them of the Holocaust, regardless of whether the UN decides that activity fits its strict legal definition of genocide.*

Ukrainians: Around 4,200,000 were starved in 1932–33[4] (see "Joseph Stalin" for details).

The "terror famine" that Stalin created while restructuring Soviet agriculture fell most heavily on the Ukrainians, who insist that the Holodomor was an outright genocide directed specifically at them; however, this might be a good example of a brutal atrocity that was as bad as a genocide without actually being one.

Bengalis: 1,500,000 were killed by the Pakistanis in 1971.

Although everyone outside Bangladesh forgets about it, this is probably the deadliest genocide since the Holocaust.

---

* In the 1948 Convention on the Prevention and Punishment of the Crime of Genocide, the UN defines genocide as "any of the following acts committed with intent to destroy, in whole or in part, a national, ethnical, racial or religious group, as such:
  (a) Killing members of the group;
  (b) Causing serious bodily or mental harm to members of the group;
  (c) Deliberately inflicting on the group conditions of life calculated to bring about its physical destruction in whole or in part;
  (d) Imposing measures intended to prevent births within the group;
  (e) Forcibly transferring children of the group to another group."
Keep in mind that this definition was created for legal, not academic, purposes. It was enacted to enable prosecutions, not to understand the phenomenon.

For my purposes, the UN definition is too broad in theory (almost every conflict in history can be described as "intent to destroy, . . . in part, a national . . . group . . . [by] [c]ausing serious bodily . . . harm to members") and too narrow in practice (every decision to officially label an atrocity as "genocide" has to clear an almost hopeless number of political hurdles—only the Holocaust and the mass killings in Bosnia and Rwanda have been recognized by international courts as genocides).

Armenians: 972,000 were killed in 1915 (see "First World War" for details).

The Turks won't admit that they did this, and no one pressures them on it because Turkey is too important as a strategic and cultural crossroads between East and West. The Turkish version of events is that the Armenians revolted, got into ethnic fights with local Kurds, and slaughtered tens of thousands of Muslims before their rebellion was put down. The Turks explain away the million missing Armenians by claiming that they fled overseas after their defeat.

Tutsi: 937,000 were killed by Hutu in Rwanda in 1994 (see "Rwandan Genocide" for details).

Gypsies: 500,000 were killed from 1940 to 1945 (see "Second World War" for context).

Because the Gypsies had a reputation as congenital criminals, the Nazis classed them as subhuman and systematically exterminated them.[5]

Tibetans: perhaps 350,000 have been killed.[6]

Since the Chinese reconquest of Tibet in 1950, the People's Republic has systematically tried to eradicate the Tibetan people, to demolish their landmarks, and to erase their culture. Chinese immigrants have replaced the native Tibetans as the majority in most of Tibet's cities.

Serbs: 300,000 were killed[7] from 1940 to 1945 (see "Second World War" for context).

After conquering Yugoslavia in World War II, the Germans set up a puppet Croatian state under the native fascist organization, the Ustase. Not only did this puppet government happily cooperate with Nazi extermination programs directed at Jews and Gypsies, but they made a special effort to eradicate Serbs as well.[8]

Assyrians: maybe 275,000 were killed by the Turks,[9] starting in 1915 (see "First World War" for details).

Australian Aborigines: 240,000 vanished between 1788 and 1920.

In a phase of history that parallels the conquest of the Americas, the Aborigines (original population: probably 300,000,[10] possibly 750,000[11]) were caught in the teeth of white colonization and destroyed by violence, disease, and hunger. Only 60,000 were left by 1920. Maybe 20,000 Aborigines and 2,500 whites were killed directly by fighting.[12]

Chechens, Ingush, Karachai, Balkars, Kalmyks: 230,000 died in exile between 1943 and 1957 (see "Joseph Stalin" for context).

During World War II, Stalin uprooted entire nationalities that had been overtaken by the German advance because he didn't trust their loyalty. They were shipped off to the east, where hundreds of thousands died.

Asiatic Greeks: anywhere from 100,000 to 350,000 died at Turkish hands between 1919 and 1923 (see "Greco-Turkish War" for details).

Kurds: over 200,000 were killed during the 1970s, 1980s, and 1990s in several countries.

The Kurds spent most of the twentieth century as oppressed minorities in three nations—Iran, Iraq, and Turkey. The worst single period of genocide inflicted on them was in 1987–88, when Saddam Hussein had some 180,000 slaughtered in Iraq.

Darfur: 200,000 have died since 2003 (see "War in the Sudan" for details).

Carthaginians: 150,000 died in the fall of Carthage in 146 BCE.[13]

During the third and final war between Rome and Carthage, the Romans captured the mother city and burned it to the ground. They massacred the men and sold the women into slavery. Because merely killing and enslaving the entire population is just too ordinary, later legend added that the Romans plowed the land with salt so that nothing would ever grow there again.

Hutu: 125,000 were killed in Burundi in 1972–73[14] (see "Rwandan Genocide" for context).

East Timor: 102,800 died[15] between 1975 and 1999.

Indonesia invaded and conquered this former colony of Portugal, killing up to a third of the population.

Canaanites: maybe 100,000 were killed around 1200 BCE.

According to the Bible, the Israelites under the leadership of Joshua swarmed across the Jordan River into Canaan. Under direct orders from Yahweh, they systematically slaughtered the inhabitants of every town they took, beginning with Jericho. The Bible specifically mentions that all 12,000 residents at one city were killed, and then goes on to list eight more cities that were utterly destroyed in the same campaign.[16]

Dacians: as a rough guess, 100,000 may have been killed from 101 to 106 CE.

After conquering the homeland of these 800,000 people, the Romans emptied the land, hauled away a half-million captives, and replaced them with Roman settlers. Dacia ceased to exist, and the locale became "Romania," the Land of the Romans, with inhabitants that today speak an offshoot of Latin. The conquest is proudly illustrated in gory detail on Trajan's Column in Rome.

Guanches: all 80,000 were wiped out between 1402 and ca. 1520.

These native inhabitants of the Canary Islands have been called "the first people driven over the cliff of extinction by modern imperialism."[17]

Herero and Nama: 75,000 were killed from 1904 to 1907.

In putting down a rebellion in their colony of Southwest Africa (now Namibia), the Germans drove these tribes into the desert and nearly to extinction.[18]

Midianites: over 60,000 women and boys were killed around 1250 BC.

Under orders from Moses, the Israelites killed every man, boy, and married woman among the Midianites, leaving only 32,000 unmarried girls to be distributed as war booty.[19]

Trojans: 10,000?

Did it really happen? The legends tell us that when the city fell to the Greeks, old men (Priam) and young boys (Astyanax) were slaughtered, while women were either enslaved (Cassandra) or died in the sacking (Creusa).

Erie: maybe 5,000 were killed from 1654 to 1656.

This Indian tribe of the Ohio valley was wiped out by the neighboring Iroquois.

Tasmanians: 5,000 were killed after 1803.

In one of the most thorough genocides in history, every pure-blooded native of the island of Tasmania was hunted down and exterminated by white settlers. A handful lingered under the protection of charities, but the last one died in 1877.[20]

Greenland Norse: 3,000 died (?) in the early 1400s.

For several centuries, 3,000 to 5,000 Norse colonists lived on the coast of Greenland, but then without explanation, they were all gone—forgotten, dried up, and absorbed by the cruel northern wilderness. Although most modern scholars prefer to blame an act of God (a plague or a new ice age) or the victims themselves (a stubborn refusal to adapt to the harsh environment), the few remaining records clearly describe fights with hostile natives—Skraelings. In the fourteenth century, a Norse visitor, Ivar Bardarson, reported to the bishop of Bergen that "now the Skraeling have [destroyed] the whole of the Western Settlement. There are only horses, goats, cattle, and sheep all wild, but no inhabitants, neither Christian nor Heathen." Soon afterward the Eastern Settlement was under attack, and eventually visitors arriving from Europe found no survivors.[21]

Chatham Island: 2,000 died.

Maori invaders from New Zealand conquered this South Pacific island in 1835, killing, eating, or enslaving the native Moriori people. Only 101 Moriori were left alive by 1862, and the last pure-blooded Moriori died in 1933.[22]

Easter Island: 2,000 died.

In 1862, Chilean slave raiders kidnapped 1,000 native Rapanui, half the population, most of whom soon died. Disease, murder, and overwork further reduced the number of remaining natives to only 110 in 1877.[23]

Banu Qurayza: 600 were killed in ca. 624 CE.

Muhammad accused this tribe of Arab Jews of betrayal. All of the men were killed, and the women and children were sold into slavery.[24]

Melos: ca. 500 were killed or enslaved in 478 BCE.

The Athenians completely wiped out this Spartan colony during the Peloponnesian War. This is not the first genocide in recorded history, but it may be the first to be recalled with regret and shame by the perpetrators.[25] The ancient historian Xenophon reported that when the Athenians ultimately lost the war to Sparta, "there was mourning and sorrow for those that were lost, but the lamentation for the dead was merged in even deeper sorrow for themselves, as they pictured the evils they were about to suffer, the like of which they themselves had inflicted upon the men of Melos."[26]

BURMA-SIAM WARS

Death toll: "many millions"[1]
Rank: 54
Type: hegemonial wars
Broad dividing line: Burma (Myanmar) vs. Siam (Thailand)
Time frame: 1550–1605
Location: Southeast Asia
Who usually gets the most ~~blame~~ glory: Bayinnaung, Naresuan

A WEB OF LARGE RIVERS FLOW SOUTHWARD THROUGH THE JUNGLES OF the Southeast Asian mainland. Traditionally each river valley was the center of an ethnically and culturally distinct kingdom of rice paddies and pointy Buddhist temples. These were lands where the women wore colorful sarongs and the kings rode elephants. Listing them from west to east (left to right on a map), the Burmese live along the Irrawaddy River; the Karen and Shan, along the lower and upper Salween River; the Thai, along the Menam River; the Khmer, along the Mekong River. Beyond that is the Pacific coast, home of the Vietnamese. Upstream lie mountains and wilderness inhabited by barbarians.

There's more geography than that—including alternative names for everything—but that's enough to get through this chapter and most others set in Southeast Asia.

Burma Ascendant

An alien dynasty of Shan (mountain people from the border between Siam and Burma) had run Burma for many generations, until the native Toungoo dynasty threw them out. The first two Toungoo kings consolidated control over Burma and set up a new capital at Pegu. The third Toungoo ruler, Bayinnaung, spent his first year suppressing rebellions in the kingdom he inherited. Once that was settled, he attacked north and conquered all of the Shan states inland from the Burmese heartland. He systematically attacked in every direction, eventually establishing an empire that reached across inland Southeast Asia, from Manipur in the west to Laos in the east.

In 1567 Bayinnaung sent his army (said to number a million and a half) to take Ayutthaya, capital of Siam. The siege took two years and cost him a third of his force.[2] In the end, he reduced Siam to vassaldom and installed an allied Thai king, Phra Maha Thammaraja from the independent upriver city of Phitsanulok, on the throne of Ayutthaya, but he took the king's children back with him to Pegu as hostages in 1569.

Bayinnaung stiffened his army with Portuguese mercenaries, who had trouble pronouncing his name and called him "Braginoco." He is renowned as the most glorious empire builder in Burmese history, but the Burmese didn't get much of a chance to enjoy being masters of Southeast Asia because as soon as Bayinnaung died in 1581, Siam got *their* most glorious empire builder right next door.

Siam Ascendant

The Black Prince, Naresuan, son of the king of Siam, spent his youth as a hostage in Pegu to be executed if his father got out of line. Legend says he became the best friend of Bayinnaung's principal grandson, a boy his own age named Min Chit Swa; however, after many years of rivalry in various contests of strength, skill, and endurance, they had a final falling out when Naresuan's game bird beat Min Chit Swa's in a prestigious cockfight.

At the age of sixteen, Naresuan returned to Ayutthaya to rule as a vassal of Bayinnaung. Then in 1583, two years after the death of Bayinnaung, he declared himself sovereign and drove out the Burmese garrison. The Burmese army returned in full force under the crown prince, his childhood friend Min Chit Swa. Legend has the two of them fighting a climactic duel on war elephants. After the great beasts rammed and toppled each other, the two princes stood face-to-face with swords. The fight continued until Naresuan split Min Chit Swa in half from shoulder to waist. With their prince killed, the Burmese army broke and ran, leaving 200,000 men dead on the field.[3]

Naresuan's older sister, Princess Suphankalaya, had remained in Pegu as a hostage and member of the royal harem.[4] When news of Prince Min Chit Swa's death arrived, his grief-stricken and angry father, King Nanda Bayin of Burma, had her brought to him and killed, even though she was pregnant with the king's child.[*]

Naresuan invaded Burma several times during his reign, devastating the countryside and spreading famine. During his siege of Pegu in 1596, starvation drove the defenders to cannibalism, and King Nanda Bayin ordered all Siamese residents of the city butchered to feed the Burmese. Even as Pegu's population plunged from 150,000 to 30,000, Naresuan camped outside with dwindling supplies and lost 100,000 of his own soldiers to hunger. Eventually, he had to retreat before the city fell. By 1600, a Jesuit visiting Burma reported

---

[*] Nanda Bayin has become legendary for his dangerous mood swings. There are Internet claims (for example, Wikipedia and Snopes as of September 2008) that he literally died laughing in 1599 when a visiting Italian merchant told him that Venice was a kingdom without a king, but according to George Sale's *Universal History* (1759, vol. 7, p. 111), the hilarity of this discovery merely caused a coughing fit that "for some time hindered him to speak."

seeing "the ruins of gilded temples and stately edifices, lying along the banks of rivers; the roads and fields full of the skulls and bones of wretched Peguers, killed or famished; and their bodies thrown into the streams in such multitudes as to hinder the passage of vessels."[5] As Burma deteriorated and descended into civil war, Pegu was abandoned as the capital.

Meanwhile, Naresuan secured independence for the Shan as a buffer state against potential Burmese aggression. He and his brother had befriended the Shan prince of Hsenwi when all three of them were hostages in the Burmese court. The Siamese brothers were leading two columns of troops totaling 200,000 against the Burmese in Shan territory when Naresuan died, either covered in pustules from a skin disease (the Thai version) or rushing to save the life of the prince of Hsenwi in battle (the Shan version).[6]

FRENCH WARS OF RELIGION

Death toll: 3 million[1]
Rank: 30
Type: religious conflict
Broad dividing line: Catholics vs. Protestants
Time frame: 1562–98
Location and major state participant: France
Major non-state participants: Huguenot League, Catholic League
Number of Henrys: 4
Who usually gets the most blame: Catholics, Huguenots, Catherine de Medici

Reform

The late Middle Ages had been good to the Roman Catholic Church, which had become a transnational corporation that could stare down secular monarchs and make them blink. In addition to stirring up crusades, Rome could dodge taxes, force arrogant emperors to kneel penitently in the snow, and send out inquisitors to terrify the locals. They had armies of fighting monks such as the Templars, Hospitallers, and Teutonic Knights. Guilt-riddled noblemen had bribed God with tax-free donations of land, cash, art, and building funds. The details don't matter here. All you need to know is that by 1500, the Papacy was on top of the world.

With the flood of wealth and power, the Catholic Church had become monumentally corrupted, but it always managed to squash reform movements before they got out of hand. The Czech reformer Jan Hus was captured and burned at the stake in 1415. Although the English reformer John Wyclife died of natural causes in 1384 before the church could get its hooks into him, the church had his corpse dug up and burned a few years later to show its disapproval. Finally, one reformer, Martin Luther, survived its wrath, and the Reformation was launched in 1520.

With the door thrown open, people all across northwest Europe defected from the Catholic Church. Many monarchs took their countries out of the Catholic sphere and established new national churches tailored to local needs; however, the older, more powerful nations—France and Spain especially—had long ago forced the Catholic Church to share its wealth and power with the state. Now, as full partners with a stake in the well-being of the church, these monarchs had no reason to allow the Reformation to undermine its power. In these countries, dissenters had to meet in secret if they wanted to practice the newer varieties of Christianity.

Among the new reformers shouting back and forth across Europe was John Calvin, a Frenchman who was quickly chased out of that country to a safe haven in Geneva. Whereas Lutheranism was Catholicism after the auditors have been through—cleaned up, simplified, and adapted to local needs—Calvinism was Lutheranism squared—austere, populist, and decentralized. Called the Huguenots in France and the Puritans in England, Calvinists believed in the absolute sinfulness of man, which could be redeemed only by God's mercy. They denounced the frivolity and corruption of the human world and encouraged the godly to live in strict, smug holiness, without compromise.

Wherever Calvinism took root, civil war followed.

France on the Brink

International relations in western Europe at this time were simple: everyone hated his or her neighbor. Spain opposed France, which opposed England, which opposed Scotland. This made alternating countries into allies whose monarchs were occasionally married to each other. King Philip II of Spain was married to Queen Mary Tudor of England, while Prince (soon to be king) Francis of France was married to Mary, Queen of Scots. All of these monarchs were Catholic, although the population of Great Britain was mostly Protestant.

This unusual convergence of ruling queens—especially Catholic queens in countries that God meant to be Protestant—infuriated the Scottish evangelist John Knox into sounding *The First Blast of the Trumpet against the Monstrous Regiment of Women* in 1558. France was about to join the regiment.

The current French king, Henry II, hated "Lutheran scum." Crowned in 1547 at the age of twenty-eight, he had the political strength and will to keep his Protestant minority in line. With a young, healthy king raising four sons and three daughters, the future of Henry's Valois dynasty looked secure, but then King Henry had his eye socket pierced in a jousting contest in 1559. After lingering in agony for several days, Henry died, leaving France to his fifteen-year-old son, Francis.*

---

* A second outcome of Henry's jousting accident is that a few lines of mystic gibberish by an astrologer visiting at court seemed to have predicted it. This brought the author of the verse, who went by the name Nostradamus, instant fame as everybody scrambled to search his verses for other useful predictions such as winning lottery numbers.

First War

Like so many monarchs, King Francis II depended on his wife's family to help him maintain power. His queen, Mary Stuart of Scotland, was connected on her mother's side to the Guise family, powerful French Catholics.

In 1560, French Protestants hatched a scheme to kill as many Guises as they could and kidnap the king in order to force him to shed the remaining Guises. The Huguenots were so proud of their plan that they told everybody about it. When the coup was launched, the Guises were prepared. The conspirators were repelled and then hunted down, hanged, and dismembered, sometimes after a trial. The king and court watched fifty-two rebellious heads chopped off in the castle courtyard.[2]

Never healthy, Francis died in December 1560 after only a year on the throne. His ten-year-old brother, the quiet, melancholy Charles IX, took the crown, but Catherine de Medici, his mother and King Henry's previously subordinate wife, held the real power as regent. Catherine was the daughter of Lorenzo de Medici, the cold and cunning ruler of Renaissance Florence to whom Machiavelli had dedicated *The Prince*; however, she failed to learn from the master. Over the decades of her dominance, she hatched a series of clumsy schemes and weak compromises that steadily made the situation worse. On the plus side, Catherine was a trendsetter who introduced Italian novelties like forks, snuff, broccoli, sidesaddles, handkerchiefs, and ladies' drawers to the relatively frumpy nation of France.

In order to cultivate support among prominent Protestant families—the Bourbons especially—and to counteract the growing power of the Guise family, Catherine legalized Protestant worship, which annoyed the Catholic majority of France. She kept it on a tight leash, which annoyed the Protestant minority.

The wars began when another Francis, the duke of Guise, was passing through the town of Vassy and stopped at the local church to hear mass. Protestants were praying and singing at a nearby barn, which served as a church because the Crown forbade the Protestants from building real churches. A scuffle broke out between rival parishioners and drew in the duke's entourage. The fight escalated, and finally the Catholics ended up burning the Protestant barn and killing as many worshippers as they could catch.

Pretty soon Frenchmen of both religions were fortifying their towns and rushing militia into the region. The sectarian armies fought several pitched battles, but eventually, the duke of Guise was assassinated, and the leader of the Huguenots (Louis de Bourbon, prince of Conde) was killed in battle, which left both sides floundering and ready to negotiate. Gaspard de Coligny, an admiral who had served alongside Conde, emerged as the new leader of the Protestants.

Second War (1567–68)

The rivalry between France and Spain had intensified in 1494 when the heir to the Spanish throne married the heir of the house of Burgundy, uniting Spain with all of the territories that had caused the French kings so much trouble during the Hundred Years War (Burgundy, Flanders, the Netherlands). This put Spanish armies all around the edges of France. Then Calvinists in the Netherlands revolted against Spanish rule in 1567, pushing Spain and France toward a common front against Protestantism.

With the Huguenots jumpy, Catherine de Medici picked the wrong time to travel to Bayonne and visit her daughter Elizabeth, who had recently married the widowed King Philip II of Spain. To the Huguenots, this family gathering looked like scheming. It sparked a rumor among the Huguenots that the large new Spanish army that was moving to put down the Dutch Revolt was actually coming to assist the French Catholics in eradicating them.

The Huguenots launched a preemptive attack, trying to steal the king away from the Guises and keep him among the Protestants, but word leaked out, and the court reached safety. Six thousand Huguenot soldiers camped outside Paris—too few men to bring it under siege, but at Saint-Denis they beat 18,000 men of the royal army that came to chase them away. Even so, as the royal forces swelled to 60,000, the Huguenots pulled back and negotiated a cease-fire.[3]

Third War (1568–70)

Within a few months, royal forces tried to sneak up and surprise the Protestant leaders at home, but the Huguenots escaped north where they could connect with their Dutch and English supporters. The Guises made contact with Spain and set out to crush the Protestant strongholds across southern France. Although the Protestants took a beating in the ensuing war, the Crown couldn't afford to keep at it. Peace broke out in 1570 and the Huguenots were allowed to fortify and garrison four towns as safe havens in case of renewed Catholic aggression.[4]

Massacre of Saint Bartholomew's Day

Trying to patch things up, Catherine de Medici married her daughter Margaret to the highest-ranking nobleman among the Huguenots, Henry, head of the Bourbon house and king of the small kingdom of Navarre in the Pyrenees. Catherine de Medici also tried to bring Huguenots into the government, which of course infuriated the Catholics.

When everyone gathered in Paris for Margaret's wedding, someone tried to assassinate the military leader of the Huguenots, Gaspard de Coligny. As Coligny walked down the street, a sniper shot him from a window. No one really knows who planned it, but history has traditionally blamed Catherine. The wound was not serious, and it did nothing more than make the Huguenots angry.

Even though King Charles and his council had nothing to do with the assassination attempt, Catherine explained to them that now the Huguenots would retaliate, making a preemptive strike the only possible survival strategy. On the eve of Saint Bartholomew's Day, August 24, 1572, Guise and his men burst into Coligny's house and murdered him in his sickbed, while other death squads went hunting. In all likelihood, Catherine wanted only to decapitate the Huguenot cause by killing the leaders, but Paris exploded in hatred of the Protestants. Mobs all over Paris chased down any Huguenots they could find, killing anywhere from 2,000 to 10,000 of them by whatever means were handy. Adults were hanged, beaten, hacked, and stabbed; children were pitched out windows or into the river. Over the next few weeks, Protestants were massacred in other cities all over France, boosting the body count tenfold, into the neighborhood of 50,000.

The Bourbon leader and bridegroom, Henry of Navarre, survived only by converting to Catholicism on the spot. He was moved into the palace to be closely watched; his movements were restricted.

The Saint Bartholomew's Day Massacre horrified Europe. Even Ivan the Terrible in Russia denounced it. It changed the nature of the French Religious Wars from a gang fight to a war of extermination.

Fourth War

When war resumed, the king's younger brother, Henry, led a Catholic army to break the Protestant stronghold of La Rochelle. A fierce siege stretched for months, from 1572 into 1573. Sappers tried to undermine the fortifications and explode barrels of gunpowder, while artillery pounded the walls without effect. It started to look like the army outside the walls would run out of food and ammunition before those inside would. Then Prince Henry was elected king of Poland,* which gave him an excuse to lift the siege without losing face.

Fifth, Sixth, and Seventh Wars

King Charles had been haunted by guilt since authorizing the Saint Bartholomew's Day Massacre, and his health deteriorated. When he died in 1574 at the age of twenty-three,

---

* The nobility of Poland preferred to choose weak foreigners as their kings in order to keep any local family from gaining a political advantage. Catherine de Medici had lobbied to get her unemployed son this cushy job.

the throne went to his twenty-two-year-old brother, King Henry of Poland. Henry snuck out of Poland with the Polish national treasury hidden in his baggage train and escaped to Paris to accept his promotion.

The new King Henry III was Catherine de Medici's favorite and most intelligent son. He was a devout, cross-dressing Catholic who sometimes showed up at official functions in drag. Henry had an entourage of handsome young men called his Darlings (Mignons). He collected little dogs and hid from thunderstorms in the cellar.[5] Catherine unsuccessfully tried to tempt Henry into heterosexuality by offering him naked serving girls at special parties she arranged for his amusement, but that didn't work.

More dangerous, however, was Henry's intermittent tendency toward Catholic fanaticism when he sought atonement for his sexual eccentricities. At those times, Henry endangered his health with extreme fasting and mortification. Finally Catherine had the friend (and suspected Spanish agent) who encouraged her son in these rituals murdered in an alley.[6]

In the manner of most leaders facing civil wars all across history, everything King Henry did seemed to backfire. When the king restored freedom of worship for the Huguenots, Henry of Navarre took advantage of this new climate of legal tolerance to flee the court and reconvert to Protestantism once he was safely out of reach. Meanwhile Henry of Guise, angered at the king's weakness, formed an independent Catholic League with Spanish support.

King Henry III was running out of money, so the king summoned parliament in hopes of a tax hike. Parliament refused to raise taxes, but King Henry scraped up enough soldiers for a few small campaigns around the Loire River.[7]

Too Many Henrys

Because the current king was so very gay, the next king would probably not be springing from his loins. The succession pointed to the youngest Valois brother, Francis, but in 1584 he died of fever while plotting against Protestants in the Netherlands. With no further males descended from King Henry II, the law backed up to find some other direct male line branching off from an earlier king. When royal genealogists followed the new branch forward to find the senior-most descendant, it turned out that the next in line for the throne of France was the king's brother-in-law, Henry of Navarre, leader of the Huguenot Bourbon family.

Thus began the War of the Three Henrys, in which King Henry III and Henry of Guise tried to force Henry of Navarre to renounce his right of succession. Because the throne was at stake, the battles were especially bloody. Two thousand Catholics were killed at the Battle of Coutras, another 6,000 at the Battle of Ivry. The Huguenot losses were comparable, and neither side gained an advantage.

By now the endless wars had cut the population of France by 20 percent.[8] In a report home, the Venetian ambassador described the state of France after a generation of fighting: "Everywhere one sees ruin, the livestock for the most part destroyed . . . stretches of good land uncultivated and many peasants forced to leave their homes and to become vagabonds. Everything has risen to exorbitant prices . . . people are no longer loyal and courteous, either because poverty had broken their spirit and brutalized them, or because the factions and bloodshed have made them vicious and ferocious."[9]

The Catholic League hated King Henry for not crushing the Huguenots. As far as the league was concerned, a moderate Catholic was no better than a Protestant. It agitated the Parisian citizenry, who piled up barricades and drove Henry III from the city. In rural exile, the king was forced into calling parliament for advice on the succession. When parliament suggested an heir who was obviously a puppet of the Guises, King Henry decided to work out his problems with Guise once and for all.

Two days before Christmas, King Henry III invited Henry of Guise to stop by for a chat, but when Guise stepped in the room, the doors were suddenly slammed and bolted shut behind him. Soldiers rushed up; Guise drew his sword and fought gamely, but the king's soldiers still cut him down. His brother, a Catholic archbishop also visiting the king, was killed the next morning. They were cut apart and shoved into a roaring fireplace. The king then allied with the Bourbons against the Catholic League.

More War

Catherine de Medici died in 1589, and her last son followed shortly thereafter. In July of the same year, a Dominican friar angered by King Henry's betrayal of Catholicism stabbed him in the stomach. After Henry III's slow, lingering death from internal bleeding and infection, the Protestant Henry of Navarre became king of France. "I rule with my arse in the saddle and my gun in my fist," he declared and rode out to take his capital back from the Catholic League.[10]

The siege of Paris that began in May 1590 was brutal. For month after month, the 220,000 residents of the biggest city in Europe were locked inside with dwindling supplies. As time pressed on, dogs, cats, and rats disappeared from the streets. "Little children disguised as meat" showed up in the markets.[11] Before it was over, 40,000 to 50,000 Parisians had starved to death. Navarre bombarded the city with cannon from the high ground,[12] but in the end the city held and the siege was lifted in early September.

The Catholic League then called a parliament in Paris to pick a Catholic king to set up against Henry of Navarre, but when the Spaniards offered up their own princess, daughter of a Valois sister, many Frenchmen were appalled. It started to dawn on them that being French was probably more important than being Catholic. Maybe a Bourbon king was better than allowing France to become a Spanish satellite.

Suddenly, in 1593, Henry of Navarre, who had led the Protestant armies through many hard battles, announced that, well, if it really meant that much to them, he would go ahead and convert to Catholicism. He didn't want to cause a fuss.

"Paris is worth a mass," he is rumored to have explained.

This cleared the way for him to be a properly accepted and consecrated king, and before anyone could come up with any new objections, peace broke out. In 1598, King Henry IV issued the Edict of Nantes, declaring toleration for all Christian faiths. His new Bourbon dynasty wanted to start with a blank slate: "The recollection of everything done by one party or the other . . . during all the preceding period of troubles, remain obliterated and forgotten, as if no such things had ever happened." Or in the words of Monty Python's King of Swamp Castle, "Let's not bicker and argue over who killed who."[13]

RUSSO-TATAR WAR

Death toll: 500,000[1]
Rank: 70
Type: clash of cultures
Broad dividing line: Russians, Tatars
Time frame: 1570–72
Location: Russia
Major state participants: Crimean Khanate, Muscovy
Who usually gets the most blame: Tatars
Another damn: Mongol invasion

I N 1570, WHILE TSAR IVAN THE TERRIBLE WAS BUSY FIGHTING A WAR NEAR the Baltic, Tatars of the Crimean Khanate raided the southern borderlands of Russia and found them lightly defended. The next May, they launched a full invasion to plunder Russia for everything they could carry off. They looted and burned the towns and sent 150,000 residents southward into slavery.[2] The Tatars wiped out all of the small, scattered garrisons that Ivan had stationed there.

Arriving in the outskirts of Moscow, the Tatars set fire to the suburbs, and these individual fires fused and swept into the city. The inhabitants of Moscow fled in panic, crowding against the farthest gate of the city wall, pressing and trampling one another, compacting into a mass of corpses three layers deep. Others jumped into the river to escape the fire and drowned instead. The powder magazine in the Kremlin exploded.

The city was in ruins, and tens of thousands of people were dead. The Moscow River was choked with more bodies than it could hold, and it took more than a year to clear all of the corpses out of the city. For ten days, the Russian nobles were afraid to tell Ivan of the disaster.[3]

Finally, in July, Ivan's army caught up with the Tatars at Molodi, south of Moscow. The 60,000 Russians thoroughly defeated the 120,000 Tatars and deterred them from invasion for a long time to come.

THE TIME OF TROUBLES

Death toll: 5 million[1]
Rank: 22
Type: failed state, dynastic dispute
Broad dividing line: peasants vs. nobility
Time frame: 1598–1613
Location: Russia
Major state participants: Muscovy (Russia), Polish-Lithuanian Commonwealth, Kingdom of Sweden
Number of Dmitris: 4
Who usually gets the most blame: Russia's cutthroat nobility, Poland-Lithuania, Sweden, and Cossacks
Lesson learned: Always insist on seeing a photo ID before you proclaim someone emperor.

John the Fearsome

When it comes to insane tyrants, Ivan the Terrible is the standard against which all others are measured. He was short-tempered, superstitious, and erratic, and few of his inner circle outlived him. With the death of his father in 1533, Ivan became tsar of Russia at the age of three and spent the next ten years as a pawn of the boyars (noblemen). Over the course of Ivan's childhood, various close confidants were beaten to death, skinned alive, imprisoned, and starved by rival factions of nobles. His mother was poisoned. Ivan himself remained withdrawn and helpless, amusing himself by torturing dogs and cats. Finally, the thirteen-year-old Ivan asserted his authority and threw the top boyar, Prince Andrei Shuisky, to a pack of hungry hunting dogs.

For a while, Ivan's marriage to Anastasia Romanov calmed his erratic behavior, and his enlightened rule brought peace and prosperity to Russia for the first time in many years. Then, when Anastasia died, Ivan went fully mad. He accused the boyars of having poisoned his beloved Anastasia, and many were killed in revenge by slow and ingenious torture.

Among some of his more notable monstrosities, he killed one of his wives when he discovered she had lied about her virginity. He personally killed his eldest son and heir in a fit of anger. Ivan once accused the city of Novgorod of treason and started to systematically wipe out the inhabitants, day after day, week after week, giving his personal attention to many of the deaths, but then he changed his mind halfway into it and just went away. At one point in his reign, he tired of power and arranged to retire to a monastery, but no one believed it, and he soon changed his mind anyway. He empowered a special class of thugs, the *oprichniki*, to kill, rape, or steal with absolute impunity. Ivan died suddenly in 1584, and a Soviet-era autopsy revealed too much mercury in his system, suggesting that he was poisoned either by an enemy or by the mercury in the medicines commonly used at the time to treat advanced syphilis.[2]

The death toll of Ivan's reign is unknown—certainly tens of thousands, possibly a hundred thousand—but it doesn't qualify for my top one hundred list. Ivan concerns us only because when his mad reign was over, Russia's great families had been devastated, and the only sons to survive him were too young or feeble-minded to have attracted his anger.

The Last Real Dmitri

When Ivan died, the throne went to his simple-minded son Fedor. Always popular with the people, Tsar Fedor presided over sixteen welcome years of peace and calm. The real power in the land, however, was Boris Godunov, the brother of Fedor's wife Irina.

One potential glitch in the imperial succession was the existence of Fedor's younger half-brother Dmitri. He was the son of Ivan's fifth or maybe seventh wife (everyone lost track), but Eastern Orthodoxy allowed only three wives before they figured enough is enough, so there was some doubt as to whether Dmitri was illegitimate or not. It shouldn't have mattered, but Fedor and Irina were not producing children that survived.

Although Fedor was quite fond of Dmitri, Godunov found an excuse to exile Dmitri to the town of Uglich, about one hundred miles north of Moscow on the Volga River. Dmitri was already starting to take after his father and torture small animals. After a few years, in 1591, word came back to Moscow that nine-year-old Dmitri had died mysteriously of a cut throat. Rumor and Dmitri's mother fingered Godunov, and a rioting mob in Uglich lynched Dmitri's Boris-appointed guardian in anger.[3]

Godunov himself seemed authentically baffled by Dmitri's death. He secretly sent Vasily Shuisky, a young Russian nobleman, to investigate. Shuisky was no flunky of the court. He had only recently been released from prison, where he had been held for plotting against Godunov. He reported back that Dmitri had accidentally cut his own throat by having an epileptic seizure while playing with a knife, a story no one believed. Dmitri's mother was then stashed in a convent before she could complain.[4]

This left no obvious heirs, so when Fedor died in January 1598, the Rurik dynasty that had ruled Russia since the dawn of recorded history went extinct. In the shock that accompanied this terrible news, Boris Godunov stepped up and volunteered to be tsar. He gathered an assembly of compliant nobles who voted him into power. At first, his nation hated him because they suspected that he had done away with their beloved Dmitri. Then some Mongols invaded, and he drove them back from the gates of Moscow against all odds, so he was a hero. Temporarily.

The First False Dmitri

Around 1600, the dead Prince Dmitri reappeared, healthy and ready to take back his rightful throne. No one knows who this young man was, but it really doesn't matter. He's gone down in history as Dmitri, and that's good enough for now. After he attracted a large following, neighboring Poland took him under its wing and invaded Russia on his behalf.

By this time, the Russian people had forgotten the details of how Ivan the Terrible earned his nickname. All they remembered was that he had crushed the boyars without mercy, and the average Russian hated living under the oppressive thumb of the boyars. They also remembered that Ivan had gloriously attacked all of Russia's enemies, but they seemed to forget that his wars were costly and not always successful. Regardless, the Russians thrilled and rallied to the idea of a true son of Ivan coming to Russia's rescue.

Russia at the time was in the grips of a deadly famine as one bad harvest followed another, from 1601 to 1604. "Dead bodies were found with hay in their mouths and human flesh was sold in pies in the markets."[5] Boris started relief programs for the hungry in Moscow, and the cities were flooded with refugees. He also paid for burial shrouds for the dead when the food ran out. In Moscow alone, 100,000 died of starvation. Many considered the famine to be divine punishment of the usurper Boris.[6]

Dmitri's army fought a tough, bloody campaign toward Moscow, but he showed mercy to defeated enemies, while Boris's armies were prone to inflict cruel reprisals against communities that welcomed the pretender. Then, in April 1605, Boris fell ill and died. Some people say he was poisoned, but some people say that about everyone. His twelve-year-old son, Fedor, then inherited the cursed throne of Muscovy.

Almost all of the support for the Godunovs evaporated with Boris gone, so a popular uprising of Muscovites seized the Kremlin and imprisoned the royal family. As Dmitri took control of the city, Tsar Fedor II and his mother were quietly strangled in their cells.

Tsar Dmitri ascended the throne in 1605. Vasily Shuisky disavowed his earlier investigation into the Dmitri's death and signed off on the new official version, which was that Dmitri had evaded Godunov's assassins, who had killed a substitute child instead.

When Dmitri married the Polish princess Marina Mniszech in May 1606, too many Catholic Poles for Russian tastes attended the wedding. Orthodox Muscovites quickly soured on the imperial couple and their odious foreign entourage. Quarrels, fistfights, and riots escalated between the foreigners and natives in the capital. Finally, on May 17, a mob attacked the palace and burst into the tsar's bedroom. Dmitri broke his leg as he scrambled out of the window, and they shot him dead as he tried to hobble away. His carcass was dragged off by a rope tied around his feet and genitals, and then put on display for the people to poke with sticks. Dmitri was then buried, exhumed a week later, and burned. His charred corpse was blown from a cannon back toward Poland, where he belonged. During a general purge of Poles in the city, about 420 were killed and the rest were chased away.[7]

The Second False Dmitri

The leader of the assassination conspiracy was Vasily Shuisky, who had led the investigation of Dmitri's first death. He then became Tsar Vasily. In order to prove that the previous tsar had been an impostor, Tsar Vasily acquired the corpse of a young boy and declared it to be the real Dmitri from the grave in Uglich. He hauled it to the capital, and after the remains were credited with the requisite number of miraculous cures of lepers and cripples, Vasily bullied the church into declaring the boy to be definitely Dmitri, dead and a saint.[8]

In 1607, a well-educated drifter was jailed for impersonating a nobleman. Under torture, however, he recanted his claim of being that particular nobleman, and instead claimed to be the lost Dmitri. He was unchained, brushed off, and proclaimed tsar. The Poles arranged a mercenary army to carry him to Moscow. As the army won battle after battle, Russians hailed the return of Dmitri. Russian noblemen abandoned Tsar Vasily and joined Dmitri, but then, he was stopped short of his goal by Muscovite resistance.

Dmitri established a temporary court in the city of Tushino, a few miles from Moscow. The court of Tsar Vasily began to bleed supporters as more and more boyars moved from Moscow to Tushino. Trying to undermine support for the pretender, Tsar Vasily released Marina Mniszech, widow of the first false Dmitri, from prison on the condition that she absolutely not throw her support to the new Dmitri. For a while she complied, but as the winds shifted away from Vasily, she escaped to Dmitri's camp, where she publicly acknowledged him as her dead husband Dmitri, now recovered from his earlier injuries.

At this point, Shuisky arranged an alliance with the Swedes to rescue his failing throne.

I know what you're thinking: Swedes? The Volvo-driving, snowy blond socialists who hand out Nobel prizes and avoided both world wars? Those Swedes? This gives you an idea of how much Europe has changed since the seventeenth century when Russia was being kicked around by Poland and Sweden rather than vice versa, but both countries were much larger in those days. Sweden controlled most of the Baltic region, including Finland, Latvia, and Estonia. Poland was united with Lithuania, and it sprawled halfway into Belarus and Ukraine.

In any case, Poland took this open intervention by an outside state as an affront. For the Swedes to conspire behind the scenes was perfectly acceptable diplomatic practice, but actually sending an army into battle crossed the line. Now the Poles entered the fray officially and directly instead of hiding behind Dmitri. Their army crossed into Russia in September 1609 to break the alliance with Sweden and elevate a new Polish candidate to the Muscovite throne. This in turn undermined much of Dmitri's support, both among Russians (who blamed him for the Polish invasion) and among his Polish entourage (who left him and rejoined the real Polish army). Dmitri broke his camp at Tushino and retreated.

In the south, while Moscow was distracted by Dmitri, Cossacks pillaged unhindered. Cossacks originated as a mix of runaway Slavic peasants and Tatar renegades who formed into bandit gangs along the frontier between the European settlements and the nomadic herdsmen of the steppe. As the Time of Troubles progressed, their numbers were boosted by more and more Russian serfs running away to join the Cossacks with their free and easy lifestyle. Cossacks were hard to control in the best of times, but they were also a useful military buffer between the Christian (Polish, Russian) and Muslim (Turkish, Tatar) empires, so the European rulers allowed them a privileged autonomy. Unfortunately, their bandit nature came out during ages of chaos. We will meet them several times in this book.

In 1607, Cossacks were raiding around the lower Volga River. One of the younger Cossacks had visited Moscow once, so the other Cossacks decided that this qualified him to be tsar. They proclaimed him to be Petr, lost son of Tsar Fedor. The mere technicality that Fedor had no son, Petr or otherwise, was of no consequence. Rumor filled in the details. An army formed around him. Many Dmitrists joined to support "Petr," but the cruelty of Petr's Cossacks disillusioned many supporters.

Tsar Vasily Shuisky was overthrown in 1610 by a conspiracy of Russian nobles who turned Moscow over to the Poles. Vasily was forcibly tonsured and shoved into a monastery, which disqualified him from ever holding office again. Shortly after that, he was hauled off to Poland and imprisoned for the rest of his life. Meanwhile, at a new headquarters far away, Dmitri was assassinated while drinking mead on a sleigh ride. He had become increasingly bad-tempered and paranoid—scolding, beating, and killing his followers with unpredictable frequency. Finally one of his entourage, a Tatar prince he had once flogged, shot him and took his head as a souvenir.[9] The Russian throne remained vacant.

The Third False Dmitri

In 1611, a new Dmitri appeared. He spurned a Swedish offer of sponsorship and hooked up with the Cossacks instead. He was captured in May 1612, shackled, and dragged back to Moscow to be hanged.

Let's back up for a minute and trace the career of a second-tier nobleman who had drifted in and out of various court intrigues. Fedor Romanov was the nephew of Tsar Ivan the Terrible's beloved wife Anastasia, and first cousin to the simple-minded Tsar Fedor. A victorious general who fought the Swedes on behalf of Tsar Fedor, Fedor Romanov was purged from power and exiled to a monastery as Brother Philaret when Boris Godunov got the throne. When the first false Dmitri was swept into power by popular revolution, Philaret was allowed back into the world, but, trapped by his monastic vows, he could reinsert himself into Russian politics only as a clergyman. He rose in rank with each passing pseudo-Demetrius, but when Dmitri number 2 fell in 1610, Patriarch Philaret was hauled off and imprisoned in Poland. The main reason this concerns us is because it left his teenage son, Michael, as the leader of the Romanov clan.

Russia by this time was split in three. Moscow and westward were held by the Catholic Poles. Novgorod and the north were occupied by the Protestant Swedes. The rest belonged to anyone who had a local force powerful enough to hold against everyone who challenged them. Both the Swedish and the Polish royal families were now hoping to put their own unemployed princes on the throne of Russia. This in turn threatened to drag Russia into the religious wars of Europe; however, in 1612, a Russian militia out of the city of Nizhni Novgorod drove the Poles out of Moscow, giving the Russian people a brief window of opportunity to set their own destiny.

Boyars from all across Russia quickly gathered for a conclave in Moscow in 1613. The ambitions of the Swedes and Poles canceled each other out, and the Russians succeeded in setting a vital ground rule for the conference: the new tsar, whoever he might be, had to be an authentic Russian. They chose Michael Romanov, the sixteen-year-old son of the Patriarch Philaret, to be the new tsar, beginning a dynasty that would last until the Russian Revolution in the twentieth century. Moscow had been so ravaged by repeated conquests and riots that Tsar Michael ruled from far away, at Orthodox Christianity's holiest monastery, the Trinity–Saint Sergius, until Moscow could be rehabilitated.

Marina Mniszech, widow of two false Dmitris, had been trying to put her baby son Ivan* on the throne as the true heir of Tsar Dmitri, but as Michael Romanov began to consolidate his hold over Russia, jittery locals expelled her from her haven in Astrakhan before the tsar's armies arrived. She fled into the wilderness, toward the protection of some sympathetic Cossacks; however, she was intercepted by unsympathetic Cossacks who sold her back to Moscow. The boy Ivan was executed, and Marina died in prison within a year.

So What the Hell Happened?

The Time of Troubles is just one mystery after another. For starters, how did Ivan the Terrible die? Originally, he was said to have dropped dead during a chess game, but the mercury found in his system has been interpreted as the result of either assassination or accidental poisoning. It's also possible that the mercury level, though high, was not enough to kill him, and he died of something else entirely. If his death was murder, Godunov is a favorite suspect. His motive is sometimes given as a preemptive strike against his paranoid

---

* God only knows who his father was.

master, although the more colorful story is that Godunov had burst in and stopped Ivan while he was raping Irina, Godunov's sister and Fedor's wife.

How did Tsarevich Dmitri die? There's the official story (running with scissors, or whatever), the common rumor (murdered by Boris Godunov), and the later official story (escaped Godunov's assassins to become Tsar Dmitri). Two other explanations sometimes surface: suicide (the church originally buried him as such) and murder, by enemies of Godunov in order to frame and discredit him (suggested by the historian Chester Dunning).[10] Let's also consider the possibility that he was murdered for entirely nonpolitical reasons, but instead because he was turning into an extremely unpleasant "little monster" (Dunning's words).

Who was the first false Dmitri? Many accounts of the Time of Troubles answer this question with more certainty than the evidence permits. It is common for the first pseudo-Dmitri to be positively identified as Grigory Otrepiev, a defrocked and debauched monk. The beleaguered Tsar Boris first spread this identification, based on political necessity rather than actual evidence. *Boris Godunov*, both Pushkin's play and Mussorgsky's opera, in which Otrepiev is a major character, popularized it. Other suggestions include the illegitimate son of a former Polish king, or a child raised by an ambitious clan of boyars to believe he really was Dmitri, a conspirator in a Polish or Jesuit plot, or the real Tsarevich Dmitri as advertised.[11]

When we try to identify the second false Dmitri, we can at least rule out a couple of candidates. Everyone nowadays agrees that he didn't look like the first false Dmitri, and no modern historian has ever seriously suggested that the original Tsarevich Dmitri was still alive by this time. He was either a priest's son or a converted Jew or someone else entirely.

We forget the certainty that the modern world has brought to our lives. Until the development of reliable biometrics, especially fingerprints, in the late nineteenth century, there was no way to positively identify a person. Without photography, only fading memories and inaccurate drawings would be available for reminding us of someone's appearance. A person could disappear from one community and easily become someone new somewhere else. Slaves and criminals were often scarred, branded, or mutilated so they couldn't pretend to be something else, but a free man could, with luck and the right attitude, reinvent himself without all of the bureaucratic paperwork that follows us around nowadays.

Properly identifying a cause of death is a modern phenomenon as well. Life and death have always been the great mysteries, especially how we go from one to the other. For most of history, medical science was so primitive that unless the deceased died in the middle of a battle or with his head on the chopping block, he probably had only a few vague symptoms—fever, nausea, delirium—that could point to anything. When a person simply sickened and died, there was no telling what had killed him—dangerous miasmas, planetary influences, eating too many cherries with chilled milk, or standing in the rain without a hat. Because every person worth noting in history books has had enemies who wanted him dead, poison has been suspected in virtually every nonviolent death across history.

Rather than getting bogged down in the messy details of who killed whom, it might be more useful to step back and see the Time of Troubles as a massive peasant revolt. A powerful tsar was the only counterweight capable of lifting the oppressive fist of the boyars off the Russian people. The Rurik dynasty, for all its faults, had been divinely ordained to protect Russia from her enemies, foreign and domestic. When the Ruriks went extinct, the boyars saw it merely as an opportunity to elevate their own candidates to the throne (Godunov, Shuisky). The ordinary Russians, however, could not accept that God would allow his chosen line to die out. In the end, they simply refused to believe it, and they invented the heir they needed.[12]

THIRTY YEARS WAR

Death toll: 7.5 million
Rank: 17
Type: religious conflict
Broad dividing line: Protestants vs. Catholics
Time frame: 1618–48
Location: Germany
Major state participants: Bohemia, Brandenburg, Denmark, France, the Palatinate, Sweden, and Saxony vs. Austria, Bavaria, Spain, and Saxony, which switched sides
Quantum state participant: Holy Roman Empire
Who usually gets the most blame: Catholics, Calvinists, Hapsburgs, France, mercenaries

Neither Holy nor Roman nor an Empire

The Holy Roman Empire began as a medieval attempt to reunite Christendom, but by the Early Modern Era it was just a patchwork of little countries all bundled together into a nominal whole. At the start, it had encompassed diverse lands throughout central Europe that spoke Czech, Dutch, French, German, and Italian, but by the seventeenth century, it had eroded at the edges and was mostly just Germany. In theory, all of the little kings, dukes, bishops, and counts in Germany owed allegiance to the emperor, but in practice, less so.

The Thirty Years War was not the first holy war to rip through Germany after the Reformation. In the first wave of Lutheranism, many princes of Germany had seized all of the tax-free estates that the church had accumulated during its centuries of privilege. Frequent Anabaptist peasant revolts also swept the region only to be brutally suppressed by the authorities of both religions.* Finally, a major war ended in 1555 with the Treaty

---

* Anabaptism is exactly the kind of Christianity you would expect from peasants. It preaches equality, peace, simplicity, sharing, and other ideas that appeal to people on the bottom of the social pyramid. Obviously the authorities can't allow dangerous notions like this to spread. Anabaptists are rare today. We met them in an earlier chapter as the Mennonites, one of the first groups to speak out against slavery. Only a million or so Mennonites exist worldwide.

of Augsburg, which established a new balance by allowing German princes to select any religion they wanted, as long as it was either Catholic or Lutheran.

By tradition, the Holy Roman Empire was ruled by one of the Hapsburgs, a family based in Austria that had married into a vast collection of holdings scattered all over Europe. As the old emperor tottered into the twilight of his life without a son, the Hapsburg family began to line up his replacement. Eventually, palace intrigues settled on Archduke Ferdinand of Styria as his heir. Bit by bit, Hapsburg lands were transferred to Ferdinand's control. While the old emperor had been forced into compromises with the Protestants under his rule, Ferdinand had been raised by Jesuits and took a hard line in support of Catholicism. In Styria, his home fiefdom, he gave the residents a simple choice: be Catholic or get out. One-third of the residents fled. As he took more Hapsburg possessions under his control, he insisted on religious conformity in larger parts of the empire.[1]

The Defenestration of Prague

Although tradition gave the empire to the Hapsburgs, the law put the official choice of Holy Roman Emperor in the hands of seven electors. Three electors were archbishops who naturally supported the Catholic Hapsburgs. The remaining four votes belonged to secular rulers of small countries within the empire—Brandenburg, Saxony, the Palatinate, and Bohemia. The first three of these had converted to Protestantism and might have preferred a Protestant emperor who would protect their interests. The remaining vote belonged to the traditionally Catholic king of Bohemia, a position that had become one of the heirlooms that passed along the House of Hapsburg. As you can see, the Catholics had the election locked up with 4 votes to 3.

Although the Hapsburgs were Catholic, the general populace of Bohemia had become Calvinist. Bohemia, like the empire itself, was an elective monarchy, but when the Bohemian nobility gathered in Prague to rubber-stamp the new Hapsburg as their king, they began to wonder if maybe a fellow Protestant might be a better choice. They tried to get a renewed guarantee of religious freedom from Ferdinand, but on May 23, 1618, negotiations broke down—badly. The Bohemians tossed the Hapsburg officials out the window into a dung heap and chose Frederick, the Calvinist elector of the Palatinate, to be king. In one stroke, the House of Hapsburg had lost its only electoral vote, and Count Palatine Frederick now had two votes of his own, plus the theoretical backing of the other two Protestant electors, which made a majority.

The Bohemian and Danish Phases

In practice, the other Protestant princes of the empire were not about to risk everything in support of the Count Palatine, so they cast their votes for the Hapsburg Ferdinand and left

Bohemia to its fate. A Catholic army led by the Bavarian general Johannes Tilly set out to reclaim Bohemia and punish the rebellious Protestants. A scorched-earth policy of vengeance reduced Bohemia to a smoking wasteland. Of the 35,000 villages that had existed before the war, only 6,000 remained after the destruction. The population plummeted from 2 million to 700,000 as peasants starved or fled the onslaught of armies.[2] Finally, the Battle of White Mountain in November 1620 dealt a crippling defeat to the Palatine forces. King Frederick was chased away, and Albrecht von Wallenstein was installed as the Hapsburg's military governor of Bohemia. The ringleaders of the rebellion were executed in Prague's town square. The devastated estates of the rebellious nobles were confiscated and allocated to Hapsburg loyalists.

Then the Catholic armies turned against the Palatinate to punish Frederick for trying to take Bohemia away. His principal city, Heidelburg, was taken and looted, while Frederick fled into exile in Holland. The Hapsburgs gave the Palatinate to their ally, the Catholic duke of Bavaria. This scared the other Protestant states into action. While they had been willing to sit back and let the Catholics restore the status quo in Bohemia, the erasure of the Palatinate was not part of the deal.

As Protestant fortunes ebbed, outside kingdoms were called in to support the Lutheran side. King Christian of Denmark led his army into Germany in 1625, but it was badly beaten by the Catholic army of Wallenstein, while Tilly crushed a new army assembled by the Protestant princes of Germany. The Catholics then rolled over northern Germany and peninsular Denmark. The Danes fled to their islands, saved only by the lack of any imperial fleet in the Baltic.

Riding the high tide of victory, Austria set out to undo the Reformation. Their 1629 Edict of Restitution ordered that all of the property seized by Protestant princes from the Roman Catholic Church in the past seventy-seven years had to be returned to the church. Calvinism was outlawed throughout the empire.

Swedish Phase

With imperial armies marching and camping along the Baltic Sea, the Hapsburgs were now encroaching on Swedish turf. First Sweden boosted its army threefold thanks to subsidies from the French, who did not want to see a Holy Roman Empire that actually functioned as an empire. Then the Swedes crossed the Baltic and took to the field in July 1630.

Students of military history know this phase of the war as the era of Gustavus Adolphus, energetic king of Sweden and legendary military genius. Having already proved his mettle in a string of wars against Denmark, Russia, and Poland, he was turning into one of those legendary warlords like Frederick the Great and Napoleon who fought battles like a chess master.

In the spring of 1631, a Catholic army under Tilly tried to crack the Protestant fortress city of Magdeburg, which guarded the crossing of the Elbe River. After a lengthy siege, the city was taken and utterly destroyed. Of the 30,000 inhabitants, no more than 5,000 survived the sack, mostly women who were dragged away by the soldiers for later use. The city burned for three days, leaving a nightmare scene of carnage: "The living crawling from under the dead, children wandering about with heart-rending cries, calling for their parents; and infants still sucking the breasts of their lifeless mothers."[3] Six thousand bodies were dumped into the river as part of the cleanup for Tilly's triumphal entrance.[4]

In September 1631, Gustavus Adolphus inflicted a major defeat on the Catholics at Breitenfeld, pushing the war away from the Protestant north into the Catholic south. The Swedish victory put the Protestants back in the game and kept peace from breaking out eighteen years too early. In the spring, the Swedes beat the imperial army again, killing Tilly in the process. Finally, in November 1632, Gustavus scored his greatest triumph against Wallenstein in the Battle of Lutzen, but he was killed while scouting too far ahead of his line. The Catholics got a chance to catch their breath.

The death of Gustavus Adolphus stalled the renewed Protestant momentum, but Wallenstein held back from taking advantage of this change in fortunes. Instead, he began to play his own game, opening tentative negotiations with the enemy and fighting them only when they proved reluctant to take his offers seriously. He was clearly angling to bypass the Hapsburgs and put himself in charge of Germany. The emperor got wind of this and enlisted a couple of Wallenstein's senior officers to assassinate him.

Style of War

The backbone of an army during the Thirty Years War was an integrated block of musketeers and pikemen. The pikemen used long spears to hold the enemy at a safe distance while the musketeers killed them. To break a block of infantry, squads of horsemen in steel armor would ride up, fire pistols into the mob, then wheel about and trot out of range to reload. These tedious assaults were repeated over and over, usually without much impact. Artillery at the time was large and cumbersome, and cannoneers might still be arriving and setting up by the time the battle ended.[5]

Gustavus Adolphus changed all that. He reduced the size of field cannon and made them light enough to be deployed more quickly in battle and to break apart the big blocks of infantry. He also trained his cavalry to attack at a gallop with lances and sabers; he stretched his infantry into a line instead of a block to make it less susceptible to bombardment from cannon, and used his pikemen offensively. The Battle of Breitenfeld was the first victory for these new-style formations, which would dominate the battlefield for the next two centuries.[6]

Uniforms were uncommon in armies of the Early Modern Era, and most soldiers dressed like ordinary tradesmen in sturdy, comfortable work clothes, supplemented by whatever armor, kit, or ornamentation they could scrounge. The only way to tell friend from foe was by the giant battle flags each unit carried. Every army was trailed by a mob of women to cook, launder, and nurse. Gustavus Adolphus and many Calvinist generals insisted that these women be exclusively the wives of soldiers. Camp followers have since earned a reputation as nothing but prostitutes, but they were much more, and no army could survive without them.

Armies on independent operations numbered maybe 10,000 to 20,000, although they would sometime coalesce into forces two or three times that size for big battles. They were generally assembled from mercenary units that were hired and discharged as a group. The individual soldiers owed their primary allegiance to their captain, not to whichever prince had hired them, and they might freely switch sides if the pay was better or if they were taken prisoner. The only military personnel that most nations had on full-time salary were the palace guards and a few staff officers who knew where to hire mercenaries in a hurry—usually Scotland, Italy, and Switzerland. Unemployed mercenary units tended to stick around and live off the land while waiting for another government to hire them.

About 350,000 soldiers died in the Thirty Years War,[7] but civilian deaths outnumbered these by 20 to 1. Compare that to World War II, where civilian deaths outnumbered military deaths by a mere 2 to 1 even though the extermination of peoples and the destruction of cities was open policy. How was it possible for so many civilians to have died in the Thirty Years War when the number who died in the Sack of Magdeburg, 25,000, stands out as uniquely horrible? Simple. Armies lived off the land.

Seventeenth-century Europe was extremely rural, and most people lived off what they grew themselves. Farmers produced a slight surplus to sell in market towns, so only a few tradesmen in any community could survive without growing their own food. Introducing an army into an area disrupted this delicate balance of producer and consumer. It was like the spontaneous eruption of a brand new town inhabited entirely by 15,000 hungry but unemployed hoodlums. They confiscated food, slaughtered the livestock, abused the women, and ripped apart buildings for firewood. Afterward, they destroyed any leftovers or surplus to keep them out of enemy hands. Every army, both friend and foe, left starving peasants in its wake.

Desolation was everywhere. Jesuits investigating the smoking ruins of Eichstatt found unclaimed children in the cellars, eating rats, so they bundled them up and carried them away to feed, house, and educate them. An English ambassador reported arriving at the deserted town of Neunkirchen and finding one house burning and two bodies in the street but no one else. As he traveled farther he found more ghost towns; Neustadt was "pillaged and burnt miserably"; at Bacharach, the starving people were found dead with grass in their mouths.[8]

Columns of refugees were thinned by starvation and the plague, and they were barred from entry into one town after another. In cities that accepted refugees, the citizens stepped over fresh bodies every morning. Eventually refugees would be expelled—7,000 from Zurich, for example—because there was no food or room for them. Often the only available food was taboo. At one gypsy camp, feet and hands were found in a cauldron. Near another town fresh human bones were found, flesh scraped away, cracked for the marrow. Fresh corpses disappeared from graveyards.[9]

As if war and famine weren't enough, witch burning peaked around the time of the Thirty Years War. The bishop of Wurzburg is said to have burned 9,000 witches between 1625 and 1628. A thousand were burned in the Silesian principality of Neisse in 1640–41.[10] Contrary to common perception, the great witch hunts were not a relic of medieval superstition and ignorance. They grew mostly from the passions inflamed by religious conflict in the Early Modern Era. Over the centuries of holy wars, communities all across Europe rooted out and exterminated the dangerous infidels among them, both real (Protestants, Catholics) and imagined (witches, demons).

French Phase

Like most big, messy civil wars throughout history, the war in Germany was sucking in all of the neighboring states, and it eventually became part of a larger contest between the two alpha nations of Europe at the time, Spain and France. Spain was run by a side branch of the Hapsburg family, and its holdings included Belgium, Burgundy, and about half of Italy. Spain was willing to assist its Austrian cousins in crushing their Protestant enemies in Germany, but in exchange they wanted Austrian assistance in crushing the Protestant enemies of Spain in the Netherlands. The French, being natural enemies of Spain, subsidized all of the enemies of the Hapsburgs, regardless of race, religion, or national origin.

The Swedish army designed by Gustavus Adolphus continued scoring victories on autopilot for the next few years, until the empire smashed them at Nordlingen in 1634. Since the Scandinavians had failed to win the war in Germany, the French now intervened directly. Although they were Catholic, the French feared the emergence of a strong united Germany (on their eastern border), dynastically linked to Spain (on their southern border), which had armies in the Netherlands (on their northern border). In fact, the intervention of the French into the Thirty Years War in 1634 represents probably the exact moment that the Age of Religious Wars ended, and Europe went back to fighting wars just for the heck of it.

Although the Swedes continued fighting throughout the center of the empire, the focus of the war now shifted to the Spanish Road, the path of possessions and allies that Spain used to move troops from the Mediterranean and the Catholic mercenary recruiting grounds in Italy, across the Alps and down the Rhine to the battlefields in the Spanish Netherlands (now Belgium). Cardinal Richelieu, the chief minister of France, set out to break this pathway once and for all, but it was a hard war. With annual convoys of silver steadily arriving from mines in its New World colonies, Spain was the only country in Europe capable of maintaining a full-strength, full-time national army.

War sputtered through the Rhineland for a few years as French-subsidized German and Dutch armies harried the Spaniards, and small French forces nibbled at the southern border of the Spanish Netherlands. Finally, in 1643, a French army that had been built up to Spanish standards cornered and destroyed the main Spanish force at the Battle of Rocroi. It took a full day of grim and systematic killing, but when it was done, the Spanish army was in no condition to lend soldiers to its Austrian cousins. Spain needed to keep its remaining forces close to home to keep the advancing French at bay.

Results

Estimates of the number killed in the Thirty Years War have been falling over time. Shortly after the war, it was said that Germany was almost depopulated, and that over 12 million inhabitants, or three-fourths of the population, had disappeared. Then, as historians studied church, tax, and court records, they often discovered that the people who had disappeared from one section of Germany turned up somewhere else, alive and well—or at least alive. By the 1930s, the preferred estimate was that one-third of the population, or 7 to 8 million people, had died.[11] An estimate that has become popular in the past few decades gives a death toll of half that—3 or 4 million.[12] Even so, the middle estimate is still the most common. This would make the Thirty Years War the deadliest event ever to hit Germany, killing more Germans than the two world wars combined.[13]

The final Treaty of Westphalia signed in 1648 made a lot of adjustments to the borders and relationships among the princes of Germany, but most of those have faded into irrelevance. It was a long time ago, and you don't have to worry about them. The most long-lasting outcome of the Thirty Years War is that Europe finally realized how stupid it was to fight over religion. In less than a century, religious conflicts had devastated France, Germany, England, and Holland. Eventually, many exhausted nations decided to allow the choice of faith to be a private matter, and this became one of the cornerstones of Western Civilization.

Nowadays fighting over religion is considered so ridiculous that many Western historians are too embarrassed to admit it even happened. It's like having a great-grandfather who owned slaves. Probably half of the historians in recent generations have preferred to describe the Wars of Religion as secular power struggles hiding behind a pretense of religion; however, this projects modern sensibilities backward onto the past. Most human societies don't separate religion from public policy. Belief governs how people act. Religion structures their society and guides their decisions. Doubting the nation's religion is an insult against the core values of the nation, and impiety risks annoying whichever god watches over the people. Western Civilization is unique in making religion a private matter, and this is based on the hard lessons learned in the era of religious wars.[14]

COLLAPSE OF THE MING DYNASTY

Death toll: 25 million
Rank: 5
Type: failed state
Broad dividing line: every man for himself
Time frame: 1635–62
Location: China
Who usually gets the most blame: two rebels (Li Zicheng and Zhang Xianzhong), a rogue general (Wu Sangui), and Dorgon the Barbarian
Another damn: Chinese dynasty collapsing

T O MANY IN THE WEST, THE MING DYNASTY IS KNOWN PRIMARILY FROM slapstick comedy as producers of expensive and fragile vases, but historically they were producers of fine everything—porcelain, silk, art, and poetry. Although nowadays it's considered bad manners among historians to pass judgment on the past, the Ming ("Brilliant") dynasty is widely considered the peak of Chinese civilization. It was the most culturally and technologically advanced era before the Europeans interfered, and the last time China was ruled by an ethnically Chinese emperor.

Den of Thieves

Li Zicheng had trouble finding the right career before he settled on warlord. After a childhood spent herding sheep, he worked awhile in a wine shop; then he apprenticed to an ironworker. Later, he was laid off from a job as a post-station attendant. Finally, in 1630, he signed up with the Chinese army.

At the time, north China was in the grips of a deadly famine. Even the army was living at the edge of starvation, so one day, when supplies failed to arrive as scheduled, Li Zicheng's unit mutinied and went into business for itself as bandits. The government eventually captured several of the renegades—Li among them—in 1634. They worked out a deal to go back to duty with the frontier army, but then the local magistrate went ahead and executed thirty-six of the rebels. Li and his men struck back and then took to the hills.

Many bandit gangs infested the Chinese foothills in those days, and the bigger ones were virtually sovereign. Eventually Li Zicheng became the crime boss of three provinces in the highlands that backed up against the northern edge of the Tibetan plateau, stretching from the Yangtze to the Great Wall. He was called the "Dashing King," not for being especially debonair, but for the speed of his attacks.

Li squabbled with other bandits as much as he did with the authorities. Several of the gangs looted the Ming dynasty's tombs and imprisoned the attendants. As they were splitting the loot, Li demanded the eunuch musicians as part of his share, and the rival rebel Zhang Xianzhong complied but smashed all of the instruments just out of spite. Li then spited Zhang one better and killed the musicians.[1]

Zhang Xianzhong had also turned to banditry during the famine of 1628. He marauded a bit and then moved into the big inland valley of Sichuan, where he took Chengdu, the provincial capital, with a general slaughter of the population. He was known by the nickname "Yellow Tiger." Eventually, Li and Zhang made a deal that split China between them.

Li Zicheng set out to expand his holdings eastward into Hunan with an army that numbered between 60,000 and 100,000. In April 1642, he besieged the city of Kaifeng for several months, driving the defenders to desperation and cannibalism. Finally, an imperial army arrived in September. Afraid to meet Li head-on in battle, the army tried instead to drive him away by breaching the dikes that held back the Yellow River. The plan worked after a fashion; Li abandoned the siege, but the resulting flood devastated the city. Of the 370,000 residents of Kaifeng, only 30,000 survived.[2]

In any case, the setback at Kaifeng did nothing to stem Li's ambition. On New Year's Day, February 8, 1644, Li Zicheng proclaimed himself lord of the Shun dynasty, which certainly didn't go over well with the current ruler of China, Emperor Chongzhen of the Ming dynasty.

The Last Emperor

On April 22, 1644, frantic courtiers found the door to the emperor's suite mysteriously jammed shut. After breaking inside, they discovered Emperor Chongzhen in tears. Not only was Li's army closing in on the capital at Beijing, but also the government was bankrupt and couldn't pay the imperial armies. A combination of famines, epidemics, bandits, pirates, and frontier wars had drained the treasury, while a naval war between the Catholic Portuguese (China's major trading partner) and the Protestant Dutch and English disrupted the influx of silver and left the imperial exchequer without ready cash.[3]

Emperor Chongzhen couldn't decide whether to flee Beijing southward for the safer city of Nanjing. If he ran, he would lose legitimacy, and the crown prince would take this as an abdication, but if he stayed, one of his opportunistic kinsmen could rally the southern lands and declare himself emperor instead. Two days later, Li's rebel army entered the suburbs of Beijing.

The emperor's panic may have been unnecessary. Li apparently was willing to accept vassalage rather than the throne itself. Li even sent a message ahead, offering to bypass the capital and throw his army against the Manchus north of the Great Wall if the emperor would only recognize and legitimize Li's rule of the southern provinces. The message apparently did not reach the emperor, who never responded. Li kept coming.

Eventually, Emperor Chongzhen decided to stay and await his fate. He got drunk and stumbled around the palace with a sword, killing his chief concubine and youngest daughters to keep them from falling into the hand of the rebels. Then he tried to kill his oldest daughter, but he only chopped off her arm when she tried to block the blow. She ran down the hall trailing blood.

Disguising himself as a eunuch, the emperor tried to slip out of the capital, but his guards fired on him as he approached the gates. He retreated to his chambers and rang a bell to summon his ministers for advice. When none came, he calmly walked out to the garden and hanged himself from a tree below a hill.[4]

Barbarians at the Gate

Let's introduce another set of characters. The Manchus were a Jurchen people, closely related to several other barbarian peoples who hovered in the lands north of China and occasionally came crashing down against the Great Wall; however, they were not the same branch of the Jurchens that established the Jin ("Golden") dynasty in north China in the twelfth century, which later fell to the Mongols (see "Genghis Khan").

If this is confusing, think of the Jurchen as being like the Australians, New Zealanders, English, and Scots. To us, it's obvious that these Anglophonic white people are entirely dissimilar, but in four hundred years few will remember or care what the differences between the Americans and Canadians used to be.

In their native state, the Manchus lived as nomadic herdsmen and fought as horse archers like the Mongols before them. Eventually, however, contact with the Chinese rubbed off on them, and they padded their armies with Chinese-style battalions of massed pikemen and musketeers. Because these forces required less training and could be raised as needed, they were more suitable to peasant societies.

In 1584, a twenty-five-year-old barbarian named Nurhachi inherited leadership of one of the four subordinate tribes of the Manchus. Through the usual combination of charisma, cunning, and ruthlessness, he united the four tribes into one mighty federation. He then embarked on a lifetime of war against every neighbor he could reach. Finally, his invasion of the neighboring Yehe tribe put him in direct conflict with the Ming. Now a grizzled fifty-nine-year-old veteran, Nurhachi beat the Chinese in their first encounter at Sahu in 1619. Soon he was plunging toward the Chinese capital at Beijing, until he ran up against an entrenched garrison with artillery. Nurhachi died shortly thereafter from a festering cannon wound.

Firearms

Yuan Chonghuan, the Chinese general who beat Nurhachi, had picked up his knowledge of Western firearms from his cook, who had been hanging around with Europeans.[5] Although the Chinese had known the principles of gunpowder for centuries, a new invention from the West, the matchlock musket, was strengthening infantry's return to the battlefield.

Although inferior to bows and arrows in almost every way—weight, accuracy, range, and rate of fire—these primitive muskets had one crucial advantage. They required almost no skill to operate: just load, point, and ignite. Fighting a battle using bows—even if you won—would erode the number of skilled archers, and it would take years to train a replacement for each one killed. On the other hand, after winning a battle using muskets, an army could just pick up all of the guns lying scattered among the dead musketmen, then take a few days to train replacement peasants to load, point, and ignite.

General Yuan Chonghuan had handed the Manchus a temporary setback, but he would not remain in their way for long. In a fit of jealousy, General Yuan had recently executed a talented subordinate, so friends of this subordinate conspired with palace eunuchs for payback. Yuan was accused of treason, dragged away, and executed by the traditional Chinese manner of having many pieces systematically sliced off in the central market of Beijing.

New Alien Overlords

Several traditionally Chinese provinces beyond the Great Wall in Manchuria were demarcated from the surrounding barbarians by the Willow Palisade, which, as you can probably guess from the name, was not quite as formidable a barrier as the Great Wall. After Nurhachi conquered these lands, the Manchus acquired a few decades of experience ruling Chinese.*

---

* This is an important, though often overlooked, aspect of empire-building. History is replete with uprisings that could have been avoided if the conquerors had simply known in advance all of the odd little taboos and quirks of their subject population and thereby avoided unintentionally offensive behavior such as exposing the wrong body part or trying to feed the wrong kind of animal to a native. It's always a good idea to get some practice running a small starter colony before you set out for world domination.

Among the little rules that would become important later, Nurhachi required his male Chinese subjects to shave their heads but keep a long braided queue, the traditional Manchu sign of servitude. Of more immediate usefulness, the Manchus learned the sacred importance of the emperor to the Chinese, so Nurhachi's son and successor, Hong Taiji, proclaimed a proper new dynasty, the Qing (pronounced "ching" and meaning "pure").

Hong Taiji also added to earlier acquisitions—Inner Mongolia in 1632, Korea in 1638. These were impressive conquests certainly, but they only added more barbarians. To earn a name in the history books, a conqueror has to overrun the center of the civilized world. Although the Manchus had been at constant war with China for several decades, they hadn't been able to decisively crack the frontier defenses.

In 1643, Hong Taiji died, and the surviving members of his house began to jostle for position. A complicated compromise between the factions produced a child khan and two rival co-regents. One of the regents, Nurhachi's sixteenth son, Dorgon, was really the man in charge.*

The bandit revolts of Li and Zhang in Ming China opened up an excellent opportunity for the Manchus to invade, but they weren't sure whether to pillage and ride back home with saddlebags stuffed with loot or to settle in for a long, profitable stay. Dorgon is said to have offered Li Zicheng a deal dividing China between them, but nothing came of it. Maybe this messenger was lost in transit as well.

Li Zicheng's bandit army camped in the palace, enjoyed the emperor's harem, and looted Beijing, while two hundred miles away, along the Great Wall, the last Ming army in the north hesitated. Ming General Wu Sangui was torn between avenging his dead emperor or advancing his career by recognizing Li as the new emperor of China, but ultimately his duty was to guard the northern frontier. He remained at his post. Li discovered General Wu's father, an elderly courtier, among his prisoners from the Ming court and tried to negotiate a deal. Wu the Younger agreed to surrender in exchange for the release of his father, and rode south toward Beijing; however, Li grew tired of waiting. He executed Wu's family, raped Wu's favorite concubine, and marched north with his army. When Wu heard the awful news, he went back to the Great Wall and flung open the gates for the Manchus to pour through.[6]

Li met Wu's forces at Shanhaiguan, where the Great Wall meets the sea. Wu lined up his forces and traded unsuccessful frontal assaults with Li's rebels for several exhausting

---

* I'm trying to keep these narratives readable by not naming every place or player in the story. I wouldn't want you to get overwhelmed. Sometimes it's a tough call deciding whether to label "the chief minister" or "the general's wife" generically, or to give them names.

In any case, the most important thing to remember about Dorgon is that, unlike his fellow Manchus, he has a great name for a barbarian warlord. Go on; say it out loud: "Dorgon the Barbarian."

hours. Then Dorgon's Manchu cavalry suddenly attacked out of a blinding sandstorm on Li's left flank. The surprise and the defeat were total.

Li retreated in good order for a few hundred miles back toward his original base of operations, fighting several large defensive battles against his pursuers. Eventually, the strain was too much for the rebels and Li's army disintegrated. Li was reported dead in the summer of 1645, either by suicide or by being beaten to death by some peasants he was trying to rob—although other stories have him escaping to live out his life as an anonymous monk.[7]

In December 1644, the other major rebel, Zhang Xianzhong, the Yellow Tiger, pulled back into Sichuan, and set up the Great Western Kingdom, headquartered at Chengdu.[8] Left on his own, Zhang grew increasingly cruel and capricious. He mutilated and beheaded thousands of scholars and their families. He decimated regiments of his army as punishment for imagined insults. His cruelty was so well known that, in 2002, when workers excavating the foundation of a new building in Chengdu uncovered one hundred very old skeletons jumbled together in the dirt, the archaeologist who investigated the site immediately suspected that Zhang was the one who put them there.[9] Zhang abandoned Chengdu in late 1646, burning much of it to the ground. He retreated deeper into the mountains, devastating the countryside behind him, until the Manchus caught and killed him in January 1647.

Mopping Up

The surviving Mings regrouped in the south, at Nanjing, the secondary capital in central China. At first Dorgon offered to split China with them provided the Mings renounced their claims on the north. No deal.

The Manchu armies moved out. At the southern terminus of the Grand Canal, the supremely rich city of Yangzhou put up a stiff resistance when the Manchus arrived, so the city was thoroughly and bitterly pillaged for ten days after it finally fell. Learning a lesson from this, Nanjing surrendered without a fight in June, and for once the city changed hands *without* a massacre, which, as we shall see, is unusual in Nanjing's long unhappy history. The Qing hauled the current Ming emperor into oblivion.

Ming royalty, however, had bred like bunnies, so the Qing were forced to hunt and execute a long string of princes who tried to establish rival kingdoms in the south. The last of the Mings was the youngest grandson of an earlier emperor, his mother's baby who had been pampered and coddled throughout childhood, so you know his story will end badly. Known as the prince of Gui, he established a rival court in the deep south, filled with "all manner of betel nut chewers, brine-well workers, and aborigine whorehouse owners."[10] Eventually, beginning in December 1650, the Qing armies chased him all over the southern borderlands and finally into Burma. The Burmese promised him sanctuary, but then changed their minds and massacred most of the renegade court. The prince was imprisoned in a small estate until a few years later when the turncoat General Wu Sangui invaded. The Burmese bought off General Wu by surrendering the last of the Mings. The prince of Gui and his only son were taken back to China and discreetly strangled in 1662.[11]

With the final demise of his masters, the last Ming admiral, Zheng Chenggong,* gathered his fleet and sailed off to a life of piracy. In 1661, he seized Taiwan from the Dutch and probably would have moved against the Spanish in the Philippines if he hadn't died shortly thereafter. This was the last throe of the Ming dynasty's glorious maritime traditions, which had once sent massive fleets all over the world, as far as East Africa. After the passing of Zheng Chenggong, the oceans became the exclusive domain of the Europeans.

Plague and Pestilence

How many people died in this age of chaos? A hint of the devastation can be found in the *Ming Shi*, the official history of the era compiled a century later, which accused Zhang the Yellow Tiger of killing 600 million people during his insane rule. As this is more people than were alive in the world at the time, the impossibly large number is probably just their way of saying "a lot."[12]

The most common estimate from modern demographers, based on tax records and archaeology, is that the original Chinese population of 150 million fell by one-sixth (or 25 million) in the mid-seventeenth century.[13] As always, famine and disease swept through the plundered and battered population, killing huge numbers of anonymous civilians.

You may have noticed that a disproportionate number of my top one hundred events occurred in the late 1500s and the1600s. In Europe, the Thirty Years War was the deadliest conflict until World War I (see "Thirty Years War"). Russia sank into the chaotic Time of Troubles. The Manchu conquest of China was responsible for one of the top population collapses in East Asian history, while Aurangzeb's invasion of south India (see "Aurangzeb") caused the highest single-war body count in South Asian history. Even in the smaller, outlying islands off the continental coasts, the dogs of war were barking louder than they ever had before. Britain was being torn apart by the English Civil War, and Japan's shoguns were vying for power in what would later become the setting for just about every film by Akira Kurosawa.[14] All of this was ravaging a world with a population of 500 million, only one-fifth the number of people alive in the middle of the twentieth century. In fact, the seventeenth century is a serious contender for worst century in human history.

The main cause of this was a quantum leap in military technology. The development of efficient muskets and artillery brought entire civilizations under the command of single

---

* Zheng Chenggong is known in Western literature as Coxinga, based on his nickname, Guoxingye, "Imperial Namekeeper."

dynasties, creating so-called gunpowder empires. Although in later centuries these new empires would be a stabilizing influence, they began by destroying ancient power balances and unleashing chaos.

Of course the Four Horsemen of the Apocalypse do their best work when they cooperate, and seventeenth-century body counts were boosted by a resurgence of bubonic plague. The most famous outbreak was the London Plague of 1665, but the plague also swept all of the trade routes of Eurasia, wherever the rat populations were big enough to support it. It wasn't nearly as bad as the Black Death three hundred years earlier, but China was hit particularly hard: "At first the bodies were buried in coffins, and next in grasses, but finally they were left on the beds." An eyewitness described a town ravaged by the plague: "there were few signs of human life in the streets and all that was heard was the buzzing of flies."[15]

This era was also the peak of the Little Ice Age. World temperatures had been falling for a few centuries and would not begin to climb again for many decades. This was squeezing agriculture into shorter, drier growing seasons, and famines followed.

On the other hand, no matter how fascinating it is to study the impact of disease and weather on history, we can get carried away trying to match every historic upheaval to a concurrent natural event. In the long term, societies adjusted to the new weather patterns, and in the short term the climate change was sporadic. Weather is always erratic, so when we talk about, for example, drier summers, we don't mean there was no rain for years on end. We mean less rain than average in most years, but perfectly normal rain the rest of the time. Drought and famine have been so common in human history that most societies have emergency plans and plenty of old-timers who remember how they got through it the last time. Only when compounded by an extra dose of bad luck or human stupidity does bad weather destroy the fabric of society.

CROMWELL'S INVASION OF IRELAND

Death toll: 400,000[1]
Rank: 81
Type: ethnic cleansing
Broad dividing line: English vs. Irish
Time frame: 1649–52
Location: Ireland
Major state participant: English Commonwealth
Who usually gets the most blame: Cromwell

I N THE ESCALATING QUARREL BETWEEN KING CHARLES OF ENGLAND AND THE Puritans of Parliament, the Catholics of Ireland were Royalists. In 1641, just before the outbreak of hostilities in England, a rumor swept through the Irish Catholics that Parliament was planning to crack down on them at any minute. The Catholics decided to strike first and destroy the Ulster Protestants who would be the foot soldiers in any such oppression. Three thousand Protestants were massacred in a sudden uprising, and another 8,000 died after they were driven homeless out into the cold.

Civil war broke out in England before any retaliation could take place. Unfortunately for the Irish, the English Civil War ended with the king dead and the commander of the parliamentary army, Oliver Cromwell, as dictator of England. In August 1649 Cromwell crossed over to Ireland to settle scores. "Misery and desolation, blood and ruin . . . shall befall them," Cromwell promised, "and [I] shall rejoice to exercise the utmost severity against them."[2]

He besieged the town of Drogheda on the east coast of Ireland, and when the English breached the walls after several fierce assaults, Cromwell's Roundheads gave no quarter. The English massacred 3,500 people, including all of the soldiers in the garrison and 1,000 government officials, priests, and other dangerous civilians. The royalist governor of the town was beaten to death with his own wooden leg by soldiers who had heard a rumor that the leg would split open and spill hidden gold coins. Survivors of the massacre were shipped out and sold to plantations in Barbados.

"This is a righteous judgment of God upon those barbarous wretches that have imbued their hands in so much innocent blood," Cromwell declared. "And that it will tend to prevent the effusion of blood for the future."[3]

Cromwell then moved south, where resistance from the port city of Wexford led to another slaughtered garrison and plundered town. As more towns fell to English sieges, the Irish people turned to guerrilla warfare. Called "tories," from the Irish *tóraidhe*, meaning "pursued man" (and later applied as an insult to all opponents of progress, such as American supporters of the Crown or the most conservative English political party),[4] these insurgents stretched the war out until 1652. Cromwell left his army to clean up and returned to London.

Parliament now decided to break the Catholic hold on Ireland once and for all. English commissioners arrived to jail or execute rebels and priests and to confiscate their lands. Public practice of Catholicism was outlawed. The English drove the Irish off the fertile land, westward into the rocky part of the island, and redistributed the best land to Protestant landlords and retired veterans from England. Almost 40 percent of the farmland switched hands.[5] The island's population plummeted by 20 percent as hundreds of thousands of Irish died of hunger and disease during this upheaval. For the next three hundred years, Ireland remained a world of landless native peasants under the thumb of alien gentry.

AURANGZEB

Death toll: maybe 4.6 million in the Deccan War[1]
Rank: 23
Type: despot
Broad dividing line: Muslims vs. Hindus
Time frame: ruled 1658–1707
Location: India
Major state participant: Mughal Empire
Who usually gets the most blame: Aurangzeb

Presumptive Heir

When Shah Jahan, the Mughal emperor of India and builder of the Taj Mahal, was unable to urinate for three days, the backup in his system sent him into a serious sickness. His oldest and favorite son, Dara, kept the illness secret and his father hidden so as not to panic the empire. Palace rumors quickly reached the ears of Shah Jahan's other sons. They suspected that Dara was scheming. He was clearly behind their father's mysterious disappearance, and they assumed that they were next, so they fled and began to raise armies in the provinces.

Shah Jahan recovered from his illness soon enough, but his sons were in open civil war by then. Dara easily beat the youngest in battle and chased him into exile, which left Aurangzeb (third) supporting Murad (second) for the throne. As these two gradually gained the upper hand, Aurangzeb invited Murad to his tent to work out the details of their partnership. Murad dined and drank fine wines while his strict Muslim brother stayed sober. Murad dozed pleasantly while a slave girl gave him a massage. Then he woke up imprisoned.

Aurangzeb eventually captured the capital and locked his father in his suite in the palace. After a hard campaign, Aurangzeb captured his brother Dara and put him on trial. As far as Aurangzeb was concerned, Dara had always seemed too tolerant of Hindus, so Dara was found guilty of apostasy and beheaded. The head was taken to his imprisoned father to prove that Aurangzeb was now completely in charge.

Aurangzeb was always mindful that he had come to power by overthrowing his father, so he kept a tight leash on his own children. Every one of them was imprisoned for a few years at some point or another during his long reign.

Faith-Based Initiatives

The Mughal dynasty had begun in Afghanistan as an offshoot of Timur's dynasty, which swept over the mountains into India. In a steady line from father to son for five generations, one glorious conqueror after another expanded and consolidated the empire; however, the Mughals preferred to show off with magnificent art and architecture rather than martial prowess. The Mughals invested heavily in public works such as roads, postal carriers, and granaries as a precaution against famine.

Although generous and pious patrons of Islam, the Mughals traditionally had been tolerant of Hinduism. Throughout their domain, Hindus had been allowed to freely practice all their rites and customs. Previous Mughals had even entrusted Hindus with the command of armies and high offices at the palace.

Aurangzeb, however, was a Muslim ascetic who banned every vice he could, and personally avoided almost everything else. He did not wear silk. He prohibited music wherever he could. Unlike previous Mughals, Aurangzeb adhered to the Muslim prohibition of images, so without the patronage of the court, painters had to leave the country to find work. Having no interest in any writing other than scripture, Aurangzeb also withdrew imperial patronage of poets and scholars.[2] He prohibited Hindus from riding horses or litters. He reintroduced the head tax non-Muslims had to pay.

Aurangzeb relentlessly destroyed Hindu temples all across India. In 1661, he demolished the Kesava Deo temple in Mathura that marked the birthplace of Krishna. The Kashi Vishwanath temple in the holy city of Varanasi, one of the most famous temples dedicated to Shiva, was demolished in 1669. He destroyed the Somnath Temple in Saurashtra in 1706.[3] This list probably means nothing to you, but it leaves Hindu historians wincing just as Westerners do whenever they read about a great landmark of Greco-Roman civilization being destroyed. All you need to remember is that thousands of Hindu holy sites were flattened throughout India and replaced with mosques. To this day, Hindu nationalists are itching for an opportunity to burn down these mosques and rebuild the lost Hindu temples.

When Guru Nanak Dev founded the Sikh religion in the 1500s, he had originally hoped to bring peace to India and reconcile Islam and Hinduism by reducing the rival faiths to their common moral elements and fusing them into a single pacifistic religion. Unfortunately this only created an awkward third religion for everyone to fight over. The Sikhs infuriated Aurangzeb by converting Muslims, and he swore to put a stop to this poaching. In 1675, he threw Guru Tegh Bahadur, leader of the Sikhs, into jail and tortured him a bit to see if he would change his mind about religious tolerance. When the guru stuck to his original opinion, Aurangzeb had him beheaded. After this, the Sikhs shifted away from their original pacifism and withdrew to mountain fortresses, where they became a warrior people who carried ritual swords and daggers at all times.[4]

Marathas

During the seventeenth century, a motley collection of Hindu highland clans called the Marathas evolved into a warrior nation bent on resisting Muslim encroachment. The chief Maratha, Shivaji, became the legendary leader of the resistance, a hero to generations of Hindus, famous for his daring escapades. During a parley with one Muslim general, he unexpectedly disemboweled the general with hidden steel tiger claws; then his troops rushed out of hiding to massacre the leaderless enemy. Later, he snuck into a fortress by blending into a royal wedding procession. He then killed the guests in their sleep. In 1663, he topped that by breaking into Aurangzeb's harem and causing mayhem.

Aurangzeb fired the general in charge of hunting Shivaji and sent his own son south. It didn't help. Shivaji stayed one step ahead of the Mughals, and he seized and looted the city of Surat in 1664. Finally, a new Mughal general, Jai Singh, took over and beat Shivaji into submission in three months. Shivaji agreed to travel to the capital, Agra, and offer his personal allegiance to the emperor, so Aurangzeb sent a magnificent caravan of elephants, litters, and attendants at Mughal expense to bring him to the city in 1666. Once there, however, Shivaji felt snubbed by the emperor and ran away to resume the war. He promoted himself to king and expanded the reach of his raids.[5] In 1680, Shivaji died of dysentery, and leadership of the Marathis went to his son Sambhaji.

In the same year, Aurangzeb sent one of his sons, Akbar, south to put down a rebellion of Rajputs (Hindu aristocratic clans), but Akbar joined the revolt instead. He declared himself emperor and unsuccessfully attacked northward. Akbar had a large enough army that he should have won at least a few of the preliminaries, but he blew the first battle and had to flee farther south, beyond the reach of his father. He eventually hopped a ship to Persia.

Deccan War

Finally deciding that he had to conquer the south himself, Aurangzeb rode out with an army reputed to number a half million. Not just an army, the traveling party included his entire court and a tent city of colorful pavilions, animal herds, wagons, corrals, and bazaars. For the remaining twenty-six years of his life, he would never again return to the north.

In 1686–87 he overran the independent Muslim kingdoms of Bijapur and Golconda, whom he considered decadent and hedonistic. Then he turned his full attention against the Marathas on the mountainous rim of the Deccan plateau in west-central India. When the Mughals finally captured the Maratha king Sambhaji in 1689, Aurangzeb had him gradually dismantled over the next three weeks—cutting out his tongue the first day, eyes the next, then his limbs one by one. Finally Sambhaji was reduced to an unrecognizable fraction of his former self and was beheaded.

Although Aurangzeb systematically captured one Maratha hill fort after another, new ones continually sprang up somewhere else. Maratha forts usually surrendered as soon as Aurangzeb arrived, but then resumed their revolt as soon as he was safely gone.[6] The Marathas became experts at guerrilla warfare, so Aurangzeb tried to root them out by destroying the villages and crops that supported them.

As the war dragged on, southern India was devastated. According to contemporary sources, 100,000 of Aurangzeb's men and 300,000 beasts of burden (horses, camels, asses, oxen, and elephants) died every year during the quarter century of war in the Deccan. When drought, plague, and famine hit the war-torn lands in 1702 to 1704, two million civilians died within a few years.[7]

The long war never quite accomplished its ultimate purpose. By the end of Aurangzeb's life, the Mughals had come close to conquering the entire subcontinent of India, but the farthest tip of the peninsula still remained outside their grasp. Mughal power reached its peak under Aurangzeb, but the problem with a peak is that it's all downhill after that. Years of fighting had exhausted the empire. The treasury was depleted. The Mughal Empire quickly crumbled away after Aurangzeb died.

GREAT TURKISH WAR

Death toll: 384,000[1]
Rank: 89
Type: clash of cultures
Broad dividing line: Turks vs. Holy League
Time frame: 1682–99
Location: southeastern Europe
Major state participants: Austria, Ottoman Turkey
Minor state participants: Venice, Poland, Papacy, Russia
Quantum state participant: Hungary
Who usually gets the most blame: Kara Mustafa

Siege of Vienna

When its king and nobility were wiped out by the Turks at the Battle of Mohacs in 1526, Hungary ceased being a viable nation. The leaderless land was partitioned between the Austrians in the northwest and the Ottoman Turks in the southeast, but a century later, Hungarians under Imre Thokoly tried to drive the Austrians out of their half of Hungary. After suffering a string of defeats, Thokoly realized he couldn't do it alone. Hoping to play one great power against the other, he turned to the Turks for help.

His request came at the right time. The elite Turkish infantry, the Janissaries, were looking for a war in order to pick up some quick loot, and a twenty-year truce between Turkey and Austria was set to expire. Kara Mustafa, the latest vizier produced by the Koprulu family and the power behind the throne of Ottoman Turkey, seized the opportunity. He organized a massive spearhead to drive against Vienna. Although the Turks issued their declaration of war in August 1682, preparing their invasion force of over 140,000 troops and four hundred cannon delayed the offensive until the next spring.

Although they knew the Turks were coming, the Austrians dithered about preparing Vienna for a siege. A hundred years of peace had led them to neglect their fortifications. Bastions had eroded. Houses and trees had sprung up in what was supposed to be an open field of fire. At first, Emperor Leopold I couldn't decide whether his place was with his troops or safe from harm, but he finally snuck out of the city just before the Turkish vanguard arrived, leaving a mere 12,000 regular troops to coordinate the militia's defense.

Fortunately for Christendom, the Turks dithered as well. When they surrounded Vienna in July 1683, they dug trenches and waited, occasionally raiding but never attacking in force, even on a couple of occasions when a useful breach appeared in the enemy defenses. Under the laws of war at the time, common soldiers could legally plunder a city seized by assault for three days without restraint, but a peacefully surrendered city belonged to the sultan. Kara apparently preferred to wait and take Vienna intact for the empire, rather than taking it quickly and seeing his soldiers destroy it. Instead, the Turks stayed busy by terrorizing the surrounding countryside, such as massacring 4,000 villagers in nearby Perchtoldsdorf.

The siege dragged on long enough for the emperor to hire 81,000 east European mercenaries to save Vienna. The backbone of this army was 25,000 men under King John III Sobieski, the last great king of Poland. Sobieski and his Polish Winged Hussars* swooped down on the rear of the Turkish camp. Overconfident of their success, the Turks hadn't fortified their rear against such an attack, and their camp was overrun. The entire host fled, abandoning huge stockpiles of supplies, provisions, and treasure.[2]

Damage Control

Looking to find someone to blame for his defeat, Kara Mustafa arrested Imre Thokoly, the Hungarian rebel who had talked him into this mess. The arrest of their leader insulted the Hungarian troops, who now switched over to the Austrian side, taking all of the fortresses in Turkish Hungary with them. Only Imre's wife stayed on the Turkish side to prove her husband's loyalty, and she held her lone fortress against the Austrians for a three-year siege until she finally surrendered and was hauled off to captivity.[3]

Ottoman Sultan Mehmed IV, however, had another scapegoat in mind. He ordered Kara Mustafa strangled for his failure, and the vizier's stuffed head was sent back to the sultan in a velvet sack to prove that the order had been fulfilled. The head traveled around for several centuries until eventually it ended up in a trophy case at Vienna's city museum, but in 1970 the city fathers got all delicate and moved the head to the basement where tourists couldn't gawk at it.

The sultan barely outlasted his vizier. The failure at Vienna sparked a coup in Constantinople, and Mehmed was locked in a dungeon while his brother was raised to the throne; however, the new sultan soon died (natural causes), as did the next. Eventually the empire came up with a sultan who lived long enough to negotiate peace.

With the Turkish side in chaos, the Austrians surged forward across the Hungarian plain. They took Budapest in 1686 and scored a major victory at Mohacs in 1687, which erased the stain of the Christian defeat on the same site so many generations earlier.

The Serbs and other Balkan Christians welcomed liberation from the Turks; however,

---

* These cavalrymen actually wore gigantic wings as part of their uniform. It was the era in which looking awesome was more important than practicality.

before the Austrians could fully consolidate their new territory, their troops were withdrawn and sent west to fight France in an unrelated war. Undefended, Kosovo fell to the Turks again, and the native Serbs fled Turkish retaliation. Then the Turks moved Muslim Albanians into the empty land, which would lead to another war, three hundred years later in 1999.[4]

While the Austrians advanced overland against the Turks, a Venetian fleet conquered southern Greece from the Ottomans. When the Venetians besieged Athens, the Turkish garrison stored its gunpowder in the largest, driest, sturdiest building in town—the Parthenon. Graceful, perfectly proportioned, and decorated with superb sculptures, this temple had survived the previous two millennia largely intact, but now a Venetian mortar hit the Turkish powder magazine, detonating a massive explosion that destroyed most of the building, leaving only the outer colonnade still standing.

Atlantic Ocean

North Sea

Baltic Sea

KINGDOM OF SCOTLAND

IRELAND

KINGDOM OF ENGLAND

KINGDOM OF DENMARK

KINGDOM OF

Elbe

Brandenbu

Spanish Netherlands

Holy Roman Empire

SAXONY

SILESIA

Paris

Palatinate

Prague

AUSTRI

Loire

Blenheim
(battle 1704)

BAVARIA

Vienna

KINGDOM OF FRANCE

Dijon

Besançon

SWISS CANTONS

Salzburg

SAVOY

MILAN

Milan

VENICE

HUNGARY

Po

Venice

Mohác.
(battles 1526, 1687

Genoa

Florence

Adriatic Sea

PYRENEES

TUSCANY

Corsica

PAPAL STATES

Ragusa

KINGDOM OF PORTUGAL

SPAIN

Rome

Naples

Majorca

Tyrrhenian Sea

KINGDOM OF NAPLES

Sardinia

Mediterranean Sea

Sicily

Tangier

Malta

SHARIFATE OF MARRAKESH

EUROPE

ca.1675

| 0 | 200 | 400 | 600 | 800 | 1000 | kilometers |
| 0 | 100 | 200 | 300 | 400 | 500 | 600 | miles |

SWEDEN

• Novgorod

Trinity–Saint Sergius •

Tushino •• Moscow

• Nizhny Novgorod

R u s s i a n   E m p i r e

KINGDOM OF POLAND

rsaw

⚔ Poltava
(battle 1709)

Volga

Cossacks

Astrakhan •

CARPATHIANS

Principality
of
Transylvania

Crimea

C A U C A S U S   M T S.

*Caspian
Sea*

Wallachia

Danube

Black Sea

O
t
t
o
m
a
n

Aegean Sea

• Constantinople/Istanbul

E m p i r e

A s i a   M i n o r

Athens •

Crete *Rhodes*

Mediterranean Sea

Cyprus

PETER THE GREAT

Death toll: 3 million[1]
Rank: 30
Type: despot
Broad dividing line: Peter against the past
Time frame: ruled 1682–1725
Location: Russia
Who usually gets the most blame: Peter I

PETER THE GREAT WAS LARGER THAN LIFE IN SO MANY WAYS. STANDING AT a full two meters (six feet seven inches), he is the tallest major player in this book, and he stands out from the pages of history as a man who accepted no limits and shaped the world to fit his vision. Peter rudely dragged Russia into the modern world, no matter who resisted or how badly it hurt. He shuffled populations from where they were to where he wanted them, created a new capital at Saint Petersburg, and boosted his army to unprecedented levels. He fought almost continuous wars with his neighbors.

Modernism

When he first came to the throne upon the death of his father in 1682, the ten-year-old tsar Peter I had to share the throne with his half-witted older brother Ivan, while his mother ruled as regent. It wasn't until after these two died (brother in 1696 and mother in 1694, both—surprisingly for the Russian court—of natural causes) that Peter was free to do as he pleased.

Peter wanted most of all to make Russia a world-class power. It hardly seemed right that tiny countries like Holland and Denmark had more clout than gigantic Russia. He set off on a grand tour of the West, where he investigated and tested every aspect of its culture. He worked in a Dutch shipyard under a false name. He dined with scholars in England.

Peter started his improvements with superficial modernization, figuring that if the Russians looked civilized maybe they would act it. Traditionally, Orthodox Russians wore long beards with religious pride; God had put beards on men's faces, and it was impious and vain to shave them off. Upon his return from the West, Tsar Peter immediately ordered all Russians to shave and look more Western. He himself often pulled out a razor and forcibly shaved bearded men in the street. Eventually he relented and allowed the stubbornly religious to pay a beard tax instead, but even then, they had to wear a visible beard permit as a medallion or risk being shaved.*

Peter studied every technology he could get his hands on. He especially liked dentistry, and if anyone even hinted at a toothache in Peter's presence, the poor suffering soul would be held down while Peter whipped out his pliers and yanked out the offending tooth.

Power

While Peter was off in western Europe trying to learn its clever ways, his half sister Sophia raised a rebellion among the strelsky (palace guards). Peter hurried home and bloodily reasserted control. Over a thousand ringleaders were publicly executed by humiliating and agonizing torture, while Sophia was stashed in a convent.

While concentrating all power into his own hands, Peter tried to break the power of the Russian church and confiscate its wealth for the state. When the patriarch (head of the church) died in 1700, Peter prevented the church from electing a new one. He stalled long enough for the church leadership to get used to the idea of being without a patriarch, and in 1721, Peter turned the church into a branch of the Russian civil service under the authority of the tsar. He also changed the Russian year 7208 (after creation) to 1699 (after Christ), and moved New Year's Day from September 1 to January 1 to bring it in line with the Western calendar.

Originally, Russian boyars ranked in importance according to the prestige of their ancestry, but Peter imported Western-style feudalism in which the nobility was assigned equal privileges or obligations across the class. The boyars were abolished as a class in 1711 and reordered with Western titles.

About the same time, Peter refashioned the Russian system of free peasants and household slaves into Western-style serfdom, which elevated the slaves but degraded the peasantry. The ex-slaves were now subject to taxation, while a whole string of new Russian laws forbade peasants from traveling without a passport or signing contracts without government approval.

Every year, a new levy replenished the ranks of his army, and each new census helped Peter utilize every last citizen he could get his hands on. Noblemen were required to pro-

---

* There's a tendency by later generations and by foreigners at the time to treat Peter's beard laws as a joke, but hair and clothing are key expressions of culture. Forty years ago, long hair on a male was a stomping offense in some places, and more recently I heard that "a Nevada school district agreed to pay $400,000 to a Muslim girl and her friend over allegations that other students threatened to kill her in the stairwell for wearing a religious head scarf and the staff did nothing to stop it." (Fox News, April 8, 2009)

vide one soldier per 100 inhabitants of their lands and one cavalryman per every 150 inhabitants. Before Peter, the Russian government had counted only households, but the new census tried to count individual taxpayers, a category that was expanded by the addition of several previously exempt classes.

War

When Peter began his rule, Russia's only seaport was Archangel on the White Sea just below the Arctic Circle, which froze half of the year. Peter soon launched Russia's endless quest for a warm-water port. He constantly tried to expand northward against the Swedes, who held the Baltic coast, and southward against the Turks, who held the Black Sea coast.

Every year saw a war (usually bungled) somewhere. He fought the Turks over Azov on the Black Sea in 1695 and 1696. He fought them again on the Pruth River in 1711–12, but the offensive went badly, as usual. In 1722–23, Peter fought the Persians south of the Caspian Sea. Meanwhile, revolts needed to be put down and Siberia needed to be brought under control. In each of these wars, Peter relied on what would come to be the characteristic strength of the Russian army—the stubborn ability to absorb incredible punishment and staggering loss of life to simply outlast their opponents.

Even in peacetime, soldiers weren't allowed to idle away in forgotten garrisons. Conscripted labor, both soldiers and civilians, dredged rivers and built roads, factories, and canals all over Russia. This is probably where Peter racked up his biggest body count. Peter's relentless maintenance of a huge standing army was just as deadly as his wars. Disease, malnutrition, neglect, and brutal discipline cut through his troops; so did the frigid cold of an empire that stretched all the way across the north of Asia. The draft was so dreaded that peasants mangled themselves to be ineligible. They knocked out their own teeth so they couldn't bite open cartridges to load their muskets. They severed their own toes so they couldn't march and fingers so they couldn't shoot.

Peter's attempt to open an outlet to the Baltic Sea was bloody enough to earn a chapter all by itself (see "Great Northern War"), but he didn't wait for the war to be settled in his favor to start building a new coastal capital as his gateway to the west. He rounded up criminals, prisoners, and peasant conscripts, and moved construction teams to the coast to begin building Saint Petersburg on land that technically still belonged to Sweden. He forbade the construction of stone buildings throughout Russia in order to leave all of the masons in the country free to work on his new city. When the first 40,000 workers died of fevers in the swamps, he rounded up another 40,000 to replace them. Those died as well, so he found more. All in all, as many as 100,000 workmen were sacrificed in the building of Saint Petersburg.

And Peace

To maintain his enormous army in peacetime, Peter dispersed his soldiers throughout Russia and shifted the cost of their upkeep to local taxpayers. In 1718, to determine how many soldiers each community could support, Peter decreed a new census to be taken the next year. Anyone who ducked this census would have all of his property confiscated and turned over to whomever informed on him.

Local citizens panicked whenever a new convoy of officials approached and needed to be fed and housed at local expense. Soldiers billeted in the community served as police, informers, and enforcers for Peter's officials. Peter's soldiers and agents were a constant drain on local resources, and the only useful task they performed for the local nobility was keeping peasants from escaping.[2]

Favors were issued to any investor who voluntarily helped with Peter's projects. To promote industry, Peter allowed investors to buy entire villages and put the peasants to work in factories, bound by all of the duties of serfdom toward their new masters. Most peasants were still tied to the land as serfs and hunted down if they ran away, but now Peter exempted runaways who found work in factories. They could stay at their new jobs.[3]

If Peter felt that any resource was not being thoroughly put to use, he simply decreed that it would be developed. The state took control of it; workers were rounded up and resettled. Among the new communities Peter founded, Yekaterinburg, named after his empress and built in the Urals by 25,000 drafted serfs, became the center of the iron industry.[4]

Anyone who tried to hide assets from the tax collector would have that property seized. In fact, wealth was so easily seized by government officials and landlords on one pretext or another that most Russians hid their assets. Peasants buried whatever cash they had, which inhibited commerce. Any gold and silver that Peter's agents discovered being hoarded rather than invested was declared a parasitical drain on the economy and grabbed by the state, and the cycle began again.[5]

Court Life

Peter was ostentatiously relaxed around all people regardless of rank—peasants, priests, servants, soldiers, boyars, foreigners, and so on—and he didn't hold with strict protocol; however, he became sulky when he felt he was offended, and was prone to cruel and ribald practical jokes, many involving dwarfs. He expected his courtiers to drink as enthusiastically as he did, although no one had his stamina. He disliked pomp and luxury and happily dined on the simplest food and slept in the humblest beds. He was proud of being able to endure any hardship he inflicted on his own soldiers and sailors.[6]

Peter groomed his son Alexis for the succession, but Alexis snapped under the pressure from his hyperactive father. After Alexis took a peasant girl as his full-time mistress and shot himself in the hand to avoid military duty, Peter turned cold toward his son. Expecting punishment for his disobedience to arrive at any moment, Alexis fled Russia, taking refuge in Austria first, then Italy. Peter tracked him down and ordered him to return, promising to forgive him if he came back, but to hunt him forever if he didn't. Alexis fell for it and returned.

For a while all seemed well, until Peter had a chance to brood over his son's betrayal. Who in the palace had aided Alexis's escape? Who would have disobeyed the tsar? He had Alexis seized and tortured into revealing the names of his accomplices. Then under Peter's personal supervision Alexis was whipped bloody and raw for several days until he died in agony.[7]

Nobody stayed on Peter's good side forever. In 1724 one of Peter's principal advisers, Willem Mons, fell from favor and was accused of taking bribes. He was tortured into confessing and publicly cut apart as punishment. According to legend, however, Mons's real crime was having an affair with Peter's second wife, Catherine, so Peter had his freshly severed head put in a jar of alcohol, which was placed on her bedside table to keep her company. For many years, Mons's pickled head and that of his sister Anna (the alleged matchmaker in the affair) could be seen in the cabinet of curiosities at the Kunstkamera, Peter's science museum, along with Peter's dwarf collection.

GREAT NORTHERN WAR

Death toll: 370,000[1]
Rank: 90
Type: hegemonial war
Broad dividing line: everyone against Sweden
Time frame: 1700–21
Location: eastern Europe
Major state participants: Sweden vs. Russia, Poland, Denmark, Saxony
Minor state participants: Turkey, Brandenburg, Hanover
Who usually gets the most blame: Peter and his friends
Another damn: European balance-of-power war fought with muskets

W HEN AN UNTESTED TEENAGER BECAME THE NEW KING OF SWEDEN, THE ambassadors from Denmark and Saxony came to Peter the Great with a scheme to break Swedish hegemony in the Baltic once and for all. They figured that it should be pretty easy to beat this child if every nation in northern Europe got involved. They were wrong. Sixteen-year-old King Charles XII of Sweden proved to be a natural at warfare, and he managed to stretch the war out for twenty-one years.

After coming up with a handy excuse and issuing all of the proper declarations of war, each ally attacked the nearest bit of Swedish territory. King Charles of Sweden went straight for the Russian army that had invaded Estonia. At Narva in November, Charles attacked 40,000 Russians with 8,000 Swedes during a sudden snowstorm, which hid his approach and small numbers. The Russians crumbled and fled in panic, leaving 8,000 dead on the field. Meanwhile, 15,000 Swedes occupied the Danish capital and forced the Danes out of the war.

Peter immediately began to rebuild the shattered Russian army along western lines so that it wouldn't be beaten so easily. Also, with characteristic stubbornness, Peter moved back into Swedish territory on the Baltic and began building his new capital, Saint Petersburg.

King Augustus of Saxony was also the king of Poland, so the Swedes marched into Poland next. After beating a couple of armies that got in his way, Charles put his own puppet on the throne in Warsaw. In August 1706, Charles turned against Saxony itself and occupied its capital at Dresden. Charles then forced Augustus to renounce the throne of Poland as the terms of peace.

In 1708, Charles took his army of 40,000 out of Poland into the heart of Russia, but the vast distances proved disorienting. At first, he was planning to link up with 16,000 Swedes under General Lowenhaupt, who was coming out of the Baltic region with much-needed supplies, but Charles turned abruptly south instead in order to connect with some rebellious Cossacks among the wheat fields of Ukraine. This left Lowenhaupt's force stuck in the middle of nowhere, where Peter wiped it out at Lesnaya in September 1708.

Trapped by the severe Russian winter, Charles's Swedish army melted away to 18,000. In June 1709, Peter and 80,000 Russians caught up with him as the Swedes were attacking the Russian fortress of Poltava in central Ukraine. Charles turned around and attacked the new army and came close to defeating it, but Peter had fresh reserves while Charles didn't. Admitting defeat, Charles abandoned his smashed army and escaped into Turkey.

Poltava is usually held up as another classic example of why you shouldn't invade Russia (see also "Napoleonic Wars" and "Second World War"), but the war didn't end right away. Because all of the direct routes back to Sweden were blocked by his enemies, Charles didn't get home for five years. Since the Turks were happy to see the war drag on as long as possible, they held on to Charles and refused the Russian extradition request. When the Russians sent a force to take him back, the Turks arrested the Russian ambassador and declared war, but their counteroffensive banged uselessly against Russia until they gave up. Finally, the Turks released Charles, who wended his way home through small, friendly German states.

In the meantime, Charles's enemies had whittled away his rudderless empire. Peter took the war into Finland, which at the time was an integral part of Sweden. In order to deny Charles the use of Finland's resources, the Russians devastated the countryside. Finns remember this as the Great Wrath, when the Russians looted crops and livestock and burned what they couldn't carry. As hunger set in, the population of Finland plunged from 400,000 to 330,000.[2]

By the time Charles got home, nothing remained of the Swedish empire but Sweden itself. Charles scraped up a new army and attacked Norway (a Danish territory at the time) but was killed in battle in 1719. With Charles out of the way, peace became a possibility. The new Swedish king was willing to become a second-rate power. Over the next couple of years, diplomats arranged peace treaties in which all of the allies' territory expanded and Sweden's contracted.[3]

WAR OF THE SPANISH SUCCESSION

Death toll: 700,000[1]
Rank: 61
Type: dynastic dispute
Broad dividing line: everyone against France
Time frame: 1701–13
Location: western Europe
Major state participants: France, Spain vs. Austria, Britain, Holland
Minor state participants: Piedmont, Bavaria (French allies) vs. Denmark, Portugal (Austrian allies)
Who usually gets the most blame: Louis XIV
Another damn: European balance-of-power war fought with muskets

SOMETIMES A NATION'S LUCK RUNS OUT. SPAIN HAD HAD A GOOD RUN, but centuries of Hapsburg inbreeding had finally produced a king barely able to function as an adult—King Charles II of Spain. The sole surviving son of a marriage between an uncle and niece,* Charles was dysfunctional on far too many levels. He was unable to speak until he was four, and unable to walk until he was eight; the only adult activity he performed enthusiastically was shooting. Because of a massive, deformed jaw he was barely able to speak coherently or chew, and because of uncontrollable premature ejaculation, he produced no children. He was nicknamed "Charles the Hexed" because it was obvious that something awful had happened to him.

Charles's archnemesis was also his brother-in-law. King Louis XIV of France had married Charles's half sister, the oldest daughter of the previous king of Spain. As the "Sun King," Louis set Europe's standards of magnificence with his new palace at Versailles. By 1700, he had already fought four wars against the rest of Europe, trying to take the Spanish territories in Flanders and Burgundy along the eastern border of France. To keep France

---

* More examples of a family tree that didn't branch: his mother's parents were first cousins; his mother's father's parents were first cousins; his father's father's parents were uncle and niece. I found eleven distinct paths (probably more) by which he was descended from Joanna the Mad of Castille, which couldn't have been a good sign.

from gaining too much power, Austria, Britain, and Holland had established the ongoing Grand Alliance against him.

Charles the Hexed had always seemed doomed to a short life. Most people expected him to die in childhood, but he lasted a lot longer than anyone thought possible. Even so, with the extinction of the Spanish Hapsburgs imminent, the rest of Europe haggled at several conferences over who should get the inheritance. Several claimants and partition schemes were floated. It was finally decided to reboot the Hapsburgs in Spain using another Charles, the brother of Emperor Joseph of Austria, while France would be placated with stray Hapsburg lands scattered around the continent.

Charles the Hexed grew annoyed at the way the other great powers talked about him as if he were already dead, carving up the Spanish Empire without even consulting him. Out of spite, in 1700 on his deathbed, Charles altered his will to prevent the partition of his vast and magnificent empire. He gave the whole thing to the French claimant, his half sister's grandson, who was also the grandson of King Louis XIV of France. This would link the two primary powers in Europe, leaving everyone else a distant second, so the rest of the world decided they had to stop this union.[2]

Style of War

By this time, warfare had reached a plateau of development, which stabilized tactics and equipment for the next century. Flintlock muskets, which slammed a flint down to spark the gunpowder, had replaced the less reliable matchlocks, which dipped a smoldering rope against a touchhole. Bayonets had removed the need for pikemen to support the firing line. Uniforms became standardized to reflect nationality, although soldiers were still recruited from far and wide. Less than half of the army of Louis XIV was French.

European armies of this era had also gotten larger—too large for the main battle force to forage for food. Louis began this war with 375,000 soldiers and 60,000 sailors at his disposal—although individual field armies were usually around 60,000. These big armies were tied to supply lines anchored at fortified strongpoints. This slowed down the overall pace of warfare as armies focused on defending or capturing these forts one siege at a time.

Civilian camp followers still furnished most support functions. For example, the 26,500-man Swedish army campaigning in Russia at this time (see "Great Northern War") was followed by 4,000 male servants, 1,100 nonmilitary administrators, and 1,700 women and children. They cooked, laundered, kept records, mended clothes, gathered firewood, hauled water, tended and butchered livestock, drove wagons, guarded the baggage while the army was fighting, nursed the wounded, and buried the dead.[3]

The Spanish Succession

Louis XIV quickly moved into Spanish territory to stake his claim, and the Grand Alliance moved to stop him. Austrian forces under Prince Eugene of Savoy (a veteran commander of the Great Turkish War) invaded Italy to take the Spanish territories of Milan and Naples. The English general John Churchill, duke of Marlborough, fought the French to a standstill in the Low Countries. Marlborough had only recently been restored to the English king's favor after having spent a few weeks in the Tower of London on charges (probably false) of plotting to overthrow the king.

The war came to a climax in 1704, when Marlborough marched to the Danube and joined with Eugene to take on the French army that was then rampaging through Germany. Although both armies were roughly equal in size at fifty-some thousand, the Franco-Bavarian army had a strong position with their right wing anchored on the Danube. Their infantry was solidly imbedded in three villages, each about a mile apart (notably Blenheim on the river), with lines of cavalry stationed between these three strongpoints.

With a stealthy night march, the Anglo-Austrians got within striking distance undetected, so when morning came, the French had to scramble into line. Allied skirmishers and artillery bombardments against the villages tied down the French infantry, while Marlborough drove the bulk of his force against the cavalry in the center. After the French cavalry was driven off, their infantry was left isolated and surrounded. English musketry and bombardment then destroyed these pockets. By the time it was over, the French and Bavarians had lost 80 percent of their army to death, injury, or captivity, while the Grand Alliance had lost a mere 20 percent. This was the first major defeat of the French in over fifty years.

The Battle of Blenheim ended all combat on the Danube and removed the direct threat against Austria; however, the tide of war accidentally turned back to France's favor in 1711 when Emperor Joseph I of Austria died without having produced any children who lived past childhood. His brother suddenly became the new emperor, Charles VI of Austria, in addition to his earlier position as the Austrian claimant to the Spanish throne. England and Holland panicked. An outright union of Spain and Austria was almost as bad as a union of Spain and France, so they worked out a deal with the French.

The final treaty signed at Utrecht split the inheritance. All of the Spanish territories in Europe, bar Spain itself, went to the Austrian Hapsburgs. Spain and the overseas colonies went to a side branch of the French Bourbons, which was to remain separate from the French throne.

WAR OF THE AUSTRIAN SUCCESSION

Death toll: 500,000[1]
Rank: 70
Type: hegemonial war
Broad dividing line: everyone against Austria
Time frame: 1740–48
Location: central Europe
Major state participants: France, Prussia vs. Austria, Britain
Minor state participants: Bavaria, Saxony-Poland
Who usually gets the most blame: Frederick the Great
Another damn: European balance-of-power war fought with muskets

THE HAPSBURG EMPEROR CHARLES VI OF AUSTRIA NEVER PRODUCED A SON, and unfortunately, each of his territories had its own peculiar inheritance laws for dealing with this. Some lands had no problem passing ownership to, say, a daughter or brother-in-law. Others forbade titles to pass anywhere close to a woman; they preferred to pass inheritance through uncles or cousins. The emperor, however, wanted everything to go to his eldest daughter, Maria Theresa, so he put a lot of effort into convincing all of the European powers to sign an agreement (the Pragmatic Sanction) saying that they would go along and not make a fuss. It wasn't supposed to be a problem.

However, the new young king of Prussia, Frederick II (soon to be Frederick the Great), was looking for an excuse to go conquering gloriously across Europe. After Emperor Charles died, Frederick scrounged up a medieval agreement between dead princes that gave the Austrian province of Silesia to Prussia before they would allow it to go to any female.

No one else in Europe found this convincing, and they dismissed his invasion of Silesia (now in western Poland) as foolish adventurism, doomed to fail against the greatest power in central Europe. In the first clash at Mollwitz, the Austrians easily chased off the Prussian cavalry, Frederick among them, and then turned against the isolated Prussian infantry; however, the Prussians' discipline and training surprised everyone when their infantry stood firm and slaughtered the attacking cavalry. Then a Prussian counterattack overwhelmed the Austrian infantry as well. Maria Theresa was forced to accept the loss of Silesia.

The conquest of Silesia boosted the Prussian population by a million German Protestants in fertile farmland along a navigable river. Frederick withdrew from the war to enjoy his new territory; however, with Austria knocked down, France realized that now was the perfect opportunity to administer kicks to the ribs, face, and groin of its fallen enemy, so the French declared war. Bavaria and Saxony—itching to break Austrian hegemony in Germany—joined in as well. Meanwhile, Britain was already fighting France on the high seas and beyond, and the British were dynastically linked to the German state of Hanover, so they subsidized the Austrians.

War boiled over all of the usual battlegrounds and pathways in central Europe, but each of the allies had different war aims, so they never quite coordinated their strategy. In the end, the Austrians managed to hold off the circling scavengers and to keep their losses down to only Silesia.

SINO-DZUNGAR WAR

Death toll: 600,000[1]
Rank: 67
Type: conquest
Broad dividing line: China vs. Dzungars
Time frame: 1755–57
Location: central Asia
Who usually gets the most blame: Qianlong

SOMEWHERE OUT IN THE MIDDLE OF NOWHERE, A LONG TIME AGO, THE Chinese wiped out a tribe few people have heard of. Most of history is like this.

The Dzungars were a species of Mongol. The nomadic horsemen of the central Asian steppe whom we've seen so far—such as Huns and Mongols—had been a continuous threat to civilization. Only a few chapters ago, horsemen such as the Manchus and Tatars were terrorizing China and Russia. Now guns had turned the tide against these nomads, and their independence was being squeezed by advancing civilization.

The soldiers on the leading edge of civilization who pushed into the steppe were themselves usually only a few generations removed from the steppes—Turks, Cossacks, and, in the case of China, the Manchus (see "Collapse of the Ming Dynasty"). Emperor Qianlong brought the Qing empire of China to its widest extent by conquering all around the periphery of China, notably into the western desert in Xinjiang and the land of the Dzungars.

People and Places You've Never Heard Of

Until he died in 1745, Galdan Tsereng, khan of Dzungaria, had maintained tight control over all of the component tribes in his empire. His son and successor, however, was cruel and degenerate, so the Dzungar nobility blinded and imprisoned him. He was followed by a monkish weakling who let several tribes drift into independence before he was killed in a coup. While the new khan, Dawaji, was consolidating control, several losers in the power struggle took refuge in Chinese territory and asked for help. Emperor Qianlong was happy to oblige.

A Chinese army took the Dzungar capital at Kuldja and put Galdan Tsereng's fugitive son-in-law, Amursana, in charge. After a chase across the desert, the former khan Dawaji was captured by the Chinese, but they tucked him away in a comfortable retirement rather than killing him.

Because the Chinese did not want a strong Dzungar state on their border, they recognized the autonomy of individual tribes rather than restoring the unified Dzungar empire, but Amursana had been hoping to inherit his father-in-law's grand empire, so he rose in rebellion.

Qianlong felt personally betrayed by this disloyalty so he insisted on wiping the Dzungars from the face of the earth. The details of this ethnic cleansing are pretty standard: anyone who didn't get out of the way was killed; anyone who did get out of the way starved.[2]

SEVEN YEARS WAR

Death toll: 1.5 million[1]
Rank: 40
Type: hegemonial war
Broad dividing line: everyone against Prussia
Time frame: 1756–63
Location: Europe, the oceans, the colonies
Major state participants: Austria, France, Russia vs. Prussia, Britain
Minor state participants: Sweden, Saxony
Who usually gets the most blame: Frederick the Great
Another damn: European balance-of-power war fought with muskets

Junkers

Scattered in pieces all across the northern European plain, the Kingdom of Prussia lacked natural boundaries. There was Prussia itself on the eastern Baltic, Brandenburg around Berlin, Pomerania on the central Baltic coast, and a few pinpricks like Kleve and Ravensberg over by the Netherlands. Countries like these tended to get trampled by armies passing through on their way to attack the countries that mattered. Only by building up a world-class army could such a country convince marauding generals to respect their neutrality and go the long way around.

Frederick the Great's father, Frederick William, had achieved this through personal frugality. Instead of building magnificent palaces, he financed an army. Instead of servants, he had soldiers. The rest of Europe consider this to be a personal eccentricity rather than a national policy, and joked about it instead of worrying.

The single-minded fanaticism with which the Prussians built their army paid off by producing soldiers who were superior to whomever they fought. The Prussians didn't waver or delay. Their drill and discipline allowed them to fire five shots for every two fired by the Austrian infantry.

Prussian armies of this era continued to evolve away from the mercenary bands of the previous century. They were becoming true national armies filled by beating the drum from village to village and luring bored farm boys into signing up. Each unit was permanently billeted in a district from which they gathered new recruits. Three-fourths of the Prussian army was actually Prussian.

This manpower certainly was not the best that Prussia had to offer. Armies were usually the dregs of society. Useful people like craftsmen, shopkeepers, and artisans were too important to the national economy to be recruited. Instead, armies were assembled out of expendable people—criminals, landless peasants, teenagers, vagrants, drunkards. Since the Prussian aristocracy—the Junkers—had nothing better to do, they were made the officers.

The shiftless rabble that filled the ranks could be controlled only by the most brutal discipline. Heavy whipping was the standard punishment for almost any offense, unless it was serious enough to require something worse. The Prussian army had standing orders to not make it too easy to desert—no camping near woods, no night marches, no unsupervised foraging. Cavalry patrolled the edges of the army, mostly to keep the Prussians in, rather than to keep the enemy out.[2]

War Begins

After losing Silesia in her first war against the Prussian juggernaut (see "War of the Austrian Succession"), Queen Maria Theresa of Austria spent the following peace wooing away all of Frederick's allies. It proved to be remarkably easy since none of the other great powers wanted a dynamic new player like Prussia to replace a comfortably declining old power like Austria. Maria Theresa's major success in this diplomatic revolution was befriending France, Austria's mortal enemy for over a hundred years. Empress Elizabeth of Russia also signed on to the anti-Frederick team.

When it became obvious that the new alliance was gearing up to attack as soon as warm weather arrived in the spring of 1757, Frederick launched a preemptive attack in August 1756 against what he assumed would be their jumping-off spot, the independent Duchy of Saxony. Unfortunately, Saxony had not officially joined the coalition against Prussia, so Frederick had just invaded a neutral nation without warning or provocation. This made it a lot easier for the rest of Europe to declare war on him.

This new lineup brought all of the Catholics together, so Frederick tried to persuade England and other northern European countries to join him in Protestant solidarity, which everyone spotted as a cynical ploy. According to one Englishman of the time, Frederick "cried out *religion* as folks do *fire* when they want assistance." In any case, it didn't matter to England which side they were on, as long as France was on the other.[3]

The 4.5 million people of Prussia now faced 70 million enemies.[4] But cash, not population, was the deciding factor for how large an army a country could put in the field. Frederick began the Seven Years War with a war chest of 11 million thalers, and once the war got going, the British subsidized him with 4 million yearly, plus occupied Saxony could be squeezed for another 5 or 10 million each year as well.

Frederick the Great became known for the oblique order of battle. He withheld one wing of his army, threatening but disengaged from the enemy. Then he loaded up the other flank and threw it against the smaller enemy wing that faced it. This overwhelmed the enemy wing and forced a progressive collapse of the enemy line as each piece was attacked in turn from both the front and the side. At each point of contact, the Prussians would have a local superiority of numbers, knocking aside the enemy line bit by bit. Other countries tried to emulate Frederick's tactics, but they wouldn't work without soldiers as disciplined as the Prussians or a mind as sharp as Frederick's.

The Seven Years War was a reckless, hyperactive affair that zigzagged around central Europe, blasting apart armies whenever they caught up with each other. Frederick's ability to attack in every direction and fend off practically the whole of Europe for seven years has always amazed military historians, and his tactics have been eagerly studied and analyzed. He won important battles against astounding odds and miraculously recovered from his occasional defeats; however, the final twist that gave the victory to Frederick was a matter of luck rather than skill.

In January 1762, as the Russians were closing in on the Prussian capital at Berlin, Empress Elizabeth of Russia suddenly died, leaving the throne to her young son, Peter III, who had admired Frederick ever since Peter was a little boy playing with toy soldiers. Peter III pulled Russia's troops out of the war zone and signed a treaty in May, preparing to intervene on Frederick's side; however, Tsar Peter was soon overthrown and assassinated by his wife, Catherine (the Great), who withdrew Russia completely from both sides of the war.

By this time, the armies were in no shape to launch another major offensive. Manpower was down to burnt-out veterans and green recruits. In the autumn of 1762, the French were driven back over the Rhine, which finally convinced everybody that further fighting would be futile. The peace treaty was signed in February 1763 in Paris.

Worldwide War

Because the Europeans carried their fight all over the world, some writers—Winston Churchill, for instance—have argued that the Seven Years War deserved the credit for being the *real* first world war.

Two of the major colonial powers, France and England, used the European war as an excuse to fight each other elsewhere. In North America, the French won the first battles in the Appalachian wilderness that separated their settlements, but then a fresh British army captured Quebec, which put England in control of the entire American mainland. In India, the British decisively defeated the native ally of the French at the Battle of Plassey, which set them on the path to ruling the whole subcontinent.

NAPOLEONIC WARS

Death toll: 4 million (3 million soldiers and 1 million civilians died, including the French Revolutionary Wars)[1]

Rank: 26

Type: world conquest

Broad dividing line: Supporters of Napoleon would say it pitted the virtues of the Enlightenment against the decadent Ancient Regime. The rest of Europe would just call it Napoleon against the world.

Time frame: 1792–1815

Location: Europe, Levant, Caribbean

Major state participants: Austria, France, Prussia, Russia, United Kingdom

Minor state participants: Bavaria, Brunswick, Denmark, Egypt, Naples-Sicily, Netherlands, Ottoman Turkey, Piedmont-Sardinia, Portugal, Saxony, Spain, Sweden, United States, Wurttemberg

Who usually gets the most blame: Napoleon Bonaparte

Another damn: European balance-of-power war fought with muskets

Liberty, Equality, Etc.

By the end of the 1780s, France was clearly heading toward bankruptcy. The legendary extravagance of the big-wigged courtiers at Versailles was part of it, but the bulk of the Crown's debt had been racked up in foreign wars, which had been financed by borrowing from the emerging entrepreneurial class. The way things were heading, the middle class was going to get bled coming and going—first as the only wealthy class that actually paid taxes, and then again if the Crown defaulted on its loans. The middle class agitated for reform.

Finally, in order to calm the overtaxed commoners and to straighten out his messy finances, King Louis XVI was forced to call the first meeting of the French parliament in over a century. The first two legislative houses (or *estates*), the nobility and the clergy, refused to budge on their tax exemptions, so the Third Estate—representing the commoners, both rich and poor—declared itself the only legitimate legislative body.

A liberal agenda was quickly enacted. Privileges of the upper classes and the clergy were revoked. Finances were fixed, and the budget was balanced. After fierce debate, church lands were confiscated, and the clergy was bundled into the civil service.

Unfortunately while all this was going on, scattered mobs of angry poor rampaged through the streets of Paris, lynching random nobles and royal officials who crossed their paths. The royal family panicked and tried to flee to the safety of their Austrian in-laws (the French queen, Marie Antoinette, was the daughter of Maria Theresa), but they were caught, paraded back to Paris, and imprisoned. Horrified by this nasty outbreak of liberalism, and afraid it might be contagious, the monarchs of Europe banded together into the First Coalition and set out to rescue the king of France.

This backfired. With foreign armies converging on the homeland, politics in France turned even more radical, and the Jacobin faction of Maximilien Robespierre took control. The nobility was abolished as a legal class, and to make it final, the king was beheaded. His wife, Marie Antoinette, soon followed him to the guillotine, while the dauphin, their son and heir, disappeared mysteriously into the dungeons of the new republic. His fate remained the nineteenth century's greatest mystery, with several claimants making the salon circuit a few decades later.*

Now that the sacred taboo against killing the king had been broken, France erupted. Nobles were dragged from their homes and slaughtered in a variety of horrible and imaginative ways. The Reign of Terror saw the decapitation of some 40,000 enemies of the state, most without the bother of a trial.

In the Vendee region of west-central France, peasants counter-revolted against the central government in favor of the king and church, and Paris dispatched commissioners to restore order by any means necessary, which often meant mass executions of entire families. Disposing of so many state enemies required perverse ingenuity. In Nantes condemned prisoners of all ages and genders were stuffed naked aboard river barges, sealed below decks, and then sunk into the Loire River. After sitting underwater long enough to rinse out all of the air pockets, the barges were raised again, emptied out, and loaded with more prisoners for another round.

All in all, a quarter million people died in this civil war.[2] Eventually, however, the anger subsided. Robespierre himself was shoved into the guillotine, and sensible, middle-class rule returned to France.

---

* Now it looks like the most boring answer has been right all along, and the missing dauphin had simply died in prison. In 2000, a desiccated heart that had been spirited away during a 1795 prison autopsy of a young prisoner and passed around royalist circles for two centuries proved to have the same mitochondrial DNA as a preserved lock of the queen's hair. This should have clinched it, except that gaps in the chain of evidence have left enough room for suspicions that the heart might have once resided inside some other member of the royal family instead. (Jan Bondeson, *The Great Pretenders: The True Stories behind Famous Historical Mysteries* [New York: W. W. Norton, 2004]; Nadya Labi, "Requiem for a Dauphin. DNA Analysis Reveals That the Young Heir to the French Throne Left to Die in Prison Was No Impostor," *Time*, May 1, 2000)

The Revolutionary Wars

Although every nation in Europe was swept up in the wars that followed the French Revolution, you need to know only the five great powers: France at one end of Europe; Russia at the other end; Prussia and Austria now backed up flush against Russia after dividing up Poland among themselves. England hovered off the coast. No other nation mattered because none could field an army capable of standing up to one of the great powers all by itself. The lesser nations of Europe were at best pawns, and at worst the chessboard.

The First Coalition that invaded France in 1793 from almost every direction on behalf of monarchism figured that France would be an easy conquest. The revolutionaries had executed or exiled all of their officers and sent an undisciplined rabble out to defend the homeland. What the old monarchies didn't realize was that now that Frenchmen ran France, the country was worth fighting for. For the first time in generations, authentic patriotism motivated an army. The French turned back the invaders and rolled forward over all of the little lands beyond the eastern border, spreading the gospel of revolution.

The revolutionaries were serious about remaking the world into a rational order, down to the smallest detail. All of the odd little measurements that varied from village to village were standardized into a new decimal system of meters, liters, and grams. All of the random and arbitrary medieval laws that varied from province to province were recodified along sensible lines that incorporated logic, mercy, and the rights of man. The calendar was reformed into sensible decimal units with equal months, natural names, and the year of the revolution set as Year One. Churches were reconsecrated as temples of reason. It was a new world where anyone was allowed to rise as high as his talents could take him. The downside of this quickly became apparent when a dangerously talented individual showed up.

Enter Napoleon

Born to a large, respectable, influential family on the small, disreputable, inconsequential island of Corsica in the Italian part of France, Napoleon Bonaparte never really fit in. Although Napoleon originally was hoping for the priesthood like his brother, his father sent him to military school in France instead, where he learned his trade and made very few friends. He dreamed of someday liberating Corsica from France, but as the French Revolution unfolded, he was swept up into grander visions of liberating the whole world.

In his first major combat experience, Bonaparte commanded the artillery that drove the royalists and their British allies from the Mediterranean port of Toulon. His skill and determination at scrounging and deploying enough artillery to challenge the British guns impressed his superiors. Bonaparte and his sponsors narrowly survived the purge of the radicals, but his patrons deftly tacked to follow the new winds and finagled appointments to the new government. Bonaparte followed them to Paris as the commander of the capital's artillery. When his cannon shredded an angry mob that was storming the main government building, it became obvious that his ruthlessness was just as impressive as his generalship. Here was a man the government could use.

At the age of twenty-six, and newly wed to his patron's mistress, Josephine, Bonaparte was given command of the ragged French army that was battling the Austrians in the north Italian plain. He quickly endeared himself to his soldiers by admitting that the government in Paris had failed them, had left them unpaid and unfed, and had sent a succession of incompetent political generals out to have them killed in humiliating defeats. Bonaparte instead offered his soldiers the wealth of Italy to be plundered, and they loved him for it.[3] Rather than rely on erratic supplies from France, his army would live off the land, but to do that, he would have to break up into smaller scattered corps and keep on the move. In the hands of a lesser general this would have invited disaster, but Bonaparte proved a master juggler, always keeping his scattered corps close enough to support any strategic opening that presented itself.

The Italian people had originally been tempted to welcome the French as liberators from the Austrians and their puppets, but they now suffered rape and pillage at the hands of a conquering army. Even when Milan surrendered without a fight, Bonaparte let his men loot unhindered for several days, and when the locals rose up, he sent troops into the nearby village of Binasco. They burned the houses, lined up all of the men and boys, and shot them down.[4] Very quickly, Bonaparte began to ship enough loot back to the French treasury for the invasion to turn a profit. By April 1797, he had outclassed all of the armies that Austria had thrown at him and was closing in on Vienna. It was either a bluff or sheer audacity because he clearly did not have enough men left to take and hold the city, but the enemies of France blinked first and sued for peace.

Bonaparte's career path was never smooth, and during the two decades of his dominance, Europe was dragged along on his wild oscillations depending on whether he gambled and won, or gambled and lost. At the close of the Italian campaign, Bonaparte had reached a dizzying peak. He returned to a hero's welcome in Paris and basked in the adulation of the French people. Then he gambled and lost.

The Egyptian Campaign

No one really knows why Bonaparte invaded Turkish-controlled Egypt. Ostensibly, it was to be the first step in attacking the British in India. Publicly, it was the announced policy of the French to bring rational, republican civilization to the backward peoples of the Orient. Bonaparte's enemies in the French government (and there were more enemies all the time) wanted to get him as far away as possible, and Bonaparte himself wanted to play Alexander and Caesar. The planning, however, went poorly, with many supplies and troops failing to materialize as promised at the embarkation ports. In the only bit of luck that fell his way, the French armada managed to slip all the way across the Mediterranean without being caught and captured by the superior British fleet.[5]

In July 1798, after a nauseating landing on the beach, Bonaparte pulled his wobbly soldiers up off their knees and led them into the desert without enough water or any current maps, aiming vaguely for Cairo. Harassed the whole way by Bedouin guerrillas, the column finally stumbled into the suburbs of Cairo, and Bonaparte declared Egypt liberated from centuries of Turkish misrule. Meanwhile, the British fleet under Lord Nelson found the French ships at Aboukir Bay, in the Nile Delta, and bloodily reasserted British naval superiority, leaving Bonaparte's expeditionary force stranded a thousand miles from home.

The thirteen months Bonaparte spent in Egypt would open this ancient and mysterious land to European scholarship, but it had almost no effect on the course of Bonaparte's career. The hopeless isolation of his army meant that no one back in France heard about the deteriorating condition of his army, the outbreaks of bubonic plague, the massacres of unruly natives, a futile raid into Palestine, and the suicides of desperate officers. All that Paris heard was that Bonaparte had vanquished the dreaded and exotic Mameluke cavalry under the pyramids. It didn't matter that the Egyptians quickly learned to avoid open battle in favor of hit-and-run tactics that whittled away the army's morale; Bonaparte had proved himself to be the new Caesar.[6]

In August 1799, Bonaparte abandoned his battered army to its fate and snuck back to France—to yet another hero's welcome. His country needed him. All of the foreign enemies he had beaten had rejoined as the Second Coalition and attacked.

1799: Coup d'etat c'est moi

But first things first. The French Republic was still sputtering along in its usual chaos, facing schemes and uprisings from internal enemies on both the left and the right. Royalists were trying to restore a king, while radicals wanted to redistribute property to the poor. Then Bonaparte arrived triumphantly from Egypt, and no one asked why his army wasn't with him.

After much scheming behind the scenes, and with the backing of the home army, a cabal of conspirators supplemented the weak and quarrelsome elected body that ran the republic (the Directory) with three powerful chief executives ("consuls")—Bonaparte and two others who thought they could keep up with him. When Bonaparte asked the citizenry to approve this change, the French people overwhelmingly supported the idea with 99 percent of the vote. Technically, only 30 percent of the voters actually supported the idea, but since Bonaparte's little brother, in his position as interior minister, was the one counting the votes, the reported vote was 99 percent in Bonaparte's favor.[7]

Now Bonaparte was ready to fight off the Second Coalition. Against all expectations, he slipped over the Alps during the winter. Then a quick, deadly campaign in Italy convinced the rest of Europe to leave France alone for the time being. An unparalleled five years of peace ensued.

In 1804, at the age of thirty-five, Bonaparte was secure enough in his position to drop the pretense of republican rule. He decided that consul was a silly title, so he transformed from Citizen Bonaparte to Emperor Napoleon. To gain respectability in the eyes of his fellow monarchs, he restored the official role of the Catholic Church, put Sunday back into the calendar, and returned to counting the years starting from the year of the birth of Christ. He also reestablished slavery in the Caribbean colonies. In 1809, Emperor Napoleon dumped Josephine, the exciting little tart he had married in his youth, and married the teenage daughter of the emperor of Austria, who was not enthusiastic about her new job, considering what the French had done to her great aunt, Marie Antoinette. In time, however, she grew to love and cling to him desperately, often distracting him at pivotal moments in history.

When war resumed against the Third Coalition in 1805, it unleashed the Napoleon of legend, leading his armies across Europe, steamrolling everyone who stood in his way. He fought big, bloody battles against the Russians, Prussians, and Austrians at Austerlitz and Ulm (1805), Jena and Auerstadt (1806), Eylau and Friedland (1807), Aspern and Wagram (1809), to name just a few. If you're a total nerd for tactics, this is your favorite part, but the rest of you need to know only that Napoleon proved unstoppable, no matter how many countries ganged up on him, no matter how big their armies. He beat them all with dazzling skill. The whole of Europe west of the Elbe River ended up under Napoleon's rule—either directly or through his family, whom he appointed as kings of satellite nations. Austria and Prussia were allowed to remain as free kingdoms, but they were trimmed down to a less threatening size.

Peninsular War

Napoleon's only setbacks during his zenith were in and around Spain. In 1800 he had bullied the Spanish into an alliance that joined their fleet to his. On paper, it was beginning to look like Napoleon might be able to challenge British control of the seas; however, in 1804, Nelson destroyed the Franco-Spanish fleet at Trafalgar, which ended any hope Napoleon had of expanding his empire beyond Europe. Playing to his remaining strengths, he tried to break Britain by prohibiting all trade between the continent and the United Kingdom. Any countries that broke the embargo were occupied by French troops and bundled into the empire. To tighten control over the ports, he directly annexed much of the European coastline, to the Baltic Sea in the north and to the Croatian coast in the south.

Portugal, however, stubbornly stayed outside this Continental System. Napoleon sent an army to remove this pro-British blemish from the map of Europe, but this required a long supply line across Spain. Heavy military traffic across their country led to friction with the Spaniards, which led to brawls, then riots, and eventually rebellion. A full French invasion in 1808 replaced the Bourbon king in Madrid with Napoleon's brother, but the natives continued to fight using a nasty style of hit-and-run tactics that came to be called *guerrilla*, the Spanish word for "little war." The French routinely tortured and executed any suspected rebels who fell into their hands (and vice versa), which provided the subject for a haunting series of Goya drawings but did nothing to break the rebellion. Eventually, regular British troops under the duke of Wellington fought their way out of Portugal to support the rebels.

Style of Warfare

The most significant difference between warfare under Napoleon and that of earlier generations was the nationalistic passions unleashed by the French Revolution. France was able to fight the whole of Europe because it rallied the entire homeland to defend the ideals of equality and reason against the sullen peasant levies under gentlemen officers that characterized the monarchial way of war. With the whole nation involved, the size of the armies escalated, from 60,000 who fought on both sides at Marengo in 1800, to 165,000 at Austerlitz in 1805, to 300,000 at Wagram in 1809.[8]

Napoleonic warfare represented the peak of the musket era, which meant that armies lined up, blasted away at each other, and then charged. This may sound stupid to us, but Napoleonic firepower was so inefficient that the only way to make a dent in the opposition was to concentrate hundreds of muskets together, firing in calm, steady volleys.

Instead of carefully aimed shots, the infantry relied on rapid mass fire to erode the enemy line. Muskets were designed to be loaded and fired quickly, not accurately. Powder, ball, and wadding were shoved down the muzzle in disciplined, unthinking motions. A smooth bore left a loose fit between the ammunition and the barrel, which made it easier to load but weakened the blast, reduced the range, and spoiled the aim. Rifles, which had a tighter, spiraled bore, were more accurate than muskets, but they were too slow and difficult to load to have much effect on the battlefield aside from scattered sniping and harassment.[9]

To allow officers to distinguish friend from foe on a smoky battlefield, soldiers wore uniforms of bright, distinctive colors and fought in geometric formations under giant banners. Every unit of a Napoleonic army had precise mathematical characteristics—speed of movement, length of front, rate of fire, stamina—which good generals could calculate at a glance. With careful maneuver, a line might be able to bring a little extra firepower on the enemy line. If a regiment could catch the enemy infantry from the side, it could bring more muskets to bear than the enemy could. Better yet, a regiment might be able to catch the enemy between two firing lines. Then, when the enemy has been shaken, the regiment could fix bayonets and charge, hoping to cover the open ground before the enemy could fire more than a couple of volleys.

Attacking in line (strung out across a wide front, but with no depth) was difficult because a thin line could easily lose its cohesion. Some soldiers would move faster than others; others would fall behind; some might veer a bit left, others a bit right. Gaps would form quickly. Most generals preferred to attack in a column (fewer men across the front, but many more in depth). Gaps were less of a problem for a column, because plenty of replacement soldiers stood behind any opening that might appear.

Exploding artillery shells make for exciting cinema, but simple, solid cannonballs were more commonly used to break up infantry formations. These would rip a gash through any line of soldiers who stood in the way and inflict horrible wounds, easily pulping any body part they hit and scattering jagged bone fragments like shrapnel into the neighboring ranks. At closer range, grapeshot and canister (the cannon equivalents of shotgun shells) would be sprayed into infantry formations. A column took heavier casualties from cannon than from muskets because it was deeper and more crowded. A line was the opposite. Cannon shot hitting a line might tear apart one or two soldiers before skidding to a halt in the mud behind it.

For all of the dangers of standing stiffly in formation as a target for artillery, it was still safer than trying to run. Cavalry was always ready to swoop in with sabers and spears to cut down any stray foot soldiers they spotted. This included not only enemy cavalry but friendly cavalry as well, which usually had orders to make an example of shirkers and deserters.

Improvements in musketry had reduced cavalry's impact on battle and pushed the horsemen off to the sidelines. Attacking a block of infantry was almost impossibly deadly, but cavalry could easily scatter and slaughter loose formations of skirmishers, hunt down snipers, or massacre infantry that broke formation and ran. When attacking artillery, cavalry would chase gunners away from their cannons and then hammer iron spikes into the touchholes, rendering them useless. The best defense for infantry against horsemen was a tight square, bristling with bayonets in every direction, but that made a better target for artillery.[10] Like a deadly game of rock, paper, scissors, no single formation was best against all enemies.

The point of a Napoleonic battle was not to simply slaughter the opponents willy-nilly. Rather, it was to wreck the discipline and cohesion of the enemy, regiment by regiment; to blunt its attacks, to rip open its line with artillery, chase enemy soldiers from the field with an infantry charge, and keep them running with a cavalry pursuit. Toward the end of the day, generals on both sides would have plenty of useless units, not measured purely in terms of casualties, but in the numbers scattered, exhausted, lost in the smoke, plundering the dead, hiding, or evacuating the wounded. Generals would feed fresh reserves into sectors where the enemy might be vulnerable to one last punch. It didn't always work. At Waterloo, the slaughter of Napoleon's last reserve (the Old Guard) at the end of the day destroyed any hope Napoleon might have had of recovering the upper hand.[11]

Away from the Battlefield

Medicine was still largely based on folk cures and Greco-Roman theory, so more soldiers died from disease than from battle. Gathering thousands of young men from all over the continent into army camps often exposed them to childhood diseases, such as measles and smallpox, which they had never developed immunity against. Poor rations led to scurvy. Wounds led to infection. Poorly designed latrines and wells spread waterborne diseases such as typhoid fever and dysentery, while wearing the same uniform day after day allowed thriving colonies of lice and fleas to spread typhus and bubonic plague. In especially unhealthy environments, strange new diseases could cripple an army. When Napoleon tried to reestablish control over the rebellious island of Haiti, the French had to abandon their invasion after losing half their men to yellow fever.

On the plus side, vaccination was just coming into practice, and the field of public health got a major boost during the Napoleonic era as nations scrambled to keep enough children alive to restock the armies. It was probably no coincidence that Prussia established nationwide free vaccination in 1806, right after its army was wiped out by Napoleon at the Battle of Jena.[12]

Civilians rarely came under direct fire. Armies needed open ground on which to deploy, so they avoided fighting in cities. Battlefields were usually small enough to allow any local farm families to scurry out of range at the first sign of trouble. On the other hand, besieged cities were commonly bombarded. The British fleet killed 1,600 civilians during its shelling of Copenhagen in 1807.[13]

The reach of Napoleonic campaigning was restricted by the appetites of draught animals. If the army traveled more than a few days from a river or seaport, the wagons would have no room for anything more than the hay to feed the animals that pulled the wagons. The only way past this was for foraging parties to constantly scrounge ahead of the main army, confiscating the forage that peasants had set aside for their own animals.

As unprecedented numbers of soldiers tramped back and forth across Europe, they requisitioned food from the farms they passed. They killed livestock for their own use, including chickens that would have been better used laying eggs and cows that would have been better used producing milk. The armies seized horses and oxen for transport. They conscripted the able-bodied and left the old, the young, and the feeble to fend for themselves. This continued year after year, without letup. It has been reckoned that a million civilians across northwest Europe died as a result of these wars.

While armies easily foraged in the rich farmlands of northwest Europe, countries on the rough edges of the continent were too rugged or primitive to support the huge armies Napoleon needed for victory. In Spain and Russia, Napoleon found his armies scouring the countryside and failing to turn up enough provisions to support the long, grim campaign necessary to crush the locals.

Russian Campaign

Napoleon's invasion of Russia was the most ghastly single campaign of the Napoleonic Wars, possibly of the entire nineteenth century. When Russia refused to stop trading with Britain, Napoleon gathered 611,900 soldiers and 25,000 civilian support personnel from all across occupied Europe into the Grand Army. He personally led 250,000 in June of 1812 along the main axis of advance toward Moscow, while smaller armies under his marshals followed in reserve or covered his flanks.[14] Napoleon's army was too large for the Russians to even consider trying to stop it, but the retreating Russians devastated the countryside ahead of the French, leaving nothing to feed them. Disease thinned the French ranks, as did the need to leave French garrisons to protect the route home, so the Grand Army was reduced by almost half when the Russians finally stood against Napoleon in September at Borodino. Napoleon bludgeoned them out of the way in a messy battle that left Moscow free for the taking.

However, soon after the French moved into Moscow to wait out the winter, wildfires swept across the empty city. Knowing he could never survive the Russian winter in the ruins, Napoleon began his retreat in October, but now the earlier scorched-earth tactics of the retreating Russians took their toll a second time. As the retreating French staggered homeward on reduced rations, the snows arrived early. Horses were eaten and cannon abandoned. "Our lips stuck together," a survivor wrote. "Our nostrils froze. We seemed to be marching in a world of ice."[15] Cossacks swept along the wake of the retreating French, killing stragglers with imagination and delight. Only some 70,000 ragged survivors of Napoleon's army crossed the last river to safety in December, leaving a half million dead, captured, or deserted behind them.

The French Empire was now mortally wounded, and the wolves awoke and circled in for the kill. Previously pacified nations like Austria and Prussia raised new armies, and having learned from the French, they rallied their nations with passionate appeals to patriotism. Napoleon hurried back to France and rounded up all of the young men who had come of age since he had left for Russia. He stripped the empire of garrison troops and recalled retired veterans. With an army that, on paper, was back to pre-Russian levels, Napoleon plunged into the heart of Germany to stop the allies from dismantling his empire.

The battle they fought at Leipzig for four days in October 1813 is the first battle in reliably recorded history with more than a half-million combatants, and one of the only battles that Napoleon fought on the defensive or in a city. Napoleon's untested and outnumbered army got the worst of it, and his Saxon allies switched sides in the middle of the battle. Napoleon started to pull back behind the Elbe River; however, the bridge was blown up before he finished, and tens of thousands of Frenchmen were stranded on the wrong side of the river.

Despite the defeat, he was still Napoleon, and he made his enemies fight every step of the way back to France. The allied armies gradually pushed him across France and took Paris in March of 1814. Finally admitting defeat and abdicating in April, Napoleon was exiled to the tiny Mediterranean island of Elba, where he would be free to rule over his tiny court and parade his tiny army. Then the monarchs of Europe sent their representatives to the Congress of Vienna to create a new status quo that would guard against resurgent liberalism.

Like the end of a horror movie, where the villain is beaten and left for dead, only to stealthily reemerge wet, bloody, and angry from the bottomless pit or churning waterfall and suddenly attack one last time after the hero has put his weapon aside or the heroine has undressed for bed, that's what Napoleon did. He crashed through the window and tried to strangle a screaming teenager in her nightie—metaphorically speaking.

After sneaking back into France in February 1815, Napoleon rallied his supporters and led the French army into Belgium, hoping to knock out the approaching allied armies one at a time before they coalesced into an unbeatable horde. He knocked the British back at Quatre Bras, then the Prussians at Ligny, and then turned back against the British before they could recover from the first blow. At Waterloo, Wellington's Britons stood their ground against the full fury of the French attack all day, until the Prussians arrived to chase away the exhausted French. The battle wrecked Napoleon's army beyond repair, and there was no other choice but to retreat and come to terms with the victors.

Napoleon's original plan was to escape to America, but British control of the seas put a stop to that. Most of his enemies wanted him dead, but Great Britain had never been overrun by Napoleon, so the British proved a bit more flexible on the last point than, say, the Russians. Napoleon was taken aboard a British warship and safely stashed in a heavily guarded cottage in one of the world's most remote inhabitable places—the tropical Atlantic island of Saint Helena. He would remain a private citizen under house arrest for the final six years of his life.

Worldwide Legacy

Lacking control of the seas, Napoleon couldn't impose his will outside of Europe, but for someone who never got any further than the Mediterranean basin, he caused disruptions on a global scale. The Western Hemisphere was almost totally transformed by the career of a man who never even set foot there.

The French occupation of Spain left the Spanish colonies in America adrift. Forced to look after themselves while Spain was in turmoil, they resisted when the restored Spanish monarchy tried to reassert control. It took a decade of bloody colonial wars, but eventually these Latin American communities would establish their independence.

In the United States foreign policy split along party lines, with the Jeffersonians fully in favor of killing kings and supporting America's old ally France against the hated British, while the Federalists were swayed more by America's traditional ethnic and economic ties to Britain and a general middle-class fear of revolution. The debate turned so angry that the Speaker of the House was stabbed over it after Congress approved a favorable treaty with Great Britain.

While the Federalists were in power, America fought an undeclared naval war against France, but in 1800, the election of Thomas Jefferson to the presidency restored America's friendship with France and hostility to Britain. When Napoleon needed to raise cash, he sold his North American holdings to Jefferson, doubling the size of the United States and putting the Pacific coast of the continent within reach. Ten years later, in 1812, while Napoleon trudged across Russia, America went to war with Britain over its blockade of Napoleonic Europe. The American attempt to conquer Canada was beaten back, but British assaults against Baltimore and New Orleans likewise failed, so the war was officially a draw. At least America got a national anthem out of it.

Even the farthest tips of Africa and Asia got knocked around by the wars in Europe. After France annexed the Netherlands, the British seized the Dutch colony at Cape Town, which would eventually evolve into the troublesome nation of South Africa. The British also took the strategic Malacca Strait from the Dutch, where they would soon build the city of Singapore.

Compared to the other events on my list, the Napoleonic Wars stand out for two reasons. They are one of the few giant megadeaths that ended when the perpetrator was actually caught and locked away, and among the few that killed more soldiers than civilians. In fact, if we count only the deaths of soldiers and ignore civilians, the Napoleonic-Revolutionary Wars would collectively count as the third bloodiest conflict in history, behind the two world wars.

WORLD CONQUERORS

W E CAN'T JUST HAND THE COVETED TITLE OF "WORLD CONQUEROR" TO anyone who marches up and asks for it. We need standards. Obviously, no one has ever succeeded in conquering the entire world, but a few have tried. Here are the men and women—okay, men—who have gone out of their way to attack every country within reach and beaten most of them. These are the deadliest conquerors of history:

Hitler: 42 million dead in Europe

Chinggis Khan: 40 million dead across Asia

Timur: 17 million dead in Asia

Napoleon: 4 million dead in Europe

Frederick the Great: 2 million dead in two wars over Silesia and hegemony in Europe

Louis XIV: 1.5 million dead from his wars[1]

Shaka Zulu: 1.5 million dead in southern Africa

Gaius Julius Caesar: claimed to have killed 1,192,000 foreign enemies in battle[2]

Alexander the Great: 450,000 killed in the Middle East

Perhaps it's also worth mentioning a couple of the least successful world conquerors in history. These warlords attacked all of their neighbors and were badly beaten every time:

Saddam Hussein: around 740,000 dead from his wars, not including the 300,000 Iraqis he killed by internal tyranny

First he invaded Iran, hoping to take advantage of the Iranian revolution to conquer a few oil-rich provinces. After a promising start, the tide turned and Saddam was forced to defend his own oil provinces. (Seven hundred thousand were killed in that war.)

Then he invaded Kuwait, but was kicked out by an international coalition. (Twenty-five thousand were killed in that war.) Finally, the United States invaded and removed him entirely. (Thirteen thousand were killed in the invasion itself.)

Solano Lopez: 480,000 dead from the War of the Triple Alliance, in which Paraguay fought all of its neighbors.

HAITIAN SLAVE REVOLT

Death toll: 400,000 (350,000 Haitians, 50,000 European troops)[1]
Rank: 81
Type: slave revolt
Broad dividing line: slaves vs. masters
Time frame: 1791–1803
Location: Saint-Domingue (now Haiti)
State participants: France, Britain, Spain
Who usually gets the most blame: A surprising number of people blame the slaves.
Economic factors: slaves, sugar

TWO CLEARLY DEFINED CLASSES INHABITED THE FRENCH COLONY OF SAINT-Domingue in the Caribbean Sea—a tiny white minority of citizens who had full civil rights and a huge black majority of slaves who had none. A vague third class of free mulattos every bit as numerous as the whites held a more awkward position. They were allowed to own property and form families, but they had no voice in law or politics.

All of the liberal revolutions following the Enlightenment had to face the contradiction of slavery being legal in a free nation. Some abolished it; some compromised; the French went back and forth on it, depending on who was in charge at the moment. After the French Revolution, Paris decided to slip a little more democracy into Haiti by granting full voting rights to any free man in Saint-Domingue with property, even among the biracial. Naturally the whites in the colony wouldn't accept a law that cut their political clout in half, so protests led to riots, and sporadic fighting broke out over it in 1790.

Then suddenly, in August 1791, that seemed unimportant when the slaves in the northern part of the island rose up, slaughtering 2,000 of their white masters with farm tools and burning over twelve hundred coffee and two hundred sugar plantations. The surviving whites retaliated, killing 10,000 slaves. Soon everyone was killing everyone else.[2]

Meanwhile, Paris rescinded its original franchise law. The free mulattos under Jean-Jacques Dessalines joined the slaves and pushed the whites into three defensive enclaves. The rebels usually slaughtered any whites who didn't escape in time, regardless of age or sex.

In 1793, commissioners arrived from France to sort things out. These were radicals, more inclined to side with the slaves than their masters, so they began to fulfill the mulattoes' wish list. Meanwhile, the white population began evacuating to other, less volatile islands and the United States.[3]

The chaos left Saint-Domingue vulnerable to the other colonial powers, so Spanish and British troops arrived in September 1793 to partition the French colony. With the British navy in control of the sea, France couldn't send troops to stop it, but as a parting shot the French government declared all of the slaves free in the hopes that they would fight the British and Spanish for them. It actually worked. With the Spanish forces had come an army of former French slaves under Toussaint Louverture. When the French government completely abolished slavery in the colonies in 1794, Toussaint tossed in with them. This made the island French again.[4]

A brief break in the global hostilities between France and Britain gave Napoleon the chance to ship an army over to crush the Haitian rebels, who were now slaves again. (Napoleon had restored slavery.) He sent his brother-in-law, Charles Leclerc, with 20,000 men to retake the island in February 1802. After a few defeats, Dessalines and several of the lesser warlords recognized French authority, but Toussaint stubbornly continued his fight. Finally Leclerc gave up and recognized Toussaint as the lawful ruler of Haiti. In June 1802, Leclerc invited Toussaint to a celebratory dinner, where he was congratulated, ambushed, arrested, and shipped back to France in chains. The French stashed Toussaint in a dungeon in the Jura Mountains of France, where he died of cold and neglect within a year.[5]

Back in Haiti, disease accomplished what the rebels could not. Eventually half of the French invasion force—including Leclerc—died of yellow fever. Even though Napoleon continued to ship reinforcements, those who survived the tropical fevers were in no condition to contest control of the colony. As the Haitians came to realize the growing weakness of the remaining French, the rebellion intensified. Dessalines resumed his fight against the French.

When war between France and Britain resumed in May 1803 and interrupted French shipping, Napoleon finally caved. Abandoning their ambitions, the French army and eighteen hundred civilian refugees left the island under a truce in November 1803, with the agreement that eight hundred sick and wounded who were too weak to move could be left behind and sent back to France after they recovered. Instead, a few days later, the Haitians loaded the hospital patients on boats, took them out to sea, and dumped them overboard.[6]

The main legacy of the Haitian slave revolt, aside from establishing America's second independent nation, was to terrify slave owners up and down the Western Hemisphere into refusing to even consider freeing their slaves. Look at what happened in Saint-Domingue, they said. Do you want that to happen here? In the United States right after the American Revolution, emancipation societies had been equally as common in slave and free states, but after Haiti, no true southerner would allow the merest discussion of it, which sharpened the sectional divide.

MEXICAN WAR OF INDEPENDENCE

Death toll: 400,000[1]
Rank: 81
Type: colonial rebellion
Broad dividing line: Spain vs. New Spain
Time frame: 1810–21
Location: New Spain (Mexico)
Who usually gets the most blame: Spain

The Cry of Delores

Proper hierarchies were important to the Spanish colonials. Their society was rigidly arranged such that the *peninsulares* (born in Spain) were on top, lording it over the *criollos* (Creoles, born in Mexico but of pure Spanish ancestry), followed by the *mestizos* (mixed Indian-Spanish ancestry), with the pure Indians on the bottom. After Napoleon conquered Spain in 1808 and imprisoned its Bourbon king, the colonials of Spanish America had no idea who to take orders from—the new king of Spain (Napoleon's brother) or the renegade national legislature that the Spanish rebels established. With so much confusion over who was in charge, Creole power brokers began to wonder if this was the moment to declare independence from the arrogant *peninsulares*.

In September 1810, authorities in Mexico began to crack down on a list of scheming revolutionaries, so Father Miguel Hidalgo, a Catholic parish priest in the city of Dolores and the next person on their list, took matters into his own hands. Afraid that the anticlerical attitude of the French Revolution might take hold in Mexico, Father Hidalgo inflamed the poor into a frenzied mob that demanded racial equality, land reform, and severing ties between Mexico and decadent Europe. In the name of Our Lady of Guadeloupe, the mob began a march toward Mexico City and soon grew to an army of 25,000 men and women, mostly poor Indians armed with clubs, bows, lances, and machetes. Fewer than 1,000 were equipped as real soldiers.

Both sides fought dirty. The royalist commander in charge of crushing the revolt, General Felix Calleja, burned villages, shot hostages, and executed any prisoners he took. On the other side, when Hidalgo's rebels took the wealthy city of Guanajuato, they massacred all of the leading citizens, which caused the Creole middle class to rethink its support for the independence movement.

Even so, the rebel army soon swelled to 80,000, and Hidalgo punched through the enemy line at Monte de las Cruces; however, 2,000 rebels died in that fight, and the royalists retreated in good order. As the offensive dragged on, the rebel force eroded. Forty thousand rebels deserted before the next confrontation, a battle that reduced Hidalgo's force to 7,000 men with only six hundred muskets. Finally, in January 1811, the royalists solidly defeated the rebels in a battle near Guadalajara. As Hidalgo fled toward the United States, he was caught and hauled back to face the Catholic Church (which excommunicated him) and the government (which stood him up and shot him). His severed head was stuck on a pole in Guanajuato until Mexico achieved its independence a decade later.

Iturbide

Phase two of the war was more scattered and confusing. Rebel leadership passed to another parish priest, José María Morelos y Pavón. Reality had dashed the hope that a spontaneous uprising would drive the oppressors from power, so Morelos avoided confrontation. Royalist forces, mostly Mexican creoles, numbered 80,000, and their strategy focused on reducing the pockets of resistance one by one. In January 1812, General Calleja destroyed the town of Zitacuaro at the center of a particularly troublesome rebel area and laid waste to the Indian villages around it.

The Creole general Agustin de Iturbide captured Morelos in November 1815, and the rebel leader was excommunicated and executed before the end of the year. With the main rebel force broken and its leaders dead, the war devolved into five years of guerrilla warfare that gradually diminished.

Back in Spain, the Bonapartes were gone and the Bourbons returned, but parliament had forced King Ferdinand IV to accept a liberal constitution. This alienated and worried the conservatives who ran Mexico, and one by one the generals in charge of crushing the rebellion began to switch sides. The royalist General Rafael de Riego declared for the republic in January 1820.

In February 1821, General Iturbide announced that he would no longer follow the orders of the Spanish viceroy. After negotiating with leaders of the revolution, Iturbide joined their side and marched against the viceroy's army, which he beat in a series of battles. The new independent government that Iturbide set up left much of the status quo intact, except that it declared the criollos and peninsulares to be legally equal.

The republican ideals of the early revolution didn't last very long. Within a couple of years, Iturbide declared himself emperor. That didn't last long either, and he was deposed in 1823. The political history of Mexico bounced around erratically after this.[2]

SHAKA

Death toll: 1.5 million died because of his rule
Rank: 40
Type: conqueror
Broad dividing line: Zulus vs. everyone else
Time frame: ruled 1816–28
Location: South Africa
Who usually gets the most blame: Shaka

Total Bastard

When Chief Senzangakhona of the Zulus heard that he had gotten a girl named Nandi pregnant, he tried to shrug the pregnancy off as nothing more than an intestinal beetle throwing her menses out of whack. When the pregnancy kept developing and produced an illegitimate baby boy around 1787, the chief's new son was sarcastically named Beetle, or Shaka. Because Nandi was too closely related to the chief to become a full wife, she was shamefully tucked away in the back of his harem as a lesser wife. Eventually, Nandi was sent back to her family's village, where Shaka spent the rest of his childhood in fatherless exile, scorned, bullied, and teased by other children.[1]

In later years, when Shaka rose to power, his army surprised his old village with a stealthy night march. After assembling the villagers, Shaka killed all of the bullies from his childhood by impaling them up the rectum on the sharpened stakes of the walls of their kraals (cattle stockades) and then setting fires beneath them. The villagers who had merely stood by while the others had teased Shaka were shown mercy: their skulls were cracked open with a club for a quick death. Only one man who could prove an earlier act of kindness to Nandi was spared.[2]

Impis and Assegais

By the beginning of the nineteenth century, the various clans of the Nguni people were consolidating into two large confederations: the Ndwandwe (led by Zwide) and the Mthethwa (led by Dingiswayo). Don't get too attached to either of these since they will be gone by the end of this chapter.

The Zulus began as one subordinate clan of the Nguni under Dingiswayo. When Shaka reached adolescence and his age group was called up for military service, Dingiswayo noticed the young boy's courage and audacity and groomed him for leadership. Stories were told of how Shaka stood calmly and killed a charging leopard, and how he slew a giant warrior face to face. When Shaka's father died in 1816, Dingiswayo arranged that Shaka, rather than his more legitimate half brothers, would take control of the Zulus.

Tribal battles in those days were ritual contests of bravado fought with light javelins (assegais) at a distance. There was a lot of jeering and posturing from the men in the battle and from the women on the sidelines, but few deaths. These were loud, festive occasions with dancing, singing, and shouting.

Shaka, however, took war-making more seriously. He trained his warriors in grim, unemotional killing at close quarters. Shaka increased the size of his men's oval ox-hide shields and armed them with heavy iron stabbing spears of his own design, called an *ixlwa*, supposedly from the sound it made when being thrust into and pulled out from an enemy's gut.

Zulus learned to run and fight at the very limits of human speed and endurance. Shaka's soldiers gave up their loose, floppy sandals and fought barefoot instead. Their soles were toughened by long runs across thorns and rocky ground, and any who hesitated during these training exercises would be killed on the spot.[3]

Shaka deployed his impis (regiments) as a dense phalanx rather than a long skirmish line. Each impi was instilled with great pride, and Shaka encouraged them to maintain a fierce rivalry with each other. They often had to be maneuvered into battle separately because they would fight each other if they got too close. Men who had "washed their spears"—drawn blood in battle—were allowed to wear a distinctive and prestigious head ring.

His regiments attacked in the "buffalo" deployment: a solid head that smashed directly into the enemy front line, a body reinforcing the first wave, and two curving horns of swift runners that swept around the flanks and behind the enemy to prevent escape. It was designed to annihilate anyone who stood in the way.[4] In the first battle using this formation, the Zulu horns enveloped both the enemy warriors and their cheerleading women, all of whom were butchered without mercy.

No one could stand up to the Zulus once they unleashed these new tactics on their neighbors. Shaka fought to annihilate and took few prisoners. Only an instant, utter, and abject surrender could spare a target tribe from merciless destruction. Enemy tribes were usually exterminated to the last living soul, except that young boys were often taken into the Zulu military and young girls into their harems.[5] During his career, Shaka conquered more than three hundred chiefdoms, the full list of which is both impressive and boring.[6] Because the Zulu usually absorbed the defeated clans, you are unlikely to hear their names anywhere outside of a biography of Shaka. Even the clans that keep a separate identity today are still hidden in the shadow of the Zulus.

Around 1817, Dingiswayo was killed in a battle with Zwide of the Ndwandwe Confederation. Shaka eventually avenged the death of his mentor and crushed the Ndwandwe army at the Battle of Mhlatuze River in 1820. Zwide escaped the battle with a handful of his men, but Shaka found the confederacy's women and children and slaughtered them. As a special revenge, he locked Zwide's mother, a powerful witch, in a hut full of hungry hyenas.

On the Genitalia of Tyrants

Believe me, I don't want to discuss Shaka's penis any more than you want to read about it, but the subject comes up unavoidably in his biographies—especially in those written by scholars of a Freudian outlook. During his childhood, the other children in the village teased Shaka mercilessly for his tiny penis ("like an earthworm"), but in later years he often walked around casually naked to show everyone that his penis had grown quite normally now, thank you very much. However, his childhood torment probably scarred his psyche. A common pattern throughout Shaka's tyranny is a fanatic attention to the sex life of his subjects.[7]

Shaka organized Zulu girls into non-fighting regiments parallel to the regiments of men. He forbade his soldiers to marry until they were forty, but when it was time, he would assign them wives from the corresponding women's regiment.

Sex outside marriage was now absolutely forbidden. Any unmarried woman who became pregnant by one of his warriors was put to death, as was her lover. In fact, Shaka killed his own wives if they became pregnant, but no one knows why. Among the possibilities that have been suggested are (a) he feared the birth of a son who would become a rival (Shaka's own excuse), or (b) Shaka was impotent so his wives could become pregnant only through infidelity, or (c) same thing but he was gay, not impotent. However, Zulu sexual practices were alien enough from Western practices to make words like *gay* and *impotent* meaningless. Shaka probably indulged exclusively in *uku-hlobonga* (there's no easy translation) with his wives, which meant none would get pregnant without cheating.[8]

When his mother, Nandi, died, Shaka imposed strict laws of mourning while he wallowed in grief. No crops could be planted, no cows could be milked, and obviously no one was allowed to have sex. If a woman got pregnant during the period of mourning, both she and the baby's father were killed, even if they were properly married.[9] Eventually 9,000 Zulus were killed for showing insufficient sadness.

With every new episode of bloodthirsty madness, Shaka lost support, until finally his half brothers assassinated him while he was in his kraal. As he was being cut down, every courtier, servant, neighbor, and villager fled the town in terror, figuring that they would get blamed for it. Shaka's body lay abandoned in the empty town throughout the night; the only protection from prowling hyenas was one favorite wife from his adolescence who stayed behind. The next morning, he was hurriedly buried with minimal ceremony. His bones are probably somewhere under a street in the South African town of Stanger.

Mfecane

Shaka sparked a massive upheaval called the Mfecane, the "Crushing." As the weaker peoples of southern Africa fled to escape Shaka's fury, they created ripples of instability that disturbed the status quo halfway up the continent. The first ripples were often Zulu freebooters setting out to build their own kingdoms by defeating people unaccustomed to the new Zulu tactics. Then those defeated tribes ran into the next circle of neighbors, until eventually everyone was on the move. Nations jostled one another for the next generation, and communities descended from South African fugitives are today found as widely scattered as Kenya, Malawi, Tanzania, Uganda, Zambia, and Zimbabwe.[10]

Among the notable movements:

- The Swazi were driven into the rugged mountains that are now Swaziland, a small independent kingdom surrounded on all sides by South Africa.
- One of Shaka's generals, Mzilikazi, had a quarrel with his boss and fled with his clan, the Khumalo, on a five-hundred-mile journey and established themselves as the Ndebele (Matabele) state in Zimbabwe.
- Soshangane, one of the fugitive leaders of the defeated Ndwandwe Confederation, formed the Gaza state in Mozambique and overran several Portuguese settlements. The Portuguese had to flee to their ships while they watched their towns burn.
- Another refugee Ndwandwe band under Zwangendaba migrated a thousand miles over the next twenty years before it came to rest in Tanzania.

Cobbing

Shaka passed his entire career beyond the horizon of the literate world, so we have only secondhand accounts of his life. European visitors to Shaka's court returned with blood-curdling stories of a mad savage king sowing death and destruction wherever he went. Local tribes passed along legends, rumors, and oral histories that were written down only long after the fact. This leaves a lot of room to rewrite history any way you want.

White Afrikaners have long claimed that the Mfecane left the South African interior emptied of natives, littered with bones, conveniently free for the taking when their Boer ancestors arrived a couple of decades later. Black Africans swear the Mfecane was nowhere near as destructive as that, and it was the encroachment by white slave traders that set it off anyway. The theory that the horrors of the Mfecane are mostly white propaganda (called the Cobbing hypothesis after the scholar who published it in 1988) has gained ground, but it is still the minority view. The debate is far from settled, driven by political winds more often than by solid proof.[11]

In 1838, Henry Francis Fynn, one of Shaka's white visitors whose diary is a major source for what is written about him, offered the first body count of 1 million dead at Shaka's hands.[12] Within a year of Fynn's publication, military intelligence from Cape Town passed this number back to London.[13] In 1900, historian George McCall Theal bumped the body count up to 2 million, and since then, most modern historians either repeat these numbers without much doubt[14] or avoid numbers altogether.

Although there is no compelling evidence for a death toll of a million or more, the fact that so many historians accept it is persuasive in itself. If they were truly dissatisfied with this estimate, they have had two centuries to replace it. They haven't.

FRENCH CONQUEST OF ALGERIA

Death toll: 775,000[1]
Rank: 57
Type: colonial conquest
Broad dividing line: French vs. natives
Time frame: 1830–47
Location: Algeria
Who usually gets the most blame: France

FRANCE ALREADY HAD A STANDING QUARREL WITH ALGIERS OVER THE BARbary pirates (see "Mideast Slave Trade"). Then in 1827, while negotiating payment for a debt the French owed some North African merchants from the Napoleonic Wars, Hussein, the ruler of Algiers, testily whapped the French consul with his fly whisk. Back in Paris, King Charles X of France was widely disliked, but he decided that avenging this insult to French dignity would boost his popularity, so he sent French warships to blockade Algiers. When the Algerians fired on one of the French ships, the French retaliated by occupying all of the cities on the Algerian coast. Critics inside and outside France denounced the conquest as pure aggressive adventurism.

Even conquering Algeria failed to make King Charles popular, and in 1830 the French people threw him out and put a more liberal king on the throne. The new King Louis-Philippe was hoping to get out of North Africa, but his throne was too shaky to risk alienating imperialists in France by abandoning the war, so he reluctantly continued to escalate the fight against the native Arab opposition.

In 1831, faced with a shortage of citizens willing to fight in the war, France created a special army, the French Foreign Legion, to fight the Bedouin in the desert. The legion was stocked with the toughest, meanest cutthroats and scoundrels recruited from all over the world, lured with promises of sanctuary, citizenship, regular pay, and adventure.

For several years, the French couldn't decide whether they wanted to keep Algeria, so they didn't spread beyond the few coastal towns they occupied. Finally, in 1834 they officially accepted Algeria as their colony and began to organize an administration for it. By this time, tribal elders had selected Abd el-Kader, the twenty-five-year-old son of a prominent holy man, to rule the unconquered interior region of Algeria from a new capital at Tlemcen. As the resistance solidified, the Algerians harassed the French forces with raids and ambushes. The French, unaccustomed to this kind of war, were easy targets.

The inland city of Constantine withstood several years of French attention. Perched on a rocky plateau, Constantine was difficult to reach, and the first French offensive in 1836 was easily driven off. The Arabs hounded the retreating French with sniper fire and night attacks that whittled them down to a weary, miserable fraction of their original size. In 1837, the French tried again and took Constantine after bombardment, house-to-house street fighting, and angry massacres, all of which left 20,000 Arab civilians dead in the streets.[2]

By May 1841, the number of French troops deployed in Algeria reached 60,000, but equipment and tactics that had been designed to blow away large armies on the fields of Europe could make no headway against the mobile skirmishing used by the local Arabs and Berbers. Then the new French commander appointed in 1841, Marshal Thomas-Robert Bugeaud, overhauled the entire operation. He lightened the packs carried by the average French soldier and loaded their baggage on mules instead of wagons. Bugeaud left behind the heavy artillery that encumbered his army on the march. He also left behind his irregular native auxiliaries because their presence made it too difficult to tell friend from foe, causing too many French units to not fire on unidentified natives for fear of slaughtering their own troops. Bugeaud redesigned the marching formation, placing combat troops all around the perimeter, ready at a moment's notice to fend off a native ambush. His flying columns were now able to hunt Abd el-Kader as fast as he could retreat, giving him no rest.[3]

Bugeaud encouraged his subordinates to deal mercilessly with hostile tribes. In June 1845, a rebel tribe took refuge with their families in a cave at Dahra in the northwest and refused to surrender. French Colonel Aimable Pelissier ordered a bonfire set at the mouth of the cave that consumed all of the oxygen in the cave and replaced it with carbon monoxide. The soldiers that he sent inside afterward to investigate "came back, we are told, pale, trembling, terrified, hardly daring, it seemed, to confront the light of day. . . . They had found all the Arabs dead—men, women, children, all dead!"[4] At least 500 people suffocated that day. Pelissier's official report to Paris proudly and luridly described the incident as a fine example of clever tactics, and he was shocked when French public opinion erupted in protest at his brutality. His career continued to advance anyway.

His colleague, Colonel Armand-Jacques Saint-Arnaud, learned the lesson, so when he sealed up another 500 natives who took refuge in another cave in August, he kept it secret. He lied to his men and his superiors, telling them that these caves were empty and were being blown up only as a precaution. Saint-Arnaud's career also continued to rise, eventually to war minister and commander of the French army in the Crimean War.[5]

It took several tries before the fighting in Algeria ended. In 1836, Abd el-Kader looked beaten, so he agreed to a peace treaty splitting Algeria between direct and indirect French rule, but in 1839, the French encroached on the region of indirect rule and the war started up again. The French chased Abd el-Kader into Morocco in 1843. Although Abd el-Kader kept up border raids from his base in Morocco, he finally surrendered in December 1847. The French allowed him to peacefully retire to Lebanon.

TAIPING REBELLION

Death toll: 20 million[1]
Rank: 6
Type: messianic uprising
Broad dividing line: Taiping rebels vs. Manchu dynasty of China
Time frame: 1850–64
Location and major state participant: China
Major non-state participants: God Worshippers, Taiping Tianguo, the Ever-Victorious Army
Who usually gets the most blame: Hong Xiuquan, the decadent Manchu dynasty
Another damn: Chinese peasant revolt
The important question no one ever asks: What if Hong Xiuquan really *was* the son of God?

THE STANDARD SHORT VERSION OF THE TAIPING REBELLION SOUNDS LIKE science fiction: Space-faring humans land on a primitive world, disturbing the peaceful society with their advanced weaponry, odd scientific notions, and magical technologies. The humans violate the Prime Directive by speaking indiscreetly of many strange things, including their all-powerful God who sent his son to save mankind, and who will one day come again. Amid these confusing rumors, a native falls into a fever and has delirious visions that he himself is this new Son of God whom everyone has been expecting. He confides this to his friends. He rallies followers and launches a crusade that convulses the planet in the most destructive frenzy in its long history. In order to set things right again, the humans must now use their superior technology to crush this uprising and return the world to its previous status quo.

Prelude: The Opium War

For much of recorded history an impartial observer would have considered China to be the most technologically advanced civilization on earth. The Chinese were self-sufficient, self-contained, and self-satisfied. To keep alien contamination to a minimum, the ruling Manchus of the Qing dynasty confined Westerners to a few ports. European merchants had to pay cash on the barrelhead in the form of silver if they wanted any Chinese goods—mostly tea, silk, and porcelain. The Chinese certainly didn't want any shoddy Western goods from the seafaring barbarians of Portugal, Holland, or England. In the long run, China was draining too much hard currency out of Europe, so the West had to find something to sell the Chinese to get their money back.

Opium was the perfect solution. The British had a steady supply of it coming out of India, and Chinese demand for narcotics was growing as the onslaught of alien ideas and technologies battered their social structure. Unfortunately for the West, the Chinese government completely and utterly banned opium—unless there was a suitable bribe attached. This wasn't a big problem at first. The bribes were usually less than the import duties the Europeans would have to pay on legal trade, but then, almost by accident, the Chinese court appointed an honest commissioner to stamp out opium addiction. Unlike his predecessors, Lin Zexu actually used his authority to fight opium instead of to shake down merchants. Lin locked down the foreign community and destroyed ten thousand chests of opium, so the British and French declared war.

Although China had spent much of history as the most advanced civilization on earth, the Europeans had long ago passed the Chinese where it counted—military technology. In the First Opium War, the Anglo-French forces shattered the Chinese fleet and destroyed their army with hardly a scratch to themselves. Under the peace treaty of 1842, the Chinese legalized the opium trade and established diplomatic relations with the Europeans on a level of equality; they promised to stop calling the Europeans barbarians, and they allowed them trading posts ("factories") in treaty ports up and down the coasts and navigable rivers. Along with the merchants came Christian missionaries, who fanned out over the countryside.

The Opiate of the Masses

The battering of their society was driving many Chinese to reconsider ancient spiritual certainties, and Christianity was making substantial gains. This was not entirely new. Christians had been poking around China for centuries. The Nestorian variety of the religion had arrived in caravans from Persia long, long ago. Jesuit missionaries came with the Portuguese navigators in the 1500s. Both types had limited success, but until the Opium War, Christianity never progressed beyond the level of an interesting alien cult that eccentrics sometimes converted to.

Hong Xiuquan would come to be one of those eccentrics. He lived in the far south, deep in the hinterland of Hong Kong and Canton (Guangzhou), where he scraped along as a school teacher. One night in 1837, while Hong recovered from a serious illness, a golden-haired man in a black robe appeared to him in a vision telling him to purify the land. Because the vision made no sense, Hong tucked it away in the back of his mind for a few years and got on with his life. Then, his career stalled after he repeatedly failed the civil service exam that was required to move ahead in Chinese society.

QING CHINA
1850–1873

	kilometers
0 200 400 600 800	
0 100 200 300 400 500	miles

ALTAI SHAN

MONGOLIA
(Qing vassal)

Gobi Desert

Approximate area of
the Hui Rebellion, 1863–73

Yellow

Ordos Desert

QILIAN SHAN

Great Wall

Lanzhou

GANSU

Beijing
Tientsin

Mukden
(Shenyang)

MANCHURIA

Po Hai

Yellow

Yellow Sea

Luoyang

Kaifeng

Grand Canal

HONAN

Chang'an
(Xian)

Taiping northern
expedition
1853–54

Yangzhou

Nanjing
(Taiping capital)

Shanghai

TIBET
(Qing
protectorate)

Approximate area of Taiping control, early period, 1853–57

Chengdu

Yangtze

Wuhan

Hangzhou

Ningbo

ZHEJIANG

SICHUAN

East China Sea

Taiping expedition
into Sichuan
1856–63

HUNAN

Dali

Kunming

Taiping advance
1850–53

Approximate area of
Taiping control,
later period,
1857–63

YUNNAN

Tropic of Cancer

Chin-t'ien
(origin of the Taiping Rebellion)

Canton

Taiwan

BURMA
(Qing
tributary)

ANNAM
(Qing
tributary)

Hanoi

Hong Kong

Approximate area of the Panthay
Rebellion, 1855–73

Tonkin Gulf

Hainan

South China Sea

SIAM

One day in 1843, while moping around the big city after failing the civil service exam yet again, Hong was given Protestant pamphlets. He converted to Christianity and began to study under American Baptist missionaries. Soon he recognized the Christian elements of his half-forgotten vision. He realized that God himself was the man in his vision, and remembered now that God had declared Hong to be his second son, the younger brother of Jesus.[2]

Some time later, he set up the God Worshippers' Society. At first, Hong kept his kinship to the Messiah secret and simply preached a safe fusion of Confucian and Christian principles with a heavy emphasis on the Ten Commandments. As his following grew, he struck out against the worship of idols, destroying Confucian and ancestral shines. Hong set up communities in the local countryside, baptizing more and more converts until the God Worshippers numbered 20,000 followers in 1850.[3]

The God Worshippers gained their strongest foothold among Hong's specific ethnic group, the Hakka. Who were the Hakka? Let me oversimplify a complex matter. The people whom most outsiders call "Chinese" are not really an ethnic group; they are more a cultural grouping of peoples who share a common heritage and written language, but not a common spoken language. They call themselves the Han. Because Chinese writing is not phonetic, it exists independently and is used for several diverse tongues that are similar but largely unintelligible to one another when spoken. The most widely spoken and prestigious of the Han languages is Mandarin. It is rooted in the north and is the official tongue of China. South China has several large Han languages such as Cantonese, which is common among Chinese immigrant communities worldwide.

The Hakka people are Han Chinese who fled from north to south in the 1200s during the Mongol conquest, becoming a northern enclave in the southern cultural region. They kept a lot of old traditions and avoided newer customs, such as foot-binding. Their name means "guest people."

If it helps, think of the Hakka like the Amish or Cajuns—alien to the surrounding area, old-fashioned, but not aboriginal. The main difference from the peoples in those examples is that there are many millions of Hakka. Although Hong's God Worshippers gained followers among Chinese of all kinds, the core leadership was Hakka, which made them seem slightly foreign to most southerners.[4]

Kingdom of Heaven

Can the Chinese still consider themselves men? Ever since the Manchus poisoned China, the flame of oppression has risen up to heaven, the poison of corruption has defiled the emperor's throne, the offensive odor has spread over the four seas, and the influence of demons has

distressed the empire while the Chinese with bowed heads and dejected
spirits willingly became subjects and servants.

—Taiping pamphlet[5]

The God Worshippers drifted so far from traditional Chinese behavior that friction was inevitable. They organized into paramilitaries and first clashed with the Qing authorities in December 1850. In January 1851, a God Worshipper army, 10,000 strong, beat the Qing at the battle of Jintian. With victory at his back, Hong declared himself messiah of the Taiping Tianguo or "Great-Peace Heavenly-Kingdom." He elevated five of his closest followers to kings of the East, West, South, North, and (after running out of directions) Wing. Hong took the title of Heavenly King and granted messiahood to his baby son as well.

In the face of imperial assault, the Taipings abandoned their base and went mobile, eventually marching fifteen hundred miles northward across hostile territory. By the time they seized Yongan, their numbers had swollen to 60,000. The movement continued to snowball. Converts among miners brought skills at tunneling and setting explosives, which helped in assaulting walled cities. A force of 120,000 Taipings attacked Changsha in September 1852. There were a half-million Taipings when they seized Wuchang in January 1853. They broke through encircling lines of the Qing armies in April 1853, and when they took Nanjing in September 1853, the Taipings had 2 million followers scattered throughout their territory.

At the fall of Nanjing, the Taipings hunted down and massacred the 40,000 Manchu residents of the city, only 5,000 of whom were troops. Manchu men, women, and children were speared, hacked apart, tied up and thrown into the river, or set on fire.[6]

Soon after, the Taiping momentum stalled. A column of 70,000 that was sent to take Beijing was repulsed and chased south over the course of several months in 1853–54—harassed, eroded, and eventually wiped out by the Qing. After this setback, Hong abandoned the offensive in order to consolidate control of the Yangtze River and establish a proper court in Nanjing.

The Taipings were not the only group in opposition to the Manchus, but they failed to coordinate with two neighboring uprisings—the Nian in the north and the Red Turbans in the south. At times, the Taipings tried to partner with bandits and river pirates who hated the authorities and were adept at fighting, but the Taipings tended toward puritanical asceticism, so the criminal classes inevitably lost interest.

The Taipings outlawed opium, prostitution, homosexuality, and alcohol. Men and women were kept entirely apart, although both genders were recruited into the armies. The new society was structured along military lines into a kind of holy army.

All land was shared in common. A surplus in the harvest of one village would be used to alleviate the deficiency in another village; "thus, all the people in the empire may together enjoy the abundant happiness of the Heavenly Father, Supreme Lord and Great God. There being fields, let all cultivate them; there being food, let all eat; there being clothes, let all be dressed; there being money, let all use it, so that nowhere does inequality exist, and no man is not well fed and clothed." And that went for "wheat, pulse, hemp; flax, cloth, silk, fowls, dogs, etc., and money, the same is true; for the whole empire is the universal family of our Heavenly Father, the Supreme Lord and Great God."[7]

As befitted an earthly paradise "all young boys must go to church every day, where the sergeant is to teach them to read the Old Testament and the New Testament, as well as the book of proclamations of the true ordained Sovereign. Every Sabbath the corporals must lead the men and women to the church, where the males and females are to sit in separate rows. There they will listen to sermons, sing praises, and offer sacrifices to our Heavenly Father, the Supreme Lord and Great God."[8]

The new movement abolished foot-binding, in which the feet of girls were crushed into the small, delicate, and impractical shape that was considered beautiful among the Chinese. They also abolished the hair braid that all Chinese men were required to wear as a sign of servitude to their Manchu masters. This gave the Taiping armies a savage appearance as both men and women charged into battle with defiantly big feet and long, wild hair.

For all of the utopian ideals of Taiping society, hypocrisy abounded. For most members of the movement, men and women were kept strictly separated, but the leaders gathered harems fit for Old Testament kings, not to mention attendants, servants, and pomp appropriate to their positions.

The People You Meet in Heaven

By 1853, Hong had started to withdraw from the secular business of his Heavenly Kingdom and devote himself to spiritual growth. Although both the West King and South King had been killed in the battles that brought the Great-Peace Heavenly-Kingdom into power, there were still three lesser kings to handle the minutiae of running the empire.

One of them, Yang Xiuqing, the East King, had begun as an orphaned charcoal maker, but he had an instinct for military tactics that secured many of the Taiping successes. Yang now started to have his own visions from God, and if you know anything about messiahs, you can guess the nature of these visions. Apparently, God was totally disenchanted with Hong, and now wanted to promote Yang to messiahood in his place.

In September 1856, rumors of Yang's ambition reached Wei Changhui, the North King, so he marched his army back from the front and attacked Yang's palace, slaughtering Yang and his family. Wei's troops triumphantly paraded Yang's head on a pole through the streets of Nanjing, until Hong emerged from seclusion to denounce this atrocity. Hong seized Wei and sentenced him to be publicly flogged to death. He invited the survivors of

Yang's clan to watch. After the witnesses arrived, however, a trap was sprung. It turned out that Hong and Wei were in collusion, and now that the remaining Yangs had come out of hiding and gathered in one place, Wei and Hong finished wiping them out.

Shi Dakai, the Wing King, was out campaigning in the field at the time. He had originally come from a wealthy family and had convinced many rich kinsmen to contribute money and property to the nascent Taiping movement. Upon returning to Nanjing, Shi expressed some doubt to Wei about the propriety of wiping out the Yangs. Wei took this criticism as a challenge, and Shi barely escaped the city alive. Even so, Wei caught and killed Shi's wife and mother. After taking refuge with his army, Shi marched back toward Nanjing with 100,000 troops, hungry for revenge. Hong quickly bought him off by making him a gift of Wei's severed head.

Shi Dakai was now the last of the lesser kings, and probably the least crazy. Satisfied with Wei's head, he returned for a short while to Hong's entourage, but he eventually broke from the Taiping movement altogether. He took his army into the Sichuan basin and established his own independent enclave.

Western Response

The Qing government, meanwhile, ruthlessly worked to contain the revolt. Officials kept it out of Canton by having over 32,000 suspected Taiping sympathizers beheaded by May 1856. An eyewitness reported that "thousands were put to the sword, hundreds cast into the river, tied together in batches of a dozen. I have seen their putrid corpses floating in masses down the stream—women too among the number. Many were cut to pieces alive. I have seen the horrid sight, and the limbless, headless corpses, merely a mass of flayed flesh . . . that lay in scores covering the whole execution ground."[9]

The Taipings hoped to reach an agreement with the countries of the West. Not only did they share a nominal Christianity with the Europeans, but since 1856, the Anglo-French had been fighting a Second Opium War against Qing China. By the time that war ended in 1860, the Europeans had taken and destroyed the emperor's Summer Palace outside Beijing.

The West considered its options. Maybe it was time to take complete control of China and replace the corrupt and xenophobic Qing dynasty with Westernized puppets. For several years, the West had considered the Taipings to be proper Christians worthy of moral support at least. When Hong's strange heresies became more apparent, the West returned to supporting the devil they knew, the imperial Qing. They accepted a peace treaty that left China unchanged.

It wasn't just the Western statesmen and clergy who changed their minds about the rebels. In London, Karl Marx grew disillusioned as well. In 1853 he had hoped that "the Chinese revolution will throw the spark into the overloaded mine of the present industrial system and cause the explosion of the long-prepared general crisis." (Marx with a metaphor was like a dog gnawing a bone—determined to get everything he could from it.) By 1862, however, he considered the Taipings "an even greater abomination for the masses of the people than for the old rulers [only capable of] destruction in grotesquely detestable forms, destruction without any nucleus of new construction."[10]

Hoping to connect with their presumed sympathizers in the West, a Taiping column set out in 1860 for Shanghai, which had become an international protectorate under Western control in 1854. Unaware of the shifting winds in Western attitude, the Taipings were startled to find European security forces firing at them in the outer defenses of the city. Because they assumed it was a mistake, 300 Taipings were killed without even returning fire.

Soon, the Europeans were aiding the Qing government more openly. The port city of Ningbo had fallen to the Taipings in 1861 with no opposition, and the residents had easily acclimated to their new rulers. In 1862, an Anglo-French expedition retook the city and turned it over to the Qing forces, who retaliated against the city with the torture and killing of random inhabitants as an example to the rest.[11]

Independent contractors also helped the Chinese government by training and equipping government armies with the latest weaponry. The Ever-Victorious Army, a band of mercenaries raised mostly on the docks of Spanish-controlled Manila, fought under an American commander, Frederick Ward, against the rebels.[12] When Ward was killed in battle, command went to a veteran British officer, Charles Gordon, who would gain even greater fame many years later when he was besieged in Khartoum by the screaming dervishes of the Sudan (see "Mahdi Revolt").

More important than foreign mercenaries, however, were the native Chinese armies that were being trained and equipped like Western armies. The Qing deployed modern gunboats on their rivers to bring heavy artillery to bear on the walled cities of the Taipings. Manchu generals chipped away at the Taiping kingdom during the 1860s with new, modernized armies, but the reconquest was slowed by the Qing policy of taking no prisoners. This forced even the most disillusioned Taipings to fight to the last.

Qing forces overran the Sichuan enclave of Shi Dakai, the former Wing King, in July 1863. Shi was captured and publicly killed by slicing, while his followers were massacred despite a promise that this wouldn't happen. Finally, the Qing brought Nanjing itself under siege.

Hong Xiuquan became sick and died in May 1864, but no one knows how this happened. Poison is the most likely culprit, most historians lean toward suicide, but assassination has its proponents as well. Another possibility is that he was accidentally poisoned by some lethal combination of elixirs and potions he was taking to strengthen his mojo. In any case, his untimely death occurred only a couple of months ahead of his followers'.

Nanjing fell to the government in July 1864, followed by a general massacre of its inhabitants. According to the Qing general on the scene, "Not one of the 100,000 rebels in Nanjing surrendered themselves, but in many cases gathered together and burned themselves and passed away without repentance."[13]

Hong's fourteen-year-old son, who had been proclaimed the new King of Heaven, fled after the fall of Nanjing, but his younger brothers were among the thousands killed when the city fell. The young Hong tried to disappear into the countryside, but he was caught, imprisoned, and executed by slicing.

Legacy

The game of mah-jongg was probably invented by bored Taiping soldiers. Beyond that, the Taiping Rebellion has faded into forgotten history. When Hollywood began to explore the possibility of a movie based on Caleb Carr's *Devil Soldier*, the story of the American mercenary Frederick Ward in the Taiping Rebellion, one of the first things to change was the setting.[14] The interested parties eventually filmed the basic concept as *The Last Samurai*, the story of a nineteenth-century American mercenary caught up in a civil war in, well, Japan obviously.

The Taiping Rebellion is the perfect example of the old adage that the winners write the history books. Most writers treat the Taipings as poor deluded peasants following a madman's hallucinations, but when you get right down to it, that's how most religions begin (not *your* religion obviously, but all the other ones). The only difference between Hong and history's successful prophets is that if a professor, novelist, or cartoonist disrespects Hong Xiuquan, angry mobs won't call for his head.

Is fear of its followers really the best test of a religion's authenticity? I'll admit that's the standard I use, but it's probably a good idea to remember that if the Taipings had won their rebellion, they might today be considered totally legit and every bit as Christian as the Mormons ("mostly, sort of").

CRIMEAN WAR

Death toll: 300,000[1]
Rank: 96
Type: international war
Broad dividing line: everyone vs. Russia
Time frame: 1854–56
Location: Black Sea
Major state participants: Russia vs. Turkey, France, Britain
Who usually gets the most blame: everyone except the Turks
Another damn: war of trenches and idiotic frontal assaults

THE ONE THING EVERYONE SHOULD KNOW ABOUT THE CRIMEAN WAR IS THE mind-boggling incompetence displayed by everyone involved. This war gave us "The Charge of the Light Brigade"—possibly the best-known poem in the English language—which describes the dumb courage of a futile frontal assault. The Crimean War was the first war to be photographed and reported on by war correspondents for the daily newspapers. It was also the first war to shock and horrify the people back home. The only individual whom history remembers kindly was a civilian woman, Florence Nightingale, who took it upon herself to nurse sick and wounded soldiers after the army proved incapable of the task.

The war began stupidly as well. Orthodox and Catholic clergy in Jerusalem were bickering over which of them had priority at the holy shrines. The Orthodox clergy appealed to Tsar Nicholas I of Russia to plead their case with the Ottoman sultan, the ruler of Palestine. The Russians overreacted and insisted that they be recognized as the protectors and spokesmen for all of the Christian minorities under Turkish rule. This would, in effect, make Turkey a Russian protectorate, unable to take any action without Russian permission. To make matters worse, as their negotiator, the Russians sent a man who absolutely detested the Turks ever since a Turkish cannonball castrated him in an earlier Russo-Turkish War.

When the Turks refused the tsar's demands, the Russian army moved against Turkish vassals in the Balkans, the Romanian principalities of Wallachia and Moldavia, to force the issue. The Russian fleet from Sevastopol in Crimea caught and destroyed the Turkish fleet near Sinope on the Turkish coast.

Of course the rest of the world couldn't let Russia conquer the Ottoman Empire unchallenged, so the British and French assembled an armada and expeditionary force, which they sent to back up the Turks.

The Turkish army, meanwhile, had moved up the Black Sea coast to meet the Russians head-on, and just south of the Danube, they fought the Russians to a standstill. Then Austria issued an ultimatum to Russia to quit now or be attacked by them as well. Grumbling and fuming, the Russians pulled back behind their border.

The war was over.

Except that the British and French allies had come all this way and didn't want to go home without blowing up something. They had been languishing in camp along the Dardanelles strait, dying of typhus and cholera, waiting for their chance to attack, and they certainly weren't going to let the war end without a fight. They decided to nip across the Black Sea and destroy the Russian naval base in Sevastopol on the Crimean Peninsula.

In September 1854, the allies landed north of the city and beat the small Russian field army at Alma. This left Sevastopol wide open for the taking, but the allies settled into siege lines and waited instead. At the Battles of Inkerman and Balaklava, the allies held off two Russian attempts to drive them away, and then winter set in.

No one had prepared to survive a Russian winter, and the allied army withered away from frostbite, chills, and hunger. By the time spring returned, the survivors were in no condition to press the siege toward a conclusion so the opposing armies just sat there, month after month, dying of dysentery and typhoid fever.

After almost a year, the allied armies had finally fixed enough of their problems to get the war moving again. In September 1855, a French assault took a critical fort in the Russian line, and the Russians abandoned Sevastopol, destroying the naval installations and scuttling the fleet on the way out. Treaty negotiations dragged on, but despite everyone's best efforts, peace returned in March 1856.[2]

Dynamo

The Crimean War was the first big war to be fought after the onset of the Industrial Revolution. Factories churned out mass quantities of identical guns, boots, bullets, tents, caps, and canteens. Railroads and steamships kept larger and larger armies resupplied at a greater distance. With the invention of the first mass-produced, easily loaded rifle ammunition (the Minie ball) in 1848, rifles quickly replaced smoothbore muskets on the battlefield, improving the range and accuracy of infantry fire. At Waterloo (see "Napoleonic Wars") musketry had scored only 1 hit for every 459 shots fired, but in the Crimea, 1 bullet in 16 hit someone.[3]

The Crimean War was probably the first great-power war that couldn't be fought with tactics from the previous war, although that didn't stop plenty of stubborn generals from trying to attack entrenched riflemen with Napoleonic charges. From here on out, every new war had to be figured out from scratch, usually after the first wave sent into battle had been torn apart.

With the massive increase in firepower, it became more difficult for attacking regiments to reach the enemy lines. There was a tendency for wars of this era to begin with maneuver and attack in the open countryside, but after all of the soldiers standing upright were swept off the field by improved firepower, the wars ended with deeply entrenched infantry waiting month after month in muddy sieges around key transportation hubs. Wars of movement slowed and stopped as armies hunkered down around cities like Sevastopol (1854), Petersburg (1864), and Paris (1871). This trend would eventually climax in the trench warfare of the First World War.[4]

PANTHAY REBELLION

Death toll: 1 million[1]
Rank: 46
Type: religious uprising
Broad dividing line: Han (Confucian) vs. Hui (Muslim)
Time frame: 1855–73
Location: Yunnan Province
Major state participant: Qing China
Major quasi-state participant: Nanping Guo
Who usually gets the most blame: too little known for that
Another damn: Chinese peasant revolt
Economic factor: silver

THE SILVER MINES IN THE INTERIOR SOUTHERN PROVINCE OF YUNNAN WERE gradually being exhausted. In the winter of 1855, several Han miners abandoned their depleted mine and tried to get jobs at a still-active mine run by Chinese converts to Islam, called Hui. Despite the fact that there is no difference between Hui and Han other than religion, this difference is enough to have built up generations of resentment. When the Han miners were turned down for jobs, hundreds of local Han went on a rampage through the Muslim community and tried to seize its mines. Some 700 Hui families were assaulted, their livestock stolen, their homes burned, their people killed. The Qing government ignored this until the Hui retaliated with their own attacks against the Han. Now the government ordered severe reprisals to punish the Hui. Han militia under the local magistrate hunted and slaughtered 2,000 to 3,000 Muslims of all ages and genders.

The Hui community rallied under the leadership of Du Wenxiu, who declared the independent Kingdom of the Pacified South (Nanping Guo). Ruling as Sultan Suleyman, Du established his capital in Dali (Xiaguan). As Hui armies became larger and more organized, the rebellion spread, and the Hui overran the major city of Kunming in 1863.

Ominous signs and portents began to appear in the war zone. The rats of Kunming started to appear in daylight, running around wildly and falling down dead. Apparently, in the chaos of the rebellion, the rats of Yunnan connected with the rats of upper Burma near the headwaters of the Salween River, which had long been one of the major centers of bubonic plague. In 1871, people began dying in Kunming, and armies and refugees were soon spreading the plague throughout Yunnan.

In 1894, the epidemic arrived at the ports on the Gulf of Tonkin and spread quickly across the globe on steamships and railroads. This was the start of bubonic plague's third pandemic, which killed 13 million people over the next few decades, mostly in Asia. The third pandemic only lightly brushed against the West, mostly in seaports; however, infected fleas easily hitched a ride inland, and the plague established new foci all over the world among previously untouched rodent populations, such as the squirrels of the American West, where it waits for another opportunity to break out.[2]

For a long time, the Manchu rulers of China were too busy reeling from the Taiping Rebellion to worry about the lesser treason of the Hui, but after the Taipings were all dead, Beijing was able to deal with the Panthay Rebellion. The rulers appointed the experienced and ruthless Cen Yuying as governor-general of rebellious Yunnan. He systematically reduced the Kingdom of the Pacified South and slaughtered the traitors. As the imperial armies closed in on the capital, Sultan Du Wenxiu attempted suicide with a heavy dose of opium, but it failed and he fell into the hands of the Qing field general, Yang Yuke. Du begged his captors to show mercy on his people, and they agreed.

Then they changed their minds. Massacres started in Dali three days later. Du was executed. Eventually Cen and Yang sent ten thousand pairs of ears to Beijing as proof of their victory.[3]

AMERICAN CIVIL WAR

Death toll: 620,000 soldiers[1] and 75,000 civilians[2]
Rank: 65
Type: ideological civil war
Broad dividing line: North vs. South
Time frame: 1861–65
Location and major state participant: United States of America
Major quantum state participant: Confederate States
Who usually gets the most blame: southern slaveholders
Another damn: war of trenches and idiotic frontal assaults
Economic factors: cotton, slaves

Summary

The debate over slavery in the United States became so intense that the old political alliances shattered. Both political parties split into northern and southern wings, and four presidential candidates ran in the 1860 election. When Abraham Lincoln of the antislavery Republican Party was elected, the slave states of the South stomped off in a huff. As the renegade states were setting up their independent Confederacy, they seized federal property all across the South, climaxing with the April 1861 bombardment of the federal garrison in Fort Sumter in Charleston Harbor, which officially opened hostilities.

Recruitment and training took awhile, but by spring of 1862, the two sides had big new armies manned, equipped, and ready for glory. A glacial advance brought the Union army from Washington to within a few miles of the rebel capital of Richmond, Virginia, when the new Confederate general, Robert E. Lee, attacked and drove them back in the Seven Days Battle, a rolling firefight across several counties east of Richmond (July 1862). Suddenly, the war picked up speed. For the next year, the land between the two rival capitals saw a bloody seesaw of offensives, without either side gaining an advantage. A new federal attack southward was stopped at Manassas (August), followed by a rebel attack northward that was stopped at Antietam (September). Then two federal thrusts were stopped at Fredericksburg (December) and Chancellorsville (May 1863), followed by a rebel attack that was stopped at Gettysburg (July 1863). Tens of thousands of dead soldiers littered the battlefields around Virginia.

"It was thought to be a great thing to charge a battery of artillery or an earthwork lined with infantry," one Confederate general recalled. "We were very lavish of blood in those days."[3]

West of the Appalachian Mountains, however, the war progressed solidly southward, with each confrontation resolving in favor of the federals. In the same years that the eastern war had rolled back and forth, federals in the west under Ulysses S. Grant had captured two entrenched rebel armies (Fort Donelson and Vicksburg), stood off a determined counteroffensive (Shiloh), scattered a third army in panic (Chattanooga), and consolidated control over the Mississippi River and several key railroads.

In 1864, Grant took command in the east to break Lee's army, and the conflict quickly became a war of attrition. Throughout May and June, the rebel army in Virginia was ground down and pushed back into siege lines at the railroad junction of Petersburg, while the last major Confederate army in the west was battered and cornered in Atlanta. After several months of sniping, bombardment, direct assaults, and flanking attacks, these rebel armies were pried loose from their trenches and destroyed.

Legacy

The Civil War was a battle between two competing visions of America—one defined by nationality (white Anglo-Saxon Protestants) against one defined by ideology (all men are created equal). This is probably the central conflict of American history, and if you understand this war, you will be a long way toward understanding the United States.

Obviously, the main outcome of the war was the freeing of the slaves, but that was coming down the road anyway. A war of some sort was probably inevitable—not many slave-owning countries avoided it—but even at its most stubborn, the United States would not have held onto slavery much longer than Cuba (1886) or Brazil (1888).

More remarkable were the Fourteenth and Fifteenth Amendments to the Constitution, granting full citizenship and equal protection under the law to the former slaves. No one would have dared to suggest these before the war, but with the nationalist definition of America defeated and the ideological definition triumphant, the supermajorities necessary to vote these into law were easy to find.

The entire political structure of the country was rebuilt by these amendments. Before the war, the individual states were autonomous and not bound by the federal Bill of Rights. This worked to the advantage of local elites, not only allowing blacks to be enslaved but also allowing free blacks to be expelled or disenfranchised. State governments were free to support an official religion or prohibit publication of unpopular ideas.

Then the Fourteenth Amendment made the states subordinate to the federal government on matters of human rights for the first time, an ideological victory that has annoyed conservatives for a century and a half. Although the partisans of a nationalist definition of America have gradually and grudgingly expanded their definition of American to include occasional non-whites, non-Anglo-Saxons, or non-Protestants, the conflict still shapes American political debate. Should English be America's official language, or merely its most common? Is America a Christian nation, or just a nation with a lot of Christians? Every time the Fourteenth Amendment is used to impose federal jurisdiction over criminal rights, education, employment, capital punishment, or religious favoritism, we hear echoes of the Civil War.

HUI REBELLION

Death toll: 640,000[1]
Rank: 66
Type: religious uprising
Broad dividing line: Han (Confucian) vs. Hui (Muslim)
Time frame: 1862–73
Location: Gansu Province
Major state participant: China
Who usually gets the most blame: it depends
Another damn: Chinese peasant revolt
Economic factor: bamboo poles

MUSLIM CHINESE, THE HUI (SEE "PANTHAY REBELLION"), HAD BECOME rather common in the northwest along the caravan routes to the Middle East, abutting the Turkic lands of Central Asia.

During the Taiping Rebellion, Qing officials had formed local militias all over the country to defend small communities from Taiping raiding, but in the western province of Shaanxi, the Hui formed militias to protect themselves from their Han neighbors, with whom they had an ongoing feud.

Some Hui soldiers on their way home from fighting the Taipings got to arguing over the price of bamboo poles in the marketplace of Huanzhou. Fighting broke out and several Hui were killed.[2] That night, the local Han set the Hui quarter on fire, and from there it became a full-fledged civil war. As the war ravaged the countryside, supplies of food, fuel, and fodder ran out and prices rose beyond the reach of most inhabitants. Famine followed.

Hui militias brought the cities of Tongzhou and Xian under siege, but the Qing troops inside held out. Within a few months, Qing armies forced the rebels to retreat westward into the Gansu Corridor, a narrow strip of fertile land tucked between the western mountains and deserts that traditionally had connected China with the Silk Road to the Middle East. Here the war stalemated.

In 1868, a new Chinese commander, Zuo Zongtang, arrived in Xian. A former scholar, Zuo had come to prominence putting down the Taiping Rebellion. He was a meticulous organizer and took his time training, supplying, and planning his offensive. Finally, he fought his way outward town by town along the Gansu Corridor, eventually homing in on one specific Hui leader, Ma Hualong, as the man he needed to break first.[3]

Ma Hualong was besieged in the Hui capital at Jinjibao for sixteen long, hungry months. After the Hui rebels surrendered in March 1871, General Zuo had Ma, his family, and over eighty of his officials put to death by slicing.* The last major Hui city, Suzhou, fell in November 1873 followed by a general massacre, but the war continued in the countryside for several years more. Many tens of thousands of survivors fled west, into lands under Russian control.

Confucian Confusion

I hate to admit this, but it took me a long time to realize that this uprising of Chinese Muslims in Gansu is not at all the same as the earlier chapter's uprising of Chinese Muslims in Yunnan. Most books combine all of the uprisings against the Qing in the middle of the nineteenth century into one humongous mess, but let's try to keep them separate for now.

Another possible source of confusion: the Russians call the Hui of this region who came under their control through migration and conquest by the name Dungans, so this war is often called the Dungan Rebellion. This has nothing at all to do with the Dzungars we encountered in an earlier chapter (see "Sino-Dzungar War").

And finally, even though I've dedicated three distinct chapters to nineteenth-century pandemonium in China, this doesn't exhaust the list. The Nian Rebellion, the Red Turban Rebellion, and the Punti-Hakka Clan Wars all erupted around this same time, but they probably didn't kill enough people to make this list.

---

* If you're American, you've heard of Zuo Zongtang (Tso Tsung-t'ang in old-style transcription). He's General Tso of take-out fame. No one knows why little chunks of deep fried chicken are named after this Qing general. The more entertaining but less likely possibility is that Chinese refugees settling in America in the late nineteenth century displayed a bit of gallows humor concerning the traditional Chinese form of execution—the Death by a Thousand Cuts. (You would look like this chicken when General Tso was done with you.) Unfortunately, it's more likely that the dish was invented in Manhattan in the 1970s and named randomly after a famous Chinese hero. (Michael Browning, "Who Was General Tso and Why Are We Eating His Chicken?" *Washington Post*, April 17, 2002)

WAR OF THE TRIPLE ALLIANCE

Death toll: 480,000[1]
Rank: 79
Type: hegemonial war
Broad dividing line: Paraguay vs. everyone
Time frame: 1864–70
Location: South America
Major state participants: Argentina, Brazil, Paraguay, Uruguay
Who usually gets the most blame: Francisco Solano Lopez
Another damn: war of trenches and idiotic frontal assaults
Economic factor: trade access

N O LIST OF MAD CONQUERORS ROLLING OVER THEIR NEIGHBORS IN A quest for glory and treasure is complete without Francisco Solano Lopez, dictator of Paraguay. The bad-tempered son of the previous dictator, Lopez had inherited South America's largest army along with its poorest country. Unfortunately, some of the best stories you hear about Lopez's self-destructive insanity were merely propaganda spread by his Brazilian and Argentine enemies. His story gets less interesting the more you look into it. (Damn you, research!)

For starters, the conflict erupted because of boring geopolitical intrigues rather than wild blood lust. The Río de la Plata is a broad estuary leading into the heart of South America, where wide, navigable rivers connect the trade of four nations: Paraguay, Argentina, Brazil, and Uruguay. It's the only place in South America where countries adjoin one another near well-populated areas, so naturally this is where you will find the bloodiest interstate war ever fought in the Western Hemisphere.

During a border dispute between Brazil and Uruguay, the Uruguayan opposition party, the Colorados (Reds), joined Brazil for a coup against the ruling Blancos (Whites). This made Uruguay a Brazilian satellite, jeopardizing inland Paraguay's access to the sea. Lopez decided to march in and throw out both the Brazilians and the Colorados.[2]

At first, a really satisfying war seemed out of reach because Paraguay couldn't get to Uruguay. The first shots were fired between warships off the coast of Uruguay, but Lopez failed to get control of the sea, so an amphibious attack was out of the question. The only road between the warring sides went through a panhandle of Argentina. When Argentina refused Lopez's request to pass along this road, he attacked anyway in December 1864, bringing Argentina into what now became the Triple Alliance against Paraguay—11 million people in three countries against a single nation of a half million.

The Paraguayan offensive penetrated deep into Brazil, but Brazil is a vast country that chewed up and spit out the Paraguayan army in a hard campaign. The allies drove the survivors back to Paraguay in 1866. Meanwhile, the allies had already begun their counteroffensive elsewhere. By 1865, Brazil had bought so many ironclad warships from Europe and North America that it now had the largest modern navy in the world. The Brazilians destroyed Lopez's wooden fleet in the Río de la Plata, opening the estuary and rivers to attack.

Allied armies and gunboats pushed up the Parana River until they stalled at the Paraguayan trenches covering the junction of the Paraguay River and the Parana, around the town of Humaita. It took three years and over 100,000 lives for the allies to slug across the next thirty miles, attacking each new line of Paraguayan trenches, one after another. Month by month, year by year, Lopez scoured the country for enough conscripts to fill his lines, progressively lowering his standards in desperation. Naturally he shot any of his men who failed to perform his duty to the utmost, and he planted spies throughout his army to report any treasonous utterances by his soldiers. In May 1868, the allies finally broke the stalemate and drove away the remaining 20,000 Paraguayan soldiers—emaciated teenagers, cripples, and old men mostly.

As his enemies closed in, Lopez lashed out against the conspiracies he knew had brought him down. Several hundred Paraguayan citizens—his brothers, brothers-in-law, cabinet ministers, bishops, and judges among them—were seized and executed. He killed over 200 foreigners including many diplomats. He had his own mother flogged and sentenced to die.

By December the allies had taken Paraguay's capital, Asuncion, and installed their own puppet government. They declared the war won and went home, leaving a small force to clean up. Lopez remained at large somewhere in the jungle, "raising another army of 13,000, including eight-year-old boys wearing false beards and armed with sticks."[3] He embarked on a guerrilla war and grew more insane as time passed. Finally, defeated and down to his last 200 men, Lopez was speared by a Brazilian grenadier while fleeing across a river.

His mistress, Eliza Lynch, a former Parisian courtesan who had horrified Asuncion high society with her arrogant manners, her reckless extravagance, and her low Irish birth, stuck with Lopez to the bitter end. Her Brazilian captors forced her at gunpoint to personally dig his grave after their last battle out in the wilderness.

In addition to territorial changes that shifted a lot of swamps, mountains, and jungles from Paraguay to its enemies, the war had reduced the population of Paraguay from 525,000 to 221,000, leaving only 28,000 men alive. Informal polygamy became commonplace among the surviving Paraguayans as the only way to care for the huge numbers of widows and orphans.[4]

FRANCO-PRUSSIAN WAR

Death toll: 435,000 (185,000 soldiers[1] and 250,000 civilians[2])
Rank: 80
Type: hegemonial war
Broad dividing line and major state participants: France vs. Prussia, obviously
Time frame: 1870–71
Location: France
Minor state participants: Bavaria, Wurttemberg
Who usually gets the most blame: Bismarck, Napoleon III
Another damn: war of trenches and idiotic frontal assaults

SPAIN NEVER REALLY RECOVERED FROM THE NAPOLEONIC OCCUPATION. During the half century following the restoration of the old regime, Spain was torn by one civil war after another, interspersed with shaky cease-fires. Finally, in 1868, the queen was chased away, and the Spaniards began shopping for a new monarch.

Ironically, Spain was not an actual participant in this chapter's multicide, but Spanish troubles have a tendency to radiate outward and disrupt the rest of the world (see also "War of the Spanish Succession" and "Spanish Civil War"). Its vacant throne was offered to a Prussian prince. France absolutely forbade it, so Prussia grumbled and backed down. France then insisted that King Wilhelm II of Prussia promise to never consider such an offer again, a demand that Wilhelm considered ridiculous. The crisis was almost settled diplomatically, but Chancellor Otto von Bismarck of Prussia noticed that hatred of the French was the only thing all of the little nations in Germany agreed on. A large enough crisis might be used to unite the smaller princes of Germany under Prussian rule if everybody got angry enough, so Bismarck taunted the French about the Spanish throne until their emperor, Napoleon III, declared war.

Within a few weeks, both armies were drawn up for miles in the open country along the border west of the Rhine. To outside analysts, the war seemed to be a toss-up. The French had better rifles and primitive machine guns, but the Germans had better artillery. The French army was more professional (400,000 volunteers), but the German army was larger—1.3 million regulars and reservists, mostly draftees, mobilized within the first few weeks. In practice, the Germans were in total control from beginning to end.

In the opening battle, the Germans loaded up their left wing and attacked the French right wing, driving it southward in disorder. As the Germans wedged open the breach and aimed for Paris, the French left wing also pulled back, but in the opposite direction, northward. The main German force then shepherded that half of the French army into Metz, where it was isolated and besieged. The former French right wing now rallied and reassembled between the Germans and Paris. Militarily this half army had no chance of beating the Germans, but politically the French had to give it a shot. When they moved forward to free their besieged countrymen at Metz, the Germans enveloped and captured them at Sedan, taking Napoleon III prisoner.

With their emperor in the hands of the Germans, the French people proclaimed the return of the republic and danced in the streets, until they remembered that the Germans were still coming. The French offered to negotiate, but the German price was too high. The French government withdrew to the safer city of Tours in the Loire Valley and scrambled to raise a new army in the provinces. Parisians raised the militia, herded livestock into the city, and braced for the arrival of the German army.

The Germans surrounded Paris so completely that the government was forced to send messages and officials by pigeon and balloon. The siege of Paris dragged on for month after month as the inhabitants ate through their stockpiled supplies, then ate vermin, zoo animals, and pets. German artillery bombarded the city.

While the capital starved, the French government scoured the hinterlands for enough spare men to assemble another army. They actually cobbled together two new armies to throw against the Germans, one on the Loire River and one near the Swiss border. Neither made any dent, so France finally gave up.[3]

Europe may have lost one emperor with the fall of Napoleon III, but it gained a new one as King Wilhelm of Prussia was promoted to emperor of all of the Germans. Meanwhile, political chaos in France saw Europe's first socialist government, the Paris Commune, come to power in the city. When the national government tried to disarm the Parisian militia, the Commune refused, so the French army moved in and eradicated the Communards block by block. As each pocket of resistance surrendered, the rebels were lined up and shot. Two thousand prisoners were summarily executed during the fighting, and up to 25,000 random Parisians were dead in the rubble.[4]

FAMINES IN BRITISH INDIA

Death toll: 26.6 million famine deaths[1] (not including the Bengal famine of World War II)
Rank: 4
Type: commercial exploitation
Broad dividing line: British oppressing India
Time frame: major famines in 1769–70, 1876–79, 1896–1900
Location: India
Major state participant: United Kingdom, which ruled about half of India directly as a colony
Minor state participants: native princes who ruled the other half as autonomous vassals
Who usually gets the most blame: Most people have never heard of this, so no one gets blamed.
Economic factor: grain

The Dismal Science

Famine seems so easy to explain. If there's not enough food, people starve. If it doesn't rain, crops fail and people starve. If frost or locusts show up at the wrong time, people starve. The problem is that starvation never distributes itself evenly across a society. Even in the face of a bad harvest, the rich and powerful remain fat and happy.

A relatively new theory among political scientists states that deadly famines don't occur in democracies. Amartya Sen won the Nobel Prize for this in 1999. "No famine has ever taken place in the history of the world in a functioning democracy," he wrote in *Development as Freedom*.[2] At first glance, the simple, boring explanation for this would seem to be that democracies are usually rich countries where food is plentiful. But Sen notes that a nation's wealth doesn't matter, "be it economically rich (as in Western Europe or North America) or relatively poor (as in post independence India, or Botswana)." The deciding factor seems to be that elected governments have to keep the voters happy, and letting citizens starve to death results in a loss of votes in addition to the obvious loss of voters.

The experience of India tends to support Sen's theory. A poor country that often hovers on the edge of starvation, India has never experienced a full famine since independence in 1947 despite several spells of hardship; however, while the British ruled India, famines occurred quite frequently.

Underlying the theory is the assumption that government action can always prevent famine deaths—at least in the modern era. If that's true, then whenever famine strikes, the people in charge allowed it.

Sen's theory is in direct conflict with the teachings of Adam Smith, the revered eighteenth-century philosopher of free-market capitalism. Smith wrote in 1776 that famines happen only when governments interfere with natural market forces. "Famine has never arisen from any other cause but the violence of government attempting, by improper means, to remedy the inconvenience of dearth."[3]

In imperialist England, the word of Adam Smith was the word of God.

1769–70

With their victory at Plassey (see "Seven Years War"), the British (in the form of the East India Company) ended up ruling Bengal, but right away they got off to a bad start. In 1769, the seasonal rains failed to come to India, and the resulting famine of 1769–70 killed some 10 million people, a quarter of the population of Bengal.

Whose fault was it? A Dutch naval captain in the area at the time wrote, "This famine arose in part from the bad rice harvest of the preceding year; but it must also be attributed principally to the monopoly the English had over the last harvest of this commodity, which they kept at such a high price that the most unfortunate inhabitants . . . found themselves powerless to buy the tenth part of what they needed to live."[4]

It was a deadly prologue to the next couple of centuries of British rule.

1876–77

Let's jump ahead a hundred years to a time when the whole of India had been brought under British control, and the East India Company's authority had been transferred to the Crown. In 1874, a drought in the northeastern Indian provinces of Bengal and Bihar ruined the harvest. Starvation loomed for millions of unlucky peasants, but the local official, Sir Richard Temple, leapt into action and set up a model welfare system to ease hunger. Importing a half-million tons of rice from Burma, he distributed it freely to the poor. Thanks to Temple's prompt action, only twenty-three people starved to death in that famine. It has been called "the only truly successful British relief effort in the nineteenth century."[5]

Temple was severely reprimanded for his extravagance in feeding the hungry natives in his charge. The *Economist* scolded him for teaching the Indians that "it is the duty of the government to keep them alive." He was scorned all across the governing class for spending public money and meddling in the natural order of things.[6]

Humbled by the criticism, Temple learned his lesson and wanted to make amends. The opportunity came quickly, in 1876, when the monsoon rains failed to arrive across a much larger area. The earth dried up and died. Crops shriveled; livestock wasted away.

When Temple took the job of supervising the relief effort of this new famine, he was desperate to prove that he could stay within budget. "Everything must be subordinated," he promised, "to the financial consideration of disbursing the smallest sum of money consistent with the preservation of human life."[7]

This went over well with the viceroy of India, Robert Bulwer-Lytton, who needed all of the cash in the treasury to fight a new war of conquest into Afghanistan. Prime Minister Benjamin Disraeli had assigned Bulwer-Lytton to India specifically to get the frontier moving forward again after an earlier defeat, and both men were determined that the cost would be covered by Indian taxpayers, not the British public.

Meanwhile, Queen Victoria had just been proclaimed empress of India,* and Lord Lytton spent much of 1876 planning an extravaganza to celebrate the queen's promotion. All of the native lords of India were brought together to see the magnificence of their new overlord. The festival climaxed in a weeklong feast for 68,000 native rulers—the largest such celebration in history.

Famine relief, therefore, was a distant third on the British government's list of priorities in India.

Native rulers in India such as the Mughals had traditionally stockpiled the harvest from good years as a buffer against lean years, but under British rule, the previous good harvests had been exported to England. When the crops failed in India in 1876, there was nothing to replace them. The scarcity drove prices up beyond the reach of the ordinary Indian. Merchants hoarded their grain supplies in hopes that the prices would rise even further.

As hungry peasants took to the road to find food, roadblocks kept refugees out of the cities of Bombay and Poona. Police in Madras (now Chennai in southeast India) expelled

---

* The earth was crawling with emperors in those days. They ruled Russia, Brazil, Japan, Austria, China, and other places, which meant that a mere queen like Victoria, ruler of the most powerful nation on earth, wouldn't be allowed to sit at the big table if they all got together. It got even worse in 1871, when the lowly king of Prussia was proclaimed emperor of a freshly united Germany. As Victoria fell further behind in the title race, this insulting state of affairs had to be corrected, but they couldn't just bump England from kingdom to empire with a snap of the fingers. Disraeli had to find Victoria something big and impressive to become empress of. Aha! India! It took effect on January 1, 1877.

25,000 hungry squatters. The colonial government finally set up work camps where the hungry would build canals and railroads in exchange for a meal.

The guiding philosophy at the time was that relief should be difficult to obtain in order to discourage the poor from becoming dependent on government handouts.[8] Recipients were expected to work hard for their supper, digging ditches and breaking stones. The camps accepted only the able-bodied and healthy into their public works projects, and they hired only workers from at least ten miles away, on the theory that a long walk would weed out the weaklings. Hundreds of thousands were turned away as too weak to be of any use.

Most British authorities agreed that helping the poor only created a cycle of dependency. The finance minister declared, "Every benevolent attempt made to mitigate the effects of famine and defective sanitation serves but to enhance the evils resulting from overpopulation." Lytton argued that the Indian population "has a tendency to increase more rapidly than the food it raises from the soil," and that any relief would simply be absorbed in further unrestrained breeding.[9] A later government report concluded, "If the government spent more of its revenue on famine relief, an even larger proportion of the population would become penurious."

The ration that Richard Temple distributed to each inmate of these labor camps was only two-thirds of what he had given out during his successful relief in 1874—1,627 calories per day instead of 2,500. In fact, the new daily ration for the starving Indians of 1876 had 123 fewer calories than the ration for an inmate in the Nazi concentration camp at Buchenwald in 1944. The Temple ration of one pound of rice a day—no meat, no vegetables—was half of what felons in Indian prisons received.[10]

Temple and Lytton imposed the Anti-Charitable Contributions Act of 1877 on all of the lands under their control, which outlawed any private relief donations that might undercut the price of grain set by the open market. The law was backed up by the threat of imprisonment. Meanwhile, as the people of India starved, over 300,000 tons of grain was exported from India to Europe.[11]

Futurists and modernists had hoped that the bright new technology of the modern era, particularly railroads, would make famine obsolete by rushing food into the stricken areas, but in practice, technology had the opposite effect. The areas best served by railroads suffered the most because this allowed merchants to export local crops to more lucrative markets.[12]

Lord Salisbury, the secretary of state for India, waffled on the proper response to the hunger. On the one hand, he tried to distance himself from countrymen who "worshipped political economy as a sort of 'fetish' " and who considered "famine as a salutary cure for over-population." On the other hand, he congratulated Disraeli for not being fooled by "the growing idea that England ought to pay tribute to India for having conquered her."

Salisbury denigrated the idea "that a rich Britain should consent to penalize her trade for the sake of a poor India" as a "species of International Communism."[13]

Among the large native potentates, only the Nizam of Hyderabad in south-central India offered charitable help. Hungry thousands hiked many miles to get to his distribution centers and often died along the way.

An English publisher tried to get his fellow journalists to investigate what was going on in India. "For long weary years have we demanded the suspension of [the land tax] when famine comes and in vain. With no poor law in the land, and the old policy once more set up of letting people pull through or die, as they can . . . we and our contemporaries must speak without reserve or be partakers in the guilt of multitudinous murders committed by the men blinded to the real nature of what we are doing in the country."[14]

An 1878 government report on the famine absolved the government of all responsibility and blamed it entirely on the weather. The official estimate was that 5.5 million died in the British territory, not counting the native states, but various scholars later estimated that either 10.3, or 8.2, or 6.1 million died across India during the 1876 famine.

1896–97

After it became clear that many millions of Indians had died during the 1876 famine, the government put together reports, plans, and a special Famine Fund to make sure it never happened again. Then twenty years later, it happened again, and it turned out that much of the Famine Fund had already been spent when no one was looking.[15]

The government in London had financed the Famine Fund with revenues from India, not Britain. Following the usual pattern of politics, Liberals in Parliament tried to maintain the insurance fund by placing an income tax on the wealthy and cutting military expenditure, while the Tories preferred filling the fund by raising the salt tax and restoring a license fee on petty merchants, which fell more heavily on the Indian poor. The Tory plan passed Parliament, but, as usual, this influx of ready cash got redirected toward the politicians' pet projects, rather than set aside for future famines. The extra money allowed Lytton in 1879 to remove the tariff on cotton goods entering India from Britain, thereby helping the British textile companies of Lancashire while impoverishing the local Indian cotton industry. And there was still plenty of money left over to invade Afghanistan.[16]

By 1892, a quarter of India's total government revenue went to maintain the burden of the government itself: supporting British pensions, the India Office, and interest on the debt. Very little of this was put back into the local economy; most went to banks and retirees in Britain. These home charges drained off whatever surplus the peasant economy could produce, including the grain from good harvests that normally would have been set aside to cushion against bad years.[17]

Then, in 1896, the monsoon rains failed to come, and the crops failed. Once again, the price of grain shot up beyond the reach of the common Indian. Once again, people starved.

One witness described a child of five he found among starving peasants: "Its arms were not so large around as my thumb; its legs scarcely larger; the pelvic bones were plainly shown; the ribs, back and front, started through the skin like a wire cage. The eyes were fixed and unobservant; the expression of the little skull face solemn, dreary and old. Will, impulse, and almost sensation, were destroyed in this tiny skeleton, which might have been a plump and happy baby. It seemed not to hear when addressed. I lifted it between my thumbs and forefingers; it did not weigh more than seven or eight pounds."[18]

A missionary described a Muslim farmer who sold his land, then his house, then his cooking utensils to buy food for his family. When that ran out, he gave his son to the missionaries to keep. After tearfully assuring the boy that this didn't mean he didn't love him, and that he had no choice, the man walked away, leaving his son to be raised as a Christian.[19]

1899–1900

Today we know that these droughts were caused by the El Niño Southern Oscillation, a sporadic warming on the surface of the South Pacific Ocean off the coast of Peru, which throws weather systems all over the world out of whack, bringing rain where it's usually dry and drought where it usually rains. After a brief break in the drought, El Niño returned in 1899 for an even longer dry spell.

In spite of all of the past practice the authorities had had before, this new famine went just as badly as the previous ones. The new viceroy of India, Lord Curzon, repeated most of the policies that had killed so many in the earlier famine. Native princes did no better. The maharaja of Indore vetoed all expenditures for relief, while Curzon deported refugees who arrived from the autonomous princely states.[20] In the affected regions, as many as one out of every seven peasants was bankrupt and evicted. As the Indian peasantry became broken and driven into the cities, the British hold on the subcontinent strengthened.[21]

With the local scarcity of grain, food prices soared. A Methodist in Hyderabad wrote, "The people had no reserves either of strength or grain to fall back on, the debts of the previous famine still hung around their necks, money was impossible to get, for lenders tightened their purse strings when they saw no chance of recovering their loans."[22]

British authorities saw cheaters everywhere and suspected that many of the Indians applying for relief had "buried hoards of grain and ornaments."[23] Tests designed to keep as many Indians as possible off the dole prevented a million people from collecting relief in the Bombay Presidency.[24]

Three-fourths of a million bushels of grain was exported from Berar province in the north even as 143,000 people starved to death there.[25] When Kansas Populists in the United States shipped 200,000 bags of grain to ease the famine "in solidarity with India's farmers," British officials taxed the shipment.[26] The standing order among officials was that "the revenue must at all costs be gathered in."[27]

Cholera swept through the starving refugees. A Western doctor described one camp: "Millions of flies were permitted undisturbed to pester the unhappy victims. One young woman who had lost every one dear to her, and had turned stark mad, sat at the door vacantly staring at the awful scenes around her. In the entire hospital I did not see a single decent garment. Rags, nothing but rags and dirt."[28]

In spite of the worldwide population explosion that characterized the nineteenth and twentieth centuries, the population of India suffered an absolute decline between 1895 and 1905—the only time this has happened since the first census was taken in 1872.[29] The mortality of the 1899–1900 famine has been estimated at either 19.0, or 8.4, or 6.1 million—in the same level of magnitude as the 1876 famine. This time, however, the British government report written after the fact recognized that the famine came from the failure of the economy more than a failure of weather. There had been plenty of grain in Burma and Bengal that could have been sent south and west to feed the starving:

> Owing to the excellent system of communication which now brings every person of [India] into close connexion with the great market, the supplies of food were at all times sufficient, and it cannot be too frequently repeated that the severe privation was chiefly due to the dearth of employment in agriculture and other industries, but the failure of the harvests caused loss of ordinary income in an enormous area and to an "unprecedented extent."[30]

RUSSO-TURKISH WAR

Death toll: 500,000[1] (208,000 or 283,000 soldiers)
Rank: 70
Type: clash of cultures
Broad dividing line: Turks vs. Christians
Time frame: 1877–78
Location: Balkans
Major state participants: Russia, Ottoman Turkey
Minor state participants: Austria-Hungary, Wallachia, Moldavia
Major non-state participants: Bosnians, Bulgarians
Who usually gets the most blame: Turkey

WHEN A REVOLT AGAINST TURKISH RULE ERUPTED IN BOSNIA IN 1876, IT quickly spread to all of the Christian subjects of the sultan in the Balkans as well—Macedonians, Serbs, and Bulgarians. The most distant rebels, the Bosnians, were taken under the protection of Austria. Unfortunately, the nearest, the Bulgarians, were within easier reach of Ottoman retribution, and when Turkish troops arrived to put down the revolt, they swept through the rebellious villages and slaughtered 30,000 Bulgarians of all ages and genders.

The massacres horrified Europe, and everyone insisted that someone *do* something. At first the Russian government hesitated. It was an internal matter after all, and no one wanted to start a general European war over some damn fool thing in the Balkans. Treaties forbade Russia from interfering in Turkey, but many idealistic Russian army officers resigned and joined the rebels to fight on behalf of their fellow Slavs anyway.

With European opinion in their favor, the Russians finally launched a surprise attack in April 1877 south along the Black Sea coast and liberated Bulgaria from Turkish rule. This soon became the only popular war in Russia's history, and for a few years volunteers outnumbered draftees in annual recruitment. The Russians pressed on and knocked aside several Ottoman attempts to stop them. As the Russians closed in on Constantinople in July, they got bogged down facing the trenches just outside the Turkish city of Plevna. Months of fruitless assaults chewed up the Russian army, and by the time Plevna surrendered in November, the war had stalled long enough for pragmatism to replace idealism in the capitals of Europe. Public opinion in the West shifted away from stopping the Turks in favor of saving them. As the British fleet steamed toward the war zone, a rerun of the Crimean War seemed inevitable until everyone backed away from the brink.[2]

In the end, the Ottoman Empire was taken down a notch in favor of local nationalities. The first treaty imposed by the Russians attempted to create a big Bulgarian nation that included just about everything the Turks still had in Europe, but the other powers would not allow it. Another treaty negotiated in Berlin trimmed Bulgaria down to just the south bank of the lower Danube, and then split this into two countries. The Turkish vassals Serbia and Romania were granted full independence, and Austria was allowed to occupy—though not own—Bosnia. The Turks also gave the island of Cyprus to Britain as thanks for being a friend in their time of need.[3] To purify their lands of all traces of the enemy, the Bulgarians expelled more than a half-million Muslim residents with considerable brutality, uncounted thousands of whom died in the exodus.

Pop Culture

The sons of the Prophet are brave men and bold
And quite unaccustomed to fear,
But the bravest by far in the ranks of the shah,
Was Abdul Abulbul Amir.

Now the heroes were plenty and well known to fame
In the troops that were led by the Czar,
And the bravest of these was a man by the name
Of Ivan Skavinsky Skavar.

One day this bold Russian, he shouldered his gun
And donned his most truculent sneer,
Downtown he did go where he trod on the toe
Of Abdul Abulbul Amir . . .

—Percy French, "Abdul Abulbul Amir," 1877

Even though the British stayed out of the war, the Russo-Turkish conflict left an odd relic in their vocabulary. In addition to the song "Abdul Abulbul Amir" written by a student at Trinity College, Dublin, another hit in the music halls based on current events was a proud little song written by G. W. Hunt and performed by G. H. "The Great" MacDermott:

We don't want to fight but by Jingo if we do,
We've got the ships, we've got the men, we've got the money too,
We've fought the Bear before, and while we're Britons true,
The Russians shall not have Constantinople.

From this chorus came the English word for enthusiastic warmongering—*jingoism*.

These two songs nicely represent the two sides that seem to emerge in every debate about foreign intervention. There's the attitude that we can't just sit by and watch while those foreigners do something awful, and the attitude that these foreigners have been killing each other for years and will continue to do so, regardless of what we do about it.

Casualties

After most of the battles in this book so far, armies usually left wounded soldiers unattended and groaning where they fell until the army got a good night's sleep. Fighting battles was exhausting. Gathering and patching the wounded took too much time and too many resources for armies to make more than a token effort while the enemy was still in the neighborhood threatening to resume the attack. In fact, helping to evacuate the wounded to the rear was widely seen as a coward's trick to get out of harm's way and armies often had rules against it.[4] During the decade and a half preceding the Russo-Turkish War, humanitarians in the West had been busy organizing a neutral organization dedicated to getting wounded soldiers off the battlefield and into hospitals without waiting for generals to get around to it. As long as they didn't take sides, the Red Cross would be allowed to travel freely in hostile territory to fulfill its mission.

After a promising start in a small war between Prussia and Denmark in 1864, the movement gained wider acceptance in the 1870 Franco-Prussian War, but it hit its first snag in the Russo-Turkish War. In a war between Muslims and Christians, Turkish soldiers had trouble believing that strangers marked with a big red cross weren't the enemy. To calm their suspicions, from this point forward the Red Cross would be the Red Crescent in Muslim lands.

Death Toll

The Russian military recorded some 35,000 battle deaths and 83,000 deaths by disease and accident.[5] Turkish military deaths have been estimated at 90,000[6] or 165,000.[7]

None of the civilian death tolls I've encountered inspire great confidence. Soviet demographer Boris Urlanis estimated some 300,000 to 400,000 excess civilian deaths *in Russia* even though the war wasn't fought there.[8] Turkish nationalists swear that the Bulgarians massacred 260,000 Turks while purging their new country of their former oppressors, but this estimate began with Justin McCarthy, who is outside the mainstream.[9] Although the specifics are debatable, an authentic civilian death toll of a couple hundred thousand is probably hidden somewhere in these confusing numbers, but we can't say who, how, or where.

> *A splash in the Black Sea one dark moonless night*
> *Caused ripples to spread wide and far,*
> *It was made by a sack fitting close to the back,*
> *Of Ivan Skavinsky Skavar.*
>
> *A Muscovite maiden her lone vigil keeps,*
> *'Neath the light of the cold northern star,*
> *And the name that she murmurs in vain as she weeps,*
> *Is Ivan Skavinsky Skavar.*

MAHDI REVOLT

Death toll: 5.5 million
Rank: 21
Type: messianic uprising
Broad dividing line: Mahdists ("dervishes") vs. everyone else
Time frame: 1881–98
Location: Sudan
Major state participant: Mahdiyah (the domain of the Mahdi)
Minor state participants: Ethiopia, Britain, Darfur, Egypt
Who usually gets the most blame: the Mahdi and Khalifah
Economic factors: slaves, debt
The unanswerable question everyone asks: Why have so many holy men had absolutely no problem with slavery?*

The Root of All Evil

In 1879, the government of Egypt lurched unsteadily toward bankruptcy because of the usual combination of senseless wars and a profligate ruler. Concerned about the security of the Suez Canal, the British and French jointly jumped in to straighten out Egypt's finances. Soon afterward, nationalists inside the Egyptian army rebelled against these foreign bean-counters. Because the French couldn't get there in time, the uprising was put down exclusively by British troops. This turned an international protectorate into a British colony, which had massive diplomatic reverberations that will have to wait until the next chapter (see "Congo Free State").[1]

For this chapter, all you need to know is that the British were suddenly in charge of Egypt. They only wanted their loans paid back and the canal kept safe, so they tried to keep a low profile and quietly supervise the native government behind the scenes. Unfortunately, the Egyptian government already annoyed Arab traditionalists in so many ways. Cairo was corrupt and decadent. The inhabitants openly drank alcohol and played music. The upper class studied Western languages, science, and medicine at their schools. Now Egypt was

---

* Two possible explanations would be the cynical and the theological. Cynically, we might say that large religions are part of the ruling class, so *of course* they support keeping everyone in their place. Theologically, religions usually emphasize that we are all subservient to God regardless of our rank here on earth—slaves or kings, it doesn't matter. We are all equally humble in God's eyes.

under the thumb of European overlords. The last straw came when Cairo—under British prompting—tried to abolish the slave trade, which was the economic mainstay of the upriver Arabs in the Egyptian province of Sudan. The Sudanese rebelled in 1881.

The Guide

Sudan rallied around Muhammad Ahmed, a wandering holy man who had been defying the authorities for years. Born and raised along the upriver Nile, he preferred the study of Islam to the family business of carpentry. As a teenager, he followed the dervishes—Sufi mystics. Over time, he joined the entourages of several of the Sudan's holiest men until he decided that he was holier than all of them put together. He split off and began to gather disciples himself. He soon hinted—and eventually declared—that he was the Mahdi, the "Guided One," a messianic title. The Muslim calendar was coming up on the turn of a century (1882/1883 CE = 1300 After the Hegira), and apocalyptic worries permeated society.

At first the Egyptian authorities in the provincial capital of Khartoum tried to buy him off, but when Muhammad Ahmed proved dead serious and unbribable, they sent soldiers to bring him in. Two companies of Egyptian troops raced each other all night along different routes to be the first to capture the Mahdi and claim the reward. Near dawn, they arrived at their destination simultaneously from opposite directions and ended up accidentally shooting at each other until the Mahdi's army appeared and slaughtered them both.[2]

The next force—4,000 men under Yusef Pasha—was so poorly disciplined and so confident that they could beat the savages that they didn't even post sentries. The Mahdists attacked in the night and wiped out this well-equipped army to the last man using little more than spears and swords.

A better Egyptian force of 8,000 men under Hicks Pasha, a British mercenary and convert to Islam, attacked Mahdist territory from Khartoum, but after they aimlessly chased the enemy across the open desert for several weeks, the rebels cut the Egyptian supply line. Soon, the column stumbled, straggled, and disintegrated with heat and thirst, until the dervishes sprang an ambush and slaughtered them all. Hicks's head was taken to the Mahdi, and his body was left behind to be speared over and over by the triumphant dervishes.[3]

Running low on soldiers, the Egyptian government gave up and sent Charles Gordon, the British mercenary who had helped put down the Taipings in China (see "Taiping Rebellion"), to Khartoum in February 1884 with orders to evacuate all of the Europeans and Egyptians in the city—7,000 soldiers and 27,000 civilians. Once he got there, he decided it would be cruel to abandon the outlying Egyptian garrisons to the mercy of the dervishes, so he settled down to wait for those garrisons to withdraw to Khartoum. In May, while he was still waiting, the Mahdists sealed off the city. Gordon was trapped.

When the British public learned of Gordon's heroic predicament, they insisted that their government rush out and rescue him. In October an expeditionary force of 10,000 under Lord Garnet Wolseley was thrown together in Cairo and sent eight hundred miles to Khartoum and into the heart of the rebellion.

Dispatches sent back to Britain thrilled newspaper readers as the column approached, but then the day came when Wolseley reached his destination, only to find dervishes on the walls of Khartoum. Two days earlier, January 25, 1885, with British relief imminent, the Mahdi had ordered a do-or-die assault on Khartoum. The city fell, followed by a general rape and massacre of the trapped population. The women were distributed among the harems of the privileged Mahdists. Gordon's severed head was presented to the Mahdi, although he hadn't asked for it.

The Caliphate

The failure to rescue Gordon brought down William Gladstone's Liberal government in Great Britain. Meanwhile General Wolseley abandoned the Sudan to its fate and took his army home.

Most history books skip the next fifteen years because the British weren't involved, but Sudan under the Mahdists fared badly. The dead from the Anglo-Sudanese Wars alone aren't enough to put this event anywhere near my list, but with wars on every front, famine, and intensified slave raids, the population of the Sudan plummeted. Of the 8 million people in the Sudan before the uprising, only 2.5 million were left to be counted by the Egyptian government after the reconquest.[4]

Khartoum was left in ruins, overgrown with weeds, littered with bones, and looted of anything useful, while a new capital grew up across the river around the Mahdi's compound in Omdurman, swelling to 150,000 inhabitants.

The Mahdists imposed strict Muslim law. Whippings, mutilations, and beheadings became increasingly common. The almsgiving that Islam suggested was a virtuous goal now became a mandatory tax, much of which went to maintaining the lavish lifestyle of the movement's leaders.

The Mahdi outlawed everything alien to Arab culture—European education, industry, and medicine—even wearing a fez, which looked too Turkish. In June 1885, shortly after prohibiting Western medicine and expelling or executing all doctors, the Mahdi fell ill with typhus and died. Leadership of Mahdiyah went to his close associate, Khalifah ("Deputy") Abdullahi.[5]

The nomadic Baqqarah (Arabic: Cattlemen) of Kordofan, especially Abdullahi's Taaisha clan, formed the backbone of Abdullahi's caliphate. His claim to succession, however, was contested by kinsmen of the Mahdi who felt that one of them deserved the title, and this rivalry drove a low-grade civil war. In this era, the Sudan was still very much a tribal society. Most clans kept to themselves inside their own territories, but others pursued blood feuds with neighbors that stretched back generations; however, the only modern weapons on hand were the thousands of rifles collected from dead Egyptians that the Khalifah issued only to his friends.

Abdullahi brought the whole of Sudan under his control. He slaughtered the Kababish Arabs of Kordofan, who had rejected the Mahdi and sold camels to Gordon. He massacred the Juhaina of the Blue Nile (the eastern branch that joins the White Nile at Khartoum), hardly caring that until then they had grown most of Omdurman's grain. A rebellion in Darfur brought Abdullahi's wrath and two years of savage fighting to that region as well.[6] Slave raids into pagan territory resumed.

When the Batahin tribe of Arabs rebelled, Abdullahi ordered every male of the tribe rounded up and hauled to Omdurman for punishment. Dozens died in jail before the surviving seventy were sentenced to public execution. The rope broke after eighteen had been hanged, so Abdullahi switched to beheadings for the next couple of dozen. Finally, he ordered that the last twenty-seven have their hands and feet chopped off and be turned loose to bleed to death or beg in the marketplace.[7]

The Khalifah forbade the traditional Muslim pilgrimage to Mecca and now insisted that pilgrimage to the Mahdi's tomb in Omdurman was the new sacred duty.

When the rains failed in 1888, the general scarcity of grain created by the massacre of the Juhaina and relentless war became a full famine. Under orders from the Khalifah, Sudanese soldiers scoured the countryside. They confiscated all of the grain they found and brought it back to the capital to be redistributed to the population according to their loyalty. As famine gripped the country, it became difficult to keep the streets of Omdurman clear of bodies.

In 1887 the Mahdists invaded the Christian empire of Ethiopia (also called Abyssinia at the time) and laid waste to its frontier provinces. When Emperor Yohannes IV of Ethiopia led his army out to stop them, a Mahdist force got behind him and took his capital at Gondar. The Sudanese raped and killed the inhabitants and burned the city.

In 1889 Yohannes found the Sudanese army in fortifications at the border town of Metema and attacked. It was the last big battle in history fought primarily with muscle power and sharp weapons. Although the Ethiopian attack began well, Yohannes was mortally wounded and carried back to camp. This took the spirit out of the Ethiopian troops and their attack fizzled out.* As the Ethiopians prepared the emperor's body for a funeral, his relatives began to squabble over the throne and they all hurried home to get a head start on their upcoming civil war. Taking advantage of the confusion, the Mahdists attacked out

---

* Worried by the loss at Metema, the Europeans began supplying modern weapons to the Ethiopian army to hold back the Mahdists. The side effect of this is that the Ethiopians were well armed enough to fight off European encroachment, becoming the only native state to survive the Scramble for Africa (ca. 1880-1900).

of Metema, scattering the remaining Ethiopians, who abandoned the jewel-encrusted coffin holding the emperor's body. After finding this trophy in the empty camp, the Mahdists sent the emperor's head back to Omdurman, where it was proudly paraded through the streets on a pole and added to the collection.[8]

Reconquest

After a decade and a half of ignoring the Sudan, the British worried that the French, who had been consolidating an empire across the African interior, were now approaching the Nile. This could not be allowed. If the French got a foothold on the upper Nile, the British feared they could use modern engineering to divert all of its precious water away from Egypt.

In 1898 an army of 17,000 Egyptians and 8,000 British set out to retake Sudan, led by Sir Herbert Kitchener. Awesomely mustached and fluent in Arabic, Kitchener had been a subordinate officer in Wolseley's campaign of 1884–85. Since he had no besieged compatriot to rescue, he now could move at a more leisurely pace than Wolseley had done.

The British killed 3,000 Mahdists at their first clash in April, when a dervish column tried to destroy the railroad the British were building at Atbara to support their offensive. The Mahdists had a reputation of being unstoppable and fanatically impervious to pain, which led British riflemen to use dumdum bullets, soft lead projectiles that expanded, blew away entire body parts, and left gaping holes wherever they hit. The British often shot wounded dervishes on the ground rather than risk being killed with their last stubborn burst of strength. The Sudanese have never forgiven them for this.

After a methodical march toward Khartoum, the British were hit by the full Mahdist army outside Omdurman in September. The British had brought along a marvelous new invention—the Maxim machine gun—so when the screaming dervishes attacked, they were cut down by the thousands. Omdurman was one of the most lopsided battles in history. Ten thousand dervishes were killed; 20,000 more were wounded too seriously to flee. The British lost only a half a percent of that, forty-eight killed, most of them when one glory-seeking British cavalry officer led his men in a totally unauthorized, unsupported, and unnecessary charge into the massed enemy. It was the last cavalry charge the British army ever attempted.

The British blew up the Mahdi's tomb and swept his bones into the Nile, except for his skull, which was offered to Kitchener, then to a museum in England, and finally was reburied with full Muslim rites after a disgusted Queen Victoria heard about it and ordered her troops to leave that man's remains alone.

The last glimmer of the Mahdist state was finally extinguished when the fugitive Khalifah Abdullahi was hunted down and killed in battle in November 1899.

CONGO FREE STATE

Death toll: 10 million
Rank: 14
Type: commercial exploitation
Broad dividing line: Europeans exploiting natives
Time frame: 1885–1908
Location: Congo basin, central Africa
Major state participants: none
Major non-state participants: Congo Free State
Who generally gets the most blame: King Leopold II of Belgium
Economic factors: rubber, timber, ivory

> By this time [Africa] was not a blank space any more. It had got filled
> since my boyhood with rivers and lakes and names. It had ceased to
> be a blank space of delightful mystery—a white patch for a boy to
> dream gloriously over. It had become a place of darkness. But there was
> in it one river especially, a mighty big river, that you could see on the
> map, resembling an immense snake uncoiled, with its head in the sea,
> its body at rest curving afar over a vast country, and its tail lost in the
> depths of the land. And as I looked at the map of it in a shop-window,
> it fascinated me as a snake would a bird—a silly little bird. Then I
> remembered there was a big concern, a Company for trade on that
> river. Dash it all! I thought to myself, they can't trade without using some
> kind of craft on that lot of fresh water—steamboats! Why shouldn't I try
> to get charge of one? I went on along Fleet Street, but could not shake
> off the idea. The snake had charmed me.
>
> **—Joseph Conrad, *Heart of Darkness***

The man who put the Congo River on the map was the jungle-whacking journalist Henry Stanley. After earning his fame by presumably discovering Dr. Livingstone in 1871, he returned to Africa to settle all of the big questions of geography. Carrying the *Lady Alice*, a fold-up boat, inland from Zanzibar along the Arab slaving routes of East Africa, he first circumnavigated Lake Tanganyika, then Lake Victoria, and thereby determined the source of the Nile once and for all. Having solved the great geographic mystery of the era, he launched his portable boat—along with canoes bought locally—down a big mystery river that flowed westward from the lakes. It turned out to be the Congo River. Henry Stanley's fabled expedition down the Congo River brought modern firepower to the exploration of Africa, blasting away any native opposition he encountered. When Stanley emerged from the Congo onto the Atlantic coast in 1870, the golden age of African exploration was over.

His dispatches from Africa stirred the imagination of the West. Unfortunately, via letters that had been waiting patiently for him for several years, Stanley learned the horrible news that his fiancée, Alice, whose memory had cheered and inspired him while he rode her namesake boat in darkest Africa, had married someone else about a year after Stanley disappeared. He moped around, inconsolable, and edited his journals into a best seller about his adventures in the Dark Continent.

Impressed by the vast richness of the country, Stanley had hoped to get the British government to set up a colony there, but it wasn't interested. He was only the latest major explorer to fail to get a government interested in the Congo basin. These advocates arranged meetings and wrote passionate editorials that expounded on the value of having markets for European goods, on the number of heathen souls that needed saving, on the rich natural resources free for the taking, on the savage cannibals that needed dietary reform, and on the wretched slave markets that needed to be shut down.

No one was interested. The European governments took the sensible middle-class attitude that colonies cost more than they were worth. As late as 1870 the only northern European officials south of the Sahara were in South Africa—where the climate was suited to white settlement—and in coastal towns like Libreville and Freetown that had been established as part of the anti-slavery movement. Missionaries prowled deep into the heart of Africa, but they did so at their own risk, without the protection of their governments.

A Man of Wealth and Taste

Among those failing to convince a government to take up the "white man's burden" was King Leopold II of Belgium, a hedonistic and dangerously clever person who was looking around for stray lands to take over. Born in 1835, he was only five years younger than his little country, but he had big ambitions.

"There are no small nations," Leopold said, "only small minds." Would Spain be willing to sell the Philippines? No one seems to be using that desolate stretch of Argentina—how about letting us have it? Maybe Borneo is available, or New Guinea. Unfortunately, the Belgian parliament was no more interested in taking on colonies than its British counterparts had been. Leopold's ambitions were going nowhere.

After reading Stanley's book, Leopold tried to woo a reluctant Stanley into a partnership. As Stanley traveled around Europe promoting his books, he received a number of pleasant invitations to lunch and tea whenever the king was in the same town. Leopold was floating an idea to bypass the governments of Europe entirely and create an independent colony, the Congo Free State. He pointed to the older, smaller settlement of former slaves in Liberia as his model. The Congo Free State would prohibit the importation of guns and alcohol. It would impose peace on all of the tribes, abolish the slave trade, and establish a protected zone of free trade where the three C's—commerce, Christianity, and civilization—could flourish.

Leopold sponsored a conference in September 1876 in Brussels, during which scientific and anthropological papers about Africa were presented, and then he created a front organization called the Association Internationale Africaine. This group met once more, a year later, and faded away. No matter. It had served its purpose. It had lasted long enough to convince the world that Leopold was on the up-and-up.

Stanley agreed to return to the Congo and build a road around Livingstone Falls, the long stretch of cliffs and rocky water that separated the coastal estuary from the wide, sluggish sweep of navigable river that penetrated a thousand miles into the heart of Africa. Beginning in 1879, he established posts along the river and negotiated with local chiefs, exchanging trade goods for rights-of-way.

Rubber Stamp

The British occupation of Egypt in 1879 did more than anger the natives and stir up the revolt described in the last chapter (see "Mahdi Revolt"). It also annoyed the rest of Europe.

Although no one in Europe actually wanted Africa for themselves, they'd be damned if they would let anyone else have it, so as soon as the British made their tentative grab, the rest of Europe jumped up and demanded their share. With the British in control of Egypt, everyone else—France, Germany, Portugal, Italy—wanted a piece of the action. In 1884, representatives of over a dozen nations gathered in Berlin to divide Africa fairly among all of the claimants. Of course, none of the nations represented at the conference were African, but did I really need to tell you that? Even Westernized African states like Transvaal and Liberia were shut out.

In addition to parceling out national spheres of influence, the delegates formally backed Leopold's scheme. The Congo would become a private colony under the personal rule of King Leopold—not a possession of the state of Belgium. Partly, Leopold was allowed to take the Congo as a compromise. No major power wanted to let it fall into the hand of another major power, but giving it to the king of neutral little Belgium seemed safe.

During that era of unbridled capitalism, allowing corporations to function as sovereign nations had solid precedent. The Dutch East India Company had operated colonies and navies in the Far East without government oversight throughout the seventeenth and eighteenth centuries. The British East India Company conquered India and governed independently until the Crown took over in 1858. Hudson's Bay Company controlled one-sixth of North America until 1868. The Congo Free State was just one more private colony.

Red Rubber

The Free State was not a successful operation at first. As skeptics in the Belgian parliament had predicted, colonies cost more and produced less than Leopold had originally imagined. After ten years, the Free State was heading toward bankruptcy, and Leopold was about to ask the Belgian government to take it off his hands. He was saved by a worldwide surge in demand for rubber. In 1888, Dunlop had invented the pneumatic rubber tire for bicycles, and in 1895, Michelin did the same for automobiles. Suddenly, Leopold had something that everyone wanted.[1]

In many ways, the Free State operated by elaborate sleight of hand. On paper, an incredibly complex organization could be charted with boxes and arrows that only served to disguise the fact that all of the money was being funneled directly into Leopold's pocket.

His colony was divided into two parts. The lesser was designated as a free trading zone, in which investors would be granted leases that guaranteed exclusive commercial rights over a specific service, product, region, or industry. One syndicate was sold the contract to build the railroad around Livingstone Falls. Another was granted exclusive rights to develop the minerals of Katanga, while another developed the diamond fields of Katai. Leopold almost always managed to own substantial stock in these operations, such as the 50 percent he owned of the Anglo-Belgian India-Rubber Company.[2]

The greater part of the colony was designated the private property of the state (the Private Domain). Government officials were paid low salaries, but they earned lucrative commissions based on how much they could wrest from their district. The money they sent upward went back into the state treasury to cover operating expenses.

Once expenses were covered, a third zone (the Crown Domain) was established as the personal property of Leopold himself. It was run on the same lines as the Private Domain, but this money went directly to Leopold.

In addition to the natural resources of the Congo basin, the Free State plundered the abundant local labor. The entire population of any nearby town could be drafted to cut a road or lay rails through the jungle. Inhabitants could be taken away as porters for as long as the company needed them, and if these overworked porters died of exhaustion, there were plenty more to be found at the next stop on the trail.

Villages were given regular quotas of rubber, ivory, or timber to harvest from the jungle. Any workman who failed to produce his quota of rubber was liable to be punished. A heavy flogging with a hippopotamus whip was just the start. His wife might be seized and held for ransom in rubber.[3] Most company outposts had any number of dirty, emaciated women chained outside to posts waiting for their husbands to bring their quota of rubber to the post commander. When corporate security squads were sent on punitive raids, they were told not to waste ammunition—one bullet, one kill. They were not supposed to use company ammunition hunting big game for sport. As proof of their frugality, they were expected to bring back one severed human hand for every bullet expended.[4]

One eyewitness described soldiers returning from a raid:

> On the bow of the canoe is a pole, and a bundle of something on it. These are the hands (right hands) of sixteen warriors they have slain. "Warriors?" Don't you see among them the hands of little children and girls? I have seen them. I have seen where the trophy has been cut off, while the poor heart beat strongly enough to shoot the blood from the cut arteries at a distance of fully four feet.[5]

Severed hands became a kind of currency—proof that orders were being obeyed. A basket of smoked hands covered any shortfall in production, and if there was no rubber to be had, the Free State's security forces, the Force Publique, would go out to collect a quota of hands instead. Natives quickly learned that willingly sacrificing a hand might save their life.

And not just hands. After one commander grumbled that his men were shooting only women and children, his soldiers returned from the next raid with a basket of penises.

News of the atrocities didn't reach Europe because travel to, from, and throughout the Free State was tightly regulated. If a bitter and disgusted employee hoped to get away, he "will probably never get out of the country alive, for the routes of communication, victualling stations, etc., are in the hands of the Administration, and escape in a native canoe is out of the question—every native canoe, if its destination be not known and its movements chronicled in advance from post to post, is at once liable to be stopped, for the natives are not allowed to move freely about the controlled water-ways."[6]

The Story Leaks Out

In 1899, a Polish expatriate, writing in English under the name Joseph Conrad, serialized his novella, *Heart of Darkness*, in a British literary magazine. Based on the year Conrad had spent as a riverboat pilot on the Congo River, it told the story of a corporate agent traveling up a dark and mysterious African river to bring a rogue ivory trader back to civilization. The terrifying story of Mr. Kurtz, worshipped as a wrathful god by local natives, his station surrounded by a palisade topped with severed heads, was widely acclaimed when it first appeared. The readers assumed it was fiction.

Old-fashioned humanitarians from the anti-slavery era had been hearing and reporting horror stories from the Congo for years, but no one took them seriously. They were too closely aligned with radicals in the British Parliament, and their appeals to morality and goodwill were either ignored or ridiculed. Then an insider blew the whistle on the Congo Free State.

Of mixed Anglo-French parentage, Edmund Morel had become a clerk for Elder Demster Shipping in 1890, when he was seventeen. Operating out of Liverpool—long the center of the Africa trade—Elder Demster had a shipping contract to the Congo. For ten years Morel worked diligently as a clerk while moonlighting as a business journalist. His reputation as an expert on investment opportunities in Africa grew, and he handily defended the Congo Free State from all those annoying accusations of cruelty that hounded every colonial venture.[7]

Then in 1900, in his job as shipping clerk, Morel finally noticed the scarcity of exports to the Congo. The balance of trade was too good, the profits too easy. All that rubber was coming back to Europe, but nothing was going out to pay for it—only ammunition. The only available conclusion was that the trading companies were stealing it. He also noticed that the official books were doctored to hide this.[8]

He wrote an anonymous exposé that brought him to the attention of the professional do-gooders that everyone had been ignoring. He advised them to forget philanthropy and attack Leopold for creating monopolies, which violated the Berlin agreements that mandated free trade. He advised them to stir up resentment for excluding Britain from the lucrative commerce. Once they got people looking into the Congo, they'd see the atrocities for themselves.[9]

In 1903 Morel founded his own journal, and also started publishing a series of books, beginning with *Red Rubber*. He was not allowed into the Congo, but whistle-blowers soon came to him. Since mail out of the Congo was censored, his informants had to wait until they returned to Europe before they could get word to him.

The pressure paid off when the British foreign office asked its consul in central Africa, Roger Casement, to prepare a report. A thirty-eight-year-old Irishman, Casement had been bouncing around the Congo for nearly ten years, working awhile with Stanley, working for Elder Demster Shipping, moving ivory, joining Baptist missionaries, sometimes just disappearing into the jungle with his dogs for long stretches.[10]

"He could tell you things!" his friend Joseph Conrad said of Casement. "Things I have tried to forget, things I never did know."[11] But no one outside the Congo had been interested in what Casement had seen, until now. As British consul in the Congo, Roger Casement issued a report carefully based on reliable eyewitness accounts that revealed massive atrocities.

In 1904, Morel and Casement founded the Congo Reform Association. It quickly became the trendy cause among the celebrity activists of that era. Anatole France, Arthur Conan Doyle, Booker T. Washington, and Mark Twain lectured and wrote on the subject. Quaker chocolate millionaire William Cadbury contributed money.

Leopold struck back. In the early days of the exposure, a guest at a dinner party took Morel aside. He later described the conversation.

What were the Congo natives to me? I was a young man. I had a family—yes? I was running serious risks. And then, a delicately, very delicately veiled suggestion that my permanent interests would be better served if . . . "A bribe?" Oh! dear, no, nothing so vulgar, so demeaning. But there were always means of arranging these things. Everything could be arranged with honour to all sides. It was a most entertaining interview, and lasted until a very late hour. "So nothing will shake your determination?" "I fear not." We parted with mutual smiles.[12]

All of the enemies of Leopold soon found themselves pressured. Morel was accused of being in the pay of Leopold's business rivals. Several prominent German newspapers suddenly stopped criticizing conditions in the Congo and began to offer a more ambiguous viewpoint. No one could explain this surprising twist until Leopold accidentally failed to reimburse his bagman for the bribes he had paid these papers. A series of confused telegrams back and forth about who was supposed to pay whom for what soon became public.

One crusading journalist was discovered vacationing with his mistress, so Leopold invited the two of them to lunch. Despite his great personal charm, the king failed to discourage this journalist from reporting on the Congo, so Leopold exposed the man's secret with a subtle touch. The king simply sent flowers to the man's wife—and a note explaining how lovely it was to have had the pleasure of her company for lunch. There's no telling what might have happened if Leopold had discovered that Casement was a closeted homosexual, this being only a few years after Oscar Wilde had been imprisoned for the same offense.[13]

The king visited America and connected with leaders of Congress and industry. He donated three thousand artifacts from the Congo to the Smithsonian and offered huge concessions to American businesses operating in the Free State. Although President Theodore Roosevelt favored Morel and the Congo reformists, Congress resisted when he tried to send investigators into the Congo.

Leopold made a big mistake hiring Henry Kowalsky, the flashiest lawyer in San Francisco, to improve his public image and generously lobby Congress. When Leopold began to realize how dangerously eccentric Kowalsky was, he tried to cut him loose. Angry and betrayed, Kowalsky sold Leopold's letters to William Randolph Hearst, who now took up the cause of the Congo for his newspaper chain.[14]

The beloved explorer, Henry Stanley, died in 1904. Although he had long ago retired from public life, his reputation as a hero and visionary had shielded the Congo Free State from criticism. As long as Stanley vouched for Leopold, that was enough for many people. When Stanley died, Leopold was left unprotected.

By 1908, it had become undeniable how badly the people of the Congo had been abused, and the outcry was overwhelming. The international community finally forced Leopold to let go of the Congo. The Belgian parliament reluctantly bought the Congo from their king at an exorbitant price and promised to administer it openly and fairly. Leopold died a year later.

Death Toll

When Casement traveled through the rubber-producing districts preparing his report, it was obvious how badly these villages had suffered in the decade since he had first passed this way. As he noted in his diary:

June 5: The country a desert, no natives left.

July 25: I walked into villages and saw the nearest one—population dreadfully decreased—only 93 people left out of many hundreds.

August 6: Took copious notes from natives. . . . They are cruelly flogged for being late with their baskets [of rubber]. . . .

August 22: Bolongo quite dead. I remember it well in 1887, Nov., full of people then; now 14 adults all told. . . . 6:30 passed deserted side of Bokuta. . . . Mouzede says the people were all taken away by force to Mampoko. Poor unhappy souls.

August 30: 16 men women children tied up from a village Mboye close to the town. Infamous. The men were put in the prison, the children let go at my intervention. Infamous. Infamous, shameful system.[15]

Casement's original report estimated that some 3 million Congolese had died. Morel estimated that the Congo's population began with an original 20 or 30 million, and then collapsed and bottomed out at a mere 8 million. This became the most commonly quoted death toll through much of the twentieth century.[16] In 1977, journalist Peter Forbath, in *The River Congo*, set the death toll at 5 million.[17] The consensus nowadays follows the estimate offered by Adam Hochschild in *Leopold's Ghost*, that the Congo's original population of 20 million was cut in half by the atrocities.[18]

All anyone can say for certain is that the population of the Congo plummeted horribly in the two decades of the Free State. Most of the deaths were caused by diseases that spread as populations were shuffled around, starved, and overworked. Smallpox, originally endemic to the coasts, spread into the interior. Sleeping sickness, endemic in the interior, spread outward. Direct oppression also took its toll. In just one year in just one of the rubber districts, it was recorded that soldiers expended 40,000 rounds of ammunition, for which, presumably, they would have had to produce an equal number of severed hands to prove they weren't wasting bullets.

CUBAN REVOLUTION

Death toll: 360,000[1]
Rank: 93
Type: colonial rebellion
Broad dividing line: Spain vs. Cuban rebels
Time frame: 1895–98
Location: Cuba
Major state participant: Spain
Quantum state participant: Cuba
Winner: United States
Who usually gets the most blame: Spain
Economic factor: sugar

The Second War of Independence

The first attempt by the Cuban people to throw off Spanish rule had been beaten down in the Ten Years War, 1868–78, at a loss of 200,000 lives. The next generation decided to have another go at it. The industrialization of sugar processing was concentrating the milling into fewer hands, causing widespread unemployment and bankruptcy, which in turn radicalized the poor.

In exile in New York, the poet and journalist José Martí declared Cuban independence in 1895 and returned home to lead the fight, but he was ambushed and killed within a few months. His followers pressed onward and scored tremendous success in 1896. Sympathetic peasants spied on the Spanish forces, whom the rebels harassed with raids and ambushes. The rebels tried to make Cuba worthless to Spain by suppressing sugar production. They destroyed isolated plantations and avoided open battle with well-armed regulars. To help contain the rebellion, the Spaniards split the island with the Trocha (the "Trench"), a chain of ditches, moats, barbed wire, and fortified blockhouses across Cuba that prevented free movement between the east and west halves of the island.

In January 1897, the Spanish government turned the rebellion over to General Valeriano Weyler, who was about to invent a brand new horror to let loose on the world—concentration camps. Within a month of arriving in Cuba, Weyler rounded up some 300,000 peasants in the war zone and stashed them in fortified camps, after which any Cubans caught at large would be considered rebels and killed. Weyler hoped to dry up the support for the rebels. Meanwhile, disease, hunger, and neglect swept through the camps, killing thousands.

In August 1897, an anarchist assassinated Canovas del Castillo, the conservative prime minister of Spain, and General Weyler lost his main supporter. He submitted his resignation to the new liberal government of Prime Minister Praxedes Mateo Sagasta.

Spanish-American War

One of the few things both sides agreed on was the need to keep the United States out of the war. Both Spain and the rebels knew that once provoked, the Americans would simply swoop down and take Cuba for their very own. American investors dominated the Cuban economy, and the United States had discussed annexing Cuba ever since American expansion had reached the Gulf of Mexico some eighty years earlier. It was vitally important not to give them an excuse to go through with it. The only major segment of the Cuban population that looked toward the United States for salvation were Cuban landowners. They just wanted the war to end and stability to return.

The American people generally sympathized with the rebels. American newspapers stoked hatred of the Spaniards by eagerly splashing every new atrocity across their front pages. The United States hovered on the edge of intervention and sent the USS *Maine* to Havana harbor to keep an eye on American interests during riots in the city. Then suddenly, on the night of February 15, 1898, an explosion ripped apart the American battleship, obliterating the front end and killing two-thirds of the crew. The explosion probably started as an accidental fire in a coal bunker, but at the time there was no doubt that those accursed Spaniards had attacked the *Maine*. War fever boiled over, and America issued an ultimatum to Spain to leave Cuba. The Spaniards refused.

The war was quick and to the point. In both the Philippines and Cuba, American warships easily destroyed the outdated and outgunned Spanish fleets from a safe distance with hardly a scratch to themselves. A hastily assembled American expeditionary force took Cuba in ten weeks, and the whole war cost the United States a mere 385 combat deaths.

The Americans had made such a big deal about supporting Cuban independence that they couldn't annex their new conquest outright. They had to give Cuba the appearance of sovereignty, but they wrote clauses into the treaties to guarantee American control of the Cuban government for many years to come.[2]

THE WESTERN
WAY OF WAR

T HE FIRST HALF OF THE TWENTIETH CENTURY WOULD SEE THE PEAK OF THE
West's dominance over the rest of the world. Many reasons drove the rise of the
West—capitalism, geography, monotheism, smallpox, and lactase (the enzyme for digest-
ing milk)—but only war concerns us here. At first glance, it may seem that superior
weaponry gave the West its edge, but in many fights, the Western armies were more
poorly armed than the enemy. Native Algerian gunsmiths built rifles that were better
than the arsenals of the French who conquered them, and wealthy Oriental armies often
purchased the newest guns from Western manufacturers like Krupp, Enfield, and Win-
chester long before the poorly funded European armies they faced. Western armies won
their wars because they were consistently superior in attitude, support, and discipline.

The way the West fights its wars is distinctive and coldly efficient, and you can trace
a common tradition that began with the Greek phalanx, progressed through the Roman
legion and the British bayonet line, and continued with the American landings at Normandy and Iwo Jima. First, war is openly declared. Then soldiers go into battle under banners or in uniform, with weapons visible, in massive force. The fighting aims to overwhelm
the enemy and achieve a clear, decisive victory as quickly as possible. The war ends with
a formal peace treaty.[1]

Western soldiers are expected to be disciplined professionals. They are drilled repeatedly so that coordination between all of the men becomes mechanical. Courage is not
defined by reckless single combat, man-to-man, but by standing unflinchingly beside one's
comrades.

It's no coincidence that World War I and the Napoleonic Wars are the only giant megadeaths on my list in which more soldiers died than civilians. The Western way of war is so
horribly destructive of armies that it takes an extra-special effort to even get close to killing
that many civilians. In fact, Western warfare historically has been so deadly that a Western
army often lost more soldiers winning a battle against another Western army than losing

a battle against native forces. For instance, the United States lost more soldiers winning a battle against poorly equipped Southern rebels at Nashville than when it was wiped out by the Sioux at Little Bighorn. In successive South African wars, the Boers (1899–1902) killed more than five times as many British in battle as did the Zulus (1879), despite the latter's legendary ferocity and stunning victory at Isandlwana.

Although European soldiers are probably no more or less merciful than those of any other culture, Western philosophy of war-making tries to avoid killing civilians and focuses on getting rid of combatants first. Killing civilians is considered a distraction, a minor injury against the enemy, like stepping on someone's foot instead of going for the jugular. Showing mercy to prisoners of war is also encouraged for practical if not moral reasons. It gets huge numbers of enemy soldiers out of the way without the trouble of cornering and killing every last one. The goal in a Western war is to neutralize the threat, not to kill for the sake of killing.*

The rules by which civilized countries are supposed to wage war were codified by the Hague Convention in 1899, which tried to cleanly divide everyone in the war zone into the belligerent and the harmless. As long as the former fought in uniform, and the latter— civilians, prisoners, wounded, doctors, and reporters—kept their heads down and did not fight back, then nonbelligerents were considered off-limits.

Articles 25 through 27 of the Hague Convention allow the bombardment of defended cities, which was fine in 1899 when bombardment meant lobbing a few shells randomly into a besieged town in order to pressure the defenders into surrendering. Civilians were usually too far away to be hit, so cannon fire killed far fewer people than hunger did in a city under siege, but then the invention of aircraft made it possible to rain fire and death down on any city that contained a militarily useful object—a radio tower, rail yard, factory, or power plant—anywhere behind enemy lines, far from troop concentrations.

Under the Western way of war, the 1945 atomic bombing of Hiroshima is justified as a legitimate act of war, while the 1983 suicide bombing of the U.S. Marine barracks in Beirut is condemned as terrorism. The key difference is that one was performed openly

---

* "The most important point in this massive body of law is that war is not legally about killing. It is about compelling an enemy to submit. To achieve this it is lawful to incapacitate the enemy's military forces and damage or destroy valid military objectives. But you can never kill or further injure an enemy who offers to surrender or who is already incapacitated by illness, wounds, or previous capture. . . . We could kill or wound them only when they were combatants at large and there was a military necessity to disable them from conducting further military operations against us. As soon as they were incapacitated, they became protected under both longstanding customary principles, enforced through literally thousands of war crimes convictions post-WWII, and the more familiar law of war." (Dave Glazier, professor at Loyola Law School, quoted in Marty Leder-man, "John Yoo Appears to Confirm CIA Waterboarding," March 17, 2007, http://balkin.blogspot .com/2007_03_11_balkin_archive.html)

against a declared enemy who had the opportunity to fight back or surrender, while the other was sneaky. Other philosophies of war-making would condemn Hiroshima as an attack against a mostly civilian target and justify Beirut as a military target.

The Western way of war faded during the late twentieth century because the West has never figured out how to beat guerrillas. From Napoleonic Spain, to Algeria and Vietnam, the most effective way to beat Western armies has been to avoid fighting them on their terms.

The traditional response to guerrilla war has been to drop all of the protections that noncombatants are guaranteed by the laws of war. If you can't tell the difference between rebels and civilians, then *everyone* is the enemy. An army facing guerrillas will shoot hostages, burn houses, arrest family members, destroy property, torture prisoners, and herd entire populations into heavily guarded camps in the hopes that the people realize that supporting the insurgency is too dangerous. It rarely works.

THE DEADLIEST GREAT-POWER WARS FOUGHT AMONG EUROPEANS (MILITARY DEATHS ONLY)

Second World War	1939–45	France, Britain, Russia, America vs. Germany, Italy	14 million in the European Theater
First World War	1914–18	France, Britain, Russia, America, Italy vs. Germany, Austria, Turkey	8.5 million
French Revolutionary and Napoleonic Wars	1792–1802 and 1802–15	France vs. Prussia, Britain, Russia, Austria	3 million
Seven Years War	1755–63	France, Austria vs. Prussia, Britain	ca. 650,000
War of the Spanish Succession	1701–13	France vs. Austria, Britain, Holland	400,000–700,000
War of the Austrian Succession	1740–48	France, Prussia vs. Austria, Britain	450,000
Thirty Years War	1618–48	France, Sweden vs. Austria, Spain	ca. 350,000
Crimean War	1854–56	France, Britain, Turkey vs. Russia	ca. 300,000
Great Northern War	1700–21	Sweden vs. Russia, Poland	ca. 300,000
War of the Grand Alliance	1688–97	France vs. Austria, Britain, Holland	233,000
Franco-Prussian War	1870–71	France vs. Prussia	188,000
Franco-Dutch War	1672–78	France vs. Austria, Britain, Holland	175,000

MEXICAN REVOLUTION

Death toll: 1 million[1]
Rank: 46
Type: failed state
Broad dividing line: poor vs. rich
Time frame: 1910–20
Location: Mexico
Assassinations: Carranza, Madero, Villa, Zapata
Last man standing: Alvaro Obregon
Who usually gets the most blame: everyone

Scratch Díaz

In his three decades as dictator of Mexico since 1876, Porfirio Díaz had turned the country into his personal estate. The army answered only to him. All business depended on his good graces and passed through his hands one way or another.

The only potential rivals to Díaz were big rural landowners who operated as feudal lords. The son of one of the largest estates, Francisco Madero, had been educated abroad and now had all sorts of liberal notions. The 1910 election for president was just for show. It was not supposed to be contested, but Madero entered the race, which forced Díaz to fight back. Díaz arrested five thousand known malcontents—Madero included—before they could ruin the election. Díaz announced his overwhelming reelection, and exiled Madero to the United States, where he called for the people of Mexico to rise up and throw out Díaz.[2]

They didn't need much encouragement. Revolution was in the air, and the election fight had highlighted the vulnerability of the Díaz regime. The hacienda system of agriculture kept Mexican peasants indebted, landless, and hopeless, which sparked a revolt in the southern state of Morelos under the Indian anarchist Emiliano Zapata. A northern uprising coalesced under the flamboyant bandit Pancho Villa, supported by small ranchers, unemployed cowboys, and other flotsam and jetsam of the cattle-herding economy. The northern uprising spread through the state of Chihuahua, until the rebels took the border town of Ciudad Juarez after a hard battle in May. Then, as everyone geared up for a tough fight toward the capital, Díaz surprised them by resigning and going into exile.

Scratch Madero

After Francisco Madero returned and took his place as president, he proved to be more conservative than his supporters had hoped. Mexico was now filled with huge numbers of armed peasants and workers who had hoped to see the wealth of Mexico redistributed to its people, but Madero wanted only to bring elections and free-market capitalism to the country. The revolution splintered. Zapata maintained his own socialist enclave in Morelos beyond the reach of the central government. Meanwhile, annoyed at how slight Madero's reforms were, one of the principal generals of the revolution, Pascual Orozco, rebelled in the north in March 1912.

Victoriano Huerta, a protégé of the former dictator Porfirio Díaz, was in charge of the army sent to put down Orozco. By October, a brutal campaign of attrition had broken Orozco and sent him fleeing to the United States, so Huerta returned to the capital to scheme with Mexican conservatives and the U.S. ambassador (who was probably acting without authority from Washington). After watching President Madero flounder incompetently for about a year, Huerta led a military coup against him in February 1913. Madero surrendered to the junta, so Huerta had no excuse to kill him publicly and legally, but as Madero was being transferred between jails, his car overshot its destination and stopped. Madero's escort dragged him outside and shot him dead, then peppered the car with bullets to make it look like a rebel ambush.[3]

Scratch Huerta

In November 1913, a rebel alliance against Huerta formed in northern Mexico between Governor Venustiano Carranza of Coahuila, Pancho Villa, and Alvaro Obregon, a small-time planter and politician who was starting to display natural military talent and rise through the ranks. For the next half year, rebel armies consolidated and expanded their territory.

The new American president, Woodrow Wilson, refused to recognize the legitimacy of the Huerta government and supported the rebels instead. Tensions escalated between the two governments such that when local authorities in Tampico insulted some American sailors in April 1914, American troops seized the port of Veracruz, which cut off Huerta from the lucrative customs duties that supplied around a quarter of the government's revenue.

As the rebel armies closed in, Huerta resigned in July 1914 and fled abroad. A few years later, he arrived in the United States and hooked up with his previous enemy and fellow exile, Pascual Orozco, to plan a comeback; however, as they were scheming, Texas Rangers moved in, killing Orozco and arresting Huerta for violating American neutrality laws. Huerta died in jail before the Americans figured out what to do with him.[4]

Convention

With Huerta gone, Obregon occupied Mexico City on behalf of the revolution in August 1914. Carranza declared himself president, but now that they had beaten their common enemy, all of the revolutionaries started squabbling. Eventually, factions from all over Mexico gathered in neutral territory at the resort town of Aguascalientes to iron out their differences. The convention filled the office of president with a harmless nonentity and enacted much of Zapata's radical agenda, which aimed to redistribute the large landed estates to the poor.

Everyone but Carranza fell into line with the Aguascalientes Convention, which was unfortunate because the United States really wanted Carranza, a moderate centrist, to be president. Although the American people had a certain fondness for Pancho Villa, the U.S. government decided that Carranza would be more likely to stabilize Mexico—plus he had no plans to confiscate and redistribute foreign-owned property. In November 1914, the American troops pulled out of Veracruz and gave it to Carranza, who used it as his base to resume the civil war.

In December 1914, Zapata arrived in Mexico City from the south, and Villa arrived from the north to hold the city for the Conventionists. The contrast between the two rebel forces became obvious during this joint occupation of Mexico City. Zapata's men were well behaved and disciplined. Then Villa's bandit army arrived and began dragging prominent citizens out of their homes to be shot against any convenient wall. After a few such examples, they extorted money from everyone who wanted to escape a similar fate.

In January 1915, Carranza moved out of Veracruz and won a convincing victory against the Conventionist forces at Puebla, which seems to be where every army on the road from Veracruz to Mexico City fights a decisive battle. Carranza arrived in Mexico City and claimed the presidency in July 1915.

Obregon switched sides, bringing a large new force to fight for Carranza against Villa. Zapata took his army and returned home to hunker down in Morelos, so the new government focused on getting rid of Pancho Villa. In a string of battles, Obregon pushed back Villa, until finally Villa gambled everything at Celaya in central Mexico. Convinced that dash and courage would be enough, Villa sent wave after wave of his troops charging uselessly against Obregon's trenches, which broke Villa's Division of the North beyond all hope of repair. The survivors were driven hundreds of miles across mountains and scrubland back to Villa's home turf, eroding his thousands down to mere hundreds. After the federals had chased Villa all over the northern desert without catching him, Carranza decided to ignore him.

Scratch Villa

Sooner or later, every phase of the war seemed to converge on the northern border. Controlling the towns along the U.S. border let the rebels contact outside supporters, raise hard cash, and smuggle guns. Because so many border towns were split down the middle between Mexico and the United States, Americans often gathered on rooftops to watch the Mexicans fighting in the southern half of town, and the Mexicans had to be especially careful not to accidentally shoot across the border and provoke a massive American response.

In November 1915, Villa attacked Carranza's forces in the heavily fortified border town of Aqua Prieta, but this time the Americans allowed the Mexican government to move reinforcements along railroads in the United States where Villa couldn't stop them. Then when Villa tried to overrun the federal trenches with a night assault, his men were exposed and blinded by enemy searchlights plugged into power stations on the American side.[5] Infuriated by these violations of strict neutrality, Villa stopped a random passenger train at Santa Isabel in Mexico, pulled all of the Americans off, lined them up, and shot them.[6]

In 1916, Villa crossed the border to raid the United States and ended up in a firefight with the U.S. Army garrison in Columbus, New Mexico. After stocking up on American weapons and provisions, he retreated back to Mexico. To put an end to this menace once and for all, a large American expeditionary force invaded Mexico. They chased Villa all over the northern desert without catching him and finally gave up after about a year.

Villa remained at large but became increasingly irrelevant until a 1920 pardon allowed him to peacefully retire. Three years later, his enemies ambushed his car and riddled him with machine-gun fire.

Scratch Zapata

During the Mexican Revolution, soldiers routinely changed sides whenever the mood struck them. Sometimes they switched quickly in order to escape the summary executions that all sides usually inflicted on captured officers. At other times it was more of a carefully considered career move. When Colonel Jesus Guajardo, one of the federal army's star cavalry officers, was thrown in jail for drinking on duty, Zapata sent a note asking if he'd like to come over to his side. The federal commander intercepted the note and threatened Guajardo into conspiring with the government. So far, Zapata had kept to himself, but he was still a rebel who needed to be eradicated. Guajardo pondered the situation and came up with a surefire plan.

When Guajardo returned to duty, he staged a mutiny with his cavalry. To boost his credibility with Zapata, Guajardo attacked his own side, the federal garrison in the town of Jonacatepec, killing several and driving the rest into headlong retreat. To prove he was serious, he even followed his victory with the massacre of fifty prisoners. Impressed by his ruthlessness, Zapata now trusted him and agreed to a meeting. As Zapata rode into town among Guajardo's men, they raised their rifles to fire a salute but shot him dead instead.

Scratch Carranza

In March 1920, Obregon mutinied against Carranza and marched on the capital. Carranza fled toward Veracruz on twenty-one trains with 20,000 soldiers and a fortune in gold coins. The loyal General Guadalupe Sanchez in Veracruz was supposed to protect the government after they arrived, but he switched to the winning side and set out to intercept Carranza. After Sanchez ambushed, derailed, and destroyed the fugitive government's trains, Carranza fled with a small squad on horseback. That night, exhausted and lost, he was discovered and shot dead while he slept in a peasant's hut.

With everyone but Obregon dead, the war finally ended, and Mexico stabilized as a single-party state. Obregon brought all of the major factions into the government and bought them off with a share of power. Anyone who stayed outside and refused to cooperate was shut off from the government, and no independent opposition party could break the Institutional Revolutionary Party's firm grip on power for several generations, until 2000.

FIRST WORLD WAR

Death toll: 15 million (8.5 million soldiers[1] + 6.6 million civilians,[2] rounded off; not including postwar flu deaths or deaths from various postwar civil wars)

Rank: 11

Type: hegemonial war

Broad dividing line: Germany vs. everyone

Time frame: 1914–18

Locations: Europe, Near East, North Atlantic

Major state participants: Austria-Hungary and Germany vs. France, Italy, Russia, and the United Kingdom (each of these mobilizing more than 5 million troops and losing more than a half-million dead)

Minor state participants: almost everybody else; it's probably easier to list the countries that stayed out.

Non-participants: in Europe: Denmark, Netherlands, Norway, Spain, Sweden, and Switzerland. In the Orient: Afghanistan, China, Ethiopia, and Siam. Most of Latin America.

Who usually gets the most blame: No one in particular, just the international system of militarized nation-states in general. Kaiser Wilhelm and the military aristocracy of Germany are often blamed for escalating it from a regional squabble to a world war.

Another damn: war of trenches and idiotic frontal assaults

The unanswerable question everyone asks: Was it really as stupid as it sounds?

ALTHOUGH THE FIRST WORLD WAR RANKS ONLY ELEVENTH ON MY LIST BY overall body count—including civilians—it would easily rank second if I counted only soldiers. The war was a meat grinder that killed more soldiers than any other four wars you can name—except of course for its sequel and namesake, World War II.

The exhaustion of this war sparked the overthrow of four of the world's most powerful dynasties—our old friends the Hapsburgs, the Romanovs, and the Ottomans, plus the Prussian Hohenzollerns. At least three local wars continued to rage even after an armistice brought peace between the major participants. World War I destroyed a cooperative international order based on interrelated monarchs and multinational investment, replacing it with a world of competing ideologies. All of the conflicts, struggles, and tragedies that became the hallmarks of the twentieth century were rooted in the destruction of the First World War.

Why?

Taking a lesson from the gigantic national armies that had conquered Europe on behalf of Napoleon (see "Napoleonic Wars") and France on behalf of Bismarck (see "Franco-Prussian War"), most regimes in Europe adopted universal conscription in the nineteenth century. The draft was popular with politicians on both sides of the aisle. The left wing approved of conscription because modern armies erased class distinctions and promoted by merit, putting arms into the hands of the people instead of the aristocracy. Reserve duty gave the nation an opportunity to provide a small measure of education, health care, and income to the working classes. The right wing liked national service because it promoted obedience, collected the masses to be washed and disciplined, and gave the government a tool to bully foreigners and dissidents. All across the continent, conscription created enormous armies that faced each other across disputed borders.[3]

Supplying, collecting, and deploying these giant national armies required railroads, and doing it right required carefully planned timetables. In case of war, reserve units would have to gather at the village train depot at the exact time to catch the exact train that was assigned to collect them. These trains would converge on the enemy's border at fixed intervals to be unloaded quickly and then sent back for more troops—all without stalling or crashing into trains arriving from the wrong direction at the wrong time. In the event of a real war, speed mattered. Whoever got their armies mobilized and placed on the disputed border first could strike and penetrate many miles into essentially undefended territory for every day the enemy delayed.[4]

For years, contested borderlands had divided nations all over Europe. Germany and France squabbled over Alsace-Lorraine. Austria and Serbia both felt entitled to Bosnia; Italy and Austria quarreled over Tyrol, as did Bulgaria and Greece over Thrace, as did Germany and Denmark over Schleswig-Holstein. The ethnic boundaries of Europe were so convoluted that every nation had little alien enclaves that would prefer to belong to a neighboring country. It all sounds terribly complicated, but it created a very simple foreign policy: your neighbor was your enemy; your neighbor's neighbor was your neighbor's enemy and, therefore, your friend.

On the larger scale, nations also competed for mastery in the international pecking order. By beating France in 1871, Germany had become top dog of Europe, and the Germans had recently embarked on a massive shipbuilding program to challenge British dominance of the seas. Austria and Russia competed to replace the fading power of Turkey as lord of the Balkans. To pursue these rivalries each nation sought allies to back them up in a time of crisis. France, for example, needed someone on the other side of Germany to make the Germans think twice before invading again. The French could hook up with either Russia or Austria—it didn't really matter—but whichever they picked, the other would attach itself to Germany by default. After a generation of shuffling, nudging, and posturing, Europe had divided into two power blocs—the Triple Alliance of Germany, Austria, and Italy versus the Triple Entente of France, Britain, and Russia.*

A small war between any two of these countries could easily escalate to a six-power war within weeks. If one side failed to mobilize before the other attacked, it was screwed. This doesn't mean that foreign policy was a predestined, hair-trigger mousetrap. At any time, human intervention could have interrupted the process and averted war. For example, Italy—or rather, the men who made decisions on behalf of Italy—decided that their country didn't really need to get involved in the initial quarrel, so they sat out the opening declarations of war despite Italy's obligation by treaty to assist Germany and Austria.

The Spark

Gavrilo Princip created the twentieth century on June 28, 1914. Almost every geopolitical trend that unfolded across the globe for the next eight decades traces back to the day this Serbian terrorist assassinated the Hapsburg heir to the Austro-Hungarian throne in the provincial capital of Bosnia-Herzegovina. After he was hustled off by police, his Austrian interrogators learned that the assassination had been planned in Belgrade. They issued an ultimatum to Serbia: let us follow up our leads or else.

Serbia refused, and Austria-Hungary declared war on Serbia. Russia couldn't let Austria destroy a fellow Eastern Orthodox, Slavic nation and gain another piece of the Balkans, so the Russians declared war on Austria. Germany couldn't let a fellow German nation that shared its longest border get crushed by Russia so the Germans took the plunge as well.

Then the Germans demanded an assurance from France that the French wouldn't be jumping on Germany while the Germans were busy invading Russia. They even wanted the French to allow German troops to occupy key French border fortifications so that France would be unable to cause any trouble. France, of course, refused, so Germany declared war on it as well.[5]

The Germans had long realized that the alliance between France and Russia would put them in a vise, so the General Staff had already worked out all of the details and filed the plan away for just such an occasion. Faced with a two-front war, the Germans needed to knock one of these enemies out of the game quickly and decisively.

---

* Confusingly, when the war arrived, the Triple Alliance didn't become the "Allies." It was the Entente that came to be called the "Allies," while the Alliance came to be called the "Central Powers," after their place on the map.

But which one? Russia was too big and deep for a lightning invasion, which made France a more tempting target. Its capital was closer (the distance between the German border and Saint Petersburg was twice the distance between Germany and Paris),[6] and the French armies would be mobilized much sooner, so Germany should act fast. Fortunately it would take the large and sluggish Russian Empire awhile to mobilize, which should give Germany enough time to go after France first. Unfortunately the German border with France was short and the Germans would never find a gap to punch through. They would have to go around the French line. That meant going through neutral Belgium, which would almost certainly enrage the British, but if everything went smoothly, Paris would be taken before the British could mobilize and cross the English Channel.

The Germans quickly moved into Belgium. To ensure speed, they ruthlessly suppressed every hint of resistance they spotted in the Belgian populace. A single potshot from a sniper was often punished with the execution of all of the men in town. They shot 211 Belgian civilians at Andenne, 384 more at Tamines, and 612 at Dinant. At the city of Louvain, they executed 209 civilians and destroyed eleven hundred buildings, including the library with 230,000 books. In all, the passing Germans killed some 5,500 Belgian civilians to quiet the population.[7]

Having penetrated the entire depth of Belgium, the German army wheeled left and flooded across the border into France along a wide front, only to discover that modern weapons favored the defensive even more than prewar planners had suspected. Machine guns mercilessly cut through attackers; hence, one phase of the opening campaigns became remembered in German history as the Kindermord—the "Massacre of the Innocents." The German army had to throw more and more soldiers at each position just to compensate for the soldiers being slaughtered charging across open ground. This meant they had to tighten up and shorten their offensive lines.

The French were discovering the flip side. Because machines guns were so good at piling up German bodies, defensive lines could be stretched thinner and longer. By the time the forward elements of the German advance reached the Marne River, just short of Paris, the French had outflanked them, and a counterattack stopped them.

As the principal armies dug in outside Paris, their flanks swept outward, looking to turn the enemy's flank while keeping the enemy from turning theirs. This race to the sea ended when there was no further flank to turn.

Stuck in the Mud

Most history books make this war sound stupider than it really was, which is not easy. Charging into the face of entrenched machine guns sounds pretty stupid, but eventually many generals learned to not do that.

Perfected in the late 1880s, a machine gun sprays out bullets so quickly that it is physically impossible for soldiers to attack across open ground without being cut down—no matter how many soldiers rush at it, and no matter how quickly they run. Within the first few months, the armies realized that the days of pure, gutsy frontal assaults were over. The only thing left to do was to dig in and figure out Plan B.[8]

The trenches of the First World War were a marvel of engineering, proving once again that war is what people do best. Thicker and more impenetrable than the Great Wall of China, created by more digging than went into a major canal, and fed by more railroad mileage than you would find in most countries, the trench network was a long, thin, underground city of over a million residents, backed up by rail yards, hospitals, theaters, churches, warehouses, pubs, and whorehouses—split between two rival street gangs.

Dug deep enough for soldiers to move freely without crouching, and too narrow to be an easy target for artillery, trenches were never straight, but kinked and notched into bays and traverses so that no single enemy could drop in and machine gun down the entire length of the firing line. Bomb blasts were also confined to small stretches by these zigzags. Given enough time on a static front, soldiers might add an elevated plank floor and makeshift stick or plank walls to keep the earth in place. Heavily reinforced burrows were planted deep underground as living quarters and bomb shelters. Periscopes kept an eye on the enemy.

Steps and platforms were cut into the dirt so soldiers could climb up to ground level and fire into attackers. Piles of sandbags along the rim of the parapet extended cover above ground, but were arranged to leave tiny loopholes through which to aim and fire. A tangle of barbed wire was strung out front in no-man's-land to slow the enemy advance and snag enemy soldiers long enough for the defenders to rake them with machine-gun fire. Uniforms were changed to drab, inconspicuous colors that blended with the dirt, and steel helmets replaced cloth caps to protect soldiers in trenches from shells bursting overhead and shrapnel raining down.[9]

Behind the firing line, communication trenches zigzagged up from the rear to move supplies, casualties, messengers, and reinforcements back and forth. Buried telephone lines kept commanders in touch with the front. A second line of defense was built safely beyond the range of enemy artillery, making the capture of the front trench only one small step on a long ugly road. A third line of defense backed up the second.

Once the trench network was complete, it was almost possible to walk below ground level all the way from Switzerland to the English Channel. Not the whole way, of course. Rivers and cliffs broke the line here and there, and fortifications in soggy terrain had to be built upward, rather than dug downward into the water table. Forts on solid rock were also built upward rather than down, but it would still be possible to walk mile after mile with your head below where your feet belonged.

It was hoped that other technology could be used to counteract the defensive advantage of the machine gun. The Germans tried choking British troops with chlorine gas at

Ypres in 1915. They later tried mustard gas, which raised blisters on any contaminated tissue. This created a horrible new way to die (drowning in the fluids released by blistered lungs) but failed to break the enemy lines. The British deployed primitive tanks in 1916, which crawled on treads over most obstacles. Armored hulls protected the crew, and machine guns and light cannon bristled from the sides to clear the enemy trenches.[10] Unlike most modern tanks, the first models had no turret for fear that the extra weight would tip the tank over.

The wisdom at the time declared that "artillery conquers; infantry occupies."[11] The preferred method of breaking the trenches began with a curtain of covering artillery fire, called a barrage after the French word for barrier. This would rip apart barbed-wire obstacles and drive the defending troops to seek safety deep underground, where they were unable to fire into the attacking lines. With proper timing, the attackers would arrive just as the last scheduled artillery shell came crashing down. As the barrage shifted downfield to cut off reinforcements, the attackers would hop into the enemy trenches and take possession before the defenders came rushing out of their bombproof shelters. It was so simple.

Unfortunately any number of snags could throw a barrage off schedule. If the attackers advanced too quickly or the barrage didn't stop in time, the artillery could easily end up shelling their own troops, but if the barrage was lifted too early or the attackers were delayed, the defenders could redeploy and mow down the attackers caught out in the open. Lacking reliable portable radios, World War I foot soldiers had no way to change plans based on the realities at the front.[12]

As cannons became more powerful, shells landed far beyond the line of sight, so airplanes had to fly overhead to spot targets. These frail biplanes were unable to carry heavy weapons that might directly affect the battle on the ground, but on general principle, enemy pilots began to shoot at each other whenever their paths crossed. This soon developed into flashy, formal, but ultimately useless aerial dogfighting.

The Germans pioneered defense in depth. They realized that there was no point in packing your whole army into the front trenches, within easy reach of enemy artillery. All you needed was a skirmish line to sound the alarm and enough machine gunners to delay an infantry attack long enough for your own artillery to be brought to bear. The bulk of the army could be kept safely beyond artillery range in a second line of trenches and be sent forward only when necessary.

The Big Battles

The years of trench stalemate produced some actual battles in which armies made plans, attacked, retreated, regrouped, and counterattacked. Generally, the hope was to punch through the trenches and reach open country beyond, where maneuver and cleverness could be brought back into the tactical equation. If that failed, the hope was that you would kill more of theirs than they killed of yours, until finally the last man standing won the war. Here's a list of big battles just in case you see a name in a book or on a test.

BATTLE	DURATION	KILLED	FARTHEST ADVANCE	RESULTS
Second Artois	May 9–June 16, 1915	50,000	3 miles	Nothing
Gallipoli	February 19, 1915–January 19, 1916	125,000[13]	2 miles	Zilch
Somme	July 1–November 18, 1916	306,000[14]	8 miles	Zip
Verdun	February 21–December 16, 1916	305,000[15]	6 miles	Bupkes
Passchendaele	July 31–November 16, 1917	150,000[16]	4 miles	Nada

The only absolutely vital detail you need to know about any of these battles is that 19,240 British were killed on July 1, 1916, the first day of the Battle of the Somme, most of them in just a few minutes charging across no-man's-land.[17]

As a purely practical matter, the number of British dead on the first day of the Somme accounted for maybe 1,400 tons of rotting tissue and bone littering the battlefield. Disposal on that scale would have been a logistical nightmare even in peacetime, but in wartime it was too dangerous for burial parties to collect bodies from no-man's-land. Eventually it was discovered that a thriving population of rats in the trench zone would clean the flesh off the skeletons very quickly, so it became the official policy to leave the rats alone and let them do their thing.[18]

Because the war was fought by educated societies, thousands of letters sent home have been collected in books and archives across Europe, documenting the harrowing experience of battle. Open any history of the war and you'll find dozens of small stories describing what it was like to be in the middle of it.

We crawled on our bellies to the edge of the forest, while the shells came whistling and whining above us, tearing tree trunks and branches to shreds. Then the shells came down again on the edge of the forest, flinging up clouds of earth, stones, and roots, and enveloping everything in a disgusting, sickening yellowy-green vapor. . . . I jumped up and ran as fast as I could across meadows and beet fields, jumping over trenches, hedgerows, and barbed-wire entanglements, and then I heard someone shouting ahead of me: "In here! Everyone in here!" There was a long trench in front of me, and in an instant I had jumped into it . . . under me were dead and wounded Englishmen. . . . Now I knew why I had landed so softly when I jumped in. . . . An unending storm of iron came screaming over our trench. At last, at ten o'clock, our artillery opened up in this sector. One—two—three—five—and so it went on. Time and again a shell burst in the English trenches in front of us. The poor devils came swarming out like ants from an antheap, and we hurled ourselves at them. In a flash we had crossed the fields in front of us, and after bloody hand-to-hand fighting in some places, we threw them out of one trench after another. Most of them raised their hands above their heads. Anyone who refused to surrender was mown down. In this way we cleared trench after trench.

. . . Four times we went forward and each time we were forced to retreat. In my company only one other man was left besides myself, and then he also fell. A shot tore off the entire left sleeve of my tunic, but by a miracle I remained unharmed.[19]

And the young letter writer, Adolf Hitler, survived the war.

Elsewhere

More than most wars, the First World War killed people you might encounter in other contexts. Henry Moseley, the physicist who had discovered the secret behind atomic numbers, was shot down at Gallipoli. Umberto Boccioni, the Italian sculptor of the Futurist movement, died in a training accident. The British writer H. H. Munro and the American poet Joyce Kilmer were killed in combat. The French cubist sculptor Raymond Duchamp-Villon died of typhoid fever in camp. George Llewelyn-Davies, one of the children who inspired J. M. Barrie's *Peter Pan*, was shot through the head in Flanders. This was probably the most democratic war in history. The nations of Europe sacrificed an entire generation, regardless of individual talents, accomplishments, or connections.*

It's easiest to think of the First World War as a black hole or bonfire of a war—a static line of trenches cutting across western Europe, hungrily devouring the resources of an entire world. It wasn't just the nations close to the front—Germany, France, England—that shoveled their sons into the flames. Young men were imported from all over the world—America, Australia, India, Senegal—to feed the monster.

Obviously that's not the whole story, and the world war certainly lived up to its name. Ottoman Turkey, which controlled most of the Middle East, jumped in to prevent its old enemy Russia from gaining any advantage in the Balkans. This attracted small, mostly

---

* *Peter Pan was shot through the head in Flanders.* That's the war in a nutshell. Most soldiers killed in wars are either too young to have had much impact other than as someone's son or else they are known to history primarily for their military accomplishments. Civilians killed in war are even more faceless, usually disappearing without a trace, without even a regimental paymaster to take note of their passing. Among the few people known for nonmilitary achievements who died in wars other than the First World War are Archimedes, Lord Byron, and Glenn Miller.

British, colonial armies to nibble at the edges of the Ottoman Empire, trying to punch through and hook up with Russia. The British pushed into Palestine from Egypt, capturing Jerusalem and incidentally fighting a battle at Armageddon (yes, it's a real place). An army from British India invaded Mesopotamia but was cornered and besieged at Kut. After several months of eating horses, rats, and belts, this force surrendered to the Turks.

The most ambitious effort against Turkey began with a British naval attack directly into the Dardanelles strait to capture Constantinople and to open access to Russian ports on the Black Sea (February 1915). The plan failed right from the beginning, mostly because the British had not considered the possibility that this crucial pathway through the heart of enemy territory might be heavily guarded. Maritime minefields and shore batteries sank three warships and damaged all the rest coming and going. The Allies then decided that they needed to land a full army on the Gallipoli Peninsula and take the Turkish shore batteries, but unfortunately they had brought only enough troops to parade through Constantinople after it fell. The fleet popped across the Mediterranean to pick up untested Australian troops training in Egypt, and then waited while veteran British troops were shipped over from the western front. This delay gave the Turks a chance to reinforce and dig in. The Allies were slaughtered while landing on the beaches, then slaughtered some more as they tried to break out of the beach head, and slaughtered again as they crept uphill against the defenders. After banging uselessly against the Turks for several months, the Allies gave up and sailed away.

After about a year of neutrality, Italy shopped around for the best offer and joined the Allies when they offered Italy the Alps and Adriatic coast from Austria-Hungary. Because so much of the short border between Italy and Austria was rugged mountains, this front quickly collapsed into another static line that chewed up armies in one shallow offensive after another.

Most of the Balkans were eventually overrun by the Central Powers. Serbia, Montenegro, Albania, and Romania were battered, looted, and starved as the war rolled over them and occupation forces followed. Greece almost joined the Central Powers, but an Allied-sponsored coup removed Greece's pro-German king.

The Russian front was wider than the western front (approximately one thousand miles north to south versus three hundred miles),[20] spreading the troops more thinly and making it easier to outflank or penetrate the enemy line. For the first several years, the front oscillated back and forth as one side or another gained a brief advantage and scooped up huge hauls of prisoners. These fluctuations on the eastern front chewed up the civilian populations much more than the static western front. Armies on the move stirred up and overran columns of refugees, trampled crops, and looted towns. They slaughtered livestock; they spread disease. A third of all of the civilian deaths in the First World War occurred in Russia, mostly from hunger and typhus.

Armenians

In 1915, a Turkish offensive against the Russians in the Caucasus Mountains failed badly, and they had to blame someone for it. As Turkish generals looked around for a convenient scapegoat, they spotted the Christian Armenians living right beside the war zone. Obviously, Armenian treason had undermined the Turkish war effort. Further proof came when these Christian subjects of the sultan welcomed the Russian counterattack as liberation.

As the Ottoman Empire weakened, the Turks had become increasingly paranoid about nationalism among their subjugated minorities, and any suspicious activity could bring down an overwhelming preemptive massacre. The Turks had slaughtered 200,000 Armenians for no reason in 1894, and then killed another 30,000 in 1905, but now they decided that allowing a disgruntled Christian minority this close to the front lines was too dangerous. They had to get rid of the Armenians completely, once and for all, so they moved in and systematically erased the Armenian presence from the Ottoman Empire. They also rooted out the Assyrian (Syriac Christian) community while they were at it.

Armenians who had been conscripted into the Turkish army were disarmed and reassigned to labor battalions, where they were worked to death. In April 1915, the Armenians were cleared out of Constantinople. In June, 15,000 Armenians in the city of Bitlis were rounded up, taken out to the countryside, and killed; another 17,000 were collected from the city of Trebizond and massacred in July.[21] Then the Turkish soldiers began to empty the Armenian villages in the northeastern provinces and the Assyrian villages to the south. The men were rounded up and shot. The women, children, and elderly were herded southwest to be resettled, although children and pretty girls were sometimes taken into Turkish households to be raised as Muslims or kept as servants or wives. The major population movements became death marches across mountains and deserts, with Armenians shot, bayoneted, clubbed, or simply abandoned in the wilderness when they stumbled.[22] Recently uncovered Turkish records show that 972,000 Armenians died in this ethnic cleansing.[23]

Civilians

To break the military deadlock, the warring powers put the squeeze on civilian populations. Out of pure spite, the Germans deployed a gigantic cannon to lob shells randomly into Paris, seventy-five miles away, killing a total of 250 hapless citizens. They also sent zeppelins to drop bombs on England, killing 550 civilians. Neither of these came close to affecting the outcome of the war; however, the German naval blockade did.

Hoping to starve the British into submission, German U-boats sank any ship they caught approaching the British Isles. For a time, the strategy almost worked because of new technologies developed over the previous decades. Submarines made it possible to creep within striking distance, and torpedoes made it possible to sink ships with a single well-placed shot.

Like the air war of World War II, the sea war of World War I existed in a murky gray zone of moral ambiguity. International law had developed complex rules of engagement between warships and civilian craft. For example, unarmed merchant ships had to be stopped and searched; crews had to be evacuated; but mounting defensive weapons on a civilian ship made it fair game for immediate attack. It all sounded good in theory but was largely unworkable in practice. Submarines were far inferior to surface ships in speed, armaments, range—everything but surprise. If they surfaced, challenged, and delayed their attacks in order to search a suspect ship for contraband, they lost their single advantage. Therefore, they had to sink any suspicious ship immediately, whenever the opportunity arose.

Naturally, the indiscriminant sinking of any ship approaching British waters sent many harmless passengers to the bottom of the ocean. On May 7, 1915, the ocean liner *Lusitania* arriving from New York was sunk near Ireland, killing 1,200 passengers and crew. The outrage among the neutral Americans was strong enough to shut down the U-boat program for a while.

Eventually the British started moving in convoys, making it more difficult for the German submarines to find targets because the ships were in a few clusters rather than strung out all across the Atlantic. Even if a submarine encountered a vulnerable convoy, the U-boat probably couldn't fire more than a couple of shots before the faster surface ships fled out of range. More important, the Germans overestimated the extent to which the British relied on imports. As oceanic trade became riskier, the British brought more land into cultivation to make up the food deficit.

The British blockade of German ports was mostly imposed by minefields and patrolling surface ships. Because it generally obeyed the laws of the sea, there was less international outcry, but in the grand scheme it was far deadlier. Germany's position inside the North Sea offered some useful choke points to the British, who were more effective at creating a food shortage. The official estimate is that 763,000 German civilians died from wartime hunger, especially in the final months of the blockade after Germany lost access to the farms of occupied eastern Europe. After the armistice, despite peace on the ground, the Allies kept the blockade in place in order to keep the pressure on German diplomats negotiating at Versailles.

The warring powers did all they could to undermine the stability of their opponents. When the Russian government began to totter unsteadily in 1917, the Germans shipped the Communist leader Lenin back to Russia from his Swiss exile just so he could make trouble. As Churchill put it, "They transported Lenin in a sealed train like a plague bacillus from Switzerland to Russia." The Germans also supported Irish rebels, spawning the Easter Rebellion of 1916. Among the British subjects caught cooperating with the Germans in the cause of Irish freedom was Roger Casement, hero of the Congo (see "Congo Free State"). He was hanged for treason.[24] Working in the opposite direction, the British colonel Thomas Lawrence—known to folklore and film as the dashing "Lawrence of Arabia"—hooked up with Arab rebels to undermine the Ottoman position in the Near East.

Collapse

After three miserable years of war, French troops being marched into battle would sometimes bleat like sheep when they passed a cluster of generals. They knew they were being sent to slaughter. In May 1917, after another senseless offensive killed or wounded 100,000 Frenchmen, the soldiers refused to go any further. Tens of thousands of French soldiers deserted, and half of the army—fifty-four divisions—refused to take any more orders from above.

The French mutiny was resolved by a combination of executions and reforms. The ringleaders were shot or imprisoned at Devil's Island, while many ordinary soldiers were sent home to rest for a while. The high command eventually restored the army's confidence with smaller offensives that guaranteed limited success, rather than the colossal, bloody gambles they had been accustomed to.

For years, the Italian front had seen nothing but one useless battle after another over the Isonzo River—four in 1915, five in 1916, three in 1917. In the twelfth battle of Isonzo, begun in October 1917, the Austro-German forces finally broke the Italian line, scattering the defenders in panic and scooping up huge numbers of prisoners. Within a month, 280,000 Italians were captured; 350,000 deserted. Even though the front stabilized again sixty miles away before any vital piece of Italy was lost, the Italian army no longer mattered to the course of the war.[25]

The situation in Russia, however, was the worst. The Russians had thrown away about a million lives in one losing battle after another, and brought back many millions more wounded. The government's finances were shot and food wasn't getting to the cities. A series of mutinies and rebellions tossed out the emperor in March 1917, and the nation crumbled into a savage civil war that earns an entire chapter of its own (see "Russian Civil War"). German troops occupied huge sections of the country and began shipping food and supplies back home.

With the fall of Russia, the Germans shifted their combat divisions westward, boosting their manpower enough to resume the offensive with newly developed infiltration tactics.* Slowly, bloodily, but effectively, a renewed German offensive pushed the Allied

---

* Rather than sending out human waves under cover of artillery, these new tactics depended on small squads creeping close enough to seize strategic strongpoints behind the front lines without the warning that a lengthy, preparatory bombardment would give.

lines back toward Paris. As the weeks progressed, however, the Allies learned to counter the new German tactics, and this offensive fizzled out just as fresh troops from the United States launched a counterattack.

For years the United States had been trying to steer clear of the European insanity. Economic ties connected the United States to both sides. General historic kinship nudged the country toward Britain, but substantial German and Irish immigration in the generations before the war nudged it away; however, repeated German attacks against civilian shipping outraged American opinion.

Fortunately for Germany, the European war wasn't the only war in town. The Mexican Revolution was on full boil, and American troops had just come home from hunting Pancho Villa deep inside Mexico. The Germans offered a secret alliance to the Mexican government, hoping to keep the Americans busy in their own hemisphere, but when the offer became public, the Americans angrily declared war on Germany (April 1917).[26]

It took almost a year for the Americans to mobilize their full potential. They didn't fight their first major action until March 1918, but the steady influx of 2 million fresh troops proved to be more than Germany could stand. The Germans slowly fell back in the face of renewed Allied attacks. With the German lines driven relentlessly backward, Berlin panicked. Conquest loomed in their future. Waiting until the army was completely destroyed would leave Germany with no bargaining power. In October, the government began to explore the possibility of a cease-fire.

As the telegrams flew back and forth, Germany's allies abandoned the cause. An Allied offensive out of Greece was unexpectedly rolling over the enemy armies in the Balkans. Bulgaria, Turkey, and Austria-Hungary called it quits in September, October, and November, respectively. The Austrians even tossed out their emperor while they were at it. As Germany delayed, the Allies made it clear that the German emperor would have to abdicate before any cease-fire could take effect. Kaiser Wilhelm quit on November 9, and two days later, the fighting stopped.

More or less. "The War of the Giants has ended," Churchill declared. "The quarrels of the pygmies have begun."[27] Embers smoldered in the aftermath of the war. Russia was being battered by civil war. Finland was having one as well. Hungary and Romania fought a new war over where their common border would fall, as did Russia and Poland. Greece and Turkey started fighting over their common border, while two rival regimes in Turkey squabbled over whether to remain a monarchy or become a republic. In 1919, the warring powers gathered in quiet estates around Paris to negotiate the exact details of the peace treaties, but peace would last only long enough for the rival nations to grow a new generation of soldiers.

Legacy

The major lesson of World War I is that war is bad. This may seem like the obvious lesson of most wars, but the previous generation of Europeans had seen an unprecedented era of peace, and they had forgotten what war was like. Most wars in recent memory had been easy victories or clean defeats. World War I reminded world leaders that wars don't always go as planned. Almost every scheme backfired, and most nations came out of the war broken and shattered.

In upcoming chapters, we will see that many of my top one hundred deadliest multicides easily trace back to the First World War. The Second World War was a rematch. The Russian Civil War was a spin-off. Other multicides are rooted in World War I one step removed. Stalin emerged from the Russian Revolution, and the Korean War grew out of World War II.

Even today, the shockwaves are being felt. Osama bin Laden's first public comment on the attacks of September 11, 2001, announced an end to the eighty years that the Muslim world had suffered at the hands of the West, most likely a reference to the postwar partition of the Ottoman Empire and the British occupation of Palestine, which began (coincidentally?) on September 11, 1922.[28] In fact, some of recent history's most troubled countries came into existence when the empires of the losers were parceled out by the winners:

Burundi, Rwanda: Two bites of German East Africa were given to the Belgians, putting Tutsi and Hutu in the same country even though they hate each other. There have been countless massacres back and forth for the past half century.

Czechoslovakia, Poland: Two new polyglot nations were carved out of the Slavic borderlands of Austria, Germany, and Russia. The hope was that these would form a safe buffer between implacable enemies, but they lasted only long enough to spark a new world war and get quickly conquered.

Darfur: In Muslim solidarity, the sultan of Darfur in the Sahara switched his allegiance from the British to the Ottoman Turks during World War I. The British then occupied and abolished the sultanate, attaching it to Sudan. Today, Darfur is facing genocide by its Sudanese overlords.

Iraq: All of the oil-producing provinces of the Ottoman Empire were bundled together and given to the British, even though this arbitrarily mixed Sunni Arabs, Shia Arabs, and Kurds into one country. These three groups have been fighting an ongoing civil war over who gets control of the country and its oil revenue.

Israel: This slice of the Ottoman Empire was handed to the British and soon set aside for Jewish immigration. The neighboring Arab states have been trying to remove this ethnic blemish for over a half century.

Lebanon: Local Christian enclaves of Syria were carved out of the Ottoman Empire in order to create a little country with a Christian majority. During the 1970s and 1980s, the local Muslims fought a civil war with the Christians over power sharing.

Soviet Union: When war-weary Russia turned to Communism, it created a monstrously powerful nation, ideologically opposed to the West. It took three-quarters of a century and the daily threat of nuclear annihilation to get Russia back on the same page as the rest of Europe.

Yugoslavia: All of the Balkan Slavs of the Austrian Empire were combined with Serbia into one big, polyglot nation. During the 1990s, they all fought a series of civil wars to get out of it.

RUSSIAN CIVIL WAR

Death toll: 9 million[1] (including 1 million military deaths, 5 million famine deaths, and 2 million deaths by epidemic disease; the rest are civilian deaths by terror, crossfire, and so on)
Rank: 16
Type: ideological civil war, failed state
Broad dividing line: Reds vs. Whites
Time frame: 1918–20
Location: Russia
Full state participants: France, Germany, Great Britain, Japan, United States
Quantum state participants: Armenia, Estonia, Finland, Georgia, Latvia, Lithuania, Poland, Russian Provisional Government, Soviet Russia, Ukraine
Quasi-state participants: Czech Legion, Don Cossacks, Free Territory, Green Army, Komuch, Provisional Government of Autonomous Siberia, Volunteer Army
Who generally gets the most blame: The Left blames the Right, and the Right blames the Left.

Fall of the Romanov Dynasty

The First World War was such a monumental mess for everybody involved that many participants came out of it with their governments wrecked beyond repair. The first major country to crack under the strain was Russia. Food shortages and strikes disrupted urban life. Supply shortages and boneheaded strategy shattered the army. As the years of endless slaughter continued, thousands of Russian soldiers simply gave up and went home, carrying their guns in case anyone tried to stop them.

The February Revolution (actually in March 1917) started when protests in the capital at Petrograd turned violent.* Soldiers sent to put down the strike joined it instead. Tsar

---

* Every account of the Russian Revolution is required by law to have a footnote where the author tries to clear up confusing nomenclature. For starters, the February and October Revolutions took place in March and November because the Russians were using the Julian calendar that was ten days out of sync with the Gregorian calendar used by the rest of us. Also, during World War I, the Russians called Saint Petersburg "Petrograd" because "Saint Petersburg" sounded too German. Later they called it "Leningrad" because "Petrograd" sounded too imperialist. Nowadays they call it "St. Petersburg" because "Leningrad" sounded too Communist. "Soviet," by the way, doesn't mean anything special. It's just the Russian word for council.

Nicholas was on a train hurrying to Petrograd to restore his authority when it became obvious that events had passed him by. Still outside the city, he formally abdicated. The crown was offered to relatives, but no one else in the Romanov family wanted to inherit the basket case that Russia had become. For the moment the parliament was in charge, although the local workers' group, the Petrograd Soviet, controlled most of the workers, making it the noisiest faction in the capital. One leader of the Soviet, Aleksandr Kerensky, formerly of the Socialist Revolutionary Party,* became the most influential power broker in Russia. For a few months, the new government tried to muddle through with a minimum of changes to the social and political fabric of Russia. The war against Germany continued without an end in sight.

In 1903 a schism had split the Russian socialists between a moderate minority and a radical majority. The radicals are therefore known to history as Bolsheviks, from the Russian word for majority, while the moderates were known as the Mensheviks, from the word for minority.

The leader of the Bolsheviks was a hard-working, intense, and humorless intellectual who was born Vladimir Ulanov, but was long known by the alias Lenin. Exiled from Russia for revolutionary activity, he had been bouncing around western Europe for many years. At the outbreak of the First World War, socialist parties all over Europe had lined up behind their various national governments in support of the war rather than uniting across national boundaries to force an end to the madness. Lenin cursed them for their spineless patriotism, and he quickly became unwelcome across the continent, until he found a safe haven in neutral Switzerland.

After the February Revolution, political prisoners and exiles of the tsar's regime found themselves welcomed home. The Germans allowed Lenin and his entourage to travel across Germany to the Baltic Sea, where he returned to Petrograd via neutral Sweden. Lenin immediately began to agitate for a radical agenda, and getting Russia out of that senseless war was right at the top of the list. As the Russian battlefront continued to deteriorate, the Bolsheviks under Lenin gained more supporters and a stronger hand. Finally they seized control of the government in the October Revolution (in November 1917). Over the next few months, they consolidated their hold over the government and then

---

* The Socialist Revolutionaries tend to get forgotten in the confusion of the revolution, but they were Russia's major radical party until the rise of the Bolsheviks. They were the driving force behind the unsuccessful revolution in 1905. Their main policy called for confiscating and redistributing land to the peasants. Most Socialist Revolutionaries opposed the Bolsheviks, whom they easily beat in the first parliamentary elections following the Bolshevik takeover, which is why the Socialist Revolutionaries were quickly banned and parliament closed.

moved the capital deep inland to Moscow to avoid the German armies and unruly mobs that endangered the government in Petrograd.

In December, Lenin called a cease-fire with Germany and began to negotiate terms. Under the final Treaty of Brest-Litovsk, signed in March 1918, Soviet Russia accepted defeat and gave up the Baltic, Ukrainian, and Byelorussian provinces to German occupation.

The Civil War

Most history books stop here and fast-forward through the next few years of Russian history. Everything that would affect the rest of the twentieth century had already happened by this time. Russia was Communist and out of the war. In the vast sweep of history, that's all that really mattered. The rest is pointless and depressing, so let's get right to it.

Not everyone was willing to roll over and accept the Bolshevik power play. The other factions of Russian government fled Petrograd after the October Revolution and started gathering armies in the provinces. The capitalist countries of the West obviously weren't happy to welcome the first Communist government in history to the community of nations. Ethnic minorities in the Russian Empire wanted to take advantage of the chaos to stake out new nations. It was going to get messy.

The timeline of the civil war can be reduced to a few simple landmarks, each about a year apart:

> From November 1917 to November 1918, the Germans were dominant and the Bolsheviks subservient.

> From November 1918 to November 1919, the Germans were gone and the Bolsheviks were on the defensive against anti-Bolsheviks.

> From November 1919 to November 1920, the Bolsheviks were on the offensive against anti-Bolsheviks.

> After November 1920, the anti-Bolsheviks were gone and the Bolsheviks consolidated power.

The map of the Russian Civil War is both simple and complex. The simple part is that the Communists (the Reds) held the center, and they were being attacked on all sides by hostile forces, generally known as the Whites. The complex part is that just about every direction was being attacked by a completely different hostile force—not just home-grown Whites, but Germans, Poles, Cossacks, British, French, Americans, and Japanese too.[2] Let's describe them in a clockwise spiral, starting with 4:30:

Cossacks (Southeast)

Almost from the start, the Don Cossacks refused to acknowledge the authority of the Bolsheviks, and they asserted their independence by force of arms in July 1918, which is usually considered the official beginning of the Russian Civil War. The Reds tried to enforce their authority during the early months of 1919 by sweeping through Cossack territory and systematically executing some 12,000 Cossack counterrevolutionaries. A renewed Cossack uprising against this terror aided the offensive of the nearby White Army under General Anton Denikin.[3]

Germans (Southwest)

The German occupation did not reach much of the ethnic heartland of Russia, but the Germans seized almost all of the European lands inhabited by non-Russians—those that would become independent republics in 1991. Germany started to organize these into vassal states, but the worldwide armistice in November 1918 led to a hasty withdrawal. Most of the occupied territories then tried to stake out an independent existence. Finland, Estonia, Latvia, Lithuania, and Poland succeeded. The Ukrainians and the peoples of the Caucasus Mountains didn't.

Whites (Northwest)

After Germany was out of Russia, General Nikolai Yudenich led a small army of Whites out of Estonia toward Petrograd in October 1919. For a few weeks, this was a deadly spearhead pointing at the tottering Bolshevik regime, but they were driven off about the same time that the White offensives elsewhere collapsed.

Allies (North)

A few thousand British and American troops began arriving at the subarctic ports of Archangel and Murmansk in July 1918 to guard stockpiles of Allied war materiel and prevent them from falling into either German or Bolshevik hands. As Russia became more chaotic, this force grew. Because every country in the West wanted to earn a seat at the eventual peace conference and maybe pick up valuable trade concessions and colonies inside the new Russia, all of the other allies—Australians, French, Canadians, Italians, Serbs, and so on—sent small units as well. As the Allies began to stake out defensive perimeters around the ports, they found themselves in open but sporadic combat with the Bolsheviks, although reluctantly. No one seriously expected these Allied forces to affect the outcome of the civil war, so after a couple of years, when they saw which way Russia was heading, the Allies finally abandoned the northern Russian ports.

The battle against the Bolsheviks killed 304 Americans—more than twice the number of Americans killed in combat during the 1991 Gulf War—but Americans don't like to talk about it, probably because they lost, but also because the intervention seemed to justify Russian paranoia during the Cold War. You never see the Russian Civil War on the official list of America's wars.[4]

Whites (East)

Probably the most confusing label on any map of the Russian Civil War is the appearance of a Czech army under a Russian admiral campaigning in the middle of Siberia, thousands of miles from both Prague and navigable oceans.

During the First World War, the Allies had organized 60,000 Slavic prisoners and deserters from the Austro-Hungarian army on the Russian front into the Czech Legion to help liberate Bohemia from the Austrian Empire, but after pulling Russia out of the war, the Bolsheviks didn't need them, and the Czech Legion was sent to connect with Allies elsewhere. The plan was for the Czechs to return to the war the roundabout way, out the Trans-Siberian Railroad to the Pacific, which was the only way the Germans didn't block.[5]

At one Siberian railroad station, the local Soviets tried to disarm the Czechs, but this only made them angry. The Czechs turned around and started fighting their way back into Russia along the railroad. They eventually became the backbone of the White forces in the east.[6]

The admiral on the maps of Siberia was Aleksandr Kolchak, former commander of the Russian Black Sea fleet who resigned in June 1917, before the Bolsheviks came to power. He drifted around Russian émigré communities for a while and finally ended up organizing anti-Bolshevik forces in Manchuria. He then moved inland to Omsk, where he became war minister of the conservative government of Russia.

In November 1918, Admiral Kolchak seized power in Omsk by coup d'etat.[7] For the next year, he was regarded internationally as Russia's official head of state; however, after his offensive against the Bolsheviks collapsed in November 1919, Kolchak abandoned Omsk. By January 1920, the Whites had retreated out the Trans-Siberian Railroad to Irkutsk, where they were trapped when the local government switched hands. The Czech Legion turned Kolchak over to the new authorities in exchange for safe passage home, and the Reds shot him and dumped his body into the nearest river.[8]

Allies (Far East)

Another Allied expeditionary force of French, British, and Americans occupied the Pacific port of Vladivostok and its Siberian hinterland. The first engineering units had arrived during the First World War to help operate the Trans-Siberian Railroad, and more arrived later. Seventy thousand Japanese soldiers also came along to help. Japan was spending the first half of the twentieth century trying to conquer the Pacific coast of Asia. The Japanese had already taken Korea and Taiwan and would soon go after China. In the meantime, they took advantage of the chaos by invading Siberia. The Japanese finally had to abandon this foothold in 1922, a year after the other Allies had pulled out.

Komuch (Southeast)

For a while, the city of Samara hosted a socialist government, called Komuch, which is compressed Russian for the *Com*mittee of something that begins with *uch*.* The Komuch collected enough refugee members of the Petrograd legislature to claim to be the legitimate government of all Russia. Although it took over most of the Volga river basin, it was too moderate to fire up mass support. After the Bolsheviks broke up this Samara government, the Provisional Government of Autonomous Siberia in Omsk swallowed up the retreating remnants.[9]

Turkestan (Far Southeast)

The Central Asian lands of the Russian Empire had their own civil war for a few months in late 1917 and early 1918, as Muslim nationalists and Communists fought over which direction to take to get away from their imperial Russian past. When the Reds emerged victorious from that struggle, White and British forces attacked out of Iran without success. A temporarily independent Communist state was set up in Bukhara until it was absorbed back into Russia.

Blacks (South)

As if the metaphorical anarchy ripping apart Russia wasn't enough, one faction tried to establish a true anarchist society, a stateless state of absolute equality among the peasants of east-central Ukraine. Between autumn 1918 and summer 1919, the anarchist Black Army under Nestor Makhno carved the Free Territory out of a chaotic Ukraine. Forced to pick sides, the Blacks eventually tossed in with the Reds against the Whites, but once the

---

* It doesn't matter what it was the committee of.

Whites were out of the way, the Reds turned against the Blacks. Luckily, anarchist agents intercepted the secret orders from Moscow, and forewarned, Makhno fled to the West.[10]

Greens (South)

Ukrainian peasants fed up with both the Whites (too many former landlords) and the Reds (who were shooting priests and confiscating property) formed into the Green Army under a Cossack named Nikifor Grigoriev. After the Greens spent about a year fighting both the Reds and the Whites, the Bolsheviks drove the Greens into the territory of the Blacks. The anarchists captured Grigoriev, and Makhno's wife personally executed him.

Whites (South)

Generals Lavr Kornilov and Anton Denikin, the two chief commanders of the Russian front, were arrested in August 1917 for scheming to seize control in Petrograd. After the Bolsheviks took over, however, the generals escaped and fled to southern Russia to organize the White Army. When Kornilov was killed in April 1918, Denikin assumed command.

From May to October 1919, Denikin was on the offensive, but a Red victory at Orel sent him reeling back, leaking deserters the whole way. By March 1920, the remnants of his army were cooped up in the Crimea, so in April, Denikin turned his army over to his assistant, Pyotr Wrangel, and retired to France. Finally admitting defeat, Wrangel and the last of the Whites scrambled out of Crimea in November 1920 aboard French and British ships.

Pogroms (South)

Ideology aside, most Russians at this time hated the Jews, so the armies of the Whites, Reds, Greens, and Blacks abused Jews wherever they found them. The persecution was worst in the Ukraine. Rumors circulated widely among the Whites that the Bolshevik Revolution was, at its heart, a Jewish plot, so throughout 1919, Whites, Cossacks, and Ukrainian nationalists destroyed around five hundred Jewish communities in their path. Between 60,000 and 150,000 Jews were shot down, burned alive, drowned, beaten to death, or hacked apart in one massacre after another, the deadliest outbreak of anti-Semitism that occurred between Bar Kokhba (see "Roman-Jewish Wars") and the Holocaust (see "Second World War").[11]

Poles (West)

After the White armies in Ukraine collapsed, the Poles surged forward to take their place. They captured Kiev in May 1920, but a Bolshevik counteroffensive quickly drove them back. For a while, it looked like Poland was going to be taken back into the Russian Empire, but this counteroffensive was finally stopped just short of Warsaw in August 1920. To hear the Poles tell it, this battle at the gates of Warsaw is one of the most important turning points in modern history. Had it not been for the valor of the Polish army, then the Communist hordes would have rolled over the whole continent of Europe. Another way of describing it would be that the Red Army was so worn out that *even the Poles* could beat them.

As it was, the Polish counter-counterattack cleared the Reds entirely out of Polish territory and got halfway back to Kiev before the Russians stopped it again. It was here that the new border between Russia and Poland was drawn, putting a few million Ukrainians and Byelorussians into Poland as difficult minorities.[12]

Reds (Center)

Faced with a crumbling nation, Lenin's answer to all his problems was to shoot someone. In January 1918 he ordered "shooting on the spot one of every ten found guilty of idling." Later he decreed "the arrest and shooting of takers of bribes, swindlers, etc."[13]

For our purposes, the most important single event of this chapter happened in December 1917, shortly after the Bolsheviks came to power, when Lenin set up a commission inside the interior ministry to fight sabotage and counterrevolutionary activities. The full nine words of its official name were too much trouble to say, write, or even remember, so most of the time the name was whittled down to the innocuously vague Extraordinary Commission, and more commonly reduced even further to its two-letter Russian initials: Che Ka.

The name of this organization would change over the years, but the terror it instilled would remain constant. Surviving records show that the Cheka executed almost 13,000 counterrevolutionaries over the course of the civil war—and those are just the killings we can prove. They shot many more spontaneously, without leaving a paper trail. In all, the Cheka killed anywhere from 50,000 to 200,000 citizens during the civil war.[14]

At first, the Bolshevik government shared power with the Left Socialist-Revolutionaries (a cooperative splinter group from the original Socialist Revolutionaries), who had strong support among the peasantry, but the LSRs were infuriated by the surrender terms of the Brest-Litovsk treaty. In July 1918, the LSR assassinated the German ambassador, making it look like a Cheka hit in the hopes of driving a wedge between Lenin and Germany. Lenin smoothed things over with Germany, and then set out to arrest members of the LSR. The LSR took the leader of the Cheka hostage.[15] Lenin called out the troops, who freed the leader and broke the LSR, removing the last outsiders from the Bolshevik government.

While cleaning house in Moscow, the Bolsheviks addressed another pressing problem.

The royal family had been imprisoned in various rural estates since the revolution, and was now stashed in Yekaterinburg in the Ural Mountains. As advancing Whites eroded the encircled territory of the Reds, something had to be done. Tsar Nicholas, his wife, five children, and their loyal servants were taken into a small room, where they were sloppily shot, bayoneted, beaten with rifle butts, and shot until they were clearly dead. Then the bodies were carted out to the woods, disfigured with acid, and buried in an unmarked grave.[16]

In August 1918, an assassin previously affiliated with the Socialist Revolutionaries wounded Lenin, which sparked the Red Terror and intensified mass executions. As orders went out to clamp down on dissent and antisocial behavior, Lenin instructed one local soviet, "You must . . . instantly introduce mass terror, shoot and transport hundreds of prostitutes who get soldiers drunk, ex-officers, etc. Not a minute to be wasted." The same month, he instructed the leaders of another town, "Hang no fewer than a hundred well-known kulaks [prosperous peasants], rich-bags and blood-suckers (and make sure that the hanging takes place in full view of the people)."[17]

In late 1919, Leon Trotsky, another Communist intellectual who had originally been exiled to the West by the tsar, turned the tide of battle in favor of the Bolsheviks. With the revolution, Trotsky returned to Russia, and Lenin assigned to him the job of negotiating peace with Germany. Now he was given command of the army. He cranked the Red Army up to a million men via a massive conscription of peasants in Soviet territory. Political commissars who were assigned to bully or rally the troops as necessary hardened these uncertain new recruits. Behind his frontline troops, Trotsky positioned special political units to shoot down fleeing soldiers just in case someone tried retreating. As he explained in his autobiography:

> An army cannot be built without reprisals. Masses of men cannot be led to death unless the army command has the death-penalty in its arsenal. So long as those malicious tailless apes that are so proud of their technical achievements—the animals that we call men—will build armies and wage wars, the command will always be obliged to place the soldiers between the possible death in the front and the inevitable one in the rear.*[18]

Unlike many other Bolshevik leaders, Trotsky was willing to use former tsarist officers as advisers and occasionally as commanders—as long as he had political commissars to keep an eye on them.

The Russian Revolution led to one of the largest redistributions of wealth ever seen,

---

* To be fair, Trotsky went on to say, "And yet armies are not built on fear. The Czar's army fell to pieces not because of any lack of reprisals. . . . Upon the ashes of the great war, the Bolsheviks created a new army. . . . The strongest cement in the new army was the ideas of the October revolution."

but for the most part the Communists didn't go door to door seizing property. They simply refused to enforce the laws of property when ordinary people stole it from the wealthy. Peasants farmed whatever land they wanted, knowing that the government wouldn't drive them off. Workers took control of factories, and the police would not chase them out. People would take livestock or move into abandoned buildings, and there was nothing the owners could do about it. Anyone who objected would be lynched by the mob, or summarily executed by the Cheka.

In the aftermath of the First World War, Soviet republics also sprang up in Bavaria and Hungary, and for a brief moment Lenin hoped—and the rest of the world feared—that this would lead to a cataclysmic wave of revolution all across the world. Then Bavaria collapsed in May 1919 and Hungary in August 1919, and the epidemic of Marxism was quarantined inside of Russia.

By the time the smoke cleared, five new countries around the shores of the Baltic Sea had managed to establish their independence from a weakened Russia. Elsewhere, Bolshevik forces pushed outward to absorb the other little republics that had been staked out in the tsar's former domain. In December 1922, all of the local Communist governments that had taken root across the old Russian Empire were officially bundled together into the Union of Soviet Socialist Republics, or the USSR.

Legacy

A generation ago the Russian Revolution stood out as the most important geopolitical event of the twentieth century. All of the great dictators had fallen. The two world wars were over and fading in importance. History's more recent wars had been long and fruitless, but the Soviet Union still loomed inescapably over the whole century, threatening, struggling, growing, and evolving. The upheaval that brought the USSR into being was central to modern history.

Nowadays the Russian Revolution is an elective course in ancient history. It's an excellent example of how changes in the present echo backward and change the past. With the Soviet Union gone, all of the ins and outs of the Bolsheviks, Mensheviks, Reds, and Whites have become mere trivia.

On the other hand, a lesser event that was largely ignored in history classes when I went to school has grown more important. The 1922 decision to organize the former Russian Empire into a federation of theoretically autonomous ethnic republics used to look like window dressing. No one seriously believed that those "republics" were anything other than provinces of a Russian empire, so their names and borders didn't matter. We always called citizens of the USSR "Russians," rarely "Soviets." Everyone knew who really ran the show.

Then, in 1991, these "republics" declared their independence, and suddenly it mattered whether Crimea was in the Russian or Ukrainian republic, or whether the home-lands of the Chechens, Byelorussians, and Tatars had the status of full republics, or how many Armenians lived inside the borders of Azerbaijan. Fifteen countries came out of the Soviet Union, and the break-up could have been a lot messier without these convenient dotted lines along which to cut. Even so, five little wars erupted because someone didn't like the way the borders of the former Soviet republics had been drawn.

GRECO-TURKISH WAR

Death toll: 400,000[1]
Rank: 81
Type: failed state
Broad dividing line: Greece vs. Turkey
Time frame: 1919–22
Location: Turkey
Who usually gets the most blame: Greeks by the Turks and Turks by the Greeks—
never put them in the same room

THE OTTOMAN TURKS LOST WORLD WAR I VERY BADLY, SO THE SULTAN IN Constantinople now lived under the thumb of the victorious Allied powers who forced him to sign away his empire. The French and British grabbed most of the Arab provinces for themselves, and the Italians landed an occupation force in southern Anatolia (the peninsula of Asian Turkey). The Greeks wanted to expand onto the coast of Turkey where Greek minorities still lived under Ottoman rule. Unfortunately, the Greeks and Turks were intermingled throughout Anatolia, so it wasn't easy to draw a clean border between them.

Greek Prime Minister Eleftherios Venizelos, chief architect of the palace coup that put Greece on the winning side of World War I, landed an army at Smyrna (Izmir nowadays) in May 1919 to annex this mostly Greek city in Turkey. About the same time, however, the Turkish general Mustafa Kemal (later called Ataturk) renounced the sultan and his treaties, and tried to revive the sagging nationhood of Turkey. He set up an opposition government inland, at Ankara.

In the summer of 1920, the Greek army invaded inward from Smyrna toward Ankara, but their soldiers turned undisciplined and brutal as they crossed Turkish territory. As reports of Greek behavior toward Turkish civilians filtered out of the war zone, Greece lost a lot of the international support it had enjoyed at the beginning of the war.

In October 1920, King Alexander of Greece died of an infected monkey bite,* so the throne passed back to his father, King Constantine, who had been overthrown in 1917 for being pro-German. About the same time, Prime Minister Venizelos lost his reelection.

---

* "It is perhaps no exaggeration to remark that a quarter of a million persons died of this monkey's bite." (Winston Churchill, *The World Crisis*, vol. 5 [London: Butterworth, 1929], p. 409)

King Constantine was still rather annoyed at having been overthrown, so he purged the government of his son's friends. Most Greek officers in the field were immediately fired and replaced by inexperienced officers loyal to the new regime.

"The subsequent display of military incompetence was stunning, and [war correspondent Ernest] Hemingway reported that the new artillery officers 'massacred their own infantry.' "[2]

During 1921, the Turks blunted every Greek offensive and fought them to a standstill. The tide turned at the bloody Battle of the Sakarya River in August 1921.[3] A year later, in August 1922, Mustafa Kemal launched an offensive that broke the Greeks and drove them back to the coast. Bitter in defeat, the Greeks "set fire to village after village as they fled through them, leaving a trail of burning ruins."[4]

The Greeks retreated to the port of Smyrna, trailing thousands of refugees behind them as Greek civilians fled Turkish retaliation. The Greek army scrambled out of Smyrna, but there wasn't enough shipping to evacuate the civilians. Soon the Turkish army arrived and began to loot and shoot up the Armenian quarter. Fires they set here consolidated and spread, driven into the Greek quarter by the wind and the Turks. As the fire swept across the city from September 13 to 15, desperate Greeks and Armenians swarmed over the docks, looking for ships to take them to safety. Throughout the night, Turks arrived to rape refugees or shove them off the pier into the sea, and they stopped only when ships in the harbor shone their searchlights over them and threatened to fire their guns. The Turks rounded up all of the Armenian males of fighting age and herded them inland, which was the last anyone heard of them.

Officially, 2,000 people died in the fire, but as many as 200,000 Greeks and Armenians disappeared and were never accounted for. The Turks swear the fire was accidental and beyond their control, but coincidentally the Turkish quarter was spared the devastation that destroyed the rest of Smyrna.

Once military events determined that the border was going to stay put, the two countries shoved people around to fit it. In order to remove any excuse for another Greek invasion in the future, Turkey roughly rounded up and expelled all of the Greeks. Greece then decided to make room for the incoming Greeks by expelling all of the Turks. Because the Turks ended up in control of all of the disputed territories, three times as many Greeks as Turks were on the wrong side of the border.

Approximately 375,000 Turks and 1.25 million Greeks were uprooted and exiled, making it the largest mass resettlement in history up to that point. The Greeks definitely got the worst of the ethnic cleansing, and they were tossed out with less preparation and less room aboard the ships. Greece had difficulty absorbing all these new people. Athens and Salonika were packed with twice their normal population, and 875,000 Greek refugees—almost three-fourths of the total—required government support to survive. By 1923, mortality among new arrivals was approaching 45 percent, as malaria, dysentery, and typhoid fever swept over the displaced. [5]

CHINESE CIVIL WAR

Death toll: 7 million (5 million killed in the first phase + 2 million killed in the second phase, not including the 10 million killed in the Sino-Japanese War)

Rank: 19

Type: ideological civil war, failed state

Broad dividing line: warlords vs. Communists vs. Nationalists vs. Japanese

Time frame: 1926–37, 1945–49

Location: China

Quantum state participants: Republic of China, Manchukuo

Major state participant: Empire of Japan

Who usually gets the most blame: Chiang Kai-shek and Japan

Summarized in 25 words or less: "All Political Power Comes from the Barrel of a Gun"—Mao Zedong

Another damn: Chinese dynasty collapsing

Exit the Dragon

By the beginning of the twentieth century, the Chinese Empire was dying. The endemic corruption of the imperial government, combined with the colonial feeding frenzy of the Western powers, had undermined the credibility of the ruling Manchu dynasty. The only thing holding it together was the iron will of Dowager Empress Cixi, a former concubine who had been running the empire as regent through a string of child emperors she had handpicked for their compliance. Cixi was almost single-handedly responsible for keeping the empire afloat after the rebellions of the nineteenth century, but when she died in 1908, the new child emperor was adrift in a hostile world.

In October 1911, while the reform movement was still dithering over the details of how to ease into a modern republican government, a bomb being built by a cell of revolutionaries in the city of Wuhan accidentally exploded in their faces. When the police investigated, they discovered extensive files and lists of revolutionaries. Facing arrest for being on those lists, republicans inside the city's army garrison mutinied and took over the local government. Soon garrisons all across China joined the mutiny, dragging their provincial governments along with them. Finally, Emperor Puyi abdicated, although he was probably too young to even know what that meant.

The first president of the republic was supposed to have been Sun Yat-sen, an American-educated Christian and the intellectual and spiritual leader of the republican movement. Since the army had started the revolution, however, it was the commander in Beijing, General Yuan Shikai, who ended up in charge.

For a while, Yuan ruled as an upright president with a national legislature, but over the next few years, he hoarded more and more power until he became a full-fledged dictator. Of course, the more he tried to boss around the provincial governments, the more they ignored him. Tibet and Mongolia openly declared their independence. By the time Yuan died of cancer in 1916, the central government was largely fictitious.

Thus began the age of warlords, but it may not have been quite as bad as that sounds. The warlords rarely fought each other in pitched battles. The average Chinese citizen still paid the same taxes, bribes, and protection money to the same local officials for the same lack of services, just as he had always done. The local officials passed a cut up to the provincial boss, as always. The only difference was that now the provincial boss kept the whole thing instead of sharing some with Beijing.

But a broken China was worse than a stable empire, no matter how corrupt. The breakdown of the central government allowed bandits to become more brazen in plundering the countryside. An official report noted that ten thousand towns and villages in one district of Honan Province had been held to ransom, and one thousand had been looted. "When they capture a person for ransom they first pierce his legs with iron wire and bind them together as fish are hung on a string. When they return to the bandit dens the captives are interrogated and cut with sickles to make them disclose hidden property."[1]

The Northern Expedition

While the rest of the world was busy fighting the First World War, Japan tried to bully China into becoming a protectorate. The Beijing government—such as it was—tried to stand firm, but it eventually caved in. When the agreement became public in 1919, angry students marched and clashed with police (on May 4), among them a student librarian at Beijing University, Mao Zedong, who was just starting to take an interest in politics.

Riding the upsurge of nationalism in the May Fourth Movement, Sun Yat-sen was elected head of a government of sorts. His Guomindang (Nationalist) Party set up a rival regime in the southern city of Guangzhou (Canton). Then, in 1925, Sun Yat-sen died of cancer, and the Guomindang government passed to his army commander and posthumous brother-in-law, Chiang Kai-shek.*

In July 1926, the Guomindang army launched several columns northward from Guangzhou with the goal of reunifying China. After a year of battling through all of the

---

* Sun and Chiang married two sisters of the Soong family, a wealthy and powerful dynasty of American-educated Christian Hakkas.

warlords in its way, Chiang Kai-shek's army arrived at the Yangtze River, where it stopped for the winter to catch its breath.[2]

At the mouth of the Yangtze River was Shanghai, the industrial heart of China. The Nationalist army had to approach Shanghai carefully because the foreign enclaves that covered most of the city were sovereign territory. In March 1927, undisciplined Nationalist troops had robbed and killed several foreigners in Nanjing, so Western warships were getting ready for trouble.[3]

Shanghai accounted for half of the manufacturing in China, which meant the city contained half of China's industrial proletariat as well. The Guomindang at the time headed a broad coalition that included the Communists, who now called a general strike in March in support of the approaching Nationalist army. As the city was brought to a halt, Chiang Kai-shek took control of the Chinese sector of Shanghai and reassured Westerners that life would soon return to normal; however, party factions began to fight over the spoils, and the coalition broke apart when Nationalist troops machine-gunned participants at a Communist protest rally.[4]

This break in the coalition in 1927 is considered the formal beginning of the Chinese Civil War. The Left separated and established a rival regime in Wuhan, and Communists rose up in the streets of Guangzhou. Chiang Kai-shek took a few weeks to crush the rebellions, killing thousands of rioters in the streets of cities all over southern China. Then he extorted protection money from the foreign community of Shanghai, which financed the next step of the Northern Expedition beyond the Yangtze.

By the time the Nationalist columns entered Beijing in June 1928, they had either broken the warlords or made convenient alliances. After Chiang Kai-shek established the new capital of this theoretically reunified country at Nanjing, the name *Beijing*, which means "Northern Capital" in Chinese, had to be changed back to its older name, Beiping, "Northern Peace."

With the Guomindang government safely settled in Nanjing, its reach contracted to just the Yangtze River valley. The warlords who had run for cover when the Nationalist army passed through now poked their heads up cautiously and resumed running their provinces. Rural Communists carved out backwater enclaves and organized their peasants into soviets. Western gunboats patrolled the rivers to protect trade and missionaries.

The Rising Sun

Among the parts of China under foreign control were the railroads. Most had been built by foreign capital, so foreign soldiers patrolled the tracks against bandits. The Japanese owned and guarded the lines that cut across Manchuria in the far northeast.

Over the previous sixty years, the Japanese had been doing everything they could to become just like the Europeans. They built factories and warships and dressed in suits and ties. They elected a parliament and tried to conquer all of the native peoples up and down the Pacific edge of Asia. Just like their European mentors, the Japanese had coaling stations, colonies, and concessions scattered throughout China.

Although liberals in the Japanese parliament opposed the automatic conquest of every neighbor, the militarist factions tended to assassinate anyone who spoke too openly against their empire-building. Pretty soon, the remaining opposition leaders learned to keep their heads down and their mouths shut. In many ways, however, the debate in Tokyo didn't matter. The army was going to do whatever was necessary to enhance the glory of the emperor, with or without permission.

In 1931, a mysterious explosion destroyed a few feet of railroad track in Mukden (now Shenyang), so Japanese soldiers immediately seized all of the critical nerve centers in Manchuria and declared it the independent country of Manchukuo. They installed Puyi, the unemployed Manchu ex-emperor of China, as the ruler of this new nation and left their troops in place to make sure he did what he was told. Although it was widely suspected that the Japanese army had planted the bomb that caused the explosion, to create an excuse to respond in force, the rest of the world sputtered and raged without much effect.[5]

The Long March

In 1927 Mao Zedong abandoned his second wife and their three children and set out into the countryside to stir up a peasant rebellion. His wife, Yang Kaihui, never saw him again. She had begun with a Communist compassion for the poor but had grown disillusioned by the realities of civil war. She dropped out of politics and tried to make sense of her world by writing her memoirs. "Kill, kill, kill! All I hear is this sound in my ears!" she wrote at the end. "Why are human beings so evil? Why so cruel?" In 1930, at the age of twenty-nine, a year after she wrote these words, her husband's guerrilla activities came too close to home, so the local officials took her away and shot her.[6]

Chiang Kai-shek tried to root out the Communist infestation in the countryside by launching several campaigns of annihilation, each larger than the last, but it wasn't until the fifth annihilation campaign that the main force of the Communists, the Jiangxi Soviet, was shaken loose. In October 1934, all able-bodied Communists, 100,000 strong, pulled out and began a long, legendary withdrawal to a safer base of operations, far to the north and west. The Communists abandoned the weak, the sick, and the wounded, among them Mao's feverish younger brother, who was subsequently killed by the Guomindang, and Mao's infant son (by a third wife), who was mislaid and simply disappeared into the mass of nameless, rootless children the war was churning up.[7] The Reds slipped out of the Guomindang encirclement and retreated the hard way, eventually crossing eighteen mountain ranges, twenty-four rivers, and 6,000 miles in a year. Only 8,000 arrived at their new sanctuary in a dusty, mountainous loop of the Yellow River in October 1935.

Does the Long March live up to its name? How do other military movements compare? Sherman's march through Georgia and the Carolinas barely gets its boots muddy at 700 miles.[8] Hannibal's invasion of Italy across the Alps was a stroll in the park at a mere 1,000 miles. The journey of Lewis and Clark's Corps of Discovery squeaks past with 8,000 miles to the Pacific and back, as does Stanley's crossing of Africa, 7,000 miles coast to coast.

The importance of the Long March is not that it saved Communism in China—there were plenty more Reds where those came from. More important is that it thinned the ranks with intensely concentrated natural selection. Setbacks and mistakes in the first few months ignited a power struggle among the leaders of various branches and factions. When the retreat began, Mao Zedong was one of a dozen prominent leaders, but he was not a member of the governing committee; he emerged at the other end as the unquestioned leader of the party. Only the most indestructible, hard-hearted, and dedicated revolutionaries survived the Long March, and these formed the core around which the movement would grow again. With these people in charge, there would be no half measures or compromise.

Sino-Japanese War

In 1937, Mao wrote *On Guerrilla Warfare*, the textbook every insurgent movement studies for lessons on how to defeat overwhelming force: "In guerrilla warfare, select the tactic of seeming to come from the east and attacking from the west; avoid the solid, attack the hollow; attack; withdraw; deliver a lightning blow, seek a lightning decision. When guerrillas engage a stronger enemy, they withdraw when he advances; harass him when he stops; strike him when he is weary; pursue him when he withdraws. In guerrilla strategy, the enemy's rear, flanks, and other vulnerable spots are his vital points, and there he must be harassed, attacked, dispersed, exhausted and annihilated."

The publication was timely. A powerful new enemy had attacked into the heart of China.

In July 1937, along the Yongding River outside Beijing, Guomindang soldiers exchanged shots with Japanese soldiers who were conducting maneuvers across the river. Although no one was killed, one Japanese soldier was missing at roll call the next day. The Japanese accused the Chinese of holding him and cranked their forces up to full alert. By the time the missing soldier returned from his visit to the local brothel and asked what all the fuss was about, Japanese intelligence had spotted Nationalist Chinese troops heading for the border.[9] Scattered fighting broke out, and after a few weeks, the Japanese army surged into China proper across the Marco Polo Bridge.[10]

Communists and Nationalists quickly stopped fighting each other in order to focus on the invaders. Month after month, the Japanese pushed Chiang Kai-shek's forces southward. In August 1937, the battle lines moved to Shanghai after a hard-fought campaign where Chiang lost 250,000 troops to death or wounds, while the Japanese had 40,000 casualties. Even with so many people to draw from, a six-to-one exchange ratio was more than the Nationalist army could take. As the Japanese pressed on, the Guomindang were driven in confusion from their capital in Nanjing.[11]

The general slaughter of civilians and prisoners after the Japanese took Nanjing in December 1937 may be the bloodiest well-documented single massacre in history. Almost all of the Chinese prisoners of war taken in and around the city were slaughtered, some machine-gunned beside the river for easy disposal, others strapped up and bayoneted to train and amuse Japanese recruits.

Over the next two months, the citizens of Nanjing faced death daily as they were assaulted on the street, rounded up, shot down, beaten, stabbed, drowned, and burned without mercy. Women by the tens of thousands were gang-raped, often killed afterward, mutilated, and left on display to terrify the locals. Any Chinese man of military age was assumed to be an escaped prisoner and shot down. Western witnesses reported seeing bodies lying on every block, along with occasional piles of severed heads. It got so bad that even the Nazis begged Japan to show some mercy, and a local German businessman, John Rabe, set up a safe zone where Chinese refugees could hide under international protection.

Private charities in Nanjing recorded the burial of 155,000 victims, and unrecorded tens of thousands more were dumped into the river or mass graves under Japanese supervision. According to the International Military Tribunal for the Far East that tried the Japanese leaders after the war, 260,000 civilians and prisoners were killed in the Rape of Nanjing. Although some Japanese shrug off the evidence and refuse to acknowledge much more than the sporadic shooting of guerrillas, looters, and escaping prisoners, even *they* usually admit to some 40,000 dead, which makes it as bad as any individual massacre of the Jews by the Nazis.

To slow the Japanese onslaught in 1938, the Nationalist Chinese blew apart the dikes on the Yellow River and flooded the land in the path of the Japanese. The river jumped into a new course, flowing into a completely different sea hundreds of miles from its old outlet. The rushing waters destroyed eleven large towns and four to five thousand villages, leaving 2 million people homeless. Although Chinese peasants had advance warning of the flood and were told to get out of the way, evacuation was haphazard and famine followed, with the loss of life estimated to be in the hundreds of thousands.[12]

In October 1938, the Chinese government retreated to Sichuan, the mountain-rimmed basin on the upper Yangtze that was the last refuge of losers in so many previous chapters. Here the Nationalists established a new capital at Chongqing. The rest of the world tried to save the Guomindang as best they could without actually going to war. The British built the Burma Road to move supplies from India to Chongqing. Soviet and American pilots formed the backbone of the Chinese air force (unofficially, of course). The British renegotiated the unequal trade treaties that had crippled previous Chinese governments, agreeing now to give China a fair shake. If Chiang Kai-shek could pull through, China might get a chance to become an equal partner in world affairs. At the moment, that was a big if.

With China knocked down, the Japanese organized their conquests into four puppet states to keep order, and then they began to consider new avenues for growth. Just to the north, big empty Siberia with its timber and gold mines was just begging to be conquered. The Japanese had tried once before, during the Russian Civil War, and now they tried again. The Japanese army poked outward across the Manchurian border to see whether Stalin was all that attached to the place. As it turned out, yes, Stalin wanted to keep it. A full armored counterattack by the Soviets in 1939 convinced the Japanese to look elsewhere for expansion opportunities. The two countries signed a non-aggression pact in order to concentrate on crises elsewhere.

When the Japanese struck out against the Western powers in December 1941, bringing themselves and the Americans into the Second World War, they seized the foreign concessions in Hong Kong and Shanghai. After the Japanese diverted their attention to the Pacific war against the West, the Chinese front settled into a stalemate. Its main contribution to the global war effort was tying down two-fifths of available Japanese manpower and providing airfields for long-range American bombers.[13]

As a full partner in the grand alliance against the Axis (the coalition of fascist countries), Chang Kai-shek received money, guns, and a permanent seat on the Security Council of the United Nations; however, as the war dragged on, the American mission to China grew disgusted at the corruption and incompetence of the Nationalist government. Although this disillusion had little impact on American assistance during World War II, it squashed Western enthusiasm for supporting the Nationalists much longer than necessary.

With the fall of Germany in May 1945, the Soviets declared war on Japan and shifted their units east. Over a million veterans fresh from beating Hitler massed along the border of Manchuria, facing a garrison that had been stripped of its best troops for the Pacific war. On August 9, after a short devastating bombardment, the Red Army rolled over the Japanese and conquered Manchuria within a week, taking 600,000 prisoners. Together with the simultaneous atomic strikes by the Americans against the home islands, this convinced Japanese Emperor Hirohito that further resistance was useless. Over the objections of his military staff, he commanded his nation to surrender to the Americans.

Chinese Civil War, Second Phase

The fall of Japan left Manchuria in the hands of the Soviets, who dawdled long enough to put their own people in charge. Although the Soviets had a history of cooperating with and supporting the Nationalists, the opportunity to put real Communists in control was too tempting to pass up. With Soviet encouragement, Mao's army struck north on a forced march to establish Communist control over the countryside as quickly as possible. The

Soviets allowed all of the captured Japanese armaments to fall into the hands of the Red Chinese, including hundreds of aircraft and tanks and thousands of artillery pieces and machine guns.[14]

Even without the increase in weaponry, the Communists had done quite well in the war with Japan. Appealing to patriotism and freed from harassment by the Nationalists, they had boosted party membership from 100,000 to 1.2 million between 1937 and 1945.

As part of the surrender terms, the Americans instructed the Japanese in China to surrender only to the Nationalist forces. To expedite this, the Americans airlifted Nationalist forces into the big cities, while U.S. marines landed in Tianjin and hurried inland to take Beiping for the Nationalists. The United States advanced loans to Chiang and sold him weaponry at bargain prices, but the old frustration over wartime corruption had seriously eroded Western sympathy. The American Mission that coordinated military aid was closed in 1947, effectively leaving China to its own fate.

The Communists kept the Nationalist cities in Manchuria under loose siege for a couple of years without causing great hardship. Finally the Reds became serious and cut the railroads supplying them.

In May 1948, the Communists isolated the Manchurian city of Changchun in a merciless siege, trapping a half-million citizens, only 170,000 of whom survived to the end.[15] As more sieges sprouted all over north China, the trapped Guomindang soldiers were forced to lower their expectations. Tree bark was a good meal, and a dead rat was "Delicious! It was meat." In Changchun, where 500 civilians starved to death every day, human flesh sold for $1.20 a pound.*[16]

The Manchurian war kicked up 30 million refugees who flooded south, away from the battle lines. A reporter for *Time* magazine traced the long, tortured path many had to make to safety. Those who fled Changchun were gladly sent on their way by the defending Nationalists because it reduced the strain on provisions, but only after the refugees were searched for salt, hard currency, and any metal objects that could be melted down for bullets. Then they passed the outer line of defending pillboxes to enter the no-man's-land called *san-pu-kuan*, "three-don't-care," where neither Communists nor Nationalists nor local governments bothered with enforcing order. Here bandits—usually deserters—preyed on the refugees and removed anything useful or valuable, even untattered clothes. Those who resisted—or were discovered trying to hide a bracelet or earring in a seam of clothing—were beaten or shot. Eventually, the refugees arrived back in Nationalist lines at the besieged city of Mukden, where they were registered and searched, this time for opium, weapons, and Communist currency. Loaded on cattle cars, they were shipped southward. Beyond the end of the rail line was another three-don't-care, where the refugees were stripped of whatever valuables could be shaken loose. Frustrated bandits left many more

---

* For comparison, beef chuck roast sold for $0.43 per pound in Illinois in 1947.

shot and beaten. Finally, the Daling River, last barrier before the end of the war zone, loomed ahead. To prevent Communist infiltration, Guomindang soldiers fired on boats, swimmers, and waders trying to cross the river, only allowing the refugees to walk over the twisted girders of a blasted railroad bridge. Finally, in Shanhaiguan, where the Great Wall meets the sea, the refugees were safely stashed in a proper camp.

"Its restroom is bare earth covered with canvas to keep out the rain. The washroom is one pipe of running water. The cloakroom will mend patched garments, or exchange better rags for those beyond mending. A free milk line serves half a bowlful to each child under five; then, if the child does not vomit from an unaccustomed stomach, he may have another half bowlful."[17]

Finally, in October, the two Nationalist armies defending Changchun planned a break-out. The Seventh Army, American-trained veterans of the Burma front, attacked outward, but the dispirited Yunnanese conscripts of the Guomindang's Sixtieth Army mutinied instead. When the Seventh Army failed to break the Communist lines and retreated back to Changchun, the Sixtieth opened fire on them and then surrendered the city to the Reds. Mukden surrendered the same month.

The loss of the Nationalists' urban garrisons destroyed some of the army's best combat units, which hadn't been all that impressive to begin with. The Communists then closed in on Beiping, took it in January 1949, and advanced south. Between April and November, the Communists rolled over most of China's cities without much resistance. Chiang Kai-shek fled Nanjing to take refuge on the island of Taiwan, while Mao proclaimed the People's Republic of China in the restored capital Beijing.

Within a year, the Red Chinese had mopped up most of the warlords and quasi-independent splinters of the old empire. They overran Tibet in 1950, but grudgingly acknowledged the independence of Communist Mongolia, now a Soviet protectorate. They also ignored Taiwan for the time being.

Death Toll

No one knows how many people died in the Chinese interregnum, but reading through the literature, one gets a clear sense of a million here, a million there, tossed out almost casually. Among the bits and pieces:

> The Guomindang admitted that 1 million civilians were killed or starved in the fifth annihilation campaign.[18]

> The population of northern Szechwan was reduced by 1.1 million from war, in 1932–34.[19]

> The population of Hubei Province is said to have fallen by 4 million, in 1925–30, with very little emigration and no natural famine.[20]

According to one common database of war statistics, the war between the Communists and Nationalists, in 1930–35, killed 200,000 in combat. A Muslim rebellion against the government in 1928 killed another 200,000.[21] An earlier version of this database estimated that the war between the Communists and Nationalists had killed 500,000.[22]

Overall, it would not be unreasonable to suppose that something like 5 million Chinese died as a result of the first civil war.[23]

The civilian death toll of the Sino-Japanese War is any number you care to pick. Open any three books on the subject and you'll probably see three different numbers falling somewhere from 2 to 15 million.[24] The median of the guesses seems to be 8 million civilian deaths.

Because armies keep better track of their own soldiers than they do of collateral damage, we have better numbers for military deaths than we do for civilians. The total body count of the Sino-Japanese War, in 1937–45, comes to about 2.5 million soldiers:

Nationalists: 1,310,224[25]

Communists: 446,736[26]

Japan's Chinese allies: 240,000[27]

Japanese: 388,600 killed in China[28]

During the second phase of the Chinese Civil War, 263,800 Communist troops were killed. The Nationalists lost 1,711,110, both killed and wounded, with maybe a fifth of those (some 370,000) dead.[29] I see occasional estimates of totals somewhere between 1 and 3 million deaths—military plus civilian—during the second phase, but none jump out as being hugely authoritative.[30] Let's split the difference and say 2 million, all told.

JOSEPH STALIN

Death toll: 20 million (including famine and a few million atrocities committed during World War II)
Rank: 6
Type: Communist dictator
Broad dividing line: Stalin on top
Time frame: ruled ca. 1928–53
Location and major state participant: Soviet Union
Who usually gets the most blame: Stalin personally and Communism generally
The unanswerable question everyone asks: How did he end up as one of the good guys in World War II?

Rise to Power

At first glance, Joseph Stalin was one of the least likely people to become leader of Soviet Russia. Born in Georgia in 1879 under the name Ioseb Dzhugashvili, he only learned Russian later, in school. He was sent to a Jesuit seminary but expelled for reasons that remain something of a mystery. Speculation abounds, but none of it has been proved, so let's just say he was expelled for being Stalin.

After the seminary, he did all of the things an aspiring rebel was supposed to—writing and printing revolutionary pamphlets, organizing strikes, robbing banks, getting arrested, escaping from custody, and serving two terms in Siberian exile. In 1913 he took the pseudonym Stalin from the Russian word for steel, which was an improvement over his childhood nickname of Chopura ("Pocky") from the smallpox scars on his face.[1]

He was still in Siberia when World War I broke out. In 1917, the new republican government of Russia pardoned all of the tsar's political prisoners, and Stalin returned to civilization. Unimportant in 1917, Stalin worked his way up during the Russian Civil War. His sycophantic subservience earned him the derisive nickname "Lenin's Mouthpiece." Stalin's main rival for Lenin's favor was the charismatic intellectual and civil war savior Leon Trotsky.

In 1922 Lenin made Stalin head of the Communist Party because no one else wanted to do it. A minor, tedious post at the time, being head of the party gave the detail-oriented Stalin the ability to purge membership rolls of Trotskyites and to advance his own people. After the Communists took control of Russia, party membership expanded. The urban intellectuals who had formed the backbone of the movement during its underground phase were overwhelmed by the influx of members who were not as well schooled in the subtleties of Marxist theory. These new members identified more strongly with the earthy Stalin than with urbane Jews like Trotsky.

Shortly after this, Lenin was weakened by a stroke, which left the government in the hands of rival flunkies arguing about what Lenin really wanted. As Lenin's mouthpiece, Stalin controlled much of Lenin's dialog with the outside world; however, when Lenin finally died in 1924, he had soured on Stalin. His last testament would have disowned Stalin in favor of Trotsky, but Stalin intercepted and suppressed it.

For the next few years, the Soviet Union was run by committee rather than dictatorship. Stalin hooked up with a couple of radicals—Grigory Zinoviev and Lev Kamenev—in a ruling triumvirate that shut out Trotsky. Once Trotsky was completely removed from government in 1925, Stalin dumped his original partners and took up with two moderates—Nikolay Bukharin and Aleksey Rykov. He kept this troika active only long enough to strip power from everyone else. You really don't have to know these four people, but I mention them so that you'll recognize the names later when Stalin has them all killed.

In any case, the upshot of this maneuvering was that Trotsky was exiled in 1929 and Stalin reigned supreme.*

Stalin's personal life was thrown into turmoil in 1932 when he had an argument at a party with his wife, Nadya, who then stepped away for a moment and committed suicide. Some biographers say that this destroyed Stalin's last vestiges of humanity and turned him from a simple bastard into a monster.

Liquidation of the Kulaks

Beginning in 1929, Stalin tried to bring agriculture in line with Communist theory by abolishing private farms and bringing all of the peasants into collective farms. Here they could share modern equipment and be forced to sell crops at government-mandated prices. Peasants who resisted were shot or, more likely, deported to unhealthier climates where they labored on government projects without anyone knowing.

Rather than surrender their animals, peasants slaughtered and ate them. Stalin retaliated against any defiance by withholding food from disobedient communities. He rationed

---

* The exile of Trotsky was the fork in the road of Western Communism. Ever since then, Communists in the West could put a comfortable distance between themselves and the horrible events happening in the Soviet Union by calling themselves Trotskyites. Being a Trotskyite implied an ideological purity that was clearly missing from the Stalinists. Obviously, *anyone* would have been an improvement over Stalin, but it's worth noting that Trotsky's behavior during the Russian Civil War showed that he wasn't exactly Mr. Cuddly either.

food to families according to their loyalty to the state. Prosperous peasants (kulaks) became the universal scapegoats for everything wrong in the Soviet Union. Not only was every food shortage blamed on their profiteering, but everyone knew the kulaks spread venereal disease, had loathsome hygiene, and exploited the labor of others. Whole kulak families were uprooted and shipped off to deadly exile. Battered, deprived, and exhausted by their long journeys, kulak corpses piled up at rural train stations.[2]

The shake-up of Soviet agriculture disrupted the whole infrastructure—not just farms, but transport and mills as well, especially in the breadbasket of Ukraine. The system stressed and finally snapped. In 1932, a massive famine erupted all across the Soviet Union, and anywhere from 7 to 10 million people died within a couple of years. Although millions of peasants were already starving in Ukraine, Soviet commissars still seized their grain to fill rigid quotas. Even seed grain needed for next year's planting was taken away, while 5 million Ukrainian peasants died.[3] Anyone in the stricken areas who didn't show the swollen bellies and stick-thin limbs of starvation was assumed to be hoarding food and punished.[4]

Taking Life Five Years at a Time

When Stalin first came to power, Russia was still operating under Lenin's New Economic Policy, which was trying to rebuild the war-ravaged economy by allowing small-scale capitalism. Not only did this annoy the hard-core Communists on a philosophical level, but also it clearly would not restore Russia to full strength in time for the next world war.

"We are 50 to 100 years behind the advanced countries," Stalin said in 1931. "We must cover this distance in 10 years. Either we do this or they will crush us."

Under a series of Five-Year Plans, huge new industrial cities were built among the coalfields of Ukraine and on the Asian side of the Ural Mountains. Railroads and canals connected them with their vital resources. Dams and reservoirs tamed some of the world's largest rivers to generate power and water crops.

To develop these projects, Stalin expanded Lenin's political prisons into a network of slave labor camps under the "Main Camp Administration"—Glavnoe Upravlenie Lagerei in Russian—"Gulag" for short. The system was packed with outcasts, troublemakers, complainers, dissidents, and other dangerous enemies of the state, along with their family members and anyone else who got on the wrong side of someone powerful. The NKVD, or secret police,* suspected anyone who had come into contact with alien ideas, whether by traveling abroad, being captured in the World War, or even collecting stamps. Merely

---

* The Soviet Secret Police were constantly being reorganized and renamed. Cheka, OGPU, NKVD, and KGB are the four most notorious manifestations, but you don't have to know what all those letters stand for because it's just bland bureaucratic jargon in Russian. The agents were commonly called Chekists, after the first version.

showing up late to work too often might get someone branded a saboteur and hauled away. If more labor was needed, the NKVD arrested random individuals to fill strict quotas. By 1939, the network of forced labor camps, prisons, and colonies held 2.9 million people.[5]

Even though millions died in the Gulag, "labor camp" was not a mere euphemism. "The vast secret police bureaucracy . . . was far likelier to arrest, sentence, and forget about people for a decade or two than to gouge their eyes out. For the most part, the 'meat-grinder,' as Solzhenitsyn called the system of Soviet repression, was not intended to kill or torture people but to reduce them to the status of cattle, who were worth feeding only as long as they could help boost production figures. For the most part, the horror of Soviet camp guards lay not in their sadism but in their indifference to the prisoners' fate."[6]

The Kolyma River valley in the coldest, farthest reaches of the Arctic was a rich geologic basin stuffed with gold, coal, and uranium. Here an enormous complex of concentration camps stretched across the neck of Siberia, extracting the resources of the basin. Prisoners died daily from collapsing mines and subzero temperatures. Food was limited to the minimum necessary to support work, with perhaps a bonus for good behavior. Escape into the arctic wilderness was impossible, although the lucky ones might eventually be paroled from prison and sent to live in the squalid district capital of Magadan. Anywhere from 250,000 to 1,000,000 people died at the Kolyma complex.[7]

Twenty-four hundred miles away—but still above the Arctic Circle where trees don't grow—were the coalfields of the Vorkuta labor camp, where perhaps 100,000 prisoners died. "For 15 years I shoveled coal into the furnaces," said one former inmate. "At night we used to sleep on hard wooden shelves. So many people died of hunger and cold."

"We had no proper winter clothes, our boots were full of holes and to eat we had crushed, salted fish and a small, frozen potato a day. All my teeth fell out because of lack of vitamins," said another. "They made us work 14 hours a day in the mines and many men simply died. At night we slept with our clothes on, on a mattress stuffed with wood chips."[8]

The Great Purge

Sergei Kirov is more notable dead than he was alive. This up-and-coming party boss of Leningrad looked like Stalin's eventual successor until he was shot dead in his office in December 1934. The assassin, your customary troubled loner, was apprehended nearby in a state of confusion and hustled away.

Stalin immediately assumed that the assassin was part of a larger conspiracy and issued orders to neutralize anyone suspected of being an enemy of the people. Every problem from the past decade—shortages, famines, accidents, even natural disasters—was now to be blamed on counterrevolutionary saboteurs undermining Soviet society. Trotsky was assumed to be at the center of this conspiracy, deliberately creating chaos that would open the door for his return.

Stalin's unrestrained paranoia became the guiding principle of the government. The assassin was accused of being in league with Trotsky and shot.[9] Two dozen associates of the assassin were shot. Almost every loser in Stalin's earlier climb to power (Bukharin, Kamenev, Rykov, and Zinoviev, for example, see above) was arrested, beaten into confessing, paraded through show trials, and shot.[10] An assassin was dispatched to hunt down Trotsky in his Mexican exile. Trotsky was tricked into trusting him, and then brained with an ice axe.*

Stalin also turned his attention to the army, culling 43,000 officers and executing 3 out of 5 marshals, 15 out of 16 army commanders, 60 out of 67 corps commanders, and 136 out of 199 division commanders. In all, one-third of all officers were taken away and shot, more than the number of officers who would die in the upcoming world war.[11]

The purge also took out the head of the NKVD, Genrikh Yagoda. A former pharmacist, his specialty was quietly poisoning highly visible Soviets whom Stalin needed to disappear without a big fuss. In 1936 Stalin fired Yagoda for failing to uncover enough evidence to convict Nikolai Bukharin—and how incompetent do you have to be to *not* get a conviction in a totalitarian show trial? Regardless, he and his staff were arrested and shot at the same time as Bukharin's retrial.

Yagoda was replaced by Nikolai Yezhov, who became synonymous with the Great Purge, or as it is sometimes called in Russia, Yezhovshchina. A tiny, genial, and hardworking bureaucrat, Yezhov was probably responsible for 7 million arrests, 1 million executions, and 2 million deaths in prison camps in just a couple of years. He fell out of favor with Stalin and was replaced by Lavrenty Beria in 1938. Beria executed Yezhov in 1940 and outlived Stalin as a likely successor, but he was arrested and shot shortly after Stalin's death.[12]

The Great Purge spread into all segments of society. In forests near all of the big cities, the NKVD established massive secret graveyards that would begin to yield their secrets fifty years later. In the forest of Bykivnia, near Kiev, as many as 200,000 bodies have been discovered in mass graves.[13] Outside Leningrad (Saint Petersburg), 30,000 victims were buried at Rzhevsky and 25,000 at Levashevo. At Butovo, near Moscow, investigators have found the remains of 25,000 victims.[14] Skeletons have even been discovered under the Moscow zoo.[15]

At Kurapaty, near Minsk, scores of burial pits have been found containing around 100,000 bodies. Old-timers report that between 1937 and 1941, gunfire was heard every

---

* The Great Purge followed the assassination of Kirov so closely that some scholars suspect that Stalin planned the shooting as an excuse; however, an official search through newly opened secret Soviet archives in 1989 found no evidence for this. (David Aaronovitch, *Voodoo Histories: The Role of the Conspiracy Theory in Shaping History* [New York: Riverhead Books, 2010], p. 84)

day and every night coming from the woods. Enemies of the people were lined up along freshly dug ditches, gagged, and killed with a pistol shot to the back of the head.[16]

The Great Purge wasn't all ideology and power struggles. Beria used his position as head of the NKVD to have young—often underage—girls who caught his eye kidnapped, then brought to his house for him to rape.

Great Patriotic War

By 1938, it was obvious that Germany was cranking up for a war of conquest. The First World War had shown that it took at least three great powers to keep Germany in line, but France and Britain couldn't bring themselves to deal with Communist Russia, and the United States wasn't interested, so Hitler did whatever he wanted while the French and British railed impotently.

Stalin took the snubbing by the West personally. When France, Britain, Germany, and Italy signed the Munich Agreement whittling down Czechoslovakia without even consulting him, he took it as a sign that the West would sell him out in a heartbeat. He had to beat them to it. The next year, Germany and the Soviet Union signed a secret agreement partitioning eastern Europe between them. A couple of weeks after Hitler invaded Poland, Stalin's soldiers moved in and took half of the country as their payoff. Polish leaders were rounded up and stashed in the Gulag until the next spring, when 15,000 Polish military officers and 7,000 prominent civilians were taken out to local forests and shot.

In 1940, Stalin seized the three Baltic republics, Estonia, Latvia, and Lithuania, and the Soviets immediately arrested anyone who might give them trouble; 85,000 Balts were deported, of which 55,000 were killed or died.[17] Then Stalin tried to bully the Finns into adjusting their shared border to his advantage, and when they refused, he invaded. This war showed just how badly the Soviet army had deteriorated when Stalin purged its officer class. The Finns held against the full might of Russia and even scored a successful counteroffensive. In the end, however, sheer size won the day, and the Soviets hammered the border back a few dozen miles. The whole war had cost at least 127,000 Soviet lives versus only 23,000 Finnish lives.[18] Finland kept its independence but nursed a grudge that made it the only democracy in the world to join Hitler in the subsequent world war.

The German invasion of Russia on June 21, 1941, caught the Soviets entirely off guard. In battle after battle, Russian armies were annihilated. Stalin himself fell numbly into shock for the first week of the war, too shaken to even address the nation by radio until July. Eventually he regained his grip and reemerged to rally his people and issue orders allowing no retreat and no surrender. Every position had to be defended, and he routinely executed any officers suspected of wavering, complaining, or incompetence. In just a few months of war, the Soviets lost millions of soldiers, killed, wounded, or captured. Soviet factories in the path of the Germans were hurriedly dismantled and shipped east, beyond the Ural Mountains, to resume production of war materiel.

Among the prisoners of war taken in the first rush was Stalin's son, Yakov Dzhugashvili. Hitler offered to trade him back for a German general but Stalin refused. Yakov eventually died in German custody, running into an electric fence while attempting either an unsuccessful escape or a successful suicide.

Eventually, the endless space, resources, and manpower of Russia turned the tide and crushed the Germans, but the cost was staggering. Men and women* were thrown against German positions with little training, few weapons, and minimal planning. Some 8.7 million Soviet soldiers died stopping the Nazi invasion.

It's hard to argue that 8.7 million deaths isn't a monumental waste of life, but history is never simple. "One awkward fact makes it difficult to accept that the Soviet system as such squandered its manpower in war: the Tsarist armies between 1914 and 1917 averaged 7,000 casualties a day, compared with 7,950 a day between 1941 and 1945. . . . This strongly suggests that the explanation lies not in Soviet system, but in the traditions of Russian life, military life in particular."[19]

Stalin pushed his people without mercy. Official records show that over the course of the war, 158,000 Soviet soldiers were sentenced to be executed for cowardice, desertion, or similar failings.† Another 442,000 offenders were forced to serve in penal battalions, which were assigned suicidally dangerous tasks such as marching through minefields ahead of the far more valuable tanks. The most likely way out of a penal unit was death or wounds, but a few regained their freedom by acts of special heroism.[20]

Ultimately, it wasn't Stalin's leadership that drove the Soviets to fight with such tenacity. It was the knowledge that living under Hitler would be—you won't believe this—even worse. The Germans massacred hundreds of thousands of Russian Jews, allowed millions of Soviet prisoners of war to die of neglect, shot thousands of hostages in revenge for partisan attacks, and confiscated so much food, livestock, vehicles, and farm equipment that the local peasantry starved. Some 18 million Soviet civilians died in the German invasion.

Even so, picking sides was a tough call. As the Germans penetrated into Soviet territory, they began to uncover evidence of Stalin's cruelty. Outside Smolensk, in the Katyn forest, the Germans unearthed a mass grave containing 4,000 of the Polish officers captured in 1939. At Vinnitsa, they discovered pits with 10,000 dead Ukrainians. It might have

---

* The Red Army was the first modern army to make extensive use of women, mostly (but not entirely) in support units.

† For comparison, the British executed 306 for cowardice in the First World War and none in the Second. (Richard Norton-Taylor, "Executed WW1 soldiers to be given pardons," *Guardian*, August 16, 2006) The Americans executed only one deserter in the world wars.

given them a valuable propaganda point to justify their invasion of Russia, except the Nazis had spread so many lies that no one believed them anymore.

As many as 1 million Soviet nationals, including a quarter-million Cossacks, served with the German army.[21] Most of these Hiwis (from Hilfswillige, "volunteers") were released from POW camps to perform servile duties such as supply and support. Up to 50,000 Hiwis were trapped with the German Sixth Army in the Stalingrad Pocket. Records are scanty, but it's unlikely that many survived. Any who were recaptured by the Russians were sure to be executed.

Perhaps a quarter-million Soviet nationals were recruited as Osttruppen, fully accepted combat soldiers. How did the Nazis square this with their racial bigotry? The easiest way was to not tell Hitler about it.[22]

Enemy soldiers captured by the Red Army were shoveled into the Gulag system as slave labor. Most of them were not released and repatriated until after Stalin died in 1953. Of the approximately 4.1 million prisoners taken by the Soviets, some 580,000 died in captivity.[23]

As soon as the Soviets began to retake their lost territory, Stalin turned his attention to the people who had collaborated with the conquerors. Actually, collaboration wasn't necessary to earn his mistrust. Merely surviving the German occupation tainted millions in the eyes of Stalin. What kind of deals had they made with the fascists? What dangerous ideas had they been contaminated by? Obviously, even Stalin couldn't kill every person polluted by contact with the enemy, but some of the smaller nationalities could be punished as an example to the rest. In 1943, the Chechens and several other Caucasus peoples were shipped en masse to Siberia, and they weren't allowed to return until after Stalin was posthumously denounced in 1957. Approximately 231,000 of these exiles died of their hardships.[24]

Stalin punished any of his people who had fallen into German hands. As part of a wartime deal among the Allies, all Soviet nationals discovered in German custody— exiles, refugees, prisoners of war, and slave laborers—were repatriated, whether they wanted to be or not. The Western Allies forced tens of thousands to go back at gunpoint to almost certain death, especially those who were suspected of collaboration with the Germans, although countless innocent laborers and exiles were caught in the same net and shipped off. Perhaps 1.5 million liberated Soviet POWs—all that remained of the more than 5 million taken by the Germans—were not welcomed back to their homes; instead they were sent to the Gulag to be punished for failure and to be cleansed of dangerous ideas. They were accompanied into the camps by 2.7 million Soviet civilians who had been taken away by the Germans as slave labor. Many would not be freed until well after Stalin was gone.[25]

Iron Curtain

After World War II ended in 1945, Stalin was determined to control all of the buffer states between Russia and Germany to prevent another attack from the West. The war had left the Soviets occupying eastern Europe and the northern zones of China, Korea, and Iran, where they set about installing their own puppets. Stalin purged moderates from the local Communist parties, tolerated no half measures, and installed the most brutal local protégés he could find as the nominal leaders of the conquered countries.

Germany and Austria were partitioned among the winning powers, with Soviet garrisons remaining in the eastern quadrants for the rest of Stalin's life. All across their occupation zone in East Germany, the Soviets rounded up new political prisoners—both former Nazis and likely anti-Stalinists—65,000 of whom would die in Soviet hands over the next five years. The old Nazi concentration camp of Buchenwald remained open a while longer, now as a Soviet concentration camp, where 8,000 to 13,000 new political prisoners died.[26]

Stalin's solution to disputed borders under Soviet control was brutally simple—draw the borders and move the people to fit them. Italians were expelled from Yugoslavia. Poles were expelled from the Soviet Union, and Turks from Bulgaria. Magyars living in Romania were deported into Hungary.

Soviet control of the occupied countries was not always a foregone conclusion. Czechoslovakia had deep democratic traditions that tried to reemerge in peacetime. In the 1946 elections, the Communists polled a minority, but they got control of the police courtesy of the occupying Soviet army. Strikes destabilized the non-Communist coalition government. Riots endangered the moderates. Many Czech politicians fled; most were forced to resign. One of the last holdouts, Foreign Minister Jan Masaryk, mysteriously plummeted to his death from a high window in 1948. Similar struggles accompanied Communist takeovers in Poland, Romania, Bulgaria, and Hungary, but Communist power plays in Greece, Italy, and Finland failed, mostly because these countries were outside the Soviet occupation zone and the Red Army wasn't on hand to tip the balance.

The full reach of Soviet influence was in flux during much of the postwar era as Stalin continued to test the limits of what he could get away with. The Soviets and British had occupied neutral Iran in 1941, deposing the pro-German shah in favor of his more cooperative son, but in 1946, when Stalin tried to organize his occupation zone into a pair of independent Communist states, the United States pressured him into returning these provinces to Iranian control. In 1949, Stalin tried to block the West's access to its occupation zones in Berlin, but a determined Allied airlift of supplies kept West Berlin in operation long enough for Stalin to give up. The stakes in this East-West rivalry were raised when the Soviets tested their first atomic bomb in 1949. The next year, Stalin approved and supplied the North Korean invasion of South Korea. It took a major commitment of Western troops and 3 million lives, but in the end, South Korea survived.

By late 1952, Stalin began to eye his inner circle and wonder how many of them were actively plotting his downfall. He started to maneuver into a position to clean house, but on March 1, 1953, before he could initiate this new purge, he was felled by a stroke. As he lay helpless on the floor, his terrified staff dared not knock on his door for a full day. Even after he was discovered and doctors were summoned, his cronies suspected a trick and hovered nervously by his bedside, afraid to say anything that might later come back to bite them. Luckily, it wasn't a trick, and Stalin died on March 5.[27]

Killing the Messenger

When Stalin conducted the new Soviet census in 1937, he expected to find the population bursting with socialist prosperity. Instead, the count fell 16.7 million short of where it was supposed to be.[28] In a totalitarian state where every inhabitant was carefully watched, no one could use the excuse that the census takers had simply missed 16 million people. Whether they were exiled, dead, or simply failed to be born, losing that many people reflected badly on Stalin's stewardship of the country. To keep the bad news under wraps, the census was suppressed and the heads of the census bureau were shipped off to the Gulag on charges of slandering the nation.

How many people did Stalin kill? There are three schools of thought when it comes to the number of Soviet citizens who died at his hands.

At the high end, we find estimates of 40 to 60 million. Many of these began as wild guesses during the Cold War when Soviet records were sealed and any number was possible. Estimates were pieced together from whatever scraps and stories could be uncovered. Although recent research in newly opened Soviet archives doesn't support the highest numbers, many people have become too fond of these numbers to let them go. The big problem with these estimates is that they come close to asserting that Stalin killed every adult male in the Soviet Union during the 1930s.[29]

At the other end, we find historians who will acknowledge a victim only if an actual body or death warrant turns up. During the Cold War, when Soviet history was closed to investigation, Stalin had many apologists who openly ridiculed the high numbers. In the absence of hard evidence, these apologists could get away with admitting only a few tens of thousands of deaths at his hands. Nowadays, the evidence for a few million deaths is too strong, so the minimalist camp will reluctantly admit to some 786,098 officially recorded executions[30] and 1,590,378 officially recorded camp deaths,[31] but that's as far as they'll go. Many of them consider the famine to be accidental and entirely beyond Stalin's control, so those deaths don't count.[32]

Historian Robert Conquest's estimate of 20 to 30 million dead was originally derided as another wild guess when it was first proposed in 1968,[33] but now it has become the third category—the consensus figure. It's not that Conquest's estimate was originally based on sounder evidence than any other Cold War–era estimates, but newer research has converged on it. Once you start adding all of the documented nastiness and rounding the totals upward to fill in the gaps, you find that 20 million or so seems to cover it nicely without straining credulity.[34]

CRAZED TYRANTS

Who's Worse: Stalin or Hitler?

I'm sure the question you *really* want answered is "Who was the single most evil person in history?" Unfortunately, there's no easy answer to that. You'll sometimes see the bald assertion that Stalin killed more people than Hitler, but rational debate stumbles on two squishy problems. First, obviously, is that all of the numbers are rough guesses. Stalin killed anywhere from 3 to 50 million. Estimates for Hitler's murders range anywhere from 11 to 25 million. Cherry-picking the right two numbers can make Stalin five times the killer Hitler was or Hitler three times as bad as Stalin.

The second problem is that no one can agree on which deaths should count as indictable homicides. Should we tally only the callous murder of the helpless? Or is starting a war a crime against humanity? Does causing a famine count as criminal negligence? Stalin and Hitler killed a comparable number of victims with their camps and secret police, but if we add the number of war dead, then Hitler surges ahead. If we count famine deaths, then Mao's our man; however, if we stick to a narrow definition and count only the cold-blooded murder of helpless victims outside of battle, then an incomplete and debatable list of bloodthirsty tyrants might look something like this:*

- Hitler (Germany, 1933–45): ca. 15,500,000 outright murders of Jews, Slavs, Gypsies, mental patients, hostages, and prisoners of war[1]
- Stalin (Soviet Union, 1928–53): 13,000,000 executions and camp deaths, but not including famine
- Mao Zedong (China, 1949–76): as many as 10,000,000 murders, not including famine
- Leopold II (Belgium,1865–1909): 10,000,000 natives dead in the Congo Free State
- Idi Amin (Uganda, 1972–79): 300,000 murders

---

* This list isn't declaring these to be the seventeen worst tyrants in history. These are merely seventeen that we have some numbers for.

- Francisco Franco (Spain, 1939–75): 175,000 political opponents executed[2]
- Vlad Dracula (Wallachia, 1456–62): 100,000 impaled or otherwise murdered[3]
- Murad IV (Ottoman Empire, 1611–40): 100,000 offenders against the sultan's authority put to death[4]
- Ezzelino da Romano (Padua, 1236–59): 55,000 citizens, rivals, prisoners of war, beggars, and others killed[5]
- Francisco Macias Nguema (Equatorial Guinea, 1969–79): 50,000 murders[6]
- Sekou Toure (Guinea, 1958–84): as many as 50,000[7]
- Hissene Habre (Chad, 1982–90): 40,000 murders[8]
- François Duvalier (Haiti, 1957–71): some 30,000 people murdered[9]
- Ivan the Terrible (Russia, 1533–84): at least 3,700 random individuals killed in anger; another 18,000 to 60,000 people massacred at Novgorod in 1570[10]
- Hastings Banda (Malawi, 1966–94): 18,000[11]
- Tiberius (Roman Empire, 14–37): 10,000 paranoid executions[12]
- Cornelius Sulla (Roman Republic, 82–79 BCE): 4,700 killed in his purges
- Augusto Pinochet (Chile, 1973–90): 3,000 deaths and disappearances

But as they say, a single death is a tragedy; a million deaths is a statistic.* Numbers aside, the West generally considers Hitler worse than Stalin because Hitler's evil disgusts more successfully on a gut level. The human face of the Holocaust is Anne Frank, an innocent little girl hunted down and exterminated because of dangerous racist pseudoscience. The human face of the Gulag is Aleksandr Solzhenitsyn, a cranky old guy in a wild beard who survived.

Hitler also makes a much better morality tale: By appealing to people's fears and hatreds, he whipped the mob into a frenzy and became leader of a free democracy, which he quickly twisted to his own desires. While trying to conquer the world, he committed unparalleled atrocities. Finally, Hitler overreached and was taken down by the wrath of a unified world in a final apocalyptic fury. It's a more satisfying narrative that people enjoy telling over and over again.

Stalin, however, is more typical of tyrants throughout history. He lurked in the shadows, manipulated his way to the head of a preexisting autocracy, consolidated power brutally, and expanded his empire by cleverly playing both sides of the fence. At a fine old age, he died in bed, undefeated, unpunished, mourned by a loving nation.

---

* This saying is commonly attributed to Stalin, but (a) no one can point to a time and place, (b) the quote wasn't attached to Stalin until he was long gone, and (c) Erich Maria Remarque said it earlier.

ITALO-ETHIOPIAN WAR

Death toll: 750,000[1]
Rank: 59
Type: colonial conquest
Broad dividing line and major state participants: Italy vs. Ethiopia
Time frame: 1935–41
Location: Ethiopia (sometimes called Abyssinia at the time)
Who usually gets the most blame: Mussolini

AS THE LEADING EDGE OF WESTERN CIVILIZATION SHIFTED TO NORTHERN Europe, Italy fell one step behind on most modern trends. Italy didn't even become a unified country until the mid-nineteenth century, and it almost missed getting a slice when the Europeans carved up Africa. As a latecomer, Italy was given only a few coastal stretches of desert that no one else wanted. When the Italians tried to enlarge their holdings by conquering Ethiopia in 1896, their army was badly beaten, making Ethiopia the only native state in Africa to survive European ambition—also making the Italians the laughingstock of imperialists everywhere.

When Benito Mussolini took power in Italy, he tried again, bringing modern firepower to the situation. In 1935 two columns thrust into Ethiopia from the Italian colonies on either side, Somaliland in the south and Eritrea in the east. Italian aircraft bombed and strafed Ethiopian troops, villages, and cities. Ethiopian soldiers were mowed down by machine guns and choked with mustard gas. Although it wasn't quite the naked spearmen charging tanks that Western imagination made it out to be, the Ethiopian army was completely outclassed and overwhelmed, losing almost twenty of their own soldiers for every Italian they killed. Even so, the Ethiopians went on the offensive in December and January.

Because blatant imperialism had grown unfashionable since the nineteenth century, the world condemned Mussolini. Ethiopian Emperor Haile Selassie delivered an impassioned plea in Geneva to the League of Nations to rescue his ancient land, so the league imposed economic sanctions against Italy. One of the first times this tactic was ever used, it became an early example of sanctions failing miserably. Many statesmen and strategists suggested that extending the embargo to oil or closing the Suez Canal to Italian shipping would have more teeth, but these were dismissed as impractical or needlessly provocative. No one really wanted to make the Italians angry.

In May 1936, the Italians took the capital at Addis Ababa, and Ethiopia stayed quiet for a short time while the remnants of the native armies organized an underground resistance. In February 1937, guerrillas tried to kill Italian General Rodolfo Graziani, and the Italians launched a three-day retaliatory massacre in Addis Ababa in which thousands of citizens were killed. In May, the Italians destroyed the Shawan monastery of Dabra Libanos and executed several hundred resident monks. The guerrilla war continued, as did the Italian retaliation.

Finally, World War II brought Ethiopia into the larger fight between Italy and Britain, which made the Italian colonies fair game for an Allied offensive. The British flew Haile Selassie into the Sudan to wait while British troops cleared the Italians out of East Africa in 1941. When all was safe, he was allowed to reclaim his throne.[2]

SPANISH CIVIL WAR

Death toll: 365,000[1]
Rank: 91
Type: ideological civil war
Broad dividing line: Nationalists (right wing) vs. Republicans (left wing)
Time frame: 1936–39
Location and major state participant: Spain
Minor state participants: Germany, Italy
Major non-state participants: Falange, International Brigades
Who usually gets the most blame: Nationalists

S PAIN WAS GOING THROUGH ONE OF ITS OCCASIONAL DEMOCRATIC INTER-ludes in the early 1930s when the Popular Front, a coalition of leftists ranging from moderate liberals to hard-core Communists, set aside their bickering long enough to win the elections as a solid bloc. The king quit rather than sign the leftist legislation the coalition started churning out, which suited the Popular Front just fine since it didn't like kings anyway (hence its name in the upcoming war: Republican).

Spain had been a mess for over a hundred years, now made worse by the Great Depression. Political murder had become a common part of Spanish life, with journalists, policemen, labor leaders, and priests from all parties being gunned down, blown up, or beaten to death with frightening regularity. After the right wing lost an especially notable victim, it also lost patience with the government's inability to keep order. In league with the Falange, the Spanish fascist party, the army garrison in Spanish Morocco mutinied, followed quickly by army units all over Spain. The commander in North Africa, Francisco Franco, was declared leader of a renegade Nationalist government that held scattered towns all over Spain.

With the army against it, the government's only armed support came from militias raised by the trade unions; however, this tipped the Republican side from center-left to a full-fledged Communist revolution. Workers seized factories, and peasants seized land. Churches were burned and priests murdered in retaliation for the Catholic Church's support of the military uprising.

The fascist rebels, meanwhile, rounded up and murdered anyone deemed Marxist or anti-Spain. Members of the Popular Front, union officials, Freemasons, and left-wing journalists were summarily executed. The poet Frederico García Lorca was hauled off and shot for being a homosexual. In August 1936, the Nationalists shot almost 2,000 Republican prisoners in the bullring of Badajoz following the capture of Extremadura in central Spain.

In the first chaotic days of the uprising, towns under the control of one faction or another were scattered haphazardly all over the country. Soon the Nationalists consolidated control over the center of the country and drove straight for Madrid. By this time, however, the Republican government had scrounged up enough troops to hold off the Nationalist attacks.

The fascists now shifted their efforts elsewhere and began to erase the Republican enclaves that clung to the edges of Spain. First, the south around Seville was mopped up, then the Basque region on the north coast. Fellow fascist regimes sent troops—40,000 to 50,000 Italians, at least 10,000 Germans—to help the Nationalists and to test their latest equipment and tactics. As part of this joint effort, German dive-bombers helped to punish and terrorize the enemy population with a devastating air raid against the Basque city of Guernica. One of the first urban air raids in history, this slaughter of over a thousand helpless civilians at Guernica horrified the world, but it might have been forgotten by now, overshadowed by later, larger atrocities, except that its savagery was frozen forever by Pablo Picasso in probably the most famous and powerful work of art in the twentieth century.

The Nationalists then invaded the Ebro River valley, homing in on the coastal city of Barcelona. Finally, all that was left in Republican hands was Madrid and the roads back to the coast. Soon Madrid fell, and the roads to the coast were choked with the last refugees of the Republican government, trying to escape the country.

The Big Picture

As one democracy after another collapsed during the Great Depression, the survivors had difficulty deciding whether the extreme right or extreme left was the greater danger to civilization. Liberals often denied and whitewashed the sins of the Communists, while conservatives did the same for the fascists; however, trying to overthrow the democratically elected government of Spain crossed the line, and fascism lost most of its sympathizers in the democracies. The beleaguered leftists of Spain became the world's tragic heroes.

The Spanish Civil War was the last romantic conflict of Western Civilization where idealistic young men volunteered to fight for a great and noble cause. The International Brigades, sponsored by Communist parties worldwide, recruited 40,000 volunteers from all over the world to defend the Popular Front. Ten thousand Frenchmen fought for the cause, as did 5,000 Germans and 5,000 Poles. Twenty-seven hundred Americans volunteered for the Abraham Lincoln Brigade, and one-third of them died in the war.

The literary world especially rallied to the cause. French author André Malraux organized the Republican air force and negotiated the purchase of aircraft from France; Ernest Hemingway was imbedded as a journalist with the International Brigades; the writer Arthur Koestler spied on the Nationalists while posing as a journalist sympathetic to their side; the poet W. H. Auden drove an ambulance. Both the English poet Stephen Spender and the American novelist John Dos Passos tried to arrange the release of political prisoners. George Orwell fought in the Republican infantry, until he ran afoul of the Soviet military advisers provided by Stalin and had to flee.[2]

SECOND WORLD WAR

Death toll: 66 million (20 million soldiers and 46 million civilians, including the Sino-Japanese War, the Bengal famine, the Holocaust, and Stalin's wartime atrocities, but not including any of the postwar purges and conflicts)[1]
Rank: 1
Type: world conquest
Broad dividing line: Axis (mostly fascist) vs. Allies (mostly democratic or Communist)
Time frame: 1939–45
Locations: Europe, East Asia, North Africa, Pacific Ocean, North Atlantic Ocean
Major state participants: China, France, Germany, Italy, Japan, Soviet Union, United Kingdom, United States (each of these mobilizing more than 4 million troops)
Minor state participants: everybody else—with only about a dozen holdouts
Non-participants: In Europe: Ireland, Portugal, Spain, Sweden, and Switzerland. In the Orient: Afghanistan, Nepal, Tibet, Turkey, and Yemen
Who usually gets the most blame: the Axis, especially Hitler
Economic factors: oil, steel, grain, the Great Depression

Why Did They Have to Have a *Second* World War?

The Germans had come so close to winning the First World War that they couldn't believe they didn't. By 1917, they had knocked Russia, Serbia, and Romania out of the war, driven the French army to mutiny, and pushed within a few miles of Paris. Even after being driven back by the final Allied offensive, they had retreated in good order, without panic or surrender. Because they had never really grasped that they had been fairly and completely beaten, many German soldiers blamed their defeat on "a stab in the back" by unpatriotic elements back home in Germany—Jews, war profiteers, or Communists depending on the complainer's leanings. After all, it had been the civilian government that sued for peace, not the army. Once a new generation of young men had grown up, ready to fill out the ranks, and new technologies were developed that could overcome entrenched machine gunners, the German militarists were eager for a rematch. All they needed was an excuse and a cooperative government.*

---

* You probably think I'm kidding when I say that the main reason for World War II was "because they could," but John Keegan comes pretty close to suggesting the because-they-could explanation in *The Second World War* (pp. 10–11).

Among the disgruntled veterans bumming around Germany and complaining about backstabbing Jews was Adolf Hitler. Born in Austria in 1889, he passed a brief, unpleasant period of his youth in the polyglot and cosmopolitan capital at Vienna. He failed to gain admittance to art school because of his inability to draw people, which is probably a metaphor—if not an actual symptom—for a deep psychological flaw. He made a meager living painting postcards and then moved to Munich, Germany, to escape poverty, multiculturalism, and the Austrian draft; however, when the First World War broke out, he enlisted in a local German regiment. After the western front bogged down into trench warfare, he took a job as a message runner, a dangerous job that got him gassed and earned him some medals.[2]

In postwar Munich, Hitler fell in with the fascist movement and helped form the National Socialist (Nazi) Party. Fascism had originated in Italy under Mussolini (who ruled in 1922–43). Unlike traditional conservatism, which defended the ruling class of nobility, church, and capitalists against the radical populism of the poor, fascism was itself radical populism in favor of conservative ideals. Like the Communists, fascists rallied the masses with promises of full employment, consumer gratification, and national unity of purpose, but were very un-Communist in their support of the homeland, God, and the natural order of things. Like other radical parties of postwar Germany such as the Communists, the Nazis fielded paramilitary squads (the Brown Shirts) to terrorize the opposition.

At first, the Nazis did poorly in Germany's elections, but the collapse of the world economy in 1929 turned unemployed voters toward parties with radical agendas. This was happening almost everywhere, and the number of democracies in the world plummeted as quickly as the economic indicators. For a time it was uncertain whether Germany would swing hard left or hard right, but when it came down to choosing sides, the right wing offered the most (a return to the good old days) and made fewer demands (no confiscation of property). When the Nazis emerged as the leading party in the hopelessly divided German parliament in 1933, Adolf Hitler became chancellor. Within a matter of months, he broke, scattered, or arrested the opposition. He established the first concentration camp at Dachau, outside of Munich, to hold the growing numbers of political prisoners. Fascism soon infiltrated every aspect of society, from the big urban rallies to the Hitler Youth that replaced the multinational Boy Scouts.

Springtime for Hitler

After coming to power in Germany, Hitler set about establishing the Third Reich, German hegemony over Europe, while assuring France and Britain that this wasn't his intention at all. He began to build the German army (the Wehrmacht) back up to pre-1914 levels, incorporating all of the latest technology. The Rome-Berlin Axis of 1936 established a partnership with Italy. In 1938, Austria was annexed, and Czechoslovakia was neutralized and partitioned. Still shaken by the senseless bloodbath of the Great War, the Western powers hesitated about starting another conflict with Germany, but they finally stiffened their spines and declared that they would allow no further encroachment on neighboring countries. This worried Hitler not in the least. A secret treaty with the Soviet Union secured a free hand in the east, and in September 1939 he launched a massive invasion of Poland, sweeping over it in a matter of weeks. The French and British declared war.

Rather than attacking France immediately, Hitler secured his northern flank by overrunning Denmark and Norway. Then he shifted his attention west and swept over the Netherlands, Belgium, and France in six weeks, while the broken remnants of the British army fled from the port of Dunkirk. Meanwhile, Stalin was taking advantage of these distractions to expand into the smaller neighbors of the Soviet Union, taking parts of Poland, Romania, and Finland and completely devouring Lithuania, Latvia, and Estonia. Mussolini also tried to expand Italy's holdings, this time from Albania (annexed in 1937) into Greece, and from Libya into Egypt, but he met unexpected resistance. Unable to leave an unstable situation on his southern flank, Hitler had to hurry to his ally's assistance, rolling over an uncooperative Yugoslavia while he was at it.

The score at this point: in a little over three years, Germany had taken ten countries, Russia had annexed three and shared one of Germany's, while Italy had annexed one. The whole of continental Europe had fallen into German hands, either directly or through allies like Hungary and submissive neutrals like Spain. The only countries still in the game against any of these aggressors were the scattered dominions of the British Commonwealth.

And the Chinese. As you'll recall (see "Chinese Civil War"), the Japanese had begun reducing China to subjugation in 1937, and within a couple of years, they had consolidated their hold over the coast and the north. Chiang Kai-shek maintained his refugee Nationalist government deep inland, at Chongqing, supplied by the British and Americans.*

---

* And that's probably all we need to say about China for now. It's not easy to fit the Sino-Japanese War neatly into my top one hundred multicides. The killing of some 10 million Chinese clearly earns it a place on my list, but where? Alone as Number 14? Included as part of World War II? As part of the Chinese Civil War? I consider it best to count all of the dead in China between the Japanese invasion in 1937 and their surrender in 1945 as part of the worldwide conflict; however, the flow of events is easier to explain as an episode of the Chinese interregnum, as I did in the chapter on the Chinese Civil War.

War in Russia

Now came the showdown that Hitler had been planning all along, the crusade against the Jewish-Slavic-Bolshevik stronghold of Soviet Russia. Although this invasion is considered a mistake in hindsight, the First World War had seen France survive while Russia collapsed, so if Germany could beat France now, then Russia should be a breeze. The opening attack in May 1941 proved this, as the Soviets were caught completely off guard. The Germans bombed Soviet airplanes on the ground and easily pierced and bypassed Russia's frontline units. Eventually, the rout had reached the point where entire Russian armies were being scooped up and destroyed. In July and August, German forces killed 486,000 Soviets and captured 310,000 in the Smolensk pocket east of Belarus. In September, they encircled and took Kiev in Ukraine after killing 616,000 Soviet soldiers and capturing 600,000.[3]

As the Wehrmacht pushed into Russia, it was followed by the Einsatzgruppen, special units designated to kill Jews, Communists, and other undesirables. The fall of every big Soviet city was soon followed by a massacre. In late September 1941, the Jews of Kiev were taken to the ravine of Babi Yar, stripped, shot, and buried. The officer in charge reported a meticulous tally of 33,771 killed in three days.[4] Another couple of days in October were enough for Germany's Romanian allies to kill 39,000 Jews in and around Odessa.[5] In November and December, 28,000 Jews were taken by the Germans into the Rumbula Forest outside Riga, stripped, lined up, and gunned down.[6] By April 1942, the Einsatzgruppen had reported killing a total of 518,388 victims.[7]

Within the first few months, around 3.9 million Soviet prisoners of war were shipped back to German territory, some destined for hard labor, some for turncoat battalions, some for medical experiments, but most for starvation, frostbite, and typhus in squalid prison camps. All but 1.1 million were dead by spring.[8] Of the 5.7 million Soviets taken prisoner during the whole course of the war, 3.3 million died of neglect and brutality in a deliberate policy by the Nazis to eradicate the subhuman Slavs. Prisoners taken from racially kindred nations like Britain and America were treated far better, and most survived.[9]

Because of the vastness of Soviet territory,* beating the Russians was taking longer than the few weeks it took to crush the French, but by December the German armies had almost enveloped Moscow. However, the months of continuous combat had exhausted

---

* The Soviet Union encompassed some 8,400,000 square miles, roughly one-sixth of the habitable land surface of the earth, and it contained 164 million people in 1937. Germany on the eve of war covered some 226,000 square miles with a population about half of Russia's: 80 million. The population of France was only half of *that*: 42 million. (Edgar M. Howell, *The Soviet Partisan Movement* [Bennington, VT: Merriam Press, 1997], p. 13; Nick Smart, *British Strategy and Politics during the Phony War* [Westport, CT: Praeger, 2003], p. 43)

the fighting efficiency of the German army, so it failed to close the circle before winter set in. The momentum shifted back to the Red Army, which had drawn on the vast reserves of Soviet manpower and industry to build itself back into a competent fighting machine. The Soviets pushed the Germans back from the suburbs of Moscow, but they made no serious dent in the fighting abilities of the German army. With spring, the Germans resumed the offensive, now in a southern drive toward the oilfields of the Caucasus Mountains.

In order to cover their advance into the Caucasus, the Germans needed to anchor their line at Stalingrad (Volgograd now). Not only would this cut off the southern Soviet armies from reinforcement, but also it would give the Germans a foothold across the Volga River, the last natural barrier before the Ural Mountains at the eastern edge of Europe. In August 1942, after sweeping through the outskirts of the city, they were stopped a few blocks short of the river by a desperate Soviet defense. The Russians turned the rubble of buildings into fortresses, and the fighting bogged down into intimate, intense firefights, street by street, block by block, and—in large factories and department stores—room by room. By day snipers patiently waited in the ruins to put a bullet into any visible German body part. By night Siberians and Tatars crept into isolated German positions with knives and bayonets to butcher an enemy unprepared for hand-to-hand fighting.[10]

The urban warfare chewed up German manpower with such ferocity that the rural flanks of its Stalingrad line were being held by Italian and Romanian allies. The Russians launched two big pincers against these flanks in November, smashing them and snipping off a pocket that trapped 275,000 men in the devastated city. This pocket was starved, pounded, and assaulted over the next few months until finally, in February 1943, the pitiful remnants surrendered. Most were so haggard, frostbitten, and malnourished that they didn't even survive the trip to Soviet POW camps. Fewer still survived those.

Possibly 750,000 soldiers and 140,000 civilians died in the Battle of Stalingrad, making it the second bloodiest battle in human history.[11] Yes, it was only the second. History's bloodiest battle was the simultaneous battle for Leningrad, in which some 1.5 million soldiers and civilians died.[12] In September 1941, after the Germans had advanced to the suburbs of Leningrad (Saint Petersburg), their Finnish allies closed the circle from behind and isolated the Soviet Union's second largest city. Because the Soviet high command had made little effort to evacuate the city's population, 3 million civilians were trapped with no hope of resupply. Unlike the battle for Stalingrad, there are no tactical oscillations to describe. The Soviet army dug in and held on for nine hundred days under the worst punishment Germany could offer.

Cut off from outside help, the people of Leningrad stretched their rations as thin as possible, then ate their animals, then ate grass, belts, and bark, then each other, and finally just starved by the hundreds of thousands.[13] During winter, the Soviets built a road across the frozen surface of Lake Lagoda to get supplies into the city and civilians out, but it was vulnerable to air attack, and it sank into the lake at the first thaw. Although the official death toll of civilians is set at 632,000, more than 1 million Leningraders may have disappeared in the siege.[14] Eventually the Red Army cleared a narrow overland corridor into the city, but this roadway was still within easy range of German artillery and aircraft. It wasn't until January 1944, when battles elsewhere dragged the front lines back toward Germany, that the siege safely ended.

Pacific War

After France fell, the Japanese tried to grab their orphaned colonies in Indochina. The Americans were trying to stay out of the war, but they kept tightening the economic screws to make Japan back off. First the Americans banned Japanese shipping from the U.S.-controlled Panama Canal, followed by an oil and steel embargo that threatened to cripple the Japanese war machine. The only solution that planners in Tokyo could see would be to seize the oil-rich East Indies from Britain and the Netherlands, both of which were busy fighting the Nazis. In 1941 Japan moved troops, planes, and warships into French Indochina.

By now it was obvious to everyone that Japan was setting up to strike across the archipelagoes of Southeast Asia, but when the attack finally came in December, the Japanese surprised everyone and reached halfway across the Pacific to smack the American fleet with a crippling air attack on Pearl Harbor in Hawaii. In the several months that followed, Japanese fleets and troops scooped up the resource-rich archipelagoes that had originally been held by the Dutch, British, and Americans.

To everyone's surprise, the 85,000-man British garrison at Singapore (mostly Indians under British officers) surrendered almost immediately—the largest defeat in British history. This was followed by several lawless months in which the Japanese massacred perhaps 25,000 Chinese inhabitants of the city.

Also a surprise, the 125,000-man American garrison in the Philippines (mostly native Filipinos) held on longer than anyone expected. In the end, they too surrendered—the largest defeat in American history. Enraged by the delay, the Japanese herded their prisoners up the Bataan Peninsula without water or rest, shooting, bayoneting, or clubbing to death any who stumbled. Thousands died.

Having established control of the East Indies, the Japanese needed to install a defensive perimeter among the small islands of the central Pacific and drive the last of the Americans out; however, by intercepting and decoding Japanese radio transmissions, the Americans learned the target and timetable of the Japanese offensive against Midway Island. Scout planes and radar confirmed the approach of the Japanese fleet, which the Americans attacked on the open ocean with wave after wave of carrier-based aircraft. The Japanese retaliated in kind, but luck and planning were with the Americans, who sank four enemy aircraft carriers—more than the Japanese could easily replace. The momentum of the Pacific war shifted to the Americans.

Europe in the Balance

After the British had been chased entirely off the continent of Europe, they had no easy way to maintain an active role in the war and were forced onto the defensive. Hitler tried to break British stubbornness with a submarine blockade and relentless air raids. In the Battle of Britain, German aircraft attacked England directly for several months in 1940, eventually killing 60,000 civilians without gaining uncontested control of the sky or shifting the military balance in any way. German U-boats hunted along the shipping lanes around Britain to cut the island off from vital supplies. As in the First World War, the German blockade caused friction with the theoretically neutral Americans, leading to open but undeclared naval warfare between the two powers. Finally, in December 1941, a few days after Pearl Harbor, Hitler formally declared war on the United States. Eventually, British code-breakers figured out how to track German U-boats, and British and American aircraft based on the islands of the North Atlantic provided effective cover for convoys along much of the route.

For a few years, the British could only nibble at the edges of fascist Europe. The British easily blocked the Italian attempts to seize Egypt and Greece, but German forces arrived to stiffen the Italians and push the British back again. In Greece, this ended matters in favor of the Axis, but in Egypt, the British defense eventually firmed up and stopped the enemy offensive. Then the counterattacks began. Eventually, the British and Americans cleared North Africa and attacked into Italy. This knocked the Italians out of the war, but German forces dug in halfway down the peninsula and proved difficult to budge.

By 1943 the Russian front had developed a predictable pattern. The Russians attacked in winter, and the Germans attacked in summer. For the summer of 1943, the German high command planned Operation Citadel to crush the Kursk salient between two powerful tank offensives and grind the local Soviet army group out of existence. The July battle was the largest armored battle in history, but the German thrusts slowed, then stopped, then fell back in the face of a counteroffensive. For the first time in two years of war, the Russians won a battle without snow. This three-week battle had killed 325,000 soldiers all told, but significantly, the Russians had lost only three and a half times as many as the Germans.[15] This was a sixfold improvement over the first year of the war, when twenty times as many Soviets died as Germans.[16]

Holocaust

As with all empire builders, the Nazis exploited the cheap manpower of conquered enemies. By 1944, eight million foreigners, mostly civilians, had been brought to Germany as slave labor.* Another two million were working under German command in the territories. They were assigned jobs as farmers, factory hands, and domestic servants. Foreign workers supplied a quarter of the labor in the chemical industry and a third in the armaments industry.[17]

However, Hitler had bigger plans for the Third Reich. To purify his new European empire, he classified anyone who didn't fit into conventional society as subhuman and scheduled them for extermination. Homosexuals, Jehovah's Witnesses, Freemasons, and mental patients were jailed, gassed, shot, and castrated by the tens of thousands.

Jews were at the top of the list of Hitler's targets. On top of the traditional European mistrust of the Jews as an alien religion and the paranoid suspicion that Jews were controlling society with their banks and media empires, the Nazis added a pseudoscientific fear of genetic pollution by the Jews living among them. Upon taking control of Germany, Hitler restricted the civil liberties of Jews. They were forbidden from one profession after another and banned from the company of decent folk. On the night of November 9–10, 1938 (Kristallnacht or the "Night of Broken Glass"), mobs went out to beat Jews and loot their property. By the time the war began, two-thirds of the Jews in Germany and Austria had seen which way history was heading and fled to other countries.[18]

The conquest of Europe, however, brought millions more Jews under Hitler's control. Not only was this more Jews than could be simply expelled, but also it was proving to be more than could be easily massacred. In January 1942, much of the Nazi middle management gathered in a villa at Wannsee outside Berlin to plan the Final Solution to the Jewish problem.

Whenever the Germans conquered new territory, they immediately registered all Jews. Some would be shot on the spot, but most were herded together into local ghettos. Smaller ghettos were eventually wiped out or consolidated into larger ghettos, and the largest anywhere was the Warsaw ghetto. Walled off from the rest of the city, Jews might be let out to work, but otherwise, they were kept quarantined. Disease and malnutrition cut the population drastically, but even that wasn't fast enough, so the Germans began shipping them off to concentration camps to be used as slave labor.[19]

The Nazis realized that simply shooting the Jews was inefficient. It tied up troops and trucks and wasted ammunition. A spray of machine-gun fire into a line of Jews left too

---

* For perspective, notice that this is two-thirds the number of African slaves shipped across the Atlantic and over twice the number held in the Gulag under Stalin.

many wounded who had to be dispatched with pistol shots to the head. Burial added more work to the process, and the noise alerted the neighborhood to what was happening.

Cyanide gas was the answer. It took awhile for the Nazis to iron out the difficulties, but eventually it all came together in death camps scattered around Poland. With cover stories about resettlement in the East, the Jews were collected at train stations in the ghettos and shipped out in boxcars. Upon arriving at the death camps, they were quickly sorted by age, sex, and labor potential.

Jews who weren't needed for hard labor were stripped of their belongings and sent to the showers. Instead of water, crystals of Zyklon-B, the trade name for hydrogen cyanide, would be dumped through vents in the roof, vaporizing into poisonous gas. After a frantic several minutes of screaming and scrambling, the victims would fall silent. The gas would be pumped out, and the corpses would be carted off to high-capacity crematoria.

From mid-1942 to mid-1943, in just over a year, 600,000 people were killed at Belzec—and Belzec ranked only third in capacity. The largest camp, Auschwitz, was open for three years, during which 1.1 million people were killed. In the single year that Treblinka was in operation, 800,000 were killed. A third of a million were killed at Chelmno and a quarter million at Sobibor. The system was so efficient that Treblinka operated with fewer than 150 camp personnel, supplemented by inmate labor that could be liquidated when the job was done. By the end of 1943, most of the Jews under German control were dead, and all of the death camps but Auschwitz were shut down.[20]

Some German allies (Croatia, Romania) were perfectly happy to cooperate with the Final Solution and established their own concentration camps, while others (Bulgaria, Finland, Hungary, and Italy) tried to stay out of it. Regardless, most Axis countries registered native Jews, limited their participation in public life, and willingly deported alien Jews back to countries under Hitler's control. For the Italian and Hungarian Jews, the reluctance of their governments to murder them was only a temporary reprieve. As the war turned against Germany, both these countries tried to pull out of the Axis, but German troops swooped in and deposed the wavering governments. Hundreds of thousands of local Jews were then crated up, shipped off, and gassed with stunning efficiency.[21]

The Roma people, or Gypsies, were another rootless minority reviled and targeted by the Nazis. Long slandered as thieves and sorcerers, the Gypsies were hunted down and exterminated as thoroughly as the Jews. The most common estimate is that 250,000 Roma died, but no one really knows. It may have been more than 1 million.[22]

Asian Mainland

Meanwhile, in order to cut the supply route between the Nationalist forces in China and the outside world, the Japanese conquered Burma from the British, but they soon found that the overland transportation lines in this part of the world ran unhelpfully north to south, from the interior to the coast, while the shipping lanes ran perilously around the Malay Peninsula, where Allied submarines lurked. With their army now fighting its way westward toward India, the Japanese needed to connect their staging ground in Thailand directly with the Burmese front. They rounded up native labor to cut a railroad through the jungles, over the mountains and across rugged river valleys, against the geologic grain of the country. Fifty to a hundred thousand Burmese civilians and 16,000 Allied POWs were worked to death in this project.[23]

At the same time, the British army in India scrambled troops and ordinance eastward into the path of the approaching Japanese army. Unfortunately, when the Japanese took Burma, the rice bowl of Southeast Asia, they cut off the food exports that had sustained much of the population of India. The British army commandeered all of the local transportation for military needs and sent only troops and ammunition into eastern India. Without transportation, civilian imports stopped, while grain merchants hoarded local crops for profitable resale. Showing their customary lack of concern for the Indian people (see "Famines in British India"), the British refused to interfere with the skyrocketing price of food as set by the free market, and they left the people of Bengal to starve. At least 1.5 million Indians, possibly 3 or 4 million, died of hunger before anyone cared.[24] Prime Minister Winston Churchill shrugged the famine off as the natives' fault for "breeding like rabbits."[25]

Meanwhile the Japanese were settling in to exploit the captured peoples of Asia. Millions of natives starved in Indochina and Indonesia after their crops were confiscated to feed Japan. Chinese and Korean sex slaves—"comfort women"—were rounded up and shipped out to amuse Japanese garrisons.

In Manchuria, the Japanese set up a secret biological warfare lab, Unit 731. Prisoners were deliberately injured so doctors could test risky surgical procedures. Others were strapped down and vivisected without anesthesia to reveal the mysterious inner workings of the body. Experimental germs were developed using prisoners of war as guinea pigs. In 1940, Japanese aircraft spread plague-infected fleas on the central coastal Chinese city of Ningbo. In 1942, Japanese war planes dropped cholera on Chinese villages along the Allied supply line in Yunnan Province on the border of Burma, killing an estimated 200,000 civilians in the resultant epidemic.[26]

The Shrinking Reich

It took a couple of years for the Americans to fully mobilize their enormous manpower and industry, but by 1944 they were ready to attempt a full-scale assault against the continent of Europe. They gathered a strike force in England and launched a massive amphibious attack against the German fortifications on the French coast at Normandy on June 6, 1944. By the end of the first day—D-day—the Anglo-American allies had successfully landed 133,000 troops and 20,000 vehicles on the beaches, dropped another 23,500 airborne troops behind enemy lines, and fought their way inland to seize key crossroads, at a loss of around 3,000 fatalities.[27]

After about a month, the Allies had boosted their forces enough to break free of the Normandy peninsula. British and American armored divisions swept across the French countryside toward the German border and the Rhine River. A German counterattack in December—called the Ardennes Offensive by somber historians and the Battle of the Bulge in American memory—delayed the crossing of the Rhine for a couple of months, but chewed up the last German reserves. By spring, the American forces had their bridgeheads across the Rhine. They poured into the German heartland.

In the east, the Soviets launched their own offensive in June 1944—Operation Bagration. Four massive columns of tanks and infantry punched through the German line in Belarus and quickly converged deep inside of old Poland. It was probably the largest Soviet victory on the eastern front. Scores of German divisions were trapped and annihilated. After three years of war, the fighting quality of the Red Army had finally surpassed the Wehrmacht.

As the Germans fell back into Poland, they dug a new defensive line along the Vistula River, anchored at Warsaw. Then, with the Red Army grinding to a halt as they outran their supply lines, the underground Polish Home Army launched a partisan uprising against the Germans, hoping to establish an independent government in Warsaw before the Soviets arrived with their own puppets in tow. Since neither the Germans nor the Russians wanted to see Polish nationalists running Poland, the Soviets stopped their advance and watched from across the Vistula River while the Germans moved in. The Nazis systematically reduced Warsaw to rubble and massacred the population in what's been called the largest single atrocity of the war.[28] Some 225,000 Poles died in the Warsaw uprising.*

To understand the difference between the two fronts, contrast the fate of Warsaw with that of Paris. The Americans' original plan was to bypass Paris completely and concentrate on destroying the German armies in the field, rather than diverting precious resources to feed and tend the several million civilians they would be responsible for if they took the city. Hitler's original plan was to destroy Paris rather than let it fall. Just as in Warsaw, the French underground rose up against the German garrison, but the western front was so much more civilized than the eastern that the outcome was far different. The German commander balked at destroying such a magnificent city, while the Allies allowed the Free French troops to move in and take the city under Allied protection as quickly as possible.[29]

The two approaching fronts, Anglo-Americans from the west and Soviets from the east, had already decided to meet on the Elbe River in eastern Germany, leaving the final bloody battle for Berlin to Stalin. As the Red Army plowed through the German lands of

---

* This Warsaw uprising (August 1944) is not the same as the Warsaw Ghetto uprising (April 1943), in which the Jews of the ghetto made a last-ditch effort to resist being hauled off to the death camps.

East Prussia, payback for the German invasion became official policy. Not only was all portable property looted or shipped back to Russia, but almost every woman in the path of the onslaught was raped, then tossed aside, then raped again whenever a new unit of the Red Army arrived.[30]

German civilians scattered in panic from the oncoming front lines, and hundreds of thousands of refugees died in the scramble to escape Soviet brutality. German ships were packed with civilians and wounded soldiers and launched from ports in the Baltic toward the West, often to be torpedoed by Soviet submarines. The converted cruise ship *Wilhelm Gustloff* was sent to the bottom with over 9,000 passengers and crew, the deadliest single shipwreck in history. The overstuffed freighter *Goya* was sunk, taking along over 6,000 refugees.

German soldiers held the line with no expectation of victory, only a desperate hope that they could stall the Soviets long enough to escape and surrender to the more merciful British and Americans. Hitler, though, had other plans. Commanding now from his bunker under the Chancellery building in Berlin, Hitler had no intention of meeting the same fate as Mussolini, who had recently been captured by partisans, shot, and strung up in the town square like a slaughtered hog. Hitler intended to die in a blaze of glory and take his unworthy nation with him.

The Soviets were willing to help with that. The Red Army pulled up to the Oder River, the last barrier before Berlin, and opened a massive bombardment on the Seelow Heights overlooking the river. Shining antiaircraft searchlights into the German positions to blind the defenders, the Soviets assaulted the bluffs, and after a brief bloody day of fighting, the way to Berlin was wide open.

A week of savage street fighting across Berlin killed 100,000 civilians[31] and tightened the noose around Hitler's bunker. Soviet advances were measured by blocks and buildings. The German army at this point was filling its ranks with old men and boys who were no match for the veterans of the Red Army. Maybe 225,000 German soldiers died defending Berlin, as opposed to the 78,000 Soviets killed attacking them.[32] Finally, the war had narrowed to just the few blocks around the Chancellery. Unable to delay any longer, Hitler committed suicide with a gunshot to the head after poisoning his dog and new wife. His followers set fire to his body and scattered before the Russians got there.*

---

* The Soviets found Hitler's corpse pretty quickly, but they kept the discovery a secret to worry the West. They hoped that the mystery of his disappearance and the nightmare of a resurgent Hitler could be used to bluff more concessions out of Western leaders. Hitler was buried in an unmarked grave at a Soviet base in East Germany until 1970, when the base was transferred to East German control. Hitler was then exhumed, cremated, and flushed into the neighboring river to prevent him from ever becoming the focus of a pilgrimage site.

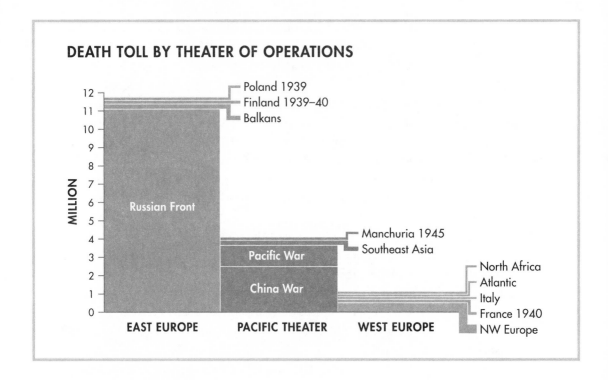

DEATH TOLL BY THEATER OF OPERATIONS

(Chart showing death toll in millions by theater of operations. Y-axis labeled MILLION, ranging from 0 to 12. Categories along X-axis: EAST EUROPE, PACIFIC THEATER, WEST EUROPE.)

EAST EUROPE: Russian Front (large bar), with Poland 1939, Finland 1939–40, and Balkans at top.

PACIFIC THEATER: Pacific War and China War, with Manchuria 1945 and Southeast Asia.

WEST EUROPE: North Africa, Atlantic, Italy, France 1940, NW Europe.

Island Hopping

With the Japanese offensives in the Pacific Ocean halted by the defeat at Midway, the United States faced the problem of how to counterattack across the world's largest ocean. One step at a time was the only possibility. Rather than clearing every island in the ocean, the United States bypassed the big Japanese bases, cut off supply routes, and left their garrisons to starve. Instead, the Americans went after secondary islands that were large enough to be developed as forward bases, but too small for major Japanese troop concentrations.

This made for a more intermittent war than was found elsewhere on solid ground. American submarines and aircraft carriers would first isolate a target island by destroying local Japanese shipping. Then the American carriers and their escort battleships would soften up the Japanese garrison with air raids and artillery barrages. Finally ground forces would storm the beaches and fight their way through Japanese defenses. After a few weeks, even before the last Japanese on the island had been hunted down and exterminated, the Americans would build air bases on the island and launch heavy bombers to soften up the next target on the list. They would assemble fresh troops and supplies on the island, and do it all over again, one step closer to Japan.[33]

Even these lesser Japanese garrisons were tough targets, and each amphibious assault cost thousands of American and tens of thousands of Japanese lives. The Japanese code of honor did not allow surrender, so when the situation turned hopeless, rather than ask for terms, soldiers launched suicidal charges against the American positions in order to die gloriously in battle. This refusal to surrender was so deeply rooted in the national psyche that even civilians killed themselves by the thousands rather than suffer the humiliation of being taken alive. Some stubborn Japanese soldiers took to the jungles and refused to surrender as late as the 1970s.[34]

The only big city destroyed by street fighting in the Pacific war was Manila in the Philippines. American General Douglas MacArthur wanted the Japanese to declare it an open city (meaning that all defense and attacks were to take place outside the city) but instead the Japanese dug into the city center. Even as MacArthur delayed rooting the enemy out, Japanese frustration turned against the civilian inhabitants. Thousands of prisoners and civilians were bayoneted, beaten, shot, or strapped down inside buildings that were then set on fire. During January and February 1945, almost 100,000 residents of Manila were massacred. When the Americans attacked, the Japanese fought to the last man and took the city with them.[35]

In the spring of 1945, the battle for the island of Okinawa—the last stop before Japan itself—became the Second World War's bloodiest battle outside the Russian front. By the time it was all over, the Americans had lost 12,000 of their own troops, killed on land and sea, and they counted the bodies of 110,000 Japanese soldiers scattered around the island in parts and pieces. The final 20,000 Japanese soldiers retreated into caves for a last stand, only to be sealed in by American explosives.

It's been estimated that as many as 160,000 civilians—one-third of Okinawa's population—died in the crossfire, or by mass suicide, or (among the less fanatical) by forced suicide. Okinawa became legendary for the large number and variety of Japanese suicides. The war had been chewing up Japanese pilots so quickly that their replacements could not be trained in the subtle skills of aerial dogfighting and precision bombing, so the Japanese turned instead to blunt suicide attacks against American shipping. Kamikaze pilots crashed planes loaded with explosives into the American fleet. The ferocity of the Japanese defense convinced American war planners to reconsider invading their home islands and instead try bombing them into submission.[36]

The War of the Machines

The major innovation in ground tactics of World War II was the deployment of armored divisions. Under the doctrine of *blitzkrieg*—lightning war—tanks supported by aircraft would punch holes in the line, followed by mobile artillery and mechanized infantrymen in trucks to exploit the breakthrough. Often paratroopers would drop from the sky to seize strategic landmarks ahead of the advancing columns. In open country like Russia, France, and North Africa, an enemy breakthrough could strand tens of thousands of foot soldiers a hundred miles behind the rapidly moving front lines, where they would have little choice but to dig in and hope for a change in fortunes. The destruction of these pockets produced many of the horrendously huge body counts associated with the Second World War. Because mechanized transport could easily outpace any fleeing foot soldiers, battles of annihilation became a regular part of warfare for the first time in centuries.

The increase in the use of machinery took its toll. During the American Civil War, U.S. Army personnel suffered one accidental death for every eleven deaths in battle. By World War II, that was up to one accidental death for every four battle deaths.[37] Soldiers were now being crushed in jeeps, smashed in airplanes, burned in trucks, scalded and poisoned by strange new chemicals, mangled and electrocuted by heavy equipment, and blown apart by mishandling heavy munitions.

World War II produced the first naval battles in history in which the opposing fleets never laid eyes on one another. Instead of cannons, it was radar-directed fighter planes that delivered the killing blows between ships across miles of empty ocean.

The experience of World War II reinforced the truism that war sparks technological innovation. Radar, jet aircraft, computers, sonar, antibiotics, and guided missiles were some of the new technologies first deployed in World War II. Secret labs all over the world— American nuclear physicists at Los Alamos, British code-breakers at Bletchley Park, German rocket scientists at Peenemunde—helped determine the outcome of the war.

On the other hand, we can go too far in focusing on the technology. Only the American army came close to fighting a completely mechanized war. Aside from specialized Panzer divisions, the Wehrmacht still slogged through the mud with horses pulling their artillery pieces and supplies. Even the cold industrial efficiency of the death camps can be overstated. Most victims of the Holocaust died in ways that have worked for centuries— disease, overwork, hunger, and face-to-face massacres.

Aside from the occasional breakthroughs achieved by armored thrusts, most armies fought much as they had during the First World War—with riflemen digging in or attacking and machine gunners defending under cover of artillery. On the Russian front, where most of the fighting happened, field artillery firing by map coordinates into targets out of sight did more killing than other weapons. The artillery expended 80 percent of the total ammunition fired and caused 45 percent of deaths in battle. Examination of the dead and wounded showed that heavy infantry weapons (machine guns, mortars, and light artillery aimed by sight) killed another 35 percent. Aircraft caused 5 percent of battle deaths; armored vehicles killed another 5 percent. The light infantry weapons that are the staple of war movies (rifles, pistols, grenades) were essentially for self-defense; these inflicted 10 percent of battle deaths.[38]

Air Power

Airplanes became major agents of destruction during World War II. Precision bombing of military and industrial targets was the most effective use of aircraft, and it was completely legal under the international laws of war. This, however, required a better-than-average mix of intelligence, reconnaissance, and bomber design. It also required bombers to approach on a straight path in clear daylight directly into a curtain of antiaircraft fire and swarms of defensive fighter planes.

Because of these difficulties, air forces were tempted into the indiscriminant destruction of softer targets. Early in the war, cities were attacked with a random scattering of bombs to terrify the inhabitants, but as the size of air forces increased, so did the body counts. The German bombing of Rotterdam on May 14, 1940, which killed around 850 civilians, horrified the world.[39] A year later, on April 6, 1941, the first German air raid against Belgrade killed 17,000 civilians.[40] The opening air raid against Stalingrad killed 40,000 civilians on August 23, 1942.[41]

Soon the annihilation of cities became a science. Over the course of a night, as many as a thousand planes would be sent against a target. The first waves of bombers would drop explosives all over the city to splinter wood buildings into kindling, followed by later waves that scattered incendiaries to start little fires. Soon, the various fires consolidated into one gigantic firestorm, which created its own weather system with hurricane winds and a heat so intense that it warped metal, cracked masonry, and carbonized bodies. A firestorm could sweep a city clean off the face of the earth and suck the oxygen out of underground shelters, suffocating all of the people who thought they were safe. The British launched the war's first major firebombing on the night of July 28–29, 1943, against Hamburg, incinerating 42,000 residents.[42] On the night of February 13–14, 1945, Allied bombers destroyed Dresden and 35,000 civilians.* On March 9–10, 1945, American bombers destroyed Tokyo, killing 84,000 inhabitants.[43]

Since the beginning of the war, physicists all over the world had been reporting to their

---

* The bombing of Dresden has become a metaphor for senseless slaughter, largely as a result of two books published in the 1960s. Kurt Vonnegut's *Slaughterhouse-Five* (1969) is one of the great novels of the twentieth century and a vivid eyewitness description of World War II, so it will shape our perceptions of the event for a long time to come. The other book, David Irving's *The Destruction of Dresden* (1963) was the definitive nonfiction description of the firebombing for a generation. Unfortunately, Irving has turned into the world's foremost defender of Hitler's reputation, and it's now known that he repeated a lot of false Nazi propaganda uncritically in *The Destruction of Dresden*, such as a death toll of 135,000 and a total lack of military targets in the city. The newer book by Frederick Taylor, *Dresden: Tuesday, February 13, 1945* (2004), clears up a lot of Irving's most outrageous mistakes.

governments that splitting radioactive atoms would release a massive pulse of energy that could be used to obliterate entire armies with the flick of a switch—so God help us if the enemy gets this first. Secret research programs were established in Germany, America, Russia, and Japan to explore this potential. As the world's primary industrial power, the United States was the first to work out all of the technical problems. On August 6, 1945, a single airplane dropped a single atomic bomb on Japan, and the city of Hiroshima was blasted out of existence, taking along 120,000 of its inhabitants.[44] Three days later, another nuclear strike destroyed Nagasaki and 49,000 of its inhabitants.[45]

Because the war was almost over anyway and the bombs were used against cities rather than armies or fleets, debate rages over whether these attacks were necessary; however, two other facts stand out. The Japanese stopped their dithering and surrendered unconditionally a few days after the bombing of Nagasaki, and since that time, nations armed with nuclear weapons have carefully avoided fighting big wars with each other.

Aftershocks

The fall of the Axis did not stop the killing. Many countries had come out of enemy occupation with their political systems wrecked, so chaos replaced oppression. In China, the Communists and Nationalists resumed the civil war that had been interrupted by the Japanese (see "Chinese Civil War"), while Left and Right also fought a civil war over who would inherit Greece. In East Asia, a couple of colonies that had been occupied by the Japanese—French Indochina (see "French Indochina War") and the Dutch East Indies—seized the moment and rebelled to prevent their former masters from reclaiming control. In Eastern Europe, the nations that had been (liberated? conquered? trampled?) by the Soviet Union tried to set up multiparty democracies, but Soviet-sponsored Communist parties quickly gained the upper hand and put an end to that.

The recently liberated nations had plenty of scores to settle. The Communist partisans (mostly Serbs) who took control of Yugoslavia killed over 100,000 compatriots (mostly Croats) tarnished by association with the wartime fascist government. The French killed 10,000 collaborators after liberation, only about 800 of them after the formality of a trial. The Italians killed from 10,000 to 15,000 war criminals. The Netherlands executed 40 collaborators, while Norway executed 25.[46] The formal trials of high-ranking Nazi war criminals at Nuremberg and other similar trials in occupied West Germany led to 486 executions.

Unlike the Nazis, the Japanese militarists had never centralized power in the hands of one omnipotent dictator. General Tojo Hideki seemed to be near the center of power for most of the war as general, war minister, or prime minister, so he was duly tried and hanged by the Americans, along with six other generals and ministers. Lesser trials led to another 900 or so executions;[47] however, the Americans allowed Emperor Hirohito to keep his throne in order to calm the Japanese resentment of the American occupation.

Tens of thousands of surviving Jews fled Europe to make a new life in the British colony of Palestine, which shortly became the independent state of Israel. The immediate war between Israel and its Arab neighbors in 1947 was the first of many that would continue to erupt, about one per decade, for a long time to come.

Mind-Numbing Numbers

The Second World War killed the most people in history by several different criteria. As a whole, it was the deadliest event in history. It was also history's deadliest event for many individual nations—Russia, Poland, Japan, Indonesia, and the Netherlands, to name a few—and for several non-national groups of victims—such as soldiers, POWs, and Jews.

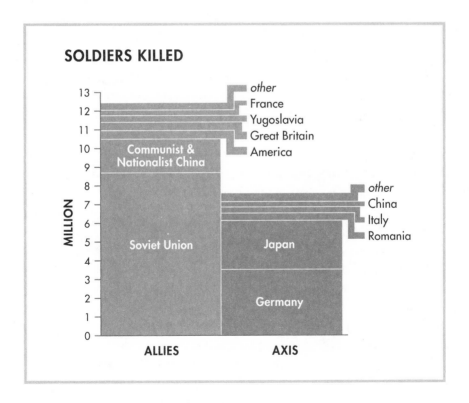

The U.S. Strategic Bombing Survey claimed that "probably more persons lost their lives by fire at Tokyo in a 6-hour period [March 9–10, 1945] than at any time in the history of man."[48] This may be true, depending on which numbers you accept, but I'm more inclined to count the 120,000 killed almost instantly at Hiroshima as the most people killed in the shortest time by human agency in history.* The killing of 1.1 million at Auschwitz took longer, but it probably counts as the most people killed in the smallest place. The bloodiest battle in history was probably the Siege of Leningrad (if you count both soldiers and civilians) or Stalingrad (if you only count soldiers), but even if they weren't, then the other likeliest candidates were also fought on the Russian front.

The following chart shows the relative evil and suffering of the participants of World War II by listing how many millions of noncombatants died. The chart shows only death tolls that exceed 250,000 because on the scale of the Second World War, mere tens of thousands was small change. Numbers don't add up exactly because there's overlap and a lot of unknowns. The columns under "TOTAL" include everything—murders, negligence, accidents, and innocent bystanders caught in the crossfire—while the columns under "Perpetrators" tally only the deaths that are widely considered to be deliberate, avoidable, or excessive.

Looking at the big body counts isn't the only way to see how monumentally destructive the war was. You might also want to peek into the little, forgotten corners, and see how many deaths occurred among people that no one ever notices, like New Zealanders.

New Zealand is about as far from anywhere as you can possibly get. It was not under any kind of threat. Even if the Axis Powers had conquered the rest of the world, they probably would have left New Zealand alone, just as they had ignored Sweden and Switzerland. A small country whose contribution to the war hardly tipped the scale, New Zealand could have sat out the war without shifting the balance, but instead the country jumped in and lost 12,000 men in a war it wasn't required to fight. How many is 12,000? Think of it as sinking eight *Titanic*s.

The war put so many people in deadly situations that unprecedented numbers of people died in surprising and unusual ways. When the British trapped a Japanese force on Ramree Island in Burma, the Japanese tried to flee through impenetrable swamps. It is said that a thousand Japanese went in, but only twenty emerged on the other side. The missing hundreds had been eaten by crocodiles.

The largest shark attack in history occurred when the USS *Indianapolis* was torpedoed by a Japanese submarine. The ship went down too quickly for an adequate distress call to go out, delaying rescue for several days. Of the 900 stranded sailors who bobbed in the water in their life vests, only 316 survived the circling sharks.

---

* "by human agency": A few sharp, sudden natural disasters, such as the 2004 Indian Ocean tsunami, killed more people just as quickly.

VICTIMS	PERPETRATORS								TOTAL NON-BATTLE DEATHS	
	Germans	Japanese	Soviets	British	Americans	Nationalist Chinese	Romanians	Croats	Civilians	POWs
Soviets	17.0[49]		2.0						16.9	3.3
Chinese		4.0[50]				0.6[51]			8.0	0.5
Poles (pre-war)	5.5[52]								6.0	
Jews (all nations)	5.5[53]						0.3[54]		5.5	
Indonesians		4.0[55]							4.0	
Indians				1.5[56]					3.0[57]	
Vietnamese		2.0[58]							2.0	
Germans			1.4	0.3*	0.3*				1.6	0.4
Yugoslavians	0.5							0.3[59]	1.2	
Gypsies	0.5								0.5	
Japanese					0.4[60]				0.4	
French	0.3[61]								0.4	
Romanians									0.3	
Greeks	0.3								0.3	
Hungarians	0.3								0.3	
Czechoslovakians	0.3								0.3	
TOTAL	24.0	11.0	4.0[62]	2.0	1.0	0.6	0.5	0.3	46.0	4.2

* The official estimate is that Allied bombing killed 593,000 in Germany (Keegan, *Second World War*, p. 590). Both the United States and Britain share responsibility, so I've given them each half.

Revisionism

No aspect of World War II is without controversy, but some debates burn more energy than others. For a previous generation of scholars, the hottest debate was whether Hitler had a strategy of world conquest and genocide all planned out, or did he merely seize whatever opportunities presented themselves. That was a more polite era. Nowadays, people are willing to challenge fundamental features of the war.

Everywhere you look, Holocaust deniers simply refuse to admit that the Nazis tried to eradicate the Jews of Europe. In some Muslim countries, this is actually taught in schools as the mainstream view. On the other hand, in some European countries, it is forbidden to express this view in public. Emotions over the issue have grown so polarized that, for all practical purposes, the Holocaust has been removed as a topic for constructive disagreement worldwide.

Because you would be hard-pressed to find a historical event with stronger documentation than the Holocaust,* you might wonder how *anyone* can doubt it. Well first, you have to *want* to doubt it. After that, it's easy. If your ideology fails to arouse support because it sounds too much like Nazism, then you will want to rewrite history to make the Nazis less frightening. You acknowledge that some Jews died—disease swept ghettos and labor camps, German troops executed partisans, and so on—but war is hell, and such things were happening everywhere. Holocaust deniers argue that there was no *systematic* effort directed at Jews, and that the death toll was no worse than, say, the bombing of German cities. The deniers are assisted by the fact that retreating Germans deliberately destroyed much of the forensic evidence—gas chambers, bodies, witnesses, for example.

In Germany, the big controversies center around how much support the Nazis had among ordinary German citizens. Most Germans would like to be able to blame the Holocaust on a narrow clique of fanatics, but pesky facts keep showing that a disturbing number of ordinary citizens—from civil servants to common soldiers—assisted in the process. Every prominent person who has emerged from the German-speaking world in the past half century—whether rocket scientist, secretary-general of the United Nations, governor

---

* For the record: The proof begins with thousands of eyewitness accounts detailing all parts of the process. Then we can illustrate these accounts with photographs taken of the events as they happened. We can dig through census and tax records to show that millions of Jews who existed in the 1930s had disappeared under German occupation. And finally, we have boxes of official documents produced by the perpetrators, including orders, memos, reports, schedules, and invoices. The entire history of the ancient world is based on far less evidence than that. (For more, see chapters 12–14 of Michael Shermer's *Why People Believe Weird Things* [New York: W. H. Freeman, 1997]. For even more, see, Richard Evans's *Lying About Hitler: History, Holocaust, and the David Irving Trial* [New York: Basic Books, 2001].)

of California, Nobel literature laureate, or pope—has faced awkward revelations about past associations with Nazism.

The big controversies in the English-speaking world challenge the Allies/good, Axis/bad stereotypes of official history, either by minimizing the sins of the Axis (the Holocaust, starting the war, for example) or maximizing the sins of the Allies (Stalinism, Dresden, for example). In fact, a significant minority openly suggests that the Western democracies fought on the wrong side.

Patrick Buchanan, a ubiquitous American commentator, wrote in his 1999 book, *A Republic, Not an Empire*, that the Western democracies should have stood by and let Hitler and Stalin duke it out. "By redirecting Hitler's first blow upon themselves, Britain and France bought Stalin two extra years to prepare for Hitler's attack—and thus saved the Soviet Union for Communism. . . . Had Britain and France not given the guarantee to Poland, Hitler would almost surely have delivered his first great blow to Russia. . . . [H]ad Hitler conquered the USSR at enormous cost, would he then have launched a new war against Western Europe, where his ambitions never lay?"[63]

Even George W. Bush denounced his predecessors' decision to ally with Stalin: "The agreement at Yalta followed in the unjust tradition of Munich and the Molotov-Ribbentrop pact. Once again, when powerful governments negotiated, the freedom of small nations was somehow expendable."[64]

In this case, revisionists seem to forget that the world went to war against Hitler because he was *dangerous*, not because he was *evil*. This is an important distinction in international relations. You can do whatever you want inside your own country, but when you start invading your neighbors, the rest of the world gets jumpy. No matter how brutal Stalin may have been to his own people, he was content to stay inside the borders of the Soviet Union. By the time Stalin began grabbing small countries for himself, the West was already committed to war with Hitler. The choice wasn't between fighting Hitler or Stalin. The choice was to fight Hitler or both of them.

Furthermore, the Soviets beat the Germans fair and square. They produced 96 percent of their own munitions and 66 percent of their own vehicles, while inflicting 80 percent of all German fatalities in the war.[65] They had already turned the tide at Stalingrad at a time when Britain was stalemated and America was still mobilizing. It was a close call, and Western assistance tipped the balance, but the West needed Stalin more than Stalin needed the West. Without the Soviets, the Western allies would have had to face several million more Germans all by themselves. This gave Stalin a better negotiating position throughout the war.

EXPULSION OF GERMANS FROM EASTERN EUROPE

Death toll: 2.1 million[1]
Rank: 36
Type: ethnic cleansing
Broad dividing line: Poles and Czechs vs. Germans
Time frame: 1945–47
Location: Eastern Europe
Major state participants: Poland, Czechoslovakia
Minor state participants: Soviet Union, United States, Britain, France
Who usually gets the most blame: Poland, Czechoslovakia
The unanswerable question everyone asks: Can you really blame them?

POLAND SUFFERED THE MOST DURING THE SECOND WORLD WAR. IT WAS the first nation to be conquered; then it was partitioned, then subjected to massacres, which escalated to genocide; then the war returned from the other direction and plowed over Poland yet again. When it was all over, one-sixth of the Polish people—three million Jews, three million others—were dead. The victors sensed that Poland deserved some compensation for all of its troubles, especially since Stalin was keeping the eastern territories of Poland for himself, where local Ukrainian and Belorussian majorities were being incorporated into the Soviet Union.

After the war, the border between Germany and Poland was shifted westward, to the Oder River. Unlike the border changes after World War I, in which Germany was stripped only of districts with a non-German majority, these new border changes were clearly punitive. Lands that had been German for centuries—East Prussia, Pomerania, Silesia—were handed over to Poland, and the local inhabitants were kicked out.

A small sliver of East Prussia containing the port of Konigsberg was attached to Russia. Under the new name of Kaliningrad, it became the forward base for the Soviet Baltic fleet. Russians so completely replaced the Germans that today this district is more Russian than Russia itself.

This was happening everywhere. Hitler had used alleged mistreatment of German minorities across Eastern Europe as an excuse to invade, so everyone decided to get rid of their Germans once and for all. The second largest German minority was in Czechoslovakia, a country that Germany had dismantled and occupied even earlier than Poland. German villages and urban minorities in Hungary, Romania, and Croatia remained from the days when the Austrian Empire sprawled across Eastern Europe. These had to go as well.

The expulsions went through three phases. In the first phase, 5 million Germans fled the Soviet advance during the war, often with only a few hours' preparation. Of the nearly 2.4 million Germans in East Prussia, 1.9 million abandoned this outlying enclave of Germany and fled westward. Probably 20 percent of these refugees died along roads and in villages—in air raids, shipwrecks, artillery barrages, and gang rapes—as the war caught up and rolled over them.

Breslau, the capital of Silesia and the largest city to change hands in the postwar reduction of Germany, had already seen huge shifts in population under Nazi rule as Polish and Jewish minorities were shipped out. Then the Red Army arrived in January 1945, while the Wehrmacht dug in to defend it. The German government ordered all noncombatants to leave immediately. Half a million civilians were forced to flee through snow and ice toward collecting centers many miles away. Eighty thousand died in the cold.

The second phase saw the "wild" expulsions. After the fighting stopped, angry mobs spontaneously and brutally drove away the local German minorities. They stripped the Germans of their property and forced farmers to abandon their houses, crops. and livestock. They lynched suspected collaborators and their families, and the occupying Soviet soldiers ignored all of it.

In July 1945, a mysterious explosion at a factory in the Czech town of Usti nad Labem was rumored to be sabotage, and the townspeople attacked their German neighbors. In the first assault, the mob swarmed over a German family on the bridge and tossed their baby into the river. By the time the riots were over, anywhere from 1,000 to 2,500 Germans had been shot dead, beaten to death, or drowned.[2] In June, 2,000 Sudeten Germans in Postoloprty were rounded up and shot or beaten to death in a few days. Two years later, in August 1947, Czech authorities quietly dug up the mass graves and burned all of the bodies so that "Germans [would] have no memorials to which they could point as a source of suffering by their people."[3]

The third phase entailed the formal resettlement by the governments of Europe. While in exile during the war, the past and future Czech president Edvard Benes submitted his plan for clearing the Sudeten Germans out of the mountainous borders of Czechoslovakia. "We must get rid of all those Germans who plunged a dagger in the back of the Czechoslovak state in 1938," Benes declared. The Churchill government had officially endorsed this policy by August 1942, and the Americans and Soviets followed in 1943.[4]

The major powers authorized final action at the postwar Potsdam Conference among the Allies in August 1945. Within weeks, Benes stripped ethnic Germans of their Czech citizenship unless there were mitigating circumstances, such as marriage to a Slav or a record of fighting the Nazi occupation. In November 1945, the Allied Control Council in charge of postwar Europe ordered the 3 million Germans living in Czechoslovakia and the 3.5 million inside Poland's pre-war borders to be resettled in Germany. Then 6 million Poles were removed from the 70,000 square miles in the east taken by the Soviet Union and resettled in the 48,000 square miles that Poland got from Germany.

Eventually Churchill would have second thoughts. In his 1946 speech that gave the world the phrase "iron curtain," he now denounced the brutality of the policy. "The Russian-dominated Polish Government has been encouraged to make enormous and wrongful inroads upon Germany, and mass expulsions of millions of Germans on a scale grievous and undreamed-of are now taking place."[5]

Meanwhile, the expulsion and transit were only half the problem. These eastern German deportees were being dumped into the middle of a major famine. Forced to abandon their original livelihoods back home, they found themselves in a bombed-out and ravaged land swarming with cripples, vagrants, and refugees. Because the German cities were in ruins, the newcomers were stashed on farms, in army barracks, and even in former concentration camps. Anyone with a spare room was ordered to take in a refugee. Unfortunately, the Germans from the East spoke alien dialects that sounded almost foreign to West German ears, and they were insulted with the name *Polacken*. Natives resented immigrants as competitors for scarce housing and food; the displaced were often left to fend for themselves and likely starve.

When it was all done, 12 to 14 million Germans had been expelled from the East. So many Germans arrived from the East that West Germany's population in 1950 was 20 percent higher than it had been before the war, despite war casualties. The population boost was especially noticeable in rural areas, which rose by as much as 60 percent in some districts.[6]

In 1967, Germany's federal statistical office estimated that 267,000 of the Germans expelled from Czechoslovakia had died in those harsh years.[7] An estimated 1,225,000 of those expelled from Poland and 619,000 from Hungary, Romania, Yugoslavia, and the Baltic nations died. All in all, the total number of deaths among the eastern refugees is estimated as 2,111,000.[8]

FRENCH INDOCHINA WAR

Death toll: 393,000
Rank: 88
Type: colonial rebellion
Broad dividing line: France vs. Viet Minh
Time frame: 1945–54
Location: French Indochina
Major state participant: France
Major quasi-state participants: Cambodia, Laos, Viet Nam
Major non-state participant: Viet Minh
Who usually gets the most blame: France

NGUYEN SINH CUNG WAS BORN IN 1890, THE SON OF A VIETNAMESE teacher, and he spent his youth bouncing around all of the major centers of Communist thought—university in Paris, Moscow after the revolution, and Shanghai before Chiang Kai-shek cracked down. In 1919, he tried to convince the victorious allies at the Versailles peace conference to free his people from French rule. When that failed, he returned to his homeland to organize an independence movement. Before anything came of that, East Asia was thrown into turmoil by the Japanese occupation of the West's colonies, but regardless of who was in charge, Nguyen was ready to launch a nationalist resistance; he merely directed the effort against Japan instead. He established a rebel force called the Viet Minh, from which he took his new alias, Ho Chi Minh.

The fall of Japan in August 1945 left Vietnam in limbo. Without any Allied troops to tell them otherwise, Japanese garrisons began to cooperate with the Viet Minh on local administration, and after settling into the colonial capital of Hanoi, Ho Chi Minh declared Vietnam's independence. Then, in September, Nationalist Chinese forces—the nearest Allies on hand—arrived to take control, but mostly they just looted Hanoi and left the rest of the colony to look after itself. Indochina sank into chaos as discharged troops, released prisoners, deserters, and crime bosses scrambled to grab whatever they could before anyone could stop them. In some regions, the harassed and outnumbered French authorities—recently released from Japanese prisons—reached agreements with Ho Chi Minh's rebels to restore order. Back in Paris, General Charles de Gaulle of the provisional government announced that France was not going to abandon any of its colonies. As far as he was concerned, independence would never happen.[1]

When Ho Chi Minh heard this, he turned less cooperative about letting more French troops and officials into Vietnam. With a cease-fire in place, negotiations dragged on, and tensions escalated. In November 1946, the French demanded full control of the port city of Haiphong, but the Viet Minh refused to evacuate. French warships bombarded Viet Minh neighborhoods and blew apart 6,000 civilians. French tanks and aircraft attacked rebel positions in the city. Door-to-door fighting finally cleared the Viet Minh from the city.[2]

As more troops arrived from Europe, France took firm control of all of the cities in Indochina. The Viet Minh, however, dominated the remote countryside and ambushed any French troops who ventured too far into their territory.

The French tried to deflate the independence movement by reorganizing their colony into autonomous but cooperative vassals. They put local monarchs into each piece of the colony and gave them nominal independence under an umbrella organization called the French Union.

In 1949, the Communist takeover of China finally reached the borders of Vietnam, which gave the rebels access to a major supplier of weapons. The war now shifted to these border regions as the Viet Minh tried to keep in contact with the Red Chinese and the French tried to break this contact. In December 1953, French paratroops seized and fortified Dien Bien Phu (now in Laos), a major station on the Communist supply line, hoping to draw the rebels into an open battle that favored the French. Instead Vietnamese General Vo Nguyen Giap brought the strongpoint under siege. By March 1954, rebel combat troops numbering 70,000 and 100,000 support personnel isolated 15,000 entrenched French, and General Giap opened his attacks. After fifty-six days of relentless raiding, sniping, and bombardment wore down the French and squeezed them into a shrinking enclave, Dien Bien Phu surrendered.

This defeat convinced the French government that further fighting was futile. Peace negotiations started shortly afterward and granted independence to French Indochina in the form of four countries—Laos, Cambodia, and a Vietnam divided into two parts, one for the Communists and another for the non-Communists.

That wouldn't last long.

Death Toll

The French side lost around 93,000 soldiers dead, but the French *people* lost only 20,700 of those. The rest were Indochinese allies (18,700), Indochinese colonials (26,700), African colonials (15,200), and Foreign Legionnaires (11,600). Obviously one of the advantages of having an empire is that you can use the colonials to do most of your fighting for you.

Estimates of casualties among the Vietnamese are sketchy. Probably 175,000 Viet Minh were killed fighting the French, while 125,000 civilians were killed as well.[3]

PARTITION OF INDIA

Death toll: 500,000[1]
Rank: 70
Type: ethnic cleansing
Broad dividing line: Hindus and Sikhs vs. Muslims
Time frame: 1947
Location and major state participants: Pakistan, India
Who usually gets the most blame: Hindus, Muslims, especially Jinnah

THE END OF COLONIAL RULE IN INDIA WAS SUPPOSED TO BE A TRIUMPH OF the human spirit. The second most populous political entity on the planet, a free India would liberate one-sixth of the human population. Just as inspiring, the liberation had been accomplished without violence. Mohandas Gandhi had staged massive marches, fasts, boycotts, and strikes to convince the British to leave. This was no replay of the long bloody rebellions that had liberated the Western Hemisphere.

The one small snag in the independence movement was that many of India's Muslims did not want to be a minority under Hindu control. Their leader, Mohammed Jinnah, demanded a separate country carved out of those regions where Muslims were the majority. Gandhi, on the other hand, was horrified at the idea of a fractured India, and even offered to accept Muslim rule over all Hindus if that would keep India intact. Other Hindu nationalists, however, were just as horrified by Gandhi's solution.

In the mid-1930s, when the British finally began to consider the idea of eventual independence for India, they had put the actual day a long way off into the vague future, but then the Second World War exhausted Britain into abandoning its empire much sooner. The first plan called for a federation of autonomous states, but just as they were putting the finishing touches on the plan in 1946, Jawaharlal Nehru, leader of the Hindus, casually mentioned that it was subject to change. Feeling they were tricked, the Muslims in Calcutta rioted. Within three days, 5,000 people had been killed in pogroms launched back and forth between Muslims and Hindus in the city. After the riots spread throughout the country, the body count quadrupled. Corpses piling up in the streets snarled traffic.

Tempers eventually cooled long enough to devise a new plan. The Muslim-majority regions of British India were bundled together to form the sovereign country of Pakistan. The frontier provinces abutting Iran and Afghanistan were so thoroughly Muslim that they could be easily assigned to Pakistan, but two inner provinces, Bengal and Punjab, were especially tricky because both religions were equally common and interwoven throughout the area. These provinces would have to be split into Hindu and Muslim majority regions. A British commissioner named Sir Cyril Radcliffe was given the thankless and impossible task of carving out fair boundaries. His main qualification was that he had never been to India and presumably had no bias. He was locked away with socio-ethnic census maps, a pencil with an eraser, and absolute authority to do whatever he wanted. The exact borders weren't even announced until August 14–15, 1947, the evening of independence.[2]

Lord Louis Mountbatten was appointed to be the final viceroy of India, and he wanted to get it over with. While advisers suggested a gradual timetable with sovereignty progressively handed over one piece at a time, Mountbatten insisted on cutting the subcontinent loose all at once, within a year. Mountbatten did not want to get caught in the civil war that was looming in India.[3]

Even before independence arrived, mob violence began to purge communities of their minorities, trying to remove any excuse for getting assigned to the wrong country. Hindus angry at Muslims for forcing the split committed the first murders, but the killing soon went in both directions as each side sought revenge for whatever atrocity the other side had just committed.

Millions of Indians tried to escape the violence, which continued even as the day of independence came and went. Columns of refugees fleeing their former homes were often ambushed and slaughtered. Trains often had to run a gauntlet of gunfire from machine guns set up alongside the tracks. If the trains stopped, passengers were dragged off screaming and butchered by the dozens, hundreds, and eventually thousands.[4] Silent "ghost trains" pulled into stations hauling boxcars loaded only with the dead and dying, moaning in congealed pools of blood.[5]

Gandhi camped out in Calcutta, fasting in protest over the ethnic violence and growing ever weaker with hunger. His spiritual hold over the Indian people was so great that they obeyed him, and Bengal was spared the worst of the violence.

In November 1947, once all of the people who had been caught on the wrong side of the border were either dead or exiled, the slaughter abruptly stopped. Over those chaotic months, more than 14 million people had fled their homes—7.3 million Hindus and Sikhs from Pakistan, 7.2 million Muslims from India.[6] For what it's worth, the fact that a roughly equal number of each were stuck in the wrong country probably means that Radcliffe had drawn the border as fairly as was humanly possible.

However, the partition violence still had one more victim left to claim. In January 1948 a Hindu fanatic assassinated Mohandas Gandhi for betraying his side and caring about the lives of the enemy.[7]

MAO ZEDONG

Death toll: 40 million
Rank: 2
Type: Communist dictator
Time frame: 1949–76
Location: China
Broad dividing line: new vs. old
Major state participant: People's Republic of China
Who usually gets the most blame: Mao personally and Communism generally
Another damn: insane people's republic

L IKE MOST OF THE PEOPLE WHO MADE THE MID-TWENTIETH CENTURY SUCH
a dangerous time to live, the life of Mao Zedong is entwined with several of my top
one hundred multicides, but he stands here as Number 2 purely as the ruler of China
for a quarter century. Mao is almost certainly the deadliest individual in history to have
wreaked havoc inside a single country.

Mao was an authentic ideologue. Rather that sitting back and enjoying being absolute
master of all he surveyed, he was constantly fiddling with the way his country worked.
Obviously this made him far more dangerous than a dictator who merely siphoned off a
percentage of government contracts or bedded the wives of ambitious flunkies. Instead,
he disrupted agriculture in a country that was hovering dangerously close to starvation
and incited angry mobs to attack anyone who lacked proper enthusiasm for his policies.

Victory of the Revolution

In April 1949, Chiang Kai-shek fled China for exile on Taiwan (see "Chinese Civil War"),
and after a bit of mopping up, Mao Zedong proclaimed the new People's Republic of China
on October 1. For the first year of this new era, China was run by a layer of Communist
watchdogs placed over top of the old Nationalist bureaucracy, but clearly that couldn't last
forever. The Korean War gave Mao both a reason and an excuse to tighten security.[1]

The 1950s saw a string of political movements that were ostensibly designed to mold
the new China along Marxist lines, but mostly they just made everybody jumpy and
prevented rival power structures from taking root. The goals of each campaign were
reduced to numbered checklists and slapped up on wall posters. Certain classes would be

targeted for a few months of accusations, betrayals, arrests, suicides, purges, and beatings, until Mao grew weary of going in that direction. Then he'd start another campaign. New enemies were decried and persecuted. The imprisoned survivors of the earlier campaigns might be turned loose and rehabilitated, while their earlier persecutors would suddenly become the new focus of Mao's denunciations.[2]

The first salvo was the Suppression of Counterrevolutionaries campaign (October 1950–October 1951), which wiped out any trace of the old Nationalist regime. "Bandits" and "spies" were hunted down—usually anyone who had actively supported the previous regime. Retired sympathizers of the Nationalists were dragged out to be publicly humiliated, beaten, or exiled. By May 9, 1951, an internal report noted proudly that the population had been cowed: "rumour-mongering [has] died down and social order stabilised."[3] All of the weapons that had piled up over a quarter century of civil war were collected, and it was forbidden for a person to change residence without a permit. Organized crime was virtually eliminated as *real* gangsters, pirates, and bandits were killed or imprisoned with little formality.

The simultaneous Agrarian Reform campaign saw the destruction of the landlord class. The peasants were encouraged to seize land and attack the owners. Mao preferred public killings for maximum impact. "A young half-Chinese woman from Britain witnessed one rally in the centre of Peking, when some 200 people were paraded and then shot in the head so that their brains splattered out onto bystanders."[4] Millions of prisoners were put to work in the newly established *laogai* ("reform through labor") camps. Most authorities estimate that these first purges killed between 1 and 3 million people.

The Three-Antis campaign (late 1951–May 1953) aimed to eliminate the misuse of government money by civil servants. The watchwords were anti-corruption, anti-waste, and anti-bureaucratism. Almost 4 million government officials were hauled in and roughly interrogated. Mao set a quota that at least 10,000 embezzlers were to be sentenced to death, but it turned out that he overestimated the degree of corruption in the old regime, and relatively few big embezzlers were uncovered. In any case, the underlying purpose of the campaign was to put government finances firmly under Mao's control, and it worked.

Next came the Five-Antis campaign (January 1952–May 1953). Businessmen were collectively accused of undermining the fiscal integrity of the state, as the Communists proceeded to stamp out (first anti) tax evasion, (second) bribery, (third) cheating in government contracts, (fourth) thefts of economic intelligence, and (fifth) stealing of state assets. At first businessmen were pulled into group criticism sessions during which they were encouraged to confess their crimes and denounce their rivals. Then workers committees paraded with drums and banners to encourage more action. The businessmen were hauled into public meetings to be yelled at some more. Although few were killed outright, the humiliation, abuse, and harassment drove many to suicide.

The Hundred Flowers Campaign

In February 1956, three years after Stalin died, the new leader of the Soviet Union, Nikita Khrushchev, was secure enough in power to denounce Stalinist repression. Mao decided to do him one better. In February 1957, he openly invited criticism of the party and the direction that society was heading. "Let a hundred flowers bloom," he announced, calling for an outpouring of new ideas. Mao wanted to let China's intellectuals discuss policy. He encouraged his people to speak their mind. He wanted suggestions and criticism. Really. It wasn't a trick. Wall posters criticizing the regime were pasted up—and they stayed up. After a few cautious voices spoke up without punishment, people slowly came to realize that maybe Mao meant it. They began to offer a few suggestions. Soon, all of the gripes that people had been keeping bottled up for eight years erupted.[5]

Or maybe it *was* a trick. Mao considered Khrushchev weak for opening Soviet society and dragging Stalin's good name through the mud. In April, Mao described to a select few, "Intellectuals are beginning to . . . change their mood from cautious to more open. . . . One day punishment will come down on their heads. . . . We want them to speak out. You must stiffen your scalps and let them attack! . . . Let all those ox devils and snake demons . . . curse us for a few months." As he later explained, "How can we catch the snake if we don't let them out of their lairs? We wanted those sons-of-turtles to wriggle out and sing and fart . . . that way we can catch them."[6] Mao's critics say this was his diabolical plan all along; Mao's defenders explain that he started with honest intentions, but was surprised, insulted, and, frankly, a little bit hurt when people started picking on him, so he had them all punished (I don't know why this is better than "he planned it all along").[7]

The hundred flowers were hit by a weed whacker when the Anti-Rightist campaign began in June 1957. Now that the government knew exactly who the malcontents were, the intellectual class could be purged. Scientists, of course—especially nuclear scientists— were exempt. But anyone else who had spoken out was shipped to labor camps to chop timber or mine radioactive ores.

Mao also used the Anti-Rightist campaign to weaken members of his inner circle who were getting dangerously well established. He encouraged fanatics to challenge the loyalty of moderates in the upper echelons of power. Under pressure bubbling up from below, old allies like Zhou Enlai and Liu Shaoqi were forced to abase themselves in front of the Party Congress. All their friends denied them, and their allies denounced them. Although they weren't purged, they were broken, and Mao would be safe from their maneuvering for a while.

Lifestyle

Mao made the most of being the master of a quarter of mankind. He had squads of beautiful women picked and assigned for his pleasure. He had over fifty rural villas built. Entire mountains and lakefronts were fenced off for his personal enjoyment. It became customary for every important city to have an opulent estate set aside specifically for his use.[8]

Mao was notoriously unhygienic. He preferred old, comfortable clothes, eventually imposing his fashion on the entire country. He never brushed his teeth but instead rinsed his mouth with tea and chewed the leaves. His teeth were covered with a green film, and slightly loose, wobbling in gums that often oozed with infection. It's been said that he did not have a bath for a quarter century. "A waste of time," he called it. Instead, he would have a servant rub him down with a hot towel. His failure to bathe wasn't an aversion to water; Mao loved swimming, even in the floating sewage of dangerously polluted rivers. He especially enjoyed swimming in private pools with his squads of naked pleasure women.[9]

Foreign Policy

By 1953 almost all non-Soviet foreigners had been cleared out of China. Missionaries were driven away. Doctors and engineers fled. Teachers, reporters, and merchants were expelled. Tourists didn't dare. For the next twenty years, China would be closed to foreign scrutiny.

Mao was a loose cannon on the world stage. Until the 1970s, the United Nations and the West continued to recognize the fugitive Nationalist government on Taiwan as the legitimate government of China. This wasn't just stubbornness on the part of the capitalists. A British offer to recognize the People's Republic was turned down flat because the United Kingdom refused to completely break relations with Taiwan.[10]

In 1950, Mao threw a couple of million troops into the Korean War against the United Nations, United States, and United Kingdom, making this the last open war between great powers in history (so far). Among the hundreds of thousands of Chinese killed was one of Mao's sons.[11] After Stalin died in 1953, Mao began to drift away from the Communist bloc as well. In 1964, after an immense research effort that gobbled up economic resources, the Chinese exploded an atomic bomb. In 1969, China fought a small border war with the Soviets. Faced with the first open war ever fought between nuclear powers, the world held its breath until the fighting safely ended with no one nuked.

The upshot of all of this was that for many turbulent years, the most populous country on earth was on the boil, removed from the world, a secret, xenophobic, and fanatic nation armed with the most powerful weapons known to man.

Great Leap Forward

Beginning in 1958, Mao tried to instantly overtake the industrial output of the rest of the world by fiat. He assured worried advisers that China had enough food—more than enough—too much, really—so peasants could easily be reassigned to work in the factories.

Communist theory didn't trust peasants. They were considered too backward to understand the historic forces at work in a revolution, and too timid to throw off their chains. Turning them into proper industrial proles would deepen the revolution.

Mao consolidated farming villages into giant communes. All private land, animals, houses, and trees had to be surrendered to the commune. A family's house could be dismantled for parts if necessary. Residents had to eat in communal canteens rather than at home. The entire population of China was made to wear the drab, baggy Mao uniforms that hid all individuality. For a while, Mao tried to break up families and make the whole nation live in barracks sorted by age and gender.

Because Mao believed that iron and steel production figures were the true measure of a nation's strength, he decreed that all of the people should make steel and double the national output in a year. If there was no factory on hand, they should smelt metal at home. To meet arbitrary quotas of steel production, communes gathered metal tools, cooking utensils, hair clips, and door handles to be melted down. By this massive effort, steel production was pushed up from 5.3 million tons to 10.7 million tons for one year, but only the steel mills already in existence had produced anything that could be put to use. Three million tons of the new homemade steel was unusable.[12]

This massive urbanization pulled 90 million peasants off the farms, stripping the land not just of its workforce but also of its experience and folk wisdom.[13] Generations of learning how to work the land disappeared, while ideologues in Beijing dictated farm policy. The amount of acreage under cultivation fell along with the number of farmers. Then a drought hit.

The combination created the worst famine in history, in which tens of millions of people died. Grain production dropped from 200 million tons in 1958 to 144 million in 1960. The number of pigs fell by 48 percent between 1957 and 1961. People scrounged meals from apricot pits, rice husks, and corn cobs, while Beijing refused to admit that anything was wrong. To prove to the world that the Great Leap was a success, China exported almost 5 million tons of grain in 1959.[14]

Was the famine really Mao's fault? Was it malice, hard-hearted negligence, or just carelessness that killed 30 million people? Admittedly, none of these reasons will earn him a satisfactory job performance evaluation, but it makes a difference as to whether historians list him among the ten most evil people of history, or merely among the ten most incompetent.

Maurice Meisner: "Mao Zedong, the main author of the Great Leap, obviously bears the greatest moral and social responsibility for the human disaster from the adventure. But this does not make Mao a mass murderer on the order of Hitler and Stalin, as it is now the fashion to portray him. . . . There is a vast moral difference between unintended and unforeseen consequences of political actions . . . and deliberate and willful genocide."[15]

Amartya Sen: "The particular fact that China . . . experienced a gigantic famine during 1958-61 . . . had a good deal to do with the lack of press freedom and the absence of a political opposition. The disastrous policies that had paved the way of the famine were not changed for three years as the famine raged on, and this was made possible by the near total suppression of news about the famine and the total absence of media criticism of what was then happening in China."[16]

Jung Chang and John Halliday: "The four-year Leap was a monumental waste of both natural resources and human effort, unique in scale in the history of the world. One big difference between other wasteful and inefficient regimes and Mao's is that most predatory regimes have robbed their populations after relatively low-intensity labour, and less systematically, but Mao first worked everyone to the bone unrelentingly, then took everything—and then squandered it."[17]

The shoddiness of the Great Leap Forward continued to kill many years after it was stopped. A massive network of poorly planned and badly built dams and reservoirs was thrown together on the rivers in Henan Province in 1961. An engineer who criticized the design and construction of this system was purged as a "right-wing opportunist." Then in August 1975, heavy rains overflowed the two principal reservoirs. As the rising waters rushed along the river channel, the entire network of sixty-two dams failed. Either 85,000 (officially) or 230,000 (unofficially) people died in this disaster.[18]

Tibet

Although the former nation of Tibet had been occupied immediately after the Chinese Civil War in 1950, the native culture was left largely untouched until March 1959, when the famine and confiscations during the Great Leap Forward sparked nationalist riots in the capital city of Lhasa. The Chinese troops who moved in to crush the insurgents had orders to eradicate any focus of Tibetan nationalism. The Chinese demolished countless temples and systematically destroyed statues, paintings, and books.

Many centuries of pristine history were erased in just a few years. Of the 2,500 monasteries in Tibet before 1959, only 70 were left two years later. The number of monks and nuns fell from 100,000 to 7,000, but only 10,000 of the missing escaped safely abroad. As resistance was ground down, countless thousands of Tibetans died at Chinese hands.[19] The population of Tibet plunged from 2.8 million in 1953 to 2.5 million in 1964.[20]

Great Proletarian Cultural Revolution

The failure of the Great Leap Forward broke Mao's iron grip on the government and dealt the moderates a stronger hand. Mao was eased out of real power and into a figurehead position, while the important posts were divvied out to various moderates. Liu Shaoqi became head of state, and Deng Xiaoping, party chairman. Rather than accept this uninvited retirement, Mao used the one weapon still left to him—his spiritual hold over the Chinese people. Unleashing a new wave of revolutionary enthusiasm could drive the moderates from power. Because the main centers of power had turned against him, he relied on his fourth and final wife, Jiang Qing, and her circle of friends. Among the most important was Lin Biao, head of the army.[21]

The opening shot of the Cultural Revolution was small and tentative. In November 1965, a literary critic trashed a popular play that contained an obvious satire of Mao in the guise of a Ming emperor.[22] Within six months wall posters in the big cities had denounced all of the major moderates in China. With the party apparatus in the hands of the moderates, Mao stirred up ideological cadres of students to do his dirty work. He himself stayed aloof from the struggles.

The first recorded death by torture was on August 5, 1966. A swarm of students denounced and set upon the headmistress of a prestigious girls school for important government daughters. They kicked and trampled her, forced her to carry bricks until she collapsed, and finally beat her with belts and sticks as she lay dying.[23]

Two weeks later, Mao dressed in his army uniform for the first time since the civil war and stood atop Tiananmen gate to review a parade of the new organization of enthusiastic students, the Red Guards. Later that week, the Red Guards hauled thirty of the nation's best-known writers, musicians, and artists into a library to scold and beat them while books, art, and other cultural artifacts were burned in a bonfire.

In Beijing alone, during August and September, thirty-four thousand homes were raided. Old manuscripts were burned, paintings slashed, musical instruments smashed. Some 1,800 people were beaten or tortured to death, and before it was all over, five thousand of the city's seven thousand registered historical monuments were destroyed.[24]

The Red Guards were encouraged to run amok during the Cultural Revolution, destroying all vestiges of the forbidden past, waving the little red book of Mao's quotations that everyone in China was required to buy. Wrong thinkers were dragged out and paraded through the streets in dunce caps. Any trace of Western influence or Confucian tradition was to be eradicated.[25] Men were beaten for merely owning neckties.[26]

In January 1967, the minister of coal became the first senior official in China to be tortured to death. He was sliced, beaten, and smashed against a concrete floor. China's head of state, Liu Shaoqi, and his wife were publicly beaten and tortured in an auditorium full of screaming Red Guards, and later the husband was killed in prison. Two of their children were also killed. Deng Xiaoping was sent to a labor camp. Zhou Enlai survived the purges only because he had remained friends with Mao's wife, Jiang Qing, when she was out of favor in the 1950s.[27]

In the south Chinese province of Guangxi, fanatic mobs tore apart and ate at least a hundred enemies of the state. Cafeterias displayed bodies on meat hooks and fed them to workers. Students killed, cooked, and ate their principals.[28]

One study has suggested that the most fanatic Red Guards were the children of previously purged middle-class parents. Whether they were trying to prove their loyalty or to get some payback is anyone's guess—probably a little of both. As a rule, however, entire families were dragged out and punished for any crimes pinned on the head of the household.

Mao began to rein in the forces of destruction after 1968. As with so many of his schemes, it became obvious after a couple of years that the Cultural Revolution was undermining China's viability. Because most of China's schools were shut down during the Cultural Revolution, an entire generation would enter adulthood distinctly undereducated. Now that the Red Guards had successfully broken the moderates, it was time to break the Red Guards. They were dispersed into the countryside, to work on the farms and reinvigorate their working-class identities. It was a successful cover story that served to dilute the concentrated power of the guards. Red Guards who tried to stay behind in the cities were then hunted down and killed by Lin Biao's soldiers.[29]

Sunset

Although Lin Biao was acknowledged to be Mao's eventual successor, there came a time in the early 1970s when outside observers realized that they hadn't seen him in a while. It was nearly a year before the Chinese government offered a terse explanation and a few unhelpful photographs.

Apparently Mao felt that Lin was becoming a bit impatient about waiting for him to die of natural causes. Mutual mistrust escalated, and by 1971, Lin sensed that the boss was about to tack right again. He planned a coup, but the plot was discovered—possibly by Mao's wife, a prominent radical who moved in the same circles as Lin but stood to lose her privileges if her husband were deposed. As Lin was trying to flee to Russia, his plane crashed before he got there, conveniently killing his entire family and entourage.[30] Maybe it was an accident; maybe not.

With the radical faction tarnished by Lin's treachery, Zhou Enlai's moderates made a comeback. The surviving moderates were gradually released from their labor camps, washed off, fattened up, and returned to positions of power. The most notable among them was Deng Xiaoping, who would eventually become leader of China during its de-Communization phase in the 1980s and 1990s. The radical faction, now under the leadership of Mao's wife, Jiang Qing, lost its primacy, but they were still safe as long as Mao was alive. Shortly after his death, however, they would be jailed as the notorious Gang of Four.

By the early 1970s, old age had caught up with Mao. During his dotage, he withdrew from the public eye, and his very existence came to be doubted unless he was periodically hauled out and displayed for the cameras. His regime coasted along for a couple of years waiting for him to die. He finally obliged in 1976.

Death Toll

No one will know for sure until the People's Republic falls and its archives become available, but the consensus is that Mao's rule was responsible for tens of millions of deaths. The 1971 Walker Report to the U.S. Congress guessed that some 32 to 59.5 million people were killed under the People's Republic.[31] In 1997, the *Black Book of Communism* estimated 65 million deaths under Mao.[32] In *Mao: The Unknown Story*, Jung Chang and John Halliday put the total at 70 million.[33] Mao's defenders (and he has them) will point out that these three sources are hardly unbiased, which is true, but obviously many reasonable people consider high death tolls quite plausible.

The death tolls of specific mass dyings are also uncertain:

- The estimates of the number of political enemies killed during the first purges after taking power are scattered, but most fall between 1 and 3 million.[34]
- Most of the excess deaths under Mao were caused by hunger during the Great Leap Forward. Jasper Becker cites several studies that put the total number of famine deaths anywhere from 19 to 46 million, but he singles out Judith Banister's 30 million as "the most reliable estimate we have."[35]
- The number killed during the Cultural Revolution is a pure guess, with at least one secondhand estimate I've seen reaching 20 million.[36] Most commentators, however, suggest between half a million to a couple of million deaths.[37]
- Just adding the number of deaths from these three episodes gives a plausible death toll ranging from 20.5 million to 51 million, most likely something in the neighborhood of 33 million.

These first purges, the Great Leap Forward, and the Cultural Revolution represent the three peaks in the death rate under Mao, but how many died in the unexceptional day-to-day tyranny of his rule? Guesses for the number of deaths in labor camps have ranged from 15 million (Harry Wu)[38] to 20 million (Jean-Louise Margolin)[39] to 27 million (Jung

Chang and John Halliday),[40] but these are largely based on presumed camp populations and presumed annual death rates extrapolated from small anecdotal samples. That's too many guesses in a row to instill confidence. Realistically, the annual death rate of everyday repression probably did not exceed the annual death rate of the really, really bad years during the first purges (1 to 2 million in four years?) and the Cultural Revolution (also 1 to 2 million in four years?). That means we should expect considerably fewer than a half-million people to have been killed in each slow year, giving us, at most, 9 million additional deaths not associated with the 1.5 to 5 million killed during the major movements listed above.

In short, the best guess would be 30 million deaths from the famine, plus maybe 3 to 4 million executed, massacred, driven to suicide, or dying in prison during the big movements, and perhaps twice that to cover the lesser purges and camp deaths—a total of around 40 million.

KOREAN WAR

Death toll: 3 million soldiers and civilians[1]
Rank: 30
Type: ideological civil war
Broad dividing line: Communists vs. capitalists
Time frame: 1950–53
Location: Korea
Major state participant: United States
Major quasi-state participants: Democratic People's Republic of Korea (North), People's Republic of China, Republic of Korea (South), and United Nations
Minor state participants: Australia, Belgium, Canada, Columbia, Ethiopia, France, Greece, Netherlands, Philippines, the Soviet Union, Thailand, Turkey, and the United Kingdom lost soldiers in the war.
Who usually gets the most blame: North Korea. (Lately there's been an effort to spread some of the blame to South Korea, but since the entire world in the form of the UN supported that side, it's a little late to be changing our minds.)
Another damn: superpower ground war in Asia

Split

World War II ended with the Soviet army in Manchuria, poised to take over the entire Japanese colony of Korea, but the Americans insisted on joint occupation instead, so the victors partitioned the peninsula along the 38th parallel into Soviet and American zones. In each one, the sponsoring powers installed compliant puppets to create a nation in their image.

The Soviets had kept Kim Il-sung tucked away in Siberia for just such an occasion. Kim had led Korean partisans against the Japanese occupiers from 1932 until 1941, when he fled to Russia. He returned to Korea with the Soviet occupation forces as a major in the Red Army.

For the southern half, the Americans brought in Syngman Rhee, a Christian Korean with a PhD from Princeton. Every post-colonial founding father needs a prison sentence on his record to foster his credibility, and luckily Rhee had been jailed in 1897 for leading demonstrations against the Japanese. After his life sentence was revoked during a general amnesty in 1904, he went to school in America but was eventually exiled from Korea forever in 1912. During a 1919 uprising against Japan, he had been proclaimed president of the Korean government-in-exile, but the uprising failed, so he never got to exercise his authority.

Cheju

Elections in the southern Republic of Korea (ROK) were scheduled for May 1948. They were expected to be less than fair and to confirm Rhee as president. As rightists fled from Communist north to capitalist south, tilting the vote further in favor of Rhee, leftists took to the streets to protest the dismemberment of Korea. Because of unrest, the island of Cheju, a stronghold of the South Korean Labor Party, was not going to be included in the May elections, further weakening the left wing in the south. Tempers boiled. Police fired on protesters in Cheju. On April 3, rebels retaliated with a raid on the local police station, killing 50 officers. The island descended deeper into chaos.

Rhee sent troops, police, paramilitaries, and thugs to Cheju to restore order by any means. They hauled away dissidents in the dead of night, burned villages, raped girls, and left unburied bodies on the beaches. By the time it was all over, maybe 60,000 people—a fifth of the island's residents—had been killed.[2] The rest were hiding in caves, nursing wounds, mourning relatives, and having nightmares.

The superpowers were only marginally involved in Cheju. For the most part, the Americans had left the response to the South Korean government. As native governments fell into place, the Soviets withdrew their occupation forces in late 1948, and the Americans pulled out early the next year.

In North Korea, Kim Il-sung had hoped that the Cheju uprising would spread and drive Rhee from power. When that didn't happen, the Communists had to do it the hard way.

Attack

The two Koreas had been trading border raids since 1948, but both their sponsoring powers tried to keep these from escalating to civil war. In fact, the Americans had deliberately avoided giving too many heavy weapons to the ROK in order to prevent Rhee from invading the North. Neither the Soviets nor the Americans wanted the ultimate conflict for the future of civilization to be fought here. Their eyes were on Europe instead.

Kim Il-sung, however, knew that his best chance was now. A few years of peace would only stabilize and strengthen South Korea. On a visit to Moscow, Kim begged Stalin for permission, but Stalin hesitated; he wanted Mao's opinion before he agreed to anything. Kim hurried to Beijing and told Mao that Dad said it's okay with him if it's okay with you, Mom. (Not his exact words.) Mao approved.[3]

The attack by 120,000 North Korean troops across the 38th parallel on June 25, 1950, took the world by surprise. The South Korean army crumbled and fled in disorder. At first, it was assumed that the Americans would not consider the defense of South Korea to be in their vital interests and would sit this one out, but President Harry Truman surprised everyone by declaring his intention to defend South Korea.

American troops were rushed over from their occupation duties in Japan and thrown into the melee. These first units were quickly chewed up and sent reeling southward. The American commanders counted an action successful if their soldiers delayed the enemy and then retreated without abandoning their heavy weapons and wounded. That was rare enough; actually stopping the North Koreans was beyond their abilities.[4]

Truman asked the United Nations to authorize international intervention. As luck would have it, this followed almost immediately on the heels of the Chinese Civil War (ended 1949), and the Soviet Union was boycotting the UN over which Chinese government deserved a seat at the table. This meant the Soviets weren't there to exercise their veto when the UN authorized a police action to stop North Korea's invasion.

Just ahead of the North Korean onslaught, South Korean soldiers and police hurriedly rounded up and shot as many leftists and dissidents as they could find rather than leave them behind to reinforce and assist the invaders. Perhaps 1,000 were killed in Suwon, 4,000 in Taejon, and as many as 10,000 in Pusan.[5] Then the North Koreans arrived and massacred class enemies and community leaders who might become the focus of resistance to Communist rule. The combined result was that any South Korean known to have opinions, education, property, or skills was liable to be shot by one side or the other.

As rumors of massacres spread, up to 2 million refugees fled the advancing battle front. Communist infiltrators sometimes blended into these columns of civilian refugees in order to sneak close enough to enemy troops to spring an ambush, so the Americans soon refused to let refugees cross into their lines. During the chaotic retreat south, American troops would warn off approaching civilians with a spray of machine-gun fire. Sometimes they fired into the air, sometimes into the dirt, sometimes into the crowd. American fighter pilots who couldn't tell one bunch of Koreans from another indiscriminately strafed every crowd they spotted.

The worst known incident occurred at No Gun Ri when hundreds of refugees were camped under a bridge just beyond American lines for several days, until the order came down to kill them all. The Americans raked the crowd with machine-gun fire until everyone stopped moving. Some 300 men, women, and children were killed that day.

The South Korean army was driven back to a last line of defense around the port of Pusan (now Busan) at the very tip of the peninsula, which held desperately against all of the Communist attacks. The North Koreans had lost heavily in their advance and were not able to push the southerners out of their last stronghold. The Communists quickly conscripted all of the young men in the captured territory—including ROK prisoners of war—but it would take awhile to train them.

Counterattack

When the front finally stabilized around the Pusan Perimeter, American planners turned to the problem of restoring the nation of South Korea. In September 1950, American troops under General Douglas MacArthur landed an amphibious assault force at Inchon, the port of Seoul. This put them behind the North Korean army and within striking distance of their supply line. As UN forces also attacked out of Pusan, the Communists scrambled back in panic, leaving tens of thousands of prisoners. The Americans chased the remnant back across the 38th parallel.

The war could have ended here, four months after it had started, but intelligence reported that 30,000 northern troops had escaped the debacle in the south, and another 30,000 recruits were almost ready for deployment.[6] MacArthur wanted to continue across the 38th parallel and destroy the North Korean army once and for all. He assured President Truman that liberating North Korea from the clutches of the Communists would be no problem. With Truman's cautious permission, MacArthur chased the retreating army beyond the old border, out of the northern capital of Pyongyang, and eventually up to the Yalu River, which separated Korea from China.

Upon retaking Seoul, the South Koreans and Americans found a lot of bodies—prisoners of war, students, police, civil servants, businessmen, teachers—often lined up in ditches with their hands bound behind them with barbed wire. Similar discoveries followed the reoccupation of almost every South Korean community, but we still aren't certain who bears the most blame. The retreating southerners may have killed as many as 100,000 political prisoners on the left, and the ROK government estimated that the conquering northerners killed 26,000 class enemies (and later re-estimated the number to be 129,000) to clear the way for Communist rule.[7]

The city of Taejon, for example, suffered dual massacres—the July massacre at the hands of the South Koreans, and the September massacre at the hands of the North Koreans. These two events killed some 5,000 to 7,500 civilians in Taejon, but the United States blamed these killings entirely on the North, and the North blamed them entirely on the South. Regardless of who killed the most civilians, the forty-two American prisoners of war found tied up and shot at Taejon were certainly the work of the North Koreans.

The retreat by the Communists added to the misery of the prisoners they had taken. North Koreans usually killed foreign prisoners unless they could be used for propaganda purposes, and in October 1950, as the fall of Pyongyang loomed, the North Koreans packed their American prisoners onto trains to be moved north. Dozens died of cold and hunger during the five-day ride, and sixty-eight were taken off the train and shot at the Sunchon tunnel in the far north. All in all, three out of every eight Americans taken captive in the war died in Communist hands.[8]

South Korean troops quickly began killing suspected collaborators in the newly reoc-cupied territories. Although the American high command usually ignored these actions, the British eventually intervened. "On Dec. 7, in occupied North Korea, British officers saved 21 civilians lined up to be shot, by threatening to shoot the South Korean offi-cer responsible. Later that month, British troops seized 'Execution Hill,' outside Seoul, to block further mass killings there."[9]

Counter-counterattack

An American army pushing toward their border worried the Communist Chinese. Mao knew there was strong sentiment in the West for crossing the Yalu River and taking care of China while they were at it, so he began shipping troops into Korea to stiffen the remnants of the North Korean army. The first waves of these troops were fanatically committed young volunteers who had known nothing but war in their lifetimes. They had grown up in the Communist enclaves that Mao had defended from the Japanese, and they had wrested control of China from Chiang Kai-shek.[10]

Within a week, 100,000 Chinese veterans of the People's Liberation Army managed to slip across the border undetected by Western intelligence. The first hint that the war had changed came when American and ROK forward units were overrun and chased into panicky flight by fresh soldiers wearing strange quilted uniforms. Then a few of these mystery troops began to show up among the North Korean prisoners, speaking an odd tonal language that confused and worried the first interrogators. Pretty soon, the Chinese forces had massed enough to counterattack in force, driving the Americans south again.[11]

The northernmost UN forces pulled back to the east coast to be evacuated by sea, while the rest began the long march south. The Chinese attackers were relentless and num-berless. The bitter cold destroyed soldiers' fingers and toes and froze the blood in wounds. In late November, the Chosin Reservoir and the swarming enemy blocked the American retreat in the far north and center of the peninsula. Twenty thousand American marines had to run a gauntlet of 200,000 Chinese; however, the previous months of combat had taught the Americans how to successfully withdraw from a bad situation. The Americans grimly fought their way out of the pocket and escaped south, orderly and largely intact—morally if not physically.

The American field commanders tried to stabilize the line near the old border on the 38th parallel, but the necessary reinforcements were being held up. Washington wor-ried that the Chinese intervention in Korea was just the first stage in an all-out Commu-nist assault across the globe. Although the United States was hastily boosting its military strength by calling up reserves and expanding the draft, the new troops were being held in reserve against possible Soviet invasions of Germany, Turkey, or Iran, rather than being sent to Korea.*

Washington even considered following MacArthur's suggestion of taking the war directly against China with a naval blockade, air strikes, and an attack from Taiwan by the Nationalist army. After much debate, the idea was dropped. President Truman certainly didn't want to expand a war the Americans were still losing. Unfortunately, MacArthur continued to push this plan in public, undermining Truman's effort to wrap up the war quickly and favorably by diplomacy. The war of words escalated until finally Truman fired MacArthur.

In the meantime, a Communist assault on New Year's Eve pushed across the old border and Seoul fell again. The Americans secretly resolved to abandon the peninsula entirely if they found themselves backed up to Pusan again. Finally, after taking half of South Korea, the Communists overreached their supply line and foundered. American patrols soon discovered how disorganized the enemy was. The United States counterattacked, inflicting heavy casualties.[12]

Stalemate

The American counter-counter-counterattack pushed the front back to the 38th parallel and then across again, until the Communists stiffened, stopped, planned, and counter-counter-counter-counterattacked. The front line eventually settled down near the old border again.

In a year of fighting, the front line had rolled up and down Korea like a windshield wiper, even sweeping the entire peninsula once from Pusan to the Yalu, so it's no surprise that there were horrendous collateral casualties. No one will ever know for sure, but somewhere around 2 million civilians died in the war, most by general hardship rather than actual malice.

It took a few months of little battles for the Americans to fine-tune the new front line, code-named Kansas-Wyoming, in their favor. This was mostly a matter of taking the

---

* Although most people didn't know it at the time, Americans were already fighting the Soviets in the air. Russian pilots were getting combat experience and testing new equipment over North Korea in jets with Chinese markings, but they had strict orders not to get shot down over UN territory. Stalin did not want anyone to find proof of Soviet involvement in the wreckage of a downed aircraft. For that matter, neither did the Americans, who had their suspicions. If it became widely known that the two superpowers were already fighting in the air, the Korean conflict could quickly escalate to World War III. (Stanley Sandler, *Korean War: No Victors, No Vanquished* [Lexington: University Press of Kentucky, 1999], p. 185; Carter Malkasian, *The Korean War, 1950–1953* [New York: Rosen Publishing Group, 2009], p. 54)

high ground from entrenched Communists. The last adjustment to the Kansas-Wyoming line was fixed by June 1951, and after that, with the South Koreans holding the tactical advantage all along the line, the UN forces just settled in and waited for diplomacy to do the rest.[13]

Peace negotiations snagged on the question of returning prisoners of war. The West did not want to repeat what had happened after World War II, when reluctant Soviet prisoners held by the Germans were forcibly repatriated, only to be punished as traitors by Stalin. It was found that many prisoners of war held in South Korea were conscripts who did not want to go back into Communist hands. North Korean soldiers were often South Koreans grabbed by the Communists during the northern occupation, and Chinese soldiers were often Nationalists captured by Mao during the Chinese Civil War and now forced to fight for the People's Republic.[14] The United Nations insisted on giving every prisoner the choice of staying. Almost half of the North Koreans in southern hands eventually chose to remain in the South.[15]

The North Koreans stalled as best they could, but after two years of arguing, they accepted that nothing was going to change. All fighting stopped on July 27, 1953, although technically, the war has merely paused, not ended. No peace treaty has ever been signed.

NORTH KOREA

Death toll: 3 million[1]
Rank: 30
Type: Communist dictatorship
Broad dividing line: the state vs. the individual
Time frame: since 1948
Location and major state participant: Democratic People's Republic of Korea
Who usually gets the most blame: Kim Il-sung, Kim Jong-il
Another damn: insane people's republic

Great Leader

Sometimes mankind has a really bad day, like April 15, 1912. On that day, the mortally wounded ocean liner *Titanic* sank into the icy waters of the North Atlantic, taking fifteen hundred passengers to their deaths. Meanwhile, half a world away in Korea, Kim Il-sung was born. Of those two events, the second was probably worse.

Originally named Kim Song Ju, he took the war name Kim Il-sung after a legendary Korean freedom fighter. Kim was one of the few survivors of an army of anti-Japanese guerrillas that had been beaten and driven into the Soviet Union in 1941. After World War II the Soviet conquerors put Kim Il-sung in charge of the northern half of the former Japanese colony (see "Korean War").

Kim was known to his people simply as the "Great Leader," and he is everywhere in North Korea. He watches from murals in subway stations, government buildings, and street corners. Quotations of his, both profound and trivial, are engraved into brass plaques or printed on posters. A sixty-foot statue of Kim towers over the plaza of the Museum of the Revolutions, and children bow before it as they pass, chanting, "Thank you, father."[2]

Kim Il-sung started the policy that required every North Korean over the age of twenty-one to wear a badge with his face on it. Eventually, there were twenty different types of badges, each one denoting the social status of the wearer. Koreans soon learned to recognize the important badges and behave accordingly whenever they encountered a stranger. In due course, a line of badges depicting his son, Kim Jong-il, became acceptable as well.[3]

Hermit Kingdom

We know very little about what's been happening in North Korea these past fifty years. In a country of 23 million, there were only three hundred foreigners as of 2003.[4] North Korea has an estimated 150,000 to 200,000 prisoners at any given time, but until very recently, only a handful escaped the country and told their stories to the Western press. For those who tried but failed, "the police who picked up fugitives held them together by putting wire through the cheeks or noses of these traitors to the nation who had dared to try to leave the fatherland. As soon as they reached their destination they were executed, and their families were sent to labor camps."[5]

North Koreans can get thrown into prison for the most trivial offenses—sitting on a newspaper photo of the president, joking about his tiny size, or idly singing a South Korean pop song they might have heard from a friend, for example. Usually an entire family is punished for the crimes of a single member. Parents are imprisoned for having a rebellious son. Sisters are hauled away when a brother they haven't seen in years is exposed as an enemy of the state. A well-connected model citizen might suddenly be hauled off to jail when a search of old records reveals that his father had committed a political crime many decades earlier.

The classless Communist society is divided into three classes—Central, Undecided, and Hostile—depending on the Communist credentials of one's forebearers. Lucky descendants of a Japanese-era freedom fighter might be granted all of the benefits due the Central class, while the descendants of bankers, landowners, or southerners are kept out of good jobs and the capital city, like all of the scum of the Hostile class. Nearly a quarter of North Koreans are stigmatized as members of the Hostile class, who are only one wrong step away from a labor camp. Most North Koreans, however, fade into the background of the Undecided class, with neither the privilege nor the disgrace of the more notable classes.[6]

The slave labor of political prisoners has become a vital part of the economy. They cut timber, dig mines, and manufacture goods for export and domestic consumption. In exchange, they get a daily ration consisting of perhaps a handful of corn meal, some cabbage leaves, and some salt.

As a Communist state, North Korea forbids the practice of religion, but the philosophy of *juche*—self-reliance—fills the gap. In theory, juche is Marxist humanism that declares that man is the master of his own destiny. In practice, juche means putting Korea first. Koreans can be self-reliant individually by not pestering the state for favors or self-reliant collectively by keeping Korea free from foreign influence. Like a child of divorce watching his parents act strangely, Kim was worried by Stalin's death in 1953 and the subsequent Sino-Soviet split. Since he could no longer trust his giant co-Communists to look out for his best interests, he adopted juche in 1955 to help North Korea stand alone.

Foreign Relations

The phrase "state sponsor of terrorism" has lost a lot of its bite because of overuse, but North Korea really *is* a state sponsor of terrorism. The killing of hated foreigners overseas is planned at the highest levels and executed by trained professionals. Great powers, of course, have always thrown their weight around and meddled in the internal affairs of lesser nations, but it's less common for a pip-squeak country like North Korea to blatantly provoke the rest of the world and dare them to do something about it.

In 1974, North Korea tried to kill South Korean dictator Park Chung Hee, but the assassins killed his wife instead. In 1983, North Korean operatives exploded a bomb at a conference in Rangoon, Burma, intending to kill another president of South Korea. They killed seventeen high officials in the president's entourage, including four cabinet officers, but missed the president. In 1987, another bomb planted by North Korean agents blew up a South Korean airliner, killing all 115 people aboard. Over the years, North Korea has kidnapped hundreds of random, ordinary South Koreans and Japanese. They are imprisoned in the North and forced to teach the subtleties of pop culture to North Korean spies so they can blend into the outside world.

Since punishing North Korea would only reignite the Korean War, the world has had little choice but to ignore these provocations. Juche means that North Korea has few imports or exports that can be stopped, plus they are the world's most militarized country, with a million armed men. Any punitive attack would likely fail and provoke an angry counterattack with screaming Commie hordes swarming over their southern neighbor.

Dear Leader

When the elder Kim died in 1994, his title was boosted to "Eternal Leader," which makes North Korea the only nation on earth whose president is a corpse. The daily operation of the government, however, was put into the hands of his son, Kim Jong-il, the "Dear Leader."

Kim Jong-il was probably born in 1943 in the Soviet Union during his father's exile, but the official story is that he was born at a secret rebel camp on Korea's sacred mountain amid glorious omens. "At the time of his birth there were flashes of lightning and thunder, the iceberg in the pond on Mount Paektu emitted a mysterious sound as it broke, and bright double rainbows rose up," according to an official biography.[7] In 1992 Kim Jong-il's official year of birth was moved to a year earlier so that North Korea could celebrate both his fiftieth birthday and his father's eightieth in the same nationwide gala.

The rest of Kim Jong-il's family died off as he got older. When Jong-il was five, his younger brother Shura drowned while they were both playing in a pond. Their mother died in childbirth a year later, along with the boy she was carrying. Jong-il also had a sister, Kim Pyong-il, but her story and whereabouts are unknown.[8] For some reason, I'm reminded of family life among hyenas, cuckoos, and other unpleasant animals, where the strongest offspring will kill its rival siblings in the nest—not that we can prove anything.

Since Communist theory favors meritocracy over monarchy, it was tricky justifying passing the throne from father to son. The younger Kim was gradually inserted into the leadership through an escalating series of positions in the government—but what he really wanted was to direct. An avid cinephile, Kim collected thousands of films. He even had his agents kidnap a prominent South Korean actress and her film director husband so that they could make wonderful movies for him.

At first, there was some hope that conditions would improve with the passing of the Great Leader. Kim Jong-il had a reputation as a lightweight and a playboy. With luck he would be corruptible and would evolve into a run-of-the-mill dictator, more interested in collecting a harem than in enforcing merciless ideology. Another possibility was that the military would overthrow him, which would deal a wild card on the table but still leave open the possibility that the new boss would prove more flexible than the elder Kim and ease off the totalitarian repression.[9] No one anticipated what really happened, which was that the new Kim would hold onto power and become a clone of his father.

Going Broke

In the original split, the urbanized North got most of the mines, dams, and factories, while the rural South got most of the crops and livestock. In fact, until the 1970s, the industrial economy of North Korea maintained a higher per capita income than did the peasant-heavy economy of South Korea. Then, over the next generation, the South Korean economy took off, producing world-class cars and electronics, crossing the threshold from Third World to First World, while the North Korean economy stagnated in the age of concrete and smokestacks.

The gap grew wider after Communist regimes all over the world collapsed in 1989–92. With fewer Communist trading partners like Russia to prop them up, the North Korean economy shrank by half in the 1990s. The government in Pyongyang, however, puts a special effort into keeping the people ignorant of how bad their life really is. They are told that things are even worse outside North Korea and that they are lucky to be living in a land where the Dear Leader will take care of them. To maintain this fiction, the people are not allowed to have any contact with foreigners. Radio dials are fixed so that they can receive only North Korean stations. All foreign visitors surrender their cell phones at the border and must keep two Korean escorts with them at all times.[10]

North Korean agriculture had been heavily industrialized and subsidized. While it had produced adequate food for decades, the tractors, combines, and harvesters were fueled by cheap gasoline from the Soviet Union. When the new capitalists of the Russian

North Sea

Arctic

German Democratic
Republic
(E. Germany)

Berlin

Baltic Sea

Finland

Barents Sea

Kara Sea

Czechoslovakia

Poland

Hungary

UKRAINE

Yugoslavia

Romania

Kiev

Albania

Bulgaria

UKRAINE S.S.R.

Leningrad
(Saint Petersburg)

Smolensk

Moscow

GULAG

Vorkuta

Norilsk

GULAG

Mediterranean Sea

Black Sea

Gorky
(Nizhny Novgorod)

Union

of Soviet

U R A L S

S I B

GULAG

Sverdlovsk (Yekaterinberg)

Volga

Stalingrad
(Volgagrad)

Kuybyshev (Samara)

Omsk

Novosibirsk

Cyprus

Euphrates

Egypt

*Caspian
Sea*

Iran

*Aral
Sea*

L. Balkash

Nile

Red Sea

Bukhara

P e o p l e'

Afghanistan

Kabul

Pakistan (West)

TIBET

Pakistan
(East)

I n d i a

Arabian Sea

Bay of Bengal

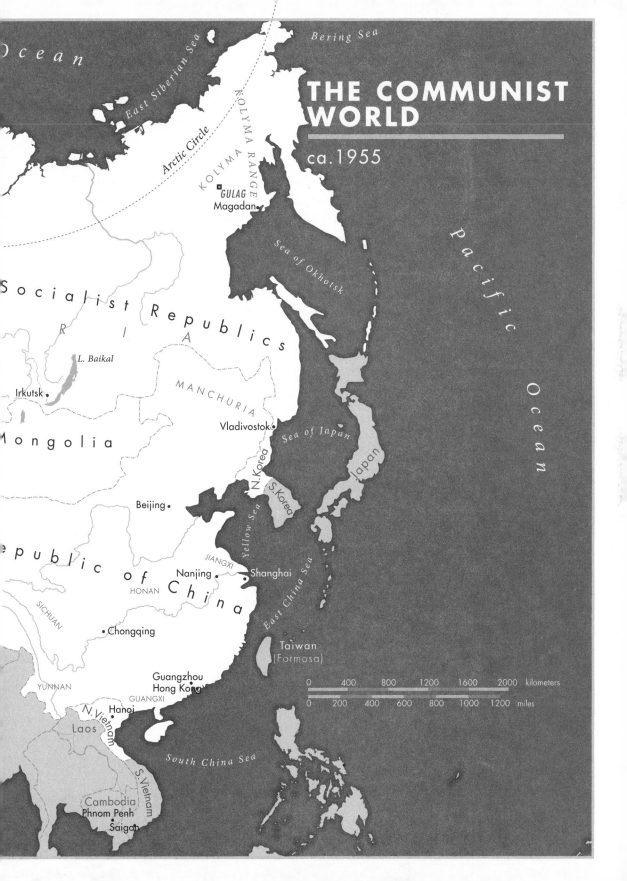

THE COMMUNIST WORLD
ca.1955

Bering Sea

Ocean

East Siberian Sea

Arctic Circle

KOLYMA RANGE

KOLYMA

■ *GULAG*

Magadan•

Sea of Okhotsk

P a c i f i c

S o c i a l i s t   R e p u b l i c s

R   I   A

• *L. Baikal*

Irkutsk•

M A N C H U R I A

Sea of Japan

M o n g o l i a

Vladivostok•

N.Korea

S.Korea

Japan

Beijing•

Yellow Sea

O c e a n

e p u b l i c   o f   C h i n a

JIANGXI

SICHUAN

HONAN

Nanjing•

Shanghai•

East China Sea

•Chongqing

Taiwan
(Formosa)

YUNNAN

Guangzhou•
Hong Kong•

GUANGXI

N.Vietnam

Hanoi•

Laos

South China Sea

S.Vietnam

Cambodia

Phnom Penh•

Saigon•

0	400	800	1200	1600	2000 kilometers

0	200	400	600	800	1000	1200 miles

Federation started letting the free market rather than ideology set prices, North Korean agriculture sputtered to a halt. All it took was one spell of bad weather (heavy rains in 1994) to turn general hardship into a deadly famine that decimated the population over the next few years.[11] Eventually, China picked up the task of subsidizing North Korea, and the famine eased.

North Korea began to pursue nuclear weapons in the mid-1950s, but it was too backward to make much headway quickly; however, persistence paid off, and by the 1990s the North Koreans were closing in on success. Faced with the prospect of yet another insane nuclear power in the world, American President Bill Clinton bought off Kim in 1994. Vital food and fuel imports were sent in exchange for a halt to nuclear activities. The crisis fizzled out, and the world sighed in relief until 2002, when the next American president, George Bush (the younger), took a hard line and cut these subsidies. Kim immediately resumed his nuclear ambitions. Washington thought North Korea was either bluffing or overreaching and largely ignored the threat. After a few years of insisting that they were going to do it—no kidding, they meant it this time—North Korea tested something in 2006 that made a big boom—probably a nuclear weapon, although the evidence is disputed. A more convincing explosion occurred in 2009.

In December 2011, Kim Jong-il's sudden death by heart attack at the age of sixty-nine brought about another toss of the dice over North Korea's future. Because Kim had had a falling out with his eldest son almost a decade earlier, the Korean leadership went to a younger son, Kim Jong-un. He is such a mystery that the most the BBC could report about him is that he "is believed to be in his late twenties" and might be Kim Jong-il's third son.

THE BLACK CHAPTER
OF COMMUNISM

NEVER TRUST ANYONE WHO ARGUES AGAINST COMMUNISM ON THEORY. Here we have one of the greatest social experiments in history failing spectacularly, yet instead of using the obvious, scientific proof that we tried Communism and it doesn't work, some people want to take the long way around and argue property rights and theories of ownership. They obviously don't care whether Communism worked or not; it's the theory of Communism that bothers them, and they'd argue against it even if it had worked perfectly.

So it failed. Is that really a big deal? Dinosaurs and Rome failed, but they flourished successfully far longer than most other species and institutions hope for. Communism lasted longer than fascism, jazz, John Wayne, *Bonanza*, and the American Motors Corporation. Unfortunately, the problem with Communism isn't the mere failure to last forever. The bigger problem is that every Communist regime in history killed huge numbers of its own people. If history had seen only one or two nasty people's republics amid a few decent ones, I might accept that a few bad apples gave the whole movement a bad name, but when death and destruction have followed every single Communist regime ever established, there would seem to be a flaw somewhere in the system.*

Generally speaking, there were five waves of mass killing associated with a Communist regime:

---

* The most benign Communist regime seems to have been Nicaragua. The worst accusations I could find directed against the Sandinista government was that dozens, possibly hundreds, of noncombatant Miskito Indians were killed in a couple of disputed incidents (massacres? battles? deliberate? unauthorized?) in 1981. This is closer to the average for a Latin American country than to the average for a Communist country.

1. It began with a civil war during which Marxist rebels wrested control from a brutal, authoritarian regime. During this first stage of regime change, the Communists were usually preferable to the status quo. They educated. They shared. They provided free medical care. They dispensed real and fair justice when arbitrating disputes. Meanwhile, the dictators they were trying to overthrow were plundering, raping, and selling justice to the highest bidder.

   It's worth noting that Communism, unlike fascism, strict Sharia, and other forms of oppression, has never taken over a free democracy. Voting seems to immunize a society against Communism.

   - Russian Civil War (1918–22): 9,000,000 deaths
   - Chinese Civil War (1927–49): 7,000,000
   - Vietnam War (1959–75): 3,500,000 in Vietnam
   - Yugoslavia (part of World War II, 1940–45) 1,400,000
   - Cambodian Civil War (1970–75): 600,000
   - Nicaragua (1972–79): 30,000
   - Cuba (1955–59): 5,000
   - Rough total: 21 million

2. After the Communist victory, the new bosses executed the power base of the old regime.

   - China (1950–53): 2,000,000
   - Cambodia (1975): 400,000 outright executions[1]
   - Yugoslavia (1945) 175,000[2]
   - Russia (1918–22): 100,000 executions during the Russian Civil War
   - Vietnam (after 1975): 65,000
   - Mongolia (1936–38): 35,000
   - Poland: 30,000[3]
   - Bulgaria: 20,000[4]
   - Cuba (1959–60): 5,000[5]
   - Rough total: 3 million

3. This was eventually followed by a redistribution of the land, relocation of the people, and restructuring of the economy, which usually turned out to be a big mistake and led to mass starvation.

   - China (Great Leap Forward, 1959–62): 30,000,000 famine deaths
   - Soviet Union (1932–33): 7,000,000

- Korea (1995–98): 2,000,000
- Ethiopia: 1,000,000
- Cambodia (1975–79): 800,000[6]
- Rough total: 41 million

4. Then the Communist Party turned on itself, purged the moderates, and focused power into the hands of a single dictator.

- Russia (Great Purge, 1934–38): 7,000,000
- China (Cultural Revolution, 1966–69): 1,000,000
- North Korea (intermittent purges): 100,000[7]
- Ethiopia (Red Terror): 80,000
- Rough total: 8 million

5. As Communist regimes came to power in more countries—particularly in the 1970s—the tables turned, and the world witnessed the outbreak of anti-Communist insurgencies, which would have been considered an oxymoron twenty years earlier.

- Afghanistan (1979–89): 1,500,000
- Mozambique (1975–92): 800,000
- Angola (1975–2002): 600,000
- Nicaragua (1981–90): 30,000
- Hungary (1956): 5,000
- Rough total: 3 million

After the purges had run their course and the first generation of ideologues died off, the average Communist regime settled into a sluggish, corrupt bureaucracy, which slowly loosened its grip on the people and eventually surrendered power without a fight.

Not every Communist regime went through these five stages. Some had simpler histories, and some more complicated. In all regimes, there was also a persistent background level of dying in labor camps and prisons. For those who prefer totals broken down by country, here are reasonable estimates for the number of people who died under Communist regimes from execution, labor camps, famine, ethnic cleansing, and desperate flight in leaky boats:

- China: 40,000,000
- Soviet Union: 20,000,000
- North Korea: 3,000,000
- Ethiopia: 2,000,000

- Cambodia: 1,700,000
- Vietnam: 365,000 (after 1975)
- Yugoslavia: 175,000
- East Germany: 100,000[8]
- Romania: 100,000[9]
- North Vietnam: 50,000 (internally, 1954–75)
- Cuba: 50,000
- Mongolia: 35,000[10]
- Poland: 30,000
- Bulgaria: 20,000
- Czechoslovakia: 11,000[11]
- Albania: 5,000[12]
- Hungary: 5,000
- Rough total: 70 million

(This rough total doesn't include the 20 million killed in the civil wars that brought Communists into power, or the 11 million who died in the proxy wars of the Cold War. Both sides probably share the blame for these to a certain extent. These two categories overlap somewhat, so once the duplicates are weeded out, it seems that some 26 million people died in Communist-inspired wars.)

Considering that the aggregate death toll from Communism probably exceeds the total for World War II, you may wonder why I don't list Communism as Number 1 in my list of horrible things. Mostly it's because I consider each regime unique, and the whole Communist movement is too broad to be counted as one event. If I bundle all Communist regimes together to make a new Number 1, I would have to drop my individual chapters on Mao, Stalin, Pol Pot, and Kim Il-sung.

The End

Contrasting with the abysmal Communist failures in agriculture was its general success in heavy industry. During the era of big manufacturing economies, when the modern world revolved around gigantic projects like dams, power plants, coal mines, and steel mills, the Communists easily mobilized enough labor and resources to catch up with the rich countries of the West. This meant that the urbanites lucky enough to survive the purges and famines found their standards of living and life expectancies steadily improving.[13]

However, once the necessities of life were provided, centrally planned economies proved too inflexible to predict and fulfill the fickle demands for consumer goods. Wasteful surpluses, shoddiness, and shortages resulted. Constant scarcities meant that only the well-connected could acquire goods and services. This bred resentment and cynicism in a system that was supposed to be based on idealism and solidarity. The collapse of Communism was delayed almost a decade because oil exports from the Soviet Union pumped hard cash from the West into the Russian economy after oil prices shot up in the 1970s, but eventually even that wasn't enough. As soon as reformers allowed the people to choose the system they preferred, no one chose to keep the status quo.[14]

ALGERIAN WAR OF INDEPENDENCE

Death toll: 525,000
Rank: 69
Type: colonial revolt
Broad dividing line: French vs. Arabs
Time frame: 1954–62
Location: Algeria
Major state participant: France
Major non-state participants: National Liberation Front (FLN), Secret Army Organization (OAS)
Who usually gets the most blame: France

Setting

In time, most European colonies overseas fell into one of two categories. Either the natives were conveniently wiped out and replaced by Europeans (Australia and New Zealand), or else European settlement never really took root (Nigeria and Burma). When the time came, the first type of colony was easy to set free because those people were just like the folks back home and they could be trusted with self-government. The second type was also easy to set free because those people were totally different, so no one cared what happened to them.

Algeria was in an awkward third category. Enough Europeans had settled there to create the desire for continued French rule, but not enough to make it very likely. There were 1 million Westerners with full civil rights in a population of 9 million Arabs and Berbers who had none. By every measure, the European settlers, the *pied noir*, had the good life. Their wealth averaged ten times that of the natives, and they were taxed at only half the rate of their compatriots back in France. Labor was cheap, and their cities on the Mediterranean coast were every bit as civilized and cultured as the rest of France.

Uprising

In December 1954, Algerian rebels of the National Liberation Front (FLN) attacked military and police targets all over the colony. The uprising intensified and turned cruel very quickly. In August 1955, the FLN inaugurated a new policy of killing French settlers and turncoat Muslims instead of soldiers, hacking apart 123 French civilians at the village of Philippeville. Angry French soldiers immediately retaliated by indiscriminately shooting any Arabs they found in the vicinity.

During the back-and-forth atrocities that erupted, the rebels routinely tortured and mutilated any French soldiers or settlers they captured, often leaving their bodies to be found with their severed genitalia stuffed in their mouths. The FLN especially targeted policemen and their families, which undermined the ability of the French to keep order. In response, the French recruited 150,000 *harkis*, irregular local forces who fought back with as much brutality as the FLN.

After a few years of terrorizing the countryside, the FLN moved into the cities. In 1957, Algerians unleashed terrorist attacks all over the city of Algiers. The French reacted by dropping all restraint and due process, instituting curfews and checkpoints, and imprisoning any suspicious characters. After beating confessions out of them, they summarily executed the most expendable. As many as 3,000 Arabs disappeared while in French custody during the Battle of Algiers.[1]

Between 1957 and 1960, the French government resettled 2 million rural Algerians into fortified camps in order to separate the rebels from their popular support. The French laid mines and built barrier fences along the borders with Tunisia and Morocco to disrupt the supplies and sanctuary that the rebels were getting from the outside world.

Originally most of the soldiers fighting on the French side were members of tough, professional units such as the Foreign Legion or the paratroopers who didn't shrink from a little torture and murder if it got results, got revenge, or at least let them blow off some steam. However, as troop levels rose to 400,000, demands on manpower increased and Paris started sending ordinary conscripts to Algeria. This meant that the general public now began to learn firsthand how savage the war had become, and the French people quickly turned against the conflict.

The bloody stalemate sparked the most dangerous political crisis to hit France since World War II. It was the closest any of the traditional democracies of Western Europe would come to dictatorship in the postwar era. In May 1958, as political support for the war eroded in Paris, hard-liners in the French army attempted a military coup in Algiers. It failed but threw the national government into chaos, and only Charles de Gaulle, retired hero of the Second World War, commanded enough respect to restore order. In June 1958, he was given the power to rule by decree until the crisis passed. Eventually, the French constitution was rewritten to transfer power from the divided and quarrelsome parliament to a strengthened presidency—the Fifth Republic.[2]

While addressing the United Nations in September 1959, de Gaulle uttered the forbidden phrase "self-determination" in reference to Algeria. This outraged the hard-line hawks who insisted that Algeria was, and always would be, an integral part of the French motherland. With de Gaulle openly discussing the possibility of independence, the Secret Army Organization (OAS)—bitter-enders inside the French military—began planning a coup or at least an assassination. Although not one to back away from a fight, de Gaulle grew understandably annoyed at the frequent attempts on his life, and he turned against the war hawks. He realized that France would remain in turmoil as long as the war continued. Since victory was impossible, he cut Algeria lose in July 1962.

Nine hundred thousand French citizens fled Algeria within a few months of independence. Then, after the French were gone, mobs of native Algerians hunted down and slaughtered tens of thousands of their own people who had supported French rule but had been left behind by the defeated French.

Death Toll

The French military lost 17,456 soldiers dead, about 7,000 of whom were colonials or Foreign Legionnaires, not French. According to official French estimates, the FLN lost 141,000 who were killed in action, plus another 12,000 killed in internal purges. A total of 2,788 French civilians were killed.

Officially, the Algerian government claims that more than 1 million Algerians died during the war, but most scholars doubt it. Historians commonly suggest a civilian death toll somewhere between 200,000 and 500,000 Algerians. I split the difference and added it to the 173,000 above. Somewhere in those numbers are the thousands of Algerians (estimated as either 30,000 or 150,000) who were lynched after the war in revenge for helping the French.[3]

WAR IN THE SUDAN

Death toll: 2.6 million (500,000 in the first war,[1] 1.9 million in the second,[2] 200,000 in Darfur[3])
Rank: 35
Type: ethnic civil wars
Broad dividing line: Muslim Arabs of the north vs. pagan and Christian blacks of the south
Time frame: 1955–72, 1983–2005, 2003–present
Location and major state participant: Sudan
Major non-state participant: Sudanese People's Liberation Army
Who usually gets the most blame: Arabs
Another damn: African civil war

AFTER BRITISH TROOPS CONQUERED THE MAHDIST STATE (SEE "MAHDI Revolt"), they set up colonial Sudan with clean borders and a joint Anglo-Egyptian administration. The British Sudan included not only the Arab core along the middle stretch of the Nile River, but also a native black region in the upriver swamps of the Sahel in the south, which had nothing in common with the rest of Sudan except for a history of the Sudanese Arabs raiding it to harvest slaves. Since slavery was now illegal and the British were in charge, it shouldn't matter that these two regions hated each other. The British were around to keep them apart.

The British treated the south like a cultural reserve, and the people here—the Nuba, the Dinka, and so on—had not been overrun by missionaries. Traditional African life-styles stayed strong here, although a Christian minority gave the region a westward slant. While Muslims grudgingly tolerated Christians, they had no similar regard for half-naked pagans.

First Sudanese Civil War (1955–72)

Fast-forward to 1955 when the Sudan was being prepared for independence. These two regions were going to end up in the same country, and it began to look like the new federal government was going to be run mostly by the Arabs, who were Britain's favorite colonials. Protests in the south turned into riots. Shots were fired. A southern military unit was called in to put down the uprising, but it mutinied instead. By the time the British handed the keys to an elected government in 1956, a civil war was already raging.

Why didn't the north just let the south go? Unfortunately, northern Sudan (where most of the people live) is just a precarious strip of farmland along the Nile River in the middle of a vast, uninhabitable desert. The south, on the other hand, has a maze of rivers that feed into the Nile, gold, more farmland, pasture, timber, and water, so naturally the north was reluctant to let the south secede and take all that wealth with it. It got even worse in 1979 when oil reserves were discovered in the south. In addition, the kidnapping and selling of slaves from the south was still a lucrative business—nominally illegal but often unenforced.

The elected government put in place by the departing British was overthrown by Sudan's first military coup in 1958. Democracy of a sort returned to Sudan with a popular uprising in October 1964, and various political parties regrouped and returned to parliament.

The war continued, and by 1969 there were 12,000 government troops in the south fighting 5,000 to 10,000 rebels. Then a 1969 coup put General Jaafar Nimeiri in power, and for the next decade, he ruled about as benignly as any dictator you will find in this part of the world. He shared power and brought opposing factions into the government. The war slowed down, and both sides started negotiating. Finally, the Addis Ababa Agreement stopped the fighting in March 1972 by granting autonomy to the south.

Second Sudanese Civil War (1983–2005)

Sudan had been a Soviet client state for many years, but in 1976, Nimeiri switched to the American side of the Cold War. In 1977, he allowed his political rivals—mostly Muslim fundamentalists—to participate openly in politics. It looked like peace and freedom were just around the corner, but the situation went downhill after that. Nimeiri changed course and became more dictatorial.[4]

In 1983, President Nimeiri declared Sudan a Muslim state under strict Islamic Sharia law, and shortly afterward, he proclaimed a state of emergency and suspended constitutional rights. The south lost much of its autonomy, and Islamic law would now apply to anyone living in the north, regardless of religion. Strikes, riots, and guerrilla activity disrupted the south.

It was hoped that the crisis would defuse in 1985 when a popular coup overthrew Nimeiri. Sharia was rolled back, and civilian rule was restored after reasonably free elections were held in 1986; however, the leader of the Sudanese People's Liberation Army (SPLA), Colonel John Garang, an American-educated Dinka, dismissed the new regime as "the hyena with new clothes" and continued the fight. By 1986, Sudan had 20,000 armed rebels of the SPLA and three quarters of a million refugees to deal with. Even so, a certain level of calm returned to the Sudan for a few years, with multiple political parties and more freedom to bicker than any other African country had.[5]

Then in May 1989 another coup put General Omar al-Bashir into power. He was the frontman for the National Islamic Front, a band of hard-core fanatics under the ideological guidance of Hassan al-Turabi. They blamed the insurgency on Americans and Zionists and refused to negotiate.

Turabi created a frighteningly efficient police state in a country that until then had been no worse than a chaotic kleptocracy. Through all the previous ups and downs, the Sudanese people had been willing and able to express contrary opinions, but now, independent press and trade unions were banned. Dissident voices were cleared out of the military, universities, and judiciary.[6]

In 1991, harsh Sharia punishments like stoning for adultery, flogging for possession of alcohol, and amputation for theft were introduced nationwide, in both north and south. In 1993, the federal government replaced all of the judges in the south with proper Muslims, and moved all of the non-Muslim judges to the north where they would be easier to control. New laws forced southerners to dress like proper Muslims even if they weren't. Converting from Islam to another religion was now a capital crime. In 2000 the government of Khartoum tried to ban women working in public places.

As the fighting intensified, the economy of the south fizzled out. Soon there were no banks, no employment, and no cash. Goods and services circulated only by barter or theft. Life support depended on charity shipments by international agencies.[7] After rebel warlords skimmed off the top, the rest might trickle down to the needy.

In 1999, Bashir (the general) and Turabi (the ideologue) butted heads over who was really in charge of the Sudan. When the dust settled, Turabi ended up in jail on charges of treason while Bashir was reelected president the next year in a rigged election, so that settled that.[8]

After years of stalemate, the warring parties signed a peace treaty in Nairobi in January 2005. Although the south got most of what it wanted on paper, for a few years it looked like the north would renege on the deal. After a cooling-off period, however, the south was allowed to vote itself independent in 2011. The subsequent partition of Sudan represents the first time that a new African nation was not delineated along old colonial boundaries.

Darfur (since 2003)

Just about the time Sudan was wrapping up the civil war in the south, a new war erupted in the west. It began as a small uprising against Arab rule in the province of Darfur, but it expanded into the world's worst humanitarian crisis when Bashir ordered the army to crush the rebels and bring back no prisoners. The army didn't bother to differentiate between combatants and civilians as they systematically eradicated the local African tribes—the Fur people mostly, along with the less numerous Masalit and Zaghawa. Like the rebellious tribes of the south, the targeted groups are black, but, like the government, the Fur, Masalit, and Zaghawa are Muslim.

To avoid blame for the escalating genocide in Darfur, the government withdrew most of its troops and turned the extermination over to local Arab militias called the Janjaweed, whom Khartoum has not-so-secretly kept supplied and funded. The Janjaweed have methodically wiped out African villages, killed the men and children, raped the women, and destroyed or looted all property. Within a couple of years, 200,000 people were dead and two and a half million Africans—almost the entire non-Arab population of Darfur—had been uprooted and driven into refugee camps.[9]

VIETNAM WAR

Death toll: 4.2 million (3.5 million in Vietnam, 600,000 in Cambodia, 62,000 in Laos, not including postwar purges)
Rank: 24
Type: ideological civil war
Broad dividing line: Communists vs. capitalists
Time frame: 1959–75
Location: Southeast Asia
Major state participants: South Vietnam, North Vietnam, United States, Cambodia, Laos
Minor state participants: Australia, Philippines, South Korea, Thailand
Major non-state participants: Viet Cong, Khmer Rouge, Pathet Lao
Who usually gets the most blame: U.S. President Lyndon Johnson
Another damn: superpower ground war in Asia
The unanswerable question everyone asks: How did the world's greatest superpower get beaten by a bunch of second-rate Third Worlders?

Two Vietnams Created

1954: The treaty establishing Vietnam's independence from its French rulers never intended it to remain two distinct countries forever. It was a stopgap measure. Although Communist rebels under Ho Chi Minh had done most of the work driving out the French, there was absolutely no way that the great powers were going to allow a brand new Communist country to emerge unchallenged. As President Eisenhower later wrote, "I have never talked or corresponded with a person knowledgeable in Indochinese affairs who did not agree that had elections been held at the time of the fighting, possibly 80 per cent of the population would have voted for the communist Ho Chi Minh as their leader."[1]

Instead, the West allowed Communist control only in the northern half, at Hanoi, while establishing a traditional constitutional monarchy in the South at Saigon. In the North, the customary Communist killing of class enemies followed, with tens of thousands of landlords and affluent peasants executed. In the South, the emperor was quickly overthrown by a military coup that established the Republic of Viet Nam (RVN), a dictatorship of a Catholic elite under Ngo Dinh Diem. One hundred thousand opponents, including both Communists and "Communists," were rounded up and imprisoned. Elections were promised for later, but you know how that goes.

Diem was neither charismatic nor clever enough to be an effective strongman. Prone to arrogance and nepotism, his closest advisers were his brothers, General Ngo Dinh Nhu and Archbishop Ngo Dinh Thuc. The first lady of the clan was the beautiful and sarcastic Madame Nhu, wife of the general.

A Communist rebellion slowly emerged in the South. During 1959, insurgents assassinated some twelve hundred government officials in South Vietnam. During 1961, four thousand officials were assassinated. Because the really important leaders were heavily guarded, the Communists focused on killing minor civil servants and bystanders. As the insurgency escalated into outright civil war, Saigon developed a plan to herd all loyal peasants into strategic hamlets. Anyone who remained outside would be considered rebels and thus fair game. These hamlets were supposed to be self-sustaining and stockaded, but they were built with conscripted peasant labor, and General Nhu ran many of these hamlets like plantations for his own personal enrichment.

The French had originally invaded Vietnam long ago to defend Christian missionaries, and the Catholic Church held a privileged position in the colony. Even after independence, Diem continued these pro-Christian policies, which increasingly brought him into conflict with the Buddhist majority. An unnecessary ban on banners during a Buddhist holiday celebration provoked the usual round of protests, escalating to beatings, shootings, arrests, murders, and riots—which you'll find in every society under strain—and climaxed with Buddhist monks setting themselves on fire—which is unusual. Madame Nhu was unimpressed and promised to "clap hands at seeing another monk barbecue show."[2]

Finally, in 1963, unhappy elements in the Vietnamese military decided to get rid of President Diem. First they cleared it with their American CIA contacts, and were *not* told to *not* do it, so the coup went forward as planned. Diem and General Nhu were taken prisoner, and for a while it looked like all parties might agree to exile, but that seemed like a lot of trouble, so Diem and Nhu were just shot instead.[3]

The coup created a leadership vacuum in which the government passed through several hands, but a viable strongman in Saigon was not put in place for many years, until Nguyen Van Thieu was elected president in 1967.

The Smell of Napalm in the Morning

In August 1964, two U.S. Navy destroyers snooping around the Gulf of Tonkin reported that they had been attacked by suspicious radar images that were either North Vietnamese torpedoes or fish. An angry American Senate authorized President Lyndon Johnson to use whatever force was necessary to get even.[4]

Johnson waited until he was safely reelected in November before he tried anything. After being told that the Saigon government was on the verge of collapse, Johnson authorized regular bombing raids against North Vietnam and then boosted American ground forces in order to defend the newly established air bases. In April 1965, Johnson committed American combat units to fight alongside the South Vietnamese in offensive operations. The numbers built up until over a half-million Americans were fighting in Vietnam by 1968, almost as many as South Vietnam's 670,000 soldiers.[5]

Two major technological innovations separated the style of fighting in Vietnam from the previous generation of superpower warfare: helicopters and assault rifles.

During the 1950s and 1960s armies began to equip their infantry with assault rifles, which could be fired as either a rifle or a light machine gun. Studies of combat in World War II had shown that most infantry firefights took place at a closer range than previously believed, which meant that soldiers did not need to fire heavy rifle bullets across long distances. Instead infantry could shift to lighter, intermediate-range ammunition. As the soldiers could now carry more cartridges, it was possible to waste ammunition in bursts of automatic fire rather than limiting fire to carefully aimed individual rounds. These same studies had also shown the effectiveness of small squads over larger formations. Small groups bonded more tightly and fought with stronger individual motivation than the large faceless mobs of the past. Assault rifles made up for the lost firepower.

More controversially, studies of World War II had also shown that the combat skills of a frontline soldier reached a peak after a few months of experience, and then went into a steady decline as burnout set in. The U.S. Army decided to rotate all soldiers home after a year in combat, a policy that was widely criticized as creating an incentive for a soldier to avoid risks and survive his year, rather than fighting to victory as the only way out.

Over the previous decade, technology had moved mechanized warfare up into the air. Helicopters proved to be more versatile than earthbound armored vehicles. They circumvented obstacles, fortifications, and obstructive terrain by operating in three dimensions. Helicopter gunships like the Cobra packed rocket launchers, Gatling guns, and cannons, which had earlier been the weapons of tanks. Transport helicopters kept combat troops supplied and reinforced, while medevac helicopters carried away the wounded.

Although the Viet Cong (the southern insurgents) and North Vietnamese (allied troops sent by Hanoi) were supplied by the Soviets and Chinese, they had less advanced weaponry and relied more on surprise to kill or demoralize the Americans. Booby traps and land mines killed and maimed Americans. Infiltration and ambush tactics could bring a brief tactical advantage before the Americans had a chance to bring their heavier firepower to bear. Viet Cong would blend quietly into the civilian population, attack suddenly, and then disappear.

The Communist supply route was as elusive as the Communist soldiers. The Ho Chi Minh Trail slipped around the Demilitarized Zone (DMZ, the border between the Vietnams), through neutral Laos and Cambodia, and into South Vietnam the back way. The Americans tried bombing it but there wasn't anything to hit, just a dirt path somewhere under the jungle canopy.

The American goal was to create a situation where the Communist forces could be exposed to overwhelming firepower and destroyed. To that end, it was necessary to clear civilians, brush, and jungle out of the war zone. Two chemical weapons helped clear vegetation, leaving the guerrillas out in the open to be slaughtered. Napalm, a jellied gasoline, spread sticky flame across a vast field of fire, and Agent Orange, a herbicide defoliant, stripped the trees of their leaves. Obviously, both were dangerous to any human who got in the way.

Americans also tried to establish free-fire zones from which all noncombatants were forcibly evacuated. By 1968, a total of 5 million of the 17 million South Vietnamese had been driven from their villages.[6] In theory, by removing all civilians in the war zone, soldiers on patrol could safely shoot anything that moved without endangering the general population they were supposed to be defending. Aircraft and artillery could pound these areas with the full military might of the world's greatest industrial power, and the only people who would get killed would be the bad guys. Of course, many peasants resisted the idea of abandoning everything they owned so that the Americans could destroy it, so they stayed behind, in harm's way.[7]

Because the Viet Cong couldn't be brought to stand and fight against the superior armaments of the Americans, the war was mostly a matter of relentless patrols. A hint, rumor, or suspicion of a vulnerable Viet Cong base would draw an American search-and-destroy mission. These patrols could just as easily turn out to be false alarms or ambushes as successful missions, and the persistent uncertainty frayed the nerves of the soldiers and made them dangerously jumpy. As military discipline broke down, angry, frustrated American soldiers took to massacring the civilian population in which the guerrillas hid.

In March 1968, the day after losing men to a Viet Cong booby trap near the village of My Lai, a company of American soldiers occupied the town and began pulling civilians from their homes. Almost a hundred villagers were herded into the plaza, where they were gunned down by soldiers. A dozen or so old women were shot in the backs of their heads as they knelt praying at a temple. Still more were lined up and shot along an irrigation ditch. Some villagers survived hidden under fallen bodies.[8] Finally, horrified by what they were seeing as they flew over the town, an American helicopter crew intervened on its own initiative, threatening to fire on the soldiers if the massacre didn't stop. As many as 500 civilians were killed that day.[9]

My Lai wasn't the only mass killing of civilians. In the fall of 1967, a special American unit called Tiger Force was given the job of pacifying a contested territory with almost no oversight. During their months in the field, they racked up over 1,000 registered kills, although many of their victims were clearly not the enemy soldiers they were reported to be. "One soldier kicked out the teeth of executed civilians for their gold fillings. [One private] slit the throat of a prisoner with a hunting knife before scalping him—placing the scalp on the end of a rifle. . . . Two partially blind men found wandering in the valley were escorted to a bend in the Song Ve River and shot to death, records show. Two villagers, including a teenager, were executed because they were not in relocation camps. . . . Platoon members strung the ears on shoe laces to wear around their necks, reports state. There was a period when just about everyone had a necklace of ears. . . . A 13-year-old girl's throat was slashed after she was sexually assaulted, and a young mother was shot to death after soldiers torched her hut."[10] A secret army investigation uncovered eighty-four obvious murders by at least eighteen soldiers, but charges were never brought.

Every bit as ineffectual as the military campaign was the parallel "Hearts and Minds" campaign, during which America shoveled money into Vietnam to build roads, clinics, power plants, and schools. The Americans bullied the Saigon government into land redistribution for the peasants. The expenditure was staggering, the results were impressive, and the effect was nil. In a popular war, these social programs would have been the crowning proof of American benevolence, but when contrasted with the bombing, the massacres, and the relocations, it was cast as a hypocritical attempt to whitewash the horrors.

Both sides operated shadowy programs for assassinating the civilian leadership of the opposition, but most of the victims were small fry or unlucky passersby. Terrorist attacks by the Communists in the 1950s had preceded open war and continued year after year. In 1967, for example, the Viet Cong killed some 6,000 local leaders. The CIA retaliated with the Phoenix program, which coordinated various RVN counterinsurgency programs under one command, and killed anywhere from 20,587 (CIA director's estimate) to 40,000 (Saigon's estimate) suspected civilian leaders and supporters of the Viet Cong with raids deep inside enemy territory. Tens of thousands more were captured and either imprisoned, turned into double agents, or released after paying their captors a suitable bribe.[11]

Tet Offensive

Saigon and Hanoi traditionally arranged a cease-fire during the massively popular Buddhist holiday of Tet; however, on January 31, 1968, Viet Cong infiltrators broke the truce and launched simultaneous surprise attacks against political targets up and down the country, even overrunning the major southern city and old imperial capital of Hue. Their greatest propaganda victory occurred when a handful of Viet Cong infiltrated the grounds of the American embassy in Saigon, even though they were eventually contained and killed. The American base at Khe Sanh in the heart of enemy territory was besieged, but it held against everything the Communists could throw at them.

After retaking Hue, the U.S. and Saigon forces began to discover fresh graves packed with bound civilians, first a few hundred, then a few thousand. During their brief occupation of Hue, the Viet Cong had rounded up anyone with a Western taint—government officials, teachers, doctors, clergy, students—and shot at least 2,800 of them. Another 3,000 missing were never found.

The Tet Offensive was clearly a tactical victory for the Americans. The enemy was slaughtered everywhere they popped up. Half of the 20,000 Communists who attacked Khe Sanh were killed or severely wounded, while the 6,000 defending Americans lost only 200 killed and 850 wounded.[12] In fact, the Viet Cong ceased to be an effective fighting force after Tet, and the war had to be continued by North Vietnamese regulars instead. However, public perception in the United States considered tactical victory irrelevant. The government had been assuring its people that the Communists were too broken and disorganized to last much longer, but now the enemy was attacking deeper into American territory with larger forces than ever before. It didn't seem to matter that the offensive had played right into the hands of the American army, allowing it to bring its massive firepower to bear against the outgunned Viet Cong. Even in defeat, the Viet Cong elicited sympathy. The image that stuck with the American public was a widely publicized photo and film of a South Vietnamese officer blowing out the brains of a weeping prisoner on the streets of Saigon.

Antiwar Movement in America

The American government faced a dilemma. There was a limit to the number of casualties the American public was willing to accept without a clear and vital national interest being at stake.[13] Because the stated purpose of the war was to bring peace and freedom to the beleaguered people of South Vietnam, turning the whole country into a smoking and cratered desert wouldn't do anyone any good. America's best chance to win militarily would be to destroy the war-making capabilities of the Communists at the source in North Vietnam, but doing so risked a war with China—which at this stage in history was a xenophobically insane nation armed with nuclear weapons—and launching Armageddon would probably kill more Americans and Vietnamese than anybody was willing to accept.

The sporadic, almost ritualistic, bombing campaigns against the North were usually designed to send messages rather than destroy the country. Pilots were given a very restricted list of approved targets. Even so, the sheer tonnage of bombs dropped on North Vietnam was over three times the total quantity dropped by the Americans during World War II. Targeting was often careless, and an estimated 65,000 North Vietnamese civilians died in these air raids.

As the war dragged on with no clear purpose and no end in sight, most Americans turned against it. The most visible category of dissidents was college students of draft age who had the motivation, social organization, and political skills to stage large, angry protests. America had been packing its military with conscripts since the Korean War, but what had once been a necessary coming-of-age duty to be endured had now turned into a nightmare to be avoided.

The Gulf of Tonkin Resolution, which had originally authorized the president to wage war, had passed the U.S. Senate with only two dissenting votes, but by the beginning of the 1968 presidential campaign, a major faction of the ruling Democratic Party was forming behind peace candidates such as Robert Kennedy. After a poor showing in the first primary, President Johnson realized he'd never be renominated to his party's ticket and withdrew from the race. Robert Kennedy was gliding toward nomination, but his assassination in June left the peace faction without a viable candidate. The Democratic nomination went to Vice President Hubert Humphrey, an old-fashioned social liberal with no stated opposition to the war. Violent street battles between antiwar protesters and local police at the Democratic convention in Chicago undermined support for the party, and in November the Republican candidate, Richard Nixon, was narrowly elected president.

A Bigger, Smaller War

A total of 30,000 Americans had been killed in Vietnam by the time Johnson left office.[14] During the course of the 1968 election, it became clear that America was going to get out of Vietnam, regardless of who won the election or who won the war. The only question was how to do it without losing face. Nixon began withdrawing troops as soon as he was inaugurated, trying to shift the burden back onto the South Vietnamese Army. Meanwhile the Communists launched another offensive. Even though Nixon was actively trying to disengage the United States from ground combat, some 10,000 Americans were killed during his first year in office.[15]

For many years, Vietnamese Communists had been operating out of sanctuaries in neutral Cambodia to the west, which the Americans began secretly bombing and raiding as soon as Nixon came to power. Cambodia's Prince Sihanouk reluctantly and quietly permitted the American incursions because he had little choice. In retaliation, the Viet Cong armed, trained, and infiltrated a force of Khmer Rouge (Red Cambodians) back into Cambodia to harass Sihanouk's government. Sihanouk tried to maintain a balanced neutrality in the face of the spreading war, but his chief minister Lon Nol pressed for a harder line against the Khmer Rouge. In March 1970, while the prince was vacationing in France, Lon Nol deposed him and declared Cambodia a republic. Rather than accept a quiet French retirement like his fellow ex-monarch from Viet Nam, Sihanouk hurried to China and connected with representatives of the Khmer Rouge, with whom he joined into a common front.[16]

With Cambodia rapidly deteriorating, American and RVN troops openly invaded in May to destroy the Viet Cong sanctuaries. The idea was to corner and destroy the Communists, but they were no more capable of destroying them in Cambodia than they had been in Vietnam. In fact, the foreign invasion stirred up Cambodian nationalism and boosted local support for the Khmer Rouge. This sudden expansion of the war also caused a new outbreak of protests in America, during which National Guardsmen fired into a crowd of protesters at Kent State University, killing four.

In 1971, South Vietnamese forces openly invaded Laos to shut down the Ho Chi Minh Trail, but they were driven back by North Vietnamese.

Back to Civil War

By the next presidential election, in 1972, America's commitment had been reduced by over 90 percent, with only 40,000 American soldiers on the ground, but the Communists still refused to let the Americans withdraw. Peace talks had been sputtering along in Paris for years and had become a farce, with petty bickering over the most trivial procedures. Nixon improved diplomatic relations with the Communist giants, China and Russia, in the hopes of returning to the calm, practical nineteenth-century way of doing things, when big powers decided the fates of little countries. Even though both of the Communist big powers were losing money on the Indochina war and had cut their support back to almost nothing, the North Vietnamese persisted. In the spring of 1972, they launched another massive offensive.[17] Out of desperation, the Americans resumed heavy bombing of North Vietnam in December 1972 in order to force the Communists to let the Americans withdraw with some dignity intact.[18] Finally, the North Vietnamese agreed, and a cease-fire took effect in January 1973.

The terms of the cease-fire were complicated—involving promises of elections, power-sharing, territorial arrangements, return of prisoners, and so on—but none of that matters. The key point was that the Communists were allowed to keep their armies in place, but they were supposed to stay quiet long enough for the Americans to withdraw without calling it a retreat.

The civil war continued unofficially, with the RVN slowly gaining ground, but it was becoming clear that both sides were on their last legs. Even though South Vietnam's wartime economy was based on bribery, theft, prostitution, and black markets, at least it was a thriving economy of *some* sort, but with the withdrawal of American soldiers, their money went with them. The masses of peasants driven into the cities now had no income at all. On the other side, the stubborn and profligate attacks by the Communists year after year had gutted and broken the North Vietnamese army. In October 1973, both Russia and China refused to resupply the North Vietnamese. The Chinese prime minister told the leader of North Vietnam, "It would be best for Vietnam and the rest of Indochina to relax for, say, five or ten years."[19] In the United States, the animosity over the war had been steadily driving politics to the edge of anarchy and dictatorship. The Nixon administration was caught trying to stifle domestic opposition with a web of illegal activities, and in August 1974, the president was forced to resign—an unprecedented event in U.S. history.

As it turned out, however, the North Vietnamese had one last offensive left in them. Their first attack broke through the Central Highlands, isolating the cities of the North. The RVN commander flew out to safety, leaving 200,000 soldiers and dependent family members to find their own way of escape.

Then the Communists turned against Hue. Remembering the massacre of 1968, the population panicked and tried to escape. Civilians overran the airport; they waded out to sea to scramble aboard boats or drown trying. Hue fell on March 25, 1975; Da Nang, shortly after. Massive columns of refugees fleeing from the Communists were caught in the crossfire and slaughtered by the tens of thousands. In scattered actions, the South Vietnamese soldiers either were beaten badly or fled without a fight, stripping off their uniforms and blending into the civilian columns in order to avoid Communist prison camps.[20]

As soon as the endgame started, the U.S. Congress voted overwhelmingly to stay out. In the United States, there's still a furious debate over the failure of the Americans to go rushing back into a country they had been driven out of, in order to rescue a failing ally, but realistically, America wasn't going back. Period.

Both Saigon and Phnom Penh fell in April 1975. A massive settling of scores followed, but that's another story altogether (see "Postwar Vietnam" and "Democratic Kampuchea").

Death Toll

The army of South Vietnam recorded 223,748 deaths among its personnel before the final offensives interrupted its bookkeeping. The United States registered 58,177 dead. For the longest time, no one had any idea how many Communists or civilians had died, but everyone knew it was a lot. In April 1995, on the twentieth anniversary of the end of the war, Hanoi announced its official estimates, which indicated that the war was twice as destructive as anyone had previously dared to guess. Hanoi declared that 1.1 million Viet Cong and North Vietnamese soldiers and 2 million Vietnamese civilians had died during two decades of conflict, 1954–75.[21] The 2008 world health survey largely confirmed this, estimating 3.8 million violent deaths in Vietnam during this period.[22]

It has been estimated that 600,000 people died in the associated Cambodian Civil War (1970–75) from all causes, among all parties.[23] An estimated 62,000 died in Laos.[24]

THE COLD WAR

East-West Confrontation

During the forty years of their bipolar global conflict, the United States and the Soviet Union had an obsession about gaining spaces on the game board. Each side tried to control as many countries as possible regardless of their strategic or economic value. In fact, when you look down the list of major hot wars during the Cold War, you'll see the most worthless collection of countries you can possibly imagine. Except for Indonesia, none stand out as major suppliers of oil, metals, food, or cash crops, and except for Indonesia, Ethiopia, and Greece, none adjoin any important shipping lanes. The fact that millions of people died for control of these places may be the best proof that both sides in the Cold War were sincerely motivated by ideology. If the Soviet Union and United States had been concerned with only economic self-interest, they would have let these countries go without a fight. As it was, they lost lives and money and gained almost nothing tangible in return.

On the other hand, wars that were unprofitable to the country as a whole could still produce a profit for certain powerful factions. The Cold War created a feedback loop in which the threat of powerful ideological enemies required large, standing armies, which then required a massive investment in the military, which created a powerful class of people whose wealth and livelihood depended on continued military spending, which could be justified only by a constant threat of war. Also, the ready availability of this military-industrial complex made it temptingly easy for the leaders of the great powers to resort to arms whenever an international dispute flared up.

Here's a quick list of the deadliest proxy wars of the bipolar era, beginning with the bloodiest:

1. Vietnam (1959–75): 3,500,000 dead in Vietnam. Direct American involvement on behalf of the government against Communist rebels.
2. Korea (1950–53): 3,000,000 dead. Direct Western involvement on behalf of South

Korea, and direct Chinese involvement on behalf of North Korea.

3. Afghanistan (1979–92): 1,500,000 dead. Direct Soviet involvement on behalf of the government against mujahideen rebels.

4. Mozambique (1975–92): 800,000 dead. Western-oriented rebels versus a Communist government.

5. Cambodia (1970–75): 600,000 dead. Direct American involvement on behalf of the government against Communist rebels.

6. Angola (1975–94): 500,000 dead. Direct Cuban involvement on behalf of the government against Western-oriented rebels.

7. Indonesia (1965–66): 400,000 dead. A Western-oriented government massacred the leftist opposition.

8. Guatemala (1960–96): 200,000 dead. Leftist rebels versus a Western-oriented government.[1]

9. Greece (1943–49): 160,000 dead. Communist rebels versus a Western-oriented government.[2]

10. El Salvador (1979–92): 75,000 dead. Leftist rebels versus a Western-oriented government.

11. Laos (to 1973): 62,000 dead. American assistance on behalf of the government against Communist rebels.[3]

12. South Korea (1948–49): 60,000 dead. Leftist rebels versus a Western-oriented government.

13. Philippines (from 1972): 43,000 dead. Communist rebels versus a Western-oriented government.[4]

14. Argentina (1976–83): 30,000 dead. Western-oriented government oppressing the leftist opposition.[5]

15. Nicaragua (1972–79): 30,000 dead. Communist rebels versus a Western-oriented government.[6]

16. Nicaragua (1982–90): 30,000 dead. Western-oriented rebels versus a Communist government.[7]

This totals some 11 million people who died in various conflicts where the Americans supplied one side and the Soviets supplied the other. Although it is far beyond the scope of this book to meticulously untangle each of these conflicts and assign blame to either the Communists or the West, if you hear someone assert that the nuclear standoff between the superpowers created an unprecedented era of international peace, they are probably forgetting these 11 million lives.

INDONESIAN PURGE

Death toll: 400,000[1]
Rank: 81
Type: ideological purge
Broad dividing line: army vs. leftists
Time frame: 1965–66
Location and major state participant: Indonesia
Who usually gets the most blame: Suharto, CIA
The easily answerable questions that everyone asks: Is Sukarno the same person as Suharto? Don't they have first names?*

The Year of Living Dangerously

On September 1, 1965, a small faction of junior officers kidnapped six of Indonesia's top generals. Details are murky, but it seems to have been the first stage in a coup d'etat. When the scheme went bad, the insurgents panicked and killed their prisoners, stuffing their bodies down a well. The sole survivor was General Abdul Nasution, who had jumped over the back wall in his yard into the yard of the Iraqi ambassador next door after an attack on his home killed his six-year-old daughter and his aide.

After escaping the abduction attempt, General Nasution reported to the senior surviving officer, General Suharto, who had somehow not appeared on the list of assassination targets. General Suharto blamed the PKI, the Indonesian Communist Party—at the time, the world's third largest Communist party and Maoist in orientation—for the attempted coup. Others find it mighty suspicious that the plotters had completely forgotten to put Suharto on their list of targets. Not only did he survive without a scratch, the attacks definitely worked out to his advantage.

The president of Indonesia at the time was Sukarno, the old freedom fighter who had taken Indonesia out of the Dutch empire after World War II. In the 1950s, Sukarno had helped found the nonaligned movement, which tried to organize a "third world" that remained outside the Soviet and American blocs. He had begun as a properly democratic president with elections and a free press, but as the years passed he spun a tight cocoon of power around himself until he emerged like a butterfly as president-for-life in

---

* Answers: No. No.

1963. To keep the opposition safely in check, members of the Indonesian parliament were appointed rather than elected under a policy Sukarno called Guided Democracy.

Indonesia stayed calm for a few weeks after the attempted coup of September 1965, but soon the military began to round up and kill anyone suspected of Communist sympathies. It drew up lists that included leftists of all kinds—Communists of course, but also trade unionists, students, and journalists—and summarily executed thousands of them. Some were killed in raids that wiped out entire families or destroyed uncooperative villages as well. Other suspects were hauled into local jails to be roughly interrogated and ignored for several weeks, until the day came when they were taken to a conveniently desolate spot and shot. According to several former U.S. officials, American intelligence personnel supplied the Indonesian military with the names of hundreds, maybe thousands, of people they wanted removed.[2] The soldiers and their vigilante assistants also targeted ethnic Chinese, members of a merchant community that had been part of Southeast Asian culture for generations, on the rumor that they were all agents of Mao.

Most of the raids took place at night as masked men whisked prisoners into oblivion. One eyewitness describes hiding in the bushes one night watching masked vigilantes drive up to the riverbank with truckloads of prisoners, many of whom he recognized as neighbors and teachers. They were dragged out and beheaded with machetes. Their heads were stuffed into bags and kept, while the bodies were pushed into the water to float away.[3]

Almost a half-million people were hunted down and killed during the purge; 600,000 were imprisoned without trial, often for years. Thousands were exiled to penal colonies across the archipelago, where many were worked to death.

President Sukarno was powerless to control his military, and he officially gave up trying in March 1966, when he relinquished control of the country to General Suharto, who then served as acting president for about a year until he promoted himself to real president. Suharto eased Indonesia away from nonaligned status and turned his foreign policy increasingly toward the American bloc.[4]

BIAFRAN WAR

Death toll: 1 million[1]
Rank: 46
Type: ethnic civil war
Broad dividing line: Nigeria vs. Biafra
Time frame: 1966–70
Location: Nigeria
Who usually gets the most blame: usually Ojukwu, sometimes Gowon, rarely both
Another damn: African civil war

Outbreak

Like most African countries, Nigeria makes no sense. It came into existence as an enclave on the Slave Coast that the British took in order to police the slave trade. Then the area was expanded inward to keep the interior from falling into French hands. Nigeria is split between a Muslim north and a Christian south, with a variety of tribes scattered throughout. In the first years following independence in 1960, it was a federation of largely autonomous provinces allotted to the major ethnic groups: notably, the Northern Region (mostly Hausa-Fulani—Muslim), the Eastern Region (Ibo, also called Igbo—Christian), and the Western Region (Yoruba—also Christian). The Ibo people had had the most success assimilating to Western ways under the British. They were richer, more educated, and had a disproportionate influence in the army.

In January 1966, Ibo officers in the Nigerian army tried to overthrow the corrupt and inefficient civilian leaders of the First Republic. A loyal Ibo general broke the coup, but he spared the plotters and then declared himself president in order to restore order. When he began to pack the government with fellow Ibos, the Muslims of the Northern Region began scheming a coup of their own. In July 1966, this countercoup put the government into the hands of Northern troops; however, to calm worries in the Christian half of the country, this new junta gave the presidency to Yakubu Gowon, a colonel from a minor Christian tribe who had not been involved in either coup.

At thirty-two years old, Gowon was Africa's youngest head of state. Handsome and charismatic, he was well liked inside and outside of Nigeria. Even though he would oversee a war that killed a million of his countrymen, history has been kind to his reputation. Most of the blame has fallen on the equally young but less charismatic military governor of the

Eastern Region, an Ibo named Chukwuemeka Odumegwu Ojukwu. Ojukwu's family was the richest in the country, and this fortune went a long way to keeping the Biafran army supplied during the upcoming war.

After the July countercoup, pogroms erupted across the Muslim north targeting Christian residents, especially Ibo. Angry at the January coup plotters, northern mobs killed around 30,000 Ibo and drove a million back to the Eastern Region. After Ibo protests and negotiations with the central government failed to protect the Ibo, Ojukwu declared a new nation, Biafra, in the southeast quarter of Nigeria.

War

The first attempt by the federal army to retake the province was easily swatted away, and the Biafran army followed the retreating federals across the Niger River into the Western Region, threatening the capital at Lagos. This raid was contained and driven back within a few weeks, and Biafra was entirely on the defensive after this.

Nigeria is Africa's most populous state, so the federal army eventually built up to 250,000 while the Biafran army topped out at 45,000. Neither army impressed observers with its martial prowess. Whenever they clashed, the most important tactical objective seemed to be to make as much noise as possible. During a typical federal offensive, artillery would first pound the living hell out of the supposed Biafran position, regardless of whether the enemy sighting was confirmed or civilians were in the way. The Biafran troops, however, usually withdrew when the first shell fell because they had no artillery of their own with which to fight back. Then the federal infantry would run forward, firing their machine guns wildly in the enemy's general direction until every round was expended. When their shooting stopped, the Biafrans might counterattack while the federal troops pulled back to wait for more ammunition.[2]

Famine

The federal army gradually whittled Biafra away at the edges. It fought its way along the border with Cameroon in the east, separating Biafra from overland contact with the rest of the world. Eventually an amphibious attack took Port Harcourt, cutting the last direct contact that Biafra had with the outside. Now only airplanes could bring supplies, but it was never enough. Starvation killed hundreds of thousands of trapped Biafrans. Photographs of emaciated children with bloated bellies stared out from the covers of news magazines worldwide.

As Nigeria surrounded Biafra and squeezed it down to a tenth of its original size, only humanitarian supplies were allowed through the blockade. Then, in June 1969, Gowon tightened the noose and banned Red Cross flights into Biafra. Although the international outcry forced Gowon to rescind his order within two weeks, the crisis started a chain reaction.

The Red Cross had to maintain a precarious balance among all sides in order to be allowed into the war zone, which meant the humanitarian organization had to play politics. Now a group of French doctors working in Biafra loudly criticized the Red Cross for playing favorites, and they began to organize medical assistance that bypassed politics. Over the next several years this became Doctors Without Borders, chartered as a nonpolitical funnel bringing medical aid to troubled countries—which, ironically, was one of the original reasons for establishing the Red Cross.

Surrender

As the enclave eroded over the next few years, Ojukwu tightened internal security and propagandized the Biafrans into believing that surrender would lead to genocide. Both sides accused the other of massacring civilians and then invited outside observers into the war zone to prove that they themselves were obeying all of the laws of civilized warfare—unlike those savages on the other side.

Biafra fought until there wasn't much left to defend, and the final stronghold was abandoned in January 1970. Ojukwu fled to the Ivory Coast, but there was none of the customary retribution that followed most Third World civil wars. No massacres, no executions, just a general amnesty and reconciliation. Sure there were rumors, but none held up to outside scrutiny. Gowon was widely praised for his unusual leniency, which shows you just how rare that really is.[3]

BENGALI GENOCIDE

Death toll: 1.5 million[1]
Rank: 40
Type: ethnic cleansing
Broad dividing line: West Pakistan vs. East Pakistan
Time frame: 267 days in 1971
Location: East Pakistan
Major state participant: Pakistan
Quantum state participant: Bangladesh
Minor state participant: India
Who usually gets the most blame: Agha Mohammad Yahya Khan

Geography

The country of Pakistan began as two distinct territories on opposite sides of India that shared nothing more than the Muslim religion and a British imperial past. The western wing of the country, West Pakistan, was the ethnically diverse center of political power, while the eastern wing, East Pakistan, was mostly Bengali in language and treated by the west as a poor, downriver colony. The fact that slightly more people lived in the East made it a dangerous mix.

When a devastating typhoon overwhelmed East Pakistan in November 1970, the federal government bungled the response. The military dictator of Pakistan, Agha Mohammad Yahya Khan, was preoccupied instead with weighty matters of global politics. As an ally of both China and the United States, Pakistan served as the go-between for arranging talks between Nixon and Mao. Yahya was in China when the disaster struck.

Even though hundreds of thousands of his people were swept out to sea by the storm surge, Yahya did little to help the survivors. Other countries—Britain, the United States, West Germany, and others—stepped in to help before the government of Pakistan did. Because of the federal indifference, the local Bengali nationalists of the Awami League gained in influence throughout East Pakistan and were set to win the upcoming elections.

Politics

It may seem odd that Pakistan had both elections and a dictator at the same time, but that's normal for them. The government of Pakistan has historically fluctuated between sort of democratic and sort of authoritarian. In fact, a little of both is not unusual. Pakistan usually has a parliament, a free press, and an independent judiciary (more or less), but the national leadership alternates between military and civilian. The top dog is either a military strong-man who lets the civil service run the country as long as nothing explodes, or an elected president who rules via bribes and kickbacks and doesn't force the army to do anything it doesn't want to. Regardless of the career path that brought the ruler into power, Pakistani government is usually focused on the personality of the leader.

During the national elections in December 1970, the Awami League led by Sheikh Mujibur Rahman won almost all of the seats from East Pakistan, giving the league a solid majority nationwide, but this only convinced Yahya that free elections had been a mistake. There was no way that the junta would turn the government over to Mujibur, but it had to face the uncomfortable side effect of restoring democracy in Pakistan. As long as the Bengalis stayed united behind the Awami League, they would have the power to run the whole country.

Meanwhile, the voting showed that the People's Progressive Party dominated in West Pakistan, but their leader, Zulfikar Ali Bhutto, refused to sit in any parliament run by Mujibur. He held out for a two-part federation, which—no surprise—would put Bhutto in charge of the western half. Three-way talks between Bhutto, Mujibur, and Yahya dragged on until tempers broke. Mujibur called a round of strikes and protests in Bengali East Pakistan, and Yahya sent soldiers to arrest him and restore order in February 1971.

"Kill three million of them," President Yahya Khan told his inner circle, "and the rest will eat out of our hands."[2] Pakistani apologists now insist that he didn't mean this *literally*.

Massacre

General Tikka Khan took command of the army in East Pakistan on March 7, and within weeks he began to massacre the Bengalis, starting at the universities. Bengali intellectuals and political leaders were hunted down. The army killed 3,000 people in Dacca the first day, March 25, and at least 30,000 within the first few days while the city emptied in panic.

"Peaceful night was turned into a time of wailing, crying and burning," a Pakistani general described in his memoirs. "Gen. Tikka let loose everything at his disposal as if raiding an enemy. Instead of disarming Bengal units and imprisoning Bengali leaders, as he was ordered, he resorted to the killing of civilians and a scorched-earth policy."[3]

At the university, Pakistani soldiers set fire to the women's dormitory and machine-gunned the students as they ran out the doors.[4] At the town of Hariharpara near Dacca, Pakistanis stashed prisoners in an abandoned warehouse. At night, roped together in batches of six or so, they were herded outside and waist deep into the river. Silhouetted by powerful electric arc lamps, they were shot and left to drift away on the current.[5]

Archer Blood, the American consul in Dacca, telegraphed his government on March

28 with details of the ongoing genocide and begged, without success, for it to intervene. "Here in Dacca we are mute and horrified witnesses to a reign of terror of the Pak military." The U.S. State Department, however, needed Yahya Khan to help hook up with Mao, so it issued orders to not annoy the Pakistanis.[6]

There had been no armed separatist movement in East Pakistan before the massacres started, but now the survivors began to band together into militias to fight back using whatever weapons they could scrounge. Meanwhile, as many as 30 million Bengalis were uprooted internally during these months, and anywhere from 6 to 10 million Bengali refugees poured into India to escape the massacres. Overwhelmed by this mass influx of starving, desperate people, India decided to make East Pakistan safe for their return. On December 3, India invaded East Pakistan, and by the sixteenth, the local Pakistani army had surrendered. This allowed the creation of independent Bangladesh.[7]

IDI AMIN

Death toll: 300,000[1]
Rank: 96
Type: despot
Broad dividing line: Idi Amin vs. everyone
Time frame: 1971–79
Location and major state participant: Uganda
Minor state participants: Tanzania, Libya
Who usually gets the most blame: Idi Amin

IDI AMIN WAS AN ENORMOUS MAN, SIX FEET FOUR INCHES TALL, WEIGHING 270 pounds, but was barely able to read or write. A champion boxer and a professional soldier down to the bone, Amin worked his way up in the British colonial army to become the army chief of staff for Uganda's first elected president, Milton Obote. Amin was widely considered a jovial brute, far too unimaginative to be much of a threat. Because he came from an insignificant Sudanic tribe, he just didn't have the connections necessary to cause much trouble.

In January 1971, Amin seized power by coup d'etat just as President Obote was thinking of getting rid of him.

Almost immediately, Amin purged the army of the Acholi and Langi tribesmen who had formed the core of Obote's support, killing some 10,000 of them in an army that wasn't very big to begin with. At the same time, he replaced them with Sudanic tribesmen recruited from north Uganda and beyond the border, in Muslim territories more akin to his own people.

In 1972 Amin expelled 70,000 Ugandans of Asian (mostly Indian) descent and confiscated their property. Although this was popular and temporarily profitable, it destroyed the economy. Their ancestors had been brought to Africa by the British to staff the civil service, and they formed the backbone of the nation's middle class.[2]

Idi Amin shifted Uganda's alignment away from British and Israeli military advisers, toward Muslim solidarity instead, and soon Libyan troops arrived to help prop up his regime. When Palestinians hijacked an Israeli airliner in 1976, they found a safe place to park at Uganda's Entebbe airport. While Amin was basking in the attention at the center of a crisis, Israeli commandos swooped in and rescued the hostages.

Of course, none of this is the reason why Idi Amin has become the most recognized name in Third World thuggery. We all know Idi Amin because he hogged the spotlight by playing the clown. During any international crisis of the 1970s, the world press could always count on outrageous commentary coming out of Uganda. Amin advised Arab states to send kamikaze pilots against Israel and offered President Richard Nixon his sincere wishes for "a speedy recovery" from the Watergate scandal. He challenged a neighboring president to a boxing match to settle a border dispute. He awarded himself Britain's Victoria Cross and volunteered to be the king of Scotland. Even Amin's rumored cannibalism was treated more as a fascinating quirk than as a human rights violation. Among the titles he awarded himself were "Lord of All the Beasts of the Earth and Fishes of the Sea" and "Conqueror of the British Empire," but his favorite was Dada, "Big Daddy."[3]

All the while, Idi Amin maintained a tyrannical regime, among the most brutal in history. Bodies were dumped into the Nile River because graves couldn't be dug fast enough to hold his victims. At one point, disposal proved too much for even the Nile crocodiles, and bloated floating bodies clogged the intake to the nation's principal hydroelectric dam, interrupting the power supply. His inner circle never stabilized, and he elevated and purged advisers and wives with erratic rapidity. Prisoners were forced to eat each other in order to stay alive.

Finally, as Uganda became too poor to plunder, Amin sent his army into Tanzania to loot disputed borderlands. The Tanzanian army replied in force, overrunning Uganda and exposing the truth about his regime. Next to Amin's favorite palace, in the headquarters of the State Research Bureau (Uganda's secret police) they found "20 to 30 bodies scattered around the room in varying states of decay and mutilation. Almost all showed signs of torture and the floors were covered with bloodstains." Ragged, broken prisoners were released from jails. Mass graves were excavated, turning up skulls bashed open by rifle butts, arms and legs bound, children impaled on stakes.[4]

Amin meanwhile escaped to Libya, then moved to Saudi Arabia, where he lived in comfortable retirement until his death in 2003.[5]

MENGISTU HAILE

Death toll: 2 million[1]
Rank: 37
Type: ethnic civil war, Communist regime
Broad dividing line: Ethiopia vs. its minorities
Time frame: 1974–91
Location and major state participant: Ethiopia
Minor state participants: Somalia, Cuba
Quantum state participants: Eritrea, Tigre
Major non-state participants: Afar Liberation Front, Ethiopian People's
Revolutionary Democratic Front, Eritrean Liberation Front, Eritrean People's
Liberation Front, Ethiopian People's Revolutionary Party, Oromo Liberation Front,
Somali Abo Liberation Front
Who usually gets the most blame: Mengistu Haile Mariam
Another damn: African civil war

A FTER WORLD WAR II, THE ITALIAN COLONY OF ERITREA ALONG THE RED
Sea coast was attached to Ethiopia as both an outlet to the sea and compensation
for all of the trouble Italy had caused the Ethiopians. Because the Eritrean people are
nothing at all like the Ethiopians, this union was supposed to be a loose federation with
a wide measure of Eritrean autonomy, but the Ethiopians got greedy and began running
their new province like they owned the place.

When Emperor Haile Selassie (see "Italo-Ethiopian War") unilaterally annexed Eritrea
in 1962, the locals rose in rebellion. For the next thirty years, the Ethiopian coast was a
war zone. Compounding the chronic warfare, a famine settled over Ethiopia in 1973–74,
killing 100,000 to 200,000 in the northern province of Tigre, as the country descended
further into chaos.

Red Terror

In September 1974, a cabal of army officers called the Derg (the "Committee") took power
in the capital, Addis Ababa, and imprisoned Emperor Haile Selassie. The first leader of
the provisional government, General Aman Andom, was Eritrean and mistrusted and

therefore was assassinated within a couple of months. His replacement was Teferi Benti, who declared Ethiopia a socialist state.

After a year under house arrest, Haile Selassie was strangled in his bed and buried under a toilet in the palace. In addition, fifty-seven former high officials, including two former prime ministers and seventeen generals, were executed without trial in the first year of Derg rule. Altogether, some 10,000 suspected opponents of the new regime were killed in the first purges.

In 1977, during a cabinet meeting, Vice President Lieutenant Colonel Mengistu Haile Mariam and his associates quietly excused themselves and left the room. A moment later, Mengistu burst in with some gunmen and began shooting everyone who remained. This turned into a running gunfight down the halls of the palace in which Benti and his supporters were killed.[2]

Mengistu then continued to purge rival factions of Marxists. In a May 1977 speech, Mengistu declared the Ethiopian People's Revolutionary Party an outlawed organization: "Death to the rebels! Death to the EPRP!" Mobs of government and factory workers were organized to go door to door, dragging suspects out to be shot or strangled with wire. During the Red Terror, bodies were dumped in the gutters with placards tied around their necks: "This will happen to you if you support the EPRP." Over the course of his reign, Mengistu had some 80,000 political enemies and prisoners killed in cold blood.[3]

War and More War

For most of modern history, Ethiopia always seems to have a couple of wars going at any given time. Some are civil wars; others are border wars. During the era of Derg rule, wars raged at two ends of the country. In addition to the Eritrean War, the Somalis in the Ogaden Desert to the east were in revolt, and hard-line Communists revolted in Tigre. In total, these wars killed 400,000 to 600,000 people by one means or another.[4]

Somalis are one of the most distinctive and numerous ethnicities in all of Africa, but during the colonial era, they were split among five different jurisdictions (hence the five-pointed star that dominates the Somalian flag). Independence brought three of these together—Italian and British Somalilands, plus the northeast corner of Kenya. This left the French enclave at the port of Djibouti and the Ogaden Desert of Ethiopia as Somali lands outside the Somali nation. With Ethiopia straining under civil war, famine, and factional infighting, the dictator of Somalia, Mohamed Siad Barre, figured that now would be a good time for a land grab. In July 1977, Somalian troops crossed into Ethiopia and occupied the Ogaden in support of local Somali rebels.

The war sent shockwaves around the world. Because the Horn of Africa could be used to choke off the flow of oil from the Persian Gulf to the Suez Canal, every superpower wanted military bases in the neighborhood. The West had befriended Haile Selassie's monarchy, while the Soviets had cultivated the radical dictatorship in Somalia.

Now, however, with Communists in charge in Addis Ababa, the Russians controlled the whole Horn, but the Ogaden War put the Soviet Union in the awkward position of supplying both sides in a war between allies. When the Soviets tried to choke off the invasion by cutting aid to Somalia, Siad Barre kicked out his Soviet advisers and became a friend of the West. By 1980, the Americans had been granted use of the air and naval facilities the Soviets had built in the Somalian capital of Mogadishu.

Meanwhile, 24,000 Cuban troops arrived to fight alongside the Ethiopians. Cuban soldiers fought as proxies for the Soviets in several African civil wars. For one thing, Cubans were more Third Worldy (that is, darker, scruffier) than the Russians and many were of African descent so there were fewer unpleasant colonial overtones. For another, deploying Soviet troops directly would have raised the stakes and elevated the conflict to a great-power war.

With Cuban help, the last Somalian invaders were driven out in March 1978.

Famine

It almost goes without saying that the Communist takeover of Ethiopia led to another famine. If we've learned anything from previous chapters, it's that previous Communist regimes learned nothing from their predecessors. As soon as Communists start fiddling with agriculture, people starve. Mengistu's government collectivized agriculture with the traditional brutality and stubbornness of Communists everywhere, and food production crashed.

It began with drought in Tigre and Eritrea, which became mass starvation in 1984–85. Of course, no one can be sure, but the famine killed anywhere from 0.5 million to 2 million.[5] Mengistu tried to conceal the extent of the famine, which kept outside help from reaching Ethiopia.

Ideology alone didn't intensify the famine. The wars stirred up thousands of refugees, while Mengistu forcibly moved hundreds of thousands of peasants from the war-torn northern provinces to the west in order to starve the rebels. It worked too well, starving both rebels and peasants and spreading the famine.

Finally the West took notice and began to send food. The most visible response was the Live Aid concert, which gathered dozens of bands and raised millions in hard cash for famine relief. This wasn't the first international rock-and-roll charity—George Harrison's Concert for Bangladesh predates it—but in many ways it was the largest.

When food finally did arrive from the outside world, Mengistu tried to distribute it according to the people's loyalty to the regime. Most Western aid agencies had seen this trick before and refused to allow it, but this still caused delays, disputes, and cancellations that a starving population could not afford.

Fall

As the Soviet Union began to back away from strict Communism in the mid-1980s, the Soviet leader Mikhail Gorbachev cut off aid to Ethiopia. Without this crutch, Mengistu's regime began to stumble. By 1988, most of Eritrea had fallen into rebel hands. Tigre followed shortly. As the rebel groups coalesced around the capital at Addis Ababa in May 1991, Mengistu fled to Zimbabwe, where he remains today in comfortable exile.

In the early afterglow of victory, all of the various factions assembled into a broad-based provisional government in Addis Ababa and held elections that were almost honest. This democratic interlude didn't last long before one faction took over, but at least they tried.

The new regime found Emperor Haile Selassie's skeleton and gave it a proper church burial.

Within a year of Mengistu's defeat, a UN-sponsored referendum finally offered Eritrea its independence, an opportunity the Eritreans overwhelmingly seized. This was the first time a secession movement actually succeeded in post-colonial Africa, making Eritrea the first second-generation African nation.

POSTWAR VIETNAM

Death toll: 365,000[1]
Rank: 91
Type: ideological purge
Broad dividing line: Communists vs. former anti-Communists
Time frame: 1975–92
Location and major state participant: Vietnam
Who usually gets the most blame: Communist government of unified Vietnam, Malay pirates
Another damn: insane people's republic
The unanswerable question everyone asks: Does this mean the Americans were right to go into Vietnam and wrong to leave?

IN THE CHAOTIC DAYS PRECEDING THE FALL OF SAIGON, THE AMERICANS managed to evacuate 130,000 Vietnamese allies who would have been the most obvious targets for retribution—government officials, army officers, and biracial children. Even with that many rescued, the new Communist government found plenty of suspiciously Americanized South Vietnamese who needed to be dealt with. Civil servants, teachers, former officers, girlfriends, and students were told to report for a one-month seminar at special reeducation camps.

The ordeal did not pass as quickly as promised. They were to be quarantined from the new society and converted to loyal Marxists. The camps were run with a sort of religious fervor dedicated to transforming these hard cases into model citizens, but first their will had to be broken, often by torture, overwork, fatigue, and hunger. Many were kept in the camps for ten to fifteen years, working hard labor on low rations. Discipline was strict. Prisoners' ankles and wrists grew scarred from chains and handcuffs.

"A lieutenant colonel tried to escape from the Lang Son reeducation camp by bribing one of the guards," one witness described. "His plan was revealed; he was shot in one leg and caught. On the next day he was buried alive. He died after four days."[2]

Almost a million people passed through these camps, where probably 65,000 people were executed, and another 100,000 died of neglect, disease, or overwork. The reeducation camps were closed during a general amnesty in 1992, and thousands of prisoners who had been held for the full seventeen years were finally freed.

Boat People

Faced with unforgiving new rulers, many Vietnamese tried to flee the country. They used all their handy cash to bribe officials and buy whatever boats were available, many of them barely seaworthy, good for maybe a single one-way trip and not always that. Political refugees were only one part of the exodus. When a border war broke out between China and Vietnam in 1979, Hanoi heavily persecuted all Vietnamese of Chinese ancestry as suspected traitors.

Probably a million boat people fled Vietnam in just a few years, and as many as one-fourth of them died at sea.[3] They drifted in the harsh sun in leaky boats, slowly sinking, often running out of food or water. The dead were thrown overboard.

Aside from the ordinary hazards of the seas, the boat people suffered from human perils. The neighboring nations didn't want them. Local coast guards chased them back into the open sea, and vigilantes attacked them when they washed ashore on foreign beaches. Many boats were seized by Malay pirates. Their possessions were stolen, the women raped, the men beaten.

Most of the boat people went to Malaysia, Hong Kong, Indonesia, and the Philippines as their first stop, where they waited in refugee camps for richer countries to take them in. The largest numbers were resettled in the United States, with France and Australia taking many thousands as well.[4]

In the late 1980s, another surge of boat people risked their lives to get out of Vietnam. Unfortunately, by this time, the world classified the boat people as economic refugees rather than political ones. They were considered a nuisance and received less sympathy.

In one 1989 incident, "seven pirates armed with shotguns and hammers stormed the refugees' boat, which had left Vietnam on April 14 with more than 130 people aboard, including 20 children. . . . The pirates shot and killed the boat's two pilots and raped most of the 15 to 20 women and girls aboard. Then they set the boat afire. In the ensuing panic, many refugees grabbed buoys, jerrycans and floats and plunged into the sea. . . . The pirates used sticks to prevent refugees from clinging to floating objects." There was only one survivor, who drifted away on floating planks.[5]

DEMOCRATIC KAMPUCHEA

Death toll: 1,670,000
Rank: 39
Type: Communist regime
Broad dividing line: Khmer Rouge vs. everyone
Time frame: 1975–79
Location: Cambodia (official name: Democratic Kampuchea)
Who usually gets the most blame: Pol Pot, Khmer Rouge
Another damn: insane people's republic

The Killing Fields

The Communist insurgency in Cambodia had been little more than bandit gangs in the countryside until the American bombings and invasion spread the Vietnam War over the border. As Cambodia became engulfed in the larger conflict, the credibility and stability of the government in Phnom Penh faltered. The capital finally fell to the Khmer Rouge on April 17, 1975.

Almost immediately, the Khmer Rouge started herding the population of Phnom Penh out to the countryside. The people were told that Americans were on their way to bomb the city, so they should hurry. Leave everything behind and get out to the country-side as quickly as possible. Anyone who disobeyed was shot, as was anyone discovered on the list of class enemies. All across Cambodia, cities were abandoned by hundreds of thousands of people who would never see their homes again.

The populace was being moved back to the farms. To a certain extent, this was a purely practical response to the food shortages crippling the cities after years of guer-rilla war, but ideology guided the move as well. The Khmer Rouge would not even consider two simpler, time-tested ways of getting food to the cities—foreign aid and free markets.[1]

The Khmer Rouge believed that the simple life of the humblest Cambodian peasant was the only acceptable lifestyle. Self-sufficient, contented, and hard-working, the peas-ant had survived the centuries without exploiting the labor of others. It represented the Communist ideal. Freed from capitalist exploitation, the peasants of Cambodia were now expected to triple their output. The average pre-war yield of 1 metric ton of rice per hectare was expected to reach the new quota of 3 metric tons per hectare. In practice, their output didn't even come close.

Shopkeepers, waiters, clerks, secretaries, and anyone else who had been too much a part of modern, urban society were classified as "New People"—the source of everything that was wrong in the world. They were taken out to the country and put to work on farms, but they were clearly expendable. If the New People adapted to the peasant life, that was fine, but if they died of exhaustion, that was fine too. Ethnic minorities were also classified as New People and systematically wiped out. A third of the Cham—a Muslim ethnic minority—died over the next few years. Half of the Chinese in Cambodia died, as did around 40 percent of the Lao and Thai who lived along the border. Probably every Cambodian of Vietnamese heritage who didn't flee or hide in time ended up dead at the hands of the Khmer Rouge. None have been found who survived the era out in the open.[2]

Every institution across the country—temples, schools, mosques, stores—was closed as the Khmer Rouge began to wipe out Cambodia's intellectuals. Obviously, teachers, students, journalists, and priests were killed right away, but anyone tainted by education was suspect. Wearing glasses or knowing a foreign language was enough to prove that a person had been poisoned by a dangerous degree of learning. These people would be killed as well, as would their parents, spouses, and children. As with the Soviet purges and Mao's Cultural Revolution, the taint of being a class enemy fell on all of the members of a family.

Tuol Sleng high school in the suburbs of Phnom Penh was adapted as a prison, S-21. The records show that only 7 of the 14,000 prisoners who entered this building survived the visit. That's seven *period*, not seven thousand.[3] The rest are now just pictures in file folders and jumbled bones in the ground. After the suspects confessed to whatever crimes they were charged with (they always confessed), they were taken to the nearby village of Choeung Ek in batches to be shot and dumped into mass graves. A quarter century later, forensic archaeologists had exhumed almost 9,000 skeletons from eighty-nine burial pits at Choeung Ek. Many more remain to be explored.

The year 1975 was reset as the year zero, with April 17 as its first day. Money was abolished; it was not needed in the new society. Farming provided everything a person needed according to a simple formula. Those who worked were fed, housed, and clothed. Those who didn't were shot.

Party cadres enforced discipline all across the countryside. On the farms, Khmer Rouge overseers summarily killed people for laziness or backtalk. They killed them for slowing down after the endless cycle of hard work, poor food, and little sleep. They killed them for stealing food to supplement their meager rations. They killed them if they showed anger or sadness when someone else was killed. Famine swept through the rest.

Refugee camps sprang up across the border in Thailand, holding as many as 600,000 frightened Cambodians by the regime's end. When stories of the atrocities began to leak out, the world was shocked—if not shocked then skeptical. No one had ever seen anything like it. No other revolution had been so thorough about wiping out every trace of the old ways so quickly. Never had such a merciless mass murder been directed against a people by their own kind.

Pol Pot

Unlike most other Communist regimes, there was no cult of personality surrounding the ruler of Cambodia. At first, Prince Sihanouk (see "Vietnam War") was the public face of the regime, but after about a year, he was arrested and kept out of sight. As far as anyone knew, the secretive Angka (the "Organization"), a shadowy cabal of faceless ideologues, ran Cambodia.[4] The leader was known publicly only as "Brother Number One."

Born under the name Saloth Sar to prosperous peasants in an undetermined year of the 1920s, Brother Number One had been educated by Buddhist monks, Catholic nuns, and Parisian professors. They had tried to teach him useful skills like carpentry and radio electronics, but he was more interested in politics and he failed at several schools. After joining the Viet Minh rebels in their fight against the French, he went to school in Paris. When he flunked out, he returned to Phnom Penh to teach (his day job) and to help organize the small Cambodian contingent of the Viet Minh into a separate movement directed at overthrowing the monarchy (his hobby). In 1963, a police crackdown in the capital forced him to flee to the countryside. There he acquired the war name Pol Pot.[5]

After rising to general secretary of the Communist party, Pol Pot proceeded to weed out the less pure among his colleagues. He cleaned out foreigners, moderates, and intellectuals. By the time the Khmer Rouge took over Cambodia, only the purest remained in the organization. This massive turnover had removed the movement's elders and experienced veterans, and filled the ranks with fanatic teenagers—often children—which might explain a lot of the impetuous cruelty of the regime.[6]

Third Indochina War

As Cambodians, the Khmer Rouge had inherited an ethnic hatred of the Vietnamese that transcended Communist solidarity. When the Cambodians tried to intimidate the Vietnamese by raiding over the border, they stirred up a hornets' nest. The Vietnamese army crossed in full force in December 1978, and it quickly became a proxy fight in the larger rivalry between China (patron of the Khmer Rouge) and Russia (patron of Vietnam). Within two weeks, the Vietnamese were in Phnom Penh, and the Angka had fled to the countryside. The Khmer Rouge were soon driven even farther back and quarantined in the boondocks where they could do less harm.

In one of those Orwellian "Oceania has always been at war with Eurasia" ironies, the United States joined China in supporting the fugitive Khmer Rouge in their fight against the Vietnamese-Soviet puppets installed in Phnom Penh. Even though everyone knew about their atrocities by now, the Khmer Rouge remained seated at the United Nations as the official government of Cambodia until 1992, when most of the factions in the ongoing civil war agreed to stop fighting and hold free elections under UN sponsorship.

After Pol Pot disappeared into the jungle in 1979, he was not seen again until a video surfaced in July 1997 showing a frail old man on trial for treason in a Khmer Rouge enclave. His former comrades sentenced him to house arrest in a hut near the Thai border.[7] After a few more months of silence, in April 1998 reporters and officials were brought to the hut and shown his corpse, dead of a heart attack.[8]

Death Toll

The Cambodian autogenocide is probably second to the Holocaust as the most studied megamurder of the twentieth century, so body counts are easy to find. At one extreme, the Cambodian government installed by the Vietnamese conquerors claimed that 3.3 million Cambodians had died under the previous Khmer Rouge regime.[9] This comes to about half of the original population, and it is the upper limit of plausibility. At the other end, Michael Vickery's estimate of 400,000 deaths is the lowest death toll ever seriously suggested by a knowledgeable historian.[10] Most authorities estimate the death toll to be in the range of 1 to 2 million, and Ben Kiernan's estimate of 1,670,000[11] (approximately one-fifth of the population) is probably the most widely accepted specific number.

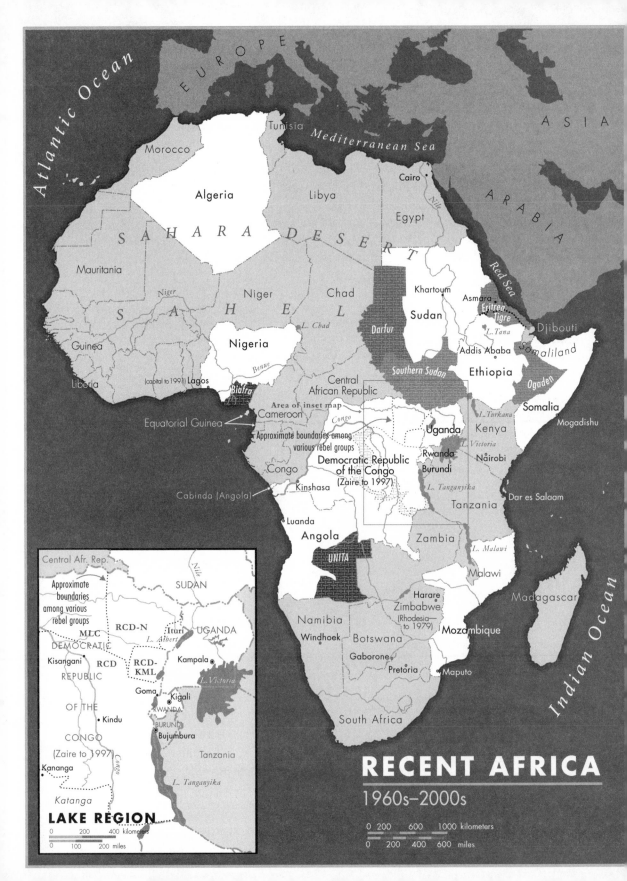

EUROPE

ASIA

ARABIA

Atlantic Ocean

Mediterranean Sea

Tunisia

Morocco

Algeria

Libya

Egypt

Cairo

Nile

Red Sea

S A H A R A   D E S E R T

Mauritania

Khartoum

Asmara

Eritrea
Tigre

Djibouti

Somaliland

Niger

Chad

Sudan

S A H E L

L. Chad

L. Tana

Darfur

Addis Ababa

Guinea

Nigeria

Benue

Southern Sudan

Ethiopia

Ogaden

Somalia

Liberia

(capital to 1991) Lagos

Biafra

Central
African Republic

Area of inset map

Congo

Uganda

L. Turkana

Kenya

Mogadishu

Cameroon

Equatorial Guinea

Approximate boundaries among
various rebel groups

Rwanda

L. Victoria

Nairobi

Congo

Democratic Republic
of the Congo
(Zaire to 1997)

Burundi

L. Tanganyika

Tanzania

Dar es Salaam

Kinshasa

Cabinda (Angola)

Luanda

Zambia

Angola

UNITA

Malawi

L. Malawi

Madagascar

Indian Ocean

Namibia

Harare

Zimbabwe
(Rhodesia—
to 1979)

Mozambique

Windhoek

Botswana

Gaborone

Maputo

Pretoria

South Africa

RECENT AFRICA

1960s–2000s

0   200   600   1000 kilometers

0   200   400   600 miles

LAKE REGION

Central Afr. Rep.

Nile

SUDAN

Approximate
boundaries
among various
rebel groups

RCD-N

Ituri

UGANDA

MLC

L. Albert

DEMOCRATIC

Kisangani

RCD

RCD-
KML

Kampala

REPUBLIC

L. Victoria

Goma

Kigali

OF THE

RWANDA

Kindu

BURUNDI

Bujumbura

CONGO

Tanzania

(Zaire to 1997)

Kananga

Congo

L. Tanganyika

Katanga

0   200   400 kilometers

0   100   200 miles

MOZAMBICAN CIVIL WAR

Death toll: 800,000[1]
Rank: 55
Type: ideological civil war
Broad dividing line: Frelimo vs. Renamo
Time frame: 1975–92
Location and major state participant: Mozambique
Minor state participant: South Africa
Major non-state participant: Renamo
Who usually gets the most blame: Renamo
Another damn: African civil war

MOST EUROPEANS DUMPED THEIR AFRICAN COLONIES BETWEEN 1955 and 1965, after which the last stubborn bastion of white rule in Africa was a bloc of lands in the south: the apartheid regimes of South Africa and Rhodesia nestled among the Portuguese colonies of Angola and Mozambique.

A broad coalition of rebels inside Portuguese East Africa organized the Front for Liberation of Mozambique (Frelimo) in 1962. They kept the pressure on the Portuguese government with a backwoods civil war for the next dozen years in the hopes that the imperialists would eventually give up and go home.

In 1974 a coup in Lisbon replaced the military dictatorship of Portugal with democrats, and the next year the new government granted independence to Portugal's overseas colonies. Frelimo took control of Mozambique, after which the government declared itself Communist and cultivated support from the Soviets. Mozambique now became a haven and staging center for rebels fighting against the neighboring apartheid regimes.

In retaliation, Rhodesia and South Africa organized and armed outcasts, malcontents, and dissidents of all stripes as a new rebel organization, the Mozambique Resistance Movement (Renamo). Renamo had no unifying ideology or political goals other than the overthrow of Frelimo. Renamo's leadership came from "traditional authorities down on their luck—petty chiefs, *curandeiros* (healers), witch doctors, spirit mediums—discarded as Frelimo laid the foundations for a pan-ethnic, socialist millennium. Magic played a useful part in keeping up Renamo's fighting spirit. If its fighters rubbed their bodies with herbs, Frelimo's bullets would 'turn to water.'"[2] Rank-and-file support came from peasants who were forced by Frelimo to give up whatever small land they had and go to work on collective farms instead.

Renamo tried to destabilize the government by terrorizing civilians and damaging the economy. The rebels destroyed bridges and power plants, bringing the country to its knees. Even worse, their attacks against the general population were designed to maximize terror. Villagers often had their ears, lips, and noses cut away, and then were let loose as a warning to others. In 1988, a report for the U.S. State Department estimated that Renamo had blatantly murdered 100,000 people during the mid-1980s with raids, kidnappings, and random shootings. Their atrocities drove 1 million refugees into exile in other countries and left another 3.5 million displaced internally.[3]

After years of war, the World Bank ranked Mozambique the poorest country in the world—not second or third, not "among the poorest," but dead last.[4] Talks between the two sides began in 1990, and soon after that, Communist Russia and apartheid South Africa were swept into the dustbin of history.* This left Mozambique entirely on its own, no longer a pawn in larger struggles. Without sponsors to supply fresh ammunition, the two sides agreed to a cease-fire in 1992. Frelimo was confirmed in power by multiparty elections held in October 1994, while Renamo emerged as a legitimate opposition party with a surprising amount of support.

---

* White-run Rhodesia had already become black-run Zimbabwe in 1979.

ANGOLAN CIVIL WAR

Death toll: 500,000[1]
Rank: 70
Type: ideological civil war
Broad dividing line: MPLA vs. UNITA
Time frame: 1975–94
Location and major state participant: Angola
Minor state participants: Cuba, South Africa
Major non-state participant: UNITA
Who usually gets the most blame: Jonas Savimbi
Another damn: African civil war
Economic factors: oil, diamonds

AT FIRST GLANCE, THIS LOOKS LIKE THE EXACT SAME WAR AS THE ONE IN Mozambique (see "Mozambican Civil War") but with different names. Marxist guerrillas (in this case, the Popular Movement for the Liberation of Angola, or MPLA) took over Angola after the Portuguese left in 1975, propped up by Soviet aid. South Africa supported an insurgency to keep them from meddling in South Africa's affairs. The war fizzled out after their foreign sponsors collapsed. Just replace "Renamo" with "UNITA," and we've got our chapter.

By the 1980s the rebels of the National Union for the Total Independence of Angola (UNITA), led by the charismatic thug Jonas Savimbi, managed to carve out one-third of the country as their own autonomous enclave. In addition to South African aid, the United States, Ivory Coast, and Mobutu Sese Seko of Zaire (Congo) supported Savimbi's fight against the MPLA government.

Unlike Mozambique, Angola has some obvious natural resources: diamonds and oil. The war kept production down, which drove prices up, so the few companies willing to risk getting caught in the crossfire earned nice profits. These companies generally had to maintain large private armies, which gave them a free hand to exploit the resources however they wanted, without competition or labor disputes. The diamond companies often shot down anyone they caught near company mines trying to dig diamonds for themselves. Even farmers hoeing their crops might be mistaken for illegal miners and shot.[2]

The Angolan war sucked in more foreign troops than the average African conflict. Fifty thousand Cuban combat troops helped to prop up the MPLA,[3] while South African soldiers often crossed the border to hunt down insurgents from South Africa's satellite country, Namibia. In 1978, at Cassinga in Angola, the South Africans massacred 600 Namibian refugees, claiming that the community harbored terrorists; however, most of them, maybe all of them, were noncombatants.

A cease-fire was negotiated in 1991, and multiparty elections were held the next year, but when Savimbi realized he was going to lose the election, he went back to fighting. Another year of conflict killed another 100,000 Angolans before Savimbi was offered a power-sharing agreement. He turned it down, but by then his former supporters had soured on him. UNITA was embargoed, and American President Bill Clinton finally recognized MPLA as the legitimate government in 1994. This is usually considered the official end of the war.

Without foreign sponsors, only diamond smuggling kept Savimbi financed, and he was pushed farther and farther away from the important parts of the country. He was finally killed in a fight with government forces in 2002, after which UNITA quieted down.

UGANDAN BUSH WAR

Death toll: 500,000[1]
Rank: 70
Type: civil war
Broad dividing line: Obote vs. Museveni
Time frame: 1979–86
Location and major state participant: Uganda
Major non-state participant: National Resistance Army
Who usually gets the most blame: Milton Obote
Another damn: African civil war

AFTER DRIVING IDI AMIN OUT OF UGANDA (SEE "IDI AMIN"), TANZANIA turned the country over to a commission of Ugandans, who tested and discarded a series of ineffective heads of state over the next few months. Finally, a rigged election in December 1980 picked Milton Obote, Uganda's very first president (1962–69), to be the new president. Although Obote had been a relatively decent and only slightly corrupt president the first time around, he had grown bitter in exile.

This time, he ran Uganda almost entirely on behalf of a handful of favored tribes—the Tesos, the Acholis, and Obote's own people, the Langis—who had suffered under Amin's tyranny. Obote quickly created a dictatorship that was every bit as bad as Idi Amin's, but less colorfully eccentric, so the world mostly ignored it.

Opposition to Obote coalesced around Yoweri Museveni and his National Resistance Army. Unlike Amin and Obote, Museveni was a southern Bantu, specifically a member of the Banyankole tribe. He was also more educated than those leaders, a graduate of a college in Tanzania.

Resistance to Obote was strongest in the Luwero Triangle, north of the capital Kampala. Obote's soldiers terrorized the Triangle and drove two-thirds of the population out. Women were routinely gang-raped. North Korean advisers taught the army the newest torture techniques. In mid-1981, the army massacred sixty people at the Red Cross center. Museveni's rebels recruited heavily among the orphans created by Obote's army's massacres, but he trained them in moderate politics rather than the usual radicalism of revolutionary fronts.

A massacre of several dozen townspeople, including an Anglican cleric, in May 1984 in Namugongo just outside Kampala proved to be the last straw. As the world condemned

Obote for such a visible atrocity, his commander in the Triangle, an Acholi named Bazilio Olara Okello, overthrew him in July 1985. Obote fled to exile in Zambia. Okello, however, got off to a really bad start when his troops ran amok in the capital, killing and looting with impunity.

Although support quickly shifted to the rebels, Museveni bided his time until the hatred for the Okello regime was overwhelming. Museveni was a student of Mao—the good Mao—the rebel Mao who moved like a fish through the ocean of the common people. When Museveni took the capital in January 1986, there were no killings, and as his rebels mopped up resistance in the countryside, there were no reported atrocities. Museveni quickly established a remarkable level of peace and security to a nation that had epitomized Third World hellholes for a generation.[2]

POST-COLONIAL AFRICA

THE CIVIL WARS IN ANGOLA, MOZAMBIQUE, AND UGANDA ARE TYPICAL OF the conflicts that have raged across Africa for the past forty years. Here's a quick list of the deadliest civil wars on the continent after independence:

1. Congo (1998–2002): 3,800,000
2. Sudan (1983–2005): 1,900,000[1]
3. Nigeria (1966–70): 1,000,000
4. Rwanda (1994): 937,000
5. Mozambique (1975–92): 800,000
6. Ethiopia (1962–92): 500,000
7. Somalia (from 1991): 500,000
8. Angola (1975–2002): 500,000
9. Sudan (1955–72): 500,000
10. Uganda (1979–86): 500,000
11. Burundi (1993–2004): 260,000[2]
12. Liberia (1989–2003): 250,000[3]
13. Darfur (from 2003): 200,000

If you find it difficult to keep all of these African countries straight, don't worry about it. Their names and outlines aren't important. African countries rarely correspond to any authentic national entity. The continent was arbitrarily sliced up among the colonial powers at the big European conferences of the nineteenth century. A coastal fort or Christian mission would be enough to justify carving a small territory out of the surrounding countryside, and drawing a straight line between any two landmarks on the map was usually the easiest way to delineate territory. These little enclaves were then assembled into vast empires that shipped rubber, ivory, gold, copper, coffee, and diamonds out across the ocean.

By the beginning of the twentieth century, these territories were being swapped around in exchange for concessions elsewhere, or else they were tossed into the pot like poker chips during each European war. In each colony, the European powers usually picked one ethnic group over all of the others to educate and hire as civil servants and sergeants, thereby creating a local minority that supported the status quo. This created a cycle of privilege and resentment that carried over into independence. The African countries that were set free in the 1960s and 1970s had no particular identity other than as former colonies of someone else. In general, each new country contained an unhappy mix of traditional enemies that quarreled like a sack of tomcats.

Imperialism, however, was only the beginning. Most African countries have now been independent almost as long as they were under colonial domination, and they have been equally abused by the native leaders that followed independence. In general, these leaders used the rhetoric of anti-colonialism, anti-Communism, or anti-capitalism—whatever worked—to drum up support at home and abroad, and to gain a free hand in looting their countries for personal gain.

The best of these might actually have been hailed as enlightened despots in eighteenth-century Europe. Sure, they've skimmed a little off the top, put relatives on the payroll, and tossed outspoken newspaper editors into jail, but on the plus side, they redirected some of the taxes back into schools, clinics, roads, and the power grid, and forced multinational corporations to pay a fair price for extracting national resources. The middling tyrants of Africa have skimmed more, oppressed more, squandered huge sums on flashy vanity projects, and happily given away national resources in exchange for bribes. The worst of them built up paranoid cults of personality and then set out to rid their domains of anyone who failed to appreciate their magnificence. Only in the 1990s did we start to see some African countries become viable democracies.*

African diplomats insist that redrawing borders is a far lower priority than fixing Africa's many social and economic problems. Even so, the future will probably see plenty more wars as Africa either adjusts its borders to fit the ethnic distribution or adjusts its ethnic distribution to fit the borders. Either way will involve armies.

---

* Except for Botswana, which has been a democracy since it started in 1966. This is so unusual it deserves a mention.

SOVIET-AFGHAN WAR

Death toll: 1.5 million[1]

Rank: 40

Type: ideological civil war

Broad dividing line: Communists vs. mujahideen

Time frame: 1979–92

Location: Afghanistan

Major state participants: Afghanistan, Soviet Union

Major non-state participants: lots of warlords

Who usually gets the most blame: Leonid Brezhnev

Another damn: superpower ground war in Asia

The unanswerable question everyone asks: Did this cause the fall of the Soviet Union?

Coups and Countercoups

Early in the Cold War, Afghanistan had been a lukewarm Soviet client state. It wasn't Communist, but the Soviets were eager to keep their next-door neighbor stable, so they happily supplied the monarchy in Kabul with all of the guns and money it needed to maintain order.

In July 1973, while the king of Afghanistan was vacationing in France, a coup by his prime minister and cousin, General Mohammad Daoud Khan, made a return trip unnecessary. Afghanistan shifted from a lazy monarchy to a lazy dictatorship with hardly a blink at the United Nations; however, this interruption of the status quo caused both sides of the Cold War to reconsider. Daoud had no specific political agenda or orientation, but when Iran (an American client state at the time, under the shah) began to pour money into the country to buy Daoud's friendship, Afghan Communists planned their own power play.

In April 1978, Communists in the Afghan army seized power and killed Daoud. The new leader, Nur Mohammad Taraki, began the usual Communist reforms aimed at dragging the country out of the Middle Ages, which ignited a small civil war between Communists and traditionalists throughout the country. Taraki began hauling rebels and dissidents into the new Soviet-built Policharki prison near Kabul, where tens of thousands would be killed and shoveled into mass graves over the next decade.

With the fundamentalist Muslim revolution taking over Iran (January to April 1979), the Russians became skittish about the Muslim minorities inside the Soviet Union, and they were anxious to keep Afghanistan from getting out of control. They cranked up foreign aid and assigned more advisers to the government.

In March 1979, Afghan workers who had recently returned from Iran with Islamist notions rioted against Communist secular programs in the west Afghan city of Herat. The local army garrison mutinied as well, taking control of the city. They hunted down and killed dozens, maybe hundreds, of Soviet advisers and their families, parading their mutilated bodies through the streets. In retaliation, Afghan tanks and Soviet aircraft flattened the city, killing as many as 20,000 Heratis.[2]

In September 1979 the Soviet leader Leonid Brezhnev met with Taraki but continued to turn down the Afghan leader's request for Soviet ground troops. Brezhnev knew that open intervention would only turn the Afghan people against their Communist government. Almost immediately following the Afghan leader's return to Kabul, Taraki was killed in a countercoup led by his deputy, Hafizullah Amin, an American-educated independent Communist. Brezhnev was shocked at the murder of his recent guest and reconsidered intervention.[*]

In December 1979, Soviet commandos swooped in out of the blue, attacking the palace and killing Amin. Then Brezhnev's preferred president for Afghanistan, Babrak Kamal, returned from Soviet exile and was put in charge. Brezhnev quickly approved Kamal's request for large numbers of Soviet ground troops.[3]

War

At this point—mere days after it had started—everyone knew that the Soviets had already lost the war. Or at least, that's what they claimed later. In their memoirs, all of the Soviet generals swore they had tried to talk Brezhnev out of invading the country. Advisers to American President Jimmy Carter claimed to have giggled and skipped happily down the halls of the White House[†] now that Russia was about to have its own Vietnam.

In practice, it took almost a decade for the Soviet Union to realize it couldn't win the war.

The Afghan war doesn't flow in any traditional narrative structure. It was mostly a matter of patrols, raids, and local offensives against a patchwork of warlords and rebel alliances. By 1984, the Soviets had 115,000 troops in Afghanistan, but only 15 percent of them were available for offensive combat. The other 85 percent of the Soviet soldiers were tied

---

[*] It didn't help Amin's reputation in Moscow that he had had fourteen suspicious meetings with Adolph Dubs, the U.S. ambassador. In February 1979, Dubs was kidnapped by mysterious assailants and killed during the rescue attempt. Most investigators suspect Taraki of planning a hit. (Harrison, "End of the Road")

[†] Not exactly, but that's the gist.

down in garrison duties, and they never really controlled more than the big cities and the roads that connected them. The rest of the country belonged to guerrillas and warlords. The mujahideen (Muslim rebels) relied on Pakistan and Iran as safe havens to train and recuperate out of Soviet reach.

The United States, in partnership with conservative Muslim states such as Saudi Arabia, funded and supplied the rebels by funneling aid through Pakistan. The new fundamentalist Islamic Republic of Iran also supported the rebels, although definitely *not* in partnership with the United States.

Rebels of the Tajik ethnic group under Ahmad Shah Masoud held the Panjsher Valley throughout both the Soviet and the Taliban era. Because it branched off the main road between Kabul and the Soviet border, control of the Panjsher Valley was vital to the outcome of the war. The Soviets launched as many as nine massive armored offensives against rebel strongholds here without ever securing it.

When the rebels proved too slippery to catch, the Communist forces often responded by just killing whomever they could find—hostages, family members, or suspicious-looking bystanders. Despite press censorship, scattered reports of atrocities filtered out of the war zone. Any rebel bombing or rocket attack could provoke a brutal Soviet retaliation. In 1979, Soviet and Afghan government forces killed 1,300 villagers in Konarha Province.[4] In early 1985, the Soviets massacred hundreds of civilians in the northern province of Kunduz.[5] As a reprisal for an attack on a convoy near Kandahar in October 1983, three nearby villages were wiped out.[6]

Winding Down

By 1985 the mujahideen were almost broken, but the Soviets didn't know it. Instead, Mikhail Gorbachev's new reformist regime in Moscow began to reconsider the whole Afghan adventure. During 1985 and 1986, the Soviets pulled back from big combat operations, leaving the major fighting to the Afghan army. At this point, the Soviets would only initiate action with small commando raids by special forces. By 1987, the Soviet policy was to fight only defensive battles and only when necessary.

President Kamal was retired to Moscow in May 1986, and the leadership of Afghanistan was handed over to Muhammad Najibullah, the head of the secret police. During 1987, he tried to be less dictatorial and bring the moderate opposition into the government in an attempt to split the rebellion.

At a private meeting in September 1987, Soviet Foreign Minister Eduard Shevardnadze tried to interest American Secretary of State George Shultz in a cooperative approach to Afghanistan. He tried to convince his American counterpart that Islamist fundamentalism would soon be more dangerous to the West than Communism would be, and that the superpowers should jointly rebuild the war-torn nation. Nothing came of this, but it's one of those missed opportunities that always looms larger in hindsight, especially on September 11, 2001, when mujahideen operating out of Afghanistan attacked the United States.

By October 1987, as the war wound down, there were 2.9 million Afghan refugees in camps in Pakistan, and 2.3 million in Iran.[7] The Geneva Accords, which normalized relations between Afghanistan and Pakistan, were signed in April 1988 and are usually regarded as the beginning of the end of the war, even though they only included sovereign nations and were not signed by the mujahideen. The Soviets started to withdraw their troops in May, with the last of them leaving in February 1989.

This was the last conflict of the Cold War, and by now it had become clear that the Soviet Union couldn't afford to keep up with its American rivals. The war in Afghanistan had cost the Soviets about the same that the 1991 Gulf War would cost the Americans ($70 billion[8] versus $61 billion,[9] respectively), but the results were radically different. For the Soviets, those billions of dollars had been scrounged and doled out over ten years, costing 13,310 Soviet lives, leaving them at the other end beaten, bankrupted, and exhausted. For roughly the same price—pocket change by Western standards—the Americans could fight a more concentrated war, winning in less than one year with a loss of only 383 lives.*

War without End

Violating every prediction made at the time, the Communist government in Kabul held on for several years after the Russians left. It successfully kept the rebels at bay, and it was only internal divisions in the government that finally brought it down. As the rebels closed in, President Muhammad Najibullah resigned and handed the government over to a subordinate who couldn't hold onto it either. In 1992, the Muslim fundamentalist Taliban militia took Kabul and imprisoned Najibullah. He languished under arrest for a few years until September 1996, when he was tossed to the crowd, castrated, shot, and strung up from a traffic light.

The lynching of Najibullah is as good a place as any to close the chapter on the war in Afghanistan. Much of Afghanistan remained under the thumb of local warlords, and the world as a whole did not recognize the Taliban as legitimate rulers, but Communism was no longer an option, so the world ignored the Afghans for several years. Since then, the war has shifted in a new direction, which—so far—hasn't killed enough people to make my list.

---

* Actually, much of this bill was paid by the oil-rich Arab countries that the United States was defending, but that only highlights the point that the West had a *lot* more money than the East and could spend a lot more on its war machine.

SADDAM HUSSEIN

Death toll: 300,000 killed internally[1]
Rank: 96
Type: despot
Broad dividing line: Saddam vs. everyone
Time frame: ruled 1979–2003
Location and major state participant: Iraq
Who usually gets the most blame: Saddam
Economic factor: oil
The unanswerable question everyone asks: Was he really as evil as the U.S. government made him out to be?

NEVER A SOLDIER DESPITE THE UNIFORM HE HABITUALLY WORE, SADDAM spent his youth as a street brawler and enforcer for the Ba'ath Party—revolutionary pan-Arab nationalists. The overthrow of the Iraqi monarchy in 1958 led to a decade of coups and countercoups, in which the Ba'ath sometimes won and sometimes lost. By 1968, Saddam was the chief deputy to the dictator, Ahmad Hassan al-Bakr, and in July 1979 he set aside his ailing boss and quickly killed anyone who seemed likely to object.

Iraq is an artificial country with borders that were drawn to suit the European colonial powers (Britain especially) rather than to reflect local allegiances. In this multiethnic mishmash, Saddam gave lucrative favors to the Sunni Arab minority concentrated in the center of the country in exchange for their help in keeping the Shiite Arab majority under control. Saddam especially promoted family and friends from his hometown of Tikrit to high positions and encouraged them to loot their various fiefdoms with near impunity, although any cronies who showed ambition beyond simple greed would be dragged away and killed.[2]

Saddam himself was the idolized apex of power. He erected statues to his glory and hung posters wherever statues wouldn't fit. Songs praising him opened television newscasts.[3] He maintained tight control over his people by propagandizing himself into a great hero and then whisking away in the dead of night anyone who dared disagree. In prisons up and down Iraq, tens of thousands of troublemakers were either tortured and killed or tortured and released as a warning to others. Mutilated bodies of state enemies were returned to their families for burial in order to spread rumors of savage treatment in prison.[4] Innocent family members of dissidents were kidnapped, raped, tortured, or killed as an additional punishment against anyone who got on his bad side.[5]

Kurds

While most dictators in the past half century have been content to stay at home and quietly brutalize only their own countries, Saddam tried twice to expand into his neighbors, first Iran (1980–88) and then Kuwait (1990–91). He failed both times and turned his wrath against his own people.

The Kurdish minority that straddled the border of Turkey, Iran, and Iraq had been sporadically resisting Iraqi rule since the country had been formed after World War I. When the Kurdish town of Halabja just inside Iraq fell to an Iranian advance in March 1988, the local Kurds welcomed the liberation. Angered by the disloyalty, Saddam unleashed hell against Halabja. Several rounds of airstrikes destroyed the town with explosives, napalm, and poison gas, indiscriminately killing 5,000 or so civilians.[6]

By this time, Saddam had focused on the Kurds as the scapegoats for the failure of his war with Iran. Between February and September 1988, Saddam's troops systematically swept through Kurdish territory, destroying the rural Kurds village by village in Operation Anfal. The men of fighting age were trucked off to be beaten, shot, and dumped into mass graves. The elderly were sent to concentration camps in the south to be starved, and the women were resettled, often sold as brides or nightclub hostesses across the Arab world.[7] Saddam killed anywhere from 100,000 to 200,000 Kurds in this operation.[8]

Americans

In 1991, as the American-led coalition drove Saddam out of Kuwait, the Americans encouraged the Iraqis to throw off the dictator who had dragged them into a war against the entire world. The Shiite Arabs of the southern marshes rose in revolt, expecting the coalition to come to their aid. The Americans were not about to get sucked into a civil war, so they held back while Saddam moved in and massacred 50,000 Shiite rebels, sympathizers, and bystanders. A simultaneous uprising of Kurds also failed to dislodge him, and Saddam drove the Kurds into the mountains of the north where American air cover eventually helped them establish an autonomous zone.

Although the world quarantined Saddam and Iraq after 1990 for disrupting international calm, that never seemed like a satisfactory solution. Leaving such a valuable supply of the world's oil sitting unused under a pariah dictator was dangerous and unprofitable. In March 2003, hoping to drag Iraq kicking and screaming back into the community of nations and the global economy, American President George Bush (the younger) invaded Iraq and clumsily replaced Saddam with what was supposed to be a lucrative and stabilizing outpost of Western Civilization in the heart of unfriendly territory, but it deteriorated into car bombs and chaos instead.

Saddam, now a prisoner, was tried and hanged by this new regime in 2006.

IRAN-IRAQ WAR

Death toll: 700,000[1]
Rank: 61
Type: hegemonial war
Broad dividing line and major state participants: Iran vs. Iraq
Time frame: 1980–88
Location: Persian Gulf
Who usually gets the most blame: Saddam Hussein
Economic factor: oil

IRAN AND IRAQ HAD DISPUTED OWNERSHIP OF THE OIL-RICH BORDERLANDS along the Shatt al-Arab River at the head of the Persian Gulf for years. Then Saddam Hussein tried to take advantage of the chaos unleashed by the 1979 Iranian Revolution by annexing the disputed territory. Iraqi armies crossed into Iran in September 1980 and rammed through the first Iranian lines of defense, but as Iranian resistance stiffened, the war stalled in the outskirts of the city of Abadan.[2]

When two of the world's leading suppliers of oil go to war, the rest of the world has to take sides, but when the war pits a brutal dictatorship against a fanatic theocracy, it's hard to know which side to take. As a purely practical matter, however, it's easier to line up with corrupt dictators because they're usually more willing to work a deal. During the Iran-Iraq War, most of the world tossed in with Iraq. Centrist Muslim states such as Egypt, Pakistan, and Saudi Arabia openly assisted the Iraqis, as did the Soviets, who were the traditional Cold War sponsors of Iraq. The United States supplied the Iraqis with intelligence, and committed the U.S. Navy to safeguarding the flow of oil out of (and the flow of money and arms into) Iraq.

The Islamic Republic of Iran was too crazy for any respectable nation to support openly, but plenty of nations operated covertly. The world's outcast states—Israel, South Africa, North Korea, and Libya, for example—supported their fellow outcast by supplying military technology and expertise in exchange for cash or oil. Iran also got secret aid from the superpowers in exchange for the Iranians using their influence with dangerous Muslim fanatics in Afghanistan (Russians) and Lebanon (Americans).[3]

In May 1982, an Iranian counterattack restored the antebellum border and shifted the momentum of the conflict. Over the next couple of years, the Iranians gradually slugged deeper into Iraq, until once again the war stalled in the suburbs of a major objective, the Iraqi city of Basra.

By now, both sides had turned desperate and were fighting dirtier than usual. To terrorize the enemy population, both sides sent warplanes and missiles screaming out of the sky into cities far behind the front lines. Iraq shelled enemy soldiers with nerve gas. Iranians took advantage of their superior numbers and fanatically religious youth to launch human waves against Iraqi positions in the hopes that some—not many—might break through.

Iran launched Operation Kheiber (Dawn) from mid-February to mid-March 1984 over control of the strategic Basra-Baghdad waterway. It was an artless slugging match of Iranian frontal assaults and Iraqi gas attacks that killed 20,000 Iranians and 6,000 Iraqis— and mutilated and scarred tens of thousands more—in less than a month.[4]

The last major offensive was the Battle of Basra, which became the bloodiest battle fought anywhere in the world since World War II. From December 1986 to April 1987, approximately 50,000 Iranians and 8,000 to 15,000 Iraqis were slaughtered for no gain on either side.[5]

None of these efforts broke the stalemate; they merely elevated this conflict to the deadliest war for soldiers since Vietnam. Finally, in August 1988, when it became clear that no one was going to win, the two exhausted countries agreed to a cease-fire negotiated by the UN.

SANCTIONS AGAINST IRAQ

Death toll: 350,000[1]
Rank: 94
Type: international standoff
Broad dividing line: Iraq vs. the world
Time frame: 1990–2003
Location: Iraq
Major state participants: Iraq, United States
Major non-state participant: United Nations
Who usually gets the most blame: United States, Saddam Hussein
Economic factor: oil

Gulf War

Foiled in his attempt to expand into Iran, Saddam Hussein turned around and conquered Kuwait in August 1990. Almost immediately, the UN imposed trade sanctions, while the United States flew troops into the region and issued an ultimatum: Saddam had to be out of Kuwait by January 15, 1991, or else. As the deadline approached, pacifists begged the United States to give the sanctions more time, but President George Bush (the elder) was in no mood to wait. When the appointed day passed, the American-led coalition opened an air attack, and two months later, a ground attack.

The war went precisely according to plan, and the Iraqis were quickly driven back into their own country. The coalition stopped short of invading Iraq and deposing Saddam because no one wanted to spend long bloody years occupying a hostile country.

The Gulf War killed perhaps 25,000 Iraqi soldiers and a couple of thousand civilians, which isn't enough to make my list.[2] Iraq's industrial infrastructure had taken a beating in the air war, but it wasn't anything that a healthy economy couldn't repair. It never got the chance.

Peace Returns

Under the terms of the 1991 cease-fire, economic sanctions would stay in place until Saddam dismantled his ability to threaten his neighbors. Saddam was supposed to surrender or destroy all of his facilities for producing and deploying weapons of mass destruction (WMDs). He had to shut down his chemical weapons labs and surrender his surface-to-surface missiles. Naturally, as a warmongering dictator, Saddam stalled as long as possible, nurturing the fear and respect that big weapons give a little country.

The blockade was enforced by coalition warships patrolling the Persian Gulf, which inspected all cargo heading for Iraq.[3] Meanwhile, with no oil exports, the Iraqi economy collapsed. Education became sporadic. Medicine became rare. People died in hospitals from trivial shortages of common supplies. With no jobs available, professionals like lawyers and architects drove cabs. Massive unemployment destroyed the standard of living. Iraq had once been among the richest and most cosmopolitan Arab countries, but now it became the most ragged and outcast.[4]

In August 1991, when it became obvious that the sanctions were devastating the ordinary people of Iraq, the UN offered to let Iraq export oil in exchange for credit that could be spent only on food, medicine, and other civilian necessities. Saddam refused to agree to these conditions until 1995. He personally was not starving and the shortages gave him a useful tool for controlling his people and rewarding his cronies.[5]

As with all famines—even artificial famines like this one—the powerful continued to live quite nicely. While his people suffered, Saddam sacrificed none of his comfort. He spent hundreds of millions of dollars "on palaces—building about a dozen since the sanctions started. . . . [H]e opened a new vacation village with an amusement park, stadiums and a bronze statue of himself. Saddam's police [got] brand new Hyundai patrol cars and the street signs [got] brand-new, well-lighted portraits of the president."[6]

Saddam stalled and shuffled his contraband one step ahead of the UN's weapons inspectors like a three-card Monte game. Finally, he kicked out the UN inspectors in 1998. The Americans then launched air strikes, which destroyed the last WMD facilities. No one outside Iraq knew the threat was actually gone, and Saddam wasn't about to admit his impotence to the world at large, so the sanctions remained in place. The standoff dragged on until Saddam was deposed by the American invasion in 2003.

Analysis

As with many deaths by hardship, we can't easily point to individuals and say he died, she died, he died, and so on. It's not like deaths in battle, where you just count the bodies strewn about. Instead, we see an increase over the ordinary death rate, and all we can say is that some of these people would have died anyway, but some would not have. It's a matter of statistics.

Over the years, the Iraqi government issued a series of escalating death tolls to highlight their suffering, from 700,000[7] to 1 million[8] to 1.5 million.[9] Each new claim was dutifully repeated by the press and international agencies, but there's no reason to believe any of them. We can be polite and point out that these high estimates "are based on faulty baseline statistics for prewar childhood mortality in Iraq,"[10] or we can impolitely suggest that bureaucrats in the pay of a dictator made them up. Various estimates by impartial outsiders are as low as 110,000[11] and top out at 500,000.[12]

Sanctions are a tempting form of nonviolent coercion, but in practice, sanctions mean bringing an entire country under siege and starving it into submission, and the process is never as clean as its proponents suggest. At the end of World War I, Germany was losing more civilians to starvation than soldiers in battle. By some estimates, the number of Japanese civilians who were dying because of wartime shortages and the American blockade in 1945 far outweighs the number killed by the atomic bombs.

Sanctions aren't really a replacement for war; they are just war fought by other means.

SOMALIAN CHAOS

Death toll: 500,000[1]
Rank: 70
Type: failed state
Broad dividing line: everyone vs. everyone
Time frame: since 1991
Location: Somalia
Minor state participants: United States, Ethiopia
Major non-state participants: Somalis
Who usually gets the most blame: warlords
Another damn: African civil war

W HEN A MILITARY UPRISING IN SOMALIA IN JANUARY 1991 CHASED AWAY
the dictator Mohamed Siad Barre, the last effective government fell with him. In
Somalia people identify more with their clan than their country, and the country quickly
broke into loose territories run by local warlords. The economy sputtered to a halt, and
armed bands seized all of the food supplies that were on hand, leaving the unarmed
population to starve. After an estimated 50,000 Somalis had been killed in fighting and
300,000 had died of hunger, the UN negotiated a cease-fire in March 1992 between the
principal warlords in order to bring food into the country.

A multinational (mostly American) peacekeeping force arrived in December 1992 to
guard the food supplies that were being imported by international charities. In October
1993, a unit of U.S. troops was trapped and cut to pieces in Mogadishu while trying to
capture associates of the warlord Mohamed Farrah Aidid. In the grand flow of history, it
was a minor battle, but it made the American leadership so gun-shy that they vigorously
avoided intervening in the Rwandan genocide the next year. The Americans pulled out of
Somalia in 1994, and the UN left the next year.[2]

A new wave of intensified fighting erupted in 1996, but after General Aidid was killed,
the top three remaining warlords agreed to a mutual cease-fire. Outside of warlord territory, the northern wing of the country has achieved stability as two new independent
nations, Puntland and Somaliland, although no one officially recognizes them as such.

Years of war have left Mogadishu looted and battered, and many of its 1.2 million
people live in rubble and tents. Schools and businesses have long ago shut down. Most
young men can find steady employment only as gunmen for the local warlords, trading

their muscle for food and khat, the local narcotic. Armed men easily rob, rape, and kill without consequences.[3] Somalia has also become a safe haven for pirates who hijack ships going through the Suez Canal.

Warlords come and go, and presumably they engage in rivalries that mean something to the participants, but these have never caught the attention of outsiders. Whenever anyone bothers to distinguish between the various warlords, they are usually classified by the degree of Islamic fundamentalism they want to impose on the country. In 2006, Ethiopian troops occupied Mogadishu in order to install a UN-approved national government, but this did little more than create yet another ineffectual local faction.

Death Toll

The only authoritative estimate floating around is the UN report that 350,000 people had died in the first year and a half of chaos. As the fighting continued, it became obvious that the growing death toll was leaving the old estimate behind. When no updated estimate appeared, reporters decided to unofficially upgrade the number, so it has become more and more common to vaguely suggest that a half-million to a million people may have died.

RWANDAN GENOCIDE

Death toll: 937,000
Rank: 53
Type: ethnic cleansing
Broad dividing line: Hutu vs. Tutsi
Time frame: 100 days in 1994
Location and major state participant: Rwanda
Who usually gets the most blame: Belgium, France, and American President Bill Clinton*
Another damn: African civil war
The unanswerable question everyone asks: Why didn't anybody stop this?

Background

Many centuries ago, tall Nilotic cattle herders from Sudan drifted south, about the same time that stocky Bantu farmers from the western hump of Africa were migrating eastward. They crashed and mingled in the Lake Region, and after struggles and adjustments across unrecorded generations, the Nilotic Tutsi aristocracy ended up ruling over the Bantu Hutu peasantry. This was the situation that the first European explorers discovered in the middle of the nineteenth century. In the colonial Scramble for Africa, the region was split between the Germans and the Belgians.

After the First World War, the overseas German colonies were quickly divvied up among the winners. Two inland bites of German East Africa adjacent to the Belgian Congo were handed over to the Belgians as a League of Nations mandate, which, by the terms

---

* Really. Popular accounts of the Rwandan genocide are more likely to blame the West for not stopping it rather than the Hutu for actually doing it. For example, in the (excellent) film *Hotel Rwanda*, two of the major characters were foreign observers complaining about international indifference, and they got more screentime than most of the native characters. At its most ambitious, White Guilt even reaches back and accuses the Belgians of dividing a single harmonious people into manufactured categories of "Hutu" and "Tutsi" when they issued those colonial ID cards.

Why does so much of the blame attach to people and institutions that weren't even involved in the killing? Mostly this is just how some people view foreign affairs: "Yes, it's sad, but how is this *my* problem?" However, other people just want to blame the UN, the West, or Bill Clinton for everything.

of the treaty, had to be administered separately from the rest of Belgium's colonies. Both the Germans and the Belgians relied on the local Tutsi nobility to help them rule, and in exchange granted them privileges that were denied the Hutu, such as an exemption from the sixty days of free labor that all natives owed the state. Because centuries of interbreeding and coexistence had worn away the physical and cultural differences between the two groups, the Belgians issued identification cards that clearly labeled each person as one or the other so the authorities would know who was entitled to preferential treatment. Those of mixed or uncertain ancestry were arbitrarily assigned their ethnicity based on the whim of the colonial officials. Hutu and Tutsi usually identified one another by subtle class differences rather than anything immediately obvious to outsiders. Both groups spoke the same language and were mostly Catholic by the time of independence.[1]

In 1962, the League of Nations mandates became the independent countries of Burundi and Rwanda. Unfortunately, this twofold split in ethnicity created an inherently unstable situation. Chronic suspicion and ill will between Hutu and Tutsi led to endemic civil war, punctuated by occasional mind-numbing massacres. For a time, the worst such massacre in memory occurred in 1972, when a ruling Tutsi regime in Burundi slaughtered some 100,000 to 150,000 Hutu and sent thousands of bitter Hutu refugees streaming over the border into Hutu-dominated Rwanda.[2]

Foreground

A later generation would see even worse. On April 6, 1994, the Hutu presidents of Burundi and Rwanda were flying back from negotiating a peace treaty with Tutsi rebels when their plane was shot down by surface-to-air missiles. No one knows by whom. Hutu leaders blamed Tutsi rebels and immediately launched retaliatory massacres, but others claim that Hutu extremists manufactured an excuse to crack down on the Tutsi by assassinating a couple of presidents who had sold them out.*

Regardless, by the next day, infuriated Hutu militias, the Interahamwe ("Those who work together"), began to massacre Tutsi all across Rwanda. The genocide was masterminded by Defense Minister Theoneste Bagosora, and it was terribly efficient. Within two weeks—before the international community even had a chance to flinch—a quarter of a million men, women, and children had been hacked apart, often with the genocide's characteristic weapon, the machete.[3]

Among the first to die was Prime Minister Agathe Uwilingiyimana, a moderate Hutu woman who was raped with bayonets and killed. The Belgian soldiers of her UN body-

---

* In Burundi, the death of its president rekindled the country's fading civil war, but the subsequent death toll (260,000) didn't reach the threshold for being on my top one hundred list.

guard were under orders not to provoke the locals by fighting back, so they surrendered without a fight, only to be castrated, gagged with their own genitalia, and killed anyway.

All across the country, in attacks coordinated and encouraged by radio propagandists like Ferdinand Nahimana, Hutu turned against their Tutsi neighbors. Teachers killed their students. Hutu babysitters killed Tutsi children left in their care. Reluctant Hutu were taken aside and threatened with death if they didn't join the killing. They were swept up by gangs, handed machetes, and ordered to kill or die. The guilt of killing was deliberately spread as widely as possible by a whole gang taking turns hacking and slashing.[4]

The hatred went so deep that there was no place the Tutsi were safe. A week into the genocide, the mayor of Nyarubuye led 7,000 militia to his local Catholic church and its adjacent convent to massacre 20,000 Tutsi taking refuge in the building complex.[5] At the Catholic church in Nyange, the priest ordered workmen to bulldoze the building on top of the 1,500 refugees gathered inside.[6] Several convents also gathered refugees together and then gave them up to the militias. At a convent in Sovu, the nuns not only locked some Tutsi in the convent's garage but also provided the gasoline to burn it down.[7]

The Interahamwe made a special effort to rape and humiliate female victims before cutting them apart. Sometimes the victims were killed immediately after the rape; sometimes they were left to die of grotesque mutilations; sometimes they were caged for another round of rape later. On one occasion, a woman was pinned to the ground with a spear thrust through her foot while her attackers ran a quick errand before returning to rape her again. Witnesses could see the proof of these atrocities months later, "even in the whitened skeletons. The legs bent and apart. A broken bottle, a rough branch, even a knife between them. . . . They died in a position of total vulnerability, flat on their backs, with their legs bent and their knees wide apart."[8]

Finally, after three months of killing, Tutsi rebels under Paul Kagame broke through the front lines and raced to rescue their surviving kinsmen. Hutu by the millions fled into neighboring countries to avoid retaliation. About the same time, the world community finally intervened for humanitarian purposes, which stopped the killing but also allowed many of the Hutu militia and armed forces to escape justice (or revenge—take your pick).

Shortly afterward the United Nations estimated that 800,000 Rwandans had been killed in just three months. The Rwandan government eventually set the official death toll of the genocide at 937,000.[9] It was the worst single episode of pure genocide in decades— five times as swift as the Holocaust.[10]

Justice, Sort Of

The Rwandan Genocide is one of the few atrocities in this book to be followed by a systematic effort to judge and punish the culprits by means of fair trials. A surprisingly stable government under Paul Kagame returned to Rwanda within a few years, but the sheer magnitude of the crime made justice difficult. Four years after the genocide, 130,000 Inter-ahamwe were locked in filthy, overcrowded prisons, still awaiting trial. By the end of the year, tribunals had tried 330 of them.[11]

By 2005, the Rwandans had decentralized the process and established village courts to pass judgment. In their first eight months of operation, these courts heard over 4,000 cases and convicted 89 percent of the defendants. By this time, however, most prisoners had already spent years in jail awaiting trial. Any sign of contrition would be enough to get them sentenced to time-served and then released.[12]

Although around 650 prisoners had been sentenced to be shot, Rwanda abolished the death penalty before very many executions had taken place. This was the only way the Rwandans could get their hands on almost 45,000 fugitive suspects who lived in countries that wouldn't extradite prisoners if they faced the death penalty.[13]

SECOND CONGO WAR

Death toll: 3.8 million
Rank: 27
Type: hegemonial war
Broad dividing line: Hutu vs. Tutsi, no matter who else gets in the way
Time frame: 1998–2002
Location: Congo Major
Major state participants: Democratic Republic of the Congo vs. Rwanda and Uganda
Minor state participants: Angola, Zimbabwe, Namibia, Chad (on Congo's side), and Burundi (on Rwanda's side)
Major non-state participants: Alliance of Democratic Forces for the Liberation of Congo-Zaire, Allied Democratic Forces, Congolese Rally for Democracy, Interahamwe, Mai-Mai, Movement for the Liberation of Congo
Who usually gets the most blame: Paul Kagame (Rwanda), Laurent Kabila (Congo), Yoweri Museveni (Uganda)*
Another damn: African civil war
Economic factors: coltan, diamonds, timber
The unanswerable question that everyone asks: This was only a few years ago. Why didn't I hear anything about it?

THE SECOND CONGO WAR LIES AT THE END OF A CHAIN REACTION THAT began in the distant mists of time and bounced around randomly until it ended up destroying millions of lives that had nothing at all to do with the beginning. The 1994 genocide in Rwanda scattered millions of refugees around the Great Lake region of Africa. Ironically, these refugees were not the Tutsi victims of the genocide, but rather the Hutu perpetrators who had lost control of Rwanda and were now fleeing the vengeful Tutsi rebels who had taken over the government. Over a million of them were holed up in refugee camps in Congo Major.

---

* I hope you noticed that two of the heroes from earlier chapters are the villains in this chapter. History is complicated.

Exit Mobutu

During the Rwandan Genocide, the larger of the two Congos (the former Congo Free State—see that chapter) was called Zaire and ruled by Mobutu Sese Seko, a thuggish old tyrant who had been systematically plundering his country for three decades, amassing a personal fortune estimated to be among the world's largest. He had survived the usual assortment of coups, border raids, and civil wars that beset every African dictator, but this massive flood of refugees pouring over the border was too much for the cancer-addled old man. He lost control of the situation, and these border provinces became, for all practical purposes, no-man's-land. While international aid agencies traveled in armed convoys and struggled to keep the refugee camps livable, the Hutu militia used them as bases to rebuild their organizations to retake Rwanda. They kept in practice by fighting with the local Tutsi of Congo Major, known as the Banyamulenge.

Fearing a Hutu resurgence, Paul Kagame's Tutsi government of Rwanda wanted to disarm the Hutu and arrest their ringleaders, but Mobutu wouldn't cooperate, so he had to be replaced. The Rwandans needed a Congolese front man to lead the charge, so they scouted out an unemployed Congolese rebel, Laurent Kabila, who had been drifting aimlessly around East Africa hoping something would turn up.

Kabila had lurked in the shadow of more charismatic men during the Congo Crisis—a collection of civil wars that immediately followed independence in 1960. He began as an associate of the beloved leftist president of the Congo, Patrice Lumumba. After Lumumba's assassination at the hands of rebels in 1961, Kabila helped to detach an eastern Congolese province as a Marxist enclave. Che Guevara himself, the legendary Latin American revolutionary, dropped in to fight on behalf of this new Communist nation, but he quickly became disillusioned. As he notes in his diary, "Every day it was the same old story; Kabila did not arrive today, but he will be here tomorrow, and if not, then the day after tomorrow."

"Kabila has not laid foot since time immemorial at the front," Che complained. Instead, he was spending much of his time in Paris, Cairo, and Dar es Salaam, staying "in the best hotels, issuing communiques and drinking Scotch in the company of beautiful women," or simply bouncing from "saloon to whorehouse."[1]

Then, after this enclave fell to the Zairian army in the 1970s, Kabila disappeared and was widely presumed dead. There were occasional sightings, usually involving a kidnapping or a shady business deal, but no one paid much attention to Kabila until he befriended President Yoweri Museveni of Uganda, who suggested him to the Rwandans as a possible president of Congo.[2]

Safely legitimized by Kabila's Alliance of Democratic Forces for the Liberation of Congo-Zaire (AFDL), Rwandan and Ugandan troops crossed the border in October 1996, to drive Mobutu from power and scatter the Hutu even farther afield. The 1.4 million Hutu refugees registered with aid agencies in Zaire fled in every direction from this onslaught, and when the region calmed down enough for the aid agencies to resume operations, over 200,000 Hutu refugees had vanished in the confusion.[3] God only knows what happened to them, but they were probably dead. Amnesty International reported that the AFDL and Rwandan army massacred many of them.[4]

Mobutu fled the capital in May 1997 and died of stomach cancer in Morocco a few months later. Kabila entered Kinshasa and victoriously proclaimed the new Democratic Republic of the Congo. This ended the First Congo War.

Africa's World War

Once he was established in the President's Palace, Kabila quickly drove away his friends. In his dying days, Mobutu had been forced to ease up restrictions on human rights and political opposition, but now Kabila reversed these tiny improvements. He tried to establish his independence from his Rwandan backers by removing the Rwandan general who now served as Congo's chief of staff and by dismissing his Rwandan bodyguard. In July 1998, he finally ordered all foreign troops from the country.

It's not certain whether Rwanda actually complied with this order or merely pretended to comply, but it didn't matter, because on August 2, 1998, two units of the Congolese army stationed along the border mutinied, starting the Second Congo War. As Kabila moved against them, Rwandan forces came to their assistance. To prevent additional outbreaks, Tutsi units of the Congolese army stationed near the capital of Kinshasa were ordered to disarm. They refused, but Congolese army units of other ethnicities attacked and wiped them out. A general pogrom against Tutsi of all kinds—soldiers, civilians, men, women, and children—erupted all across Congo.[5]

On August 4, a planeload of Rwandan and Ugandan soldiers flew completely across the country to the western tip of Congo, where they landed at an army base that held 10,000 to 15,000 former Mobutu loyalists as POWs from the First Congo War. The prisoners were freed, armed, and formed into a new strike force that set out for the capital to overthrow Kabila. Meanwhile, the whole spectrum of Congolese politicians, from former cronies of Mobutu to former enemies of Mobutu, formed the Congolese Rally for Democracy (RCD). After a couple of weeks, Kabila appeared doomed, but then, on August 28, the Mobutist-Rwandan-Ugandan expeditionary force in the west was attacked and destroyed by troops from neighboring Angola, which had endured too many border wars and intrigues with Mobutu to let his followers resume control. Zaire had interfered in Angola's civil war (1975–94), so now Angola would return the favor.[6]

Let's back up a bit. How did Uganda come into this conflict? Uganda, like so many sub-Saharan countries, had a bad case of insurgents. The Allied Democratic Forces (ADF) operating in the borderlands of Uganda and Congo were not the largest or the worst rebels in Uganda, but Ugandans realized that they would have a shot at crushing the ADF by joining the Rwandan invasion. In February 1999, Uganda organized cooperative Congolese into the Movement for the Liberation of Congo (MLC), composed mostly of former Mobutists in Mobutu's home province of Equateur. Uganda put the MLC in charge of the nearby Congolese provinces in exchange for them cracking down on the ADF.

Kabila meanwhile mobilized support among the exiled Rwandan Hutu militias, and accepted troops offered by several neighboring countries that were eager to restore stability to the region.

By mid-1999, all of the armies were in place, and there were no surprises left. Congo settled down into a painful threefold partition: Uganda held the northeast, Rwanda held the southeast, and Kabila held the west. A big scar ran down the middle of the country where the various armies raided, patrolled, and looted each other's territory.

There were at least twenty attempts by international organizations to arrange a ceasefire before one finally took hold. The Lusaka Ceasefire Agreement was signed in July 1999, which solidified the partition until something better could be arranged.

The negotiations dragged on, of course. The warring parties were in no hurry to quit since they were all making a lot of money from the war. The breakdown of law and order allowed them to plunder their occupied territories of diamonds, gold, timber, and coltan, a rare ore essential to the manufacturing of cell phones and computers. As the Congo supplies 80 percent of the world's coltan, the price skyrocketed from $30 to $400 per pound, and illegal mines popped up all across the war zone, with miners shooting endangered gorillas and elephants for food.[7] Ugandan troops and their rebel allies seized the northeast's entire stock of wood and coffee, which they hauled away to Uganda for very profitable export.[8]

Exit Kabila

On January 16, 2001, one of Kabila's bodyguards assassinated him. At first, the government denied that anything bad had happened to the president, and his chief aide appeared on television to beg the nation to remain calm. Finally, after days of speculation, they had to admit that Kabila was indeed dead. Two years later, this same chief aide was convicted of having planned the assassination as part of a failed coup, probably in cooperation with the Congolese Rally for Democracy and the Rwandans.[9]

Kabila's son, Joseph Kabila, took over as president, and (as of this writing) he seems to be an improvement over his father. He opened the government to opposition voices and began serious peace negotiations. In October 2006, nationwide elections, which outside observers generally called free and fair, confirmed Kabila as president. As the BBC declared, "Congo's war led to shady business deals, but Mr. Kabila has not been directly implicated in any."[10] That's a pretty good definition of honest in this part of the world.

Rwanda and Congo signed a cease-fire in Pretoria, South Africa, on July 30, 2002. Congo officially denied harboring any of the Hutu involved in Rwanda's 1994 genocide but agreed to turn them over to Rwanda anyway. In exchange, Rwanda agreed to withdraw from Congo. Another bilateral agreement between Uganda and Congo on September 6, 2002, ended that part of the war. The withdrawal of foreign troops left the various rebellious paramilitaries in place, but these were all given a place in the new transitional government.

In spite of the major shuffling of troops and reallocation of political power, scattered fighting has continued over the past few years. Some have already begun calling the new fighting the Third Congo War, but for the sake of time, space, and simplicity, let's stop our history of the Second Congo War here.

The Style of War

The International Rescue Committee surveyed the inhabitants of the war zone and issued a report in 2005, estimating 3.8 million more deaths than usual since the outbreak of the Second Congo War, mostly from the disease and famine that spread in the wake of the devastation. Only 10 to 15 percent of these war deaths were directly by violence.[11]

History's bloodiest wars often involve the most efficient and well-equipped soldiers available on the planet at the time. Armies at the peak of military efficiency, for example, fought the two world wars and conquered much of the world on behalf of Napoleon and Chinggis Khan. These were the most destructive armies of their era, and true to their training, they destroyed huge swaths of humanity.

The armies of the Congo war are in a different league altogether. This war was fought by poorly disciplined gangs of teenagers with outdated small arms and no loyalty to anyone other than the paymaster. They were scattered around a loose front, and they rarely committed to pitched battles that lasted more than a couple of hours. Discipline was brutal and life was cheap. They relied more on magical charms than training to protect them in combat. Bribery and looting were rife, and they spent more time terrorizing the locals than fighting the enemy. According to aid agencies, 60 percent of the combatants in the war have the virus that causes AIDS, and a third of the women they raped became infected.[12]

Singled out for human rights abuses were the Mai-Mai, a loose collection of local militias fighting in the center of Congo against the Rwandans and Ugandans, though not necessarily on behalf of the central government. The town of Kibombo changed hands several times, and each time, the soldiers would loot or extort and eventually withdraw, dragging a few women along for later. Typical is the experience of one sixteen-year-old girl:

In October, 2002, Onya and her mother were in a group of 48 women who had gone to tend the fields together, seeking safety in numbers. It didn't work: They encountered a patrol of Mai-Mai who beat them, marched them off to their camp and began to rape them. Her mother escaped after a few days, but Onya was kept as a "wife" until last March [2004], forced to farm, cook and provide sex. Finally, the Mai-Mai fled after losing a major battle, and she made her way back to Kibombo.[13]

RANKING: THE ONE HUNDRED DEADLIEST MULTICIDES

1. Second World War (1939–45) ———————— 66,000,000
2. Chinggis Khan (1206–27) ———————— 40,000,000
   Mao Zedong (1949–76) ———————— 40,000,000
4. Famines in British India (18th–20th centuries) —— 27,000,000
5. Fall of the Ming Dynasty (1635–62) ———— 25,000,000
6. Taiping Rebellion (1850–64) ———————— 20,000,000
   Joseph Stalin (1928–53) ———————— 20,000,000
8. Mideast Slave Trade (7th–19th centuries) ——— 18,500,000
9. Timur (1370–1405) ———————————— 17,000,000
10. Atlantic Slave Trade (1452–1807) ———— 16,000,000
11. Conquest of the Americas (after 1492) ———— 15,000,000
    First World War (1914–18) ———————— 15,000,000
13. An Lushan Rebellion (755–63) ———————— 13,000,000
14. Xin Dynasty (9–24) ———————————— 10,000,000
    Congo Free State (1885–1908) ———————— 10,000,000
16. Russian Civil War (1918–20) ——————— 9,000,000
17. Thirty Years War (1618–48) ——————— 7,500,000
    Fall of the Yuan Dynasty (ca. 1340–70) ——— 7,500,000
19. Fall of the Western Roman Empire (395–455) —— 7,000,000
    Chinese Civil War (1927–37, 1945–49) ——— 7,000,000
21. Mahdi Revolt (1881–98) ———————— 5,500,000
22. The Time of Troubles (1598–1613) ——— 5,000,000
23. Aurangzeb (1658–1707) ———————— 4,600,000
24. Vietnam War (1959–75) ———————— 4,200,000

25. The Three Kingdoms of China (189–280) ———— 4,100,000
26. Napoleonic Wars (1792–1815) ———— 4,000,000
27. Second Congo War (1998–2002) ———— 3,800,000
28. Gladiatorial Games (264 BCE–435 CE) ———— 3,500,000
    Hundred Years War (1337–1453) ———— 3,500,000
30. Crusades (1095–1291) ———— 3,000,000
    French Wars of Religion (1562–98) ———— 3,000,000
    Peter the Great (1682–1725) ———— 3,000,000
    Korean War (1950–53) ———— 3,000,000
    North Korea (after 1948) ———— 3,000,000
35. War in the Sudan (1955–2003) ———— 2,600,000
36. Expulsion of Germans from
    Eastern Europe (1945–47) ———— 2,100,000
37. Fang La Rebellion (1120–22) ———— 2,000,000
    Mengistu Haile (1974–91) ———— 2,000,000
39. Democratic Kampuchea (1975–79) ———— 1,670,000
40. Age of Warring States (ca. 475–221 BCE) ———— 1,500,000
    Seven Years War (1756–63) ———— 1,500,000
    Shaka (1818–28) ———— 1,500,000
    Bengali Genocide (1971) ———— 1,500,000
    Soviet-Afghan War (1979–92) ———— 1,500,000
45. Aztec Human Sacrifice (1440–1521) ———— 1,200,000
46. Qin Shi Huang Di (221–210 BCE) ———— 1,000,000
    Roman Slave Wars (134–71 BCE) ———— 1,000,000
    Mayan Collapse (790–909) ———— 1,000,000
    Albigensian Crusade (1208–29) ———— 1,000,000
    Panthay Rebellion (1855–73) ———— 1,000,000
    Mexican Revolution (1910–20) ———— 1,000,000
    Biafran War (1966–70) ———— 1,000,000
53. Rwandan Genocide (1994) ———— 937,000
54. Burma-Siam Wars (1550–1605) ———— 900,000
55. Hulagu's Invasion (1255–60) ———— 800,000
    Mozambican Civil War (1975–92) ———— 800,000
57. French Conquest of Algeria (1830–47) ———— 775,000
58. Second Punic War (218–202 BCE) ———— 770,000
59. Justinian (527–65) ———— 750,000
    Italo-Ethiopian War (1935–41) ———— 750,000
61. Gallic War (58–51 BCE) ———— 700,000
    Chinese Conquest of Vietnam (1407–28) ———— 700,000

War of the Spanish Succession (1701–13) ———— 700,000
Iran-Iraq War (1980–88) ———————————— 700,000
65. American Civil War (1861–65) ———————— 695,000
66. Hui Rebellion (1862–73) ————————————— 640,000
67. Goguryeo-Sui Wars (598 and 612) ————— 600,000
Sino-Dzungar War (1755–57) ——————— 600,000
69. Algerian War of Independence (1954–62) —— 525,000
70. Alexander the Great (336–325 BCE) —————— 500,000
Bahmani-Vijayanagara War (1366) ———— 500,000
Russo-Tatar War (1570–72) ———————— 500,000
War of the Austrian Succession (1740–48) ——— 500,000
Russo-Turkish War (1877–78) ——————— 500,000
Partition of India (1947) —————————— 500,000
Angolan Civil War (1975–94) ——————— 500,000
Ugandan Bush War (1979–86) ————————— 500,000
Somalian Chaos (since 1991) ——————— 500,000
79. War of the Triple Alliance (1864–70) ———— 480,000
80. Franco-Prussian War (1870–71) —————— 435,000
81. First Punic War (264–241 BCE) ——————— 400,000
Third Mithridatic War (73–63 BCE) ———— 400,000
Cromwell's Invasion of Ireland (1649–52) ———— 400,000
Mexican War of Independence (1810–21) ——— 400,000
Haitian Slave Revolt (1791–1803) ——————— 400,000
Greco-Turkish War (1919–22) ——————— 400,000
Indonesian Purge (1965–66) ——————— 400,000
88. French Indochina War (1945–54) —————— 393,000
89. Great Turkish War (1682–99) ——————— 384,000
90. Great Northern War (1700–21) —————— 370,000
91. Spanish Civil War (1936–39) ——————— 365,000
Postwar Vietnam (1975–92) ——————— 365,000
93. Cuban Revolution (1895–98) ——————— 360,000
94. Sanctions against Iraq (1990–2003) ——— 350,000
Roman-Jewish Wars (66–74, 132–135) ——— 350,000
96. Second Persian War (480–479 BCE) ——— 300,000
War of the Allies (91–88 BCE) ——————— 300,000
Crimean War (1854–56) ————————— 300,000
Idi Amin (1971–79) ————————————— 300,000
Saddam Hussein (1979–2003) —————— 300,000

WHAT I FOUND: ANALYSIS

WHAT CAN WE CONCLUDE FROM MY LIST OF MASS KILLINGS? IS THERE any single quality that all one hundred of them share? Aside from the horrific everyday details like torture, cannibalism, assassination, rape, castration, betrayal, and severed heads, are there any larger characteristics that all of these multicides have in common?

I don't see any. In fact, the only major characteristic that applies to most of these mass killings without applying to all of them is that four-fifths are wars. You may not consider it a startling revelation that wars kill more people than dictators—after all, the average war mobilizes more active participants and allows more indiscriminate destruction than the average police state—but there's a widespread school of thought in atrocitology that wars are *not* the leading cause of violent death. Some atrocitologists claim that oppressive government is worse. This appears to be wrong.*

A few of the one hundred incidents have some unusually specific similarities. I'll leave it up to you as to whether these are significant or mere coincidence:

Defenestrations of Prague: Twice in this book, someone was thrown out of a window in Prague. (Thirty Years War and Joseph Stalin)

---

* The argument that oppressive governments kill more people than wars is popular among extreme libertarians and supported by including the internal killing by tyrants in peacetime (such as the Cultural Revolution) with the mass murder of noncombatants during war (such as the Holocaust) and then pointing out that this total is higher than the socially approved killing of soldiers during war. (see, for example, Rummel, *Death by Government*) I hold the opposite view: *All* killing during a war should be counted as war dead. After all, the Americans would not have bombed Hiroshima in peacetime, nor would the Nazis have had access to Poland's 3 million Jews without conquering them.

Tweaking definitions to support a viewpoint occurs on the other side of the scale as well. Pacifists trying to show how deadly war is will often label institutional oppression (the Cultural Revolution, Stalin's purges, and so on) as "conflict" and include those with the more obvious war dead—even though they lack the indiscriminate reciprocal killing that characterizes real war. In these cases, I would differentiate between war and oppression by noting what it would take to end the killing. If both sides need to lay down their arms, it's a war; if one side can simply and unilaterally stop killing (without surrendering), it is oppression.

Many of the dictators came from communities slightly beyond the margin of the nations they would come to lead. Napoleon was Corsican, not French. Stalin was Georgian, not Russian. Hitler was Austrian, not German. Alexander was Macedonian, not Greek.

The United States was sucked into three European wars when the belligerents imposed blockades against their enemies. (Napoleonic Wars, World War I, World War II)

Twice the conquest of China followed the same geographic pattern: During a civil war, an army out of Manchuria took Beijing. The defending Chinese tried to regroup at Nanjing, but were beaten, and a remnant retreated to Taiwan, which they seized from foreigners. (Fall of the Ming Dynasty, Chinese Civil War [second phase])

Thuggish warlords like to be named after iron and steel. *Stalin* comes from the Russian word for steel. *Timur* and *Temujin* probably come from *temur*, the Mongolian word for iron. In alchemy/astrology the same symbol (♂) is used for Mars, war, iron, and male, and these gentlemen would probably appreciate the equivalence.

Three times the West tried to put native Christian strongmen in charge of recently created non-Christian East Asian countries. (Chiang Kai-shek in China, Syngman Rhee in Korea, Ngo Dinh Diem in Vietnam) The religious difference may be one reason why the majority of natives never rallied to their support in the subsequent civil war. (Chinese Civil War, Korean War, Vietnam War)

Saxony can never decide which side it wants to be on. (Thirty Years War, Seven Years War, Napoleonic Wars)

Even though Russia gets all of the credit for being unconquerable, armies invading Egypt get chewed up and spit out too. (Fifth Crusade, Hulagu's Invasion, Napoleonic Wars, World War II)

While we're on the subject, it *is* sometimes possible to beat the Russians on their home turf. (Mongols, World War I)

Has anybody actually *won* a war using elephants? (Timur, Second Punic War, Alexander the Great)

Vacationing in France is a bad career move for monarchs. (Cambodia, see "Vietnam War"; Afghanistan, see "Soviet-Afghan War")

Twice, backstabbing palace intrigues wiped out a ruling family, leaving the throne in the hands of a usurper. Natural disasters showed God's disapproval of the usurper, so the peasants rose against him. (Xin Dynasty, The Time of Troubles)

The taboo against cannibalism isn't quite as strong as they say it is. (Too many examples to name)

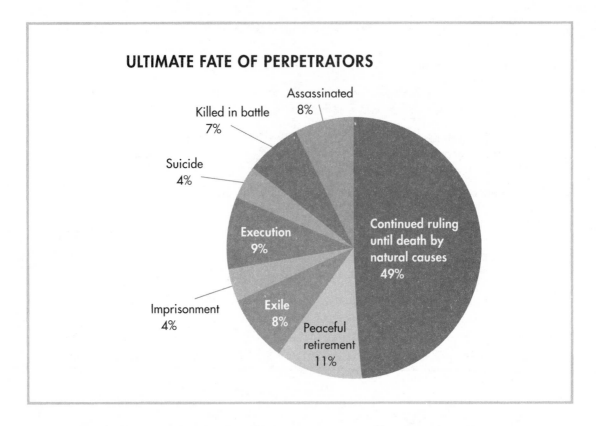

ULTIMATE FATE OF PERPETRATORS

- Assassinated 8%
- Killed in battle 7%
- Suicide 4%
- Execution 9%
- Imprisonment 4%
- Exile 8%
- Peaceful retirement 11%
- Continued ruling until death by natural causes 49%

About 60 percent of the individual oppressors and warmongers who were most responsible for each of these multicides lived happily ever after (see above chart).

Off the Hook

I'm sure that some readers (but certainly not you) will look at this list and smugly declare, "Aha! [Somebody we hate] produced six megadeaths, while [somebody we like] produced only two, which proves that [somebody we hate] is far worse than [somebody we like], so there!" Fill in the blanks however you want—Africans, Belgians, Christians, Communists, French, the godless, left-handers, Muslims, multinational corporations, racists, Russians, or white people.

Unfortunately, that line of reasoning falls apart on one very important issue. "Only" two megadeaths is nothing to be proud of. Causing *any* megadeath is bad, especially since there are a few human types and activities that don't stand out as the direct cause of my one hundred mass killings.

BIRDS AND/OR BEES

Considering that sex drives everything that people do, and drives them all crazy in the process, you might think there would be at least one real war fought over it. According to legend, the Greeks destroyed Troy in order to reclaim the fair Helen, and the bachelors of early Rome kidnapped the Sabine women as breeding stock, but I can find no large, documented war by a state-level society that was fought over sex. The closest I can find is an occasional conflict where the winner gets a useful political marriage with a huge dowry.

But that's not really sexual, is it?

This doesn't mean that sex is absent from wars. Rape is as much a part of war as killing, looting, and enslavement. Military recruiters have always lured farmboys into the ranks with the promise of adventure, and women traditionally swoon over a man in uniform, but wars don't start over sex. The fighting is always about something else. After all, you can rally mass armies with appeals to patriotism, God, revenge, glory, and greed, but citizens won't flock to the colors to help the president get laid.

Some commentators would blame sex anyway. They will talk of hidden motivations, stressed libidos, raging testosterone, macho posturing, and hormone-flooded teenagers, but this becomes the flip side of the problem we faced when discussing holy wars. To what extent do we take declared motivations at face value? Across history, people have always been willing to fight wars in the name of religion, but not in the name of sex. Some scholars ignore those declarations, and instead claim that, deep down, all wars are about sex and none are about religion. Who are we to believe?

TERRORISTS

A terrorist act sparked the First World War, but terrorism itself is small potatoes. Except for a few especially destructive operations, terrorism rarely kills more than a few dozen people per incident. Even an entire campaign of terrorism won't kill enough to get on my list. If your choice is between tolerating a few car bombings now and then, and starting a war over terrorists, probably fewer lives will be lost with the first choice.

JEWS

Throughout my studies of atrocities, I've always found a dark undercurrent of opinion that wants to blame all of the evil in the world on certain sinister minorities. One homosexual Nazi who was purged early in Hitler's regime (Ernst Roehm) is enough for some people to blame the entire Nazi movement on a supposed cabal of sexual deviants.[1] One prominent Jew among the Bolsheviks (Leon Trotsky) was enough to provoke massive pogroms during the Russian Civil War.

As tempting as it is to simply ignore people who spout these opinions, we probably should keep in the habit of refuting them whenever we find them. When you let crazy opinions pass without debate, outside observers might think that those opinions are commonly accepted.

So let's look at the statistics. Only one of these hundred multicides—the Roman-Jewish Wars—can be blamed even partially on the Jews. Go back and count. You'd be hard-pressed to find more than a couple of stray Jews who appear as minor perpetrators in any other chapter. Mostly this is because there have never been enough Jews to cause as much trouble as they get blamed for, but even so—someone's got to say it. The Jews are *not* behind everything bad that happens in the world.

GAYS

Here's another much-maligned minority that doesn't stand out among the prime movers of the multicides. When you start listing the people who have inflicted massive death and destruction on humanity, you don't find as many gays as when you list, for example, writers, artists, actors, or kings. You've got Alexander the Great from a bisexual culture. Julius Caesar, Vespasian, and Titus apparently would jump on anything. Frederick the Great and Shaka were enigmatic and childless. But none of the major perpetrators on my list have been proved to be gay—even when homosexuality is well documented among some of their contemporaries. You might think this is merely a function of the relatively small number of gays throughout history, but alcoholics, painters, giants, and cat-haters (for example) are also minorities, and several perpetrators in this book easily fit those descriptions.* The worst thing that gays have done in this book was fail, as monarchs, to ensure a smooth succession by producing sons.

Well, that and stuffing an archbishop into a roaring fire.

VIKINGS, SAMURAI, SPARTANS, SIKHS, AND OTHERS

A lot of people who have reputations as total badasses have not killed very many people, while other nations that are widely ridiculed as losers, cowards, and sissies did.

On the Hook

Some aspects of human destruction surprised me by being more common than I had originally suspected.

SIEGES

Military history usually focuses on battles; it brushes lightly over everything else as second-rate war-making. Sieges are dismissed as wasted time between battles, and no one

---

* Not an excessive number. Just in rough proportion to their presence in any collection of important people.

pays them much attention. They're boring. It's easier to find popular histories on Gettysburg than on Petersburg, on Stalingrad rather than Leningrad, on World War II rather than World War I. Sitting around in fortifications waiting for the other side to crack isn't proper war; however, in writing this book, I found that the most destructive and decisive event of many wars was a siege, not a battle.

MISTAKES

I'm amazed at how often the immediate cause of a conflict is a mistake, unfounded suspicion, or rumor. People seem to just blunder through history. A few wars that started before all of the relevant facts were available would be the First World War, Sino-Japanese War, Spanish-American War, Vietnam War, Seven Years War, Second French War of Religion, An Lushan's Rebellion, Indonesian Purge, and Time of Troubles. And these don't even include ordinary ideological and religious wars, which are fought in support of ideas that might be wrong. I'll grant you that some of these wars were coming anyway and just needed an excuse to get started, but history would be a lot more pleasant if people didn't rush into things.

WOMEN

Even though I've never entirely trusted the old truism that a world run by women would be more peaceful than our male-dominated society, I still expected this book would be mostly male: Hitler, Stalin, Chinggis Khan . . . not just men, but men advised and assisted by other men, opposed by more men, in which women only appeared as victims, trophies, or background.

Surprisingly, I found more women causing atrocities than I had originally expected. As my research progressed, I discovered Catherine de Medici, Honoria, Maria Theresa, Jiang Qing, Marina Mnieszech, and a handful of equally difficult women causing trouble throughout history. They are still a small minority among our perpetrators, but this book has more women than Hindus or homosexuals.

Which brings me to . . .

Maybe

Here are some categories that are far from blameless, but probably not as deadly as some of you might suppose.

INDIA AND HINDUISM

Wars of conquest are rarely launched from India. A naval expedition against Indonesia in the eleventh century and scattered raids into Afghanistan may be history's only attacks outward across the natural borders of India. Who else can claim to be so harmless? Certainly not the British. Nor the French. Nor the Americans, Turks, Japanese—well, we don't have enough room to continue listing nations that have been more dangerous than India historically. Even the Mongolians and Portuguese have caused more trouble.

That might be explained by geographic isolation, but there's also a notable scarcity of massive killings inside India as well. Considering that India has usually contained around one-fifth or one-sixth of the human population—as many people as either China or Europe—why doesn't India show up on my list as often as China and Europe? Even when India appears on the list, the worst megadeaths were inflicted by non-Hindus—Lytton, Yahya Khan, and Aurangzeb. This seems to make the native culture of India almost eerily nonthreatening.

Or does it mean only that no one wrote it down? Hindu philosophy has never been very interested in the real world around us, which means Hindus don't put a lot of effort into recording the chain of cause and effect that got us here. Most societies that have produced recorded megadeaths have also produced historians to record it. India, however, has no tradition of history writing. Even if some ninth-century Indian warlord had burned and slaughtered his way across the Gangetic Plain, we probably wouldn't have any record of it.

Even so, that doesn't entirely explain why there are so few recorded megadeaths after 1000 CE, when historians arrived alongside the major Muslim conquerors. I should also point out that I managed to find two megadeaths (Mayan and Aztec) in the poorly recorded history of pre-Columbian America, so why not India?

HEREDITARY MONARCHS

> Men will never be free until the last king is strangled with the entrails of the last priest.
>
> **—Denis Diderot**

Considering that hereditary monarchy has such a bad reputation among political theorists, you would expect to see more mad monarchs on my list; however, when we study the careers of the bloodiest individuals in history, we find that most are self-made men. Regardless of what they called themselves at the peak of their powers, Hitler, Napoleon, Timur, Chinggis Khan, Mao, and Stalin all had to claw their way up from the bottom. Catherine de Medici, Boris Godunov, and Wang Mang caused trouble as regents and usurpers who were connected to the royal families by marriage. Even the Crusades were started by an elected leader (Pope Gregory). None of these people inherited their position.

In 1801, almost every monarch in Europe was a gibbering lunatic. Even those who may not have been clinically insane were odd enough that later generations could find plenty of strange stories. You would think that with so many unbalanced individuals at the helm, countries like England (George III), Russia (Paul I), Portugal (Maria I), Sweden

(Gustav IV Adolf), and Denmark (Christian VII) would be a menace to society, but no. Lunatics were running every country in Europe—except one. A perfectly sane military dictator, Napoleon Bonaparte, ruled France, and *that* was the country causing all of the trouble.

Among the monarchs on my list, none rise to the same level of personal blame as Hitler and Timur. The deadliest, King Leopold II, brutalized the Congo as CEO of a company he created himself, rather than as inheritor of a sovereign state. The monarchs that blundered into World War I were followers more than leaders. The truly deadly monarchs born and raised as royal heirs don't appear until the middle levels, down around Peter the Great, Frederick the Great, and Alexander the Great.*

Is there a reason why monarchy is relatively benign? One possibility is the absence of meritocracy. In a system where the rulers inherit their positions, their individual talents are the luck of the draw. Some might be very skilled, while others are hopelessly incompetent, but most will be extremely mediocre. Meanwhile, in a republic or dictatorship, individuals rise and fall based on their strengths and talents, so talented evil can rise as easily as talented virtue.

Another reason might be that because the ruling class of monarchies is narrower, rival power structures can be destroyed with smaller massacres. Richard III of England could eliminate his rivals with a few precise murders, but when the Communists set out to destroy the capitalists, they had to kill millions.

NATURE

Well, actually Nature has killed quite a lot of people—most of them in fact. More than 95 percent of all deaths in the twentieth century were by natural causes. That said, there's a tendency in popular science writing to overemphasize the role that Nature plays in shaping history. To hear some scientists talk, mankind is constantly being knocked around helplessly by every high-pressure system over the Pacific Ocean, or cut down by every bug that lurks in the jungle. Empires rise or fall according to wavering sunshine or annual rainfall.[2] Civilizations are immortal without tsunamis to take them down.[3] It sometimes sounds like societies don't budge unless weather or disease forces them to.

Recently I read an article that blamed the Time of Troubles in Russia on a volcanic eruption in Peru.[4] The gist was that the dust cloud from the volcano changed the weather, which caused the famine that provoked the peasant revolt. This chain of events is probably more or less true, but I still doubt the overview. Weather fluctuations are quite common; more important is how people react to them.

A few years ago my state had a summer drought that ruined the local crops, but somehow that didn't provoke a farmer revolt. In fact, I'm pretty sure that every year, the weather

* Do you detect a pattern in what it takes to be considered great?

does something destructive somewhere in the world, but most of the time people just muddle through. Just about every decade in recorded history has seen a major epidemic somewhere, and most haven't launched turning points in history. Only when society is ripe for an uprising will bad weather produce an uprising. Social events have social causes. Nature merely provides the setting.

Obviously, a lot depends on your philosophy of causation. If an epidemic cuts through a population that's been uprooted and battered by a war, are those deaths caused by the war or the disease? If a drought proves to be the tipping point for a system of agriculture straining under mismanagement, which is to blame, farm policies or the weather?

Take, for example, one classic story of the weather's impact on history: the failure of the Germans to capture Moscow in 1941. If winter hadn't arrived in the nick of time, the Nazis might have taken the capital in December. But let's be realistic: if the Red Army hadn't been in the way, then the Germans would have taken Moscow a whole lot earlier, in June, after a leisurely drive from the border. We really should give more credit to the Russian army for slowing them down long enough for winter to arrive.

PROGRESS

> Our ignorance of history makes us libel our own times. People have always been like this.
>
> —Gustave Flaubert

Half of the multicides on my list occurred in the past two hundred years. One-third of them occurred in the last one hundred years. I probably don't need to belabor the point that the twentieth century saw unparalleled horror.

However, this doesn't necessarily mean that the world is getting more dangerous. Yes, weapons have been getting deadlier, and brutal ideologies have risen and fallen in recent generations. On the other hand, it's possible that more people were killed in the twentieth century simply because there were more people around to kill. It's easier to kill a half-million people when nations are fielding armies of millions rather than armies of tens of thousands.

Even that might overstate the increase in killing. Maybe the only reason why it appears that so many were killed in the past two hundred years is that we have more records from that period. I've been researching this for years, and it's been a long time since I found a new, previously unpublicized mass killing from the twentieth century; however, it seems like every time I open an old book, I find another hundred thousand forgotten people killed somewhere in the distant past. Perhaps one chronicler made a note long ago of the number killed, but now that event has faded into the past. Maybe a few modern historians have revisited the event, but they ignore the body count because it doesn't fit into their perception of the past. They don't believe it was possible to kill that many people without gas chambers and machine guns so they dismiss contrary evidence as unreliable.

A related misconception is that the killing of civilians is getting more common. This is usually demonstrated by comparing the Second World War to the First World War, or some recent Third World bloodbath to some chivalric war between gentlemen in the era before machine guns. Aside from cherry-picking the examples, this attitude is also based on simply forgetting the past. History books rarely point out that World War I, the Franco-Prussian War, the Napoleonic Wars, and the Seven Years War killed plenty of civilians even without air raids and concentration camps.

By my calculation, around 3.5 percent of all deaths in the twentieth century were caused by war, genocide, or tyranny.[5] This is certainly higher than the 2 percent who died of those causes in the nineteenth century, but less than the 15 percent that anthropologists and archaeologists have found to be the average for tribal, pre-state societies.[6]

RESOURCES . . .

It is not easy to find a solid economic cause for many of these conflicts. Yes, plenty of wars have been fought over oil, gold, loot, slaves, and trade routes, but you have to scrounge widely and pass over a lot of counterexamples to build up a list of them. Among my one hundred, I only found eighteen that are easily explained as a fight to control exploitable resources. The rest are better explained as power struggles, holy wars, ethnic squabbles, vendettas, and mistakes (to name just a few alternative reasons).

. . . ESPECIALLY LAND

Since humans are visual creatures, we focus on results that can be illustrated. A territorial change on a map is easier to portray than a change of regime, a debt, a trade agreement, or a realignment of factions. Unfortunately, when we illustrate only wars that resulted in territorial change, it looks like all wars have been about territory.

Notice, however, that the twelve most recent of my one hundred multicides involved no territorial adjustments at all. Even before that, territory didn't always change hands.

Civil wars, for instance, aren't really about land. Instead, the territory is part of a whole package of prizes that goes to the winner—including control over the nation's treasury, courts, churches, and schools. The land is the place where the prize is kept, not the prize itself, and it usually transfers all at once. In many international wars, the winners forego territorial expansion in favor of reparations and veto power over the loser's foreign policy. Even when land changes hands, the war is often about something else, and the land is just a way of keeping score. The way that Alsace-Lorraine has been traded back and forth after every war between France and Germany is a prime example of this.

EVIL DICTATORS . . .

For every cruel psychopath slaughtering hundreds of thousands without mercy, I found another ruler with a better historical reputation killing just as many. Idi Amin, Saddam Hussein, and Adolf Hitler, for example, easily fit the stereotypes of the devil incarnate, but other deadly rulers on my list left a mixed legacy as lawgivers (Justinian, Napoleon), modernizers (Peter the Great, Mao Zedong), and organizers (Qin Shi Huang Di). One of the most frightening things I discovered is that murdering huge numbers of people doesn't necessarily make you a bad person—at least, in the eyes of history.

. . . ESPECIALLY HITLER

The other day, I saw an anti-war music video in which images of horror were flashed onscreen while the band sang about the need for love. It's a fine sentiment, but my first impression was that every image was politically safe.

Injured children. Abu Ghraib Prison. The Ku Klux Klan. Adolf Hitler.

We all hate Hitler. It doesn't take courage to denounce Hitler. He's safely gone and completely discredited.

It takes more courage to denounce someone who has mainstream admirers, like Ataturk, Arafat, Mao Zedong, or Robert E. Lee. The latter two make an interesting pair because you will rarely see them denounced in the same context. American conservatives who have no problem listing Mao as history's greatest monster go strangely silent on the matter of Confederates. Leftists who would never wear a Confederate flag on their cap will gladly emblazon quotes from Chairman Mao on their T-shirts.

As someone once said, "Why do you look at the speck of sawdust in your brother's eye and pay no attention to the plank in your own eye?"

WHAT I FOUND: RAW NUMBERS

I T'S IMPOSSIBLE TO FIND A COMMON CAUSE RUNNING THROUGH ALL ONE hundred of the multicides on my list, unless I pick causes that are too vague to be much help ("hatred," "stupidity," "power"). When I tighten my criteria, I find that more specific categories rarely account for even one-eighth of the total. Naturally most of the multicides on my list can fit several types—colonial revolts can become ideological civil wars; cultural conflicts can seem religious; all wars contain a smattering of genocide—but if I assign each event only to the one or two categories that fit the whole atrocity best, I get the totals below.

The best use of these numbers is for broad comparisons of causes. For example, you may notice that religious conflicts are almost three times more common than dynastic disputes. However, if adding/subtracting one or two multicides will completely overturn a comparison, you probably shouldn't consider that comparison significant.

Specific Nature

HEGEMONIAL WAR (13 MULTICIDES):
Similar countries fought over who's Number 1.

First Punic War
Second Punic War
Third Mithridatic War
Burma-Siam Wars
Great Northern War
War of the Austrian Succession
Seven Years War
Crimean War

War of the Triple Alliance
Franco-Prussian War
First World War
Iran-Iraq War
Second Congo War

FAILED STATE (12 MULTICIDES):

The central government collapsed, and the land was broken up among warlords.

Age of Warring States
Xin Dynasty
The Three Kingdoms of China
Fall of the Western Roman Empire
Mayan Collapse
The Time of Troubles
Fall of the Ming Dynasty
Mexican Revolution
Russian Civil War
Greco-Turkish War
Chinese Civil War
Somalian Chaos

RELIGIOUS CONFLICT (11 MULTICIDES):

Followers of rival religions fight for cultural dominance.

Crusades
Albigensian Crusade
French Wars of Religion
Thirty Years War
Cromwell's Invasion of Ireland
Taiping Rebellion
Panthay Rebellion
Hui Rebellion
Mahdi Revolt
Partition of India
War in the Sudan

IDEOLOGICAL CIVIL WAR (10 MULTICIDES):

Factions fought inside a single nation over which type of government to have.

American Civil War
Mexican Revolution

Russian Civil War
Chinese Civil War
Spanish Civil War
Korean War
Vietnam War
Angolan Civil War
Mozambican Civil War
Soviet-Afghan War

WAR OF CONQUEST (9 MULTICIDES):

The primary violence is one country trying to take over another.

Second Persian War
Gallic War
Justinian's Western Wars
Goguryeo-Sui Wars
Hulagu's Invasion
Conquest of the Americas
Aurangzeb's Deccan War
French Conquest of Algeria
Italo-Ethiopian War

ETHNIC CLEANSING (9 MULTICIDES):

The perpetrators were trying to get rid of a hated ethnicity in one burst of activity.

Conquest of the Americas (one *very long* burst of activity)
Cromwell's Invasion of Ireland
Sino-Dzungar War
First World War (Armenians)
Second World War (Jews, Gypsies)
Expulsion of Germans from Eastern Europe (post World War II)
Partition of India
Bengali Genocide
Rwandan Genocide

RACISM (8 MULTICIDES):

The main perpetrators specifically targeted their victims as a physically distinct, genetically inferior race, unworthy of human decency.

Atlantic Slave Trade
Conquest of the Americas
Haitian Slave Revolt

Famines in British India
Congo Free State
Italo-Ethiopian War
Second World War
War in the Sudan

COLONIAL REVOLT (8 MULTICIDES):

The people of a distant region tried to throw off their alien overlords.

Slave Wars
Roman-Jewish Wars
Fall of the Yuan Dynasty
Haitian Slave Revolt
Mexican War of Independence
Cuban Revolution
French Indochina War
Algerian War of Independence

CLASH OF CULTURES (7 MULTICIDES):

Very different countries fought over who's Number 1.

Second Persian War
Bahmani-Vijayanagara War
Aurangzeb's Deccan War
Russo-Tatar War
Great Turkish War
Russo-Turkish War
Second World War (Pacific war, Russian front)

WORLD CONQUEST (7 MULTICIDES):

One nation tried to take over every country within reach.

Alexander the Great
Age of Warring States
Chinggis Khan
Timur
Napoleonic Wars
Shaka
Second World War

COMMUNIST DICTATORS (6 MULTICIDES): A Communist government or dictator oppressed the people.

Joseph Stalin
North Korea
Mao Zedong
Haile Mengistu
Khmer Rouge
Postwar Vietnam

MODERNISM (6 MULTICIDES): A nation is dragged kicking and screaming into the modern world.

Peter the Great
Napoleonic-Revolutionary Wars
Famines in British India
Congo Free State
Chinese Civil War
Mao Zedong

COLONIAL EXPLOITATION (4 MULTICIDES): Most of the dying came as the perpetrators drained an alien region for their own profit.

Mideast Slave Trade
Atlantic Slave Trade
Famines in British India
Congo Free State

DYNASTIC DISPUTE (4 MULTICIDES): Each side fought in order to put a different member of the ruling family on the throne.

Xin Dynasty
Hundred Years War
The Time of Troubles
War of the Spanish Succession

ETHNIC CIVIL WAR (3 MULTICIDES): Tribes fought each other inside a single country.

War of the Allies
War in the Sudan
Biafran War

HUMAN SACRIFICE (2 MULTICIDES):

Ritualized killing was performed in hopes of earning the favor of supernatural forces.

Gladiatorial Games
Aztec Human Sacrifice

MISCELLANEOUS

DESPOT (3 MULTICIDES): An oppressive ruler, without the characteristics that would put his reign into another category.

Qin Shi Huang Di
Idi Amin
Saddam Hussein

COMMON CIVIL WAR (3 MULTICIDES): Fighting inside a nation, but without the characteristics that would put it into another category.

An Lushan Rebellion
Fang La Rebellion
Ugandan Bush War

General Means

WARS (78 MULTICIDES): The violence at their core had organized armies fighting each other openly.

INTERNATIONAL WARS (48 MULTICIDES): Multiple sovereign nations fought each other.

CIVIL WARS (30 MULTICIDES): Factions fought inside one country.

INSTITUTIONAL OPPRESSION (21 MULTICIDES): These atrocities don't have enough organized conflict to count as wars. Most of the killing flows in one direction, from the oppressors to the oppressed, in the form of dictators, slavery, and genocide.

General Cause

IDEOLOGICAL MULTICIDES (32 MULTICIDES): These were driven by some sort of fanatic, utopian ideology such as Communism or religion. This point is debatable because every historic event will have some participants who are in it for themselves and others who are in it for bigger principles. But if we were to arrange my top one hundred on a spectrum, some will be more ideological than others. I'm saying that "some" is 32. Among them:

RELIGION (13 MULTICIDES): The single most important cause for the killing was a belief in god(s).

COMMUNISM (6 MULTICIDES): All the major perpetrators were Communist.

RED-WHITE CIVIL WARS (6 MULTICIDES): Communists fought anti-Communists.

MISCELLANEOUS IDEOLOGICAL CONFLICTS (7 MULTICIDES).

ETHNIC MULTICIDES (28 MULTICIDES): These conflicts were internal or external. They arose just because the other side was different. This type includes genocides, ethnic civil wars, and colonial conflicts, but not wars between sovereign nations treating each other as equals.

GREED (18 MULTICIDES): At some point, the control of a specific resource or source of wealth became an issue in the multicide, although not necessarily the most important issue. Among the most frequent resources in dispute:

SLAVES (6 MULTICIDES):

Slave Wars
Mideast Slave Trade
Atlantic Slave Trade
Haitian Slave Revolt
American Civil War
Mahdi Revolt

OIL (5 MULTICIDES):

Second World War
Angolan Civil War

Saddam Hussein
Iran-Iraq War
Sanctions against Iraq

DEBT (4 MULTICIDES):

Third Mithridatic War
Slave Wars
Mahdi Revolt
Second World War

SUGAR (3 MULTICIDES):

Atlantic Slave Trade
Haitian Slave Revolt
Cuban Revolution

GOLD (3 MULTICIDES):

Mideast Slave Trade
Atlantic Slave Trade
Conquest of the Americas

GRAIN (3 MULTICIDES):

Slave Wars
Famines in British India
Second World War

Principal Location

CHINA (14 OR 16 MULTICIDES):

Age of Warring States
Qin Shi Huang Di
Xin Dynasty
The Three Kingdoms of China
An Lushan Rebellion
Fang La Rebellion
Fall of the Yuan Dynasty
Fall of the Ming Dynasty
Sino-Dzungar War

Taiping Rebellion
Panthay Rebellion
Hui Rebellion
Chinese Civil War
Mao Zedong
(Largely but not exclusively in China: Chinggis Khan, Second World War)

EUROPE (7 OR 8 MULTICIDES): widespread and multinational inside Europe, less so outside of it.

Fall of the Western Roman Empire
War of the Spanish Succession
War of the Austrian Succession
Seven Years War
Napoleonic Wars
First World War
Expulsion of Germans from Eastern Europe (post World War II)
(Largely but not exclusively in Europe: Second World War)

RUSSIA (6 OR 7 MULTICIDES):

Russo-Tatar War
The Time of Troubles
Peter the Great
Crimean War
Russian Civil War
Joseph Stalin
(Largely but not exclusively in Russia: Second World War)

FRANCE (5 OR 6 MULTICIDES):

Gallic War
Albigensian Crusade
Hundred Years War
French Wars of Religion
Franco-Prussian War
(Largely but not exclusively in France: First World War)

ROMAN EMPIRE (5 MULTICIDES): More than just Italy or single provinces.

First Punic War
Second Punic War

Gladiatorial Games
Fall of the Eastern Roman Empire
Justinian

INDIA (5 MULTICIDES):

Bahmani-Vijayanagara War
Aurangzeb
Famines in British India
Partition of India
Bengali Genocide

MEXICO (4 OR 5 MULTICIDES):

Mayan Collapse
Aztec Human Sacrifice
Mexican War of Independence
Mexican Revolution
(Largely but not exclusively in Mexico: Conquest of the Americas)

VIETNAM (4 MULTICIDES):

Chinese Conquest of Vietnam
French Indochina War
Vietnam War
Postwar Vietnam

KOREA (3 MULTICIDES):

Goguryeo-Sui Wars
North Korea
Korean War

Historical Trends

POST-COLONIAL AFRICAN CIVIL WARS (9 MULTICIDES): Tribal enemies inside an African nation fought a seemingly endless war with small arms, little discipline, and no mercy, often funded by outside interests.

ROMAN CONQUEST AND RESISTANCE (6 MULTICIDES): The rise but not the fall of Rome.

WARS OF TRENCHES AND IDIOTIC FRONTAL ASSAULTS (6 MULTICIDES): Clueless generals of the Industrial Era sent their men charging against entrenched riflemen. After they were slaughtered, they dug in, waited awhile, and tried again.

CHINESE DYNASTIES COLLAPSING (5 MULTICIDES): Everything's plugging along just fine until all hell breaks loose.

EUROPEAN BALANCE-OF-POWER WARS FOUGHT WITH MUSKETS (5 MULTICIDES): Bewigged monarchs of the Enlightenment played a giant chess game with live ammo.

CHINESE PEASANT REVOLTS (4 MULTICIDES): Chinese peasants are stereotypically obedient and subservient, except when they aren't.

MONGOL INVASIONS (4 MULTICIDES): The barbarians are waiting just over the horizon to come crashing down on civilization.

Participants

FRENCH (18 MULTICIDES)

CHINESE (17 MULTICIDES)

BRITISH (16 MULTICIDES)

RUSSIANS (12 MULTICIDES)

GERMANS (11 MULTICIDES)

AMERICANS (11 MULTICIDES)

ROMANS (9 MULTICIDES)

AUSTRIANS (7 MULTICIDES)

SPANISH (7 MULTICIDES)

POLES (7 MULTICIDES)

TURKS (7 MULTICIDES)

TOTAL NUMBER OF DEATHS*

ONE HUNDRED DEADLIEST MULTICIDES: 455 million killed overall. This comes to about 725,000 people killed for every page of this book, or 2,000 people killed per word.

WARS: 315 million, including 49 million soldiers and 266 million civilians. On average, 85 percent of the people killed in wars have been civilians.

INSTITUTIONAL OPPRESSION: 141 million.

IDEOLOGICAL MULTICIDES: 142 million.

RELIGION: 47 million.[†]

COMMUNISM: 67 million.

RED-WHITE CIVIL WARS: 26 million.

MISCELLANEOUS IDEOLOGICAL CONFLICTS: 2 million.

ETHNIC MULTICIDES: 74 million.

ECONOMICS: 154 million.

---

* I calculated the total number of deaths only for the larger categories. The margin of error is too large with too many variables to make anything but the broadest comparisons. To go much deeper, I would have to start splitting death tolls and deciding, for example, how much of World War II was genocide or combat, or how much of the slave trade was the fault of native kings or the Europeans.

† A friend once wondered aloud how much suffering in history has been caused by religious fanaticism, and I was able to confidently tell her 10 percent, based on this number. She probably didn't mean the question literally.

APPENDIX 1: DISPUTING THE TOP ONE HUNDRED

Definition

What does it take to get on my list? I've put this off to the end because any useful definition will be so pedantic and confusing that it will scare you if I put it up front.

But here goes:

I count all of the deaths of living, breathing individuals that result from a specific outbreak of coordinated human violence and coercion, both directly (war, murder, execution) and indirectly (aggravated disease, avoidable famine), as long as they are the obvious result of the event. I count all deaths the same, whether military or civilian, malicious or accidental, negligent or authorized. I count only deaths that occur immediately or follow closely—no cancer deaths, no long-term complications from wounds, no suicides among haunted veterans, no unexploded ordinance that blows up farmers fifty years later.

I use a broad definition because I find it unseemly to bicker about whether some victims deserve more pity than others. If I counted only the deliberate killing of civilians while excluding the accidental killing of civilians, then I would be spending all my time trying to decide whether malice was intended. I might also find myself wondering why killing three thousand teenage conscripts in battle is morally acceptable while shooting a half-dozen political troublemakers in prison isn't, or why deliberately shooting a few dozen prisoners of war is illegal while haphazardly bombing ten thousand civilians isn't. That would change the subject of this book from history to philosophy. If you want philosophy, it's two shelves over that way.

Runners-up and Disqualified

Some of you will wonder why certain terrible events don't appear on my list. One of my guidelines is that I won't be the first person ever to estimate a death toll, so a mere suspicion that a lot of people died carries less weight with me than a number—any number—suggested by a previous historian.

To head off these questions, here are some candidates that I've heard about over the years, along with a few that came close but didn't make the final cut. Either they fell short of the minimum necessary death toll (300,000), or the numbers are unverified, or they simply don't belong on the same list as Hitler, Idi Amin, and Chinggis Khan.

Trojan War: According to an account supposedly written by a Trojan survivor named Dares, 866,000 Greeks and 676,000 Trojans were killed in the war.[1] Archaeology has uncovered nothing to suggest that a war that large was fought on that site.

Sack of Seleucia (167 CE): Avidius Cassius, a Roman general under Marcus Aurelius, is said to have massacred 300,000 to 400,000 residents of this Mesopotamian city; however, there are not enough supporting details.[2]

Gothic War (269 CE): Claudius II defeated the Goths, of whom 320,000 were slain.[3] This number is from the "notoriously unreliable"[4] *Historia Augusta*.

Probus's German War (277 CE): During a crisis in the Roman Empire, several tribes of Germans moved across the border into Gaul. After driving them out, the new emperor, Probus, informed the Senate that he had killed 400,000 Germans. Also from the *Historia Augusta*.[5]

Battle at Comnor (385 CE): According to Mormon tradition, 2 million men (plus their women and children, which would bring the total to at least 6 million) were killed in a battle between Shiz and Coriantumr on the hill Comnor in upstate New York.[6] There is absolutely no evidence that this event happened, or that Shiz and Coriantumr even existed. See chapter 16 of Mark Twain's *Roughing It* for a witty debunking.

Muslim Conquest of India (1000–1700): In *The Story of Civilization*, Will Durant wrote that "the Mohammedan conquest of India was probably the bloodiest story in history."[7] Koenraad Elst, "an acknowledge[d]—albeit controversial—scholar on the conservative Hindu Movements in India,"[8] has cited estimates that 50 million Hindus died in the Muslim conquest,[9] but that's probably an exaggeration. Regardless of the death toll, this conquest is too long and sporadic to count as a single event.

Reconquista (1085–1492): A long, nasty series of wars, the reconquest of Spain by the Christians of the north probably killed a lot of people; however, except for confusing references in old religious essays, I've never seen an estimate of the death toll.[10]

Battle of Rio Salado, Portugal (1340): It was said that 400,000 Moors were killed.[11]

Black Death (1347–51): Bubonic plague was introduced to Europe when Mongols flung infected corpses over the wall of a besieged city; however, that's not enough to count it as man-made.

Some Other Ghastly Thing in South Asia: A lot of history has been forgotten, so probably some events are missing from my list simply because the records have been lost. Because India is the biggest region with the most poorly recorded history, it is the most likely venue for completely unknown megadeaths that killed millions.

Some Other Dreadful Thing in Pre-Colonial Africa or America: One of the advantages of living in a society without a written language is that you don't leave a paper trail when you commit crimes against humanity.

Sengoku Jidai (Age of Warring States in Japan, 1467–1603): I looked into it, but all of the authorities describe the Samurai Wars as ritualistic, in which only the warrior caste was killed. Useful people, like peasants, craftsmen, and geishas, were left alone.[12]

Waldenses (1545): Protestant polemicists of the nineteenth century accused the Catholics of killing 900,000 Waldenses in thirty years, and the claim still shows up now and then,[13] but *The Cambridge Modern History* estimates a total of 3,000 massacred and twenty-two villages destroyed.[14]

Witch Hunts (fifteenth to eighteenth century): In the nineteenth century, it was commonly claimed that 9 million or so witches were killed across Europe in the witch hunts. This was based on taking the worst-known events in Germany and extrapolating for the entire continent. Modern research has shown that the continent-wide total was much lower, probably mere tens of thousands, but you still see the estimate of 9 million sometimes.[15]

Franco-Dutch War (1672–78): This was one of Louis XIV's wars. Jack Levy (*War in the Modern Great Power System*) estimated a death toll of 342,000,[16] but his numbers tend to be higher than most for the wars of that era. Other sources (such as André Corvisier and John Childs, *A Dictionary of Military History and the Art of War*)[17] suggest this war was one-fourth as deadly as the War of the Spanish Succession, which would indicate a death toll of 175,000 or so.

War of the Grand Alliance (aka Nine Years War, aka War of the League of Augsburg, 1688–97): This is another one of Louis XIV's wars. Jack Levy estimated a death toll of 680,000,[18] but (see above) this is probably too high. Other sources suggest this war was one-third as deadly as the War of the Spanish Succession, which would indicate a death toll around 233,000.

Circassians (1763–1864): The Russians fought a long, nasty war of conquest against the Circassians in the Caucasus Mountains, and hundreds of thousands were driven into exile. The surviving Circassians scattered around the world claim that anywhere from 300,000 to 1.5 million died, but I can't find any reliable support or widespread agreement for these claims. I ran *circassian* and *genocide* through a giant news database and got no unbiased hits—no book reviews, no background to recent conflicts, no travel features, nothing.[19]

Australian Aborigines (1788–1920): The native population of the island continent is usually estimated as 300,000 originally, which then plummeted to 60,000 by 1920. That's not quite enough to put it into my top one hundred, but less common estimates suggest that 600,000 natives may have died, most by disease.[20]

Thugs (until the nineteenth century): The traditional number of victims murdered by this Indian cult of thieves is 2 million; however, Mike Dash's recent book plausibly estimates only 50,000 victims.[21]

Turks (1821–1921): In response to Greek and Armenian accusations of genocide, the Turks have (a) denied doing anything wrong, and (b) counter-accused the Greeks and Armenians of genociding millions of Turks. Justin McCarthy[22] claims that 5.5 million Ottoman Muslims were killed by various Christian oppressors in the last century of the Ottoman Empire. The massacres certainly went back and forth in each ethnic uprising, but there's no convincing evidence that more than a few thousand noncombatant Turks were killed by angry minorities. I can find no unbiased historian who takes accusations of 5.5 million seriously. James J. Reid's *Crisis of the Ottoman Empire*[23] has a brief rebuttal.

Irish Potato Famine (1845–49): The causes of this famine are too complex to definitely call it an atrocity. I don't usually count peacetime, non-Communist famines as full-fledged atrocities unless especially coercive circumstances set one apart from the rest. As far as I'm concerned, the only stand-alone, man-made famines worth discussing in this book are the famines of British India and the Iraq sanctions, but I'm setting my limit at two—no more.

Philippine-American War (1899–1901): When the United States took the Philippines from Spain, the natives put up a fight. A few—*very* few—estimates of the death toll during the conquest/insurgency go into the neighborhood of 1 million or so. Most books on the subject blame it for something around 200,000 to 250,000 civilian deaths and around 20,000 combatants killed.[24]

Spanish Flu (1918–19): Because the first outbreaks of the disease were spread via troop movements, some people want to add all of the flu deaths to the battle deaths of World War I, thereby raising the war's death toll from 15 million to more than 35 million; however, I have never seen an actual, published history of the First World War do this. Epidemiologists seem to be the major proponents of this attitude, perhaps because it makes the flu an integral part of history rather than a sideshow, as it is usually depicted. My opinion is, yes, we should (and do) count the soldiers and refugees who died of the flu in the war zone, but obviously not the millions in China or India who died far from any battlefield long after the armistice.

Libya (1923–31): Muammar Gaddafi has claimed that 750,000 Libyans—half of the total population of Libya—were killed under Italian occupation. Scholars more commonly estimate the death toll at half the *Bedouin* population, or around 100,000.[25]

Cigarettes: I get occasional suggestions that I should include tobacco company executives among history's worst killers, but smoking lacks two critical characteristics that my top one hundred share—immediacy and coercion. A voluntary activity that might kill you thirty years down the road just isn't in the same league as getting shot, beheaded, or gassed.

Colombia (the civil war known as La Violencia: 1946–58): I found two authorities claiming that 300,000 died, as opposed to five authorities claiming that 200,000 died. This means the death toll is probably below my threshold.

Arab-Israeli Wars (since 1947): These are the most heavily publicized conflicts of the past half century, and many readers will expect to see them here; however, Israel is a small country and there just aren't enough people in this part of the world to generate death tolls at my threshold without a special effort. Estimates run from 50,000 to 100,000 deaths in total.

Tibet (ongoing since 1959): Most of the killing inflicted on Tibet is part of Mao's legacy. I include it in that chapter.

Abortion: Judging by the emails I've received over the years, this will be the most controversial absence. Let's keep it civil and note that "breathing individual" is part of my definition, which excludes the unborn.

East Timor (conquest by Indonesia: after 1975): Of the eleven estimates I found, only one put it unequivocally at my threshold of 300,000. One estimated 200,000 to 300,000, and all the rest don't come close. The median of all eleven is 200,000.

AIDS (after 1981): I am sometimes told that Ronald Reagan (or someone else) deserves condemnation as a mass murderer for allowing AIDS to get out of hand; however, no matter how badly governments bungled the response to the first appearance of AIDS, it was simply beyond anyone's control.

Starving Children in Africa: To be on my list there has to be a core of violence and coercion in which identifiable perpetrators kill, beat, or plunder identifiable victims. Otherwise, it's economics, not atrocitology.

Liberia (1989–2003): Another damn African civil war. You'll sometimes see estimates that reach my threshold, but the official death toll as reported by the Liberian Truth and Reconciliation Committee is 250,000 dead.

Burundi (1993–2004): Yet another civil war between Hutu and Tutsi. I found fifteen articles with estimates of the dead ranging from 200,000 to 500,000. The median of these is indeed at my threshold of 300,000, but the most authoritative single number is 260,000 dead, as calculated in 2004 by the UN Population Fund.[26]

Iraq War (ongoing since 2003): Since this is the most controversial war of the twenty-first century (so far), many readers will want to see it on my list. A widely publicized report in *Lancet* in October 2006 estimated that 655,000 Iraqis had died violently in the war; however, I'm more convinced by several other studies (such as one by the World Health Organization) that estimated around 150,000 deaths.[27]

Disputing Number 1

I have to admit a bias. It is pretty hard to shake my belief that the Second World War was the most destructive man-made event in history. Other candidates for the top rank have been suggested over the years—Stalin, slavery, the conquest of America, Mao—and these are all found somewhere in this book, but the horrors of World War II are so complex and well documented that I find it difficult to accept any of the other contenders without extremely good evidence.

With World War II, we have every nation on the planet, many under the rule of brutal tyrants and ideologies, pounding away at each other, back and forth across three continents, with massively destructive weapons such as atomic bombs. Compare that with what occurred in China under Mao. Yes, he was a ruthless dictator in the largest nation on the planet for a quarter century. He certainly had the means, motive, and opportunity to commit mass murder on a grand scale, but he was only one man in one country. Just at the gut level, I would suspect that an all-out war between Hitler, Stalin, Tojo, and Mao would kill a lot more people than Mao could do all by himself.

It's not just at the grand scale. The horrors of World War II are fractal—they are just as jagged up close as they are from a distance. The massacre at Babi Yar, the bombing of Dresden, and the Battle of the Bulge each killed thirty-some thousand people, and each is important enough by itself to have been the subject of individual books, yet these are not even the worst that World War II has to offer. The war produced deadlier massacres, air raids, and battles. Compared to World War II, what occurred under Mao (for example) seems smoother under the microscope, with fewer deadly events to describe. Even with a big famine, several purges, and a couple of wars, the timeline of Mao's rule just doesn't have the same density as World War II. While writing the chapter on World War II, I worked hard to trim a complicated narrative down to the basics, but with Mao, I worked hard to find enough details to fill out the chapter.

Overlap

One big difference between ranking atrocities and ranking people is that people are very clearly defined. If I drew up a list of the one hundred most important people in history, I wouldn't find that Hitler and Stalin share a leg, and that Napoleon was actually five people taking turns, and that Martin Luther was a centaur. With atrocities, on the other hand, I have to decide whether the French Revolutionary-Napoleonic Wars should count as one, two, or seven events, and whether the Armenian Genocide is its own atrocity or part of World War I. This means that another list-maker using my exact same numbers could easily reshuffle the list just by dividing some atrocities and combining others.

I have a few rules of thumb for dealing with the problem:

If the overlap between two episodes is slight, then I treat them as separate. Mao and the Korean War appear in each other's chapters, but only briefly.

If an event is entirely contained within another event on this list, the smaller event doesn't get its own chapter. For example, I treat the Holocaust as part of World War II, not as a separate event. After all, if I were to give the Holocaust its own chapter, then why stop there? Seventeen pieces of World War II have death tolls large enough to stand alone among the one hundred deadliest events in history: five battles, five theaters of operation, and seven campaigns against noncombatants. If I went around breaking every large event into its component parts, one out of every six chapters would be some aspect of World War II.

Between those obvious guidelines is a mushy middle ground: Should I bundle closely related multicides together, or treat them separately? The Napoleonic Wars and the Haitian Slave Revolt came from the French Revolution, but they definitely went in different directions. On the other hand, the two civil wars in the Sudan could earn separate chapters by body count, but I can't describe them separately because each one is incomplete without the other.

In general, I count tyrants (Saddam Hussein, Peter the Great) separate from their wars (Iran-Iraq War, Great Northern War) unless that war is the setting for almost all of their killing. (Hitler and World War II, Lopez and the Triple Alliance).

I'm more likely to combine old events and split apart recent ones. You probably don't need to know each individual conflict in the fall of the Roman or Ming empires in excruciating detail, so one chapter covering the overall event is enough. Similarly, a hundred years from now, the whole upheaval in Indochina from 1945 into the 1980s will probably be considered a single event, but for now, I treat all of the bits and pieces of recent Vietnamese history separately in order to give you more detail of an era that still affects us today.

I'm often guided by the complaints I hear in debates on comparative genocide. When people complain about the treatment of the American Indian, they mean the whole thing, from Columbus to Wounded Knee. When they ask how many Indians died, they want the grand total, not each little piece. On the other hand, the complaints about Saddam Hussein's tyranny are usually quite different from the complaints about the economic sanctions imposed on Iraq during the 1990s, so I treat those separately.

APPENDIX 2:
THE HEMOCLYSM

Death toll: 150 million

Rank: the other Number 1

Type: technological and political upheaval

Broad dividing line: Us vs. Them

Time frame: early twentieth century

Location: earth

Major participants: humankind

Who usually gets the most blame: people, technology, economics

The reason this isn't the actual Number 1 on my list: Because it combines several distinct events. If I were to include this as a fully accredited event, I'd have to drop a fourth of my chapters (Stalin, World War I, and so on) and replace them with more dynastic upheavals from medieval China. Nobody wants that.

WHEN PEOPLE SAY THAT THE TWENTIETH CENTURY IS THE BLOODIEST CENtury on record, they're really referring to the string of interconnected barbarities that stretched from the First World War to the deaths of Hitler, Stalin, and Mao.

Although each of these wars and dictators represents a distinct event, many are closely interrelated. Hitler, Stalin, and Mao were not only tyrants in their own right, but also major players in World War II, which was clearly a sequel to World War I. The Russian Civil War, which paved the way for the rise of Stalin, was also a spin-off of World War I. The anarchy that swept China following the overthrow of the monarchy brought Chiang Kai-shek to power, put Mao in conflict with him, and encouraged the Japanese invasion. The fall of the Japanese Empire following World War II left Korea up for grabs, and Mao's army was among those who tried to grab it.

It's very possible, therefore, that future historians will consider these events to be mere episodes of a single massive upheaval—the "Hemoclysm," to give it a name (Greek for "blood flood")—which took the lives of some 150 million people. All in all, over 80 percent of violent deaths in the twentieth century occurred in the Hemoclysm.

Geopolitically, the Hemoclysm arose from the decline of two old empires and divides neatly into two parts—Eastern and Western. The Western Hemoclysm began when the decline of the Ottomans left a congestion of petty states in the Balkans under the competing influence of Russia and Austria-Hungary. A war between them quickly expanded to include all of the world's powers. This war was so destructive of armies and wealth that four of Europe's most important monarchies collapsed. The resulting power vacuum was filled by the Nazis in Germany and the Communists in Russia. These two competing ideologies consolidated power brutally, and then fought each other in the Second World War, which was basically a rerun of the First World War. The death of Stalin in 1953 finally extinguished the Western Hemoclysm after the loss of some 100 million lives.

The Eastern Hemoclysm began when the fall of the Chinese emperor spawned four decades of civil war that attracted the ambitions of the Japanese. In 1949, the bloodbath of the interregnum gave way to a greater bloodbath as the Communists consolidated power under Mao, who died in 1976. When seen as a continuum, this phase of Chinese history was a sixty-five-year nightmare which took some 55 million lives.

If it weren't for the fact that the Second World War is considered to be a single event, we could probably consider the Eastern and Western halves of the Hemoclysm to be distinctly unrelated pieces of history.

Why did the world suddenly explode into this unprecedented wave of killing? The causes are complex, but after years of study, I think I've narrowed it down to three reasons:

1. Because they could.
2. Because they wanted to.
3. And because everybody else was doing it.

Or, if you'd prefer fancier academic terms for these causes, let's say:

1. Technology.
2. Ideology.
3. The escalating cycle of violence.

Because They Could (Technology)

It wasn't just machine guns scything down advancing infantry by the fistful. It wasn't just airplanes delivering death hundreds of miles behind enemy lines. It was trucks and railroads that could provision huge armies in desolate battle zones. Tanks brought movement back to armies that had stalled in front of unbreakable fortifications. Radar and sonar could locate enemies far beyond the line of sight. Radio could coordinate offensives across an entire continent. Industry produced vast quantities of munitions that could be expended in wasteful overkill. Urbanization brought huge populations together where they could be pounded by air raids or rounded up for massacre or deportation. Well-staffed and well-wired bureaucracies made it nearly impossible to hide from the tax collector, the draft board, or the secret police.

Because They Wanted To (Ideology)

One might hope to be clever and connect the major upheavals of the twentieth century ideologically:

> Nationalism (World War I) + Socialism (Stalin) = something even worse: National Socialism (Hitler).

Unfortunately, this analysis fails on two points. First, National Socialism was no more "socialist" than the Democratic Republic of (North) Korea is a "democratic republic." The Nazis called themselves "socialists" because it attracted more working-class support than calling themselves the "We'll Stomp Anyone Who Gets in Our Way Party," but they hated real socialists and supported none of the economic redistribution that is the core of authentic socialism.

Second, we can't blame the First World War entirely on nationalism. In fact, it's hard to blame the First World War on anything in particular because we're still not sure what it was all about. However, the Great War was such a catastrophic trauma for Western Civilization that it caused a massive ideological reassessment across Europe. Among the winning countries, this showed up as postwar hedonism and artistic nihilism, but among the losing countries, the rejection of mainstream philosophy was more thorough. Russia turned left, toward the hyper-modernism of Marxism, while Germany turned right, toward the hyper-primitive Nazism. Both philosophies brutally dehumanized and demonized the opposition, and casually threw away the lives of their followers in the name of a greater good.

Because Everyone Else Was Doing It (The Escalating Cycle of Violence)

Each killing created a litter of bitter orphans who would grow up to avenge their father's death. Each campaign pushed thousands of refugees into a life of scavenging and plundering. Each draft put more weapons into the hands of thousands of angry, alienated young men who were just as likely to use them against their own government as against the enemy. Every conquered nation had to be liberated. Every surprise attack brought another country into the war. Every loss had to be reversed. No victory was ever final.

It was only after the development of nuclear weapons and the prospect of the end of the world that the cycle of violence ran into a brick wall and was forced to stop.

ACKNOWLEDGMENTS

MY SPECIAL THANKS GO TO VINCENZO OSTUNI FOR GETTING ME STARTED on this project and to Steven Pinker for all his help and encouragement in getting me published. I am very grateful to my friends Jennifer, Joanna, Sarah, Gopa, Lelia, Frances, Lou, Andrew, Robert, Niki, and Brian for criticizing the early drafts and talking me through so many tricky questions. Thanks to my brother Peter for all his encouragement and his shared interest in history. I am deeply indebted to Brendan Curry, Melanie Tortoroli, and Mary Babcock at W. W. Norton for their help in finalizing the book, correcting my mistakes, helping me clarify complicated issues, and generally nudging me toward better writing. Thanks also go to Adrian Kitzinger for his excellent maps. I am especially grateful to my agent and his colleagues—Max Brockman, Russell Weinberger, and Michael Healey—for guiding me through the strange new world of publishing. Finally I'd like to thank the acquisitions departments of the Richmond Public Library and Virginia Commonwealth University's Cabell Library, whom I have never met, but their anonymous work at maintaining large history collections greatly helped my research.

NOTES

Second Persian War

1. Hanson, *Carnage and Culture*, p. 31, estimated that a quarter-million Persian soldiers died in both Persian Wars. Sorokin, *Social and Cultural Dynamics*, vol. 3, p. 543, estimated that 57,000 Greeks were killed or wounded. These are all rough estimates, but they point to something in the neighborhood of 300,000 all told, including civilians.
2. Hanson, *Carnage and Culture*; Strauss, *Battle of Salamis*.

Alexander the Great

1. Hanson, *Wars of the Ancient Greeks*, p. 178: "In the space of just eight years Alexander the Great had slain well over 200,000 men in pitched battle alone"; p. 178: "A quarter million urban residents were massacred outright between 334 and 324." I rounded upward to include Alexander's losses.
2. Keegan, *Mask of Command*, pp. 13–91.
3. Pratt, *Battles That Changed History*, pp. 17–37.
4. Rogers, *Alexander*.

Age of Warring States

1. Ancient histories claim that Qin soldiers killed a total of 1.5 million enemies in all of their battles. Modern historians don't take this total literally, but they report it as a plausible order of magnitude for the dead on all sides from all causes. Hui, *War and State Formation*, p. 87; Peers, *Warlords of China*, pp. 58–59.
2. Lei Hai-tsung, "Warring States."
3. Ibid.
4. Ibid.
5. Peers, *Warlords of China*, pp. 55–57.
6. Ibid., p. 58.
7. Peers, *Warlords of China*, p. 61.
8. Sima Qian, *Records of the Grand Historian*, p. 163.
9. Man, *Terra Cotta Army*, pp. 46–47.

First Punic War

1. Richard A. Gabriel, *The Culture of War: Invention and Early Development* (Westport, CT: Greenwood Press, 1990), pp. 110–111. "Polybius called this war the bloodiest in history, and it is probable that the loss of life on both sides, most of it Roman, approached four hundred thousand men."
2. Bagnall, *Essential Histories*, p. 34.
3. Ibid., p. 41.

Qin Shi Huang Di

1. Fitzgerald, *China*, p. 140: "Popular tradition has held his memory in undying hatred for building the Wall. . . . [T]he people repeat that a million men perished at the task."
2. Peers, *Warlords of China*, p. 66.
3. Ibid., pp. 62–64; Lesley A. DuTemple, *The Great Wall of China* (Minneapolis: Lerner, 2003), pp. 22–41.
4. Peers, *Warlords of China*, pp. 67–69; Qingxin Li, *Maritime Silk Road* (Beijing: China Intercontinental Press, 2006), p. 11.
5. Peers, *Warlords of China*, p. 69.
6. Ibid., p. 70.
7. Ibid., pp. 66–67.

Second Punic War

1. The Roman historian Appian (Pun. 20.134) recorded 300,000 Roman battle deaths. Theodore Ayrault Dodge, in *Hannibal: A History of the Art of War among the Carthaginians and Romans* (Boston: Houghton Mifflin,1891), pp. 610–611, added disease and expanded this to 500,000 Roman and 270,000 Carthaginian soldiers dead of all causes.
2. Bagnall, *Essential Histories*, pp. 50–52.
3. Ibid., pp. 54–55.

Gladiatorial Games

1. Based on the number of amphitheaters uncovered by archaeologists, the frequency of festivals, etc., Keith Hopkins and Mary Beard, in *The Colosseum* (Cambridge, MA: Harvard University Press, 2005), pp. 92–94, estimated that 8,000 deaths, including from training accidents, occurred in the arena each year all across the empire. This would multiply out to a maximum of 5.6 million deaths during all 700 years of recorded gladiatorial combat, or (more likely) to 3.2 million deaths if this death rate was sustained only during the 400-year peak of the games between the times of Spartacus and Constantine. I chose a round number at the low end of this range as my guess.
2. Kyle, *Spectacles of Death in Ancient Rome*, p. 45.
3. Ibid., p. 106.
4. Ibid., p. 51.
5. Ibid., pp. 187–194.
6. Ibid., p. 187.
7. E. W. Bovill and Robin Hallett, *The Golden Trade of the Moors* (Princeton, NJ: M. Weiner, 1995), pp. 5–7; Johnson Donald Hughes, *The Mediterranean* (Santa Barbara, CA: ABC-CLIO, 2005), pp. 37–38.
8. Kyle, *Spectacles of Death in Ancient Rome*, p. 86.

9. Ibid., p. 162.

10. Auguet, *Cruelty and Civilization*, p. 55.

11. Kyle, *Spectacles of Death in Ancient Rome*, pp. 158–165.

12. Jones, "Gladiators: The Brutal Truth."

13. Gibbon, *Decline and Fall of the Roman Empire*, vol. 2, ch. 16, citing Origen, estimated some 2,000 Christian martyrs.

Roman Slave Wars

1. Athenaeus, *Philosophers at Dinner*, 6.272 (cited in Zvi Yavetz, *Slaves and Slavery in Ancient Rome* (New Brunswick, NJ: Transaction Books, 1988), p. 78; Naphtali Lewis, *Roman Civilization*, vol. 2: *The Roman Empire* (New York: Columbia University Press, 1990), p. 245).

2. Mommsen, *History of Rome*, vol. 3, pp. 309–310.

3. Ibid., pp. 383–387.

4. Strauss, *Spartacus War*; Mommsen, *History of Rome*, vol. 4, pp. 357–364.

War of the Allies

1. Paterculus, *Roman History*, p. 79, http://penelope.uchicago.edu/Thayer/E/Roman/Texts/Velleius_Paterculus/2A*.html (accessed March 9, 2011), 2.15.3 (killed on all sides).

2. Mommsen, *History of Rome*, vol. 3, pp. 490–527.

Third Mithridatic War

1. Plutarch, "Life of Lucullus," in *Parallel Lives* (1914), http://penelope.uchicago.edu/Thayer/E/Roman/Texts/Plutarch/Lives/Lucullus*.html (accessed March 9, 2011): In the third war, 300,000 Pontics were killed fighting for Mithridates (p. 505), plus 100,000 Armenians were killed fighting for Tigranes (p. 565).

2. Plutarch says 200,000. Appian says 160,000.

3. Alfred S. Bradford, *With Arrow, Sword, and Spear* (Westport, CT: Praeger, 2001), p. 204.

Gallic War

1. The 700,000 is the average of the two contradictory death tolls that have come down to us: one million in Plutarch, "Life of Julius Caesar," in *Parallel Lives* (1919), vol. 7, para. 15, p. 479, http://penelope.uchicago.edu/Thayer/E/Roman/Texts/Plutarch/Lives/Caesar*.html (accessed March 9, 2011); 400,000 in Paterculus, *Roman History*, book 2, ch. 47, p. 153, http://penelope.uchicago.edu/Thayer/E/Roman/Texts/Velleius_Paterculus/2B*.html (accessed March 9, 2011).

2. Meier, *Caesar*, pp. 239–241.

Ancient Innumeracy

1. Catherine Rubincam, "Casualty Figures in Thucydides' Descriptions of Battle," *TAPA* 121 (1991): 181–198.

2. John Heidenrich, "The Gulf War: How Many Iraqis Died?" *Foreign Policy* no. 90, March 22, 1993.

3. Rebecca Santana, "85,000 Iraqis Killed in Almost 5 Years of War," Associated Press, October 14, 2009.

4. Tina Susman, "Poll: Civilian Death Toll in Iraq May Top 1 Million," *Los Angeles Times*, September 14, 2007.

Xin Dynasty

1. Twitchett and Fairbank, *Cambridge History of China*, vol. 1, p. 218.
2. Ibid., p. 219.
3. "Wang Mang," in *Encyclopaedia Britannica*, 15th ed., vol. 12, p. 486.
4. Gabriel R. Ricci, "Introduction," in *Cultural Landscapes: Religion and Public Life*, vol. 35, http://www.etown.edu/History.aspx?topic=Introduction+to+volume+35 (accessed March 20, 2011); H. H. Lamb, *Climate, History and the Modern World* (New York: Routledge, 1995), p. 315.
5. Twitchett and Fairbank, *Cambridge History of China*, vol. 1, pp. 241–242.
6. Ibid., p. 243.
7. Ibid., p. 245.
8. Ibid., p. 247.
9. Ibid., p. 248.
10. Ibid., p. 250.
11. Population collapse estimates, high to low:
    - Dan Usher says the population declined from 58 million in 2 CE to 15.1 million in 31 CE, for a loss of 43 million (*Political Economy* (Malden, MA: Blackwell, 2003), p. 12).
    - J. D. Durand estimates that the population of China Proper dropped from 71 million to 43 million between 2 CE and 88 CE, a loss of 28 million ("Population Statistics of China, AD 2—1953," p. 221).
    - P. M. G. Harris estimates a population of 41 million in 23 CE, which suggests a decline of 16 million since 2 CE (*The History of Human Populations*, vol. 1: *Forms of Growth and Decline* (Westport, CT: Praeger, 2001), p. 241).
    - William Leonard says that the population declined from just under 60 million in 1 CE to just under 50 million in 140 CE, a decline of approximately 10 million (*The Encyclopedia of World History* (London: Harrap, 1972), p. 51).
    - Rafe de Crespigny: In 2 CE the population of the whole empire was over 57 million; in the 140s there were 48 million, indicating a decline of 9 million ("South China under the Later Han Dynasty," 1990, http://www.anu.edu.au/asianstudies/decrespigny/south_china.html).
    - Twitchett and Fairbank suggest a population decline of 8 or 9 million between 2 CE and 140 CE (*Cambridge History of China*, vol. 1, p. 240).

Roman-Jewish Wars

1. Lester L. Grabbe, *An Introduction to First Century Judaism: Jewish Religion and History in the Second Temple Period* (Edinburgh: Clark, 1996), pp. 64–65.
2. Jona Lendering, "Messianic Claimants (18) Simon ben Kosiba (132–135 CE)," Livius.org, http://www.livius.org/men-mh/messiah/messianic_claimants17.html (accessed March 18, 2011).
3. Will Durant, *Caesar and Christ* (New York: MJF, 1971), p. 545.
4. Cassius Dio, *Roman History* (1925), 69.14, http://penelope.uchicago.edu/Thayer/E/Roman/Texts/Cassius_Dio/69*.html (accessed March 8, 2011).
5. Will Durant, *Caesar and Christ* (New York: MJF, 1971), p. 548.
6. Among the population estimates are Anthony Byatt, "Josephus and Population Numbers in First Century Palestine," *Palestine Exploration Quarterly* 105 (1973): 15 (2,265,000); C. C. McCown, "The Density of Population in Ancient Palestine," *Journal of Biblical Literature* 66 (1947): 425 (less than 1,000,000); Adolf von Harnack, *Die Mission und Ausbreitung des Christentums* (Leipzig: J. C.

Hinrichs, 1902) (500,000); Seth Schwartz, *Imperialism and Jewish Society, 200 B.C.E. to 640 C.E.* (Princeton, NJ: Princeton University Press, 2001) (500,000).

The Three Kingdoms of China

1. "Romance of the Three Kingdoms," *TV Tropes*, http://tvtropes.org/pmwiki/pmwiki.php/Literature/ RomanceOfTheThreeKingdoms (accessed March 20, 2011).
2. Andrew O'Hehir, "John Woo on 'Red Cliff' and the Rise of Chinawood," *Salon*, November 18, 2009, http://www.salon.com/ent/movies/btm/feature/2009/11/18/john_woo/index.html.
3. Etienne Balazs, *Chinese Civilization and Bureaucracy* (New Haven, CT: Yale University Press, 1965), p. 193 (imperial repression killed half a million in 184 alone).
4. Fitzgerald, *China*, p. 255.
5. Hong-Sen Yan, *Reconstruction Designs of Lost Ancient Chinese Machinery* (Dordrecht: Springer, 2007), pp. 275–277; Joseph Needham and Colin Ronan, *The Shorter Science and Civilisation in China: An Abridgement of Joseph Needham's Original Text* (Cambridge, UK: Cambridge University Press, 1994), p. 170.
6. de Crespigny, "Three Kingdoms and Western Jin."
7. There's nothing magical about this; it's just that when you're faced with two wildly different numbers (let's say, 16 and 10,000), averaging them by aritmetic mean $(16 + 10,000/2 = 5,008)$ is pretty much the same as dividing the highest in half. However, averaging them by geometric mean $(\sqrt{(16*10,000)} = 400)$ comes up with a number that's more recognizably influenced by and lying between the two levels.

   If all you know is the general order of magnitude, this trick can still help narrow it down to a single number for statistical purposes. If an event killed "hundreds of thousands," we can guess the single most likely number to be the geometric mean of 100,000 and 1,000,000, or 316,228. This is not far off from reality. By my count (see http://www.necrometrics.com), there were forty-seven multicides in the twentieth century with a death toll between 100,000 and 1,000,000. These had an average (mean) death toll of 297,766—which you'll notice is closer to the geometric mean than to the arithmetic mean (550,000).

Fall of the Western Roman Empire

1. Colin McEvedy, in *New Penguin Atlas of Medieval History*, p. 38, estimated that the Roman Empire's population on the eve of collapse was 36 million, and the territory lost 20 percent of its people between 400 CE and 600 CE—a loss of 7.2 million.
2. Ward-Perkins, *Fall of Rome and the End of Civilization*, pp. 22–23.
3. Howarth, *Attila King of the Huns*, p. 89.
4. Bury, *Invasion of Europe by the Barbarians*, pp. 114–119; Grant, *Fall of the Roman Empire*, pp. 15–17.
5. Howarth, *Attila King of the Huns*, p. 49.
6. Ibid., pp. 95–97.
7. Gregory of Tours, quoted in ibid., p. 99. You'll notice that chroniclers get especially upset whenever priests get killed—possibly because priests write the chronicles.
8. Hildinger, *Warriors of the Steppe*, pp. 69–70.
9. Ibid., p. 72.
10. Grant, *Fall of the Roman Empire*, pp. 19–20.

11. Ibid., pp. 27–34.
12. Ibid., pp. 35–47.
13. Ibid., pp. 203–204.
14. Ibid., pp. 155–162.
15. Ward-Perkins, *Fall of Rome and the End of Civilization*, pp. 3–10, 169–183.
16. Ibid., pp. 87–168.
17. "The population of Europe (west of the Urals) in c. AD 200 has been estimated at 36 million; by 600, it had fallen to 26 million; another estimate (excluding 'Russia') gives a more drastic fall, from 44 to 22 million." Francois Crouzet, *A History of the European Economy, 1000–2000* (Charlottesville: University Press of Virginia, 2001), p. 1.

Justinian

1. Ormsby, "Hidden Historian."
2. Gibbon, *Decline and Fall of the Roman Empire*, vol. 4, ch. 40.
3. Rosen, *Justinian's Flea*, pp. 74–76.
4. Ibid., pp. 137–141.
5. Ibid., pp. 148–151.
6. Procopius, "How Justinian Killed a Trillion People," in *The Secret History*, trans. Richard Atwater (Chicago: P. Covici, 1927; reprinted, Ann Arbor: University of Michigan Press, 1961), available at Medieval Sourcebook, http://www.fordham.edu/halsall/basis/procop-anec.html.
7. Thomas Dick, *The Philosophy of Religion: Or an Illustration of the Moral Laws of the Universe* (Philadelphia: Key & Biddle, 1833), pp. 260–262; George Cone Beckwith, *The Peace Manual: Or, War and Its Remedies* (Boston: American Peace Society, 1847), pp. 39–42.
8. The modern estimate of plague deaths is that Justinian's empire lost 4 million in the first two years of the epidemic. Rosen, *Justinian's Flea*, p. 261.
9. Gibbon, *Decline and Fall of the Roman Empire*, vol. 4, ch. 42.
10. McEvedy, *New Penguin Atlas of Medieval History*, p. 38.

Goguryeo-Sui Wars

1. According to Chinese sources (see below), the Chinese lost around 300,000 in each war. Although this might be an exaggeration, the Chinese were meticulous record-keepers and quite capable of fielding armies of 100,000 or more, losing most of them with hardly a second thought. Throw in the other side plus all of the collateral deaths, and 300,000 per war isn't unreasonable.
2. Graff, *Medieval Chinese Warfare*, p. 145.
3. Kenneth B. Lee, *Korea and East Asia: The Story of a Phoenix* (Westport, CT: Praeger/Greenwood, 1997), p. 16.
4. Jae-un Kang and Suzanne Lee, *The Land of Scholars: Two Thousand Years of Korean Confucianism* (Paramus, NJ: Homa & Sekey Books, 2006), p. 40.

Mideast Slave Trade

1. *Commonwealth v. Turner*, 26 Va. 678 (Va. Gen. Ct., November Term 1827).
2. Segal, *Islam's Black Slaves*, p. 146.
3. Ibid., p. 159.
4. Ibid.

5. Ibid., p. 156.

6. Alan Weisman, *The World without Us* (New York: St. Martin's Press, 2007), pp. 95–96.

7. Ibid.

8. Segal, *Islam's Black Slaves*, p. 148.

9. Ibid., p. 160.

10. Ibid., p. 167.

11. Ibid., p. 169.

12. Ibid., p. 171

13. Ibid., p. 156.

14. Milton, *White Gold*, p. 16.

15. Keegan, *History of Warfare*, pp. 32–40.

16. Davis, *Christian Slaves*, p. 23.

17. Davis, in *Christian Slaves*, estimated an annual death rate of 17 percent per year. For comparison, the death rate for a healthy preindustrial population would rarely exceed 3 percent (E. A. Wrigley, *Population History of England, 1541–1871: A Reconstruction* (New York: Cambridge University Press, 1989), p. 181).

An Lushan Rebellion

1. Newark, *Medieval Warlords*, pp. 48–51.

2. Ibid., p. 52.

3. Fitzgerald, *China*, pp. 399–400.

4. Newark, *Medieval Warlords*, p. 55.

5. Pulleyblank, "An Lu-shan Rebellion," p. 41.

6. Ibid., p. 43.

7. Graff, *Medieval Chinese Warfare*, p. 219.

8. Fitzgerald, *China*, p. 301.

9. Newark, *Medieval Warlords*, p. 63.

10. Graff, *Medieval Chinese Warfare*, p. 222.

11. Fitzgerald, *China*, p. 349.

12. Li Po, "Nefarious War," in *The Works of Li Po the Chinese Poet Done into English Verse by Shigeyoshi Obata with an Introduction and Biographical and Critical Matter Translated from the Chinese* (New York: E. P. Dutton, 1922), p. 141.

13. Fitzgerald, *China*, p. 350.

14. Tu-Fu, "A Song of War-Chariots," trans. Witter Bynner and Kiang Kang-hu, *The Bookman*, vol. 54 (New York: George H. Doran, 1922), p. 568.

15. Fitzgerald, *China*, pp. 351–352.

16. Po Chu-I, "The Never-ending Wrong," in L. Cranmer-Byng, *A Lute of Jade/Being Selections from the Classical Poets of China* (New York: E. P. Dutton, 1913), pp. 79–88. This is how the specific translation labels it, but nowadays Po Chu-I is usually called Bai Juyi and his poem is called "The Song of Everlasting Sorrow."

17. The census figures are referenced in the following places:

   • Durand, "Population Statistics of China," pp. 209, 223 (expressing major doubt over accuracy).

   • Fitzgerald, *China*, pp. 312–315 (major doubt).

- Richard Hooker, *World Civilizations*, Washington State University, 1996, http://www.wsu.edu/~dee/TEXT/chememp.rtf (apparent acceptance).
- Peter N. Stearns, ed., *The Encyclopedia of World History: Ancient, Medieval, and Modern*, 6th ed. (Boston: Houghton Mifflin, 2001), http://www.bartleby.com/67/370.html (slight doubt).
- Peter Turchin, "Dynamical Feedbacks between Population Growth and Sociopolitical Instability in Agrarian States," *Structure and Dynamics* 1, no. 1 (2005), http://www.escholarship.org/uc/item/0d17g8g9 (acceptance).

18. Durand, "Population Statistics of China," p. 223.

Mayan Collapse

1. Melanie Moran and Mimi Koumenalis, "Royal Massacre Site Discovered in Ruins on Ancient Maya City," November 18, 2005, http://www.exploration.vanderbilt.edu/print/pdfs/news/news_maya_massacre.pdf; Thomas H. Maugh II, "Maya War Crimes Scene Uncovered," *Los Angeles Times*, November 17, 2005.
2. McKillop, *Ancient Maya*, pp. 97–98.
3. Diamond, *Collapse*, p. 175.
4. Turner and Adams cited in Richardson Benedict Gill, *The Great Maya Droughts: Water, Life, and Death* (Albuquerque: University of New Mexico Press, 2000), p. 351. Other estimates: *The New York Times Guide to Essential Knowledge* (New York: St. Martin's Press, 2007), p. 495 (8 to 10 million people); John E. Kicza, *The Peoples and Civilizations of the Americas before Contact* (Washington, DC: American Historical Association, 1998), p. 12 (3 million to 5 million); Bodil Liljefors Persson, *The Legacy of the Jaguar Prophet* (Lund, Sweden: Religionshistoriska Avd., Lunds University, 2000), p. 88 (2 million).

The Crusades

1. Estimates of the number of people killed in the Crusades begin at 1 million (Fredric Wertham, *A Sign for Cain: An Exploration of Human Violence* (New York: Macmillan, 1966)) and go as high as 9 million (John M. Robertson, *A Short History of Christianity* (London: Watts, 1902), p. 278) passing through 3 million (Fielding Hudson Garrison, *Notes on the History of Military Medicine* (Washington, DC: Association of Military Surgeons, 1922), p. 106) and 5 million (Henry William Elson, *Modern Times and the Living Past* (New York: American Book Company, 1921), p. 261) along the way. I took the low middle (Garrison's estimate) as my estimate. The geometric mean of the extremes is 3 million.
2. Wheatcroft, *Infidels*, pp. 158–159.
3. Riley-Smith, *Crusades*, p. 9.
4. Wheatcroft, *Infidels*, p. 166; Maalouf, *Crusades through Arab Eyes*, pp. 3–8.
5. Maalouf, *Crusades through Arab Eyes*, pp. 15–17.
6. Ibid., pp. 31–32.
7. Wheatcroft, *Infidels*, pp. 170–171.
8. Riley-Smith, *Crusades*, pp. 32–33.
9. Maalouf, *Crusades through Arab Eyes*, pp. 39–40; Wheatcroft, *Infidels*, p. 171.
10. Tamim Ansary, *Destiny Disrupted* (New York: PublicAffairs, 2009), p. 145.
11. Maalouf, *Crusades through Arab Eyes*, pp. 93–94.
12. Riley-Smith, *Crusades*, pp. 121–130; Norwich, *Short History of Byzantium*, pp. 299–306.

13. Riley-Smith, *Crusades*, p. 141; James Harpur, *The Crusades: The Two Hundred Years War* (New York: Rosen Publishing Group, 2008), pp. 82–83; Cecil Adams, "Is the Children's Crusade Fact or Fable?" *Straight Dope*, April 9, 2004, http://www.straightdope.com/columns/read/2503/is-the-childrens-crusade-fact-or-fable.

14. Riley-Smith, *Crusades*, p. 7.

Religious Killing

1. Although likely exaggerated, the numbers in Exodus 32, Numbers 31, Joshua 10, Judges 1, Judges 3, Judges 20, 1 Samuel 4, 2 Samuel 8, 2 Samuel 10, 2 Samuel 18, and 2 Chronicles 25 are plausible. Those in Judges 8, 2 Chronicles 13, 1 Kings 20, and Esther 9, less so.

2. "Japanese Martyrs," in *Catholic Encyclopedia*, http://www.newadvent.org/cathen/09744a.htm (accessed March 20, 2011).

3. "Bosnia Marks War Anniversary," BBC, April 6, 2002.

4. Sakuntala Narasimhan, *Sati: Widow Burning in India* (New York: Doubleday, 1992), says that 7,941 widows were burned alive during the Bengal Presidency, 1815–28, and also cites Rammohun Roy that almost ten times more incidents occurred in Bengal than elsewhere. My estimate is that there were some 8.735 (= 1.1 3 7,941) satis in all of India in fourteen years, or around 62,400 in a century.

5. Charles Carlton, *Going to the Wars: The Experience of the British Civil Wars, 1638–1651* (New York: Routledge, 1992), p. 211.

6. John Daniszewski, "On 25th Anniversary of Civil War, Lebanese Rally for Account of Missing," *Los Angeles Times*, April 14, 2000; "Casualty Toll of Lebanese Civil War Put at 144,000," Associated Press, March 9, 1992.

7. "Ten Dead in Fighting in Algeria," Agence France Presse, June 23, 2003; Gilles Trequesser, "Bouteflika Aides Say Algerian Leader Ahead in Poll," Reuters News, April 8, 2004.

8. Peter C. Phan, *Vietnamese-American Catholics* (Mahwah, NJ: Paulist Press, 2005), p. 88; Bernard B. Fall, *Last Reflections on a War: Bernard B. Fall's Last Comments on Vietnam* (Mechanicsburg, PA: Stackpole Books, 2000), p. 44.

9. Lincoln, *Red Victory*, p. 319.

10. Gibbon, *Decline and Fall of the Roman Empire*, vol. 5, ch. 54; "Paulicians," in *Encyclopaedia Britannica*, 11th ed., vol. 20, p. 960.

11. John Lothrop Motley, *Rise of the Dutch Republic* (New York: Harper & Brothers, 1855), p. 497; Philip Schaff, *History of the Christian Church* (New York: Scribner, 1910), p. 180.

12. Paul Johnson, *A History of the Jews* (New York: Harper Perennial, 1988), pp. 259–260.

13. Gibbon, *Decline and Fall of the Roman Empire*, vol. 4, ch. 47.

14. Gibbons, "Recent Developments in the Study of the Great European Witch Hunt" (favoring estimates of 40,000 to 60,000).

Fang La Rebellion

1. Lieu, *Manichaeism in Central Asia and China*, p. 135, citing an old Chinese source (*Ch'ing-ch'i K'ou-kuei*). This counts only the number of deaths in the rebellion, not those in the subsequent collapse of the frontier.

2. William Hardy McNeill, *The Rise of the West: A History of the Human Community* (Chicago: University of Chicago Press, 1990), pp. 311–313.

3. Lieu, *Manichaeism in Central Asia and China*; Lieu, *Manichaeism in the Later Roman Empire and*

Medieval China; Youzhong Shi, *The Taiping Ideology: Its Sources, Interpretations, and Influences* (Seattle: University of Washington Press, 1967).

Genghis Khan

1. Loosely based on McEvedy, *Atlas of World Population History*. McEvedy states that the population of China declined by 35 million during the thirteenth century. Also, the population decline in the western regions of Mongol conquests adds up to 2.75 million. All in all, it seems that Eurasia had 37,750,000 fewer people in the wake of the Mongols. I've rounded that off to avoid faking too much precision.
2. Osborn, "Genghis Khan"; Pocha, "Once-Feared Invader's Reputation."
3. Mayell, "Genghis Khan a Prolific Lover."
4. Weatherford, *Genghis Khan*, p. 115.
5. Ibid., p. 117. Compare this to the certainty with which Weatherford reports European atrocities on the facing page. He describes Europeans playing soccer with severed heads, hanging prisoners from walls, pulling their limbs off, and worse ("The Germans then gathered captive children and strapped them into the catapults") without a "reportedly" or "supposedly" at all (p. 116). Also notice how the son-in-law's death in battle is described as "murder."
6. Hildinger, *Warriors of the Steppe*, p. 113.
7. Ibid., p. 116.
8. Keegan, *History of Warfare*, pp. 160–162.
9. Weatherford, *Genghis Khan*, pp. 113–114.
10. Hildinger, *Warriors of the Steppe*, pp. 21–23; Keegan, *History of Warfare*, pp. 162–163.
11. Man, *Genghis Khan*, p. 142.
12. Grousset, *Conqueror of the World*, p. 196.
13. Man, *Genghis Khan*, pp. 167–168.
14. Ibid., p. 174.
15. Grousset, *Conqueror of the World*, pp. 208–211.
16. Ibid., pp. 217–218.
17. Ibid., p. 235.
18. Ibid., p. 223.
19. Ibid., pp. 227–229.
20. Juvayni, *Genghis Khan*, p. 197.
21. Grousset, *Conqueror of the World*, p. 237; Man, *Genghis Khan*, pp. 174–177.
22. Grousset, *Conqueror of the World*, p. 264.
23. Man, *Genghis Khan*, p. 262; McEvedy, *Atlas of World Population History*, p. 172; Morgan, *Mongols*, p. 83, citing John D. Langlois, *China under Mongol Rule*; McFarlane, in *Savage Wars of Peace*, p. 50, estimates that the Chinese population was reduced to half in fifty years—60 million people dying or failing to be replaced.
24. Man, *Genghis Khan*, p. 180; McEvedy, *Atlas of World Population History*, pp. 78, 152–156.
25. Durand, "Population Statistics of China."
26. Grousset, *Conqueror of the World*, p. 233.
27. Morgan, *Mongols*, p. 79.
28. Ibid., pp. 79–81.
29. Weatherford, *Genghis Khan*, p. 114.

30. Ibid., p. 118.
31. Man, *Genghis Khan*, p. 177.
32. *Merriam-Webster's Collegiate Dictionary*, 10th ed. (Springfield, MA: Merriam-Webster, 1999), p. 842.

Albigensian Crusade

1. This is the traditional death toll given for the war against the Cathars. I don't know where it originated, nor have I seen it in a scholarly history of France, but this number is commonly repeated in religious studies, for example: Christopher Brookmyre, *Not the End of the World* (New York: Grove Press, 1998), p. 39; Max Dimont, *Jews, God, and History* (New York: Penguin, 1994), p. 225; Dizerega Gus, *Pagans and Christians: The Personal Spiritual Experience* (St. Paul, MN: Llewellyn, 2001), p. 195; Helen Ellerbe, *The Dark Side of Christian History* (Orlando, FL: Morningstar & Lark, 1995), p. 74; Michael Newton, *Holy Homicide* (Port Townsend, WA: Loompanics, 1998), p. 117. The number has been kicking around for at least a century; see John M. Robertson, *A Short History of Christianity* (London: Watts, 1902), p. 254 ("It has been reckoned that a million of all ages and both sexes were slain").
2. O'Shea, *Perfect Heresy*, pp. 75–87.
3. Ibid., p. 106.
4. Riley-Smith, *Crusades*, p. 137.
5. Ibid., p. 138.
6. Chalk and Jonassohn, *History and Sociology of Genocide*, pp. 114–134.

Hulagu's Invasion

1. Most accounts even today repeat that 800,000 people were killed at Baghdad. While this is clearly too large for a single city, I'll let it stand as a place holder for the war as a whole.
2. Frazier, "Destroying Baghdad"; Morgan, *Mongols*.

Hundred Years War

1. Tuchman, *Distant Mirror*, pp. 70–71.
2. Mortimer, "Poitiers," p. 41(7).
3. Joan Bos, "Charles VI of France," *Joan's Mad Monarch Series*, http://www.xs4all.nl/~monarchs/madmonarchs/charles6/charles6_bio.htm (accessed March 20, 2011); Tuchman, *Distant Mirror*, pp. 497–516.
4. Keegan, *Face of Battle*, pp. 79–116.
5. Pratt, *Battles That Changed History*, pp. 104–121.
6. Sorokin, *Social and Cultural Dynamics*, vol. 3, pp. 548–549, 560.
7. Turchin, *Historical Dynamics*, p. 180.
8. Philip Pregill, *Landscapes in History*, 2d ed. (New York: John Wiley, 1999), p. 167 (the population of France began at approximately19 million, but had declined by one-third by end of the Hundred Years War); Frederic J. Baumgartner, *France in the Sixteenth Century* (New York: St. Martin's Press, 1995), p. 65 (the population of France was 20 million in 1340, 10 million a century later); Henry Heller, *Labour, Science and Technology in France 1500–1620* (Cambridge, UK: Cambridge University Press, 2002), p. 202 (17 million at the beginning of fourteenth century; 9 million in 1440). In most countries, the Black Death killed one-third of the population, but the French population

apparently declined by half, so the extra one-sixth of deaths (about 3.33 million) may have been caused by the war.

9. Robert S. Lopez, in Edward Miller, ed., *The Cambridge Economic History of Europe from the Decline of the Roman Empire*, vol. 2 (Cambridge, UK: Cambridge University Press, 1979), p. 386.

Fall of the Yuan Dynasty

1. Mote and Twitchett, *Cambridge History of China*, vol. 7, p. 60.
2. Ibid.
3. Lorge, *War, Politics and Society in Early Modern China*, p. 99; Edward L. Farmer, *Zhu Yuanzhang and Early Ming Legislation: The Reordering of Chinese Society* (Leiden: Brill, 1995), p. 21.
4. Mote and Twitchett, *Cambridge History of China*, vol. 7, pp. 44–47.
5. S. L. Yang, J. Zhang, S. B. Dai, M. Li, and X. J. Xu, "Effect of Deposition and Erosion within the Main River Channel and Large Lakes on Sediment Delivery to the Estuary of the Yangtze River," *Journal of Geophysical Research* 112 (2007): F02005: "surface area of Lake Poyang has decreased from 5050 km² in 1949 to 3919 km² in 1995."
6. Lorge, *War, Politics and Society in Early Modern China*, pp. 102–103; Michael E. Haskew et al., *Fighting Techniques of the Oriental World, AD 1200–1860* (New York: St. Martin's Press, 2008), p. 234.
7. Herbert Franke and Denis Twitchett, *The Cambridge History of China*, vol. 6: *Alien Regimes and Border States, 907–1368* (New York: Cambridge University Press, 1994), p. 622.

Bahmani-Vijayanagara War

1. Scott and Firista, *Ferishta's History of Dekkan from the First Mahummedan Conquests*, p. 26.
2. Ibid., pp. 27–30.
3. Sewell, *Forgotten Empire*.

Timur

1. Median of eight published estimates. Allen Howard Godbey, *The Lost Tribes a Myth: Suggestions towards Rewriting Hebrew History* (New York: Ktav, 1974), p. 385 ("Genghis Khan is estimated to have destroyed twenty million people, Tamerlane twelve million"); McWilliam, "Uzbekistan Restores Samarkand" ("A ruthless conqueror who, by one estimate at least, caused the deaths of about 7 million people"); Ford, "Ex-Russian Satellite" ("Tamerlane . . . was responsible for the deaths of as many as 20 million people"); Kinzer, "Kinder, Gentler Tamerlane" ("His Turkish and Mongol army is said to have killed 17 million men, women and children in his 14th century rampage"); Carpenter, "Barbaric Tamerlane" ("His armies . . . are estimated to have massacred as many as 17 million people"); Greenway, "New Waves across the Steppes" ("He is said to have killed 15 million people"); Fenby, "Crossroads of Conquest" ("A local warrior with a limp from arrow wounds marched north, east, west and south to found an empire of his own on some 17 million corpses"); McMahon, "Rehabilitation of Tamerlane" ("an estimated death toll of as many as 17 million people").
2. Stephen Greenblatt, *Will in the World: How Shakespeare Became Shakespeare* (New York: W. W. Norton, 2004), pp. 189–192.
3. Marozzi, *Tamerlane*, p. 326.
4. Ibid., p. 65.

5. Ibid., p. 132.

6. Picton, "Tamerlane."

7. Marozzi, *Tamerlane*, pp. 113–114.

8. Ibid., p. 132.

9. Ibid., pp. 153–154.

10. Hildinger, *Warriors of the Steppe*, pp. 179–180, Marozzi, *Tamerlane*, p. 65.

11. Marozzi, *Tamerlane*, p. 190.

12. Hildinger, *Warriors of the Steppe*, pp. 179–180; Ruy Gonzalez de Clavijo and Guy Le Strange, *Embassy to Tamerlane: 1403-1406* (New York: Routledge, 2004), p. 92.

13. Marozzi, *Tamerlane*, pp. 312–316.

14. Ibid., p. 82.

15. "Clavijo's Embassy to Tamerlane," http://depts.washington.edu/silkroad/texts/clavijo/cltxt1.html (accessed March 11, 2011).

16. Hildinger, *Warriors of the Steppe*, p. 194.

17. Carpenter, "Barbaric Tamerlane"; Ford, "Ex-Russian Satellite"; Kinzer, "Kinder, Gentler Tamerlane"; McMahon, "Rehabilitation of Tamerlane"; McWilliam, "Uzbekistan Restores Samarkand."

Chinese Conquest of Vietnam

1. Geoff Wade, "Ming Colonial Armies in Southeast Asia," in Hack and Rettig, *Colonial Armies in Southeast Asia*, p. 84. Chinese historians claimed 7 million were killed and the plains turned red with blood. For the sake of ranking, I'm dividing this by ten and counting 700,000 for no good reason whatsoever. The census conducted by the Ming found 5.2 million people in Vietnam after the conquest.

2. Sun Laichen, "Military Technology Transfers from Ming China and the Emergence of Northern Mainland Southeast Asia; c. 1390–1527," *Journal of Southeast Asian Studies* 34, no. 3 (October 1, 2003), p. 495; Hack and Rettig, *Colonial Armies in Southeast Asia*, pp. 83–88.

3. Minh Do, "Le Loi's Struggle: Under the Ming Dynasty," *VietNow Magazine*, July 31, 1997, p. 15.

Aztec Human Sacrifice

1. Carrasco, *City of Sacrifice*, p. 51, quoting Bernal Díaz del Castillo.

2. Time-Life Books, *Aztecs*, pp. 99–100.

3. Harris, *Cannibals and Kings*, pp. 149–151.

4. Carrasco, *City of Sacrifice*, pp. 196–197.

5. Ibid., pp. 204–207.

6. Time-Life Books, *Aztecs*, p. 103.

7. Cocker, *Rivers of Blood*, p. 47.

8. This theory was most recently and persuasively set forth by anthropologists Michael Harner and Marvin Harris in the 1970s, but it also shows up in Edward John Payne's *History of the New World Called America*, vol. 2 (Oxford: Clarendon Press, 1899), p. 550.

9. Carrasco, *City of Sacrifice*, p. 167; Kyle, *Spectacles of Death in Ancient Rome*, p. 152.

10. Marvin Harris, *Cultural Materialism: The Struggle for a Science of Culture* (New York: Vintage, 1980), pp. 333–340.

11. Juan Antonio Llorente, general secretary of the Inquisition from 1789 to 1801, estimated that

31,912 were executed, from 1480 to 1808. Will Durant, *The Reformation: A History of European Civilization from Wyclif to Calvin, 1300–1564* (New York: Simon & Schuster, 1957), p. 215.

12. Gibbons, "Recent Developments in the Study of the Great European Witch Hunt."

13. Peter Hessler, "The New Story of China's Ancient Past," *National Geographic*, July 2003.

14. Keen, *Aztec Image in Western Thought*, pp. 96–97.

15. Cocker, *Rivers of Blood*, p. 47; Harris, *Cannibals and Kings*, p. 159.

16. Cook and Borah cited in Harner, "Enigma of Aztec Sacrifice."

17. William Prescott, *History of the Conquest of Mexico*, Montezuma ed. (London: Lippincott, 1904; originally published 1843), p. 94.

18. Keen, *Aztec Image in Western Thought*, p. 256.

19. Harner, "Enigma of Aztec Sacrifice."

Atlantic Slave Trade

1. My estimate is based on various percentages cited in this chapter. The total death toll for the trans-Atlantic slave trade would seem to be something like 14 to 18 million, which is the sum of 10 million to 12 million deaths in Africa (half the total captured), plus 1 million to 2 million deaths on the ocean (10 to 15 percent of the number who were transported), plus 3 million to 4 million deaths in the first year in America (one-third of those who arrived). This translates into a very rough guess that three slaves died for every two slaves transported across the ocean.

A few other estimates of total deaths:

Stannard, *American Holocaust*, pp. 151, 317: 30 million to 60 million.

Rummel, *Statistics of Democide*, http://www.hawaii.edu/powerkills/SOD.TAB2.1A.GIF: 13,667,000.

Rogozinski, *Brief History of the Caribbean*, p. 128: 8 million died in order to bring 4 million slaves to the Caribbean.

Drescher, "Atlantic Slave Trade and the Holocaust," pp. 66–67: 6 million.

2. Meltzer, *Slavery*, vol. 2, p. 2.

3. Thomas, *Slave Trade*, pp. 373–379.

4. Hochschild, *Bury the Chains*, p. 31.

5. Rogozinski, *Brief History of the Caribbean*, p. 127.

6. Stannard, *American Holocaust*, p. 317; Hochschild, *Bury the Chains*, p. 31 (50 percent died in forced marches and barracoons); Lloyd, *Navy and the Slave Trade*, p. 118 (50 percent, citing Buxton).

7. Alexander Falconbridge, *An Account of the Slave Trade on the Coast of Africa* (London: J. Phillips, 1788), p. 18.

8. Thomas, *Slave Trade*, caption to illustration 75.

9. Olaudah Equiano, *The Interesting Narrative of the Life of Olaudah Equiano* (Boston: Knapp, 1837), pp. 43–44.

10. Rogozinski, *Brief History of the Caribbean*, p. 127.

11. Thomas, *Slave Trade*, p. 416.

12. Ibid., p. 417.

13. Ibid., p. 804; Rogozinski, *Brief History of the Caribbean*, p. 123.

14. Philip Curtin's *Atlantic Slave Trade: A Census* (Madison: University of Wisconsin Press, 1969) is probably the most important study of shipping statistics. He estimates that 11.8 million slaves embarked and 9.4 million arrived. Other authorities: Davidson, *Africa in History*, p. 208 (10 mil-

lion to 12 million); Hochschild, *Bury the Chains*, p. 32 (11 million left, 9.6 million arrived); Meltzer, *Slavery*, vol. 2, p. 51 (10 million were imported, citing Philip D. Curtin; the older estimates of 15 million to 20 million were "flimsy guesses"); Stannard, *American Holocaust*, p. 317 (12 million to 15 million survived); Thomas, *Slave Trade*, p. 804 (13 million left African ports, and 11,328,000 arrived in America).

15. Davidson, *Africa in History*, p. 215 (10 to 15 percent); Meltzer, *Slavery*, vol. 2, p. 50 (12.5 percent died in transit in the 1700s); Rogozinski, *Brief History of the Caribbean*, p. 127 (13 percent); Stannard, *American Holocaust*, p. 317 (10 percent); Thomas, *Slave Trade*, p. 424 (9 percent reasonable estimate for eighteenth century).

16. Hochschild, *Bury the Chains*, p. 32; Thomas, *Slave Trade*, p. 709.

17. Thomas, *Slave Trade*, pp. 310–311.

18. James A. McMillin, *The Final Victims: Foreign Slave Trade to North America, 1783–1810* (Columbia: University of South Carolina Press, 2004), p. 61.

19. Hochschild, *Bury the Chains*, p. 63 (one-third died in the first three years); Meltzer, *Slavery*, vol. 2, p. 50 (4 to 5 percent died waiting in the harbor, 33 percent died being seasoned); Stannard, *American Holocaust*, p. 317 (half died in seasoning).

20. Hochschild, *Bury the Chains*, pp. 63–66.

21. Rogozinski, *Brief History of the Caribbean*, pp. 124, 138.

22. Thomas, *Slave Trade*, p. 805.

23. Jordan, *White Man's Burden*, pp. 52–68.

24. John P. Jackson and Nadine M. Weidman, *Race, Racism, and Science: Social Impact and Interaction* (Santa Barbara, CA: ABC-CLIO, 2004), pp. 24–27; Jordan, *White Man's Burden*.

25. Drescher, "Atlantic Slave Trade and the Holocaust," p. 72.

26. Mary Turner, *Slaves and Missionaries: The Disintegration of Jamaican Slave Society, 1787–1834* (Kingston, Jamaica: Press University of the West Indies, 1998), pp. 8–9.

27. Lloyd, *Navy and the Slave Trade*, p. 118.

28. James Walvin, *Black Ivory* (Malden, MA: Blackwell, 2001), p. 265.

29. McEvedy, *Penguin Atlas of African History*, p. 97.

30. Randall M. Miller and John David Smith, *Dictionary of Afro-American Slavery* (New York: Greenwood Press, 1988), p. 594.

Conquest of the Americas

1. Columbus, trans. Markham, *Journal of Christopher Columbus*, p. 38.

2. Ibid., p. 135.

3. Zinn, *People's History of the United States*, p. 1.

4. Columbus, trans. Markham, *Journal of Christopher Columbus*, p. 51.

5. Meltzer, *Slavery*, vol. 2, p. 6.

6. Zinn, *People's History of the United States*.

7. Cocker, *Rivers of Blood*, pp. 34, 63–65.

8. Meltzer, *Slavery*, vol. 2, p. 6.

9. Rogozinski, *Brief History of the Caribbean*, pp. 26–27.

10. "Unearthing Evidence of a Caribbean Massacre," *Los Angeles Times*, August 21, 1997.

11. Rogozinski, *Brief History of the Caribbean*, p. 31.

12. Ibid., p. 30.

13. Cocker, *Rivers of Blood*, p. 27.

14. Hanson, *Carnage and Culture*, pp. 173–176; Cocker, *Rivers of Blood*, pp. 53–60.

15. Cocker, *Rivers of Blood*, pp. 94–95.

16. Becky Branford, "History Echoes in the Mines of Potosi," BBC News Online, October 18, 2004, http://news.bbc.co.uk/2/hi/americas/3740134.stm. Estimates of the number who died at Potosi go as high as 8 million; however, that comes to 20,000 mine-related deaths per year, from 1549 to 1949, in a community whose population peaked at 200,000 and fell to half that once the mines were played out. That's at least 10 percent dying every year for nearly half a millennium. Even the Gulag had difficulty being that deadly, so I doubt these high estimates.

17. Thornton, *American Indian Holocaust and Survival*, p. 69.

18. Zinn, *People's History of the United States*, pp. 14–15.

19. Osborn, *Wild Frontier*, p. 243.

20. Ibid., p. 139.

21. Ibid., p. 156.

22. Utley and Washburn, *Indian Wars*, pp. 126–127.

23. Ibid., p. 129.

24. Thornton, *American Indian Holocaust and Survival*, p. 118.

25. Utley and Washburn, *Indian Wars*, p. 203.

26. Osborn, *Wild Frontier*, p. 217.

27. Ibid., p. 225.

28. Ibid., p. 240.

29. Ribeiro, "Indigenous Cultures and Languages in Brazil."

30. Stephen T. Katz, "Uniqueness: The Historical Dimension," in Alan S. Rosenbaum, ed., *Is the Holocaust Unique? Perspectives on Comparative Genocide* (Boulder, CO: Westview Press, 1996), p. 21.

31. Quoted in Kiernan, *Blood and Soil*, p. 227.

32. Stannard, *American Holocaust*, p. 58.

33. Loewen, *Lies My Teacher Told Me*, p. 82. The first sentence is quoting Karen Kupperman.

34. Diamond, *Guns, Germs and Steel*, p. 78.

35. Stannard, *American Holocaust*, p. 107. I also need to point out that 100,000 is much higher than most scholars would estimate for the original population anyway.

36. David E. Stannard, "The Politics of Genocide Scholarship," in Alan S. Rosenbaum, ed., *Is the Holocaust Unique? Perspectives on Comparative Genocide* (Boulder, CO: Westview Press, 1996), p. 178. By one estimate, 2.4 million of the 5.1 million victims of the Holocaust died of disease in ghettos and concentration camps.

37. Rummel, *Statistics of Democide*, http://www.hawaii.edu/powerkills/SOD.TAB2.1A.GIF (accessed March 20, 2011).

38. *The New York Public Library American History Desk Reference* (New York: Macmillan, 1997), p. 15.

39. Thornton, *American Indian Holocaust and Survival*, p. 23; Stannard, *American Holocaust*, pp. 266–267, 339–342.

40. Livi-Bacci, *Concise History of World Population History*, p. 31; Coe, Dean, and Benson, *Atlas of Ancient America*, p. 13; Mann, *1491*, p. 148.

41. The easiest solution would be to roughly guess that somewhere from one-third to two-thirds of the population decline can be blamed on the Europeans. That's 11 million to 24 million out of 35 million.

If we prefer to build a case-by-case indictment, let's ignore the wild guesses about pre-Columbian populations, and count only the authenticated number of natives who disappeared under European rule as recorded from one colonial census to the next. Well after the first wave of disease had done its worst and the Spaniards were running the show, 112,000 Cuban natives disappeared between 1512 and 1600, as did 5,300,000 Mexicans (1548–1605) and 700,000 Peruvians (1572–1620) (Livi-Bacci, *Concise History of World Population History*, pp. 55–56). In Hispaniola, the population dropped from 60,000 in 1508 to 500 in 1548 (Meltzer, *Slavery*, vol. 2, p. 8). According to Russell Thornton, in *American Indian Holocaust and Survival*, p. 90, the North American Indian population went from 600,000 in 1800 to 200,000 in 1890, during the advance of the American frontier. Then there are the 800,000 Indians in the Amazon region who disappeared during the twentieth century. Since governments are usually held accountable for bad things that happen on their watch, that's 7.3 million well-documented lives lost under Western domination in just a few quick calculations, which gives us a baseline to start with. And that doesn't even count Central America or the Aztecs and Incas who were killed directly during the conquest.

This suggests an outside range of 7 million to 24 million indictable deaths, which means that regardless of the exact death toll, the American conquest belongs high on my list, ranking no lower than number 19 and possibly as high as number 4.

Genocide

1. Diamond, *Third Chimpanzee*, pp. 289, 299.
2. Ibid., p. 303.
3. The median of twelve published estimates. See http://www.necrometrics.com/20c5m.htm#Holocaust.
4. The median of six published estimates. See http://www.necrometrics.com/20c5m.htm#Holodomor.
5. The death toll is the geometric mean of the high (1 million) and the low (250,000) number. Ian Hancock, "Responses to the Romani Holocaust," in Alan S. Rosenbaum, ed., *Is the Holocaust Unique? Perspectives on Comparative Genocide* (Boulder, CO: Westview Press, 1996), pp. 39–64.
6. The number is the geometric mean of the high (1.2 million deaths, estimated by Tibetan government-in-exile) and the low (100,000 deaths, estimated by Jack Nusan Porter, *Genocide and Human Rights* (Washington, DC: University Press of America,1982)) numbers.
7. Median of five published estimates. See http://www.necrometrics.com/20c5m.htm#Yugo.
8. Martin Mennecke et al., "Genocide in Bosnia-Herzegovina," in Samuel Totten et al., eds., *Century of Genocide: Critical Essays and Eyewitness Accounts*, 2d ed. (New York: Routledge, 2004), p. 422.
9. Totten, *Dictionary of Genocide: A-L*, p. 26.
10. McEvedy, *Penguin Historical Atlas of the Pacific*, p. 76.
11. "Experts Double 1788 Estimate of Aborigines," *Advertiser*, February 26, 1987, citing Derek John Mulvaney and John Peter White, *Australians to 1788* (Broadway, NSW, Australia: Fairfax, Syme & Weldon Associates, 1987).
12. Diamond, *Third Chimpanzee*, p. 283; Cocker, *Rivers of Blood*, p. 177.
13. Ben Kiernan, "The First Genocide: Carthage, 146 BC," *Diogenes* 203 (2004), pp. 27–39.
14. The median of thirteen published estimates. See http://www.necrometrics.com/20c1m.htm#Burundi72.
15. The Timor-Leste Commission for Reception, Truth and Reconciliation (CAVR), *Conflict-*

Related Deaths in Timor-Leste: 1974–1999, http://www.cavr-timorleste.org/updateFiles/english/CONFLICT-RELATED%20DEATHS.pdf (accessed March 11, 2011).

16. Joshua 8–11.
17. Alfred W. Crosby, *Ecological Imperialism: The Biological Expansion of Europe 900–1900* (New York: Cambridge University Press, 2004), p. 80.
18. Pakenham, *Scramble for Africa*, p. 615: The Nama population was reduced by 10,200 (from 20,000 to 9,800), the Herero by 65,000 (from 80,000 to 15,000).
19. Numbers 31; David Plotz, "The Bible's Most Hideous War Crime," *Slate*, August 23, 2006, http://www.slate.com/id/2146473/entry/2148272/.
20. Diamond, *Third Chimpanzee*, pp. 278–281.
21. Dale Mackenzie Brown, "The Fate of Greenland's Vikings," *Archaeology*, February 28, 2000.
22. Douglas L. Oliver, *Polynesia in Early Historic Times* (Honolulu: Bess Press, 2002), p. 255.
23. Luigi Luca Cavalli-Sforza et al., *The History and Geography of Human Genes* (Princeton, NJ: Princeton University Press, 1994), p. 366.
24. Segal, *Islam's Black Slaves*; "Muhammad and Jews of Medina," *Muhammad: Legacy of a Prophet*, PBS, http://www.pbs.org/muhammad/ma_jews.shtml (accessed March 11, 2011).
25. Chalk and Jonassohn, *History and Sociology of Genocide*, p. 65.
26. Xenophon, *Hellenica*, trans. H. G. Dakyns, book 2, ch. 2, http://www.gutenberg.org/files/1174/1174-h/1174-h.htm (accessed March 9, 2011).

Burma-Siam Wars

1. Peter Williamson Floris, an English visitor to Bangkok in 1612, described these wars as "the occasion of the almost total destruction of the kingdom of Pegu, [which] caused the loss of many millions of lives." Multiple contemporary witnesses clearly considered these wars to be extraordinarily destructive. For the sake of ranking, I'm calling the death toll for these conflicts 900,000—based on adding the body counts from individual events, which I'll admit are rather dubious case by case, but may reflect an accurate order of magnitude for the whole. Anthony Reid, in *Southeast Asia in the Age of Commerce* (New Haven, CT: Yale University Press, 1988), estimated the combined population of the two principal kingdoms at around 5 million, with 23 million people living throughout Southeast Asia.
2. Gaspero Balbi, "Voyage to Pegu, and Observations There, Circa 1583," *SOAS Bulletin of Burma Research* 1, no. 2 (Autumn 2003), http://www.soas.ac.uk/sbbr/editions/file64288.pdf (accessed March 9, 2011).
3. Fred Arthur Neale, *Narrative of a Residence at the Capital of the Kingdom of Siam* (London: Office of the National Illustrated Library, 1852), p. 208.
4. "Divine Rights," *Bangkok Post*, January 25, 2001; "Mystery of a Princess," *Bangkok Post*, February 25, 1999; "Princess to the Rescue," *Nation* (Thailand), March 1, 1999.
5. Sale, *Universal History* (1759), vol. 7, p. 108.
6. "Warrior King Remains a Very Modern Mystery," *Nation* (Thailand), April 30, 2006.

French Wars of Religion

1. Knecht, *French Religious Wars*, p. 91 ("The total of deaths during the wars has been roughly estimated at between two and four million").
2. Frieda, *Catherine de Medici*, p. 136.

3. Knecht, *French Religious Wars*, pp. 38–41.

4. Ibid., pp. 41–46.

5. "Henry III," in *Encyclopaedia Britannica*, 11th ed., vol. 13, p. 291; Horne, *La Belle France*, p. 89.

6. Frieda, *Catherine de Medici*, p. 255.

7. Knecht, *French Religious Wars*, p. 53.

8. Turchin, *Historical Dynamics*, p. 181.

9. Frieda, *Catherine de Medici*, p. 328.

10. Horne, *La Belle France*, p. 91.

11. Ibid., p. 98.

12. Ibid., p. 97.

13. *Monty Python and the Holy Grail*, directed by Terry Gilliam and Terry Jones (Sony Pictures, 1975).

Russo-Tatar War

1. Henri Troyat, *Ivan the Terrible* (New York: E. P. Dutton, 1984), p. 144.

2. Blum, *Lord and Peasant in Russia*, p. 159.

3. The English ambassador, Giles Fletcher, reported that 800,000 Muscovites died in the fire and panic, which was clearly an exaggeration even if a flood of rural refugees entered into the city. The peacetime population of Moscow had been counted as 100,000; then after the fire, in 1580, the papal ambassador reported only 30,000 inhabitants. Brian Glyn Williams, *The Crimean Tatars: The Diaspora Experience and the Forging of a Nation* (Leiden: Brill, 2001), p. 50; Isabel de Madariaga, *Ivan the Terrible: First Tsar of Russia* (New Haven, CT: Yale University Press, 2005), p. 266.

The Time of Troubles

1. Duffy and Ricci, *Czars*, p. 174: "Although no reliable figures exist, the population is estimated to have plummeted during the Time of Troubles from 14 million to 9 million." J. P. Cooper, in *New Cambridge Modern History*, vol. 4: *The Decline of Spain and the Thirty Years War, 1609-48/49* (New York: Cambridge University Press, 1979), p. 602, offers a lower estimate but in the same order of magnitude: "The Troubles had cost some two and a half million lives."

2. Henri Troyat, *Ivan the Terrible* (New York: E. P. Dutton, 1984); Joan Bos, "Ivan IV of Russia," *Joan's Mad Monarchs Series,* http://www.xs4all.nl/~monarchs/madmonarchs/ivan4/ivan4_bio .htm (accessed March 20, 2011).

3. Riasanovsky, *History of Russia*, p. 156.

4. Dunning, *Short History of Russia's First Civil War*, pp. 43–44.

5. Harold Fisher, *The Famine in Soviet Russia, 1919-1923: The Operations of the American Relief Administration* (Freeport, NY: Books for Libraries Press, 1971), p. 475.

6. Riasanovsky, *History of Russia*, p. 160.

7. Dunning, *Short History of Russia's First Civil War*, pp. 150–158.

8. Ibid., pp. 164–166.

9. Ibid., p. 277.

10. Ibid., p. 45.

11. Ibid., pp. 83–90.

12. Ibid., pp. 75–82; Riasanovsky, *History of Russia*, pp. 157–160, 172–174.

Thirty Years War

1. Pratt, *Battles That Changed History*, pp. 158–159.
2. Fuller, *Military History of the Western World*, p. 74.
3. Schiller, *History of the Thirty Years' War*, p. 144.
4. Hollway, "Thirty Years' War: Battle of Breitenfeld."
5. Britt et al., *Dawn of Modern Warfare*, pp. 44–45.
6. Ibid., pp. 47–48.
7. Fuller, in *Military History of the Western World*, estimated 350,000. Corvisier and Childs, in *A Dictionary of Military History and the Art of War*, p. 469, estimated 600,000 military deaths.
8. Wedgwood, *Thirty Years War*, pp. 399–401.
9. Ibid., pp. 399–400.
10. J. F. (John Frederic Charles) Fuller, *The Conduct of War: A Study of the Impact of the French, Industrial, and Russian Revolutions* (New York: Da Capo Press, 1992), p.15.
11. Wedgwood, *Thirty Years War* (1938): Population declined from 21 million to 13.5 million.
12. Geoffrey Parker, *The Thirty Years' War* (New York: Routledge, 1997), p. 188: Population declined from 20 million to 16 million or 17 million.
13. A glance at some tertiary sources will show the relative support for the different numbers: Davies, *Europe*, p. 568 (lost 8 million); Richard S. Dunn, *The Age of Religious Wars 1559–1715*, 2d ed. (New York: W. W. Norton, 1979) (lost 7 million to 8 million); McFarlane, *Savage Wars of Peace* (7.5 million); John Landers, *The Field and the Forge* (Oxford, UK: Oxford University Press, 2003), p. 352 (5 million to 6 million); McEvedy, *Atlas of World Population History*, p. 68, "Germany" (modern boundaries) (2 million). For what it's worth, if we use the trick discussed elsewhere, the geometric mean of the highest (12 million) and the lowest (3 million) numbers is 6 million.
14. Michael Burger, *The Shaping of Western Civilization: From Antiquity to the Enlightenment* (Toronto: University of Toronto Press, 2008), pp. 232–236; Scott A. Merriman, *Religion and the Law in America: An Encyclopedia of Personal Belief and Public Policy*, vol. 1 (Santa Barbara, CA: ABC-CLIO, 2007), pp. 84–89.

Collapse of the Ming Dynasty

1. Spence, *Search for Modern China*, pp. 21–22.
2. Paul E. Schellinger and Robert M. Salkin, eds., *International Dictionary of Historic Places*, vol. 5: *Asia and Oceania* (Chicago: Fitzroy Dearborn, 1996), p. 424; Henry Smith Williams, *The Historians' History of the World: A Comprehensive Narrative . . .*, vol. 24 (New York: Trow Press, 1909), p. 554.
3. Spence, *Search for Modern China*, pp. 20–21.
4. Frederic Wakeman Jr., "The Shun Interregnum of 1644," in Jonathan D. Spence and John E. Willis, eds., *From Ming to Ch'ing* (New Haven, CT: Yale University Press, 1979), pp. 43–52.
5. Spence, *Search for Modern China*, p. 24.
6. Clements, *Coxinga and the Fall of the Ming Dynasty*, pp. 99–108.
7. Frederic Wakeman Jr., *Great Enterprise: The Manchu Reconstruction of the Imperial Order in Seventeenth Century China* (Berkeley: University of California Press, 1986), p. 507.
8. Spence, *Search for Modern China*, p. 22.
9. "Skeletons of Massacre Victims Uncovered at Construction Site," *Shanghai Star*, April 11, 2002, app1.chinadaily.com.cn/star/2002/0411/cn8-3.html.

10. Spence, *Search for Modern China*, p. 37.
11. Ibid., p. 38.
12. "Chang Hsien-chung," in *Encyclopaedia Britannica*, 15th ed., vol. 3, p. 83.
13. McEvedy, *Atlas of World Population History*; McFarlane, *Savage Wars of Peace*.
14. See Kurosawa's *Seven Samurai*, *Kagemusha*, *Ran*, *The Hidden Fortress*, *Throne of Blood*, *Yojimbo*, and *Rashomon*. Really. Go see them. They're great films.
15. Spence, *Search for Modern China*, p. 23.

Cromwell's Invasion of Ireland

1. David Lawrence Smith, *A History of the Modern British Isles, 1603–1707: The Double Crown* (Oxford, UK: Blackwell, 1998), p. 416 (population declined from 2.1 million in 1641 to 1.7 million in 1672); Fuller, *Military History of the Western World*, vol. 2, p. 112 (500,000 lives lost).
2. *Oliver Cromwell's Letters and Speeches: Including the Supplement to the First Edition. With Elucidation. by Thomas Carlyle*, vol. 2 (New York: Harper & Brothers, 1859), p. 493.
3. *Oliver Cromwell's Letters and Speeches: With Elucidation. by Thomas Carlyle*, vol. 1 (New York: Wiley & Putnam, 1845), pp. 383–384.
4. Garth Stevenson, *Parallel Paths: The Development of Nationalism in Ireland and Quebec* (Montreal: McGill-Queen's University Press, 2006), p. 29.
5. Norman Davies, *The Isles: A History* (Oxford, UK: Oxford University Press, 1999), p. 594.

Aurangzeb

1. Two million by famine, plus 100,000 soldiers annually for twenty-six years. Originally estimated by Niccolao Manucci (*Mogul India*, p. 96), a Venetian mercenary, physician, and diplomat living in India at the time.
2. Gascoigne, *Great Moguls*, p. 229.
3. Keay, *India*, pp. 342–343.
4. Ibid., p. 361.
5. Ibid., p. 353.
6. Ibid., p. 357.
7. Manucci's estimate (*Mogul India*, p. 96) is repeated with almost no skepticism by Wolpert, *New History of India*, p. 167; Hansen, *Peacock Throne*, pp. 477–478; and Clodfelter, *Warfare and Armed Conflicts*, vol. 1, p. 56.

Great Turkish War

1. Levy, *War in the Modern Great Power System*.
2. Goodwin, *Lords of the Horizon*, pp. 228–236; Palmer, *Decline and Fall of the Ottoman Empire*, pp. 8–15.
3. "Hungarian Hero to Be Commemorated," *Turkish Daily News*, September 12, 2005.
4. Robert A. Selig, "Carlowitz, the Rakoczi Revolt, and the Origins of German Settlement in Hungary," *German Life*, March 31, 1999.

Peter the Great

1. Sequential censuses showed a decrease in the tax-paying population of Russia during Peter's reign of around 20 percent, but there's no agreement on how to turn this into absolute population figures.

According to George Vernadsky (*Kievan Russia* (New Haven, CT: Yale University Press, 1948), pp. 103–104), Russian historian Pavel N. Miliukov estimated that the population of Russia declined from 16 million in 1676 (rough guess) to 13 million in 1725 (well documented), but another Russian historian, P. P. Smirnov, disputes the beginning population of 16 million, arguing instead for a stagnant population of 13 million throughout Peter's reign rather than an actual decline.

2. Klyuchevsky, *Peter the Great*, pp. 112–120.
3. Ibid., p. 143.
4. Ibid., pp. 149–150.
5. Ibid., pp. 145–146.
6. Ibid., pp. 39–44.
7. Farquhar, *Treasury of Royal Scandals*, pp. 115–119.

Great Northern War

1. Three hundred thousand military deaths, including 70,000 killed in battle (Urlanis, *Wars and Population*, pp. 45, 226) plus 70,000 civilian Finns. Clodfelter, in *Warfare and Armed Conflicts*, vol. 1, p. 94, goes even higher and estimates that the war killed 350,000 Swedes and Finns, soldiers and civilians—plus even more among the other participants.
2. Rick Tapio and Laitala Vincent, "War and the Great Wrath," *Finnish American Reporter* 8 (February 28, 1995), p. 23; Eric Solsten and Sandra W. Meditz, eds., *Finland: A Country Study* (Washington, DC: Government Printing Office for the Library of Congress, 1988).
3. Fuller, *Military History of the Western World*, vol. 2, pp. 161–186; Fuller, *Strategy and Power in Russia*; Klyuchevsky, *Peter the Great*, pp. 62–71.

War of the Spanish Succession

1. Urlanis, in *Wars and Population*, estimated 700,000 soldiers dead (p. 226), including 235,000 killed in combat (p. 45); Corvisier and Childs, in *Dictionary of Military History and the Art of War*, estimated 700,000 military dead on all sides (p. 469), or 500,000 French lives, including both military and civilian (p. 470). Bodart, in *Losses of Life in Modern Wars* (Oxford, UK: Clarendon Press, 1916), p. 30, estimated 400,000 military dead. Clodfelter, in *Warfare and Armed Conflicts*, vol. 1, p. 73, agrees that 400,000 died.
2. Rowen, *History of Early Modern Europe*, p. 538.
3. Bell, *First Total War*, p. 25.

War of the Austrian Succession

1. Reed S. Browning, *The War of the Austrian Succession* (New York: St. Martin's Griffin, 1995), p. 377: "To the 100000 men in arms who perished as a consequence of the war must be added an additional 400000 civilians. . . . The War of the Austrian Succession killed half a million people." The same numbers (100,000 plus 400,000) appear in Armstrong Starkey's *War in the Age of the Enlightenment, 1700–1789* (Westport, CT: Praeger, 2003), p. 6. Urlanis, in *Wars and Population*, estimated 120,000 killed in battle (p. 45) and 450,000 soldiers dead of all causes (p. 226).

Sino-Dzungar War

1. John DeFrancis, *In the Footsteps of Genghis Khan* (Honolulu: University of Hawaii Press, 1993), p. 175 ("By 1755, nine-tenths of the Dzungars and their allies, some six hundred thousand people,

had been wiped out"); Douglas Carruthers, *Unknown Mongolia: A Record of Travel and Exploration in North-west Mongolia and Dzungaria*, vol. 2 (Philadelphia: Lippincott, 1914), p. 376 ("When the Chinese invaded Dzungaria, they killed off her population to a man—of six hundred thousand inhabitants not one remained").

2. Rene Grousset, *Empire of the Steppes: A History of Central Asia* (New Brunswick, NJ: Rutgers University Press, 1970), pp. 537–538.

Seven Years War

1. Estimates vary, but most scholars agree on the basic size of the conflict. Clodfelter, in *Warfare and Armed Conflicts*, vol. 1, pp. 99–100, called the conflict "the bloodiest of the eighteenth century," and he found one estimate that said 868,000 soldiers died of all causes, and another that said 460,000 Austrians and allies and 180,000 Prussians died. Other sources:

   • Dumas and Vedel-Petersen, *Losses of Life Caused By War*: 125,400 Austrians and 180,000 Prussians died.

   • Urlanis, *Wars and Population*: 140,000 killed in battle, 550,000 soldiers died of all causes (pp. 45, 226). The civilian population of Austria declined from 5,739,000 to 4,890,000 (p. 282).

   • Williams, *Historians' History of the World*, vol. 12, p. 352: "The Seven Years' War was a glorious means of personal aggrandisement to Frederick . . . yet it cost . . . 180,000 lives among his own partisans, a general diminution of Prussia's population by 500,000, and a grand total of 853,000 soldiers killed on all sides."

   This indicates that somewhere between 500,000 and 900,000 soldiers and up to 1.3 million civilians died. Although you probably could make a case for over 2 million total deaths, I didn't want to overdo it, so I rolled back to the next round number.

2. Britt, *Dawn of Modern Warfare*, pp. 102–104.

3. Rowen, *History of Early Modern Europe*, p. 500.

4. Fuller, *Military History of the Modern World*, p. 198.

Napoleonic Wars

1. Geoffrey Ellis, *The Napoleonic Empire*, 2d ed. (Houndmills, Basingstoke, Hampshire, UK: Palgrave Macmillan, 2003), pp. 121–122: "The present consensus puts the war losses in the land armies . . . within the 89 departments which remained French in 1815 [at] a total of some 1.4 million for the whole period 1792–1814. These figures include those killed in action, the much larger numbers who subsequently died of their wounds or from illness, the victims of exhaustion or exposure to the cold, and prisoners of war not later accounted for. . . . As for the total war dead among *all* the European armies during the Napoleonic campaigns, Charles Esdaile's 'intelligent guess' is a figure of nearly 3 million, and he also estimates that additional civilian losses amounted to around 1 million."

2. Bell, *First Total War*, p. 156.

3. Schom, *Napoleon Bonaparte*, p. 42.

4. Ibid., p. 45.

5. Ibid., pp. 75–106.

6. Ibid., pp. 107–188.

7. Ibid., p. 235.

8. Bell, *First Total War*, p. 251.

9. Muir, *Tactics and the Experience of Battle*, pp. 76–77.

10. Ibid., pp. 130–131.

11. Ibid., pp. 235–239.

12. Sheldon Watts, *Epidemics and History: Disease Power and Imperialism* (New Haven, CT: Yale University Press, 1997), pp. 116–117.

13. Clodfelter, *Warfare and Armed Conflicts*, vol. 1, p. 165.

14. Schom, *Napoleon Bonaparte*, p. 595.

15. David Grubin, "Napoleon at War," *Napoleon*, http://www.pbs.org/empires/napoleon/n_war/ campaign/page_13.html (accessed March 8, 2011).

World Conquerors

1. Lynn, in *The French Wars*, p. 90, estimates that 2,250,000 died in Louis's wars, based on Levy, *War in the Modern Great Power System*. Corvisier and Childs, in *A Dictionary of Military History and the Art of War*, p. 470, estimated the cost for France, both military and civilian fatalities, as follows:
   Dutch War, 1672–78: 120,000
   Nine Years War, 1688–97: 160,000
   War of Spanish Succession: 500,000
   Total number of French deaths in these three wars: 780,000
   If we double the total to account for both sides, we get around 1.5 million.

2. Pliny the Elder, *The Natural History*, book 7, ch. 25, trans. John Bostock and H.T. Riley (London: Taylor & Francis, 1855), vol. 2, p. 166.

Haitian Slave Revolt

1. Scheina, *Latin America's Wars*, p. 18.

2. Ibid., pp. 1–3.

3. Rogozinski, *Brief History of the Caribbean*, p. 165.

4. Ibid., pp. 167–168.

5. Ibid., p. 172.

6. Scheina, *Latin America's Wars*, pp. 15–16.

Mexican War of Independence

1. Scheina, *Latin America's Wars*, p. 84 ("Estimates of the number killed range from 250,000 to 500,000 individuals"); Clodfelter, *Warfare and Armed Conflicts*, vol. 1, p. 534 (400,000 to 500,000 died).

2. Scheina, *Latin America's Wars*, pp. 71–84.

Shaka

1. Ritter, *Shaka Zulu*, pp. 25–28.

2. Ibid., pp. 84–88.

3. Ibid., pp. 81–83.

4. Keegan, *History of Warfare*, pp. 28–32.

5. Chalk and Jonassohn, *History and Sociology of Genocide*, pp. 227–228.

6. Ibid., p. 223.

7. Ritter, *Shaka Zulu*, pp. 28–31.

8. Monica Hunter Wilson and Leonard Monteath Thompson, *The Oxford History of South Africa*, vol. 1 (New York: Oxford University Press, 1971), p. 344; Donald R. Morris, *The Washing of the Spears* (New York: Da Capo Press, 1998), p. 54.

9. Ritter, *Shaka Zulu*, p. 333.

10. Chalk and Johassohn, *History and Sociology of Genocide*, p. 223.

11. See, for example, Wylie, "Shaka and the Modern Zulu State," which is a good summary of the revisionist school. That article disagrees with pretty much everything I've said in this chapter, down to the smallest details.

12. "The numbers whose death he occasioned have been left to conjecture, but exceed a million." Henry Francis Fynn, *The Diary of Henry Francis Fynn* (Pietermaritzburg: Shuter & Shooter, 1986), p. 20.

13. "Chaka may be termed the South African Attila; and it is estimated that not less than 1,000,000 human beings were destroyed by him." Major Charters, Royal Artillery, "Notices of the Cape and Southern Africa, since the Appointment, as Governor, of Major-Gen. Sir Geo. Napier," *United Service Journal and Naval and Military Magazine* (London: W. Clowes & Son, 1839), part 3, p. 24.

14. See, for example, Donald R. Morris, *The Washing of the Spears* (New York: Da Capo Press, 1998), p. 60 ("At least a million people, and more likely two, died in a decade that virtually depopulated" the interior); Hanson, *Carnage and Culture*, p. 313 ("As many as 1 million native Africans had been killed and starved to death as a direct result of Shaka's imperial dreams"); "Shaka," in *Encyclopaedia Britannica*, 15th ed., vol. 10, p. 689 ("left 2,000,000 dead in its wake"); Totten, *Dictionary of Genocide: A–L*, p. 280.

French Conquest of Algeria

1. Mahfoud Bennoune, *The Making of Contemporary Algeria, 1830-1987* (Cambridge, UK: Cambridge University Press, 2002), p. 42: "As a direct consequence of this kind of colonial war of conquest the total urban and rural population declined from an estimated three million in 1830 to 2,462,000 by 1876." Kiernan (*Blood and Soil*, p. 374) claims that the war killed 825,000 Algerians. The average of those two numbers is 681,500. Adding the French losses (92,329 soldiers dead in the hospital and 3,336 killed in battle, in 1830–51) and rounding it off yields 775,000.

2. Kiernan, *Blood and Soil*, pp. 364–374.

3. Porch, *Wars of Empire*, pp. 59, 73–74.

4. John Reynell Morell, *Algeria: The Topography and History, Political, Social, and Natural* (London: N. Cooke, 1854), p. 441.

5. Porch, *Wars of Empire*, pp. 40–41.

Taiping Rebellion

1. Ho Ping-to, *Studies in the Population of China, 1368-1953*, pp. 246–247 ("Some nineteenth century Western observers estimated the total population loss during the Taiping period at 20,000,000 to 30,000,000. Their estimates, however intelligent, were the guesswork of treaty port residents"). Ho is lukewarm on these estimates and seems to consider them too *low*. The only hard evidence Ho gathers is that the provinces hardest hit by the rebellion had lost 19.2 million people between 1850 and 1953. "Although twentieth-century . . . wars must also have affected the populations of

these provinces, the . . . figures may reflect permanent wounds that the populations . . . received in the great upheaval of the middle of the nineteenth century."

In any case, the estimate of 20 to 30 million deaths is one of the most common facts found in almost any discussion of the Taiping Rebellion. See, for example, Spence, *Search for Modern China*, p. 805; McEvedy, *Atlas of World Population History*, pp. 170–173; "Taiping Rebellion," in *Encyclopedia Britannica*, 15th ed., vol. 11, p. 509; "China," in *MSN Encarta Encyclopedia*, p. 20, http://encarta.msn.com/encyclopedia_761573055_20/China.html; Robert L. Worden et al., ed., *China: A Country Study* (Washington, DC: Library of Congress, Federal Research Division, 1987).

2. Fitzgerald, *China*, p. 573.

3. Ibid., p. 574.

4. Spence, *Search for Modern China*, p. 176. Other notable Hakkas will appear in later chapters: Sun Yat-sen and Deng Xiaoping.

5. Ibid., p. 173.

6. Ibid., p. 174.

7. "Land System of the Heavenly Kingdom."

8. Ibid.

9. John Scarth, *Twelve Years in China* (Edinburgh: Thomas Constable, 1890), quoted in Newsinger, "Taiping Peasant Revolt."

10. Newsinger, "Taiping Peasant Revolt."

11. Uhalley, "Taipings at Ningpo."

12. Carr, *Devil Soldier*.

13. Spence, *Search for Modern China*, p. 178.

14. Michael Kenney, "Caleb Carr Probes Hearts of Darkness in His Novels," *Boston Globe*, November 10, 1997.

Crimean War

1. John Sweetman, *Essential Histories: The Crimean War: 1854–1856* (University Park, IL: Osprey, 2001), p. 89. Estimates range from 255,000 (Bodart, Westergaard, and Kellogg, *Losses of Life in Modern Wars*, p. 142) to 1 million (Edgerton, *Death or Glory*, p. 5), but the median of nine published estimates is 309,000. See http://www.necrometrics.com/wars19c.htm#Crim.

2. McEvedy and Woodroffe, *New Penguin Atlas of Recent History*, pp. 20–22; Edgerton, *Death or Glory*.

3. McNeill, *Pursuit of Power*, pp. 236–237; Edgerton, *Death or Glory*, p. 51.

4. Keegan, *Mask of Command*, p. 247.

Panthay Rebellion

1. Raphael Israeli, *Islam in China* (Lanham, MD: Lexington Books, 2007), p. 286; Damian Harper, *China* (London: Lonely Planet, 2005), p. 648; Clodfelter, *Warfare and Armed Conflicts*, vol. 1, p. 401.

2. Bray, *Armies of Pestilence*, p. 83.

3. Notar, "Chinese Sultanate"; Dillon, *China's Muslim Hui Community*, pp. 58–60; Spence, *Search for Modern China*, pp. 189–190.

American Civil War

1. McPherson, *Battle Cry of Freedom*, p. 854.
2. Rough guess based on the following: McPherson, *Battle Cry for Freedom*, p. 619, estimated 50,000. Roger Ransom and Richard Sutch (*One Kind of Freedom: The Economic Consequences of Emancipation* (Cambridge, UK: Cambridge University Press, 2001), pp. 53–54) estimated that 1.6 percent of African-Americans died as a direct result of the war. Based on the 3.5 million blacks in the Confederacy, this would come to around 56,000 deaths. Even worse, General Howard, the head of the Freedmen's Bureau, estimated that one-fourth of blacks died in the war zone. Cherokee Indians were divided in their loyalties, and the miniature version of the Civil War they fought in Oklahoma reduced their population from 21,000 to 14,000. Thornton, *American Indian Holocaust and Survival*, p. 107.
3. D. H. Hill, quoted in McPherson, *Battle Cry of Freedom*, p. 476.

Hui Rebellion

1. Dillon, *China's Muslim Hui Community*, p. 60. General Zuo reported to Beijing that only 60,000 of the 700,000 Muslims in Shaanxi survived the revolt. Colonel Mark Bell, a British observer, claimed that the population of Gansu plunged from 15 million to 1 million.
2. Ibid., p. 62.
3. Spence, *Search for Modern China*, pp. 191–193.

War of the Triple Alliance

1. Scheina, *Latin America's Wars*, p. 331.
2. Ibid., p. 314.
3. Wilson, "Latin America's Total War."
4. Scheina, *Latin America's Wars*, pp. 313–332; Strosser and Prince, *Stupid Wars*; Whigham and Potthast, "Paraguayan Rosetta Stone"; Wilson, "Latin America's Total War."

Franco-Prussian War

1. Bodart, Westergaard, and Kellogg, *Losses of Life in Modern Wars*, pp. 144–152.
2. Most by disease, hunger, and hardship. Among the published estimates are 590,000 excess deaths among French civilians (Bodart, Westergaard, and Kellogg, *Losses of Life in Modern Wars*, p. 152), or 300,000 to 400,000 excess deaths among French civilians and 200,000 among German civilians (Urlanis, *Wars and Population*, p. 265). Also: "Troop movements of raw unvaccinated recruits spread smallpox among the only one third vaccinated French population and 60-90,000 died. French prisoners-of-war carried the disease deep into Germany where it killed 162,000." Bray, *Armies of Pestilence*, p.120. Numbers this high are hard to believe, but facts are facts. I picked Bray as a conservative estimate. I didn't include the fight for the Paris Commune.
3. McEvedy and Woodroffe, *New Penguin Atlas of Recent History*, pp. 28–33.
4. Horne, *La Belle France*, pp. 282–287.

Famines in British India

1. The median estimates of deaths in these famines are 10 million (1769–70), 8.2 million (1876–79), and 8.4 million (1896–1900).
2. Amartya Sen, *Development as Freedom* (New York: Anchor Books, 2000), p. 16.

3. Adam Smith, *An Inquiry into the Nature and Causes of the Wealth of Nations*, book 4, ch. 5, para. 44. Available at http://www.gutenberg.org/files/3300/3300-h/3300-h.htm (accessed March 14, 2011).

4. Sheldon Watts, *Epidemics and History: Disease, Power and Imperialism*. New Haven, CT: Yale University Press, 1997), pp. 177–178.

5. Davis, *Late Victorian Holocausts*, p. 36.

6. Ibid., p. 37.

7. Ibid., p. 39.

8. Ibid., p. 58.

9. Ibid., p. 32.

10. Ibid., pp. 38–39.

11. Linden, "Global Famine of 1877 and 1899"; Davis, *Late Victorian Holocausts*.

12. Linden, "Global Famine of 1877 and 1899."

13. Davis, *Late Victorian Holocausts*, p. 33.

14. Ibid., pp. 53–54.

15. Ibid., p. 142.

16. Wolpert, *New History of India*, p. 248.

17. Ibid., p. 267.

18. Davis, *Late Victorian Holocausts*, p. 157.

19. Ibid., p. 144.

20. Ibid., p. 167.

21. Ibid., p. 162.

22. Ibid., p. 161.

23. Ibid., p. 165.

24. Ibid., p. 164.

25. Ibid., p. 315.

26. Ibid., p. 165.

27. Ibid., p. 172.

28. Ibid., p. 170.

29. Wolpert, *New History of India*, p. 267.

30. Davis, *Late Victorian Holocausts*, p. 161.

Russo-Turkish War

1. L. P. Brockett and Porter C. Bliss, *The Conquest of Turkey, or, the Decline and Fall of the Ottoman Empire, 1877–8* (Philadelphia: Hubbard Bros., 1878), p. 697.

2. McEvedy and Woodroffe, *New Penguin Atlas of Recent History*, p. 38.

3. Palmer, *Decline and Fall of the Ottoman Empire*.

4. Muir, *Tactics and the Experience of Battle in the Age of Napoleon*, pp. 203–204.

5. Dumas, *Losses of Life Caused by War*, p. 55.

6. Clodfelter, *Warfare and Armed Conflicts*, vol. 1, p. 331.

7. Sarkees, *Correlates of War Project*, http://www.correlatesofwar.org/cow2%20data/WarData/Inter State/Inter-State%20War%20Participants%20(V%203-0).csv (accessed April 10, 2011).

8. Urlanis, *War and Population*, p. 265.

9. Justin McCarthy, *Death and Exile: The Ethnic Cleansing of Ottoman Muslims, 1821–1922* (Princeton, NJ: Darwin Press, 1995). McCarthy is blindly pro-Turkish on these matters. Most notoriously,

he won't admit to the Turkish genocide against the Armenians in 1915. Even so, this estimate is working its way into mainstream works, such as Dennis P. Hupchick, *The Balkans: From Constantinople to Communism* (New York: Macmillan, 2004), p. 265.

Mahdi Revolt

1. McEvedy, *Penguin Atlas of African History*, p. 110.
2. Churchill, *River War*, ch. 1.
3. Green, *Three Empires on the Nile*, pp. 144–146.
4. Francis Mading Deng, *War of Visions: Conflict of Identities in the Sudan* (Washington, DC: Brookings Institution,1995), p. 51 (population of Sudan fell from 7 million to 2 to 3 million); Jok Madut Jok, *War and Slavery in Sudan* (Philadelphia: University of Pennsylvania Press, 2001), p. 75 (from 8 million to 2.5 million); Deng D. Akol, *The Politics of Two Sudans: The South and the North, 1821–1969* (Uppsala: Nordic Africa Institute, 1994), p. 33 (fell from 8.5 million to 3 million); Edward Spiers, *Sudan: The Reconquest Reappraised* (Portland, OR: Frank Cass, 1998), p. 12 (6 million out of 8 million died); Henry Cecil Jackson, *Osman Digna* (London: Methuen, 1926), p. 185 (population fell from 8.5 million to less than 2 million).
5. Green, *Three Empires on the Nile*, p. 207.
6. Ibid., p. 209.
7. Ibid., p. 229.
8. Ibid., p. 211.

Congo Free State

1. Hochschild, *Leopold's Ghost*, p. 159.
2. Forbath, *River Congo*, p. 370.
3. Hochschild, *Leopold's Ghost*, p. 161.
4. Ibid., pp. 164–166.
5. Forbath, *River Congo*, p. 374.
6. Ibid., p. 375.
7. Pakenham, *Scramble for Africa*, p. 590.
8. Hochschild, *Leopold's Ghost*, pp. 179–180.
9. Pakenham, *Scramble for Africa*, pp. 591–592.
10. Hochschild, *Leopold's Ghost*, pp. 195–199.
11. Pakenham, *Scramble for Africa*, p. 597.
12. Hochschild, *Leopold's Ghost*, p. 192.
13. Ibid., p. 199.
14. Ibid., pp. 245–249; Pakenham, *Scramble for Africa*, p. 597.
15. Hochschild, *Leopold's Ghost*, p. 202.
16. E. D. Morel, *The Black Man's Burden* (New York: B. W. Huebsch, 1920), ch. 9 ("When the country had been explored in every direction by travellers of divers nationalities, estimates varied between twenty and thirty millions. No estimate fell below twenty millions. In 1911 an official census was taken. It was not published in Belgium, but was reported in one of the British Consular dispatches. It revealed that only eight and a half million people were left."); this estimate also appears in "Congo Free State," in *Encyclopaedia Britannica*, 15th ed., vol. 3, p. 535; and Bertrand Russell, *Freedom and Organization 1814–1914* (New York: Routledge, 2001; first published by George

Allen, 1934), p. 453, citing Sir Harry Hamilton Johnston, *A History of the Colonization of Africa by Alien Races* (Cambridge Historical Series; Cambridge, UK: Cambridge University Press, 1899), p. 352.

17. Forbath, *River Congo*, p. 375.

18. Hochschild, *Leopold's Ghost*, pp. 225–234.

Cuban Revolution

1. Between 1895 and 1899, Cuba's population declined from about 1.8 million to 1.5 million. Hugh Thomas, *Cuba* (New York: Da Capo Press, 1998), p. 423; Anderson, *Under Three Flags* (New York: Verso, 2005), p. 146. Three hundred thousand Cubans died, 200,000 of them civilians from disease and hunger. Scheina, *Latin America's Wars*, p. 364. In addition, 62,853 Spanish soldiers died in Cuba, 85 percent by illness. Sergio Díaz-Briquets, *The Health Revolution in Cuba* (Austin: University of Texas Press, 1983), p. 199.

2. Rogozinski, *Brief History of the Caribbean*, pp. 205–207; Scheina, *Latin America's Wars*, pp. 351–364, 415–425.

The Western Way of War

1. This concept was originated and is described in detail by Victor Davis Hanson in *The Western Way of War: Infantry Battle in Classical Greece* (New York: Knopf, 1989), and in *Carnage and Culture*.

Mexican Revolution

1. The median of seventeen published estimates. See http://www.necrometrics.com/20c1m.htm# Mexican.

2. Skidmore and Smith, *Modern Latin America*, p. 234.

3. McLynn, *Villa and Zapata*, pp. 151–159.

4. Ibid., pp. 308–309.

5. Ibid., pp. 309–310.

6. Boot, *Savage Wars of Peace*, p. 188.

First World War

1. The canonical military death toll is around 8.5 million. See, for example: "World Wars," in *Encyclopaedia Britannica*, 15th ed., vol. 29, p. 987 (8,528,831); Gilbert, *History of the Twentieth Century*, vol. 1, p. 529; Overy, *Hammond Atlas of the 20th Century*; Rod Paschall, *The Defeat of Imperial Germany 1917–1918* (New York: Da Capo Press, 1994), citing Arthur Banks (8,513,000); John Ellis and Michael Cox, *The World War I Databook* (London: Aurum, 2001) (8,364,712).

2. Civilian deaths during World War I were not recorded as carefully as the deaths of soldiers, but the median of the various guesses falls at 6.6 million. From high to low: "World Wars," in *Encyclopaedia Britannica*, 15th ed., vol. 29, p. 987 (13 million); "Twentieth Century," in *Encyclopedia Americana* (Danbury, CT: Scholastic Library, 2006) (12.5 million); Overy, *Hammond Atlas of the 20th Century*, p. 36 (9 million); Spencer Tucker, et al., *European Powers in the First World War* (New York: Garland Pub., 1996), p. 172 (ca. 6.6 million); "Losses of Life," in *Dictionary of Military History* (Oxford, UK: Blackwell, 1994), p. 470 (6.6 million); John Ellis and Michael Cox, *The World War I Databook* (London: Aurum, 2001) (ca. 6.5 million); Urlanis, *Wars and Population*, p. 268 (6 million plus); Davies, *Europe* (5 million).

3. Keegan, *History of Warfare*, pp. 357–358.

4. Keegan, *First World War*, pp. 18–23.

5. Barbara Tuchman, *The Guns of August* (New York: Dell, 1963), p. 76.

6. James L. Stokesbury, *A Short History of World War I* (New York: Morrow, 1981), p. 61.

7. Keegan, *First World War*, pp. 82–83; McDougall, "Dirty Hands."

8. Keegan, *Face of Battle*, p. 230.

9. Miller, *Kelly Miller's History of the World War for Human Rights*, ch. 10.

10. Ibid.

11. Attributed to French Marshall Henri-Philippe Petain.

12. Keegan, *Face of Battle*, pp. 213–215, 248.

13. Edward J. Erickson, *Ordered to Die: A History of the Ottoman Army in the First World War* (Westport, CT: Greenwood Press, 2001), p. 94.

14. Gilbert, *History of the Twentieth Century*, vol. 1, p. 421.

15. Strachan, *First World War*, p. 188.

16. Gilbert, *History of the Twentieth Century*, vol. 1, p. 473.

17. Keegan, *Face of Battle*, p. 255.

18. John M. Barry, *The Great Influenza: The Epic Story of the Deadliest Plague in History* (New York: Viking Penguin, 2004), p. 103.

19. Adolf Hitler, "Letter from the Western Front," February 1915, at *The Holocaust Project*, Humanitas International, http://www.humanitas-international.org/holocaust/hepplett.htm.

20. James L. Stokesbury, *A Short History of World War I* (New York: Morrow, 1981), p. 61.

21. Gilbert, *History of the Twentieth Century*, vol. 1, p. 357.

22. Melson, "Armenian Genocide as Precursor and Prototype of Twentieth-Century Genocide," in Rosenbaum, ed., *Is the Holocaust Unique?*; Rouben Paul Adalian, "The Armenian Genocide," in Samuel Totten et al., eds., *Century of Genocide: Critical Essays and Eyewitness Accounts*, 2nd ed. (New York: Routledge, 2004); Chalk and Jonassohn, *History and Sociology of Genocide*, pp. 249–289.

23. Sabrina Tavernise, "Nearly a Million Genocide Victims, Covered in a Cloak of Amnesia," *New York Times*, March 8, 2009, http://www.nytimes.com/2009/03/09/world/europe/09turkey.html. "According to a long-hidden document that belonged to the interior minister of the Ottoman Empire, 972,000 Ottoman Armenians disappeared from official population records from 1915 through 1916."

24. Forbath, *River Congo*, p. 377.

25. Strachan, *First World War*, pp. 256–257.

26. McLynn, *Villa and Zapata*, p. 333.

27. Lincoln, *Red Victory*, p. 397.

28. Chris Suellentrop, "What's Osama Talking About?" *Slate*, October 8, 2001, http://www.slate.com/id/1008411.

Russian Civil War

1. The median of eleven published estimates. See http://www.necrometrics.com/20c5m.htm#RCW.

2. Kinder and Hilgemann, *Anchor Atlas of World History*, vol. 2, p. 142.

3. Figes, *People's Tragedy*, p. 660.

4. Boot, *Savage Wars of Peace*, pp. 207–230.

5. Figes, *People's Tragedy*, p. 576.

6. Ibid., p. 577.

7. Ibid., pp. 586–587.

8. Ibid., pp. 658–659.

9. Ibid., pp. 578–584.

10. Mayer, *Furies*, pp. 380–389; Figes, *People's Tragedy*, p. 662.

11. Mayer, *Furies*, pp. 523–525.

12. Lincoln, *Red Victory*, pp. 392–421.

13. Johnson, *Modern Times*, p. 69.

14. Service, *History of Twentieth-Century Russia*, p. 108.

15. Ibid., p. 103. He makes the interesting observation that Russia "was clearly not yet a properly functioning police state if this could happen to the Cheka's chairman."

16. Figes, *People's Tragedy*, pp. 635–640; Mayer, *Furies*, pp. 275–276.

17. Johnson, *Modern Times*, pp. 69–70.

18. Leon Trostsky, *My Life* (New York: Charles Scribner's Sons, 1930), p. 323. Available at http://www.marxists.org/archive/trotsky/works/1930-lif/1930-lif.pdf.

Greco-Turkish War

1. The only well-documented number is that the Greek army lost some 42,000, killed and missing. Urlanis, *Wars and Population*, p. 95. Assuming that the Turks lost about the same number brings the total number of military dead for both sides to some 85,000 soldiers. R. J. Rummel, in *Death by Government*, pp. 233–234, estimates that the Greeks killed 15,000 civilian Turks, and the Turks killed 264,000 civilian Greeks, including some 100,000 in Smyrna. Based on the number of refugees who disappeared between head counts, the Greeks claim that 353,000 Pontic Greeks were killed in communities along the Black Sea. Totten, *Dictionary of Genocide: A-L*, p. 337. All of these fragments point to a total death toll in the neighborhood of 364,000 to 453,000; however, I won't pretend that this is anything but a guess, so I'm just grabbing the nearest round number.

2. Stewart, "Catastrophe at Smyrna."

3. Marrus, *Unwanted*, p. 98.

4. Arnold Toynbee, quoted by Stewart, "Catastrophe at Smyrna."

5. Marrus, *Unwanted*, pp. 97–106.

Chinese Civil War

1. Johnson, *Modern Times*, p. 200.

2. Spence, *In Search of Modern China*, pp. 345–348.

3. Ibid., pp. 351–352.

4. Ibid., pp. 353–354.

5. Gunther, *Inside Asia*, pp. 112–115.

6. Chang and Halliday, *Mao*, pp. 81–87.

7. Ibid., pp. 124–125.

8. McPherson, *Battle Cry of Freedom*, p. 827.

9. Gunther, *Inside Asia*, p. 235.

10. Spence, *In Search of Modern China*, p. 445.

11. Ibid., p. 447.

12. Wallechinsky, *David Wallechinsky's Twentieth Century*, pp. 89–90; John K. Fairbank et al., *Cambridge History of China*, vol. 13: *Republican China 1912–1949, Part 2* (Cambridge, UK: Cambridge University Press, 1986), p. 555.

13. Spence, *In Search of Modern China*, p. 470.

14. Chang and Halliday, *Mao*, p. 297.

15. Ibid., pp. 312–313.

16. Ibid., p. 314; "Time for a Visit?" *Time*, November 1, 1948.

17. "30,000,000 Uprooted Ones," *Time*, July 26, 1948.

18. Edgar Snow, *Red Star over China* (New York: Grove Press, 1968), p. 188, citing Guomindang press releases.

19. Ho, *Studies in the Population of China*, p. 249.

20. Johnson, *Modern Times*, p. 200.

21. Sarkees, "Correlates of War Data on War."

22. Sivard, *World Military and Social Expenditures*, p. 30.

23. According to Jan Lahmeyer, "CHINA: Provinces Population," *Population Statistics*, http://www.populstat.info/Asia/chinap.htm, the sum of China's provincial populations declined by 5,643,300 between 1925 and 1936. This might be an actual decline in population or just a discrepancy between different sources. According to Lahmeyer's data, the population declined in ten notably wartorn provinces (Hunan, Shaanxi, Guangdong, Hubei, Zhejiang, Fujian, Guizhou, Henan, Gansu, Shanxi) and grew in the others.

24. Number of civilian deaths in the Sino-Japanese War, in ascending order: Sivard, *World Military and Social Expenditures*, p. 30 (civilian, 1937–41: 1,150,000; 1941–45: 850,000); Kinder and Hilgemann, *Anchor Atlas of World History*, p. 218 ("civilians . . . 5.4 mil. Chinese "); Ellis, *World War II*, p. 253 ("Total Civilian Casualties . . . 8,000,000"); both Keegan, *Harper Collins Atlas of the Second World War*, p. 205, and Overy, *Hammond Atlas of the 20th Century*, p. 103, reprint much of the same material for this subject (civilians: "up to 10,000,000"); Grenville, *History of the World*, p. 292 ("No one knows how many million Chinese died in the war; the figure may well be in excess of 10 million"; this would include both civilian and military); Werner Gruhl, *Imperial Japan's World War Two* (New Brunswick, NJ: Transaction, 2010), p. 143 (15,554,000). Ho, in *Studies in the Population of China*, p. 252, cited a survey that estimated 335,934 Chinese civilians killed in air raids and 1,073,496 killed otherwise. That would come to some 1.4 million civilians killed directly by war, in 1937–45, but his methodology specifically did not include the Nanjing Massacre and the Yellow River flood.

25. The number of Guomindang deaths in the Sino-Japanese War: "World Wars," in *Encyclopaedia Britannica*, 15th ed., vol. 29, p. 1023, 1992 printing (1,310,224); Keegan, *Harper Collins Atlas of the Second World War*, p. 205 (1,324,000); Clodfelter, *Warfare and Armed Conflict*, vol. 2, p. 412 (1,319,958); *Information Please Almanac, Atlas and Yearbook 1991*, 44th ed. (Boston: Houghton Mifflin, 1990), p. 311 (1,324,516); Ellis, *World War II*, p. 253 (1,400,000).

26. Ho, *Studies in the Population of China*, pp. 250–252.

27. Ibid. Puppet regimes lost 960,000 soldiers, killed and wounded. As a rough guess, a fourth of this would be 240,000 killed.

28. Ellis, *World War II*, p. 256.

29. Ho, *Studies in the Population of China*, p. 253.

30. Total number of deaths in the second phase of the Chinese Civil War: Dan Smith, *The State of*

War and Peace Atlas (New York: Penguin, 1997), p. 25 (1,000,000); Sivard, *World Military and Social Expenditures*, p. 30 (1,000,000); Robert L. Walker, *The Human Cost of Communism in China*, Report to the Subcommittee on Internal Security of the U.S. Senate Judiciary Committee (Washington, DC: Government Printing Office, 1971) (1,250,000); Lorraine Glennon, ed., *Our Times: The Illustrated History of the 20th Century* (Atlanta: Turner, 1995), p. 339 (3,000,000).

Joseph Stalin

1. Simon Sebag Montefiore, *Stalin: The Court of the Red Tsar* (New York: Knopf, 2004); "Joseph Stalin," in John Simkin, Spartacus Educational, http://www.spartacus.schoolnet.co.uk/RUSstalin .htm (accessed March 25, 2011).
2. Gilbert, *History of the Twentieth Century*, vol. 1, p. 761.
3. Mace, "Soviet Man-Made Famine in the Ukraine"; Green, "Stalinist Terror and the Question of Genocide."
4. Robert Conquest, *Harvest of Sorrow*, cited in Chalk and Jonassohn, *History and Sociology of Genocide*, p. 293.
5. Service, *History of Twentieth-Century Russia*, p. 224.
6. Anne Applebaum, "My Friend, the Trotskyite," *Ottawa Citizen*, August 18, 2002, p. A11.
7. Hochschild, *Unquiet Ghost*, p. 237.
8. Julius Strauss, "No Escape for Gulag's Former Prisoners," *Daily Telegraph* (London), January 3, 2004.
9. Service, *History of Twentieth-Century Russia*, p. 214.
10. Ibid., pp. 218, 221.
11. Hochschild, *Unquiet Ghost*, p. 192.
12. Simon Sebag Montefiore, "On the Man Who Unleashed Stalin's Terror," *Sunday Telegraph* (London), August 10, 2008.
13. Bykivnia: Raymond Pearson, *The Rise and Fall of the Soviet Empire*, 2nd ed. (New York: Palgrave, 2002), p. 127: "near-incredible" 200,000; Michael Hamm, *Kiev: A Portrait, 1800–1917* (Princeton, NJ: Princeton University Press, 1993), p. 235: "Perhaps 120,000 victims were buried there; another estimate puts the figure as high as 225,000"; Taras Kuzio and Taras Andrew Wilson Kuzio, *Ukraine: Perestroika to Independence* (Edmonton: Canadian Institute of Ukrainian Studies Press, 2000), p. 95: "a mass grave reputed to contain over 200,000 bodies."
14. Mark Franchetti, "Russians Discover Mass Grave of 30,000 Stalin Victims," *Times* (London), September 15, 2002.
15. Fred Kaplan, "Mass Grave Bears Stalin's Touch," *Boston Globe*, August 13, 1994.
16. Estimates of the number of dead buried at Kurapaty run anywhere from 40,000 to 200,000. Overy, *Russia's War*, p. 296; Mikhail Shimanskiy, "Whose Remains Lie in the Forest near Minsk?" *Izvestiya*, August 28, 1988, via BBC Summary of World Broadcasts, "Commission Investigating Unmarked Graves in Belorussia," September 13, 1988; "Soviet Weekly Provides Gruesome Details of Stalin-Era Massacre," Associated Press, October 7, 1988; "Belarus Police Break up Protest at Mass Grave Site," Agence France Presse, November 8, 2001.
17. Kenneth Christie and R. B. Cribb, *Historical Injustice and Democratic Transition in Eastern Asia and Northern Europe: Ghosts at the Table of Democracy* (New York: RoutledgeCurzon, 2002), p. 83.
18. Roger Reese, *The Soviet Military Experience: A History of the Soviet Army, 1917–1991* (New York: Routledge, 2000), p. 99; Clodfelter, *Warfare and Armed Conflicts*, vol. 2, p. 791.

19. Overy, *Russia's War*, pp. 214–215.

20. Ibid., p. 160.

21. Ibid., p. 128.

22. Anders and Munoz, "Russian Volunteers in the German Wehrmacht in WWII."

23. Overy, *Russia's War*, p. 297.

24. Ibid., pp. 232–234.

25. Nicholas Werth, "A State against Its People," in Stephane Courtois et al., *The Black Book of Communism: Crimes, Terror, Repression*, trans. Jonathan Murphy and Mark Kramer (Cambridge, MA: Harvard University Press, 1999), p. 231. Numbers vary. I use a different source in my chapter on World War II.

26. Adrian Bridge, "Iron Curtain's 100,000 Dead," *Independent* (London), October 27, 1991; Ray Moseley, "Buchenwald Haunts Muses' Valley," *Chicago Tribune*, June 11, 1991.

27. Hochschild, *Unquiet Ghost*, p. 113.

28. Hobsbawm, *Age of Extremes*, p. 393.

29. Among the places you'll find the highest estimates: Davies, *Europe*, p. 1329 (44 to 50 million); Roy Medvedev, *Let History Judge* (New York: Knopf, 1971); Rummel, *Death by Government*, p. 8 (42,672,000); Solzhenitsyn, *Gulag Archipelago*.

30. Alec Nove, "Victims of Stalinism: How Many?" in J. Arch Getty and Robert T. Manning, eds., *Stalinist Terror: New Perspectives* (New York: Cambridge University Press, 1993), pp. 270–271.

31. I've taken this statistic from Applebaum, *Gulag*, pp. 582–583, but please see her explanation for all of the reasons that this number is probably incomplete and should be higher.

32. Low estimates can be found in: Getty and Manning, *Stalinist Terror*; Melanie Ilic and Stephen G. Wheatcroft, eds., *Stalin's Terror Revisited* (Basingstoke, UK: Palgrave Macmillan, 2006); R. W. Davies and Stephen G. Wheatcroft, *The Years of Hunger: Soviet Agriculture, 1931–1933* (New York: Palgrave Macmillan, 2004).

33. Robert Conquest, *Great Terror: Stalin's Purge of the Thirties* (New York: Macmillan, 1968).

34. Among other places you'll find estimates of 15 to 25 million: "Stalinism," in *Encyclopaedia Britannica*, 15th ed., vol. 11, p. 205; Brzezinski, *Out of Control*; Courtois et al., *Black Book of Communism*, p. 4; John Heidenrich, *How to Prevent Genocide* (Westport, CT: Praeger, 2001), p. 7; Hochschild, *Unquiet Ghost*, pp. xv, 138; Chirot, in *Modern Tyrants*, p. 126, calls 20 million the lowest credible estimate and 40 million the highest.

Crazed Tyrants

1. The median of seven published estimates. See http://www.necrometrics.com/20c5m.htm#Hitler.

2. Median of five estimates: Gabriel Jackson, *The Spanish Republic and the Civil War 1931–39* (Princeton, NJ: Princeton University Press, 1972), p. 535 (200,000 executed by Nationalists during the Spanish Civil War and 200,000 after); Max Gallo, *Spain under Franco: A History* (New York: Dutton, 1974), p. 67 (192,684 after); Hugh Thomas, *The Spanish Civil War* (New York: Harper & Row, 1989), pp. 900–901 (75,000 during and 100,000 after); Ruiz, "Franco and the Spanish Civil War" (150,000 during and after); Stanley Payne, *The Franco Regime 1936–1975* (Madison: University of Wisconsin Press, 1987), p. 216 (35,021 during and 22,641 after).

3. Raymond T. McNally and Radu Florescu, *In Search of Dracula* (New York: Warner, 1972), p. 109, citing a 1475 report by the Bishop of Erlau.

4. "Murad IV," in *Encyclopaedia Britannica*, 11th ed., vol. 19, p. 15.

5. Londsdale Ragg, *Dante and His Italy* (London: Methuen, 1907), p. 127.

6. "Equatorial Guinea Accused," *Washington Post*, July 24, 1978; "Equatorial Guinea," in *Encarta*; Charles Hickman Cutter, *Africa 2003* (Harper's Ferry, WV: Stryker-Post, 2003), p. 83.

7. Mouctar Bah, "As Guinea Turns 50 Sekou Toure's Victims Want Recognition," Agence France Presse, October 1, 2008 (50,000).

8. AP-Reuter, "Ex-Ruler Murdered 40,000, Chad Says," *Toronto Star*, May 21, 1992.

9. Richard A. Haggerty, ed., "François Duvalier 1957–71," in *A Country Study: Haiti* (Washington, DC: Federal Research Division, Library of Congress, research completed December 1989), http://lcweb2.loc.gov/frd/cs/httoc.html.

10. Henri Troyat, *Ivan the Terrible* (New York: E. P. Dutton, 1984), p. 238. Toward the end of his life, Ivan drew up lists of all of the victims he could remember and sent them to monasteries for prayers. One listed 3,148 people killed; another 3,750.

11. Holger Jensen, "Old Style Dictator May Keep Power in Malawi," *Denver Rocky Mountain News*, May 17, 1994 ("the deaths of at least 18,000 people by torture, assassination or massacres of entire villages").

12. This is my guess based on the statement of the Roman historian Suetonius that at the height of the treason trials, not a day passed without an execution and there were as many as twenty executions on some days.

Italo-Ethiopian War

1. The Italian side suffered around 15,000 battle deaths, most of whom were African auxiliaries rather than Italians. In 1945 the Ethiopian government calculated the official death toll as 760,300 natives dead. Angelo Del Boca, *The Ethiopian War 1935–1941* (Chicago, University of Chicago Press,1965).
   - Battle deaths: 275,000
   - Hunger among refugees: 300,000
   - Resistance fighters killed during occupation: 75,000
   - Concentration camps: 35,000
   - February 1937 massacre in Addis Ababa: 30,000 (most historians believe the death toll was only 3,000, so I subtracted the difference)
   - Executions: 24,000
   - Civilians killed by air force: 17,800

2. Pankhurst, "History of Early Twentieth Century Ethiopia."

Spanish Civil War

1. Hugh Thomas, *The Spanish Civil War* (New York: Modern Library, 2001), pp. 900–901. This includes 200,000 combat deaths and 130,000 executions during the war. It doesn't include the 100,000 or so executed by Franco after the war. Most other recent estimates agree on the approximate total (with maybe 100,000 more or less), but differ widely on the specific cause of deaths. Earlier estimates had counted 1 million missing Spaniards presumed dead, but later investigation found that many of those had emigrated to escape the war.

2. Murphy, "Lincoln Brigade Survivors Relive Wartime Exploits"; Orwell, *Homage to Catalonia*; Ruiz, "Franco and the Spanish Civil War."

Second World War

1. This is my own calculation (see http://www.necrometrics.com/ww2stats.htm#ww2chart). The most common estimate of the death toll of World War II is 50 million, which is found in John Haywood, *Atlas of World History* (New York: Barnes & Noble Books, 1997), p. 109; Keegan, *Second World War*, p. 590; Charles Messenger, *The Chronological Atlas of World War Two* (New York: Macmillan, 1989), p. 242; Geoffrey Barraclaugh, ed., *The Times Concise Atlas of World History: Revised Edition* (Maplewood, NJ: Hammond, 1991), p. 132; J. M. Roberts, *Twentieth Century* (New York: Viking, 1999), p. 432; Urlanis, *Wars and Population*, p. 292.

2. Sherree Owens Zalam, *Adolf Hitler. A Psychological Interpretation of His Views on Architecture, Art and Music* (Bowling Green, OH: Bowling Green State University Popular Press, 1990), p. 138; Leni Yahil et al., *The Holocaust: The Fate of European Jewry, 1932–1945* (New York: Oxford University Press, 1991), p. 45.

3. Number of Soviets killed in action: Erickson, *Barbarossa*, table 12.4. Number of Soviets captured: Keegan, *Second World War*, p. 191; Charles Messenger, *The Chronological Atlas of World War Two* (New York: Macmillan, 1989), p. 64.

4. Gilbert, *History of the Twentieth Century*, vol. 2, p. 398.

5. U.S. Holocaust Memorial Museum, *Historical Atlas of the Holocaust*, p. 74.

6. Ibid., p. 67.

7. Mazower, *Dark Continent*, p. 168.

8. Ibid., p. 154.

9. Rolf-Dieter Müller and Gerd R. Ueberschär, *Hitler's War in the East, 1941–1945: A Critical Assessment* (New York: Berghahn Books, 2002), pp. 214–215; Hobsbawm, *Age of Extremes*, p. 43.

10. Overy, *Russia's War*, p. 175.

11. This is my own estimate of the number killed at Stalingrad. Red Army records show that around 480,000 Soviets were killed in the battle (Erickson, *Barbarossa*, table 12.4; Beevor, *Stalingrad*, p. 394; Overy, *Russia's War*, p. 212). In addition, it is commonly estimated that around 150,000 Germans of the Sixth Army were killed within the pocket. Hoyt (*199 Days*, pp. 161, 166) indicates that over 9,700 Germans were killed during the weeks of street fighting before the Soviet encirclement. Romanian losses run from 120,000 to 160,000 of all types, so a quarter of the mid-point would give us 35,000 killed. The Italians lost 85,000 to 130,000, so a quarter of the mid-point would give us 27,000 killed. Hungarian losses were comparable to the losses of Italians and Romanians, so let's estimate 30,000 killed. It's hard to say how many Germans were killed outside the pocket, but as a pure guess, let's say at least 10,000. Adding it all up and rounding it off gives us 750,000.

    As for the civilian death toll, Yevgenia Borisova ("Stalingrad Civilians Were Not Counted," *Moscow Times*, February 4, 2003) estimates that around 350,000 civilians disappeared from Stalingrad during the battle. The article offers five explanations for what may have happened to them: succumbed to starvation and cold, killed by the bombing and shelling, evacuated during the battle, sent to Germany as slave laborers, or managed to flee on their own. If we assign equal probabilities to each of these five possible fates, then the number who succumbed or were killed would be two-fifths of the total, or some 140,000.

12. Salisbury, *900 Days*, p. 516 (1.3 million to 1.5 million); Glantz, *Siege of Leningrad 1941–44*, p. 7 (1.6 million to 2.0 million).

13. Ibid., pp. 474–475; Michael Jones, *Leningrad: State of Siege* (New York: Basic Books, 2008), pp. 214–219.

14. Overy, *Russia's War*, p. 112. The number of military deaths at Leningrad are unknown but Glantz (*Siege of Leningrad 1941–44*, p. 179) reports that the Soviets recorded that 1,017,881 soldiers were lost irrevocably (that is, killed, captured, missing).

15. Overy (*Russia's War*, p. 212) estimates 253,000 Soviet dead at Kursk. Both Clodfelter (*Warfare and Armed Conflicts*, vol. 2, p. 827) and John Erickson (*The Road to Berlin* (New Haven, CT: Yale University Press, 1999), p. 112) estimate 70,000 Germans dead.

16. Overy, *Russia's War*, p. 117.

17. Mazower, *Dark Continent*, p. 155.

18. Smith, *Holocaust and Other Genocides*, p. 16.

19. Donald L. Niewyk, "Holocaust: The Genocide of the Jews," in Samuel Totten et al., eds., *Century of Genocide: Critical Essays and Eyewitness Accounts*, 2nd ed. (New York: Routledge, 2004), pp. 128–129.

20. Smith, *Holocaust and Other Genocides*, pp. 36–37.

21. Donald L. Niewyk, "Holocaust: The Genocide of the Jews," in Samuel Totten et al., eds., *Century of Genocide: Critical Essays and Eyewitness Accounts*, 2nd ed. (New York: Routledge, 2004), pp. 131–132.

22. Ian Hancock, "Responses to the Romani Holocaust," in Alan S. Rosenbaum, ed., *Is the Holocaust Unique? Perspectives on Comparative Genocide* (Boulder, CO: Westview Press, 1996), pp. 39–64.

23. Gilbert, *History of the Twentieth Century*, vol. 2, p. 527.

24. Keay, *India*, p. 504.

25. Johann Hari, "The Two Churchills," *New York Times*, August 12, 2010.

26. Jeffrey Alan Lockwood, *Six-Legged Soldiers: Using Insects as Weapons of War* (New York: Oxford University Press, 2009), p. 115.

27. "June 6, 1944: UK's Last Day as a Superpower," BBC, June 3, 2009.

28. Overy, *Russia's War*, p. 246.

29. Larry Collins and Dominique Lapierre, *Is Paris Burning?* (New York: Simon & Schuster, 1965).

30. Mazower, *Dark Continent*, p. 217.

31. Martin Sorge, *The Other Price of Hitler's War* (New York: Greenwood Press, 1986), citing Cornelius Ryan, *The Last Battle* (New York: Simon & Schuster, 1966).

32. Erickson, *Barbarossa*, table 12.4.

33. Wilmott, *Second World War in the Far East*.

34. Wallechinsky, *David Wallechinsky's Twentieth Century*, pp. 742–745.

35. Gilbert, *History of the Twentieth Century*, vol. 2, pp. 646–647; Manchester, *American Caesar*, p. 483.

36. Keegan, *Second World War*, pp. 561–573; Toland, *Rising Sun*, pp. 804–820; Gilbert, *History of the Twentieth Century*, vol. 2, pp. 692–694.

37. Technically, I mean "non-battle trauma" rather than "accidental" because that's how the U.S. Army categorizes its statistics. Non-battle trauma includes accidents, drowning, sunstroke, frostbite, murder, and suicide, but not disease. The number of Army personnel who died of non-battle trauma in 1942–45 was 60,054 (Edgar L. Cook and John E. Gordon, "Accidental Trauma," in John Boyd Coates Jr., *Preventative Medicine in World War II*, http://history.amedd.army.mil/books docs/wwii/PrsnlHlthMsrs/chapter7.htm, p. 247), compared to 234,874 Army personnel killed in battle during World War II, a ratio of 3.9 battle deaths per non-battle trauma death. In the Civil War, U.S. Army personnel suffered 10,282 deaths by accident, drowning, sunstroke, murder, and

suicide, compared to 110,070 battle deaths, a ratio of 10.7 battle deaths per non-battle trauma death. William F. Fox, *Regimental Losses in the American Civil War, 1861–1865* (1889), available at http://www.civilwarhome.com/foxs.htm (accessed March 14, 2011).

38. Staff of Strategy & Tactics Magazine, *War in the East*, pp. 165–167.

39. Gilbert, *History of the Twentieth Century*, vol. 2, p. 304.

40. Ibid., p. 366.

41. Overy, *Russia's War*, pp. 165–166.

42. Gilbert, *History of the Twentieth Century*, vol. 2, pp. 514–516.

43. Tokyo: Estimates go as high as 130,000, but variations of the U.S. Strategic Bombing Survey's lower estimate of 83,793 are the most commonly repeated numbers. You can find this death toll on both ends of the political spectrum. For examples, Johnson, *Modern Times*, p. 424; Zinn, *People's History of the United States*, p. 422.

44. Hiroshima: Estimates of the dead in the atomic blasts vary according to how many subsequent cancer deaths in the area are attributed to radiation poisoning. For example, CBS News reported on August 6, 2004, that there were 237,062 dead listed on Hiroshima's memorial cenotaph, including 5,142 who had "died from cancer and other long-term ailments over the past year." This means that they're counting people who lived another fifty-nine years after the bombing, even though most people worldwide don't even live fifty-nine years. In any case, the city government's 1946 report of 118,661 dead and 3,677 missing (*Bulletin of the Atomic Scientists*, June 1986, p. 37) is as reliable an estimate of immediate deaths in Hiroshima as we're likely to get, and all estimates of long-term radiation deaths are speculative.

45. Gilbert, *History of the Twentieth Century*, vol. 2, p. 703.

46. Mazower, *Dark Continent*, pp. 231–232.

47. Keegan, *Second World War*, p. 590.

48. *The United States Strategic Bombing Survey* (New York: Garland, 1976), vol. 10, p. 95.

49. Dominic Lieven et al., in the *Cambridge History of Russia* (Cambridge, UK: Cambridge University Press, 2006), p. 226, estimated that 7.4 million Soviets were "killed in hot or cold blood," 2.2 million were "taken to Germany and worked to death," and 4.1 million "died of overwork, hunger and disease." To this total of 13.7 million excessive civilian deaths under German occupation should be added the deaths of 3.3 million POWs.

50. Rummel, *Death by Government*, p. 148 (3,949,000).

51. Rough guess. The two major war crimes blamed on the Nationalist Chinese are the Yellow River flood and the overall brutality with which they rounded up and abused conscripts. I'm estimating a few hundred thousand apiece.

52. According to a 1947 government report, 6,028,000 civilians from inside the pre-war borders of Poland died in the war, only 521,000 of them as a direct result of military operations. Urlanis, *Wars and Population*, p. 290.

53. Median of eleven published estimates. See http://www.necrometrics.com/20c5m.htm#Holocaust.

54. Arendt, *Eichmann in Jerusalem*, p. 192.

55. UN postwar estimate: repeated by Robert B. Edgerton, *Warriors of the Rising Sun* (New York: W. W. Norton, 1997), p. 272; Werner Gruhl, *Imperial Japan's World War Two* (New Brunswick, NJ: Transaction, 2010), p. 111; Thomas G. Paterson, *On Every Front* (New York: W. W. Norton, 1992), p. 11; Sterling Seagrave, *Gold Warriors: America's Secret Recovery of Yamashita's Gold* (New York: Verso, 2003), p. 54.

56. The official death toll of the Bengal famine.

57. The unofficial death toll of the Bengal famine.

58. Famine deaths. Karnow, *Vietnam*, p. 160.

59. Martin Mennecke et al., "Genocide in Bosnia-Herzegovina," in Samuel Totten et al., eds., *Century of Genocide: Critical Essays and Eyewitness Accounts*, 2nd ed. (New York: Routledge, 2004), p. 422.

60. The official estimate is that conventional bombing killed 260,000 in Japan. An unknown number died by atomic bombing, but most guesses are close to the 140,000 needed to bring the total to 400,000. Johnson, *Modern Times*, pp. 424–426; Keegan, *Second World War*, p. 576.

61. Urlanis, *Wars and Population*, p. 290: 350,000 civilians killed, only 60,000 by military action.

62. This is the sum of the number of Axis POWs who died (580,000), Soviet soldiers who were executed (400,000), Gulag deaths (621,000; Service, *History of Twentieth-Century Russia*, p. 278), Black Sea/Caucasus minorities who were killed (231,000), Baltic minorities who died (200,000), repatriated Soviets who were killed after the war (1,000,000 more or less), and German civilians who died during the Red Army advance (1,000,000; Keegan, *Second World War*, p. 592). See the chapter on Stalin for details.

63. Ben Macintyre, "Britain to Blame for Holocaust, Says Buchanan," *Times* (London), September 23, 1999; see also Michael Kelly, "Buchanan's Folly," *Washington Post*, September 22, 1999.

64. Elisabeth Bumiller, "60 Years after the Fact, Debating Yalta All Over Again," *New York Times*, May 16, 2005, p. 18; David Greenberg, "Know Thy Allies," *Slate*, May 10, 2005, http://www.slate.com/id/2118394/.

65. Overy, *Russia's War*, pp. 195–196; Vecamer, "Germany-Soviet Military-Economic Comparison"; Dykman, "The Soviet Experience in World War Two."

Expulsion of Germans from Eastern Europe

1. Every account of this event seems to report a different death toll, but estimates fall into two clusters. Most historians claim that 2 to 2.8 million eastern Germans died or disappeared without a trace during the expulsions. A minority prefers tighter standards of proof, which produce estimates of 400,000 to 600,000 well-documented deaths. Regardless of whether it ranks Number 35 or 85, this event belongs somewhere on my list.

2. Istvan S. Pogany, *Righting Wrongs in Eastern Europe* (Manchester, UK: Manchester University Press, 1997), p. 106.

3. Hans-Ulrich Stoldt, "Revenge on Ethnic Germans: Czech Town Divided over How to Commemorate 1945 Massacre," *Spiegel Online*, September 4, 2009, http://www.spiegel.de/international/europe/0,1518,646757,00.html.

4. Dornberg, "Germany's Expellees and Border Changes"; Czech News Agency, "Transfer of Germans from Czechoslovakia."

5. Winston Churchill, "Sinews of Peace," Westminster College, Fulton, Missouri, March 5, 1946, http://www.winstonchurchill.org/i4a/pages/index.cfm?pageid=429.

6. Bell-Fialkoff, "Brief History of Ethnic Cleansing"; Krah, "Germans as Victims?"

7. Czech News Agency, "Profile: Organised Sudeten Deportations Began 50 Year Ago."

8. See Keegan, *Second World War*, p. 593.

French Indochina War

1. Karnow, *Vietnam*, pp. 161–167.
2. Ibid., pp. 171–172.
3. Clodfelter, *Warfare and Armed Conflicts*, vol. 2, p. 1123.

Partition of India

1. The median of fourteen published estimates. See http://www.necrometrics.com/20c300k.htm# India.
2. Spaeth, "The Price of Freedom."
3. Collins and Lapierre, *Freedom at Midnight*, pp. 97–98.
4. Gilbert, *History of the Twentieth Century*, vol. 2, p. 795.
5. Collins and Lapierre, *Freedom at Midnight*, pp. 314–316.
6. Counted by the 1951 censuses taken by India and Pakistan, cited in Pradeep Sharma, *Human Geography: The People* (New Delhi, India: Discovery Publishing House, 2008), p. 129.
7. Collins and Lapierre, *Freedom at Midnight*, pp. 355–360, 436–512.

Mao Zedong

1. Meisner, *Mao's China and After*, p. 69.
2. Spence, *Search for Modern China*, pp. 539–540.
3. Chang and Halliday, *Mao*, p. 325.
4. Ibid., p. 324.
5. Meisner, *Mao's China and After*, pp. 162–180.
6. Chang and Halliday, *Mao*, p. 417.
7. Chirot, *Modern Tyrants*, p. 192.
8. Chang and Halliday, *Mao*, pp. 329–333.
9. Nicholas Wade, "Method & Madness: Lust for Power," review of *The Private Life of Chairman Mao*, by Dr. Li Zhisui, *New York Times*, November 6, 1994; Chirot, *Modern Tyrants*, p. 195.
10. Spence, *Search for Modern China*, p. 525.
11. Meisner, *Mao's China and After*, p. 70.
12. Chang and Halliday, *Mao*, pp. 431–432; Chirot, *Modern Tyrants*, p. 196.
13. Chirot, *Modern Tyrants*, p. 195.
14. Spence, *Search for Modern China*, p. 583; Chang and Halliday, *Mao*, p. 428.
15. Meisner, *Mao's China and After*, p. 237.
16. Davis, *Late Victorian Holocausts*, p. 251, quoting Amartya Sen.
17. Chang and Halliday, *Mao*, p. 433.
18. Ibid., p. 430; Human Rights Watch, *The Three Gorges Dam in China: Forced Resettlement, Suppression of Dissent and Labor Rights Concerns*, Human Rights Watch Reports, vol. 7, no. 1 (February 1995), http://www.hrw.org/reports/1995/China1.htm; Thayer Watkins, "The Catastrophic Dam Failures in China in August 1975," http://www2.sjsu.edu/faculty/watkins/aug1975.htm (accessed March 14, 2011).
19. Chang and Halliday, *Mao*, pp. 453–457.
20. Margolin, "China," in Courtois et al., *Black Book of Communism*, p. 546.
21. Chirot, *Modern Tyrants*, p. 197.
22. Meisner, *Mao's China and After*, p. 313; Chang and Halliday, *Mao*, pp. 505–506.

23. Chang and Halliday, *Mao*, p. 517.

24. Ibid., pp. 520–521.

25. Spence, *Search for Modern China*, p. 606.

26. Chirot, *Modern Tyrants*, p. 205.

27. Ibid., pp. 204–205.

28. Marcus Mabry, "Cannibals of the Red Guard," *Newsweek*, January 18, 1993, p. 38; Chirot, *Modern Tyrants*, pp. 205–206.

29. Chirot, *Modern Tyrants*, p. 206.

30. Spence, *Search for Modern China*, pp. 616–617.

31. Richard L. Walker, *The Human Cost of Communism in China*, Report to the Subcommittee on Internal Security of the U.S. Senate Judiciary Committee (Washington, DC: Government Printing Office, 1971).

32. Courtois et al., *Black Book of Communism*, p. 4.

33. Chang and Halliday, *Mao*, p. 3.

34. Estimates of deaths in the first few years: Margolin, "China," in Courtois et al., *Black Book of Communism*, p. 479 (1 to 5 million); Spence, *Search for Modern China*, p. 517 ("as many as 1 million or more"); Johnson, *Modern Times*, p. 447 ("At least 2 million"), p. 548 ("may have been as high as 15 million, though a figure of 1 to 3 million is more likely"); Meisner, *Mao's China and After*, p. 72 "2,000,000 people executed during the first three years"); Chirot, *Modern Tyrants*, p. 187 ("Chou En-lai later estimated that 830,000 were killed between 1949 and 1956. Mao . . . estimated . . . from two to three million"); Chang and Halliday, *Mao*, p. 324 ("Some 3 million perished either by execution, mob violence or suicide "); Rummel, *China's Bloody Century*, table II.A, line 37 (4.5 million). The median of these seven estimates is 2 million.

35. Becker, *Hungry Ghosts*, p. 270. Other estimates of the death toll of the Great Leap Forward: Spence, *Search for Modern China*, p. 583 ("The result was . . . a famine that claimed 20 million lives or more"); Meisner, *Mao's China and After*, p. 237 ("demographers calculate . . . 15,000,000 famine-related deaths. . . . [S]ome scholars have concluded that as many as 30,000,000 people perished"); Chirot, *Modern Tyrants*, pp. 195–196 ("Some party officials later estimated that over 40 million died. The economist Nicholas Lardy . . . estimates that between 16 and 28 million died"); Chang and Halliday, *Mao*, p. 438 ("Close to 38 million people died of starvation and overwork").

36. Chirot, *Modern Tyrants*, p. 198 ("some estimates of deaths go as high as 20 million").

37. Estimates of deaths in the Cultural Revolution: Johnson, *Modern Times*, p. 558 ("The Agence France Presse, in the most widely respected figure, estimated (3 February 1979) that the Red Guards had murdered about 400,000 people"); Meisner, *Mao's China and After*, p. 354 ("a widely accepted nationwide figure of 400,000 Cultural Revolution deaths, a number first reported in 1979 by the Agence France Presse correspondent"); Palmowski, *Dictionary of Twentieth Century World History* ("half million"); Chirot, *Modern Tyrants*, p. 198 ("At least one million died"); Brzezinski, *Out of Control* (1 million to 2 million); Rummel, *China's Bloody Century*, table II.A, line 294a (1,613,000); John Heidenrich, *How to Prevent Genocide, A Guide for Policy Makers, Scholars, and the Concerned Citizen* (Westport, CT: Praeger, 2001), p. 7 (2 million); Chang and Halliday, *Mao*, p. 547 ("at least 3 million died violent deaths"). The median of these eight estimates is around 1.5 million.

38. David Aikman, "The Laogai Archipelago," *Weekly Standard*, September 29, 1997.

39. Margolin, "China," in Courtois et al., *Black Book of Communism*, p. 498.

40. Chang and Halliday, *Mao*, p. 325.

Korean War

1. The median of eight published estimates. See http://www.necrometrics.com/20c1m.htm#Ko.

2. "Cheju April 3rd Massacre to Be Unearthed" (30,000 to 80,000); Wehrfritz and Lee, "Ghosts of Cheju" (60,000).

3. Chang and Halliday, *Mao*, pp. 358–359.

4. Hastings, *Korean War*, pp. 77–82.

5. Charles J. Hanley and Jae-Soon Chang, "Thousands Killed by US's Korean Ally," Associated Press, May 18, 2008.

6. Center of Military History, "Korean War," p. 56.

7. "Thousands Perished in North Korean Outrages during War," Associated Press, October 13, 1999; Andrew Nahm, *Historical Dictionary of the Republic of Korea* (Lanham, MD: Scarecrow Press, 2004), p. 111.

8. Hastings, *Korean War*, p. 304.

9. "U.S. Allowed Korean Massacre in 1950," Associated Press, July 5, 2008.

10. Hastings, *Korean War*, pp. 138–139.

11. Ibid., pp. 128–146.

12. Center of Military History, "Korean War," pp. 561–562.

13. Ibid., p. 565.

14. Matray, "Revisiting Korea"; Chang and Halliday, *Mao*, p. 368.

15. Hastings, *Korean War*, p. 306.

North Korea

1. This is a pure guess. A million or two may have died in the famine, plus a million or two may have died of oppression. The numbers could easily be twice or half as much. One estimate (Omestad, "Gulag Nation") is that 400,000 political prisoners died between 1973 and 2003, and the regime was already a quarter century old by that time. Courtois et al., in *The Black Book of Communism*, estimate 2,000,000 deaths (p. 4), including 100,000 killed in party purges and 1,500,000 dead in concentration camps, without counting the famine (p. 564).

2. Chirot, *Modern Tyrants*, p. 248.

3. Liz McGregor, "Birthday Blues for the 'Sun of Mankind,' " *Sydney Morning Herald*, April 29, 1989.

4. Goodspeed, "Grim North Korea Breaks Its Isolation."

5. Pierre Rigoulot, "Crimes, Terror, and Secrecy in North Korea," in Stephane Courtois et al., *The Black Book of Communism: Crimes, Terror, Repression*, trans. Jonathan Murphy and Mark Kramer (Cambridge, MA: Harvard University Press, 1999), p. 561.

6. Ibid., p. 560.

7. Carol Clark, "Kim Jong Il: 'Dear Leader' or Demon?" CNN Interactive, 2001, http://www.cnn.com/SPECIALS/2000/korea/story/leader/kim.jong.il/. (accessed March 9, 2008).

8. Wallechinsky, *Tyrants*, p. 41.

9. Goozner, "World Watches North Korea."

10. Goodspeed, "Grim North Korea Breaks Its Isolation."

11. "Top Defector Says Famine Has Killed over Three Million Koreans," Agence France Presse, March 13, 1999; "North Korea Admits Its Famine Has Killed Hundreds of Thousands," Associated Press, May 10, 1999 (the official North Korean figures indicated 220,000 deaths; U.S. delegation estimated 2 million; South Korean intelligence said the population had fallen by 3 million); Tania

Branigan, "North Korea Life Expectancy Falls, Census Reveals," *Guardian*, February 22, 2010 (600,000 to 1 million).

The Black Chapter of Communism

1. Jean-Louis Margolin, "Cambodia," in Stephane Courtois et al., *The Black Book of Communism; Crimes, Terror, Repression*, trans. Jonathan Murphy and Mark Kramer (Cambridge, MA: Harvard University Press, 1999), p. 591.
2. Yugoslavia: Estimates run the gamut, with the highest being almost nine times the lowest: Mazower, *Dark Continent*, p. 235 (as many as 60,000); Chuck Sudetic, "Piles of Bones in Yugoslavia Point to Partisan Massacres," *New York Times*, July 9, 1990 (70,000 to 100,000); John R. Lampe, *Yugoslavia as History: Twice There Was a Country* (Cambridge, UK: Cambridge University Press, 2000), p. 227 (100,000); Noel Malcolm, *Bosnia: A Short History* (New York: NYU Press, 1996), p. 193 (250,000); anti-Communist emigrés as cited in Sudetic, "Piles of Bones" (ca. 500,000); R. J. Rummel, *Statistics of Democide* (Münster: LIT, 1998), p. 172 (500,000). Both the geometric mean of the high and low and the median come to around 175,000.
3. Poland: Rosenberg, *Haunted Land*, p. 145.
4. Bulgaria: Andrew Alexander, "Bulgarians Reveal Labor-Camp Fate of Those Who Criticized Government," *Orange County Register*, July 1, 1990.
5. Cuba: John Rice, "40 Years of Revolution," *Star Tribune* (Minneapolis), December 27, 1998 ("Historian Hugh Thomas estimated 5,000 people might have been executed by 1970").
6. Jean-Louis Margolin, "Cambodia," in Stephane Courtois et al., *The Black Book of Communism: Crimes, Terror, Repression*, trans. Jonathan Murphy and Mark Kramer (Cambridge, MA: Harvard University Press, 1999), p. 591.
7. Pierre Rigoulot, "Crimes Terror, and Secrecy in North Korea," in Stephane Courtois et al., *The Black Book of Communism: Crimes, Terror, Repression*, trans. Jonathan Murphy and Mark Kramer (Cambridge, MA: Harvard University Press, 1999), pp. 552–553.
8. East Germany: Reuters, "100,000 Died in E. Germany for Political Acts," *Los Angeles Times*, October 27, 1991 ("died in captivity or were executed for political offenses in 44 years").
9. Romania: Alison Mutler, "AP Photos BUC101-103," Associated Press, October 23, 2000 ("Some 100,000 peasants, intellectuals and members of the pre-Communist government are believed to have perished in prison or while building the [Danube-Black Sea Canal]").
10. Mongolia: "Expedition Unearths Mass Grave Dating to Communist Rule," Associated Press, October 22, 1991, AM cycle ("The death toll from that time has been widely estimated at 35,000"; estimates go as high as 100,000); "Mass Grave of Buddhist Massacre Reportedly Found in Mongolia," Associated Press, October 22, 1991, PM cycle.
11. Czechoslovakia: "Thousands of People Killed by Former Communist Regime," CTK National News Wire, May 28, 1991 (260 executed; 9,000 to 10,000 killed during arrest and in prison; 1,800 disappeared without a trace).
12. Albania: Jane Perelez, "Tirana Journal: A Stalinist Dowager in Her Bunker," *New York Times*, July 8, 1997 ("documents show that 5,000 political prisoners had been executed . . . during the 40-year period of Hoxha rule").
13. Hobsbawm, *Age of Extremes*, pp. 382–385.
14. Ibid., pp. 471–495; Mazower, *Dark Continent*, pp. 362–380.

Algerian War of Independence

1. Johnson, *Modern Times*, p. 500.
2. Walter Laqueur, *Europe since Hitler: The Rebirth of Europe*, rev. ed. (New York: Penguin Books, 1982), pp. 468–470.
3. Horne, *Savage War of Peace*, p. 538.

War in the Sudan

1. The median of eight published estimates. See http://www.necrometrics.com/20c300k.htm#Sudan.
2. The median of seven recent estimates. See http://www.necrometrics.com/20c1m.htm#Sudan.
3. Estimates go as high as 400,000, but among large, impartial organizations that keep track of these things, 200,000 is preferred. "Q&A: Sudan's Darfur Conflict," BBC News, May 29, 2007, http://news.bbc.co.uk/go/pr/fr/-/1/hi/world/africa/3496731.stm (200,000); Human Rights Watch, "Q & A: Crisis in Darfur," January 29, 2007, http://hrw.org/english/docs/2004/05/05/darfur8536.htm (200,000); Sam Dealey, "An Atrocity That Needs No Exaggeration," *New York Times*, August 12, 2007; Alfred de Montesquiou, "As Darfur Violence Continues, Some Question Death Estimates," Associated Press, November 29, 2006.
4. Berkeley, *Graves Are Not Yet Full*, p. 211.
5. Ibid., p. 214; Kaplan, "Microcosm of Africa's Ills; Sudan."
6. Berkeley, *Graves Are Not Yet Full*, p. 198.
7. Ibid., pp. 201–202.
8. "Country Profile: Sudan," BBC, June 1, 2007, http://news.bbc.co.uk/2/hi/middle_east/country_profiles/820864.stm.
9. "Prosecutor Accuses Bashir Forces of Murder, Rape, Pillage," *allAfrica.com*, March 2, 2009, http://allafrica.com/stories/200903020185.html; Robert Booth, "No Money, Not Enough Food, Rampant Sickness, Night-Time Raids. Darfur Today," *Guardian*, December 7, 2007; Hissa Hissa, "UN Envoy in Darfur Rebel Heartland to Muster Support for Peace Talks," Associated Press, December 8, 2007.

Vietnam War

1. Dwight Eisenhower, *Mandate for Change* (New York: New American Library, 1963), quoted in Simkin, "Vietnam War."
2. Quoted in Michael O'Brien, *John F. Kennedy: A Biography* (New York: Griffin, 2006), p. 859.
3. Karnow, *Vietnam*, pp. 313–327.
4. Ibid., pp. 382–392.
5. Boot, *Savage Wars of Peace*, p. 298.
6. Ibid., p. 308.
7. Zinn, *People's History of the United States*, p. 477.
8. Ibid., pp. 478–479; Doug Linder, "An Introduction to the My Lai Courts-Martial," Famous Trials, 1999, http://www.law.umkc.edu/faculty/projects/ftrials/mylai/Myl_intro.html.
9. Nell Boyce, "Hugh Thompson: Reviled Then Honored for His Actions at My Lai," *U.S. News & World Report*, August 20, 2001, http://www.usnews.com/usnews/doubleissue/heroes/thompson.htm.
10. Michael D. Sallah and Mitch Weiss, "Rogue GIs Unleashed Wave of Terror in Central High-

lands," *Toledo Blade*, October 19, 2003. Available at http://www.pulitzer.org/works/2004-Investigative-Reporting.

11. Karnow, *Vietnam*, p. 617.
12. Davidson, *Vietnam at War*, p. 552; Hanson, *Carnage and Culture*, p. 400.
13. Karnow, *Vietnam*, pp. 558–559.
14. Ibid., p. 616.
15. Ibid.
16. Ibid., pp. 617–621.
17. Ibid., pp. 654–656.
18. Ibid., pp. 666–669.
19. Ibid., p. 674.
20. Ibid., pp. 679–680.
21. "Vietnam Discloses 1.1 Million Died in War, 600,000 Wounded," Associated Press, April 3, 1995; Keith B. Richburg, "To Vietnamese, Fall of Saigon Started the Peace; 20 Years after War's End, Victors Looking Forward," *Washington Post*, April 30, 1995.
22. Obermeyer, Murray, and Gakidou, "Fifty Years of Violent War Deaths."
23. Kimmo Kiljunen, ed., *Kampuchea: Decade of the Genocide: Report of a Finnish Inquiry Commission* (London: Zed Books, 1984), p. 30.
24. Obermeyer, Murray, and Gakidou, "Fifty Years of Violent War Deaths."

The Cold War

1. Totten et al., eds., *Century of Genocide*, p. 321.
2. Edgar O'Ballance, *The Greek Civil War: 1944–1949* (New York: Praeger, 1966), p. 202.
3. Obermeyer, "Fifty Years of Violent War Deaths."
4. Vincent Cabreza, "43,000 Killed in 34 Years of Communist Rebellion," *Philippine Daily Inquirer*, January 29, 2003.
5. "Refusing to Forget," PBS News Hour, October 16, 1997, http://www.pbs.org/newshour/bb/latin_america/july-dec97/argentina_10-16a.html, citing Argentina Human Rights Information, http://www.derechos.org/human-rights/argentina.html: 30,000 disappearances.
6. "Central America," in *Encyclopaedic Britannica*, 15th ed., vol. 15, p. 692.
7. Kohn, *Dictionary of Wars*, p. 330.

Indonesian Purge

1. The median of nineteen estimates. See http://www.necrometrics.com/20c300k.htm#Indonesia.
2. Kathy Kadane, "U.S. Accused of Role in Massacre."
3. Robert Cribb, "The Indonesian Massacres," in Samuel Totten et al., eds., *Century of Genocide: Critical Essays and Eyewitness Accounts*, 2nd ed. (New York: Routledge, 2004).
4. Karmini, "40 Years on, Indonesian Victims"; Lekic, "Controversy over Elusive Document"; Whiting, "Indonesia Still Dealing with Carnage."

Biafran War

1. The median of fifteen published estimates. See http://www.necrometrics.com/20c1m.htm#Nigeria.
2. Edgerton, *Africa's Armies*, p. 107.

3. Ibid., pp. 103–109; "Ojukwu Blames Civil War on Gowon"; Harden, "2 Decades Later, Biafra Remains Lonely Precedent."

Bengali Genocide

1. The median of fifteen published estimates. See http://www.necrometrics.com/20c1m.htm#Bangladesh.
2. Kiernan, *Blood and Soil*, p. 574.
3. Stockwin, "East Pakistan's Bloody Death."
4. Christopher Hitchins, *The Trial of Henry Kissinger* (New York: Verso Press, 2001).
5. Robert Payne, *Massacre* (New York: Macmillan, 1973), p. 55.
6. Galloway, "We Are Mute and Horrified Witnesses to a Reign of Terror."
7. Ibid.; Jahan, "Genocide in Bangladesh," in Totten et al., eds., *Century of Genocide*; Kiernan, *Blood and Soil*, pp. 572–576; Stockwin, "East Pakistan's Bloody Death."

Idi Amin

1. The median of fourteen estimates. See http://www.necrometrics.com/20c300k.htm#Uganda.
2. Berkeley, *Graves Are Not Yet Full*, p. 230.
3. "Who Is This Man Field Marshal Idi Amin, Who Dares Do the Things He Does and Say the Things He Says," Associated Press, February 27, 1977; "Field Marshal Idi Amin Dada, Uganda's 'President for Life,'" Associated Press, April 11, 1979.
4. Chirot, *Modern Tyrants*, p. 392.
5. "Ex-Ugandan Dictator Idi Amin, 80, Dies."

Mengistu Haile

1. Fitzgerald, "Tyrant for the Taking" ("More than two million people have died in political purges and civil war, or from malnourishment that was abetted by government policies"); Rapoport, *Knives Are Out* ("More than two million people . . . died because of resettlement, imprisonment, withheld famine relief, military losses and straight execution").
2. Fitzgerald, "Tyrant for the Taking"; Henry, "Mengistu Leaves Ethiopia in Shambles."
3. Fitzgerald, "Tyrant for the Taking"; Rapoport, *Knives Are Out*.
4. Sanchez, "Victory Tempered by Sorrow" (400,000); Henry, "Mengistu Leaves Ethiopia in Shambles" (500,000); Obermeyer, Murray, and Gakidou, "Fifty Years of Violent War Deaths" (579,000).
5. Death toll of famine: 500,000 (Manthorpe, "Mengistu's Brutal Regime") or a million (Henry, "Mengistu Leaves Ethiopia in Shambles"; Sanchez, "Victory Tempered by Sorrow") or two million (Rapoport, *Knives Are Out*).

Postwar Vietnam

1. My estimate. That's 200,000 boat people (William Branigin, "Vietnam Demands U.S. Halt Rescues," *Washington Post*, August 3, 1979; Vu Thanh Thuy, "Boat People Defeat Sea . . . ," *San Diego Union Tribune*, July 20, 1986) plus 165,000 camp deaths ("Postwar Strife Survival: The Register Profiles O.C. Residents Who Once Were Prisoners in Vietnam's Re-education Camps," *Orange County Register*, April 29, 2001; Fidelius Kuo, "Fallen, but Not Forgotten: Washington's South Vietnamese Veterans," *Northwest Asian Weekly*, July 5, 1996), which includes 65,000 executions (Desbarats and Jackson, "Vietnam 1975–1982").

2. Desbarats and Jackson, "Vietnam 1975–1982."
3. In addition to the sources listed above, compare Elizabeth Becker (*When the War Was Over* (New York: PublicAffairs, 1998), p. 534), who cites the UN High Commissioner on Refugees that 250,000 boat people died at sea and 929,600 reached asylum; Hanson, *Carnage and Culture*, p. 425, reporting 50,000 to 100,000 dead; and Nayan Chanda, *Brother Enemy* (San Diego: Harcourt Brace Jovanovich, 1986), p. 247, writing that 30,000 to 40,000 died at sea (also in Marilyn Young, *The Vietnam Wars: 1945–1990* (New York: HarperCollins,1991), p. 306).
4. Butler, "Agony of the Boat People."
5. "Boat People; Their Endless Ordeal," *San Diego Union-Tribune*, June 25, 1989; Weiss, "Timing Is Everything."

Democratic Kampuchea

1. Chirot, *Modern Tyrants*, p. 223.
2. Ben Kiernan, "The Cambodian Genocide," in Samuel Totten et al., eds., *Century of Genocide: Critical Essays and Eyewitness Accounts*, 2nd ed. (New York: Routledge, 2004), pp. 345–346.
3. Ker Munthit, "AP Interview: Ex-Khmer Rouge Leader Acknowledges for First Time That Regime Committed Genocide," Associated Press, December 30, 2003.
4. Chirot, *Modern Tyrants*, p. 228.
5. Ibid., pp. 218–220.
6. Ibid., p. 229; Ben Kiernan, "The Cambodian Genocide," in Samuel Totten et al., eds., *Century of Genocide: Critical Essays and Eyewitness Accounts*, 2nd ed. (New York: Routledge, 2004), pp. 339–342.
7. Sarah Jackson-Han, "Pol Pot Said to Be Tried and Sentenced after 18 Years in Hiding," Agence France Presse, July 29, 1997.
8. Ker Munthit, "Khmer Rouge Leader Pol Pot Dies," Associated Press, April 16, 1998.
9. Denis D. Gray, "Cambodians Recall Khmer Rouge Massacres," Associated Press, May 21, 1987.
10. Chirot, *Modern Tyrants*, p. 209.
11. Ben Kiernan, "The Cambodian Genocide," in Samuel Totten et al., eds., *Century of Genocide: Critical Essays and Eyewitness Accounts*, 2nd ed. (New York: Routledge, 2004), p. 348.

Mozambican Civil War

1. Lawless, "After the Terror" (500,000); Jensen, "Peace Is as Difficult as War" (600,000); Christie, "Mozambique Celebrates Year of Democracy" (at least 800,000); Ottaway, " 'Slave Trade' in Mozambicans" (between 600,000 and 1 million); Pakenham, "Where a Million Died" (nearly a million); Edgerton, *Africa's Armies*, p. 109 (at least 1 million).
2. Pakenham, "Where a Million Died," quoting William Finnegan, *A Complicated War: Harrowing of Mozambique* (Berkeley, CA: University of California Press, 1996).
3. Lawless, "After the Terror"; Christie, "Mozambique Celebrates Year of Democracy"; Edgerton, *Africa's Armies*, pp. 109–114; Ottaway, " 'Slave Trade' in Mozambicans"; Pakenham, "Where a Million Died"; Jensen, "Peace Is as Difficult as War."
4. "U.S., Edging Higher, Ranks as World's 7th-Richest Nation," *New York Times*, December 30, 1994.

Angolan Civil War

1. Duke, "Will Peace Take Hold in Angola?" (500,000); Sieno, "Angolan Peace Talks Restart" (500,000); Salopek, "Inklings of Peace Intrude" (500,000); Marcus, "Relentless War Wears on Angolans" (more than 450,000).
2. Ray Fisman, "Diamonds Are a Guerrilla's Best Friend: Why Was War Good for Angola's Big Miners?" *Slate*, August 17, 2007, http://www.slate.com/id/2172333.
3. GlobalSecurity.org, "Cuba," http://www.globalsecurity.org/military/world/cuba/intro.htm (accessed March 15, 2011).

Ugandan Bush War

1. Williams, "Uganda Marks" (500,000); Wasswa, "Uganda's First Prime Minister" (500,000); Berkeley, "African Success Story?" (300,000); Edgerton, *Africa's Armies*, p. 155 (300,000); Marshall, "Obituary: Milton Obote" (100,000).
2. Berkeley, "African Success Story?"; Kaplan, "Starting Over"; Marshall, "Obituary: Milton Obote"; Wasswa, "Uganda's First Prime Minister"; Williams, "Uganda Marks."

Post-Colonial Africa

1. Millard Burr, *Quantifying Genocide in Southern Sudan and the Nuba Mountains* (Washington, DC: U.S. Committee for Refugees, 1998).
2. "Burundi Civil War Claims 260,000 Lives—UNFPA," Panafrican News Agency (PANA) Daily Newswire, April 25, 2004.
3. Republic of Liberia, Truth and Reconciliation Committee, *Final Report*: vol. 1: *Preliminary Findings and Determinations* (2009), p. 44, http://www.trcofliberia.org/reports/final/volume-one_layout-1.pdf (accessed March 18, 2011).

Soviet-Afghan War

1. The median of several published estimates. See http://www.necrometrics.com/20c1m.htm#Afghanistan.
2. David Zucchino, " 'The Americans . . . They Just Drop Their Bombs and Leave,' " *Los Angeles Times*, June 2, 2002; Coll, *Ghost Wars*, p. 40.
3. Mark J. Porubcansky, "Top Soviet Officer in Afghanistan Opposed Intervention," Associated Press, September 19, 1989; Gerald Nadler, "Soviets Had Hand in Overthrowing Afghan President," United Press International, May 4, 1989.
4. Soll Sussman, "CIA Almost Sure of Afghan Massacre, Senator Says," Associated Press, March 4, 1980.
5. "Soviet Military in Unconfirmed Report Linked to Massacre of 900 Civilians," Associated Press, March 27, 1985; "Hundreds of Civilians Reportedly Killed by Soviets in Afghanistan," Associated Press, February 26,1985.
6. Bouloque, "Communism in Afghanistan," in Courtois et al., *Black Book of Communism*, p. 718.
7. "Here Is a Chronology of Some of the Main Events in the War in Afghanistan . . . ," Associated Press, February 15, 1989.
8. "Afghan War Cost Soviet Union More Than 70 Billion Dollars," Reuters News, June 7, 1989.
9. Stephen Daggett, "Costs of Major U.S. Wars," Congressional Research Service Report for Congress (RS22926), updated July 24, 2008, http://www.history.navy.mil/library/online/costs_of_major_us_wars.htm.

Saddam Hussein

1. Niko Price, "Survey: Saddam Killed 61,000 in Baghdad," Associated Press, December 9, 2003, cites U.S. Government, (300,000 killed by Saddam across Iraq), "Human rights officials" (500,000), and "some Iraqi political parties" (over a million). Ken Roth, "War in Iraq: Not a Humanitarian Intervention," Human Rights Watch, January 2004, http://www.hrw.org/wr2k4/3.htm, estimates 250,000.
2. Hirst, "Saddam Hussein."
3. Chirot, *Modern Tyrants*, p. 303.
4. Ibid., p. 305.
5. Hirst, "Saddam Hussein."
6. Michael J. Kelly, *Ghosts of Halabja: Saddam Hussein and the Kurdish Genocide* (Westport, CT: Praeger Security International, 2008), p. 34.
7. Michiel Leezenburg, "The *Anfal* Operations in Iraqi Kurdistan," in Samuel Totten et al., eds., *Century of Genocide: Critical Essays and Eyewitness Accounts*, 2nd ed. (New York: Routledge, 2004), pp. 374–393.
8. "Anfal: Campaign against the Kurds," BBC, June 24, 2007; Michiel Leezenburg, "The *Anfal* Operations in Iraqi Kurdistan," in Samuel Totten et al., eds., *Century of Genocide: Critical Essays and Eyewitness Accounts*, 2nd ed. (New York: Routledge, 2004), pp. 374–393. The Kurds claim 182,000 died. Human Rights Watch estimates 100,000.

Iran-Iraq War

1. The median of nineteen published estimates (military deaths only). See http://www.necrometrics.com/20c300k.htm#Iran-Iraq. Iran officially reports that 11,000 of their civilians were killed. This is one of the few major wars of the twentieth century to kill more soldiers than civilians.
2. Bulloch and Morris, *Gulf War*; Pipes, " Border Adrift."
3. Michael Brzoska, "Profiteering on the Iran-Iraq War," *Bulletin of the Atomic Scientists* (June 1987); William Hartung, "Nations Vie for Arms Markets," *Bulletin of the Atomic Scientists* (December 1987).
4. Clodfelter, *Warfare and Armed Conflicts*, vol. 2, p. 1072.
5. Ibid., p. 1084.

Sanctions against Iraq

1. Suellentrop, "Are 1 Million Children Dying in Iraq?"
2. "Iraqi Death Toll," *Frontline: The Gulf War*, PBS, January 9, 1996, http://www.pbs.org/wgbh/pages/frontline/gulf/appendix/death.html; Carl Conetta, "The Wages of War: Iraqi Combatant and Noncombatant Fatalities in the 2003 Conflict," Project on Defense Alternatives, Research Monograph no. 8, October 20, 2003, http://www.comw.org/pda/0310rm8.html.
3. John Prescott, "Iraq's Contraband Trail Goes Inland as Sea Blockade Bites," *Lloyd's List*, October 3, 1995.
4. Johnson, "Trip to Baghdad Reveals a Nation Sagging."
5. Welch, "Politics of Dead Children."
6. Kaplow, "Consequences of Kuwait."
7. Shenon, "Washington and Baghdad Agree on One Point."
8. Leon Howell, "Churches Regret Calling for Sanctions," *Times Union* (Albany, NY), March 21, 1998.

9. Brian Nelson and Jane Arraf, "Ten Years after Iraq's Invasion of Kuwait and U.N. Sanctions Still Stand," *CNN WorldView*, August 6, 2000, 18:00.

10. Carl Conetta, "The Wages of War: Iraqi Combatant and Noncombatant Fatalities in the 2003 Conflict," Project on Defense Alternatives, Research Monograph no. 8, October 20, 2003, note 93, http://www.comw.org/pda/0310rm8.html#N_93_.

11. Kaplow, "Consequences of Kuwait."

12. Suellentrop, "Are 1 Million Children Dying in Iraq?"

Somalian Chaos

1. Bradley S. Klapper, "Internally Displaced Somalis Face Widespread Abuses: Campaigners," Associated Press, November 24, 2004; The Nation, "No Running Away from Somalia," *Africa News*, June 29, 2007; "Failed State: 15 Years of Horror in Somalia," Agence France Presse, June 5, 2006.

2. Miller, "Marines Pull Last Peacekeepers out of Somalia."

3. Hassan, "Somali Warlord Says Battle for Mogadishu Not Over"; Miller, "Marines Pull Last Peacekeepers Out of Somalia."

Rwandan Genocide

1. Kiernan, *Blood and Soil*, p. 555; Berkeley, *Graves Are Not Yet Full*, pp. 257–258.

2. Berkeley, *Graves Are Not Yet Full*, pp. 258–259.

3. Sperling, "Mother of Atrocities."

4. Berkeley, *Graves Are Not Yet Full*, p. 269.

5. "Mayor Gets 30 Years for Genocide," BBC, June 17, 2004; Fergal Keane, "Massacre at Nyarubuye Church," BBC, April 4, 2004.

6. "Rwanda Genocide Priest Given Life," BBC, March 12, 2008.

7. Sperling, "Mother of Atrocities," p. 656.

8. Ibid., pp. 644–646, quoting Lt. Gen. Romeo Dallaire.

9. Arthur Asiimwe, "Rwanda Census Puts Genocide Death Toll at 937,000," Reuters News, April 4, 2004.

10. Sperling, "Mother of Atrocities,".

11. Berkeley, *Graves Are Not Yet Full*, p. 273.

12. "Local Rwandan Courts Convict More Than 3,600 over Genocide," Agence France Presse, January 10, 2006.

13. "Death Penalty Abolition Spurs Quest for Justice," Inter Press Service, August 7, 2007.

Second Congo War

1. Casteneda, "Revolutionary's View of Kabila."

2. Mcgreal, "Worrying Past of a Rebel in Crocodile Shoes."

3. Donald G. McNeil, "In Congo, Forbidding Terrain Hides a Calamity," *New York Times*, June 1, 1997; French, "Kagame's Hidden War in the Congo."

4. Amnesty International, "Democratic Republic of Congo: War against Unarmed Civilians," AI Index: AFR 62/036/1998, November 23, 1998.

5. Weiss and Carayannis, "Reconstructing the Congo."

6. Ibid.

7. "Radio Expeditions: Coltan Mining."

8. Braeckman, "Looting of the Congo."
9. Amnesty International, "Democratic Republic of Congo: From Assassination to State Murder?" AI Index: AFR 62/023/2002, December 12, 2002; "Death Sentences for 'Kabila Killers,' " BBC, January 7, 2003, http://news.bbc.co.uk/1/hi/world/africa/2635295.stm.
10. "Profile: Joseph Kabila," BBC, last updated Wednesday, December 6, 2006, http://news.bbc .co.uk/2/hi/africa/6209774.stm.
11. International Rescue Committee, "Congo Crisis." There have been four reports by the IRC, each with revised estimates of death tolls: 2000 (1.7 million); 2001 (2.5 million); 2005 (3.8 million); 2008 (5.4 million). The 2008 study found that the mortality rate in Congo still exceeds the African average, causing over a million and a half excess deaths since the formal end of hostilities; however, deaths by violence fell sharply from 11.1 percent at the peak of the fighting, to 1.5 percent after December 2006, and the IRC has moved away from calling it a war to calling it a humanitarian crisis. For the sake of ranking, I'm blaming the war only for the 3.8 excess deaths that actually occurred during it, as determined by the 2005 study.
12. Nolen, "War on Women."
13. Ibid.

What I Found: Analysis

1. See "Homosexuality in Nazi Germany," Conservapedia, http://www.conservapedia.com/Homo-sexuality_in_Nazi_Germany, for an example of this.
2. David Biello, "Rise and Fall of Chinese Dynasties Tied to Changes in Rainfall," *Scientific American*, November 7, 2008, http://www.scientificamerican.com/article.cfm?id=monsoon-climate-change-chinese.
3. William J. Broad, "In the Mediterranean, Killer Tsunamis from an Ancient Eruption," *New York Times*, November 2, 2009.
4. Kimberly Johnson, "1600 Eruption Led to Global Cooling, Social Unrest," *National Geographic News*, April 29, 2008, http://news.nationalgeographic.com/news/2008/04/080429-peru-volcano .html.
5. Based on estimates from Carl Haub, "How Many People Have Ever Lived on Earth?" *Population Today*, November/December 2002, http://www.prb.org/articles/2002/howmanypeoplehave everlivedonearth.aspx, it appears that 5.5 billion people died during the twentieth century. Of these, I've counted some 203 million multicides.
6. Lawrence Keeley, *War before Civilization: The Myth of the Peaceful Savage* (New York: Oxford University Press, 1996), table 6.1.

Appendix 1: Disputing the Top One Hundred

1. Dares of Phrygia, *History of the Fall of Troy*, Theoi Classical E-Texts Library, http://www.theoi .com/Text/DaresPhrygius.html (accessed March 14, 2011).
2. *Putnam's Home Cyclopedia* (New York: G. P. Putnam, 1852), p. 417 (400,000); *A Military Diction-ary and Gazetteer: Comprising Ancient and Modern Military Technical Terms . . .* (Philadelphia: Thomas Wilhelm, 1882), p. 310 (300,000).
3. *Historia Augusta*, http://penelope.uchicago.edu/Thayer/E/Roman/Texts/Historia_Augusta/Clau dius*.html (accessed March 18, 2011).

4. Susan P. Mattern, *Rome and the Enemy: Imperial Strategy in the Principate* (Berkeley: University of California Press, 2002), p. 93.

5. *Historia Augusta*, http://penelope.uchicago.edu/Thayer/E/Roman/Texts/Historia_Augusta/Probus*.html (accessed March 18, 2011).

6. Book of Mormon, Ether 15:2.

7. Will Durant, *Our Oriental Heritage* (New York: MJF, 1971), p. 459.

8. Rajeev Srinivasan, "The Roots of Hindu Anxiety: An Interview with Controversial Scholar Koenraad Elst," *India Currents* 9, no. 11 (February 28, 1996), p. 21.

9. Koenraad Elst, "India's Holocaust: Belgium Scholar Analyzes 'The Bloodiest Story in History,' " *Hinduism Today*, March 31, 1999.

10. I found two books from the late nineteenth century (M. D. Aletheia, *The Rationalist's Manual* (London: Watts, 1897); William Wright Hardwicke, *The Evolution of Man: His Religious Systems and Social* (London: Watts, 1899), p. 275) with identical lists of multicides committed by Christians, which include "7,000,000 during the Saracen slaughters. In Spain 5,000,000 perished during the eight Crusades"; however, I suspect the punctuation is misplaced. As written, we have unidentified Saracen slaughters somewhere, and then we have eight Crusades in Spain, but neither of these fit easily into recorded history. However, if we move the period to after "in Spain," we get Saracen slaughters in Spain, and then 5 million killed in eight Crusades somewhere outside of Spain, which fits the well-known Crusades in Palestine. In any case, this isn't strong evidence for any number, but it *is* the most boring footnote in this book, combining obscure questions about both punctuation *and* statistics.

11. Philippe Contamine, *War in the Middle Ages* (New York: Blackwell, 1984), p. 257, citing J. N. Hillgarth, *The Spanish Kingdoms*, vol. 1 (Oxford, UK: Clarendon Press, 1978), p. 342.

12. McFarlane, *Savage Wars of Peace*, pp. 56–59; Mary Elizabeth Berry, *The Culture of Civil War in Kyoto* (Berkeley: University of California Press, 1994).

13. For example, Henry Hampton Halley, *Halley's Bible Handbook*, 24th ed. (Grand Rapids, MI: Zondervan, 1965).

14. Baron John Emerich Edward Dalberg Acton Acton et al., *The Cambridge Modern History*, vol. 2 (Cambridge, UK: Cambridge University Press, 1903), p. 290.

15. See, for example, Gibbons, "Recent Developments in the Study of the Great European Witch Hunt" (favoring estimates of 40,000 to 60,000); Davies, *Europe* (50,000); Rudolf Grimm, "Historians Take a Critical Look at Burning of Witches," Deutsche Presse-Agentur, January 5, 1999 (review of Wolfgang Behringer's *Hexen: Glaube—Verfolgung—Vermarktung*, which favorably cites estimates of 30,000 to 100,000, and unfavorably cites estimates of 6 million to 13 million).

16. Levy, *War in the Modern Great Power System*, p. 90.

17. Corvisier and Childs, eds., *Dictionary of Military History and the Art of War*, p. 470.

18. Levy, *War in the Modern Great Power System*, p. 90.

19. The most authoritative claim for high numbers is by Stephen Shenfield, "The Circassians: A Forgotten Genocide?" in Mark Levene and Penny Roberts, *The Massacre in History* (Providence, RI: Berghahn Book, 1999), p. 154 ("The number who died in the Circassian catastrophe of the 1860s could hardly, therefore, have been fewer than one million, and may well have been closer to one-and-a-half million"), but he's all alone. I found no one important who agrees with him.

20. Joseph Glascott, "600,000 Aborigines Died after 1788, Study Shows," *Sydney Morning Herald*, February 25, 1987.

21. Mike Dash, *Thug: The True Story of India's Murderous Cult* (London: Granta Books, 2005).

22. Justin McCarthy, *Death and Exile: The Ethnic Cleansing of Ottoman Muslims*, 1821- 1922 (Princeton, NJ: Darwin Press, 1995).

23. James J. Reid, *Crisis of the Ottoman Empire: Prelude to Collapse* (Stuttgart: Franz Steiner, 2000), p. 42.

24. Of the fifteen books I found giving a specific death toll, eight claimed that 200,000 civilians had died.

25. Denis Mack Smith, *Mussolini's Roman Empire* (London: Longman, 1976), pp. 40–41; John Wright, *Libya A Modern History* (Baltimore: Johns Hopkins University Press,1982), p. 42.

26. "Burundi Civil War Claims 260,000 Lives—UNFPA," Panafrican News Agency (PANA) Daily Newswire, April 25, 2004.

27. "Iraqi Official: War Dead 100,000," BBC, November 10, 2006, http://news.bbc.co.uk/2/hi/middle_east/6135526.stm; "New Study Says 151,000 Iraqi Dead," BBC, January 10, 2008, http://news.bbc.co.uk/2/hi/middle_east/7180055.stm; Jonathan Steele and Suzanne Goldenberg, "What Is the Real Death Toll in Iraq?" *Guardian*, March 19, 2008, http://www.guardian.co.uk/world/2008/mar/19/iraq; Kim Gamel, "Secret Tally Shows 87,215 Iraqis Killed since 2005," Associated Press, April 24, 2009.

SELECTED BIBLIOGRAPHY

Adams, Cecil. "Were Christians Really Thrown to the Lions?" *Straight Dope*, January 30, 2009, http://www.straightdope.com/columns/read/2841/were-christians-really-thrown-to-the-lions.

Adler, Nanci D. *Victims of Soviet Terror: The Story of the Memorial Movement*. Westport, CT: Praeger, 1993.

Anders, Wladyslaw, and Antonio Munoz. "Russian Volunteers in the German Wehrmacht in WWII," http://www.feldgrau.com/rvol.html (accessed March 28, 2011).

Applebaum, Anne. *Gulag: A History*. New York: Anchor Books, 2004.

Arendt, Hannah. *Eichmann in Jerusalem: A Report on the Banality of Evil*. New York: Penguin Books, 2006.

Associated Press. "Ethiopian Ex-Rulers Go on Trial," *New York Times*, December 14, 1994.

Atkinson, Chris. "Thirty Years War," http://www.pipeline.com/~cwa/TYWHome.htm (accessed March 28, 2011).

Auguet, Roland. *Cruelty and Civilization: The Roman Games*. New York: Barnes & Noble, 1994 (originally published by George Allen & Unwin, 1972).

Bagnall, Nigel. *Essential Histories: The Punic Wars 264–146 BC*. New York: Osprey, 2002.

Baker, G. P. *Justinian: The Last Roman Emperor*. New York: Cooper Square Press, 2002 (originally 1931).

Becker, Jasper. *Hungry Ghosts: Mao's Secret Famine*. New York: Owl Books, 1996.

Beevor, Anthony. *Stalingrad: The Fateful Siege: 1942–1943*. New York: Viking Press, 1998.

———. *The Fall of Berlin, 1945*. New York: Penguin Books, 2002.

Bell, David A. *The First Total War: Napoleon's Europe and the Birth of Warfare as We Know It*. New York: Houghton Mifflin, 2007.

Bell-Fialkoff, Andrew. "A Brief History of Ethnic Cleansing." *Foreign Affairs* 72, no. 3 (Summer 1993), p. 110.

Berkeley, Bill. "An African Success Story? Uganda." *Atlantic* 274, no. 3 (September 1994), p. 22.

———. *The Graves Are Not Yet Full*. New York: Basic Books, 2001.

Blum, Jerome. *Lord and Peasant in Russia: From the 9th to the 19th Century*. New York: Athenaeum, 1961.

Bodart, Gaston, Harald Westergaard, and Vernon L. Kellogg. *Losses of Life in Modern Wars: Austria-Hungary, France*. Oxford, UK: Clarendon Press, 1916.

Bonney, Richard. *The Thirty Years' War 1618–1648*. New York: Osprey, 2002.

Boot, Max. *The Savage Wars of Peace: Small Wars and the Rise of American Power*. New York: Basic Books, 2002.

Bos, Joan. *Joan's Mad Monarchs Series*, http://www.madmonarchs.nl/ (accessed March 15, 2011).

Bouloque, Sylvain. "Communism in Afghanistan," in Stephane Courtois et al., *The Black Book of Communism: Crimes, Terror, Repression*. Trans. Jonathan Murphy and Mark Kramer. Cambridge, MA: Harvard University Press, 1999.

Braeckman, Colette. "The Looting of the Congo." *New Internationalist*, May 1, 2004.

Bray, R. S. *Armies of Pestilence: The Impact of Disease on History*. New York: Barnes & Noble, 1996.

Bremer, Catherine. "Boiled Bones Show Aztecs Butchered, Ate Invaders." Reuters, August 23, 2006.

Britt, Albert Sydney, III, et al. *The Dawn of Modern Warfare*. Wayne, NJ: Avery Publishing Group, 1984.

Browning, Christopher R. *Ordinary Men: Reserve Police Battalion 101 and the Final Solution in Poland*. New York: Harper Perennial, 1998.

Brzezinski, Zbigniew. *Out of Control: Global Turmoil on the Eve of the Twenty-First Century*. New York: Scribner, 1993.

Buehler, Lester K. "A Study of the Taiping Rebellion," http://www.olemiss.edu/courses/inst203/taiping.txt (accessed March 15, 2011).

Bulloch, John, and Harvey Morris. *The Gulf War: Its Origins, History, and Consequences*. London: Methuen, 1989.

Bureau of Public Affairs, U.S. Department of State. "Background Note: Democratic Republic of the Congo," October 8, 2010, http://www.state.gov/r/pa/ei/bgn/2823.htm.

Bury, J. B. *The Invasion of Europe by the Barbarians*. New York: W. W. Norton, 1967 (originally published by Macmillan, 1928).

Butler, David. "Agony of the Boat People." *Newsweek*, July 2, 1979, p. 42.

Byron, Farwell. *Prisoners of the Mahdi*. New York: W. W. Norton, 1989 (originally published by Harper & Row, 1967).

Carayannis, Tatiana. "The Complex Wars of the Congo: Towards a New Analytic Approach." *Journal of Asian and African Studies* 38, no. 2–3 (August 1, 2003).

Carpenter, Dave. "Barbaric Tamerlane Anointed a Whitewashed Hero in Uzbekistan." Associated Press, January 5, 1998.

Carr, Caleb. *The Devil Soldier: The American Soldier of Fortune Who Became a God in China*. New York: Random House, 1992.

Carrasco, David L. *City of Sacrifice: The Aztec Empire and the Role of Violence in Civilization*. Boston: Beacon Press, 1999.

Castenada, Jorge G. "A Revolutionary's View of Kabila; Famed Argentine Once Joined Forces with Congo's Rebels." *Baltimore Sun*, May 25, 1997.

Center of Military History. "The Korean War, 1950–1953," in *American Military History*. Washington, DC: United States Army, 1989. Available at http://www.army.mil/cmh-pg/books/AMH/AMH-25.htm.

Chalk, Frank, and Kurt Jonassohn. *The History and Sociology of Genocide: Analyses and Case Studies*. New Haven, CT: Yale University Press, 1990.

Chang, Jung, and John Halliday. *Mao: The Unknown Story*. New York: Alfred A. Knopf, 2005.

"Cheju April 3rd Massacre to Be Unearthed." *Korea Times*, April 3, 2000.

Chirot, Daniel. *Modern Tyrants: The Power and Prevalence of Evil in Our Age.* Princeton, NJ: Princeton University Press, 1994.

Christie, Iain. "Mozambique Celebrates Year of Democracy." Reuters News, October 23, 1995.

Churchill, Winston S. *The River War—An Account of the Reconquest of the Sudan (1902).* Calicut, India: Nalanda Digital Library. Available at http://www.nalanda.nitc.ac.in/resources/english/etext-project/history/riverwar/index.htm. (accessed April 3, 2011).

Clements, Jonathan. *Coxinga and the Fall of the Ming Dynasty.* Stroud, Gloucestershire, UK: Sutton, 2004.

Clodfelter, Michael. *Warfare and Armed Conflicts: A Statistical Reference to Casualty and Other Figures, 1618–1991.* Jefferson, NC: McFarland, 1992.

Cocker, Mark. *Rivers of Blood, Rivers of Gold: Europe's Conquest of Indigenous Peoples.* New York: Grove Press, 2001.

Coe, M., Dean Snow, and Elizabeth Benson. *Atlas of Ancient America.* New York: Facts on File, 1986.

Coll, Steve. *Ghost Wars: The Secret History of the CIA, Afghanistan, and Bin Laden.* New York: Penguin Press, 2004.

Collins, Larry, and Dominique Lapierre. *Freedom at Midnight.* New York: Avon, 1975.

Columbus, Christopher. *The Journal of Christopher Columbus (during His First Voyage, 1492–93)....* Trans. Sir Clements Robert Markham. London: Chas. J. Clark, 1893.

Conquest, Robert. *The Great Terror: A Reassessment.* New York: Oxford University Press, 1992.

Corvisier, André, and John Childs, eds. *A Dictionary of Military History and the Art of War.* Cambridge, MA: Blackwell, 1994.

Courtois, Stephane, et al. *The Black Book of Communism: Crimes, Terror, Repression.* Trans. Jonathan Murphy and Mark Kramer. Cambridge, MA: Harvard University Press, 1999.

Curry, Anne. *Essential Histories: The Hundred Years' War 1337–1453.* Oxford, UK: Osprey, 2002.

Czech News Agency. "Profile: Organised Sudeten Deportations Began 50 Year Ago." CTK National News Wire, January 23, 1996.

———. "Transfer of Germans from Czechoslovakia." CTK National News Wire, January 17, 1997.

Davidson, Basil. *Africa in History: Themes and Outlines.* New York: Touchstone, 1991.

Davidson, Phillip B. *Vietnam at War: The History, 1946–1975.* New York: Oxford University Press, 1988.

Davies, Norman. *Europe: A History.* New York: HarperCollins, 1998.

Davis, Mike. *Late Victorian Holocausts: El Niño Famines and the Making of the Third World.* London: Verso, 2001.

Davis, Robert C. *Christian Slaves, Muslim Masters: White Slavery in the Mediterranean, the Barbary Coast, and Italy, 1500–1800.* New York: Palgrave Macmillan, 2003.

de Crespigny, Rafe. "Man from the Margin: Cao Cao and the Three Kingdoms." Fifty-First George Ernest Morrison Lecture in Ethnology, 1990. Available at http://www.anu.edu.au/asianstudies/decrespigny/morrison51.html (accessed March 18, 2011).

———. "The Three Kingdoms and Western Jin: A History of China in the Third Century AD." Internet edition, November 2003, http://www.anu.edu.au/asianstudies/decrespigny/3KWJin.html.

Desbarats, Jacqueline, and Karl D. Jackson. "Vietnam 1975–1982: The Cruel Peace." *Washington Quarterly,* Fall 1985.

Diamond, Jared. *The Third Chimpanzee: The Evolution and Future of the Human Animal.* New York: HarperCollins, 1992.

———. *Guns, Germs and Steel: The Fates of Human Societies.* New York: W. W. Norton, 1997.

———. *Collapse: How Societies Choose to Fail or Succeed.* New York: Viking, 2005.

Dillon, Michael. *China's Muslim Hui Community: Migration, Settlement and Sects.* New York: Routledge, 1999.

Do, Minh. "Le Loi's Struggle: Under the Ming Dynasty." *VietNow Magazine,* July 31, 1997.

Dornberg, John. "Germany's Expellees and Border Changes: An Endless Dilemma?" *German Life* 2, no. 1 (July 31, 1995), p. 18.

Drescher, Seymour. "The Atlantic Slave Trade and the Holocaust," in Alan S. Rosenbaum, ed., *Is the Holocaust Unique? Perspectives on Comparative Genocide.* Boulder, CO: Westview, 1996.

Duffy, James P., and Vincent L. Ricci. *Czars: Russia's Rulers for Over One Thousand Years.* New York: Barnes & Noble, 1995.

Duke, Lynne. "Will Peace Take Hold in Angola?" *Washington Post,* October 14, 1996.

Dumas, Samuel, and Knud Otto Vedel-Petersen. *Losses of Life Caused by War.* Oxford, UK: Clarendon Press, 1923.

Dunning, Chester S. L. *A Short History of Russia's First Civil War: The Time of Troubles and the Founding of the Romanov Dynasty.* University Park: Pennsylvania State University Press, 2004.

Durand, J. D. "The Population Statistics of China, AD 2–1953." *Population Studies* 13, no. 3 (1960), p. 209.

Durant, Will, and Ariel Durant. *The Age of Napoleon: A History of European Civilization from 1789 to 1815.* New York: MJF Books, 1975.

Dutt, Romesh. *The Economic History of India under Early British Rule.* London: Kegan Paul, Trench, Trubner, 1902.

Dykman, J. T. "The Soviet Experience in World War Two," http://www.eisenhowerinstitute.org/about/living_history/wwii_soviet_experience.dot (accessed March 17, 2011).

Edgerton, Robert B. *Death or Glory: The Legacy of the Crimean War.* Boulder, CO: Westview Press, 1999.

———. *Africa's Armies: From Honor to Infamy: A History from 1791 to the Present.* Boulder, CO: Westview Press, 2002.

Ellis, John. *World War II: A Statistical Survey.* New York: Facts on File, 1993.

Encyclopaedia Britannica, 11th ed. Cambridge, UK: University Press, 1910.

Encyclopaedia Britannica, 15th ed. Chicago: Encyclopaedia Britannica, 2005.

Epprecht, Marc. "Democratizing the Southern African Past." *Canadian Journal of History* 30, no. 2 (August 1995), pp. 323–327.

———. [Review of *Terrific Majesty: The Powers of Shaka Zulu and the Limits of Historical Invention,* by Carolyn Hamilton]. *Canadian Journal of History* 34, no. 3 (December 1999), pp. 423–426.

Erickson, John and David Dilks. *Barbarossa: The Axis and the Allies.* Edinburgh: Edinburgh University Press, 1994.

Erickson, John, and Ljubica Erickson. *Hitler Versus Stalin: The Second World War on the Eastern Front in Photographs.* London: Carlton Books, 2001.

"Ex-Ugandan Dictator Idi Amin, 80, Dies. A Bizarre, Brutal Leader, He Ruined the Economy and Killed Thousands." *Seattle Times,* August 16, 2003.

"False Dmitry I; The Unlikely Tsar." *Russian Life* 48, no. 4 (August 31, 2005), p. 18.

Farquhar, Michael. *A Treasury of Royal Scandals.* New York: Penguin, 2001.

Fenby, Jonathan. "Crossroads of Conquest." *South China Morning Post* (Hong Kong), November 20, 1999.

Ferguson, Niall. *The War of the World: Twentieth-Century Conflict and the Descent of the West.* New York: Penguin, 2006.

Figes, Orlando. *A People's Tragedy: A History of the Russian Revolution.* New York: Penguin, 1996.

Fisk, Robert. *The Great War for Civilisation: The Conquest of the Middle East.* New York: Alfred A. Knopf, 2005.

Fitzgerald, C. P. *China: A Short Cultural History*, 3rd ed. New York: Praeger, 1973.

———. *Mao Tse-Tung and China.* New York: Penguin Books, 1977.

Fitzgerald, Mary Anne. "Tyrant for the Taking." *Times* (London), April 20, 1991.

Forbath, Peter. *The River Congo.* Boston: Houghton Mifflin, 1991 (originally published 1977).

Ford, Peter. "Ex-Russian Satellite Enjoys Setting Its Own Agenda." *Christian Science Monitor*, June 3, 1997.

Frazier, Ian. "Destroying Baghdad." *New Yorker*, April 25, 2005.

Fremont-Barnes, Gregory, and Todd Fisher. *The Napoleonic Wars: The Rise and Fall of an Empire.* Oxford, UK: Osprey, 2004.

French, Howard W. "Kagame's Hidden War in the Congo." *New York Review of Books*, September 24, 2009, http://www.nybooks.com/articles/23054.

Frieda, Leonie. *Catherine de Medici: Renaissance Queen of France.* New York: Harper Perennial, 2006.

Fuller, J. F. C. *A Military History of the Western World*, vol. 2: *From the Spanish Armada to the Battle of Waterloo.* New York: Da Capo Press, 1955.

Fuller, William C. *Strategy and Power in Russia:1600–1914.* New York: Free Press, 1992.

Galloway, Joseph. "We Are Mute and Horrified Witnesses to a Reign of Terror." Knight Ridder Newspapers, November 8, 2004.

Gascoigne, Bamber. *The Great Moguls.* New York: Harper & Row, 1971.

Getty, J. Arch, and Roberta T. Manning, eds. *Stalinist Terror: New Perspectives.* New York: Cambridge University Press, 1993.

Gibbon, Edward. *Decline and Fall of the Roman Empire*, ed. Henry Hart Milman. New York: Peter Fenelon Collier, 1845. Available at http://www.sacred-texts.com/cla/gibbon/index.htm (accessed March 17, 2011).

Gibbons, Jenny. "Recent Developments in the Study of the Great European Witch Hunt." *Pomegranate: A New Journal of Neopagan Thought* (Corbett, OR) Issue 5 (1998).

Gilbert, Joshua. "The Goguryeo-Sui Wars." *Armchair General*, November 4, 2007, http://www.armchair general.com/the-goguryeo-sui-wars.htm.

Gilbert, Martin. *A History of the Twentieth Century.* New York: Avon Books, 1997.

Glantz, David. *The Siege of Leningrad 1941–44: 900 Days of Terror.* Osceola, WI: MBI, 2001.

GlobalSecurity.org. "Congo War," http://www.globalsecurity.org/military/world/war/congo.htm (accessed March 17, 2011).

Goodspeed, Peter. "Grim North Korea Breaks Its Isolation: Reclusive, Impoverished Nation Cracks Open Its Doors to Foreign Tourists, Businessmen." *Edmonton Journal* (CanWest News Service), November 6, 2005.

Goodwin, Jason. *Lords of the Horizon: A History of the Ottoman Empire.* New York: Henry Holt, 1998.

Goozner, Merrill. "World Watches North Korea; Early Signs Are 'Encouraging,' Clinton Says." *Chicago Tribune*, July 10, 1994.

Graff, David A. *Medieval Chinese Warfare, 300–900*. New York: Routledge, 2002.

Grant, Michael. *The Fall of the Roman Empire*. New York: Collier, 1990.

Grau, Lester W. "The Soviet-Afghan War: A Superpower Mired in the Mountains." *Journal of Slavic Military Studies* 17, no. 1 (March 2004). Available at http://fmso.leavenworth.army.mil/documents/miredinmount.htm (accessed March 17, 2011).

Green, Barbara. "Stalinist Terror and the Question of Genocide:The Great Famine," in Alan S. Rosenbaum, ed., *Is the Holocaust Unique? Perspectives on Comparative Genocide*. Boulder, CO: Westview Press, 1996.

Green, Dominic. *Three Empires on the Nile: The Victorian Jihad, 1869–1899*. New York: Free Press, 2007.

Greenway, H. D. S. "New Waves across the Steppes." *Boston Globe*, May 27, 1998.

Grenville, J. A. S. *A History of the World: In the Twentieth Century*. Cambridge, MA: Harvard University Press, 1994.

Grousset, Rene. *Conqueror of the World: The Life of Chingis-khan*. New York: Viking Press, 1972.

Grubin, David, director. *Napoleon*. PBS, November 2000; PBS Home Video, 2001 DVD.

Gunther, John. *Inside Asia*. New York: Harper & Brothers, 1939.

Hack, Karl, and Tobias Rettig. *Colonial Armies in Southeast Asia*. New York: Routledge, 2006.

Halsall, Paul, ed. *Sources for the Three Slave Revolts*, http://www.fordham.edu/halsall/ancient/3slaverevolttexts.htm (accessed April 3, 2011).

Hansen, Waldemar. *The Peacock Throne: The Drama of Mogul India*. New York: Holt, Rinehart & Winston, 1972.

Hanson, Victor Davis. *Wars of the Ancient Greeks*. London: Cassell, 1999.

———. *Carnage and Culture: Landmark Battles and the Rise of Western Power*. New York: Anchor Books, 2001.

Harden, Blaine, "2 Decades Later, Biafra Remains Lonely Precedent." *Washington Post*, June 27, 1988, p. A1.

Harner, Michael. "The Enigma of Aztec Sacrifice." *Natural History* 86, no. 4 (April 1977), pp. 46–51. Available at http://www.latinamericanstudies.org/aztecs/sacrifice.htm.

Harris, Marvin. *Cannibals and Kings: Origins of Cultures*. New York: Vintage, 1977.

Harrison, Selig S. "End of the Road." *Globe and Mail* (Toronto), February 11, 1989.

Hartley, Aidan. "Ethiopian 'Reign of Terror' Figures in Mass Trial." Reuters News, December 12, 1994.

Hassan, Mohamed Olad. "Somali Warlord Says Battle for Mogadishu Not Over." Associated Press, June 11, 2006.

Hastings, Max. *The Korean War*. New York: Touchstone, 1987.

Henige, David P. *Numbers from Nowhere: The American Indian Contact Population Debate*. Norman: University of Oklahoma Press, 1998.

Henry, Neil. "Mengistu Leaves Ethiopia in Shambles." *Washington Post*, May 22, 1991.

Hildinger, Erik. *Warriors of the Steppe: A Military History of Central Asia, 500 B.C. to 1700 A.D.* Cambridge, MA: Da Capo Press, 1997.

Hirst, David. "Saddam Hussein: Brutal and Opportunist Dictator of Iraq, He Wreaked Havoc on His Country, the Middle East and the World." *Guardian*, December 30, 2006, http://www.guardian.co.uk/Iraq/Story/0,,1980293,00.html.

Hobsbawm, Eric. *The Age of Extremes: A History of the World, 1914–1991*. New York: Vintage, 1994.

Hochschild, Adam. *The Unquiet Ghost: Russians Remember Stalin*. New York: Penguin, 1994.

———. *Leopold's Ghost*. New York: Mariner Books, 1998.

———. *Bury the Chains: Prophets and Rebels in the Fight to Free an Empire's Slaves*. New York: Mariner Books, 2005.

Hollway, Don. "Thirty Years' War: Battle of Breitenfeld." *Military History* (February 1996). Available at http://www.historynet.com/wars_conflicts/17_18_century/3030301.html.

Ho Ping-to. *Studies in the Population of China, 1368–1953*. Cambridge, MA: Harvard University Press, 1967.

Horne, Alistair. *La Belle France: A Short History*. New York: Vintage, 2004.

———. *A Savage War of Peace: Algeria 1954–1962*. New York: New York Review Books, 2006.

Howarth, Patrick. *Attila King of the Huns: The Man and the Myth*. New York: Barnes & Noble, 1994.

Hoyt, Edwin P. *199 Days: The Battle for Stalingrad*. New York: Tom Doherty Associates, 1993.

Hughes, Lindsey. *Peter the Great: A Biography*. New Haven, CT: Yale University Press, 2002.

Hui, Victoria Tin-bor. *War and State Formation in Ancient China and Early Modern Europe*. New York: Cambridge University Press, 2005.

International Rescue Committee. "Congo Crisis," http://www.theirc.org/special-reports/congo-forgotten-crisis (accessed March 28, 2011).

Jahan, Rounaq. "Genocide in Bangladesh," in Samuel Totten et al., eds., *Century of Genocide: Critical Essays and Eyewitness Accounts*, 2d ed. New York: Routledge, 2004.

Jensen, Holger. "Peace Is as Difficult as War in Mozambique." *Rocky Mountain News*, October 23, 1994.

Johnson, Larry. "A Trip to Baghdad Reveals a Nation Sagging under the Weight of Sanctions." *Seattle Post-Intelligencer*, May 11, 1999.

Johnson, Paul. *Modern Times: The World from the Twenties to the Eighties*. New York: Harper & Row, 1983.

Jones, Terry, director. "Gladiators: The Brutal Truth." *Medieval Lives*, BBC 1999; BBC Warner, 2008 DVD.

Jordan, Winthrop D. *The White Man's Burden: Historical Origins of Racism in the United States*. New York: Oxford University Press, 1974.

Juvaynī, Alā al-Dīn Atā Malik. *Genghis Khan: The History of the World Conqueror*. Manchester, UK: Manchester University Press, 1997.

Kadane, Kathy. "U.S. Accused of Role in Massacre. Ex-Envoys Say They Gave Indonesia Names of Its Enemies." *Chicago Tribune*, May 23, 1990.

Kaplan, Robert D. "A Microcosm of Africa's Ills; Sudan." *Atlantic* 257 (April 1986), p. 20.

———. "Starting Over; A New Government Has Brought Relative Stability to Uganda, for the Time Being." *Atlantic* 259 (April 1987), p. 18.

Kaplow, Larry. "Consequences of Kuwait: Sanctions Have Iraq Withering." *Atlanta Journal and Constitution*, June 13, 1999.

Karmini, Niniek. "40 Years on, Indonesian Victims of One of 20th Century's Worst Massacres Wait for Justice." Associated Press, September 30, 2005.

Karnow, Stanley. *Vietnam: A History*. New York: Viking, 1983.

Keay, John. *India: A History*. New York: Gove Press, 2000.

Keegan, John. *The Face of Battle*. New York: Vintage Books, 1976.

———. *The Mask of Command*. New York: Penguin, 1987.

———. *The Price of Admiralty.* New York: Penguin, 1988.

———. *The Second World War.* New York: Penguin, 1990.

———. *A History of Warfare.* New York: Vintage Books, 1993.

———, ed. *Harper Collins Atlas of the Second World War.* London: Times Books, 1997.

———. *The First World War.* New York: Vintage Books, 2000.

Keen, Benjamin. *The Aztec Image in Western Thought.* New Brunswick, NJ: Rutgers University Press, 1990.

Kiernan, Ben. *Blood and Soil: A World History of Genocide and Extermination from Sparta to Darfur.* New Haven, CT: Yale University Press, 2007.

Kinder, Hermann, and Werner Hilgemann. *The Anchor Atlas of World History.* New York: Anchor Books, 1978.

Kingsley, Sean. *God's Gold: A Quest for the Lost Temple Treasures of Jerusalem.* New York: Harper, 2007.

Kinzer, Stephen. "A Kinder, Gentler Tamerlane Inspires Uzbekistan." *New York Times*, November 10, 1997.

Klein, Shelley. *The Most Evil Dictators in History.* New York: Barnes & Noble, 2004.

Klyuchevsky, Vasili. *Peter the Great.* New York: Vintage, 1958.

Knecht, Robert J. *Essential Histories: The French Religious Wars 1562–1598.* Oxford, UK: Osprey, 2002.

Kohn, George Childs. *Dictionary of Wars*, rev. ed. New York: Checkmark, 1999.

Krah, Markus. "The Germans as Victims?" *Jerusalem Report*, June 17, 2002, p. 30.

Kyle, Donald. *Spectacles of Death in Ancient Rome.* New York: Routledge, 2001.

"The Land System of the Heavenly Kingdom," in *Modern History Sourcebook: The Taiping Rebellion, 1851–1864*, http://www.fordham.edu/halsall/mod/taiping.html (accessed March 28, 2011).

Lawless, Patrick. "After the Terror, the Sun May Rise on Bloody Mozambique." *Sydney Morning Herald*, October 22, 1994.

Lei Hai-tsung. "The Warring States," originally published in typescript by the War Area Service Corps, Kunming, March 1943, http://www.sfu.ca/davidlamcentre/nacrp/articles/leihaizong/leihaizong .html (accessed March 17, 2011).

Lekic, Slobodan. "Controversy over Elusive Document Revives Interest in 1965 Coup." Associated Press, March 30, 2000.

Lemarchand, Rene. "The Rwanda Genocide," in Samuel Totten et al., eds., *Century of Genocide: Critical Essays and Eyewitness Accounts*, 2d ed. New York: Routledge, 2004.

Leonard, Andrew. "The 'History War' in Northeast Asia." *Salon*, March 14, 2007, http://www.salon .com/tech/htww/2007/03/14/history_wars/print.html.

Levy, Jack. *War in the Modern Great Power System, 1495–1975.* Lexington: University Press of Kentucky, 1983.

Liddell Hart, B. H. *History of the Second World War.* New York: G. P. Putnam's Sons, 1970.

Lieu, Samuel N. C. *Manichaeism in the Later Roman Empire and Medieval China.* Tubingen: Mohr Siebeck, 1992.

———. *Manichaeism in Central Asia and China.* Boston: Brill, 1998.

Lincoln, W. Bruce. *Red Victory: A History of the Russian Civil War.* New York: Da Capo Press, 1989.

Linden, Eugene. "The Global Famine of 1877 and 1899." *Globalist*, September 6, 2006, http://www .theglobalist.com/DBWeb/StoryId.aspx?StoryId=5516.

Livi-Bacci, Massimo. *A Concise History of World Population.* Oxford, UK: Blackwell, 2001.

Lloyd, Christopher. *The Navy and the Slave Trade: The Suppression of the African Slave Trade in the Nineteenth Century.* London: Cass, 1968.

Loewen, James W. *Lies My Teacher Told Me.* New York: Touchstone, 1995.

Lorge, Peter Allan. *War, Politics and Society in Early Modern China, 900–1795.* New York: Taylor & Francis, 2005.

Lynn, John A. *The French Wars 1667–1714.* Oxford, UK: Osprey, 2002.

Maalouf, Amin. *The Crusades through Arab Eyes.* New York: Schocken Books, 1984.

Mace, James E. "Soviet Man-Made Famine in Ukraine," in Samuel Totten et al., eds., *Century of Genocide: Critical Essays and Eyewitness Accounts,* 2d ed. New York: Routledge, 2004.

Maddison, Angus. *Contours of the World Economy, 1–2030 AD: Essays in Macro-economic History.* New York: Oxford University Press, 2001.

Man, John. *Genghis Khan: Life, Death, and Resurrection.* New York: Thomas Dunne Books, 2004.

———. *The Terra Cotta Army: China's First Emperor and the Birth of a Nation.* Cambridge, MA: Da Capo Press, 2008.

Manchester, William. *American Caesar.* New York: Dell, 1978.

Mann, Charles C. *1491: New Revelations of the Americas before Columbus.* New York: Vintage, 2005.

Manthorpe, Jonathan. "Mengistu's Brutal Regime Lasted Surprisingly Long." *Toronto Star,* May 22, 1991.

Manucci, Niccolao. *Mogul India, 1653–1708.* London: John Murray, 1908.

Marcus, David L. "Relentless War Wears on Angolans: Many Speak of Yearning for Peace Yet Strife Persists." *Dallas Morning News,* January 23, 1994.

Margolin, Jean-Louis. "China: A Long March into Night," in Stephane Courtois et al., *The Black Book of Communism: Crimes, Terror, Repression.* Trans. Jonathan Murphy and Mark Kramer. Cambridge, MA: Harvard University Press, 1999.

Marozzi, Justin. *Tamerlane: Sword of Islam, Conqueror of the World.* Cambridge, MA: Da Capo Press, 2004.

Marrus, Michael Robert. *The Unwanted: European Refugees from the First World War through the Cold War.* Philadelphia: Temple University Press, 2002.

Marshall, Julian. "Obituary: Milton Obote: The First Leader of an Independent Uganda, He Imposed Virtual One-Man Rule, but Was Twice Overthrown." *Guardian,* October 12, 2005.

Massing, Michael. "Does Democracy Avert Famine? Amartya Sen's Famous Theory Is Being Tested by Starvation in India." *New York Times,* March 1, 2003.

Matray, James I. "Revisiting Korea: Exposing Myths of the Forgotten War." *Prologue Magazine* 34, no. 2 (Summer 2002). Available at http://www.archives.gov/publications/prologue/2002/summer/korean-myths-1.html.

Mayell, Hillary. "Genghis Khan a Prolific Lover, DNA Data Implies." *National Geographic,* February 14, 2003, http://news.nationalgeographic.com/news/2003/02/0214_030214_genghis.html.

Mayer, Arno J. *The Furies: Violence and Terror in the French and Russian Revolutions.* Princeton, NJ: Princeton University Press, 2000.

Mazower, Mark. *Dark Continent: Europe's Twentieth Century.* New York: Vintage, 1998.

McDougall, Alan. "Dirty Hands: Atrocities of World War I." Channel 4, 2002, http://www.channel4.com/history/microsites/H/history/c-d/dirtyhands.html.

McEvedy, Colin. *The Penguin Atlas of Modern History (to 1815).* New York: Penguin, 1972.

———. *The Atlas of World Population History.* New York: Penguin, 1978.

——. *The New Penguin Atlas of Medieval History.* New York: Penguin, 1992.

——. *The Penguin Atlas of African History.* New York: Penguin, 1995.

——. *The Penguin Historical Atlas of the Pacific.* New York: Penguin, 2002.

McEvedy, Colin, and David Woodroffe. *The New Penguin Atlas of Recent History: Europe since 1815.* New York: Penguin, 1998.

McFarlane, Alan. *The Savage Wars of Peace: England, Japan and the Malthusian Trap.* New York: Palgrave Macmillan, 2003.

Mcgreal, Chris. "Worrying Past of a Rebel in Crocodile Shoes." *Guardian,* May 21, 1997.

McKillop, Heather Irene. *The Ancient Maya: New Perspectives.* Santa Barbara, CA: ABC-CLIO, 2004.

McKnight, Michael. "Goguryeo: Ancient Kingdom, Modern Passions." *Invest Korea Journal,* January–February 2008, http://www.investkorea.org/InvestKoreaWar/work/journal/content/content_main.jsp?code=4540408.

McLynn, Frank. *Villa and Zapata: A History of the Mexican Revolution.* New York: Carroll & Graf, 2000.

McMahon, Colin. "The Rehabilitation of Tamerlane." *Chicago Tribune,* January 17, 1999.

McNeill, William H. *The Pursuit of Power.* Chicago: University of Chicago Press, 1982.

——. *The Rise of the West: A History of the Human Community.* Chicago: University of Chicago Press, 1990.

McPherson, James M. *Battle Cry of Freedom.* New York: Oxford University Press, 1988.

McWilliam, Ian. "Uzbekistan Restores Samarkand to Boost Nationalist Pride." *Los Angeles Times,* August 23, 1994.

Mehta, J. L. *Advanced Study in the History of Medieval India.* New Delhi: Sterling, 1996.

Meier, Christian. *Caesar: A Biography.* New York: Basic Books, 1982.

Meisner, Maurice. *Mao's China and After,* 3rd ed. New York: Free Press, 1999.

Melson, Robert F. "The Armenian Genocide as Precursor and Prototype of Twentieth-Century Genocide," in Alan S. Rosenbaum, ed., *Is the Holocaust Unique? Perspectives on Comparative Genocide.* Boulder, CO: Westview Press, 1996.

Meltzer, Milton. *Slavery: A World History.* New York: Da Capo Press, 1993.

Miller, Kelly. *Kelly Miller's History of the World War for Human Rights,* 1919. Available at http://www.gutenberg.org/files/19179/19179-h/19179-h.htm (accessed March 28, 2011).

Miller, Reid G. "Marines Pull Last Peacekeepers out of Somalia, Ending $2 Billion Mission." Associated Press, March 3, 1995.

Milton, Giles. *White Gold: The Extraordinary Story of Thomas Pellow and Islam's One Million White Slaves.* New York: Farrar, Straus & Giroux, 2004.

Mommsen, Theodor. *History of Rome.* New York: Scribner, 1908.

Morgan, David. *The Mongols.* Oxford, UK: Blackwell, 1986.

Mortimer, Ian. "Poitiers: High Point of the Hundred Years' War." *History Today* 56, no. 9 (September 1, 2006), p. 41(7).

Mote, Frederick W. *Imperial China, 900–1800.* Cambridge, MA: Harvard University Press, 1999.

Mote, Frederick W., and Denis Twitchett, eds. *The Cambridge History of China,* vol. 7: *The Ming Dynasty, 1368–1644, Part 1.* Cambridge, UK: Cambridge University Press, 1988.

Muir, Rory. *Tactics and the Experience of Battle in the Age of Napoleon.* New Haven, CT: Yale University Press, 2000.

Murphy, John. "Hopes High as Rwanda, Congo Sign Peace Pact." *Baltimore Sun,* July 31, 2002.

Murphy, William S. "Lincoln Brigade Survivors Relive Wartime Exploits." *Los Angeles Times*, April 25, 1986.

Newark, Tim. *Medieval Warlords*. Poole, UK: Blandford Press, 1987.

Newsinger, John. "The Taiping Peasant Revolt." *Monthly Review*, October 2000.

Nolen, Stephanie. "The War on Women." *Globe and Mail* (Toronto), November 27, 2004.

Norwich, John Julius. *A Short History of Byzantium*. New York: Vintage Books, 1997.

Notar, Beth E. Book review, "The Chinese Sultanate: Islam, Ethnicity, and the Panthay Rebellion in Southwest China, 1856–1873." *Pacific Affairs* 80, no. 1 (March 22, 2007), p. 98(2).

Obermeyer, Ziad, Christopher J. L. Murray, and Emmanuela Gakidou. "Fifty Years of Violent War Deaths from Vietnam to Bosnia: Analysis of Data from the World Health Survey Programme." *British Medical Journal* 336 (2008), p. 1482.

"Ojukwu Blames Civil War on Gowon." *Vanguard Daily* (Lagos), March 1, 2001.

Omestad, Thomas. "Gulag Nation." *U.S. News & World Report*, June 23, 2003, p. 12.

Ormsby, Eric. "The Hidden Historian." *New York Sun*, September 21, 2005.

Orwell, George. *Homage to Catalonia*. New York: Houghton Mifflin Harcourt, 1952.

Osborn, Andrew. "Genghis Khan: He's Mr. Nice Guy Now." *Hamilton Spectator* (Ontario), May 12, 2005.

Osborn, William M. *The Wild Frontier: Atrocities during the American-Indian War from Jamestown Colony to Wounded Knee*. New York: Random House, 2000.

O'Shea, Stephen. *The Perfect Heresy: The Revolutionary Life and Death of the Medieval Cathars*. New York: Walker, 2000.

Ottaway, David B. " 'Slave Trade' in Mozambicans Cited." *Washington Post*, November 26, 1990.

Overy, Richard, ed. *Hammond Atlas of the 20th Century*. London: Times Books, 1996.

———. *Russia's War*. New York: Penguin Books, 1997.

Pakenham, Thomas. *The Scramble for Africa*. New York: Avon Books, 1991.

———. "Where a Million Died." Review of *Harrowing of Mozambique*, by William Finnegan. *New York Times*, April 26, 1992.

Palmer, Alan. *The Decline and Fall of the Ottoman Empire*. New York: Barnes & Noble, 1992.

Palmowski, Jan. *Dictionary of Twentieth Century World History*. Oxford, UK: Oxford University Press, 1997.

Pankhurst, Richard. "A History of Early Twentieth Century Ethiopia." Series of 20 articles. *Addis Tribune*, January–May 1997.

Parenti, Christian. "Back to the Motherland: Cuba in Africa." *Monthly Review*, June 2003, http://www.monthlyreview.org/0603parenti.htm.

Paterculus, C. Velleius. *The Roman History*. Loeb Classical Library, 1924. Available at http://penelope.uchicago.edu/Thayer/E/Roman/Texts/Velleius_Paterculus/home.html.

Peers, Chris. *Warlords of China: 700BC to AD1662*. London: Arms & Armour Press, 1998.

Picton, John. "Tamerlane. The Curse of 'The Viper' Reached Right into the 20th Century." *Toronto Star*, July 12, 1987.

Pipes, Daniel. "A Border Adrift: Origins of the Iraq-Iran War," 1983, http://www.danielpipes.org/article/164.

Platonov, S. F. *The Time of Troubles: A Historical Study of the Internal Crisis and Social Struggle in Sixteenth- and Seventeenth-Century Muscovy*. Lawrence: University Press of Kansas, 1985.

Plutarch. *Parallel Lives*, Loeb Classical Library ed. New York: G.P. Putnam, multiple years. Available at http://penelope.uchicago.edu/Thayer/E/Roman/Texts/Plutarch/Lives/home.html.

Pocha, Jehangir S. "Once-Feared Invader's Reputation Gets a Revival." *Boston Globe*, July 3, 2005.

Porch, Douglas. *Wars of Empire*. London: Cassell, 2000.

Powell, Ivor. "The Butcher SA Plays Host To." *Mail and Guardian* (Johannesburg), December 3, 1999.

Prasad, J. Durga. *History of the Andhras up to 1565 A. D.* Guntur: P. G. Publishers, 1988. Available at http://www.katragadda.com/articles/HistoryOfTheAndhras.pdf (accessed March 9, 2011).

Pratt, Fletcher. *The Battles That Changed History*. Garden City, NY: Dolphin, 1956.

Pulleyblank, Edwin G. "An Lu-shan Rebellion and the Origins of Chronic Militarism in Late T'ang China," in John Curtis Perry and Bardwell L. Smith, eds., *Essays on T'ang Society: The Interplay of Social, Political and Economic Forces*. Leiden, The Netherlands: E. J. Brill, 1976.

"Radio Expeditions: Coltan Mining and Eastern Congo's Gorillas." NPR, December 20, 2001, http://www.npr.org/programs/re/archivesdate/2001/dec/20011220.coltan.html.

Radzinsky, Edvard. *Stalin*. New York: Anchor Books, 1997.

Rake, Alan. "Where Kabila Went Wrong." *New African*, March 1, 2001.

Rapoport, Louis. "Knives Are Out for a Bloodstained Ruler." *Sydney Morning Herald*, April 28, 1990.

Riasanovsky, Nicholas V. *The History of Russia*, 6th ed. New York: Oxford University Press, 2000.

Ribeiro, Darcy. "Indigenous Cultures and Languages in Brazil," in Janice Hopper, ed., *Indians of Brazil in the Twentieth Century*. Washington, DC: Institute for Cross-Cultural Research, 1967.

Riley-Smith, Jonathan. *The Crusades: A Short History*. New Haven, CT: Yale University Press, 1987.

Ritter, E. A. *Shaka Zulu*. New York: Penguin, 1955.

Ritter, Gerhard. *Frederick the Great*. Berkeley: University of California Press, 1968.

Rogers, Guy MacLean. *Alexander: The Ambiguity of Greatness*. New York: Random House, 2004.

Rogozinski, Jan. *A Brief History of the Caribbean: From the Arawak and the Carib to the Present*. New York: Meridian, 1992.

"Romance of the Three Kingdoms." TV Tropes, http://tvtropes.org/pmwiki/pmwiki.php/Literature/RomanceOfTheThreeKingdoms (accessed March 20, 2011).

Rosen, William. *Justinian's Flea: The First Great Plague and the End of the Roman Empire*. New York: Penguin, 2007.

Rosenbaum, Alan S., ed. *Is the Holocaust Unique? Perspectives on Comparative Genocide*. Boulder, CO: Westview Press, 1996.

Rosenburg, Tina. *The Haunted Land: Facing Europe's Ghosts after Communism*. New York: Vintage, 1995.

Rothenberg, Gunther. *The Napoleonic Wars*. London: Cassell, 1999.

Rowen, Herbert H. *A History of Early Modern Europe: 1500–1815*. Indianapolis: Bobbs-Merrill, 1960.

Ruiz, Julius. "Franco and the Spanish Civil War." *History Review*, December 1, 2007.

Rummel, Rudolph J. *Lethal Politics: Soviet Genocide and Mass Murder since 1917*. New Brunswick, NJ: Transaction, 1990.

———. *China's Bloody Century: Genocide and Mass Murder since 1900*. New Brunswick, NJ: Transaction, 1991.

———. *Death by Government*. New Brunswick, NJ: Transaction, 1994.

———. *Statistics of Democide*, http://www.hawaii.edu/powerkills.

Sale, George, et al. *An Universal history, from the earliest account of time. Compiled from original authors; and illustrated with maps, cuts, notes, &c. With a general index to the whole.* London: Osborne, 1747.

Salisbury, Harrison E. *The 900 Days: The Siege of Leningrad.* Cambridge, MA: Da Capo Press, 2003.

Salopek, Paul. "Inklings of Peace Intrude in Bereft Angola. Power Struggle over Oil and Diamonds May Be Near End as Government Forces Put Rebels to Rout." *Chicago Tribune*, January 14, 2000.

Sanchez, Carlos. "A Victory Tempered by Sorrow." *Washington Post*, May 26, 1991.

Sarkees, Meredith Reid. "The Correlates of War Data on War: An Update to 1997." *Conflict Management and Peace Science* 18, no. 1 (2000), pp. 123–144. Available at http://www.correlatesofwar.org/cow2 data/WarData/IntraState/Intra-State War Format (V 3-0).htm.

Scheidel, Walter. *Debating Roman Demography.* Boston: Brill, 2001.

Scheina, Robert L. *Latin America's Wars*, vol. 1: *The Age of the Caudillo, 1791–1899.* Washington, DC: Brassey's, 2003.

Schiller, Friedrich. *History of the Thirty Years' War in Germany*, in *The Works of Frederick Schiller.* Trans. A. J. W. Morrison. London: Henry G. Bohn, 1860.

Schom, Alan. *Napoleon Bonaparte.* New York: Harper Perennial, 1997.

Scott, Jonathan, and Muhammad Qāsim Hindū-Šāh Astarābādī Firišta. *Ferishta's History of Dekkan from the First Mahummedan Conquests.* Shrewsbury: J and W Eddowes, 1794.

Segal, Ronald. *Islam's Black Slaves.* New York: Farrar, Straus & Giroux, 2001.

Service, Robert. *A History of Twentieth-Century Russia.* Cambridge, MA: Harvard University Press, 1997.

Sewell, Robert. *A Forgotten Empire: Vijayanagar; A Contribution to the History of India.* Project Gutenberg, 2002. Available at http://www.gutenberg.org/cache/epub/3310/pg3310.html.

Shenon, Philip. "Washington and Baghdad Agree on One Point: Sanctions Hurt." *New York Times*, November 22, 1998.

Shi, Youzhong. *The Taiping Ideology: Its Sources, Interpretations, and Influences.* Seattle: University of Washington Press, 1967.

Shirer, William L. *The Rise and Fall of the Third Reich.* New York: Fawcett Crest, 1960.

Sieno, Casimiro. "Angolan Peace Talks Restart as Fighting Continues." Associated Press, July 29, 1994.

Sima Qian. *Records of the Grand Historian: Qin Dynasty.* Trans. Burton Watson. New York: Columbia Universtiy Press, 1993.

Simkin, John. "The Vietnam War," Spartacus Educational, http://www.spartacus.schoolnet.co.uk/VietnamWar.htm (accessed April 3, 2011).

Sivard, Ruth Leger. *World Military and Social Expenditures 1987–88*, 12th ed. Washington, DC.: World Priorities, 1988.

Skidmore, Thomas E., and Peter H. Smith. *Modern Latin America*, 4th ed. New York: Oxford University Press, 1997.

Smith, Helmut Wasser, ed. *The Holocaust and Other Genocides: History, Representation, Ethics.* Nashville: Vanderbilt University Press, 2002.

Solzhenitsyn, Alexandr I. *The Gulag Archipelago.* New York: Harper & Row, 1973.

Sommerville, J. P. "Russia's Time of Troubles." *Seventeenth Century Europe*, Spring 2006, http://history.wisc.edu/sommerville/351/351-10.htm.

Sorokin, Pitirim. *Social and Cultural Dynamics*, vol. 3. New York: Bedminster Press, 1962.

Spaeth, Anthony, et al. "The Price of Freedom." *Time*, August 11, 1997.

Spence, Jonathan D. *The Search for Modern China*. New York: W. W. Norton, 1991.

———. *God's Chinese Son: The Taiping Heavenly Kingdom of Hong Xiuquan*. New York: W. W. Norton, 1996.

Spence, Jonathan D., and John E. Willis, eds. *From Ming to Ch'ing*. New Haven, CT: Yale University Press, 1979.

Sperling, Carrie. "Mother of Atrocities: Pauline Nyiramasuhuko's Role in the Rwandan Genocide." *Fordham Urban Law Journal* 33, no. 2 (January 1, 2006), p. 637.

Staff of Strategy & Tactics Magazine, *War in the East: The Russo-German Conflict, 1941–45*. New York: Simulation Publications, 1977.

Stannard, David E. *American Holocaust*. New York: Oxford University Press, 1993.

Stewart, Matthew. "Catastrophe at Smyrna." *History Today* 54, no. 7 (July 1, 2004), p. 27.

Stockwin, Harvey. "East Pakistan's Bloody Death, 30 Years On." *Japan Times*, March 25, 2001.

Strachan, Hew. *The First World War*. London: Penguin Books, 2003.

Strauss, Barry. *The Battle of Salamis: The Naval Encounter That Saved Greece—and Western Civilization*. New York: Simon & Schuster, 2005.

———. *The Spartacus War*. New York: Simon & Schuster, 2010.

Strosser, Ed, and Michael Prince. *Stupid Wars: A Citizen's Guide to Botched Putsches, Failed Coups, Inane Invasions, and Ridiculous Revolutions*. New York: HarperCollins, 2008.

Suellentrop, Chris. "Are 1 Million Children Dying in Iraq?" *Slate*, October 9, 2001.

Thomas, Hugh. *The Slave Trade: The Story of the Atlantic Slave Trade: 1440–1870*. New York: Simon & Schuster, 1997.

———. *Rivers of Gold: The Rise of the Spanish Empire, from Columbus to Magellan*. New York: Random House, 2003.

Thornton, Russell. *American Indian Holocaust and Survival: A Population History since 1492*. Norman: University of Oklahoma Press, 1987.

Time-Life Books. *Powers of the Crown: Time Frame AD 1600–1700*. Alexandria, VA: Time-Life Books, 1989.

———. *Aztecs: Reign of Blood and Splendor*. Alexandria, VA: Time-Life Books, 1992.

Toland, John. *The Rising Sun: The Decline and Fall of the Japanese Empire 1936–1945*. New York: Bantam, 1970.

Totten, Samuel. *Dictionary of Genocide: A—L*. Westport, CT: Greenwood Press, 2008.

Totten, Samuel, et al., eds. *Century of Genocide: Critical Essays and Eyewitness Accounts*, 2d ed. New York: Routledge, 2004.

Trueman, Chris. *France in the Sixteenth Century: French Wars of Religion*. History Learning Site, 2000–2007, http://www.historylearningsite.co.uk/FWR.htm (accessed March 28, 2011).

Tuchman, Barbara W. *A Distant Mirror: The Calamitous 14th Century*. New York: Ballantine, 1978.

Turchin, Peter. *Historical Dynamics: Why States Rise and Fall*. Princeton, NJ: Princeton University Press, 2003.

Twitchett, Denis, and John K. Fairbank, eds. *The Cambridge History of China*, vol. 1: *The Ch'in and Han Empires 221 B.C.–A.D. 220*. New York: Cambridge University Press, 1986.

———. *The Cambridge History of China*, vol. 3: *Sui and T'ang China 589–906, Part 1*. New York: Cambridge University Press, 1986.

Uhalley, Stephen, Jr. "The Taipings at Ningpo: The Significance of a Forgotten Event." *Journal of the*

Hong Kong Branch of the Royal Asiatic Society 11 (1971). Available at http://sunzi.lib.hku.hk/hkjo/view/44/4401204.pdf (accessed March 23, 2011).

Umutesi, Marie Beatrice. "Is Reconciliation between Hutus and Tutsis Possible?" *Journal of International Affairs* 60, no. 1 (September 22, 2006), p. 157.

Unschuld, Paul U. *Medicine in China: A History of Pharmaceutics*. Berkeley: University of California Press, 1986.

Urlanis, Boris. *Wars and Population*. Moscow: Progress Publishers, 1971.

U.S. Holocaust Memorial Museum. *Historical Atlas of the Holocaust*. New York: Macmillan, 1996.

U.S. Senate Committee on Government Operations. *Korean War Atrocities. Report of the Committee on Government Operations Made through Its Permanent Subcommittee on Investigations by Its Subcommittee on Korean War Atrocities pursuant to S. Res. 40*, 83rd Cong., 2d sess., S. Rep. No. 84. Washington, DC: Government Printing Office, 1954.

Utley, Robert M., and Whitcomb E. Washburn. *Indian Wars*. Boston: Mariner Books, 1987.

Vecamer, Arvo L. "A Germany-Soviet Military-Economic Comparison," http://www.feldgrau.com/econo.html (accessed March 28, 2011).

Verdirame, Guglielmo. "The Genocide Definition in the Jurisprudence of the Ad Hoc Tribunals." *International and Comparative Law Quarterly* 49 (2000), p. 583 et seq.

Wallechinsky, David. *David Wallechinsky's Twentieth Century: History with the Boring Parts Left Out*. Boston: Little, Brown, 1995.

———. *Tyrants: The World's 20 Worst Living Dictators*. New York: HarperCollins, 2006.

Ward-Perkins, Bryan. *The Fall of Rome and the End of Civilization*. New York: Oxford University Press, 2005.

Wasswa, Henry. "Uganda's First Prime Minister, and Two-Time President, Dead at 80." Associated Press, October 10, 2005.

Weatherford, Jack. *Genghis Khan and the Making of the Modern World*. New York: Three Rivers Press, 2004.

Wedgwood, C. V. *The Thirty Years War*. New York: New York Review Books, 2005 (originally published by Jonathan Cape, 1938).

Wehrfritz, George, B. J. Lee, et al. "Ghosts of Cheju." *Newsweek*, June 19, 2000.

Weiss, Herbert F., and Tatiana Carayannis. "Reconstructing the Congo." *International Affairs*, 58, no. 1 (September 22, 2004).

Weiss, Lowell. "Timing Is Everything; Vietnamese Refugees in the U.S." *Atlantic* 273, no. 1 (January 1994), p. 32.

Welch, Matt. "The Politics of Dead Children: Have Sanctions against Iraq Murdered Millions?" *Reason*, March 2002, http://www.reason.com/news/show/28346.html.

Wheatcroft, Andrew. *Infidels: A History of the Conflict between Christendom and Islam*. New York: Random House, 2005.

Whigham, Thomas L., and Barbara Potthast. "The Paraguayan Rosetta Stone: New Insights into the Demographics of the Paraguayan War, 1864–1870." *Latin American Research Review* 34, no. 1 (January 1, 1999), p. 174.

Whiting, Kenneth L. "Indonesia Still Dealing with Carnage of 25 Years Ago after Failed Coup." *Los Angeles Times*, February 10, 1991.

Wilford, John Noble. *The Mysterious History of Columbus*. New York: Vintage, 1991.

Williams, Henry Smith. *The Historians' History of the World*. New York: Trow Press, 1904.

Williams, Jeremy, " 'Kill 'em All': American Military Conduct in the Korean War." *BBC History*, January 2, 2002, http://www.bbc.co.uk/history/worldwars/coldwar/korea_usa_01.shtml.

Williams, Philip. "Uganda Marks 25 Years of Chaotic Independence Today." United Press International, October 9, 1987.

Willmott, H. P. *The Second World War in the Far East*. London: Cassell, 1999.

Wilson, Colin. *Mammoth Book of the History of Murder*. New York: Carrol & Graf, 2000.

Wilson, Peter H. "Latin America's Total War: Peter H. Wilson Revisits the War of the Triple Alliance, Latin America's Bloodiest Conflict." *History Today* 54, no. 5 (May 1, 2004), p. 52.

Wolpert, Stanley. *A New History of India*, 4th ed. New York: Oxford University Press, 1993.

Wood, Michael. *Conquistadors*. London: BBC Worldwide, 2000.

Wylie, Dan. "Shaka and the Modern Zulu State." *History Today* 44, no. 5 (May 1994), p. 8.

Zinn, Howard. *A People's History of the United States: 1492–Present*. New York: Perennial Classics, 1999.

INDEX

Page numbers in *italics* refer to illustrations.